Lecture Notes in Computer Science 4349

Commenced Publication in 1973
Founding and Former Series Editors:
Gerhard Goos, Juris Hartmanis, and Jan van Leeuwen

Byron Cook   Andreas Podelski (Eds.)

Verification, Model Checking, and Abstract Interpretation

8th International Conference, VMCAI 2007
Nice, France, January 14-16, 2007
Proceedings

 Springer

Volume Editors

Byron Cook
Microsoft Research
Roger Needham Building
JJ Thomson Avenue
CB3 OFB, Cambridge, United Kingdom
E-mail: bycook@microsoft.com

Andreas Podelski
University of Freiburg
79110 Freiburg, Germany
E-mail: podelski@informatik.uni-freiburg.de

Library of Congress Control Number: 2006939351

CR Subject Classification (1998): F.3.1-2, D.3.1, D.2.4

LNCS Sublibrary: SL 1 – Theoretical Computer Science and General Issues

ISSN   0302-9743
ISBN   3-540-69735-7 Springer Berlin Heidelberg New York
ISBN   978-3-540-69735-0 Springer Berlin Heidelberg New York

Springer is a part of Springer Science+Business Media

springer.com

© Springer-Verlag Berlin Heidelberg 2007

Typesetting: Camera-ready by author, data conversion by Scientific Publishing Services, Chennai, India
Printed on acid-free paper   SPIN: 11973966   06/3142   5 4 3 2 1 0

Preface

This volume contains the papers presented at VMCAI 2007: Verification, Model Checking and Abstract Interpretation held January 14–16, 2007 in Nice. VMCAI provides a forum for researchers from the communities of verification, model checking, and abstract interpretation, facilitating interaction, cross-fertilization, and advancement of hybrid methods that combine the three areas. This years VMCAI was held in conjunction with POPL, allowing further cross-fertilization between programming language research and the areas covered by VMCAI.

There were 85 submissions to VMCAI 2007. Each submission was reviewed by at least three Program Committee members. The committee decided to accept 21 papers. The program also includes invited talks by Tom Reps, Moshe Vardi, and Hongseok Yang and tutorials by Ken McMillan, Madhusudan Parthasarathy, and Peter Revesz.

We would like to acknowledge the financial support from Microsoft Research and Andrei Voronkov for assistance with the EasyChair conference system.

November 2006

Byron Cook
Andreas Podelski

Conference Organization

Program Chairs

Byron Cook   Microsoft Research Cambridge, UK
Andreas Podelski   University of Freiburg, Germany

Program Committee

Marsha Chechik	University of Toronto, Canada
Edmund Clarke	Carnegie Mellon University of Pittsburgh, USA
Byron Cook	Microsoft Research Cambridge, UK
Radhia Cousot	CNRS/École Polytechnique, France
Javier Esparza	University of Stuttgart, Germany
Limor Fix	Intel Research Pittsburgh, USA
Roberto Giacobazzi	Università delgi Studi di Verona, Italy
Patrice Godefroid	Lucent Technologies Inc., USA
Neil Jones	University of Copenhagen, Denmark
Yassine Lakhnech	Université Joseph Fourier Genoble, France
Ken McMillan	Cadence Berkeley Labs, California, USA
Markus Müller-Olm	University of Münster, Germany
Kedar Namjoshi	Lucent Technologies Inc., USA
Peter O'Hearn	Queen Mary University of London, UK
Andreas Podelski	University of Freiburg, Germany
Jean-Francois Raskin	Université Libre de Bruxelles, Belgium
Scott Stoller	Stony Brook University, USA
Tayssir Touili	LIAFA - Université Denis Diderot Paris, France
Lenore Zuck	University of Illinois at Chicago, USA

Steering Committee

Agostino Cortesi	Università Ca'Foscari di Venezia, Italy
Patrick Cousot	École Normale Supérieure, France
E. Allen Emerson	The University of Texas at Austin, USA
Giorgio Levi	University of Pisa, Italy
Andreas Podelski	University of Freiburg, Germany
Thomas W. Reps	University of Wisconsin-Madison, USA
David Schmidt	Kansas State University, USA
Lenore Zuck	University of Illinois at Chicago, USA

External Reviewers

Eugene Asarin
James Avery
Ittai Balaban
Laurent Van Begin
Josh Berdine
Julien Bertrane
Ahmed Bouajjani
Marius Bozga
Thomas Brihaye
Véronique Bruyére
Peter Buchholz
Thierry Cachat
Gianfranco Ciardo
Christopher Conway
Dennis Dams
Dino Distefanno
Laurent Doyen
Bruno Dufour
Stefan Edelkamp
Jérôme Feret
Limor Fix
Martin Fränzle
Maria-del-Mar Gallardo
Yuan Gan
Pierre Ganty
Gilles Geeraerts
Naghmeh Ghafari
Mihaela Gheorghiu
Alex Groce
Arie Gurfinkel
Peter Habermehl
Nicolas Halbwachs
Rene Rydhof Hansen
Reinhold Heckmann
Jason Hickey
Micheal Huth
Radu Iosif
Neil Jones
Rajeev Joshi
Stefan Kiefer
Viktor Kuncak
Yassine Lakhnech
Julia Lawall

Etienne Lozes
Michael Luttenberger
Thierry Massart
Damien Massé
Antoine Miné
Torben Mogensen
David Monniaux
Madan Musuvathi
Shiva Nejati
Tobias Nipkow
Thomas Noll
Paritosh Pandya
Matthew Parkinson
Doron Peled
C.R. Ramakrishnan
Francesco Ranzato
Jakob Rehof
Xavier Rival
Oliver Rüthing
Andrey Rybalchenko
Marko Samer
Sriram Sankaranarayanan
Stefan Schwoon
Olivier Serre
Frédéric Servais
Mihaela Sighireanu
Jocelyn Simmonds
Jakob Grue Simonsen
Élodie-Jane Sims
Nishant Sinha
Viorica Sofronie
Sylvain Soliman
Fausto Spoto
Jan Strejcek
Dejvuth Suwimonteerabuth
Todd Veldhuizen
Tomas Vojnar
Ou Wei
Martin De Wulf
Hongseok Yang
Lenore Zuck

Table of Contents

Session 3

Invited Tutorial

Session 4

Invited Talk

Session 5

Invited Tutorial

Session 6

DIVINE: DIscovering Variables IN Executables

Gogul Balakrishnan and Thomas Reps

Comp. Sci. Dept., University of Wisconsin
{bgogul,reps}@cs.wisc.edu

Abstract. This paper addresses the problem of recovering variable-like entities when analyzing executables in the absence of debugging information. We show that variable-like entities can be recovered by iterating *Value-Set Analysis* (VSA), a combined numeric-analysis and pointer-analysis algorithm, and *Aggregate Structure Identification*, an algorithm to identify the structure of aggregates. Our initial experiments show that the technique is successful in correctly identifying 88% of the local variables and 89% of the fields of heap-allocated objects. Previous techniques recovered 83% of the local variables, but 0% of the fields of heap-allocated objects. Moreover, the values computed by VSA using the variables recovered by our algorithm would allow any subsequent analysis to do a better job of interpreting instructions that use indirect addressing to access arrays and heap-allocated data objects: indirect operands can be resolved better at 4% to 39% of the sites of writes and up to 8% of the sites of reads. (These are the memory-access operations for which it is the most difficult for an analyzer to obtain useful results.)

1   Introduction

There is an increasing need for tools to help programmers and security analysts understand executables. For instance, companies and the military increasingly use Commercial Off-The Shelf (COTS) components to reduce the cost of software development. They are interested in ensuring that COTS components do not perform malicious actions (or can be forced to perform malicious actions). Viruses and worms have become ubiquitous. A tool that aids in understanding their behavior could ensure early dissemination of signatures, and thereby help control the extent of damage caused by them. In both domains, the questions that need to be answered cannot be answered perfectly—the problems are undecidable—but static analysis provides a way to answer them conservatively.

The long-term goal of our work is to develop bug-detection and security-vulnerability analyses that work on executables. As a means to this end, our immediate goal is to advance the state of the art of recovering, from executables, Intermediate Representations (IRs) that are similar to those that would be available had one started from source code. We envisage the following uses for the IRs: (1) as an aid to a human analyst who is trying to understand the behavior of the program, and (2) as the basis for further static analysis of executables. Moreover, once such IRs are in hand, we will be in a position to leverage the substantial body of work on bug-detection and security-vulnerability analysis based on IRs built from source code.

One of the several obstacles in IR recovery is that a program's data objects are not easily identifiable in an executable. Consider, for instance, a data dependence from

B. Cook and A. Podelski (Eds.): VMCAI 2007, LNCS 4349, pp. 1–28, 2007.

statement a to statement b that is transmitted by write/read accesses on some variable x. When performing source-code analysis, the programmer-defined variables provide us with convenient compartments for tracking such data manipulations. A dependence analyzer must show that a defines x, b uses x, and there is an x-def-free path from a to b. However, in executables, memory is accessed either directly—by specifying an absolute address—or indirectly—through an address expression of the form "[*base* + *index* × *scale* + *offset*]", where *base* and *index* are registers, and *scale* and *offset* are integer constants. It is not clear from such expressions what the natural compartments are that should be used for analysis. Because executables do not have *intrinsic* entities that can be used for analysis (analogous to source-level variables), a crucial step in the analysis of executables is to identify variable-like entities. If debugging information is available (and trusted), this provides one possibility; however, even if debugging information is available, analysis techniques have to account for bit-level, byte-level, word-level, and bulk-memory manipulations performed by programmers (or introduced by the compiler) that can sometimes violate variable boundaries [3,18,24]. If a program is suspected of containing malicious code, even if debugging information is present, it cannot be entirely relied upon. For these reasons, it is not always desirable to use debugging information—or at least to rely on it alone—for identifying a program's data objects. (Similarly, past work on source-code analysis has shown that it is sometimes valuable to ignore information available in declarations and infer replacement information from the actual usage patterns found in the code [12,21,23,28,30].)

Moreover, for many kinds of programs (including most COTS products, viruses, and worms), debugging information is entirely absent; for such situations, an alternative source of information about variable-like entities is needed. While the reader may wonder about how effective one can be at determining information about a program's behavior from low-level code, a surprisingly large number of people—on a daily basis—are engaged in inspecting low-level code that is not equipped with debugging information. These include hackers of all hat shades (black, grey, and white), as well as employees of anti-virus companies, members of computer incident/emergency response teams, and members of the intelligence community.

Heretofore, the state of the art in recovering variable-like entities is represented by IDAPro [15], a commercial disassembly toolkit. IDAPro's algorithm is based on the observation that accesses to global variables appear as "[*absolute-address*]", and accesses to local variables appear as "[esp + *offset*]" or "[ebp - *offset*]" in the executable. That is, IDAPro recovers variables based on purely local techniques.[1] This approach has certain limitations. For instance, it does not take into account accesses to fields of structures, elements of arrays, and variables that are only accessed through pointers, because these accesses do not fall into any of the patterns that IDAPro considers. Therefore, it generally recovers only very coarse information about arrays and structures. Moreover, this approach fails to provide any information about the fields of heap-allocated objects, which is crucial for understanding programs that manipulate the heap.

The aim of the work presented in this paper is to improve the state of the art by using abstract interpretation [10] to replace local analyses with ones that take a more

---

[1] IDAPro does incorporate a few global analyses, such as one for determining changes in stack height at call-sites. However, the techniques are ad-hoc and based on heuristics.

comprehensive view of the operations performed by the program. We present an algorithm that combines Value-Set Analysis (VSA) [4], which is a combined numeric-analysis and pointer-analysis algorithm that works on executables, and Aggregate Structure Identification (ASI) [23], which is an algorithm that infers the substructure of aggregates used in a program based on how the program accesses them, to recover variables that are better than those recovered by IDAPro. As explained in §5, the combination of VSA and ASI allows us (a) to recover variables that are based on *indirect* accesses to memory, rather than just the explicit addresses and offsets that occur in the program, and (b) to identify structures, arrays, and nestings of structures and arrays. Moreover, when the variables that are recovered by our algorithm are used during VSA, the precision of VSA improves. This leads to an interesting abstraction-refinement scheme; improved precision during VSA causes an improvement in the quality of variables recovered by our algorithm, which, in turn, leads to improved precision in a subsequent round of VSA, and so on.

The specific technical contributions of the paper are as follows:

- We present an abstract-interpretation-based algorithm for recovering variable-like entities from an executable. In particular, we show how information provided by VSA is used in combination with ASI for this purpose.
- We evaluate the usefulness of the variables recovered by our algorithm to a human analyst. We compare the variables recovered by our algorithm against the debugging information generated at compile time. Initial experiments show that the technique is successful in correctly identifying 88% of the local variables and 89% of the fields of heap-allocated objects. Previous techniques based on local analysis recovered 83% of the local variables, but 0% of the fields of heap-allocated objects.
- We evaluate the usefulness of the variables and values recovered by our algorithm as a platform for additional analyses. Initial experiments show that the values computed by VSA using the variables recovered by our algorithm would allow any subsequent analysis to do a better job of interpreting instructions that use indirect addressing to access arrays and heap-allocated data objects: indirect memory operands can be resolved better at 4% to 39% of the sites of writes and up to 8% of the sites of reads.

Our current implementation of the variable-recovery algorithm—which is incorporated in a tool called CodeSurfer/x86 [25]—works on x86 executables; however, the algorithms used are architecture-independent.

The remainder of the paper is organized as follows: §2 provides an abstract memory model for analyzing executables. §3 provides an overview of our approach to recover variable-like entities for use in analyzing executables. §4 provides background on VSA and ASI. §5 describes our abstraction-refinement algorithm to recover variable-like entities. §6 reports experimental results. §7 discusses related work.

2 An Abstract Memory Model

In this section, we present an abstract memory model for analyzing executables. A simple model is to consider memory as an array of bytes. Writes (reads) in this trivial memory model are treated as writes (reads) to the corresponding element of the array. However, there are some disadvantages in such a simple model:

- It may not be possible to determine specific address values for certain memory blocks, such as those allocated from the heap via `malloc`. For the analysis to be sound, writes to (reads from) such blocks of memory have to be treated as writes to (reads from) any part of the heap.
- The runtime stack is reused during each execution run; in general, a given area of the runtime stack will be used by several procedures at different times during execution. Thus, at each instruction a specific numeric address can be ambiguous (because the same address may belong to different activation records at different times during execution): it may denote a variable of procedure f, a variable of procedure g, a variable of procedure h, etc. (A given address may also correspond to different variables of different activations of f.) Therefore, an instruction that updates a variable of procedure f would have to be treated as possibly updating the corresponding variables of procedures g, h, etc.

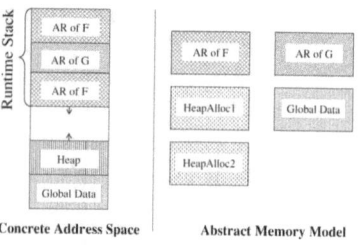

Concrete Address Space   **Abstract Memory Model**

Fig. 1. Memory-regions

To overcome these problems, we work with the following abstract memory model [4]. Although in the concrete semantics the activation records (ARs) for procedures, the heap, and the memory for global data are all part of *one* address space, for the purposes of analysis, we separate the address space into a set of disjoint areas, which are referred to as *memory-regions* (see Fig. 1). Each memory-region represents a group of locations that have similar runtime properties. For example, the runtime locations that belong to the ARs of a given procedure belong to one memory-region. For a given program, there are three kinds of regions: (1) *global*-regions, for memory locations that hold global data, (2) *AR*-regions, each of which contains the locations of the ARs of a particular procedure, and (3) *malloc*-regions, each of which contains the locations allocated at a particular `malloc` site.

3   Overview of Our Approach

Our goal is to subdivide the memory-regions of the executable into variable-like entities (which we call *a-locs*, for "abstract locations"). These can then be used as variables in tools that analyze executables. Memory-regions are subdivided using the information about how the program accesses its data. The intuition behind this approach is that data-access patterns in the program provide clues about how data is laid out in memory. For instance, the fact that an instruction in the executable accesses a sequence of four bytes in memory-region M is an indication that the programmer (or the compiler) intended to have a four-byte-long variable or field at the corresponding offset in M. In this section, we present the problems in developing such an approach, and the insights behind our solution, which addresses those problems. Details are provided in §5.

3.1 The Problem of Indirect Memory Accesses

Past work on analyzing executables [4,15] uses the addresses and stack-frame offsets that occur explicitly in the program to recover variable-like entities. We will call this the *Semi-Naïve algorithm*. It is based on the observation that access to global variables appear as "[*absolute-address*]", and access to local variables appear as "[esp + *offset*]" or "[ebp + *offset*]" in the executable. Thus, absolute addresses and offsets that occur explicitly in the executable (generally) indicate the starting addresses of program variables. Based on this observation, the Semi-Naïve algorithm identifies each set of locations between two neighboring absolute addresses or offsets as a single variable. Such an approach produces poor results in the presence of indirect memory operands.

Example 1. The program initializes the two fields x and y of a local struct through the pointer pp and returns 0. pp is located at offset -12,[2] and struct p is located at offset -8 in the activation record of main. Address expression "ebp-8" refers to the address of p, and address expression "ebp-12" refers to the address of pp.

```
typedef struct {              proc main
    int x, y;
} Point;                      1 mov ebp, esp
                              2 sub esp, 12
int main(){                   3 lea eax, [ebp-8]
    Point p, *pp;             4 mov [ebp-12], eax
    pp = &p;                  5 mov [eax], 1
    pp->x = 1;                6 mov [eax+4], 2
    pp->y = 2;                7 mov eax, 0
    return 0;                 8 add esp, 12
}                             9 retn
```

Instruction 4 initializes the value of pp. (Instruction "3 lea eax, [ebp-8]" is equivalent to the assignment eax := ebp-8.) Instructions 5 and 6 update the fields of p. Observe that, in the executable, the fields of p are updated via eax, rather than via the pointer pp itself, which resides at address ebp-12.   □

In Ex. 1, -8 and -12 are the offsets relative to the frame pointer (i.e., ebp) that occur explicitly in the program. The Semi-Naïve algorithm would say that offsets -12 through -9 of the AR of main constitute one variable (say var_12), and offsets -8 through -1 of AR of main constitute another (say var_8). The Semi-Naïve algorithm correctly identifies the position and size of pp. However, it groups the two fields of p together into a single variable because it does not take into consideration the indirect memory operand [eax+4] in instruction 6.

Typically, indirect operands are used to access arrays, fields of structures, fields of heap-allocated data, etc. Therefore, to recover a useful collection of variables from executables, one has to look beyond the explicitly occurring addresses and stack-frame offsets. Unlike the operands considered in the Semi-Naïve algorithm, local methods do

---

[2] We follow the convention that the value of esp (the stack pointer) at the beginning of a procedure marks the origin of the procedure's AR-region.

not provide information about what an indirect memory operand accesses. For instance, an operand such as "[ebp + *offset*]" (usually) accesses a local variable. However, "[eax + 4]" may access a local variable, a global variable, a field of a heap-allocated data-structure, etc., depending upon what eax contains.

Obtaining information about what an indirect memory operand accesses is not straightforward. In this example, eax is initialized with the value of a register. In general, a register used in an indirect memory operand may be initialized with a value read from memory. In such cases, to determine the value of the register, it is necessary to know the contents of that memory location, and so on. Fortunately, Value-Set Analysis (VSA) described in [4,24] (summarized in §4.1) can provide such information.

3.2   The Problem of Granularity and Expressiveness

The granularity and expressiveness of recovered variables can affect the precision of analysis clients that use the recovered variables as the executable's data objects.

Example 2. The program shown below initializes all elements of array p. The x-members of each element are initialized with 1; the y-members are initialized with 2. The disassembly is also shown. Instruction L1 updates the x-members of the array elements; instruction 5 updates the y-members.

```
typedef struct {              proc main
    int x,y;                0 mov ebp,esp
} Point;                    1 sub esp,40
                            2 mov ecx,0
int main(){                 3 lea eax,[ebp-40]
    int i;              L1: mov [eax], 1
    Point p[5];             5 mov [eax+4],2
    for(i=0;i<5;++i) {      6 add eax,  8
        p[i].x = 1;         7 inc ecx
        p[i].y = 2;         8 cmp ecx, 5
    }                       9 jl L1
    return p[0].y;          10 mov eax,[ebp-36]
}                           11 add esp,40
                            12 retn
```

Fig. 2(a) shows how the variables are laid out in the AR of main. Note that there is no space for variable i in the AR for main because the compiler promoted i to register ecx.   □

As a specific example of an analysis client, consider a data-dependence analyzer, which answers such questions as: *"Does the write to memory at instruction L1 affect the read from memory at instruction 10".* Note that in Ex. 2 the write to memory at instruction L1 does not affect the read from memory at instruction 10 because L1 updates the x members of the elements of array p, while instruction 10 reads the y member of array element p[0]. To simplify the discussion, assume that a data-dependence analyzer works as follows: (1) annotate each instruction with used, killed, and possibly-killed variables, and (2) compare the used variables of each instruction with killed or possibly-killed variables of every other instruction to determine data dependences.

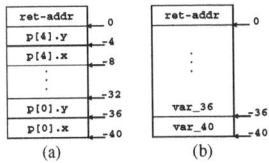

Fig. 2. AR of main for the program in Ex. 2: (a) actual layout, and (b) layout obtained from the Semi-Naïve approach

Consider three different partitions of the AR of main:

$VarSet_1$: As shown in Fig. 2(b), the Semi-Naïve approach from §3.1 would say that the AR of main has two variables: var_40 (4 bytes) and var_36 (36 bytes). The variables that are possibly killed at L1 are {var_40, var_36}, and the variable used at 10 is var_36. Therefore, the data-dependence analyzer reports that the write to memory at L1 might affect the read at 10. (This is sound, but imprecise.)

$VarSet_2$: As shown in Fig. 2(a), there are two variables for each element of array p. The variables possibly killed at L1 are {p[0].x, p[1].x, p[2].x, p[3].x, p[4].x}, and the variable used at instruction 10 is p[0].y. Because these sets are disjoint, the data-dependence analyzer reports that the memory write at instruction L1 definitely does not affect the memory read at instruction 10.

$VarSet_3$: Suppose that the AR of main is partitioned into just two (summary) variables: (1) p[?].x, which is a representative for the x members of the elements of array p, and (2) p[?].y, which is a representative for the y members of the elements of array p. The summary variable that is possibly killed at instruction L1 is p[?].x and the summary variable that is used at instruction 10 is p[?].y. These are disjoint; therefore, the data-dependence analyzer reports a definite answer, namely, that the write at L1 does not affect the read at 10.

Of the three alternatives presented above, $VarSet_3$ has several desirable features:

- It has a smaller number of variables than $VarSet_2$. When it is used as the set of variables in a data-dependence analyzer, it provides better results than $VarSet_1$.
- The variables in $VarSet_3$ are capable of representing a set of non-contiguous memory locations. For instance, p[?].x represents the locations corresponding to p[0].x, p[1].x, ..., p[4].x. The ability to represent non-contiguous sequences of memory locations is crucial for representing a specific field in an array of structures.
- The AR of main is only partitioned as much as necessary. In $VarSet_3$, only one summary variable represents the x members of the elements of array p, while each member of each element of array p is assigned a separate variable in $VarSet_2$.

A good variable-recovery algorithm should partition a memory-region in such a way that the set of variables obtained from the partition has the desirable features of $VarSet_3$. When debugging information is available, this is a trivial task. However, debugging information is often not available. Data-access patterns in the program provide information that can serve as a substitute for debugging information. For instance, instruction L1 accesses each of the four-byte sequences that start at offsets {−40, −32, ..., −8} in the AR of main. The common difference of 8 between successive offsets is evidence that the offsets may represent the elements of an array. Moreover, instruction L1 accesses every four bytes starting at these offsets. Consequently, the elements of the array are judged to be structures in which the one of the fields is four bytes long.

4 Background

In this section, we describe (1) Value-Set Analysis (VSA) [4], and (2) Aggregate Structure Identification (ASI) [23]. This material is related to the core of the paper as follows:

- We use VSA as the mechanism to understand indirect memory accesses (see §4.1) and obtain data-access patterns (see §4.2) from the executable.
- In §5, we show how to use the information gathered during VSA to harness ASI to the problem of identifying variable-like entities in executables.

4.1 Value-Set Analysis (VSA)

VSA [4] is a combined numeric-analysis and pointer-analysis algorithm that determines an over-approximation of the set of numeric values or addresses that each register and memory location holds at each program point. In particular, at each program point, VSA provides information about the contents of registers that appear in an indirect memory operand. A key feature of VSA is that it tracks integer-valued and address-valued quantities simultaneously. This is crucial for analyzing executables because numeric values and addresses are indistinguishable at runtime. Moreover, unlike earlier algorithms that analyze executables [8,11], VSA takes into account data manipulations involving memory locations also. To track the contents of memory locations, the initial run of VSA uses the variables recovered via the Semi-Naïve approach from §3.1.

For the program in Ex. 1, the initial run of VSA computes an over-approximation of the contents of the x86 registers (eax, ax, ah, al, ebx, etc.) and the memory-locations that correspond to var_12 (4 bytes) and var_8 (8 bytes). Similarly, for the program in Ex. 2, the initial run of VSA computes an over-approximation of the contents of the x86 registers and the memory-locations that correspond to var_40 (4 bytes) and var_36 (36 bytes). For both examples, the initial a-locs will be refined by our abstraction-refinement algorithm in §5. In the remainder of the paper, we overload the term "a-loc" both for the entities recovered by the Semi-Naïve algorithm (which are what we used in our previous work [4]), as well as for the entities identified by the abstraction-refinement algorithm of §5. (There should be no confusion, as it should always be clear from context which kind of a-loc is intended.)

VSA is a flow-sensitive, context-sensitive, interprocedural, abstract-interpretation algorithm (parameterized by call-string length [27]) that is based on an independent-attribute domain described below.

Call-Strings. The call-graph of a program is a labeled graph in which each node represents a procedure, each edge represents a call, and the label on an edge represents the call-site corresponding to the call represented by the edge. A call-string [27] is a sequence of call-sites $(c_1 c_2 \ldots c_n)$ such that call-site c_1 belongs to the entry procedure, and there exists a path in the call-graph consisting of edges with labels $c_1, c_2, \ldots, c_n$. CallString is the set of all call-strings in the program.

A call-string suffix of length k is either $(c_1 c_2 \ldots c_k)$ or $(*c_1 c_2 \ldots c_k)$, where c_1, c_2, $\ldots$, c_k are call-sites. $(c_1 c_2 \ldots c_k)$ represents the string of call-sites $c_1 c_2 \ldots c_k$. $(*c_1 c_2 \ldots c_k)$, which is referred to as a *saturated* call-string, represents the set $\{cs | cs \in$

CallString, $cs = \pi c_1 c_2 \ldots c_k$, and $|\pi| \geq 1$}. CallString$_k$ is the set of saturated call-strings of length k, plus non-saturated call-strings of length $\leq k$.

Value-Sets. During VSA, a set of numeric values and addresses is represented by a *value-set* that is a safe approximation of the actual set. Suppose that n is the number of memory-regions in the executable. A value-set is an n-tuple of strided intervals of the form $s[l, u]$, with each component of the tuple representing the set of addresses in the corresponding region [24]. For a 32-bit machine, a strided-interval $s[l, u]$ represents the set of integers $\{i \in [-2^{31}, 2^{31} - 1] | l \leq i \leq u, i \equiv l(\mathrm{mod}\ s)\}$.

- s is called the *stride*.
- $[l, u]$ is called the *interval*.
- $0[l, l]$ represents the singleton set $\{l\}$.

For Ex. 2, the value-sets are 2-tuples. We follow the convention that the first component always refers to the set of addresses (or numbers) in the global region and $\emptyset$ denotes the empty set. For instance, the tuple $(1[0, 9], \emptyset)$ represents the set of numbers $\{0, 1, \ldots, 9\}$ and the tuple $(\emptyset, 4[-40, -4])$ represents the set of offsets $\{-40, -36, \ldots, -4\}$ in the AR-region for main. (Although we refer to "tracking integer-valued and address-valued quantities simultaneously", the analysis makes no distinction between the two: values in the Global region could be either, and are treated appropriately according to what instruction is performed [4,24].)

VSA Domain. Let Proc denote the set of memory-regions associated with procedures in the program; AllocMemRgn denote the set of memory-regions associated with heap-allocation sites;[3] Global denote the memory-region associated with the global data area; and a-loc[R] denote the a-locs that belong to memory-region R. We work with the following basic domains:

$$
\begin{aligned}
&\mathsf{MemRgn} = \{\mathsf{Global}\} \cup \mathsf{Proc} \cup \mathsf{AllocMemRgn} \\
&\mathsf{ValueSet} = \mathsf{MemRgn} \to \mathsf{StridedInterval}_\perp \\
&\mathsf{AlocEnv[R]} = \mathsf{a\text{-}loc[R]} \to \mathsf{ValueSet}
\end{aligned}
$$

AbsEnv maps each region R to its corresponding AlocEnv[R] and each register to a ValueSet:

$$
\mathsf{AbsEnv} = \begin{aligned}
&(\mathsf{register} \to \mathsf{ValueSet}) \\
\times\ &(\{\mathsf{Global}\} \to \mathsf{AlocEnv[Global]}) \\
\times\ &(\mathsf{Proc} \to \mathsf{AlocEnv[Proc]}_\perp) \\
\times\ &(\mathsf{AllocMemRgn} \to \mathsf{AlocEnv[AllocMemRgn]}_\perp)
\end{aligned}
$$

---

[3] The implementation actually uses an augmented abstract domain that overcomes some of the imprecision that arises due to the need to perform weak updates—i.e., accumulate information via join—on fields of summary malloc-regions. In particular, the augmented domain, which is described in [5], often allows our analysis to establish a definite link between a heap-allocated object of a class that uses 1 or more virtual functions and the appropriate virtual-function table. Due to space considerations, this aspect could not be described in the present paper. The results reported in §6 are based on the augmented domain.

VSA associates each program point with an AbsMemConfig:

$$\text{AbsMemConfig} = (\text{CallString}_k \rightarrow \text{AbsEnv}_\perp)$$

In the above definitions, $\perp$ is used to denote a partial map. For instance, a ValueSet may not contain offsets in some memory-regions. Similarly, in AbsEnv, a procedure P whose activation record is not on the stack does not have an AlocEnv[P]. In addition to determining an over-approximation of the set of numeric values and addresses for each a-loc in the executable, VSA also finds a conservative estimate of the targets of indirect function-calls and indirect jumps—see [4]. Instead of describing VSA in detail, we highlight some of its features that are useful in a-loc recovery.

- *Information about indirect memory operands:* For the program in Ex. 1, VSA determines that the value-set of eax at instruction 6 is $(\emptyset, 0[-8, -8])$, which means that eax holds the offset -8 in the AR-region of main. Using this information, we can conclude that [eax+4] refers to offset -4 in the AR of main.
- *VSA provides data-access patterns:* For the program in Ex. 2, VSA determines that the value-set of eax at program point L1 is $(\emptyset, 8[-40, -8])$, which means that eax holds the offsets $\{-40, -32, \ldots, -8\}$ in the AR-region of main. (These offsets are the starting addresses of field x of elements of array p.)
- *VSA tracks updates to memory:* This is important because, in general, the registers used in an indirect memory operand may be initialized with a value read from memory. If updates to memory are not tracked, we may neither have useful information for indirect memory operands nor useful data-access patterns for the executable.

4.2   Aggregate Structure Identification (ASI)

ASI is a unification-based, flow-insensitive algorithm to identify the structure of aggregates in a program [23]. The algorithm ignores any type information known about aggregates, and considers each aggregate to be merely a sequence of bytes of a given length. The aggregate is then broken up into smaller parts depending on how it is accessed by the program. The smaller parts are called *atoms*.

The data-access patterns in the program are specified to the ASI algorithm through a data-access constraint language (DAC). The syntax of DAC programs is shown in Fig. 3. There are two kinds of constructs in a DAC program: (1) DataRef is a reference to a set of bytes, and provides a means to specify how the data is accessed in the program; (2) UnifyConstraint provides a means to specify the flow of data in the program.

```
            Pgm ::= ε | UnifyConstraint Pgm
UnifyConstraint ::= DataRef ≈ DataRef
        DataRef ::= ProgVars |
                    DataRef[UInt:UInt] |
                    DataRef\UInt₊
```

Fig. 3. Data-Access Constraint (DAC) language. UInt is the set of non-negative integers; UInt_+ is the set of positive integers; and ProgVars is the set of program variables.

Note that the direction of data flow is not considered in a UnifyConstraint. The justification for this is that a flow of data from one sequence of bytes to another is evidence that they should have the same structure. ASI uses the constraints in the DAC program to find a coarsest refinement of the aggregates.

There are three kinds of data references:

- A variable P ∈ ProgVar refers to all the bytes of variable P.
- DataRef [l:u] refers to bytes l through u in DataRef. For example, P[8:11] refers to bytes 8..11 of variable P.
- DataRef\$n$ is interpreted as follows: DataRef is an array of n elements and DataRef\$n$ refers to the bytes of an element of array DataRef. For example, P[0:11]\3 refers to the sequences of bytes P[0:3], P[4:7], or P[8:11].

Instead of going into the details of the ASI algorithm, we provide the intuition behind the algorithm by means of an example. Consider the source-code program shown in Ex. 2. The data-access constraints for the program are

$$p[0:39]\backslash 5[0:3] \approx \text{const\_1}[0:3];$$
$$p[0:39]\backslash 5[4:7] \approx \text{const\_2}[0:3];$$
$$\text{return\_main}[0:3] \approx p[4:7];$$

The constraints reflect the fact that the size of Point is 8 and that x and y are laid out next to each other. The first constraint encodes the initialization of the x members, namely, p[i].x = 1. The DataRef p[0:39]\5[0:3] refers to the bytes that correspond to the x members in array p. The last constraint corresponds to the return statement; it represents the fact that the return value of main is assigned bytes 4..7 of p, which correspond to p[0].y.

The result of ASI is a DAG that shows the structure of each aggregate as well as relationships among the atoms of aggregates. The DAG for Ex. 2 is shown in Fig. 4(a). An ASI DAG has the following properties:

- A node represents a set of bytes.
- A sequence of bytes that is accessed as an array in the program is represented by an *array* node. Array nodes are labeled with ⊗. The number in an array node represents the number of elements in the array. An array node has one child, and the DAG rooted at the child represents the structure of the array element. In Fig. 4(a), bytes 8..39 of array p are identified as an array of four 8-byte elements. Each array element is a struct with two fields of 4 bytes each.
- A sequence of bytes that is accessed like a C struct in the program is represented by a *struct* node. The number in the struct node represents the length of the struct; the children of a struct node represent the fields of the struct. In Fig. 4(a), bytes 0..39 of p are identified as a struct with three fields: two 4-byte scalars and one 32-byte array.
- Nodes are shared if there is a flow of data in the program involving the corresponding sequence of bytes either directly or indirectly. In Fig. 4(a), the nodes for the sequences of bytes return_main[0:3] and p[4:7] are shared because of the return statement in main. Similarly, the sequence of bytes that correspond to the y members of array p, namely p[0:39]\5[4:7], share the same node because they are all assigned the same constant at the same instruction.

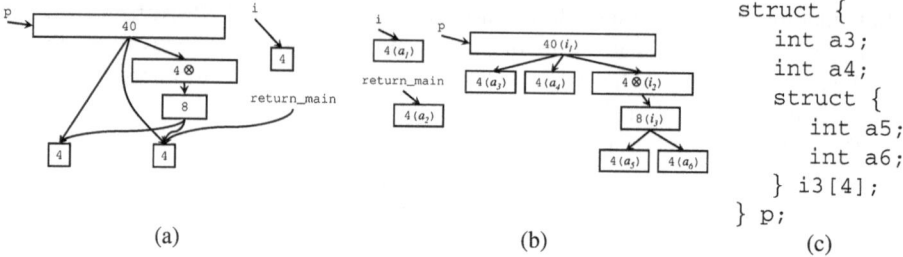

Fig. 4. (a) ASI DAG, (b) ASI tree, and (c) struct recovered for the program in Ex. 2

The ASI DAG is converted into an ASI tree by duplicating shared nodes. The atoms of an aggregate are the leaves of the corresponding ASI tree. Fig. 4(b) shows the ASI tree for Ex. 2. ASI has identified that p has the structure shown in Fig. 4(c).

5 Recovering A-Locs Via Iteration

We use the atoms obtained from ASI as a-locs for (re-)analyzing the executable. The atoms identified by ASI for Ex. 2 are close to the set of variables $VarSet_3$ that was discussed in §3.2. One might hope to apply ASI to an executable by treating each memory-region as an aggregate and determining the structure of each memory-region (without using VSA results). However, one of the requirements for applying ASI is that it must be possible to extract data-access constraints from the program. When applying ASI to programs written in languages such as Cobol this is possible: the data-access patterns are apparent from the syntax of the constructs under consideration. Unfortunately, this is not the case for executables. For instance, the memory operand [eax] can either represent an access to a single variable or to the elements of an array. Fortunately, value-sets provide the necessary information to generate data-access constraints. Recall that a value-set is an over-approximation of the set of offsets in each memory-region. Together with the information about the number of bytes accessed by each argument (which is available from the instruction), this provides the information needed to generate data-access constraints for the executable.

Furthermore, when we use the atoms of ASI as a-locs in VSA, the results of VSA can improve. Consider the program in Ex. 1. Recall from §3.1 that the length of var_8 is 8 bytes. Because value-sets are only capable of representing a set of 4-byte addresses and 4-byte values, VSA recovers no useful information for var_8: it merely reports that the value-set of var_8 is ⊤ (meaning any possible value or address). Applying ASI (using data-access patterns provided by VSA) results in the splitting of var_8 into two 4-byte a-locs, namely, var_8.0 and var_8.4. Because var_8.0 and var_8.4 are each four bytes long, VSA can now track the set of values or addresses in these a-locs. Specifically, VSA would determine that var_8.0 (i.e., p.x) has the value 1 and var_8.4 (i.e., p.y) has the value 2 at the end of main.

We can use the new VSA results to perform another round of ASI. If the value-sets computed by VSA are improved from the previous round, the next round of ASI may also improve. We can repeat this process as long as desired, or until the process converges (see §5.4).

Although not illustrated by Ex. 1, additional rounds of ASI and VSA can result in further improvements. For example, suppose that the program uses a chain of pointers to link `structs` of different types, e.g., variable `ap` points to a `struct A`, which has a field `bp` that points to a `struct B`, which has a field `cp` that points to a `struct C`, and so on. Typically, the first round of VSA recovers the value of `ap`, which lets ASI discover the a-loc for `A.bp` (from the code compiled for `ap->bp`); the second round of VSA recovers the value of `ap->bp`, which lets ASI discover the a-loc for `B.cp` (from the code compiled for `ap->bp->cp`); etc.

To summarize, the algorithm for recovering a-locs is

1. Run VSA using a-locs recovered by the Semi-Naïve approach.
2. Generate data-access patterns from the results of VSA
3. Run ASI
4. Run VSA
5. Repeat steps 2, 3, and 4 until there are no improvements to the results of VSA.[4]

It is important to understand that VSA generates sound results for *any* collection of a-locs with which it is supplied. However, if supplied very coarse a-locs, many a-locs will be found to have the value ⊤ at most points. By refining the a-locs in use, more precise answers are generally obtained. For this reason, ASI is used only as a heuristic to find a-locs for VSA; i.e., it is not necessary to generate data-access constraints for all memory accesses in the program. Because ASI is a unification-based algorithm, generating data-access constraints for certain kinds of instructions leads to undesirable results. §5.5 discusses some of these cases.

In short, our abstraction-refinement principles are as follows:

1. VSA results are used to interpret memory-access expressions in the executable.
2. ASI is used as a heuristic to determine the structure of each memory-region according to information recovered by VSA.
3. Each ASI tree reflects the memory-access patterns in one memory-region, and the leaves of the ASI trees define the a-locs that are used for the next round of VSA.

ASI alone is not a replacement for VSA. That is, ASI cannot be applied to executables without the information that is obtained from VSA—namely value-sets.

In the rest of this section, we describe the interplay between VSA and ASI: (1) we show how value-sets are used to generate data-access constraints for input to ASI, and (2) how the atoms in the ASI trees are used as a-locs during the next round of VSA.

5.1   Generating Data-Access Constraints

This section describes the algorithm that generates ASI data-references for x86 operands. Three forms of x86 operands need to be considered: (1) register operands, (2) memory operands of form "[*register*]", and (3) memory operands of the form "[*base* + *index* × *scale* + *offset*]".

---

[4] Or, equivalently, until the set of a-locs discovered in step 3 is unchanged from the set previously discovered in step 3 (or step 1).

To prevent unwanted unification during ASI, we rename registers using live-ranges. For a register r, the ASI data-reference is $r_{lr}[0:n-1]$, where lr is the live-range of the register at the given instruction and n is the size of the register (in bytes).

In the rest of the section, we describe the algorithm for memory operands. First, we consider indirect operands of the form [r]. To gain intuition about the algorithm, consider operand [eax] of instruction L1 in Ex. 2. The value-set associated with eax is $(\emptyset, 8[-40, -8])$. The stride value of 8 and the interval $[-40, -8]$ in the AR of main provide evidence that [eax] is an access to the elements of an array of 8-byte elements in the range $[-40, -8]$ of the AR of main; an array access is generated for this operand.

Recall that a value-set is an n-tuple of strided intervals. The strided interval $s[l, u]$ in each component represents the offsets in the corresponding memory-region. Alg. 1 shows the pseudocode to convert offsets in a memory-region into an ASI reference. SI2ASI takes the name of a memory-region r, a strided interval $s[l, u]$, and *length* (the number of bytes accessed) as arguments. The *length* parameter is obtained from the instruction. For example, the *length* for [eax] is 4 because the instruction at L1 in Ex. 2 is a four-byte data transfer. The algorithm returns a pair in which the first component is an ASI reference and the second component is a Boolean. The significance of the Boolean component is described later in this section. The algorithm works as follows: If $s[l, u]$ is a singleton, then the ASI reference is the one that accesses offsets l to $l+length-1$ in the aggregate associated with memory-region r. If $s[l, u]$ is not a singleton, then the offsets represented by $s[l, u]$ are treated as references to an array. The size of the array element is the stride s whenever $(s \geq length)$. However, when $(s < length)$ an overlapping set of locations is accessed by the indirect memory operand. Because an overlapping set of locations cannot be represented using an ASI reference, the algorithm chooses *length* as the size of the array element. This is not a problem for the soundness of subsequent rounds of VSA because of refinement principle 2. The Boolean component of the pair denotes whether the algorithm generated an exact ASI reference or not. The number of elements in the array is $\lfloor (u-l)/size \rfloor + 1$.

For operands of the form [r], the set of ASI references is generated by invoking Alg. 1 for each non-empty memory-region in r's value-set. For Ex. 2, the value-set associated with eax at L1 is $(\emptyset, 8[-40, -8])$. Therefore, the set of ASI references is $\{AR\_main[(-40):(-1)]\backslash 5[0:3]\}$.[5] There are no references to the Global region because the set of offsets in that region is empty.

The algorithm for converting indirect operands of the form [*base + index* × *scale* + *offset*] is given in Alg. 2. One typical use of indirect operands of the form [*base + index* × *scale* + *offset*] is to access two-dimensional arrays. Note that *scale* and *offset* are statically-known constants. Because abstract values are strided intervals, we can absorb *scale* and *offset* into *base* and *index*. Hence, without loss of generality, we only discuss memory operands of the form [*base+index*]. Assuming that the two-dimensional array is stored in row-major format, one of the registers (usually *base*) holds the starting addresses of the rows and the other register (usually *index*) holds the indices of the

---

[5] Offsets in a DataRef cannot be negative. Negative offsets are used in the paper for clarity. Negative offsets are mapped to the range $[0, 2^{31} - 1]$; non-negative offsets are mapped to the range $[2^{31}, 2^{32} - 1]$.

Algorithm 1 SI2ASI: Algorithm to convert a given strided interval into an ASI reference

---

Input: The name of a memory-region r, strided interval $s[l, u]$, number of bytes accessed *length*.

Output: A pair in which the first component is an ASI reference for the sequence of *length* bytes starting at offsets $s[l, u]$ in memory-region r and the second component is a Boolean that represents whether the ASI reference is an exact reference (true) or an approximate one (false).

> **if** $s[l, u]$ is a singleton **then**
> > **return** $\langle$ "$r[l : l + length - 1]$", true$\rangle$
>
> **else**
> > $size \leftarrow \max(s, length)$
> > $n \leftarrow \lfloor (u - l)/size \rfloor + 1$
> > ref $\leftarrow$ "$r[l : u + size - 1]\backslash n[0 : length - 1]$"
> > **return** $\langle$ref, $(s < length)\rangle$
>
> **end if**

Algorithm 2 Algorithm to convert the set of offsets represented by the sum of two strided intervals into an ASI reference

---

Input: The name of a memory-region r, two strided intervals $s_1[l_1, u_1]$ and $s_2[l_2, u_2]$, number of bytes accessed *length*.

Output: An ASI reference for the sequence of *length* bytes starting at offsets $s_1[l_1, u_1] + s_2[l_2, u_2]$ in memory region r.

> **if** ($s_1[l_1, u_1]$ or $s_2[l_2, u_2]$ is a singleton) **then**
> > **return** SI2ASI$(r, s_1[l_1, u_1] +^{si} s_2[l_2, u_2], length)$
>
> **end if**
> **if** $s_1 \geq (u_2 - l_2 + length)$ **then**
> > baseSI $\leftarrow s_1[l_1, u_1]$
> > indexSI $\leftarrow s_2[l_2, u_2]$
>
> **else if** $s_2 \geq (u_1 - l_1 + length)$ **then**
> > baseSI $\leftarrow s_2[l_2, u_2]$
> > indexSI $\leftarrow s_1[l_1, u_1]$
>
> **else**
> > **return** SI2ASI$(r, s_1[l_1, u_1] +^{si} s_2[l_2, u_2], size$)
>
> **end if**
> $\langle$baseRef, exactRef$\rangle \leftarrow$ SI2ASI$(r, \text{baseSI}, \text{stride(baseSI)})$
> **if** exactRef is false **then**
> > **return** SI2ASI$(r, s_1[l_1, u_1] +^{si} s_2[l_2, u_2], length)$
>
> **else**
> > **return** concat(baseRef, SI2ASI("", indexSI, *length*))
>
> **end if**

---

elements in the row. Alg. 2 shows the algorithm to generate an ASI reference, when the set of offsets in a memory-region is expressed as a sum of two strided intervals as in [*base+index*]. Note that we could have used Alg. 1 by computing the abstract sum

($+^{si}$) of the two strided intervals. However, doing so results in a loss of precision because strided intervals can only represent a single stride exactly, and this would prevent us from recovering the structure of two-dimensional arrays. (In some circumstances, our implementation of ASI can recover the structure of arrays of 3 and higher dimensions.)

Alg. 2 works as follows: First, it determines which of the two strided intervals is used as the *base* because it is not always apparent from the representation of the operand. The strided interval that is used as the *base* should have a stride that is greater than the length of the interval in the other strided interval. Once the roles of the strided intervals are established, the algorithm generates the ASI reference for *base* followed by the ASI reference for *index*. In some cases, the algorithm cannot establish either of the strided intervals as the base. In such cases, the algorithm computes the abstract sum ($+^{si}$) of the two strided intervals and invokes SI2ASI.

Alg. 2 generates a richer set of ASI references than Alg. 1. For example, consider the indirect memory operand [eax+ecx] from a loop that traverses a two-dimensional array of type char[5][10]. Suppose that the value-set of ecx is $(\emptyset, 10[-50, -10])$, the value-set of eax is $(1[0, 9], \emptyset)$, and *length* is 1. For this example, the ASI reference that is generated is "AR[-50:-1]\5[0:9]\10[0:0]". That is, AR is accessed as an array of five 10-byte entities, and each 10-byte entity is accessed as an array of ten 1-byte entities.

5.2 Interpreting Indirect Memory-References

This section describes a lookup algorithm that finds the set of a-locs accessed by a memory operand. The algorithm is used to interpret pointer-dereference operations during VSA. For instance, consider the instruction "mov [eax], 10". During VSA, the lookup algorithm is used to determine the a-locs accessed by [eax] and the value-sets for the a-locs are updated accordingly. In [4], the algorithm to determine the set of a-locs for a given value-set is trivial because each memory-region in [4] consists of a linear list of a-locs generated by the Semi-Naïve approach. However, after ASI is performed, the structure of each memory-region is an ASI tree.

In [23], Ramalingam et al. present a lookup algorithm to retrieve the set of atoms for an ASI expression. However, their lookup algorithm is not appropriate for use in VSA because the algorithm assumes that the only ASI expressions that can arise during lookup are the ones that were used during the atomization phase. Unfortunately, this is not the case during VSA, for the following reasons:

- ASI is used as a heuristic. As will be discussed in §5.5, some data-access patterns that arise during VSA should be ignored during ASI.
- The executable can possibly access fields of those structures that have not yet been broken down into atoms. For example, the initial round of ASI, which is based on a-locs recovered by the Semi-Naïve approach, will not include accesses to the fields of structures. However, the first round of VSA may access structure fields.

We will use the tree shown in Fig. 4(b) to describe the lookup algorithm. Every node in the tree is given a unique name (shown within parentheses). The following terms are used in describing the lookup algorithm:

- `NodeFrag` is a descriptor for a part of an ASI tree node and is denoted by a triple $\langle name, start, length \rangle$, where $name$ is the name of the ASI tree node, $start$ is the starting offset within the ASI tree node, and $length$ is the length of the fragment.
- `NodeFragList` is an ordered list of `NodeFrag` descriptors, $[nd_1, nd_2, \ldots, nd_n]$. A `NodeFragList` represents a contiguous set of offsets in an aggregate. For example, $[\langle a_3, 2, 2 \rangle, \langle a_4, 0, 2 \rangle]$ represents the offsets $2 . . 5$ of node i_1; offsets $2 . . 3$ come from $\langle a_3, 2, 2 \rangle$ and offsets $4 . . 5$ come from $\langle a_4, 0, 2 \rangle$.

The lookup algorithm traverses the ASI tree, guided by the ASI reference for the given memory operand. First, the memory operand is converted into an ASI reference using the algorithm described in §5.1, and the resulting ASI reference is parsed into a list of ASI operations. There are three kinds of ASI operations: (1) `GetChildren`(*aloc*), (2) `GetRange`(*start, end*), and (3) `GetArrayElements`(*m*). For example, the list of ASI operations for "p[0:39]\10[0:1]" is [`GetChildren(p)`, `GetRange(0,39)`, `GetArrayElements(10)`, `GetRange(0,1)`]. Each operation takes a `NodeFragList` as argument and returns a set of `NodeFragList` values. The operations are performed from left to right. The argument of each operation comes from the result of the operation that is immediately to its left. The a-locs that are accessed are all the a-locs in the final set of `NodeFrag` descriptors.

The `GetChildren`(*aloc*) operation returns a `NodeFragList` that contains `NodeFrag` descriptors corresponding to the children of the root node of the tree associated with the aggregate *aloc*.

`GetRange`(*start, end*) returns a `NodeFragList` that contains `NodeFrag` descriptors representing the nodes with offsets in the given range [*start : end*].

`GetArrayElements`(*m*) treats the given `NodeFragList` as an array of m elements and returns a set of `NodeFragList` lists. Each `NodeFragList` list represents an array element. There can be more than one `NodeFragList` for the array elements because an array can be split during the atomization phase and different parts of the array might be represented by different nodes.

The following examples illustrate traces of a few lookups.

Example 3. Lookup p[0:3]

$$[\langle i_1, 0, 40 \rangle]$$
`GetChildren(p)` $\Downarrow$
$$[\langle a_3, 0, 4 \rangle, \langle a_4, 0, 4 \rangle, \langle i_2, 0, 32 \rangle]$$
`GetRange(0,3)` $\Downarrow$
$$[\langle a_3, 0, 4 \rangle]$$

`GetChildren(p)` returns the `NodeFragList` $[\langle a_3, 0, 4 \rangle, \langle a_4, 0, 4 \rangle, \langle i_2, 0, 32 \rangle]$. Applying `GetRange(0,3)` returns $[\langle a_3, 0, 4 \rangle]$ because that describes offsets $0 . . 3$ in the given `NodeFragList`. The a-loc that is accessed by p[0:3] is a_3.   □

Example 4. Lookup `p[0:39]\5[0:3]`

$$[\langle i_1, 0, 40 \rangle]$$

`GetChildren(p)` $\Downarrow$

$$[\langle a_3, 0, 4 \rangle, \langle a_4, 0, 4 \rangle, \langle i_2, 0, 32 \rangle]$$

`GetRange(0,39)` $\Downarrow$

$$[\langle a_3, 0, 4 \rangle, \langle a_4, 0, 4 \rangle, \langle i_2, 0, 32 \rangle]$$

`GetArrayElements(5)` $\Downarrow$

$$[\langle a_3, 0, 4 \rangle, \langle a_4, 0, 4 \rangle],$$
$$[\langle a_5, 0, 4 \rangle, \langle a_6, 0, 4 \rangle]$$

`GetRange(0,3)` $\Downarrow$

$$[\langle a_3, 0, 4 \rangle],$$
$$[\langle a_5, 0, 4 \rangle]$$

Let us look at `GetArrayElements(5)` because the other operations are similar to Ex. 3. `GetArrayElements(5)` is applied to $[\langle a_3, 0, 4 \rangle, \langle a_4, 0, 4 \rangle, \langle i_2, 0, 32 \rangle]$. The total length of the given `NodeFragList` is 40 and the number of required array elements is 5. Therefore, the size of the array element is 8. Intuitively, the operation unrolls the given `NodeFragList` and creates a `NodeFragList` for every unique n-byte sequence starting from the left, where n is the length of the array element. In this example, the unrolled `NodeFragList` is $[\langle a_3, 0, 4 \rangle, \langle a_4, 0, 4 \rangle, \langle a_5, 0, 4 \rangle, \langle a_6, 0, 4 \rangle, \ldots, \langle a_5, 0, 4 \rangle, \langle a_6, 0, 4 \rangle]$. The set of unique 8-byte `NodeFragList`s has two ordered lists: $\{[\langle a_3, 0, 4 \rangle, \langle a_4, 0, 4 \rangle], [\langle a_5, 0, 4 \rangle, \langle a_6, 0, 4 \rangle]\}$.   □

Partial updates to a-locs. The abstract transformers in VSA are prepared to perform partial updates to a-locs (i.e., updates to *parts* of an a-loc) because `NodeFrag` elements in a `NodeFragList` may refer to parts of an ASI tree node. Consider "`p[0:1]` = `0x10`".[6] The lookup operation for `p[0:1]` returns $[\langle a_3, 0, 2 \rangle]$, where $\langle a_3, 0, 2 \rangle$ refers to the first two bytes of a_3. An abstract transformer that "gives up" (because only part of a_3 is affected) and sets the value-set of a_3 to $\top$ in such cases would lead to imprecise results.

The value-set domain (see §4.1, [24]) provides bit-wise operations such as bit-wise and ($\&^{vs}$), bit-wise or ($|^{vs}$), left shift ($\ll^{vs}$), right shift ($\gg^{vs}$), etc. We use these operations to adjust the value-set associated with an a-loc when a partial update has to be performed during VSA. Assuming that the underlying architecture is little-endian, the abstract transformer for "`p[0:1]` = `0x10`" updates the value-set associated with a_3 as follows:

$$\mathsf{ValueSet}'(a_3) = (\mathsf{ValueSet}(a_3) \ \&^{vs} \ 0\mathrm{xffff0000}) \ |^{vs} \ (0\mathrm{x10}).$$

5.3   Hierarchical A-Locs

The iteration of ASI and VSA can over-refine the memory-regions. For instance, suppose that the 4-byte a-loc a_3 in Fig. 4(b) used in some round i is partitioned into two 2-byte a-locs, namely, $a_3.0$, and $a_3.2$ in round $i + 1$. This sort of over-refinement can affect the results of VSA; in general, because of the properties of strided-intervals, a 4-byte value-set reconstructed from two adjacent 2-byte a-locs can be less precise than

---

[6] Numbers that start with "0x" are in C hexadecimal format.

if the information was retrieved from a 4-byte a-loc. For instance, suppose that at some instruction S, a_3 holds either 0x100000 or 0x110001. In round i, this information is exactly represented by the 4-byte strided interval 0x10001[0x100000, 0x110001] for a_3. On the other hand, the same set of numbers can only be over-approximated by two 2-byte strided intervals, namely, 1[0x0000, 0x0001] for a_3.0, and 0x1[0x10,0x11] for a_3.2 (for a little-endian machine). Consequently, if a 4-byte read of a_3 in round $i + 1$ is handled by reconstituting a_3's value from a_3.0 and a_3.2, the result would be less precise:

$$\text{ValueSet}(a_3) = (\text{ValueSet}(a_3.2) \ll^{vs} 16)|^{vs}\text{ValueSet}(a_3.0)$$
$$= \{0x100000, 0x100001, 0x110000, 0x110001\}$$
$$\supset \{0x100000, 0x110001\}.$$

We avoid the effects of over-refinement by keeping track of the value-sets for a-loc a_3 as well as a-locs a_3.0 and a_3.2 in round $i + 1$. Whenever any of a_3, a_3.0, and a_3.2 is updated during round $i + 1$, the overlapping a-locs are updated as well. For example, if a_3.0 is updated then the first two bytes of the value-set of a-loc a_3 are also updated (for a little-endian machine). For a 4-byte read of a_3, the value-set returned would be 0x10001[0x100000, 0x110001].

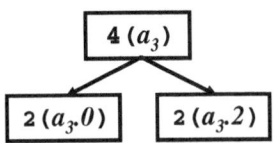

Fig. 5. Hierarchical a-locs

In general, if an a-loc a of length ≤ 4 gets partitioned into a sequence of a-locs $[a_1, a_2, \ldots, a_n]$ during some round of ASI, in the subsequent round of VSA, we use a as well as $\{a_1, a_2, \ldots, a_n\}$. We also remember the parent-child relationship between a and the a-locs in $\{a_1, a_2, \ldots, a_n\}$ so that we can update a whenever any of the a_i is updated during VSA and vice versa. In our example, the ASI tree used for round $i + 1$ of VSA is identical to the tree in Fig. 4(b), except that the node corresponding to a_3 is replaced with the tree shown in Fig. 5.

One of the sources of over-refinement is the use of union types in the program. The use of hierarchical a-locs allows at least some degree of precision to be retained in the presence of unions.

5.4 Convergence

The first round of VSA uncovers memory accesses that are not explicit in the program, which allows ASI to refine the a-locs for the next round of VSA, which may produce more precise value-sets because it is based on a better set of a-locs. Similarly, subsequent rounds of VSA can uncover more memory accesses, and hence allow ASI to refine the a-locs. The refinement of a-locs cannot go on indefinitely because, in the worst case, an a-loc can only be partitioned into a sequence of 1-byte chunks. However, in most cases, the refinement process converges before the worst-case partitioning occurs. Also, the set of targets that VSA determines for indirect function-calls and indirect jumps may change when the set of a-locs (and consequently, their value-sets) changes between successive rounds. This process cannot go on indefinitely because the set of a-locs cannot change between successive rounds forever. Therefore, the iteration process converges when the set of a-locs, and the set of targets for indirect function calls and indirect jumps does not change between successive rounds.

5.5   Pragmatics

ASI takes into account the accesses and data transfers involving memory, and finds a partition of the memory-regions that is consistent with these transfers. However, from the standpoint of accuracy of VSA and its clients, it is not always beneficial to take into account all possible accesses:

– VSA might obtain a very conservative estimate for the value-set of a register (say R). For instance, the value-set for R could be ⊤, meaning that register R can possibly hold all addresses and numbers. For a memory operand [R], we do not want to generate ASI references that refer to each memory-region as an array of 1-byte elements.
– Some compilers initialize the local stack frame with a known value to aid in debugging uninitialized variables at runtime. For instance, some versions of the Microsoft Visual Studio compiler initialize all bytes of a local stack frame with the value 0xC. The compiler might do this initialization by using a memcpy. Generating ASI references that mimic memcpy would cause the memory-region associated with this procedure to be broken down into an array of 1-byte elements, which is not desirable.

To deal with such cases, some options are provided to tune the analysis:

– The user can supply an integer threshold. If the number of memory locations that are accessed by a memory operand is above the threshold, no ASI reference is generated.
– The user can supply a set of instructions for which ASI references should not be generated. One possible use of this option is to suppress memcpy-like instructions.
– The user can supply explicit references to be used during ASI.

In our experiments, we only used the integer-threshold option (which was set to 500).

6   Experiments

In this section, we present the results of our preliminary experiments, which were designed to answer the following questions:

1. How do the a-locs identified by abstraction refinement compare with the program's debugging information? This provides insight into the usefulness of the a-locs recovered by our algorithm for a human analyst.
2. How much more useful for static analysis are the a-locs recovered by an abstract-interpretation-based technique when compared to the a-locs recovered by purely local techniques?

6.1   Comparison of A-Locs with Program Variables

To measure the quality of the a-locs identified by the abstraction-refinement algorithm, we used a set of C++ benchmarks collected from [1] and [22]. The characteristics of the benchmarks are shown in Tab. 1. The programs in Tab. 1 make heavy use of inheritance and virtual functions, and hence are a challenging set of examples for the algorithm.

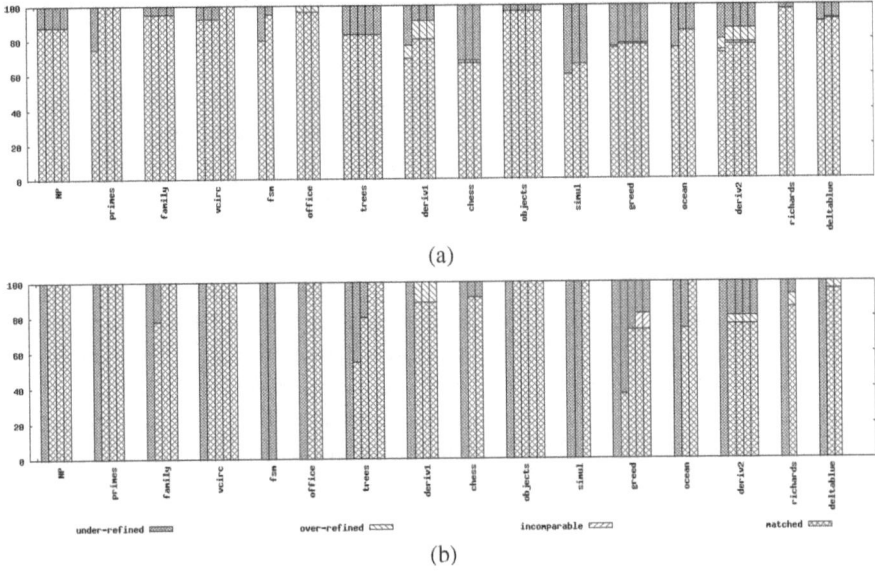

(a)

(b)

under-refined ▨   over-refined ⊠   incomparable ⊠   matched ⊠

Fig. 6. Breakdown (as percentages) of how a-locs matched with program variables: (a) local variables, and (b) fields of heap-allocated data-structures

We compiled the set of programs shown in Tab. 1 using the Microsoft VC 6.0 compiler with debugging information, and ran the a-loc recovery algorithm on the executables produced by the compiler until the results converged. After each round of ASI, for each program variable v present in the debugging information, we compared v with the structure identified by our algorithm (which did *not* use the debugging information), and classified v into one of the following categories:

- Variable v is classified as *matched* if the a-loc-recovery algorithm correctly identified the size and the offsets of v in the corresponding memory-region.
- Variable v is classified as *over-refined* if the a-loc-recovery algorithm partitioned v into smaller a-locs. For instance, a 4-byte `int` that is partitioned into an array of four `char` elements is classified as over-refined.
- Variable v is *under-refined* if the a-loc-recovery algorithm identified v to be a part of a larger a-loc. For instance, if the algorithm failed to partition a struct into its constituent fields, the fields of the struct are classified as under-refined.
- Variable v is classified as *incomparable* if v does not fall into one of the above categories.

The results of the classification process for the local variables and fields of heap-allocated data structures are shown in Fig. 6(a) and Fig. 6(b), respectively. The leftmost column for each program shows the results for the a-locs recovered using the Semi-Naïve approach, and the rightmost bar shows the results for the final round of the abstraction-refinement algorithm.

On average, our technique is successful in identifying correctly over 88% of the local variables and over 89% of the fields of heap-allocated objects (and was 100%

correct for fields of heap-allocated objects in almost half of the examples). In contrast, the Semi-Naïve approach recovered 83% of the local variables, but 0% of the fields of heap-allocated objects.

Table 1. C++ Examples

	Insts	Procs	Mallocs
NP	252	5	2
primes	294	9	1
family	351	9	6
vcirc	407	14	1
fsm	502	13	1
office	592	22	4
trees	1299	29	10
deriv1	1369	38	16
chess	1662	41	24
objects	1739	47	5
simul	1920	60	2
greed	1945	47	1
ocean	2552	61	13
deriv2	2639	41	58
richards	3103	74	23
deltablue	5371	113	26

Fig. 6(a) and Fig. 6(b) show that for some programs the results improve as more rounds of analysis are carried out. In most of the programs, only one round of ASI was required to identify all the fields of heap-allocated data structures correctly. In some of the programs, however, it required more than one round to find all the fields of heap-allocated data-structures. Those programs that required more than one round of ASI-VSA iteration used a chain of pointers to link structs of different types, as discussed in §5.

Most of the example programs do not have structures that are declared local to a procedure. This is the reason why the Semi-Naïve approach identified a large fraction of the local variables correctly. The programs primes and fsm have structures that are local to a procedure. As shown in Fig. 6(a), our approach identifies more local variables correctly for these examples.

6.2 Usefulness of the A-Locs for Static Analysis

The aim of this experiment was to evaluate the quality of the variables and values discovered as a platform for performing additional static analysis. In particular, because resolution of indirect operands is a fundamental primitive that essentially any subsequent analysis would need, the experiment measured how well we can resolve indirect memory operands not based on global address or stack-frame offsets (e.g., accesses to arrays and heap-allocated data objects). We ran several rounds of VSA on the collection of commonly used Windows executables listed in Tab. 2, as well as the set of benchmarks from Tab. 1. For the programs in Tab. 1, we ran VSA-ASI iteration until convergence. For the programs in Tab. 2, we limited the number of VSA-ASI rounds to at most three. Round 1 of VSA performs its analysis using the a-locs recovered by the Semi-Naïve approach; the final round of VSA uses the a-locs recovered by the abstraction-refinement algorithm. After the first and final rounds of VSA, we labeled each memory operand as follows:

- A memory operand is *untrackable* if the size of all the a-locs accessed by the memory operand is greater than 4 bytes, or if the value-set associated with the address expression of the memory operand is $\top$.
- A memory operand is *weakly-trackable* if the size of *some* a-loc accessed by the memory operand is less than or equal to 4 bytes, and the value-set associated with the address expression of the memory operand is not $\top$.

– A memory operand is *strongly-trackable* if the size of *all* the a-locs accessed by the memory operand is less than or equal to 4 bytes, and the value-set associated with the address expression of the memory operand is not $\top$.

Recall that VSA can track value-sets for a-locs that are less than or equal to 4 bytes, but reports that the value-set for a-locs greater than 4 bytes is $\top$. Therefore, untrackable memory operands are the ones for which VSA provides no useful information at all, and strongly-trackable memory operands are the ones for which VSA definitely provides useful information. For a weakly-trackable memory operand, VSA provides some useful information if the operand is used to update the contents of memory; however, no useful information is obtained if the operand is used to read the contents of memory. For instance, if [eax] in "mov [eax], 10" is weakly-trackable, then VSA would have updated the value-set for those a-locs that were accessed by [eax] and were of size less than or equal to 4 bytes. However, if [eax] in "mov ebx, [eax]" is weakly-trackable, the value-set of ebx is set to $\top$ because at least one of the a-locs accessed by [eax] is $\top$; this situation is not different from the case when [eax] is untrackable. We refer to a memory operand that is used to read the contents of memory as a *use-operand*, and a memory operand that is used to update the contents of memory as a *kill-operand*.

Table 2. Windows Executables. (n is the number of VSA-ASI rounds.)

	Insts	Procs	Mallocs	n	Time
mplayer2	14270	172	0	2	0h 11m
smss	43034	481	0	3	2h 8m
print	48233	563	17	3	0h 20m
doskey	48316	567	16	3	2h 4m
attrib	48785	566	17	3	0h 23m
routemon	55586	674	6	3	2h 28m
cat	57505	688	24	3	0h 54m
ls	60543	712	34	3	1h 10m

In Tab. 3, the "Weakly-Trackable Kills" column shows the fraction of kill-operands that were weakly-trackable during the first and final rounds of the abstraction refinement algorithm, and the "Strongly-Trackable Uses" column shows the fraction of use-operands that were strongly-trackable during the first and final round of the algorithm. In the table, we have classified memory operands as either *direct* or *indirect*. A *direct* memory operand is a memory operand that uses a global address or stack-frame offset. An *indirect* memory operand is a memory operand that does not use a global address or a stack-frame offset (e.g., a memory operand that accesses an array or a heap-allocated data object).

Both the Semi-Naïve approach and our abstract-interpretation-based a-loc-recovery algorithm provide good results for direct memory operands. However, the results for indirect memory operands are substantially better with the abstraction-interpretation-based method. For the set of C++ programs from Tab. 1, the results of VSA improve at 50% to 100% of the indirect kill-operands, and at 7% to 100% of the indirect use-operands. Similarly, for the Windows executables from Tab. 2, the results of VSA improve at 4% (routemon: 7% → 11%) to 39% (mplayer2: 12% → 51%) of the indirect kill-operands, and up to 8% (attrib, print: 4% → 12%, 6% → 14%) of the indirect use-operands.

We were surprised to find that the Semi-Naïve approach was able to provide a small amount of useful information for indirect memory operands. For instance, trees,

Table 3. Fraction of memory operands that are trackable after VSA. The number in parenthesis shows the number of rounds (n) of VSA-ASI iteration for each executable. (For Windows executables, the maximum number of rounds was set to 3.) **Boldface** and ***bold-italics*** in the Indirect columns indicate the maximum and minimum improvements, respectively.

	Weakly-Trackable Kills (%)				Strongly-Trackable Uses (%)			
	Indirect		Direct		Indirect		Direct	
Round	1	n	1	n	1	n	1	n
NP (4)	**0**	**100**	100	100	**0**	**100**	100	100
primes (4)	**0**	**100**	100	100	0	83	100	100
family (4)	**0**	**100**	100	100	**0**	**100**	100	100
vcirc (5)	**0**	**100**	100	100	**0**	**100**	100	100
fsm (2)	*0*	*50*	100	100	0	29	98	100
office (3)	**0**	**100**	100	100	**0**	**100**	100	100
trees (5)	10	100	98	100	25	61	96	100
deriv1 (4)	**0**	**100**	97	99	0	77	98	98
chess (3)	0	60	99	99	0	25	100	100
objects (5)	**0**	**100**	100	100	0	94	100	100
simul (3)	**0**	**100**	71	100	0	38	57	100
greed (5)	*3*	*53*	99	100	3	10	98	98
ocean (3)	9	90	99	100	6	42	98	100
deriv2 (5)	**0**	**100**	100	100	0	97	95	100
richards (2)	0	68	100	100	*0*	*7*	99	99
deltablue (3)	1	57	99	100	0	16	99	99
mplayer2 (2)	**12**	**51**	89	97	**8**	**8**	89	92
smss (3)	9	19	92	98	1	4	84	90
print (3)	2	22	92	99	6	14	89	92
doskey (3)	2	17	92	97	5	7	79	86
attrib (3)	7	24	93	98	4	12	86	90
routemon (3)	*7*	*11*	93	97	1	2	81	86
cat (3)	12	22	93	97	1	4	79	84
ls (3)	11	23	94	98	1	4	84	88

`greed`, `ocean`, `deltablue`, and all the Windows executables have a non-zero percentage of trackable memory operands. On closer inspection, we found that these indirect memory operands access local or global variables that are also accessed directly elsewhere in the program. (In source-level terms, the variables are accessed both directly and via pointer indirection.) For instance, a local variable `v` of procedure `P` that is passed by reference to procedure `Q` will be accessed directly in `P` and indirectly in `Q`.

Several sources of imprecision in VSA prevent us from obtaining useful information at all of the indirect memory operands. One such source of imprecision is widening [10]. VSA uses a widening operator during abstract interpretation to accelerate fixpoint computation. Due to widening, VSA may fail to find non-trivial bounds for registers that are used as indices in indirect memory operands. These indirect memory operands are labeled as untrackable. The fact that the VSA domain is non-relational amplifies this problem. (To a limited extent, we overcome the lack of relational information by obtaining relations among x86 registers from an additional analysis called affine-relation analysis. See §5 in [4] for details.) Note that the widening problem is orthogonal to the issue of finding the correct set of variables. Even if our a-loc recovery algorithm recovers all the variables correctly, imprecision due to widening persists. (Recently, using ideas from [7] and [13], we have implemented techniques to reduce the undesirable effects of widening, but do not yet have numbers to report.)

Nevertheless, the results are encouraging. For the Windows executables, the number of memory operands that have useful information in round n is 2 to 4 *times* the number of memory operands that have useful information in round 1; i.e., the results of static analysis do significantly improve when a-locs recovered by the abstraction-interpretation-based algorithm are used in the place of a-locs recovered from purely local techniques. Our initial experiments show that the techniques are also feasible in terms of running time.

7   Related Work

In [18], Miné describes a combined data-value and points-to analysis that, at each program point, partitions the variables in the program into a collection of cells according to how they are accessed, and computes an over-approximation of the values in these cells. Miné's algorithm is similar in flavor to the VSA-ASI iteration scheme in that Miné finds his own variable-like quantities for static analysis. However, Miné's partitioning algorithm is still based on the set of variables in the program (which our algorithm assumes will not be available). His implementation does not support analysis of programs that use heap-allocated storage. Moreover, his techniques are not able to infer from loop access patterns—as ASI can—that an unstructured cell (e.g., unsigned char z[32] has internal array substructures, (e.g., int y[8]; or struct {int a[3]; int b;} x[2];).

In [18], cells correspond to variables. The algorithm assumes that each variable is disjoint and is not aware of the relative positions of the variables. Instead, his algorithm issues an alarm whenever an indirect access goes beyond the end of a variable. Because our abstraction of memory is in terms of memory-regions (which can be thought of as cells for entire activation records), we are able to interpret an out-of-bound access precisely in most cases. For instance, suppose that two integers a and b are laid out next to each other. Consider the sequence of C statements "p = &a; *(p+1) = 10;". For the access *(p+1), Miné's implementation issues an out-of-bounds access alarm, whereas we are able to identify that it is a write to variable b. (Such out-of-bounds accesses occur commonly during VSA because the a-loc-recovery algorithm can split a single source-level variable into more than one a-loc, e.g., array p in Ex. 2.)

Other work on analyzing memory accesses in executables. Previous techniques deal with memory accesses very conservatively; generally, if a register is assigned a value from memory, it is assumed to take on any value. For instance, although the basic goal of the algorithm proposed by Debray et al. [11] is similar to that of VSA, their goal is to find an over-approximation of the set of values that each *register* can hold at each program point; for us, it is to find an over-approximation of the set of values that each (abstract) data object can hold at each program point, where data objects include *global, stack-allocated, and heap-allocated memory locations* in addition to registers. In the analysis proposed by Debray et al., a set of addresses is approximated by a set of congruence values: they keep track of only the low-order bits of addresses. However, unlike VSA, their algorithm does not make any effort to track values that are not in registers. Consequently, it loses a great deal of precision whenever there is a load from memory.

Cifuentes and Fraboulet [8] give an algorithm to identify an intraprocedural slice of an executable by following the program's use-def chains. However, their algorithm also makes no attempt to track values that are not in registers, and hence cuts short the slice when a load from memory is encountered.

The two pieces of work that are most closely related to VSA are the algorithm for data-dependence analysis of assembly code of Amme et al. [2] and the algorithm for pointer analysis on a low-level intermediate representation of Guo et al. [14]. The algorithm of Amme et al. performs only an *intra*procedural analysis, and it is not clear whether the algorithm fully accounts for dependences between memory locations. The algorithm of Guo et al. [14] is only partially flow-sensitive: it tracks registers in a flow-sensitive manner, but treats memory locations in a flow-insensitive manner. The algorithm uses partial transfer functions [31] to achieve context-sensitivity. The transfer functions are parameterized by "unknown initial values" (UIVs); however, it is not clear whether the the algorithm accounts for the possibility of called procedures corrupting the memory locations that the UIVs represent.

Several platforms have been created for manipulating executables in the presence of additional information, such as source code, symbol-table information, and debugging information, including ATOM [29] and EEL [17]. Bergeron et al. [6] present a static-analysis technique to check if an executable with debugging information adheres to a user-specified security policy.

Rival [26] presents an analysis that uses abstract interpretation to check whether the assembly code of a program produced by a compiler possesses the same safety properties as the source code. The analysis assumes that source code and debugging information is available. First, the source code and the assembly code of the program are analyzed. Next, the debugging information is used to map the results of assembly-code analysis back to the source code. If the results for the corresponding program points in source and assembly code are compatible, then the assembly code possesses the same safety properties as the source code.

Identification of structures. Aggregate structure identification was devised by Ramalingam et al. to partition aggregates according to a Cobol program's memory-access patterns [23]. A similar algorithm was devised by Eidorff et al. [12] and incorporated in the AnnoDomani system. The original motivation for these algorithms was the Year 2000 problem; they provided a way to identify how date-valued quantities could flow through a program.

Mycroft [20] gave a unification-based algorithm for performing type reconstruction; for instance, when a register is dereferenced with an offset of 4 to perform a 4-byte access, the algorithm infers that the register holds a pointer to an object that has a 4-byte field at offset 4. The type system uses disjunctive constraints when multiple type reconstructions from a single usage pattern are possible. However, Mycroft's algorithm has several weaknesses. For instance, Mycroft's algorithm is unable to recover information about the sizes of arrays that are identified. Although not described in this paper, our implementation incorporates a third analysis phase, called affine-relation analysis (ARA) [4,16,19], that, for each program point, identifies the affine relations that hold among the values of registers. In essence, this provides information about induction-variable relationships in loops, which can allow VSA to recover information about array sizes when one register is used to sweep through an array under the control of a second loop-index register.

Decompilation. Past work on decompiling assembly code to a high-level language [9] is also peripherally related to our work. However, the decompilers reported in the literature are somewhat limited in what they are able to do when translating assembly code to high-level code. For instance, Cifuentes's work [9] primarily concentrates on recovery of (a) expressions from instruction sequences, and (b) control flow. We believe that decompilers would benefit from the memory-access-analysis method described in this paper, which can be performed prior to decompilation proper, to recover information about numeric values, address values, physical types, and definite links from objects to virtual-function tables [5].

References

1. G. Aigner and U. Hölzle. Eliminating virtual function calls in C++ programs. In *European Conf. on Object-Oriented Programming*, 1996.
2. W. Amme, P. Braun, E. Zehendner, and F. Thomasset. Data dependence analysis of assembly code. *Int. J. Parallel Proc.*, 2000.
3. W. Backes. *Programmanalyse des XRTL Zwischencodes*. PhD thesis, Universitaet des Saarlandes, 2004. (In German.).
4. G. Balakrishnan and T. Reps. Analyzing memory accesses in x86 executables. In *Comp. Construct.*, 2004.
5. G. Balakrishnan and T. Reps. Recency-abstraction for heap-allocated storage. In *SAS*, 2006.
6. J. Bergeron, M. Debbabi, J. Desharnais, M.M. Erhioui, Y. Lavoie, and N. Tawbi. Static detection of malicious code in executable programs. *Int. J. of Req. Eng.*, 2001.
7. F. Bourdoncle. Efficient chaotic iteration strategies with widenings. In *Int. Conf. on Formal Methods in Prog. and their Appl.*, 1993.
8. C. Cifuentes and A. Fraboulet. Intraprocedural static slicing of binary executables. In *ICSM*, pages 188–195, 1997.
9. C. Cifuentes, D. Simon, and A. Fraboulet. Assembly to high-level language translation. In *ICSM*, 1998.
10. P. Cousot and R. Cousot. Abstract interpretation: A unified lattice model for static analysis of programs by construction or approximation of fixpoints. In *POPL*, 1977.
11. S.K. Debray, R. Muth, and M. Weippert. Alias analysis of executable code. In *POPL*, 1998.
12. P.H. Eidorff, F. Henglein, C. Mossin, H. Niss, M.H. Sørensen, and M. Tofte. Anno Domini: From type theory to year 2000 conversion tool. In *POPL*, 1999.
13. D. Gopan and T. Reps. Lookahead widening. In *CAV*, 2006.
14. B. Guo, M.J. Bridges, S. Triantafyllis, G. Ottoni, E. Raman, and D.I. August. Practical and accurate low-level pointer analysis. In *Int. Symp. on Code Gen. and Opt.*, 2005.

15. IDAPro disassembler, http://www.datarescue.com/idabase/.
16. A. Lal, T. Reps, and G. Balakrishnan. Extended weighted pushdown systems. In *CAV*, 2005.
17. J.R. Larus and E. Schnarr. EEL: Machine-independent executable editing. In *PLDI*, 1995.
18. A. Miné. Field-sensitive value analysis of embedded C programs with union types and pointer arithmetics. In *LCTES*, 2006.
19. M. Müller-Olm and H. Seidl. Analysis of modular arithmetic. In *ESOP*, 2005.
20. A. Mycroft. Type-based decompilation. In *ESOP*, 1999.
21. R. O'Callahan and D. Jackson. Lackwit: A program understanding tool based on type inference. In *Int. Conf. on Softw. Eng.*, 1997.
22. H. Pande and B. Ryder. Data-flow-based virtual function resolution. In *SAS*, 1996.
23. G. Ramalingam, J. Field, and F. Tip. Aggregate structure identification and its application to program analysis. In *POPL*, 1999.
24. T. Reps, G. Balakrishnan, and J. Lim. Intermediate representation recovery from low-level code. In *PEPM*, 2006.
25. T. Reps, G. Balakrishnan, J. Lim, and T. Teitelbaum. A next-generation platform for analyzing executables. In *APLAS*, 2005.
26. X. Rival. Abstract interpretation based certification of assembly code. In *VMCAI*, 2003.
27. M. Sharir and A. Pnueli. Two approaches to interprocedural data flow analysis. In *Program Flow Analysis: Theory and Applications*, chapter 7, pages 189–234. Prentice-Hall, 1981.
28. M. Siff and T.W. Reps. Program generalization for software reuse: From C to C++. In *Found. of Softw. Eng.*, 1996.
29. A. Srivastava and A. Eustace. ATOM - A system for building customized program analysis tools. In *PLDI*, 1994.
30. A. van Deursen and L. Moonen. Type inference for COBOL systems. In *WCRE*, 1998.
31. R.P. Wilson and M.S. Lam. Efficient context-sensitive pointer analysis for C programs. In *PLDI*, 1995.

Verifying Compensating Transactions*

Michael Emmi and Rupak Majumdar

UC Los Angeles
{mje,rupak}@cs.ucla.edu

Abstract. We study the safety verification problem for business-process orchestration languages with respect to regular properties. Business transactions involve long-running distributed interactions between multiple partners which must appear as a single atomic action. This illusion of atomicity is maintained through programmer-specified *compensation actions* that get run to undo previous actions when certain parts of the transaction fail to finish. Programming languages for business process orchestration provide constructs for declaring compensation actions, which are co-ordinated by the run time system to provide the desired transactional semantics. The safety verification problem for business processes asks, given a program with programmer specified compensation actions and a regular language specifying "good" behaviors of the system, whether all observable action sequences produced by the program are contained in the set of good behaviors.

We show that the usual trace-based semantics for business process languages leads to an undecidable verification problem, but a tree-based semantics gives an algorithm that runs in time exponential in the size of the business process. Our constructions translate programs with compensations to tree automata with one memory.

1 Introduction

Long-running business processes involve hierarchies of interactive activities between possibly distributed partners whose execution must appear logically atomic to the environment. The long-running and interactive nature of business processes make traditional checkpointing and rollback mechanisms that guarantee transactional semantics [13] difficult or impossible to implement. For example, the long-running nature makes the performance penalties associated with locking unacceptable, and the interactive nature makes rollback impossible since some parts of the transaction (e.g., communications with external agents) are inherently impossible to undo automatically. Business processes therefore implement a weaker notion of atomicity based on *compensations*, programmer-specified actions that must be executed to semantically "undo" the effects of certain actions that cannot be undone automatically, should parts of the transaction fail to complete. A long-running transaction is structured as *sagas* [12],

---

* This research was sponsored in part by the grants NSF-CCF-0427202, NSF-CNS-0541606, and NSF-CCF-0546170.

B. Cook and A. Podelski (Eds.): VMCAI 2007, LNCS 4349, pp. 29–43, 2007.

a sequence of several smaller sub-transactions, each with an associated compensation. If one of the sub-transactions in the sequence aborts, the compensations associated with all committed subtransactions are executed in reverse order.

Flow composition or orchestration languages, such as WSCL [17], WSFL [18], BPML [2], and BPEL4WS [1], provide primitives for programming long-running transactions, including programmer-specified compensations and structured control flows. For example, BPEL4WS provides the `compensate` construct that can be used by the programmer to specify actions that must be taken if later actions fail. The formal semantics for these languages (or their core features) are given as extensions to process algebras with compensations (e.g., compensating CSP or cCSP) [6,5] or transaction algebras with compensation primitives (called the *sagas calculus*) [4]. One central issue is to develop automatic static analysis techniques to increase confidence in the correctness of complex business processes implemented in these languages [14]. For example, in a business process implementing an e-commerce application, it may be desirable to verify that no product is shipped before a credit check is performed, or that the user's account is credited if it is found later that the order cannot be fulfilled. In this paper, we present model checking algorithms for the automatic verification of *temporal safety properties* of flow composition languages with compensations. We take the automata theoretic approach and specify safety properties as *regular sets* of traces of observable actions. Then, the verification problem can be formulated as a *language containment* question: check that any trace that can be produced by the execution of a saga also belongs to the set of "good" behaviors prescribed by the specification.

Our starting point is the sagas calculus [4], although our results generalize to most other languages with similar core features. We show that the safety verification problem for programs in the sagas calculus and safety properties encoded as finite word automata is undecidable in the usual trace-based semantics [6,3]. On the other hand, perhaps surprisingly, the verification problem becomes decidable (in time exponential in the size of the sagas program) if we associate a *tree semantics* with the execution. The tree semantics exposes more structure on the sequence of observable actions by making the sequential or parallel operator at each intermediate step observable. For the tree semantics, we consider safety properties encoded as regular tree languages, rather than word languages. The key hurdle is that the tree language of a sagas program is not regular: this is intuitively clear since first, the compensations are dynamically pushed on to a (possibly unbounded) stack, and second, the actions on the execution path up to an abort are related to the compensation actions thereby requiring comparisons on sibling subtrees.

Our main technical tool consists of tree automata with one memory [7], that generalize finite tree automata by allowing a memory element which is built up as the automaton walks a tree bottom-up and which can be compared across children. Specifically, we show that the tree language of any program in the sagas language is accepted by a tree automaton with one memory. Tree automata with one memory generalize pushdown automata over words and tree automata with equality tests [8]. However, their emptiness problem is decidable [7], and they are closed under intersection with finite tree automata. Our construction, together with the above properties of tree automata with one memory, provides a decision procedure for the safety verification problem. While automatic model checking techniques for web services and business process applications have been proposed before [10,11,9], to the best of our knowledge, we provide the first automatic handling of compensation stacks.

2 Sagas with Compensation

A *saga* is a high-level description of the interaction between components for web services. The building blocks of sagas are atomic actions, which execute without communication from other services. In addition, to each atomic action is attached a (possibly null) *compensation*, which is executed if the action succeeds but a later action in the saga does not complete successfully. Sagas are then built from (compensated) atomic actions, sequential and parallel composition, nondeterministic choice, and nesting. The execution order for compensating actions is determined by interpreting each sequential composition operator in reverse.

More formally, given an alphabet Σ of atomic actions containing a special *null action* 0, and a set of variable names X, the set of *transaction terms* $\mathbb{T}^{\Sigma,X}$ *over Σ and X* is the smallest set which includes the *atomic terms* $a \div b$, for $a, b \in \Sigma$, the variables $x \in X$, and is closed under binary operators for sequential composition (;), parallel composition ($\|$), and nondeterministic choice ($\oplus$), and the unary saga-nesting operator $\{\!|\,\cdot\,|\!\}$. The binary expression $a \div b$ attaches to a the compensating action b. The operators $\|$ and $\oplus$ are commutative and associative, while the sequential operator ; is defined here to be left-associative. We refer to terms of the form $\{\!|t|\!\}$ as *transactions*, and use $\mathbb{T}^{\Sigma,X}_{\{\!|\cdot|\!\}}$ to denote the set of transactions. For an atomic action $a \in \Sigma$, we abbreviate $a \div 0$ with a.

A saga is given as a tuple $\mathcal{S} = \langle \Sigma, X, s_0, T \rangle$, where $T : X \rightarrow \mathbb{T}^{\Sigma,X}_{\{\!|\cdot|\!\}}$ maps variables to transactions, and $s_0 \in X$ determines *the top-level transaction*. We frequently abuse the notation and write $x = \{\!|t|\!\}$ in place of $T(x) = \{\!|t|\!\}$, and as Σ, X, and T are usually understood from the context, we often refer to a saga by its transaction variable s_0. We refer to any term of the form $\{\!|t|\!\} \neq s_0$ as a *nested saga* or *subtransaction*.

Example 1. The sagas calculus is capable of expressing realistic long-running business transactions. Suppose ACCEPTORDER, RESTOCK, FULFILLEDOK, CREDITCHECK, CREDITOK, BOOKCOURIER, CANCELCOURIER and PACKORDER are atomic actions with the obvious meanings, and consider the saga

$$Main = \{\!| \ (\text{ACCEPTORDER} \div \text{RESTOCK}); FulfillOrder; \text{FULFILLEDOK} \ |\!\}$$

$$FulfillOrder = \{\!| \ WarehousePackaging \ \| \ \text{CREDITCHECK}; \text{CREDITOK} \ |\!\}$$

$$WarehousePackaging =$$
$$\{\!| \ (\text{BOOKCOURIER} \div \text{CANCELCOURIER}) \| \text{PACKORDER} \ |\!\}.$$

Table 1. The formal semantics for a saga $\mathcal{S} = \langle \Sigma, X, s_0, T \rangle$. The symbols P and Q range over transaction terms, a and b range over the atomic actions of Σ, x ranges over the variables of X, $\alpha, \alpha', \alpha''$ range over observations, β, β', β'' range over compensation stacks, and $\square, \square_P, \square_Q$ range over outcomes.

(NULL)
$$\langle 0, \beta \rangle \xrightarrow{0} \langle \boxdot, \beta \rangle$$

(ATOM-S)
$$\langle a \div b, \beta \rangle \xrightarrow{a} \langle \boxdot, b; \beta \rangle$$

(ATOM-F)
$$\frac{\langle \beta, 0 \rangle \xrightarrow{\alpha} \langle \boxdot, 0 \rangle}{\langle a \div b, \beta \rangle \xrightarrow{\alpha} \langle \boxtimes, 0 \rangle}$$

(ATOM-A)
$$\frac{\langle \beta, 0 \rangle \xrightarrow{\alpha} \langle \boxtimes, 0 \rangle}{\langle a \div b, \beta \rangle \xrightarrow{\alpha} \langle \boxast, 0 \rangle}$$

(SEQ-S)
$$\frac{\langle P, \beta \rangle \xrightarrow{\alpha} \langle \boxdot, \beta'' \rangle \quad \langle Q, \beta'' \rangle \xrightarrow{\alpha'} \langle \boxdot, \beta' \rangle}{\langle P; Q, \beta \rangle \xrightarrow{\alpha; \alpha'} \langle \boxdot, \beta' \rangle}$$

(SEQ-FA)
$$\frac{\langle P, \beta \rangle \xrightarrow{\alpha} \langle \square, 0 \rangle \quad \square \in \{\boxtimes, \boxast, \overline{\boxtimes}, \overline{\boxast}\}}{\langle P; Q, \beta \rangle \xrightarrow{\alpha} \langle \square, 0 \rangle}$$

(PAR-S)
$$\frac{\langle P, 0 \rangle \xrightarrow{\alpha} \langle \boxdot, \beta' \rangle \quad \langle Q, 0 \rangle \xrightarrow{\alpha'} \langle \boxdot, \beta'' \rangle}{\langle P \| Q, \beta \rangle \xrightarrow{\alpha \| \alpha'} \langle \boxdot, \beta' \| \beta''; \beta \rangle}$$

(PAR-F)
$$\frac{\langle P, 0 \rangle \xrightarrow{\alpha} \langle \square_P, 0 \rangle \quad \square_P, \square_Q \in \{\boxtimes, \overline{\boxtimes}\}}{\langle Q, 0 \rangle \xrightarrow{\alpha'} \langle \square_Q, 0 \rangle \quad \langle \beta, 0 \rangle \xrightarrow{\alpha''} \langle \square_\beta, 0 \rangle}{\langle P \| Q, \beta \rangle \xrightarrow{(\alpha \| \alpha'); \alpha''} \langle \square_P \wedge \square_Q \wedge \mathsf{force}(\square_\beta), 0 \rangle}$$

(PAR-A)
$$\frac{\langle P, 0 \rangle \xrightarrow{\alpha} \langle \square_P, 0 \rangle \quad \square_P \in \{\boxast, \overline{\boxast}\}}{\langle Q, 0 \rangle \xrightarrow{\alpha'} \langle \square_Q, 0 \rangle \quad \square_Q \in \{\boxtimes, \boxast, \overline{\boxtimes}, \overline{\boxast}\}}{\langle P \| Q, \beta \rangle \xrightarrow{\alpha \| \alpha'} \langle \square_P \wedge \square_Q, 0 \rangle}$$

(NONDET)
$$\frac{\langle P, \beta \rangle \xrightarrow{\alpha} \langle \square, \beta' \rangle}{\langle P \oplus Q, \beta \rangle \xrightarrow{\alpha} \langle \square, \beta' \rangle}$$

(VAR)
$$\frac{\langle T(x), \beta \rangle \xrightarrow{\alpha} \langle \square, \beta' \rangle}{\langle x, \beta \rangle \xrightarrow{\alpha} \langle \square, \beta' \rangle}$$

(SAGA)
$$\frac{\langle P, 0 \rangle \xrightarrow{\alpha} \langle \square, \beta \rangle}{\{\!|P|\!\} \xrightarrow{\alpha} \square}$$

(SUB-S)
$$\frac{\langle P, 0 \rangle \xrightarrow{\alpha} \langle \boxdot, \beta' \rangle}{\langle \{\!|P|\!\}, \beta \rangle \xrightarrow{\alpha} \langle \boxdot, \beta'; \beta \rangle}$$

(SUB-F)
$$\frac{\langle P, 0 \rangle \xrightarrow{\alpha} \langle \boxtimes, 0 \rangle}{\langle \{\!|P|\!\}, \beta \rangle \xrightarrow{\alpha} \langle \boxdot, \beta \rangle}$$

(SUB-A)
$$\frac{\langle P, 0 \rangle \xrightarrow{\alpha} \langle \boxast, 0 \rangle}{\langle \{\!|P|\!\}, \beta \rangle \xrightarrow{\alpha} \langle \boxast, 0 \rangle}$$

(SUB-FORCED-F)
$$\frac{\langle P, 0 \rangle \xrightarrow{\alpha} \langle \overline{\boxtimes}, 0 \rangle \quad \langle \beta, 0 \rangle \xrightarrow{\alpha'} \langle \square, 0 \rangle}{\langle \{\!|P|\!\}, \beta \rangle \xrightarrow{\alpha; \alpha'} \langle \mathsf{force}(\square), 0 \rangle}$$

(SUB-FORCED-A)
$$\frac{\langle P, 0 \rangle \xrightarrow{\alpha} \langle \overline{\boxast}, 0 \rangle}{\langle \{\!|P|\!\}, \beta \rangle \xrightarrow{\alpha} \langle \overline{\boxast}, 0 \rangle}$$

(FORCED)
$$\frac{\langle \beta, 0 \rangle \xrightarrow{\alpha} \langle \square, 0 \rangle}{\langle P, \beta \rangle \xrightarrow{\alpha} \langle \mathsf{force}(\square), 0 \rangle}$$

The saga *Main* encodes a long running business transaction where an order is deemed a success upon the success of order placement, credit check, courier booking, and packaging. If some action were to fail during the transaction, then compensations would be run for the previously completed actions. For example, if the packaging were to fail after the credit check and courier booking had completed, then the courier booking would be canceled, and the order restocked.

The operational semantics of sagas are shown in Table 1. To reduce the number of rules, we define them up to structural congruence implied by the associativity of $;$, $\|$ and $\oplus$, the commutativity of $\|$ and $\oplus$, as well as the identities $0; P \equiv P; 0 \equiv P$ and $P \| 0 \equiv 0 \| P \equiv P$, for transaction terms P. The execution of a saga leads to an *outcome* which is either success, failure, or abortion, represented by the boxed symbols $\boxdot$, $\boxtimes$ and $\boxast$ respectively. The semantics is given for a fixed set of variables X and mapping $T : X \to \mathbb{T}^{\Sigma, X}_{\{\!|\cdot|\!\}}$ from variables to sub-transactions.

An *observation* is a term constructed from atomic actions and the sequential and parallel composition operators. The semantics of sagas is given by the rule (SAGA), whose consequent $\{\!|P|\!\} \xrightarrow{\alpha} \square$ specifies that the execution of transaction $\{\!|P|\!\}$ results in outcome $\square$, emitting the observation α. The semantics relation uses an auxiliary relation $\langle t, \beta \rangle \xrightarrow{\alpha} \langle \square, \beta' \rangle$ which dictates that the execution of term t results in the outcome $\square$, while the initial compensations β

Table 2. The composition operation $\wedge$

$\wedge$	$\boxdot$	$\boxtimes$	$\boxast$	$\overline{\boxtimes}$	$\overline{\boxast}$
$\boxdot$	$\boxdot$				
$\boxtimes$	—	$\boxtimes$			
$\boxast$	—	$\boxast$	$\boxast$		
$\overline{\boxtimes}$	—	$\boxtimes$	$\boxast$	$\overline{\boxtimes}$	
$\overline{\boxast}$	—	$\boxast$	$\boxast$	$\overline{\boxast}$	$\overline{\boxast}$

are destructively replaced by the compensations β'. The observation α in these relations describes the flow of control while t is executed.

The special symbols $\overline{\boxtimes}$ and $\overline{\boxast}$ are the forced failure and abortion outcomes, and result from failure or abortion in a parallel thread of execution. When a thread encounters failure, the entire transaction must subsequently fail. When each thread can complete its compensations, the resulting outcome is $\overline{\boxtimes}$; otherwise $\overline{\boxast}$ results. The (associative and commutative) binary operator $\wedge$ over the set $\{\boxdot, \boxtimes, \boxast, \overline{\boxtimes}, \overline{\boxast}\}$ determines the outcome of two branches executing in parallel. Its definition is given in Table 2 (since $\wedge$ is commutative, only half the table is displayed). The auxiliary function force : $\{\boxdot, \boxtimes, \boxast, \overline{\boxtimes}, \overline{\boxast}\} \rightarrow \{\overline{\boxtimes}, \overline{\boxast}\}$ is given by force($\boxdot$) = $\overline{\boxtimes}$, and force($\square$) = $\overline{\boxast}$, for $\square \in \{\boxtimes, \boxast, \overline{\boxtimes}, \overline{\boxast}\}$.

We briefly describe the operational semantics given in Table 1, for a more detailed discussion, see [4]. The rule (NULL) says that the null process never fails. The rules (ATOM-S), (ATOM-F), and (ATOM-A) deal with atomic action execution. If action a succeeds, rule (ATOM-S) installs the compensation b on the compensation stack. If a fails (rules (ATOM-F) and (ATOM-A)) when the currently installed compensation is β, then β should be executed. If all compensating actions of β execute successfully (as in (ATOM-F)), then the outcome for the term $a \div b$ is $\boxtimes$; if some compensating action of β fails (as in (ATOM-A)), then the outcome for the term $a \div b$ is $\boxast$.

The rules (SEQ-S) and (SEQ-FA) execute the sequential composition of two terms. The rule (PAR-S) declares the order in which compensations from parallel branches are executed. When the terms P and Q result in the compensations β' and β'', then the term $P\|Q$ results in the compensation $\beta'\|\beta''; \beta$, where β is the compensation for actions before $P\|Q$. The associated rules (PAR-F) and (PAR-A) deal with failure on parallel branches and failed compensation after failure on parallel branches respectively. Rule (VAR) executes the term bound to a variable by T, rule (NONDET) executes one branch of a nondeterministic choice, and (FORCED) allows a thread to fail due to the failed execution of another. The remaining rules specify the semantics of nested sagas.

Example 2. Consider the saga $\langle\{a, b, c, d, e, 0\}, \{s_0\}, s_0, T\rangle$ with $T(s_0) = \{[a \div b; c \div d\|e \div 0]\}$. That is, the action a occurs before c, while e occurs in parallel. If the action c were to fail, then the completed actions a, and possibly e, are to execute their compensations. Since e has a null compensation, only b would be executed. Figure 1 shows an execution of the saga, where c fails after a and e have both executed, and a's compensation b is run successfully.

$$
\cfrac{
\cfrac{\langle b \div 0, 0\rangle \xrightarrow{b} \langle\Box,0\rangle_1}{\langle c \div d, b\rangle \xrightarrow{b} \langle\boxtimes,0\rangle_2}
}{\langle a \div b; c \div d, 0\rangle \xrightarrow{a;b} \langle\boxtimes,0\rangle_3}
\qquad
\cfrac{\langle e \div 0, 0\rangle \xrightarrow{e} \langle\Box,0\rangle_1}{\langle e \div 0, 0\rangle \xrightarrow{e} \langle\boxtimes,0\rangle_3}
\qquad
\cfrac{\langle 0,0\rangle \xrightarrow{0} \langle\Box,0\rangle_6}{\langle 0,0\rangle \xrightarrow{0} \langle\boxtimes,0\rangle_5}
$$

$$\langle a \div b, 0\rangle \xrightarrow{a} \langle\Box, b\rangle_1$$

$$\langle a \div b; c \div d \,\|\, e \div 0, 0\rangle \xrightarrow{a;b\|e} \langle\boxtimes,0\rangle_{4,*}$$

$$\{a \div b; c \div d \,\|\, e \div 0\} \xrightarrow{a;b\|e} \boxtimes_7$$

Fig. 1. An execution of saga s_0 from example 2. The corresponding rules from table 1 are (1) ATOM-S, (2) ATOM-F, (3) SEQ-S, (4) PAR-F, (5) FORCED, (6) NULL, and (7) SAGA. An additional application of (NULL) is omitted in ($*$).

3   Trace Semantics

From the operational semantics of a saga and a fixed environment, we define a *trace language*, containing all sequences of observations that may be generated from an execution. The function trace defines this language by induction over the structure of observations, as generated by the execution of a saga, as

$$\mathsf{trace}(a) = \{a\}$$
$$\mathsf{trace}(t_1; t_2) = \mathsf{trace}(t_1) \circ \mathsf{trace}(t_2)$$
$$\mathsf{trace}(t_1 \| t_2) = \mathsf{trace}(t_1) \otimes \mathsf{trace}(t_2)$$

where $\circ$ and $\otimes$ denote the concatenation and interleaving composition of languages: $L_1 \circ L_2 = \{w_1 \cdot w_2 \mid w_1 \in L_1, w_2 \in L_2\}$ and $L_1 \otimes L_2 = \{x_1 y_1 \ldots x_k y_k \mid x_1 \ldots x_k \in L_1, y_1 \ldots y_k \in L_2\}$.

Let $\mathcal{S} = (\Sigma, X, s_0, T)$ be a saga. The *trace language* $L_W(s)$ of a variable $s \in X$ is defined as $\{\mathsf{trace}(\alpha) \mid \exists \Box. \{[T(s)]\} \xrightarrow{\alpha} \Box\}$. The trace language $L_W(\mathcal{S})$ of a saga $\mathcal{S}$ is the language $L_W(s_0)$. Clearly, the language $L_W(\mathcal{S})$ may not be regular.

Unfortunately, the trace language of sagas is unsuitable for verification since, as Theorem 1 shows, language inclusion in a regular set is undecidable. While we state the theorem for sagas, a similar theorem also holds for other compensable flow composition languages such as cCSP [6].

Theorem 1. *The language inclusion problem* $L_W(\mathcal{S}) \subseteq L_R$, *for an input saga* $\mathcal{S} = \langle \Sigma, X, s_0, T\rangle$ *and regular language* $L_R \subseteq \Sigma^*$, *is undecidable.*

Proof. We proceed by reduction from the halting problem of 2-counter machines, similarly to the proof for process algebras in [15]. Let $\mathcal{M}$ be a 2-counter machine with n numbered instructions: $\langle 1 : \mathbf{ins}_1\rangle \ldots \langle n-1 : \mathbf{ins}_{n-1}\rangle \langle n : \mathbf{halt}\rangle$ where each $\mathbf{ins}_k$ for $k \in \{1, \ldots, n-1\}$ is either $c_j = c_j + 1$; $\mathbf{goto}\ \ell$, or $c_j = c_j - 1$; $\mathbf{goto}\ \ell$, or $\mathbf{if}\ c_j = 0\ \mathbf{then\ goto}\ \ell\ \mathbf{else\ goto}\ \ell'$, for $j \in \{1, 2\}$. Furthermore, let $\Sigma = \{zero_k, inc_k, dec_k \mid k \in \{1, 2\}\} \cup \{0\}$, where $zero_k$, inc_k, and dec_k stand for zero-assertion, increment, and decrement actions, respectively, where we associate (in the obvious way) traces of $\mathcal{M}$ with Σ-sequences. We construct a saga $\mathcal{S}$, whose language is the Σ-sequences corresponding to traces of $\mathcal{M}$, irrespective of $\mathcal{M}$'s control location, and a finite state automaton $\mathcal{A}$, whose language is the

Σ-sequences corresponding to traces of $\mathcal{M}$, irrespective of $\mathcal{M}$'s counter values. With these constructions, the intersection $L_W(\mathcal{A}) \cap L(\mathcal{S})$ is the language of Σ-sequences corresponding to traces of $\mathcal{M}$.

We define $\mathcal{S}$ to be the saga $\langle \Sigma, X, s_0, T \rangle$, where $X = \{C_k, Z_k \mid k \in \{1,2\}\} \cup \{s_0\}$ are the variables of $\mathcal{S}$, s_0 is the top-level transaction, and T, mapping variables to transaction terms, is given by

$$\left. \begin{array}{l} Z_k \mapsto \{[(zero_k; Z_k) \oplus (inc_k; C_k; Z_k)]\} \\ C_k \mapsto \{[(inc_k \div dec_k; C_k; C_k)]\} \end{array} \right\} \text{ for } k \in \{1,2\}$$

and $s_0 \mapsto \{[(C_1^{m_1}; Z_1) \| (C_2^{m_2}; Z_2)]\}$. Intuitively, the transaction term $T(C_k)$ defines a state of $\mathcal{M}$ which attempts to decrease the value of counter k by one, the transaction term $T(Z_k)$ defines a state which holds the value of counter k at 0, and the term $T(s_0)$ defines a state in which the counter values start at m_1 and m_2 respectively. Finite traces of $\mathcal{S}$ exist, since any action may fail, and if C_k ever fails its compensating action of dec_k, then the entire transaction s_0 aborts. Notice that traces of $\mathcal{S}$ correspond to runs of a "stateless" $\mathcal{M}$, where every step could execute any instruction.

The finite state machine $\mathcal{A}$ over alphabet Σ has states $\{1, 2, \ldots, n+1\}$, one for each instruction, and a sink state $n+1$. The transitions are given by the instructions of $\mathcal{M}$ as follows. If instruction i is an increment (resp., decrement) of counter c_j followed by a move to ℓ, then $\mathcal{A}$ has a transition $\langle i, inc_j, \ell \rangle$ (resp., $\langle i, dec_j, \ell \rangle$). If i moves to ℓ when $c_j = 0$, and ℓ' otherwise, then $\mathcal{A}$ has the transitions $\langle i, zero_j, \ell \rangle$ and $\langle i, 0, \ell' \rangle$. Each state also has a self loop on the action 0. The automaton is completed by adding a transition $\langle k, \sigma, n+1 \rangle$ for each state k in which σ is otherwise not enabled (note that this construction induces a self loop $\langle n+1, \sigma, n+1 \rangle$ for all $\sigma \in \Sigma$). Every state of $\mathcal{A}$ is accepting, however since n has no enabled actions, the language of $\mathcal{A}$ is not universal. In particular, $\mathcal{A}$'s language does not include Σ-sequences whose (proper) prefixes correspond to halting computations of $\mathcal{M}$. Notice that the traces of $\mathcal{S}$ correspond to runs of a "memoryless" $\mathcal{M}$, where every step ignores the values of the counters.

It only remains to check that $L_W(\mathcal{S}) \not\subseteq L(\mathcal{A})$ if and only if $\mathcal{M}$ has a halting computation. First suppose that $L_W(\mathcal{S}) \not\subseteq L(\mathcal{A})$, and let $w \in L_W(\mathcal{S}) \setminus L(\mathcal{A})$. Since w is not accepted by $\mathcal{A}$, a prefix of w corresponds to a halting trace of $\mathcal{M}$ (recall that $\mathcal{A}$ must have moved to state n) consistent with $\mathcal{M}$'s control. Since w is accepted by $\mathcal{S}$, w also corresponds to a trace of $\mathcal{M}$ consistent with $\mathcal{M}$'s counter values. Thus $\mathcal{M}$ has a halting computation. On the other hand, if $\mathcal{M}$ has a halting computation then $\mathcal{A}$ rejects a Σ-sequence with a prefix corresponding to a halting trace of $\mathcal{M}$, which is a trace of $\mathcal{S}$ since the counter values are necessarily consistent; thus $L_W(\mathcal{S}) \not\subseteq L(\mathcal{A})$. Thus, the language inclusion problem $L_W(\mathcal{S}) \subseteq L(\mathcal{A})$ is undecidable. $\qquad \square$

4   Tree Semantics

In this section we give an alternative interpretation to the set of observations given by a saga. Instead of interpreting executions as flattened sequences of actions, we interpret them as trees where the actions become leaves, and the composition operators become internal nodes. We then give an automata-theoretic classification of a sagas by building tree automata which recognize the set of trees representing valid executions.

4.1   Yield Language of a Saga

Trees. A (ranked) alphabet is a tuple $\langle \mathcal{F}, \mathsf{ar} \rangle$ where $\mathcal{F}$ is a finite alphabet, and ar is a map, called *arity*, from $\mathcal{F}$ to $\mathbb{N}$. The set of symbols from $\mathcal{F}$ of arity k (i.e., $\{f \in \mathcal{F} \mid \mathsf{ar}(f) = k\}$) is denoted $\mathcal{F}_k$. The set of symbols of arity zero are called constants; arity one symbols (resp. two, k) are called unary (resp. binary, k-ary) symbols. In what follows, we assume $\mathcal{F}$ has at least one constant, i.e., $\mathcal{F}_0 \neq \emptyset$. For ease of notation we write $\mathcal{F}$, omitting ar, by assuming that the arity information is encoded into each symbol in $\mathcal{F}$.

A finite ordered tree t over a ranked alphabet $\mathcal{F}$ is a mapping from a prefix-closed set $\mathrm{dom}(t) \subseteq \mathbb{N}^*$ to $\mathcal{F}$, such that (1) each leaf is mapped to a constant: for all $p \in \mathrm{dom}(t)$, we have $t(p) \in \mathcal{F}_0$ iff $\{j \mid p \cdot j \in \mathrm{dom}(t)\} = \emptyset$; and (2) each internal node mapped to symbol $f \in \mathcal{F}_k$ has exactly k children numbered $1, \ldots, k$: for all $p \in \mathrm{dom}(t)$, if $t(p) \in \mathcal{F}_k$ and $k \geq 1$, then $\{j \mid p \cdot j \in \mathrm{dom}(t)\} = \{1, \ldots, k\}$. The set of all trees over alphabet $\mathcal{F}$ is denoted $\mathsf{Trees}(\mathcal{F})$. A set of trees is a *tree language*.

Yield Language. Fix the saga $\mathcal{S} = \langle \Sigma, X, s_0, T \rangle$, and let $\mathcal{F}$ be a ranked alphabet consisting of a constant symbol for each atomic action of Σ, as well as the binary symbols $\sigma_;$ and $\sigma_\|$.

Given an observation α from an execution of $\mathcal{S}$, the set $\mathsf{yield}(\alpha)$ of *yield trees* over the tree alphabet $\mathcal{F}$ is defined inductively as

$$\mathsf{yield}(a) = \{a\}$$
$$\mathsf{yield}(t_1; t_2) = \{\sigma_;(t_1', t_2') \mid t_1' \in \mathsf{yield}(t_1), t_2' \in \mathsf{yield}(t_2)\}$$
$$\mathsf{yield}(t_1 \| t_2) = \{\sigma_\|(t_1', t_2') \mid t_1' \in \mathsf{yield}(t_1), t_2' \in \mathsf{yield}(t_2)\}$$

where $\sigma(t_1, t_2)$ denotes the tree with a σ-labeled root whose left and right children are the roots of the trees t_1 and t_2 respectively, and a is an atomic action of Σ. Informally, a yield tree considers the term α as a finite ordered tree over the alphabet of atomic actions and the sequential and parallel compositions. The *yield language* of $\mathcal{S}$, denoted $L(\mathcal{S})$, is the set

$$L(\mathcal{S}) = \bigcup_{\{\![T(s_0)]\!\} \xrightarrow{\alpha} \square} \mathsf{yield}(\alpha).$$

Example 3. The yield language of the saga $s_0 = \{\![a \div b; c \div d \| e \div 0]\!\}$ from example 2, consisting of six trees, is shown in Figure 2.

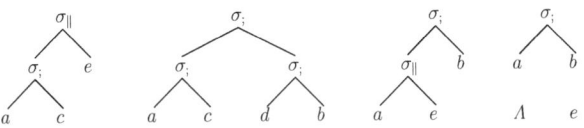

Fig. 2. The yield language of $\{[a \div b; c \div d \| e \div 0]\}$

4.2   Tree Automata with One Memory

Tree Automata. A *finite tree automaton* over $\mathcal{F}$ is a tuple $\mathcal{A} = \langle Q, \mathcal{F}, Q_f, \Delta \rangle$
where Q is a finite set of states, $\mathcal{F}$ is a finite alphabet, $Q_f \subseteq Q$ is a set of final
states, and Δ is a set of transitions (i.e., a relation) of the form $f(q_1, \ldots, q_k) \to q$
for $q, q_1, \ldots, q_k \in Q$, $f \in \mathcal{F}_k$.

A *run* of $\mathcal{A}$ on a tree t is a labeling $r : \mathrm{dom}(t) \to Q$ such that $t(\ell) \to r(\ell) \in \Delta$
for each leaf ℓ, and $t(n)(r(n \cdot 1), \ldots, r(n \cdot k)) \to r(n) \in \Delta$ for each internal node
n. A run r is *accepting* if $r(\Lambda) \in Q_f$, and we say that a tree t is *accepted* by $\mathcal{A}$ if
there exists an accepting run of $\mathcal{A}$ on t. The *language* of $\mathcal{A}$, denoted $L(\mathcal{A})$ is the
set of trees which are accepted by $\mathcal{A}$. A tree language L is *regular* if there exists
a finite tree automaton $\mathcal{A}$ such that $L = L(\mathcal{A})$.

Example 4. Regular tree languages can specify many interesting properties of
sagas. For example, the property "all b-actions occur (sequentially) after all
a-actions," over the actions $\{a, b, c\}$, is specified by the tree automaton $\mathcal{A} =$
$\langle \{q_a, q_b, q_c, q_f\}, \{a, b, c, \sigma_;, \sigma_\|\}, \{q_a, q_b, q_c, q_f\}, \Delta \rangle$, where Δ contains the transitions:

$$a \to q_a \qquad b \to q_b \qquad c \to q_c$$

$$\sigma_;(q_a, q_b) \to q_f \qquad \sigma_;(q_a, q_f) \to q_f \qquad \sigma_;(q_f, q_b) \to q_f$$

$$\sigma_\|(q_c, q) \to q \qquad \sigma_\|(q, q_c) \to q \qquad \sigma_\|(q_a, q_a) \to q_a \qquad \sigma_\|(q_b, q_b) \to q_b$$

$$\sigma_;(q_c, q) \to q \qquad \sigma_;(q, q_c) \to q \qquad \sigma_;(q_a, q_a) \to q_a \qquad \sigma_;(q_b, q_b) \to q_b$$

for $q \in \{q_a, q_b, q_c, q_f\}$. Given a tree $t \in L(\mathcal{A})$ where both a and b occur (as leaves)
in t, let r be an accepting run of $\mathcal{A}$ on t. The transitions of $\mathcal{A}$ ensure that there
is some internal node n such that every ancestor of n is labeled with q_f, and no
descendant of n is labeled with q_f. This path of q_f-labeled nodes in r divides t:
no a's (b's, resp.) can occur in a right-subtree (left-subtree, resp.) of a q_f-labeled
node. On the other hand, every such tree is accepted by $\mathcal{A}$.

Unfortunately, as Example 5 shows, the yield language of a saga may be non-
regular, and hence we must expand the expressive power of finite tree automata
to model the yield language of sagas. The extended model we consider allows a
tree automaton to use an arbitrarily large memory.

Example 5. Consider the simple saga $\mathcal{S} = \langle \{a, b\}, \{s\}, s, s \mapsto \{[s \| a \div b]\} \rangle$ for
which any finite run must reach a failure, resulting in an observation of a's
followed sequentially by b's. The yield language $L(\mathcal{S})$ consists of the set of binary trees where the root node is a sequential composition, and each subtree's

internal nodes are parallel compositions. Every leaf of the left subtree is labeled with a, while every leaf of the right subtree is labeled with b, and there are at least as many a's as b's. This tree language is not regular.

Tree Automata with One Memory. A more powerful family of tree automata can be obtained by extending the finite tree automata with a tree-structured memory for which equality of the memory built from subtrees can be enforced. Given a ranked memory alphabet Γ, define Φ_Γ as the smallest set of composition-closed functions over $\mathsf{Trees}(\Gamma)$ where (1) if $f \in \Gamma_n$ then the *constructor function* $\lambda x_1, \ldots, x_n.f(x_1, \ldots, x_n)$ is in Φ_Γ; (2) if $n \in \mathbb{N}$ and $0 < i \leq n$, then the *projection function* $\lambda x_1, \ldots, x_n.x_i$ is in Φ_Γ; (3) if $f \in \Gamma_n$ and $0 < i \leq n$, then the *pattern matching (partial) function* that associates each term $f(t_1, \ldots, t_n)$ with t_i, written $\lambda f(x_1, \ldots, x_n).x_i$, is in Φ_Γ. A *tree automaton with one memory* (TAWOM) [7] $\mathcal{A} = \langle \mathcal{F}, \Gamma, Q, Q_f, \Delta \rangle$ consists of an input alphabet $\mathcal{F}$, an alphabet Γ of memory symbols, a set Q of states, a set $Q_f \subseteq Q$ of final states, and a transition relation Δ. The transition relation Δ is given as a set of transitions of the form

$$f(q_1, \ldots, q_n) \xrightarrow[F]{c} q$$

where $q_1, \ldots, q_n, q \in Q$, $f \in \mathcal{F}_n$, $c \subseteq \{1, \ldots, n\}^2$ defines an equivalence relation of index m on $\{1, \ldots, n\}$, and $\lambda x_1, \ldots, x_m.F(x_1, \ldots, x_m)$ is a function from Φ_Γ. We often denote the function $\lambda \boldsymbol{x}.F(\boldsymbol{x}) \in \Phi_\Gamma$ simply as F, and the composition of functions $F, G \in \Phi_\Gamma$ (when F and G are naturally composable) as $F \cdot G$.

A *configuration* of $\mathcal{A}$ is a pair $\langle q, \gamma \rangle$ of a state $q \in Q$ and memory term $\gamma \in \mathsf{Trees}(\Gamma)$. Intuitively, a TAWOM constructs a configuration in a bottom-up manner, computing the new memory state from the memory states of each child. The transitions also check for equality between the children's memory states, based on the given equivalence relation.

A *run* of $\mathcal{A}$ is a labeling $r : \mathrm{dom}(t) \to Q \times \mathsf{Trees}(\Gamma)$ such that for each leaf ℓ,

$$t(\ell) \xrightarrow[r(\ell)_2]{} r(\ell)_1 \in \Delta$$

(where we use subscripts for tuple indexing), and for each internal node n with $t(n)$ of arity k, there exists $F \in \Phi_\Gamma$ such that

$$t(n)(r(n \cdot 1)_1, \ldots, r(n \cdot k)_1) \xrightarrow[F]{c} r(n)_1 \in \Delta$$

$$\text{and} \quad F(r(n \cdot 1)_2, \ldots, r(n \cdot m)_2) = r(n)_2,$$

where c is of index m, and $r(n \cdot i)_2 = r(n \cdot j)_2$ when $i \equiv_c j$, for $i, j \in \{1, \ldots, k\}$. A run r is *accepting* if $r(\Lambda) \in Q_f$, and the *language* of $\mathcal{A}$, denoted $L(\mathcal{A})$, is the set of trees on which there exist accepting runs of $\mathcal{A}$.

Example 6. TAWOM can encode pushdown automata [7]: a transition $(q, \alpha \cdot \gamma) \xrightarrow{a} (q', \beta \cdot \gamma)$ from the state q and stack $\alpha \cdot \gamma$ on letter a to the state q' and stack $\beta \cdot \gamma$ can be written (considering letters as unary symbols) as $a(q) \xrightarrow[\lambda x.\beta \alpha^{-1} x]{} q'$.

Example 7. The yield language of the saga $\{[s\|a \div b]\}$ from Example 5 is accepted by the automaton $\mathcal{A} = \langle\{a, b, \sigma_\|, \sigma_;\}, \{\gamma_0, \gamma\}, \{q_a, q_b, q_f\}, \{q_a, q_f\}, \Delta\rangle$ where Δ contains the following transitions:

$$\sigma_\|(q_a, q_a) \xrightarrow[\lambda x_1, x_2.\gamma(x_1, x_2)]{\top} q_a \qquad \sigma_\|(q_b, q_b) \xrightarrow[\lambda x_1, x_2.\gamma(x_1, x_2)]{\top} q_b$$

$$\sigma_\|(q_a, q_a) \xrightarrow[\lambda x_1, x_2.x_1]{\top} q_a \qquad \sigma_\|(q_a, q_a) \xrightarrow[\lambda x_1, x_2.x_2]{\top} q_a$$

$$\sigma_;(q_a, q_b) \xrightarrow{1=2} q_f \qquad a \xrightarrow[\gamma_0]{\top} q_a \qquad b \xrightarrow[\gamma_0]{\top} q_b$$

Note that the equivalence relation $\{\langle 1, 1\rangle, \langle 1, 2\rangle, \langle 2, 1\rangle, \langle 2, 2\rangle\}$ is here denoted by $1 = 2$, and $\top$ denotes the identity relation. An accepting run of $\mathcal{A}$ can successfully match the right subtree's memory state with the left subtree's memory state, as $\sigma_;$ is consumed, only when there are least as many a's as b's. The frequency of the memory symbol γ_0 is the exact number of b's, and a lower-bound of the number of a's.

Lemma 1. 1. *The class TAWOM is closed under intersection with finite tree automata.*
2. *The emptiness problem for TAWOM is decidable in time exponential in the size of the automaton.*
3. *For a TAWOM $\mathcal{A}$ and a finite tree automaton $\mathcal{B}$, $L(\mathcal{A}) \subseteq L(\mathcal{B})$ is decidable in time exponential in the size of $\mathcal{A}$ and doubly exponential in the size of $\mathcal{B}$.*

Proof. The first result is by a product construction. The second result is from [7], and the third is immediate from the complementation of finite tree automata [8], the product construction, and part (2).   □

4.3   Verification in the Tree Semantics

We now give an algorithm for the automata-theoretic verification of regular tree specifications. Our main technical construction is a TAWOM that accepts the yield language of a saga.

For a saga $\mathcal{S} = \langle \Sigma, X, s_0, T\rangle$, define the *reachable* terms of $\mathbb{T}^{\Sigma, X}$ from s_0, denoted $\mathsf{Reach}(\mathbb{T}^{\Sigma, X}, s_0)$, to be the smallest set which includes s_0 and is closed under $T(\cdot)$, and the inverses of $\{[\cdot]\}$, $;$, $\|$, and $\oplus$.

Theorem 2. *For every saga $\mathcal{S}$ there exists a tree automaton with one memory $\mathcal{A}$ such that $L(\mathcal{S}) = L(\mathcal{A})$.*

In our construction, the transitions of $\mathcal{A}$ encode the semantics of sagas as given in section 2. For clarity, we deal only with the transitions generating yield-trees of successfully compensated computations (including computations that need not compensate). The transitions for failed compensations, which finish with the abort outcome, are similar; the main technical difference is that the TAWOM projection functions become necessary. Because of this, and the hand-coded nature of the previous example, the automaton of example 7 does not match up exactly with the one constructed by our theorem, which is a much larger automaton.

Proof. Fix the saga $\mathcal{S} = (\Sigma, X, s_0, T)$. We define the tree automaton with one memory $\mathcal{A} = (\mathcal{F}, \Gamma, Q, Q_f, \Delta)$ in what follows. The states of $\mathcal{A}$ are the reachable terms of $\mathcal{S}$ combined with outcomes:

$$Q = \left\{ \langle t, \square \rangle, \langle t, \square \rangle^c \,\middle|\, \begin{array}{c} t \in \mathsf{Reach}(\mathbb{T}^{\Sigma,X}, s_0) \\ \square \in \{\square, \boxtimes, \boxplus\} \end{array} \right\},$$

while the final states are $Q_f = \{s_0\} \times \{\square, \boxtimes, \boxplus\}$, the input alphabet is $\mathcal{F} = \Sigma \cup \{\sigma_;, \sigma_\|\}$, and the memory alphabet is $\Gamma = \{\gamma_t \mid t \in \mathsf{Reach}(\mathbb{T}^{\Sigma,X}, s_0)\}$, where the arity of γ_t is the arity of the top level operator in t (e.g., $\gamma_{t_1;t_2} \in \Gamma_2$). The states of $\mathcal{A}$ encode the outcomes for executions of particular terms, and the superscript c of a state $\langle t, \square \rangle^c$ is used for the outcome of a compensation for the term t. The trees $\mathsf{Trees}(\mathcal{F})$ encode execution observations of $\mathcal{S}$, which can be decoded by in-order traversal, and the trees $\mathsf{Trees}(\Gamma)$ encode compensation stacks.

In what follows we present a definition schema for the transition relation, and define Δ to be the smallest relation satisfying our schema. By convention we denote an arbitrary equivalence relation with e, a state of $\mathcal{A}$ with q, and a function from Φ_Γ with φ. The function flip is defined as $\lambda x_1, x_2.x_2, x_1$. Throughout our schema, we enforce the following properties:

(P_1) For every closest $\langle \{\![t]\!\}, \square \rangle$-labeled ancestor n of a $\langle t, \boxtimes \rangle$-state in an accepting run t, $t(n \cdot 1)$ is a compensation tree of $t(n \cdot 0)$. This property ensures that when a subtransaction $\{\![t]\!\}$ fails with the observation tree $t(n \cdot 0)$, the proper compensating actions are observed in $t(n \cdot 1)$.

(P_2) A term which does not complete any action does not appear in an accepting run. This property is a technical convenience; without this, the automaton we defined would necessarily accept trees with 0-labeled leaves.

The definition schema is as follows.

Atomic actions. The atomic actions generate the leaves of memory and observation trees. For reachable atomic terms $a \div b$,

$$a \xrightarrow[\gamma_{a \div b}]{\top} \langle a \div b, \square \rangle \quad \text{and} \quad b \xrightarrow[\gamma_{a \div b}]{\top} \langle a \div b, \square \rangle^c$$

handle the execution of a, and allow for the compensation b to execute. This takes care of the rule (ATOM-S) from table 1, while the rule (ATOM-F) is taken care of by (P_1).

Sequential composition. The memory trees at $\sigma_;$-labeled nodes must be reversed when constructing the compensation's memory tree; thus we apply the flip function. For reachable sequential terms $t_1; t_2$ and outcomes $\square \in \{\square, \boxtimes\}$,

$$\sigma_;(\langle t_1, \square \rangle, \langle t_2, \square \rangle) \xrightarrow[\gamma_{t_1;t_2}]{\top} \langle t_1; t_2, \square \rangle$$

$$\text{and} \quad \sigma_;(\langle t_1, \square \rangle^c, \langle t_2, \square \rangle^c) \xrightarrow[\gamma_{t_1;t_2} \cdot \mathsf{flip}]{\top} \langle t_1; t_2, \square \rangle^c$$

partially handle rule (SEQ-S), where t_1 completes successfully but t_2 may fail after performing at least one action, whereas the transitions generated by

$$\text{if } q \xrightarrow[\varphi]{e} \langle t_1, \square \rangle \text{ then } q \xrightarrow[\varphi]{e} \langle t_1; t_2, \boxtimes \rangle \quad \text{and} \quad \text{if } q \xrightarrow[\varphi]{e} \langle t_1, \square \rangle^c \text{ then } q \xrightarrow[\varphi]{e} \langle t_1; t_2, \square \rangle^c$$

handle the cases where t_1 completes but t_2 fails before completing any action, or t_1 fails after completing at least one action, as in rule (SEQ-FA). Note that the case where t_1 fails before completing any action corresponds to an empty $\mathcal{F}$-subtree for $t_1; t_2$, and is taken care of by (P_2).

Parallel composition. With parallel threads, we get away without needing the $\boxtimes$ outcome by the invoking property (P_2). For reachable parallel terms $t_1 \| t_2$ and outcomes $\square_1, \square_2 \in \{\square, \boxtimes\}$,

$$\sigma_{\|}(\langle t_1, \square_1 \rangle, \langle t_2, \square_2 \rangle) \xrightarrow[\gamma_{t_1 \| t_2}]{\top} \langle t_1 \| t_2, \square_1 \wedge \square_2 \rangle$$

$$\text{and} \quad \sigma_{\|}(\langle t_1, \square \rangle^c, \langle t_2, \square \rangle^c) \xrightarrow[\gamma_{t_1 \| t_2}]{\top} \langle t_1 \| t_2, \square \rangle^c$$

handle rule (PAR-S) where t_1 and t_2 may complete successfully, and partially rule (PAR-F) where t_1 or t_2 fail after completing at least one action, whereas the transitions generated by

$$\text{if } q \xrightarrow[\varphi]{e} \langle t_i, \square_i \rangle \text{ then } q \xrightarrow[\varphi]{e} \langle t_1 \| t_2, \boxtimes \rangle \quad \text{and} \quad \text{if } q \xrightarrow[\varphi]{e} \langle t_i, \square \rangle^c \text{ then } q \xrightarrow[\varphi]{e} \langle t_1 \| t_2, \square \rangle^c,$$

for $i \in \{1, 2\}$, handle the other cases of (PAR-F) where one parallel branch fails before completing any action. Again the case where both branches fail before completing any action is taken care of by (P_2).

Nondeterministic choice. The rule (NONDET) of table 1 is taken care of by closing our transitions over nondeterministic terms. For the reachable terms $t_1 \oplus t_2$, $i \in \{1, 2\}$, and outcomes $\square \in \{\square, \boxtimes\}$, the transitions generated by

$$\text{if } q \xrightarrow[\varphi]{e} \langle t_i, \square \rangle \text{ then } q \xrightarrow[\varphi]{e} \langle t_1 \oplus t_2, \square \rangle$$

$$\text{and} \quad \text{if } q \xrightarrow[\varphi]{e} \langle t_i, \square \rangle^c \text{ then } q \xrightarrow[\varphi]{e} \langle t_1 \oplus t_2, \square \rangle^c$$

coincide exactly with (NONDET).

Subtransactions. For the reachable subtransaction terms $\{[t]\}$, the transitions generated by

$$\text{if } q \xrightarrow[\varphi]{e} \langle t, \square \rangle \text{ then } q \xrightarrow[\varphi]{e} \langle \{[t]\}, \square \rangle \quad \text{and} \quad \text{if } q \xrightarrow[\varphi]{e} \langle t, \square \rangle^c \text{ then } q \xrightarrow[\varphi]{e} \langle \{[t]\}, \square \rangle^c$$

take care of successful completion, as in rules (SUB-S) and (SAGA), while compensated completions of (SUB-F) and (SAGA) are handled by

$$\sigma_;(\langle t, \boxtimes \rangle, \langle t, \square \rangle^c) \xrightarrow[\gamma_{\{[t]\}}]{1=2} \langle \{[t]\}, \square \rangle \quad \text{and} \quad 0 \xrightarrow[\gamma_{\{[t]\}}]{\top} \langle \{[t]\}, \square \rangle^c.$$

The first group of transitions here helps ensure (P_1) by enforcing identical memory-trees between a partially-completed subtransaction and its compensation. The second group is used to match a completed (but locally failed, and thus already compensated for) subtransaction with a null compensation. Note that while technically we do not want to consider leaves labeled with 0, it is possible to replace the previous set of transitions with a more complicated set which introduces the memory symbol $\gamma_{\{\![t]\!\}}$ arbitrarily at any place in the tree.

For the reachable variables $x \in X$ and outcomes $\Box \in \{\boxdot, \boxtimes\}$, the transitions generated by

$$\text{if } q \xrightarrow[\varphi]{e} \langle T(x), \Box \rangle \text{ then } q \xrightarrow[\varphi]{e} \langle x, \Box \rangle \quad \text{and} \quad \text{if } q \xrightarrow[\varphi]{e} \langle T(x), \Box \rangle^c \text{ then } q \xrightarrow[\varphi]{e} \langle x, \Box \rangle^c$$

allow named subtransactions, as in (VAR).

It is not difficult to check that properties (P_1) and (P_2) are preserved in our schema, and that the language of $\mathcal{A}$ is the yield language of $\mathcal{S}$.   □

From this construction, and Lemma 1, we get the main result.

Corollary 1. [Saga Verification] *For every saga $\mathcal{S}$ and regular tree language specification (given as a nondeterministic finite tree automaton B), the verification problem $L(\mathcal{S}) \subseteq L(B)$ can be decided in time exponential in the size of $\mathcal{S}$ and doubly exponential in the size of B.*

This provides an exponential time algorithm in the size of the structure. On the other side, the problem is PSPACE-hard in both the structure and the specification, by reduction from term reachability of process algebras [16] and universality of word automata respectively.

5   Conclusions and Future Work

We have presented a first step towards automatic verification of business processes with compensations. While this paper provides a complexity-theoretic upper bound on the complexity of model checking, engineering effort is needed before we can obtain a practical tool for business process verification. Among other things, this means that our algorithms must be extended to model dataflow as well as deal with programming language features that are absent in the abstract formulation.

References

1. BPEL Specification v 1.1.http://www.ibm.com/developerworks/library/ws-bpel.
2. Business Process Modeling Language BPML. http://www.bpmi.org/.
3. R. Bruni, M.J. Butler, C. Ferreira, C.A.R. Hoare, H.C. Melgratti, and U. Montanari. Comparing two approaches to compensable flow composition. In *CONCUR 05*, LNCS 3653, pages 383–397. Springer, 2005.

4. R. Bruni, H. Melgratti, and U. Montanari. Theoretical foundations for compensations in flow composition languages. In *POPL 05*, pages 209–220, 2005. ACM.
5. M. Butler and C. Ferreira. An operational semantics for STAC, a language for modeling business transactions. In *Proc. Co-ordination 04*, LNCS 2429, pages 87–104. Springer, 2004.
6. M. Butler, C.A.R. Hoare, and C. Ferreira. A trace semantics for long-running transactions. In *Proc. 25 years of CSP*, LNCS 3525, pages 133–150. Springer, 2005.
7. H. Comon, V. Cortier, and J. Mitchell. Tree automata with one memory, set constraints, and ping-pong protocols. In *ICALP 01*, pages 682–693, 2001. Springer.
8. H. Comon, M. Dauchet, R. Gilleron, F. Jacquemard, D. Lugiez, S. Tison, and M. Tommasi. Tree automata techniques and applications. Available on: http://www.grappa.univ-lille3.fr/tata, 1997.
9. A. Deutsch, L. Sui, and V. Vianu. Specification and verification of data-driven web services. In *PODS 04*, pages 71–82. ACM, 2004.
10. X. Fu, T. Bultan, and J. Su. Conversation protocols: A formalism for specification and verification of reactive electronic services. In *CIAA 03*, LNCS 2759, pages 188–200. Springer, 2003.
11. X. Fu, T. Bultan, and J. Su. Analysis of interacting BPEL web services. In *WWW 04*, pages 621–630. ACM, 2004.
12. H. Garcia-Molina and K. Salem. Sagas. In *SIGMOD 87*, pages 249–259. ACM, 1987.
13. J. Gray and A. Reuter. *Transaction processing: Concepts and techniques.* Morgan Kaufmann, 1993.
14. R. Hull, M. Benedikt, V. Christophides, and J. Su. E-services: a look behind the curtain. In *PODS 03*, pages 1–14. ACM, 2003.
15. A. Kučera and R. Mayr. Simulation preorder over simple process algebras. *Info. and Comp.*, 173:184–198, 2002.
16. R. Mayr. Decidability of model checking with the temporal logic EF. *TCS*, 256, 31–62, 2001.
17. Web Services Conversation Language WSCL 1.0. http://www.w3.org/TR/wscl10/.
18. WSFL Specification v 1.0. http://www-306.ibm.com/software/solutions/webservices/pdf/WSFL.pdf.

Model Checking Nonblocking MPI Programs

Stephen F. Siegel*

Department of Computer and Information Sciences
University of Delaware, Newark, DE 19716, USA
siegel@cis.udel.edu
http://www.cis.udel.edu/~siegel

Abstract. This paper explores a way to apply model checking techniques to parallel programs that use the *nonblocking* primitives of the Message Passing Interface (MPI). The method has been implemented as an extension to the model checker SPIN called MPI-SPIN. It has been applied to 17 examples from a widely-used textbook on MPI. Many correctness properties of these examples were verified and in two cases nontrivial faults were discovered.

1 Introduction

Parallelism has proved remarkably effective at providing the high level of performance demanded by scientific computing. But parallel programming is notoriously difficult and, as the complexity of scientific applications increases, computational scientists find themselves expending an inordinate amount of effort developing, testing, and debugging their programs. Concerns about this level of effort—and the correctness of the resulting programs—have led to growing interest in new verification and validation approaches for scientific computing [6].

Model checking is a formal verification method that is widely-used in many hardware and software domains and in theory could be applied to scientific software. Yet significant hurdles must be overcome before model checking can be practically applied in the scientific domain. Among these is the fact that model checkers operate on a model of a program, rather than on the program itself. Hence techniques must be developed to construct finite-state models of scientific programs.

This paper describes a way to create finite-state models of programs that employ the "nonblocking" communication primitives of the *Message Passing Interface* (MPI) [3,4]. MPI is a large message-passing library with subtle and complex semantics and has become the *de facto* standard for high-performance parallel computing. The nonblocking primitives provide a precise way to specify how computation and communication can be carried out concurrently in an MPI program. For example, one may specify that a communication task is to begin at one point in an MPI process and that the process should block at a subsequent point until that task has completed; computational code can be inserted between these two points to achieve the desired overlap. An algorithm expressed

---

* Supported by the U.S. National Science Foundation grant CCF-0541035.

B. Cook and A. Podelski (Eds.): VMCAI 2007, LNCS 4349, pp. 44–58, 2007.

in this way can be mapped efficiently to hardware architectures, common in high-performance computing, that utilize distinct, concurrently-executing components for communication and computation. Because of this, nonblocking communication is ubiquitous in MPI-based scientific software and is generally credited with playing a large role in the high level of performance that scientific computing has achieved.

While previous work applying model checking techniques to MPI programs has focused on various aspects of MPI, including the basic blocking point-to-point and collective functions [9, 8, 7, 11, 10], "one-sided" operations [5] and process management [2], none has dealt with nonblocking communication. There are two reasons that might explain this. First, the semantics of nonblocking communication are considerably more complex than those of blocking communication. The nonblocking semantics involve the introduction of types, constants, and a number of functions for creating and manipulating objects of those types, as well as complex rules prescribing how the MPI infrastructure is to carry out requests concurrently with program execution. Second, it is not obvious how to represent the state of a nonblocking MPI program in a way that is amenable to standard model checking techniques. MPI blocking communication operations map naturally to primitives provided by a model checker such as SPIN [1]: SPIN *channels* can be used to represent queues of buffered messages *en route* from one MPI process to another and the send and receive channel operations correspond closely to the blocking MPI send and receive functions. No SPIN data structure corresponds to an MPI nonblocking communication request nor supports the myriad operations upon it.

We proceed with a brief summary of the MPI nonblocking primitives (Sec. 2). This is followed by a detailed description of our approach for modeling nonblocking MPI programs for verification by standard explicit-state model checking techniques (Sec. 3). Discussion of a preliminary validation of the approach follows (Sec. 4): it has been implemented as an extension to SPIN called MPI-SPIN and has been applied to the 17 examples in the popular MPI textbook [12] dealing with nonblocking communication. Many correctness properties of these examples were verified and, in two cases, nontrivial faults were discovered.

2   Nonblocking Communication

The standard mode *blocking* function used to send a message from one MPI process to another is MPI_Send. Its arguments specify a communicator object that represents the communication universe in which the processes live, the *rank* of the destination process (an integer process ID relative to the communicator), the number and type of elements to send, their location in memory (the *send buffer*), and an integer tag. It blocks until the message has been completely copied out of the send buffer—either into a system buffer or directly into the receive buffer at the destination process. In particular, the MPI infrastructure *may* block the sender until the destination process is ready to receive the message synchronously.

The *nonblocking* version of this function is `MPI_Isend`. It takes the same arguments as `MPI_Send` but in addition it allocates and returns a handle r to a *request object*. This function initiates the sending of the message and does not block. A subsequent call to `MPI_Wait` on r blocks until the message has been completely copied out of the send buffer and then deallocates the request object. In particular, `MPI_Send` is equivalent to `MPI_Isend` followed immediately by `MPI_Wait`.

The receive operations `MPI_Recv` and `MPI_Irecv` work in an analogous way. In particular, `MPI_Irecv` initiates the receiving of a message and the subsequent call to `MPI_Wait` blocks until the incoming message has been completely copied into the receive buffer, from either a system buffer or directly from the send buffer. The receive request will only be paired with a message whose destination, tag, and communicator fields match the source, tag, and communicator fields of the receive, respectively. Unlike sends, the source and tag arguments for the receiving functions can take the *wildcard* values `MPI_ANY_SOURCE` and `MPI_ANY_TAG`, specifying that the receive will accept a message from any source, and/or with any tag, respectively.

MPI makes certain guarantees concerning how receives and messages are paired (or "matched") [3, Sec. 3.5]. Fix two processes p and q. A receive r posted from q cannot be paired with a message emanating from p if there is an earlier-posted unpaired message from p to q that matches r. Similarly, a message s emanating from p cannot be paired with a receive posted from q if there is an earlier-posted unpaired receive from q that matches s.

These strictly negative guarantees are complemented by the following positive ones. If s is an unpaired send request posted by p and r is an unpaired receive request posted by q, and r and s match, then (1) s will complete unless r is paired with another message and completes, and (2) r will complete unless s is paired with another receive request and completes. In particular, at least one of r, s will complete.

The function `MPI_Test` can be invoked on r to determine whether r has completed without blocking; it sets a boolean flag to 0 if r has not completed, else it sets this flag to 1 and proceeds as `MPI_Wait`.

`MPI_Request_free` can be invoked on r to indicate that the request object should be deallocated as soon as the request completes (in which case no subsequent call to `MPI_Wait` is necessary).

A number of MPI functions operate on arrays (r_i) of request handles. The function `MPI_Waitany` takes such an array and blocks until at least one request has completed. It then chooses one of the completed requests, returns its index i, and proceeds as if `MPI_Wait` were invoked on r_i. `MPI_Waitall` blocks until all requests in the array have completed and then proceeds as if `MPI_Wait` were invoked on all r_i. `MPI_Waitsome` blocks until at least one has completed and then invokes `MPI_Wait` on all that have completed and returns the subset of indices of all completed requests. The functions `MPI_Testany`, `MPI_Testall`, and `MPI_Testsome` work in an entirely analogous way but never block.

The function MPI_Probe takes source, tag, and communicator arguments and blocks until it determines there is an incoming message that matches these parameters. However, it does not consume the message (as a receive operation would) but simply returns certain information about the message which can then be used in a subsequent receive operation. MPI_Iprobe is similar but returns a flag instead of blocking. MPI guarantees that if a send request is posted with parameters matching those passed to MPI_Probe, then MPI_Probe will eventually return, though there can be a delay between the posting and the return of the probe. Similarly, repeated calls to MPI_Iprobe must eventually return true if a matching send is posted.

MPI_Cancel is invoked on r to attempt to cancel the request. The cancellation may or may not succeed. If it does succeed then any receive buffer involved in the canceled communication should remain unchanged; if it does not then execution should proceed as if MPI_Cancel were never called. A subsequent call to MPI_Test_canceled on the status object of r is used to determine whether or not the cancellation succeeded.

Persistent requests are created by calling MPI_Send_init or MPI_Recv_init. The arguments are similar to those for MPI_Isend and MPI_Irecv but, unlike ordinary requests, a persistent request r is *inactive* until *started* by invoking MPI_Start on r. After invoking MPI_Wait (or one of the other completion operations) on r, the request object is not deallocated but is returned to the inactive state until it is re-started. A persistent request is deallocated by invoking MPI_Request_free. MPI_Startall starts all persistent requests in an array.

An example of the use of nonblocking communication is given in the MPI/C code of Fig. 1, which is extracted from [12, Ex. 2.18]. In this program, multiple producers repeatedly send messages to a single consumer. The consumer posts receive requests for each producer in order of increasing rank, and then waits on each request in a cyclic order. After a receive request completes, the message is consumed and another receive request is posted for that producer. Note that overlap between computation and communication is achieved because the consumer may consume a message from a producer while the MPI infrastructure carries out the requests to receive data from other producers.

3   Modeling Approach

We now describe our notion of a model of an MPI program that consists of a fixed number of processes and uses the functions described in Sec. 2. For this work, we make a few simplifying assumptions: the only communicator is MPI_COMM_WORLD, each process is single-threaded, there is no aliasing of request handles, and no non-zero error codes are returned by the MPI functions. In future work we expect to eliminate each of these assumptions.

Our model consists of a particular kind of guarded transition system for each process and a global array of *communication records* representing buffered messages and outstanding requests. The execution semantics are defined so that, at any global state, either an enabled transition from one process or a transition corresponding to an action by the MPI infrastructure may be selected for execution.

```
MPI_Comm_rank(comm, &rank);
MPI_Comm_size(comm, &size);
if (rank != size-1) { /* producer code */
  while (1) {
    /* produce data */
    MPI_Send(buffer->data, buffer->datasize, MPI_CHAR, size-1 tag, comm);
  }
} else { /* consumer code */
  for (i=0; i < size-1; i++)
    MPI_Irecv(buffer[i].data, MAXSIZE, MPI_CHAR, i, tag, comm,
      &(buffer[i].req));
  for (i=0; ; i=(i+1)%(size-1)) {
    MPI_Wait(&(buffer[i].req), &status);
    /* consume data */
    MPI_Irecv(buffer[i].data, MAXSIZE, MPI_CHAR, i, tag, comm,
      &(buffer[i].req));
  }
}
```

Fig. 1. Code excerpt from [12, Ex. 2.18], *Multiple producer, single consumer*

We now sketch how this can be made precise. We first fix values for the following parameters: the number $n \geq 1$ of MPI processes, an upper bound $b \geq 0$ on the total number of buffered messages that may exist at any one time, and an upper bound $r \geq 0$ on the total number of outstanding requests that may exist at any one time. We consider it an error if the outstanding request bound can be exceeded. On the other hand, if a send is posted after the buffer bound has been reached, execution can proceed but the MPI infrastructure will not be allowed to buffer messages. The difference in how our model treats these two bounds stems from the different roles these concepts play in MPI. The MPI Standard states that each request object consumes some system resources and so there must be some limit on the number of outstanding requests. (The precise limit is implementation-dependent but is expected to be reasonably high.) Furthermore, a function that allocates a new request, such as MPI_Isend, will not block if this limit has been reached—instead, an error occurs. On the other hand, a correct MPI implementation should never report an error if it has insufficient space to buffer messages; at worst, the send operations will not complete until they can be paired with matching receives or sufficient buffer space becomes available.

We begin with the definition of *communication record*, then describe the transition system for a single process, and finally define the global model and execution semantics.

3.1   Communication Records

A *communication record* is an 11-tuple

(core, source, dest, datatype, count, tag, data, handle, status, freeable, match).

For each of these components (or *fields*) we give a description and a default value. The symbol '−' will denote the appropriate default value wherever it appears. We let C denote the set of all communication records. The *null* element of C is the one for which all fields have their default values; it is also the default value for C.

The field core (or *core state*), captures the most essential information about the object: whether the record is for a request or message, a send or receive request, whether it has been canceled, completed, or matched, and so on. The core state is completely specified by the values of 9 boolean flags that answer the questions given in Fig. 2a. With a few exceptions, these are self-explanatory. A request is *active* if it is either (1) a nonpersistent request that has not been canceled or completed, or (2) a persistent request that has been started and has not been canceled or completed since last being started. A send request or message is *visible* if it can be detected by a probe on the receiver side.

At first glance it appears there could be as many as 2^9 distinct core states. But it is clear that many of the combinations are not possible, and in fact a simple reachability analysis reveals that only a small number (24, including a special *null* value) can occur. This analysis, carried out with SPIN, considers all ways in which a communication record can be created, modified, and destroyed by the 13 types of primitive state transformations described in this paper (Fig. 4). The 24 reachable core states are enumerated in Fig. 2b and the transitions between them are depicted in Fig. 3. The default value is s_0.

The integer fields source, dest, count, and tag mean exactly what one would expect; the special wildcard values may be used for the source and tag fields of receive requests. The default values are all 0.

The datatype field specifies the type of the elements comprising the message. We assume there is a fixed, finite set of datatypes numbered $0, 1, \ldots, d-1$ and that for each i we are given size(i), the size (in bytes) of datatype i. In our implementation, there are several integer types of various sizes, an *empty* type of size 0, and a *symbolic* type (of size 4) used to model floating point values as symbolic expressions. There is no reason this could not be extended in many ways, including to incorporate MPI derived datatypes. The default value is 0.

For requests, the data field is an integer referring to the location of the start of the send or receive buffer. We will see below that the local memory of a process is modeled as a finite sequence of bytes; this integer refers to the index in that sequence. For messages, this integer instead encodes the sequence of bytes comprising the message. We assume there is a fixed procedure to losslessly encode any sequence of bytes into an integer, and decode the integer back into the byte sequence. The default is 0.

Our modeling approach requires that for each process, a unique integer ID be associated to each variable that will hold a request handle (i.e., each variable of type MPI_Request in MPI/C). It is assumed that there is at most one variable containing any given handle. (While aliasing of handles is allowed in MPI, this feature is rarely used. One could incorporate aliasing into our approach using

R: Is this a request?
B: Is this a buffered message?
P: Is this a persistent request?
S: Is this a send request?
A: Is this an active request?
C: Is this a request that has completed successfully?
V: Is this a visible (but unmatched) send request or buffered message?
M: Is this a matched (but incomplete) send request or buffered message?
X: Is this a request that has been successfully canceled?

(a) Core state flags

ID	name	R	B	P	S	A	C	V	M	X
s_0	NullState	·	·	·	·	·	·	·	·	·
s_1	InvisibleSendReq	✓	·	·	✓	✓	·	·	·	·
s_2	VisibleSendReq	✓	·	·	✓	✓	·	✓	·	·
s_3	MatchedSendReq	✓	·	·	✓	✓	·	·	✓	·
s_4	CompleteSendReq	✓	·	·	✓	✓	✓	·	·	·
s_5	CanceledSendReq	✓	·	·	✓	·	·	·	·	✓
s_6	UnmatchedRecvReq	✓	·	·	·	✓	·	·	·	·
s_7	MatchedRecvReq	✓	·	·	·	✓	·	·	✓	·
s_8	CompleteRecvReq	✓	·	·	·	✓	✓	·	·	·
s_9	CanceledRecvReq	✓	·	·	·	·	·	·	·	✓
s_{10}	InactiveSendPreq	✓	·	✓	✓	·	·	·	·	·
s_{11}	InvisibleSendPreq	✓	·	✓	✓	✓	·	·	·	·
s_{12}	VisibleSendPreq	✓	·	✓	✓	✓	·	✓	·	·
s_{13}	MatchedSendPreq	✓	·	✓	✓	✓	·	·	✓	·
s_{14}	CompleteSendPreq	✓	·	✓	✓	✓	✓	·	·	·
s_{15}	CanceledSendPreq	✓	·	✓	✓	·	·	·	·	✓
s_{16}	InactiveRecvPreq	✓	·	✓	·	·	·	·	·	·
s_{17}	UnmatchedRecvPreq	✓	·	✓	·	✓	·	·	·	·
s_{18}	MatchedRecvPreq	✓	·	✓	·	✓	·	·	✓	·
s_{19}	CompleteRecvPreq	✓	·	✓	·	✓	✓	·	·	·
s_{20}	CanceledRecvPreq	✓	·	✓	·	✓	·	·	·	✓
s_{21}	InvisibleMessage	·	✓	·	·	·	·	·	·	·
s_{22}	VisibleMessage	·	✓	·	·	·	·	✓	·	·
s_{23}	MatchedMessage	·	✓	·	·	·	·	·	✓	·

(b) Reachable core states

	Prod_0	Prod_1	Cons	MPI	c_0	c_1	c_2	c_3	c_4
0					−	−	−	−	−
1			irecv$_0$		v_1	−	−	−	−
2		isend			v_2	v_1	−	−	−
3				reveal$_1$	v_3	v_1	−	−	−
4				upload$_1$	v_5	v_1	v_4	−	−
5	isend				v_6	v_5	v_1	v_4	−
6				reveal$_0$	v_7	v_5	v_1	v_4	−
7				match$_0$	v_5	v_4	v_8	v_9	−
8			irecv$_1$		v_5	v_{10}	v_4	v_8	v_9
9				match$_1$	v_4	v_8	v_9	v_{11}	v_{12}
10		wait			v_8	v_9	v_{11}	v_{12}	−
11		isend			v_2	v_8	v_9	v_{11}	v_{12}
12				synch$_0$	v_2	v_{11}	v_{12}	v_{13}	v_{14}
13		wait$_0$			v_2	v_{11}	v_{12}	v_{13}	−
14		irecv$_0$			v_2	v_1	v_{11}	v_{12}	v_{13}
15				download$_1$	v_2	v_1	v_{15}	v_{13}	−
16		wait$_1$			v_2	v_1	v_{13}	−	−
17	wait				v_2	v_1	−	−	−

	core	source	dest	handle	match
v_0	s_0	−	−	−	−
v_1	s_6	0	2	0	−
v_2	s_1	1	2	0	−
v_3	s_2	1	2	0	−
v_4	s_4	1	2	0	−
v_5	s_{22}	1	2	−	−
v_6	s_1	0	2	0	−
v_7	s_2	0	2	0	−
v_8	s_3	0	2	0	0
v_9	s_7	0	2	0	−
v_{10}	s_6	1	2	1	−
v_{11}	s_{23}	1	2	−	1
v_{12}	s_7	1	2	1	−
v_{13}	s_4	0	2	0	−
v_{14}	s_8	0	2	0	−
v_{15}	s_8	1	2	1	−

(c) An execution prefix for program of Fig. 1

(d) Communication record values used in prefix

Fig. 2. Communication records

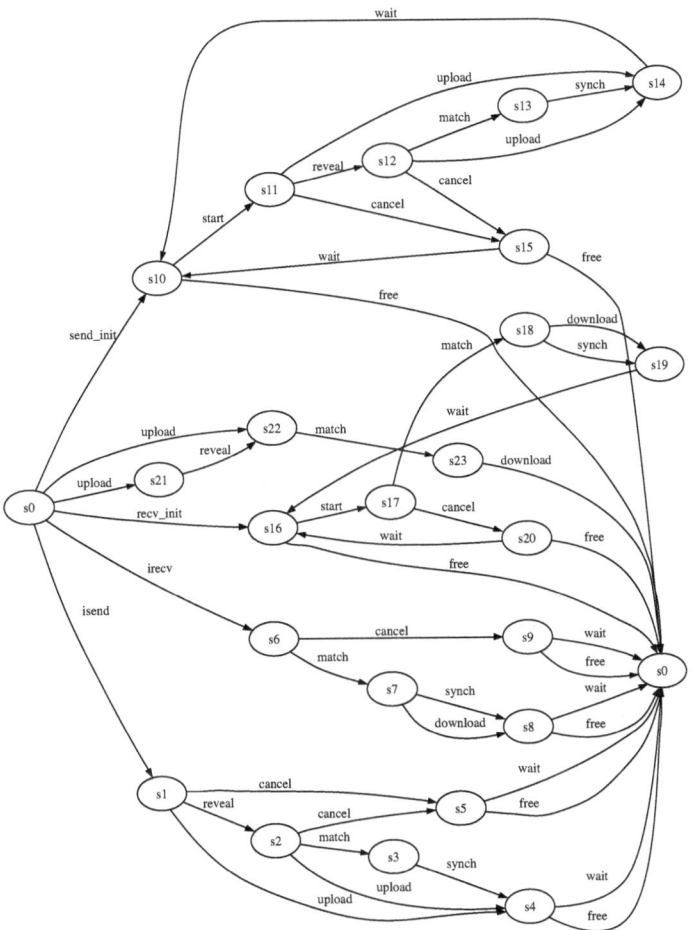

Fig. 3. Transitions between communication record core states

techniques similar to those for modeling references to heap-allocated data in Java or C, but we have chosen to defer this for future work and concentrate here on issues particular to nonblocking communication.) The integer handle field thus specifies the unique handle variable referring to that request. It is not used for messages. The default is 0.

The status field is used only for completed receive requests. It is a 4-tuple giving the source, tag, count and *status type* of the received message. (The source and tag information is redundant unless wildcards were used in the receive.) The status type can be either *undefined* (the default), *canceled* (the request was successfully canceled), *normal* (the message was successfully received), or *empty*. The last case is used in MPI to signify certain exceptional scenarios. In the default value, the status is *undefined*, and the source, tag, and count are all 0.

The boolean field freeable is 1 for a request that can be deallocated as soon as it completes (because of a user call to MPI_Request_free). Otherwise it has the default value 0. It is not used for messages.

A send request or message that has been matched with a receive request will have its integer match field set to the handle of the receive request. Since the rank of the receiver is the dest field, and we are assuming unique references to request objects, this uniquely determines the matching receive request. The match field is not used in receive requests, or in messages or send requests that have not been paired. The default is 0.

3.2   Local Process Model

A *local process model* of rank R with *global buffer bound* b and *global request bound* r is a tuple $L = (Q, q_0, T, h, l)$ where Q is a set of *local control states*, $q_0 \in Q$ is the *initial control state*, $T \subset Q \times E \times Q$ is a set of *local transitions* (the *event set* E is defined below), and h and l are nonnegative integers specifying, respectively, the number of request handle variables available to the process and the size, in bytes, of the local memory (excluding the request handle variables).

Let $X = \{0, \ldots, 255, \mathsf{UNDEF}\}$; these are the possible values for a unit of the local memory. Let $Y = \{0, \ldots, h-1, \mathsf{UNDEF}, \mathsf{NULL}\}$; these are the possible values for a request handle variable. The set $W = X^l \times Y^h$ represents all possible states of the process memory. A *local state of L* is an element of $Q \times W$. The *initial state of L* has control state q_0 and all local memory and request variables set to UNDEF.

The event set E consists of ordered pairs $\langle \gamma, \phi \rangle$, where $\gamma \colon W \times C^{b+r} \to \{\mathsf{true}, \mathsf{false}\}$ is a *guard* specifying when the transition is enabled and $\phi \colon W \times C^{b+r} \to W \times C^{b+r}$ is a *transformation function* describing the change to the local state and communication record array effected by the transition. A transformation that modifies the communication record array is required to fall into one of the 8 categories of Fig. 4a. Each of these transformations is specified by certain parameters that are functions on W; these parameters represent the expressions that occur as arguments in the corresponding MPI function. For example, at a state with process memory w, the isend transformation modifies the communication record array by inserting the record

$$(s_1, R, dest(w), dtype(w), count(w), tag(w), buf(w), req(w), -, -, -).$$

The only change to the process memory W is to set the value of the request handle variable in position $req(w)$ to $req(w)$. A wait transformation on a completed or canceled nonpersistent request removes the record from the array, sets the value of the request handle variable to NULL, sets the status object at position $status(w)$ in local memory to the appropriate value, and so on.

Each MPI function described in Sec. 2 can be modeled using suitable choices of guards and primitive transformations. For example, an MPI_Isend at control state q is modeled with two outgoing transitions t_1 and t_2. The first leads to an "error" trap state, indicating that the outstanding request bound has been

transformation	corresponding MPI function
isend(*buf, count, dtype, dest, tag, req*)	`MPI_Isend`
irecv(*buf, count, dtype, source, tag, req*)	`MPI_Irecv`
wait(*req, status*)	`MPI_Wait`
cancel(*req*)	`MPI_Cancel`
send_init(*buf, count, dtype, dest, tag, req*)	`MPI_Send_init`
recv_init(*buf, count, dtype, source, tag, req*)	`MPI_Recv_init`
free(*req*)	`MPI_Request_free`
start(*req*)	`MPI_Start`

(**a**) Primitive state transformations effected by an MPI process

transformation	effect summary
match(i, j)	match send request/message with receive request
upload(i)	copy data from send to system buffer
download(i)	copy data from system to receive buffer
synch(i)	copy data from send to receive buffer
reveal(i)	make invisible send request/message visible

(**b**) Primitive state transformations effected by the MPI infrastructure

Fig. 4. The 13 primitive MPI state transformations

violated, and has guard γ_1, which holds iff the communication record array contains r requests. Transition t_2 leads to the state for the next point of control, has guard $\neg\gamma_1$, and a transformation of the isend type described above.

The more complex MPI functions can be translated using more states and some of the local memory. Say, for example, we wish to translate a call to `MPI_Waitany` on the array of request handles that starts with the k-th handle and has length m. To do this, we introduce an intermediate state q', and add transitions $t_1 = (q, \langle\gamma_1, \phi_1\rangle, q')$, $t_2 = (q', \langle\gamma_2, \phi_2\rangle, q')$, and $t_3 = (q', \langle\gamma_3, \phi_3\rangle, q'')$, where q'' is the state for the next point of control. The guard γ_1 holds iff there exists j such that $k \leq j < k+m$ and the communication record array contains a request from process R with handle j that has completed or been canceled. The transformation ϕ_1 sets some scratch variable i (residing in some part of the local memory reserved for this purpose) to the least such j. The guard γ_2 holds iff there exists j such that $i < j < k+m$ and the array contains a request from process R with handle j that has completed or been canceled. The transformation ϕ_2 sets i to the least such j. The guard γ_3 is true and ϕ_3 is a wait transformation on the request with handle i. The effect of all this is to wait until at least one request has completed or been canceled and then nondeterministically choose one of them and apply wait to it.

3.3   Global Model

Finally, a *model of a nonblocking MPI program with n processes, global buffer bound b, and global request bound r* is an n-tuple $M = (L_0, \ldots, L_{n-1})$, where for each i, L_i is a local process model of rank i with bounds b and r. Let W_i denote the set of all local states for L_i. A *global state* of M is an element

$$(w_0, \ldots, w_{n-1}, c_0, \ldots, c_{b+r-1}) \in W_0 \times \cdots \times W_{n-1} \times C^{b+r}.$$

The initial state is one for which each w_i is initial and all c_j are null. An execution of M is a sequence of global states, starting with the initial state, such that a *global transition* exists between each pair of consecutive states. A global transition corresponds to the execution of an enabled local transition or an *MPI infrastructure transition*.

The MPI infrastructure transitions correspond to the 5 transformations in Fig. 4b. Given a global state, one match transition is enabled for each pair (i, j) for which all of the following hold: (1) $0 \leq i, j < b + r$, (2) c_i is an unmatched receive request and c_j is an unmatched send request or buffered message, (3) the parameters of c_i and c_j "match" in the MPI sense, and (4) pairing c_i and c_j would not violate the ordering rules of the MPI Standard. The effect of the transition is to change the two entries in the communication record array to indicate the two records are matched. An upload transition models the completion of a send request by copying the message data from the send buffer into some system buffer. One such transition is enabled for each send request as long as the number of buffered messages is less than b. The effect is to complete the send request record and create a new record for a buffered message. A download transition models copying a message from a system buffer to the receive buffer; this results in changing the local state of the receiver appropriately, deleting the record for the message, and completing the receive request record. A synch transition corresponds to copying the message directly from the send to the receive buffer and completes both requests. A reveal transition makes an invisible send request or message visible; it is only enabled if all preceding send requests/messages emanating from the same sender and destined for the same receiver are already visible.

An execution prefix for the example of Fig. 1 is described in Figs. 2c and 2d. In each row (other than 0) of Fig. 2c there is a transition from either one of the three processes or the MPI infrastructure. This is followed by a description of the state of the communication record array after executing the transition. The v_i refer to entries in the table of Fig. 2d. This table contains one entry for each communication record value occurring in the prefix and gives the values for the 5 most essential fields of each. The subscripts on the transitions from the consumer and the MPI infrastructure refer to the rank of the sending process.

3.4   Order

We have seen that both process and infrastructural transitions may insert, delete, and modify entries in the communication record array, but we have not yet discussed the way in which the entries of this array are ordered. It is clear that the order must reflect some information concerning the temporal order in which the requests were generated, in order to prevent violations to the MPI matching rules. On the other hand, if we maintain this temporal ordering in its full precision, we risk creating unnecessary distinctions between states and an explosion in their number. The trick is to keep track of just as much "history" as is required to prevent violations of the MPI matching rules, and no more.

Our approach is to maintain the communication record array in such a way that the $b+r$ entries always occur in the following order: (1) the send requests and messages that need to be matched (i.e., those with core state s_1, s_2, s_{11}, s_{12}, s_{21}, or s_{22}), (2) the receive requests that need to be matched (s_6, s_{17}), (3) all other non-null records, and (4) all null records. These sections are further refined as follows. Within section 1, all records with source 0 occur first, followed by those with source 1, and so on. Within each of these subsections, those with destination 0 occur first, followed by those with destination 1, and so on. Within each of these subsubsections, the records occur according to the order in which the requests were posted. Within section 2, all records with destination 0 occur first, followed by those with destination 1, and so on. Within each of these subsections, the records occur according to the order in which the requests were posted. Notice that, for receives, the further division by source is not possible because of the possible use of MPI_ANY_SOURCE. Within section 3, the records are placed in any canonical order. (In our implementation, each communication record value is assigned a unique integer ID; the canonical order is that of increasing ID.)

Each primitive MPI transformation is engineered to preserve this order. For example, in line 4 of Fig. 2c, an upload transition applied to the send request v_3 that was in section 1, at position 0, causes the send request to be completed (v_4) and moved to section 3, in position 2. A new record for a buffered message (v_5) is inserted at the original position of the send request.

4   Validation

We have implemented the approach of Sec. 3 as an extension to SPIN called MPI-SPIN. The core of the implementation is a C library for manipulating communication records. The library provides functions corresponding to the primitive MPI state transformations of Fig. 4. Because the memory required to store a single communication record is quite large, the library employs a "flyweight" pattern which (1) assigns a unique integer ID to each communication record value it encounters, and (2) stores a single copy of the record in a hash table. By using these IDs, the communication record array can be represented as an integer array in the Promela model. The library functions that operate on the array are incorporated into the Promela model using SPIN's embedded C code facility. The user can access these functions through preprocessor macros defined in a header file. There is one macro for each of the MPI primitives discussed in this paper, and their syntax corresponds closely to the syntax for the C bindings of MPI, making it particularly easy to create models of C/MPI programs (Fig. 5). The MPI infrastructure events are incorporated into the model through an additional "daemon" process that, at each state, nondeterministically selects one of the enabled infrastructure events for execution.

```
active proctype consumer() {
  MPI_Request req[NPRODUCERS];
  byte i = 0;

  MPI_Init(Pconsumer, Pconsumer->_pid);
  do
  :: i < NPRODUCERS ->
     MPI_Irecv(Pconsumer, RECV_BUFF, COUNT, MPI_POINT,
               Pconsumer->i, TAG, &Pconsumer->req[Pconsumer->i]);
     i++
  :: else -> i = 0; break
  od;
  do
  :: MPI_Wait(Pconsumer, &Pconsumer->req[Pconsumer->i],
              MPI_STATUS_IGNORE);
     MPI_Irecv(Pconsumer, RECV_BUFF, COUNT, MPI_POINT, Pconsumer->i,
               TAG, &Pconsumer->req[Pconsumer->i]);
     i = (i + 1)%NPRODUCERS
  od;
  MPI_Finalize(Pconsumer)
}
```

Fig. 5. MPI-SPIN source for model of consumer process of Fig. 1

By default, MPI-SPIN checks a number of generic properties that one would expect to hold in any correct MPI program. These include (1) the program cannot deadlock, (2) there are never two outstanding requests with buffers that intersect nontrivially, (3) the total number of outstanding requests never exceeds the specified bound r, (4) when MPI_Finalize is called there are no request objects allocated for and there are no buffered messages destined for the calling process, and (5) the size of an incoming message is never greater than the size of the receive buffer. In addition, MPI-SPIN can check application-specific properties formulated as assertions or in linear temporal logic.

MPI-SPIN includes some primitives that do not correspond to anything in MPI, but are useful for modeling MPI programs. For example, there is a type MPI_Symbolic (together with a number of operations on that type) that can be used to represent floating-point expressions *symbolically*. Previous work [11] showed how symbolic techniques can be used to verify that a parallel program computes the same result as a trusted sequential version of the program *on any input*. Another primitive, MPI_POINT, represents an "empty" MPI datatype that can be used to abstract away data completely; this is particularly useful for constructing a model of the MPI communication skeleton of a program, as in Fig. 5.

We applied MPI-SPIN to Examples 2.17–2.33 of [12], attempting to verify generic and application-specific properties of each. (The source code for MPI-SPIN and all input and output for these experiments are available at http://www.cis.udel.edu/ siegel/projects.) The symbolic technique was applied to various configurations of the Jacobi iteration examples (2.17, 2.27, 2.32; the sequential version is Ex. 2.12). Ex. 2.17 is one of the cases for which MPI-SPIN discovered a fault. The problem occurs when the number of matrix columns is less than twice the number of processes. In this case, on at least one process two send requests will be posted using the same buffer: the single column stored on that process. For configurations outside of that range, equivalence with the sequential program was verified successfully. One of the larger configurations for Ex. 2.17 involved $N = 11$ matrix columns distributed over $n = 4$ processes, $k = 2$ loop iterations, $r = 16$, and $b = 0$; its verification resulted in searching 256,905 states and consumed 30 MB of RAM. The configuration with $N = 7$, $n = 3$, $k = 2$, $r = 12$, $b = 6$ required 65,849 states and 8 MB.

For each of the producer-consumer systems (2.18, 2.19, 2.26, 2.28, 2.33) the following were checked: (p_0) freedom from deadlock and standard assertions, (p_1) every message produced is eventually consumed, (p_2) no producer becomes permanently blocked, and (p_3) for a fixed producer, messages are consumed in the order produced. Again, various configurations were used in each case; one of the largest involved the verification of p_0 for Ex. 2.18, with $n = 8$, $r = 14$, and $b = 0$, which resulted in 1.8 million states and consumed 235 MB. Some of the properties were and some were not expected to hold on particular systems and, in general, the expected result was obtained for each property-system pair. An exception was Ex. 2.19. In this program, the second `for` loop in Fig. 1 is replaced with

```
i = 0;
while(1) {
  for (flag=0; !flag; i= (i+1)%(size-1)) {
    MPI_Test(&(buffer[i].req), &flag, &status);
  }
  /* consume data */
  MPI_Irecv(bufer[i].data, MAXSIZE, MPI_CHAR, i, tag, comm,
            &buffer[i].req);
}
```

The idea is that the busy-wait loop allows the consumption of messages in whatever order they arrive, rather than enforcing a cyclic order. However, while checking p_0, MPI-SPIN discovered that i is erroneously incremented after the call to `MPI_Test` sets `flag` to `true` and before exiting the loop. This causes the consumer to consume from and repost to the wrong producer and can lead to a violation of the outstanding request bound (and other errors). After correcting this problem, the expected results were obtained.

These preliminary experiments were encouraging in several ways: (1) the tool was able to achieve a conclusive result on all of the examples to which it was applied, including some of nontrivial size, (2) the resources consumed were not excessive, at least by the standards of model checking, and (3) the tool discovered two nontrivial faults that had survived two editions of a widely-used text. However, these examples were admittedly small, and the true viability of the approach will only become apparent as we attempt to scale it to larger and more realistic scientific programs. This will be the focus of our future work.

References

1. G. J. Holzmann. *The* SPIN *Model Checker*. Addison-Wesley, Boston, 2004.
2. O. S. Matlin, E. Lusk, and W. McCune. SPINning parallel systems software. In D. Bosnacki and S. Leue, editors, *Model Checking of Software: 9th International SPIN Workshop, Grenoble, France, April 11–13, 2002, Proceedings*, volume 2318 of *LNCS*, pages 213–220. Springer-Verlag, 2002.
3. Message Passing Interface Forum. MPI: A Message-Passing Interface standard, version 1.1. http://www.mpi-forum.org/docs/, 1995.
4. Message Passing Interface Forum. MPI-2: Extensions to the Message-Passing Interface. http://www.mpi-forum.org/docs/, 1997.
5. S. Pervez, G. Gopalakrishnan, R. M. Kirby, R. Thakur, and W. Gropp. Formal verification of programs that use MPI one-sided communication. In *Proceedings of the 13th European PVM/MPI Users' Group Meeting*, LNCS. Springer, 2006.
6. D. E. Post and L. G. Votta. Computational science demands a new paradigm. *Physics Today*, pages 35–41, Jan. 2005.
7. S. F. Siegel. Efficient verification of halting properties for MPI programs with wildcard receives. In R. Cousot, editor, *Verification, Model Checking, and Abstract Interpretation: 6th International Conference, VMCAI 2005, Paris, January 17–19, 2005, Proceedings*, volume 3385 of *Lecture Notes in Computer Science*, pages 413–429, 2005.
8. S. F. Siegel and G. S. Avrunin. Modeling MPI programs for verification. Technical Report UM-CS-2004-75, Department of Computer Science, University of Massachusetts, 2004.
9. S. F. Siegel and G. S. Avrunin. Verification of MPI-based software for scientific computation. In S. Graf and L. Mounier, editors, *Model Checking Software: 11th International SPIN Workshop, Barcelona, Spain, April 1–3, 2004, Proceedings*, volume 2989 of *Lecture Notes in Computer Science*, pages 286–303. Springer-Verlag, 2004.
10. S. F. Siegel and G. S. Avrunin. Modeling wildcard-free MPI programs for verification. In *Proceedings of the 2005 ACM SIGPLAN Symposium on Principles and Practice of Parallel Programming: PPoPP'05, June 15–17, 2005, Chicago, Illinois, USA*, pages 95–106. ACM Press, 2005.
11. S. F. Siegel, A. Mironova, G. S. Avrunin, and L. A. Clarke. Using model checking with symbolic execution to verify parallel numerical programs. In L. Pollock and M. Pezzé, editors, *ISSTA 2006: Proceedings of the ACM SIGSOFT 2006 International Symposium on Software Testing and Analysis*, pages 157–168, Portland, ME, 2006.
12. M. Snir, S. Otto, S. Huss-Lederman, D. Walker, and J. Dongarra. *MPI—The Complete Reference, Volume 1: The MPI Core*. MIT Press, second edition, 1998.

Model Checking Via ΓCFA

Matthew Might, Benjamin Chambers, and Olin Shivers

{mattm,bjchamb}@cc.gatech.edu, shivers@ccs.neu.edu

Abstract. We present and discuss techniques for performing and improving the model-checking of higher-order, functional programs based upon abstract interpretation [4]. We use continuation-passing-style conversion to produce an abstractable state machine, and then utilize abstract garbage collection and abstract counting [9] to indirectly prune false branches in the abstract state-to-state transition graph. In the process, we generalize abstract garbage collection to *conditional garbage collection*; that is, we collect values which an ordinary reaching-based collector would have deemed live when it is provable that such values will never be referenced. In addition, we enhance *abstract counting*, and then exploit it to more precisely evaluate conditions in the abstract.

Keywords: Abstract interpretation, static analysis, abstract counting, abstract garbage collection, ΓCFA, higher-order languages.

1 Introduction

We are interested in analysing and verifying the behavior of programs written in call-by-value, higher-order programming languages based on the λ-calculus, such as Scheme or Standard ML. (However, techniques developed for this class of languages can be profitably adapted for other higher-order languages, such as Haskell or Java.) Our goal is to describe the construction of a model checker for higher-order programs in such a way that it is eligible to achieve precision enhancements by garbage collecting "dead" environment structure in the abstract state space traversed by the program.

We decompose building a garbage-collecting model checker for a higher-order language into four steps:

1. Convert the language's semantics into state-to-state rules of the form $\varsigma \Rightarrow \varsigma'$.
2. Axiomatize the rules by modelling control explicitly, *i.e.*, with continuations.
3. Instrument the resulting state machine with garbage collection.
4. Construct an abstract interpretation of this machine's transition relation.

The abstract state-to-state transition that results induces a finite, directed graph between abstract states, which sets the stage for model checking. However, the abstraction that makes the state-space finite and hence checkable, can obscure the property we seek, and so render the entire analysis useless. Folding states in the concrete state space together introduces spurious paths; if these spurious paths admit the possibility of "bad" behavior, then our computable abstract

B. Cook and A. Podelski (Eds.): VMCAI 2007, LNCS 4349, pp. 59–73, 2007.

analysis will erroneously conclude that a correct program might give rise to incorrect behavior. The program succeeds, but the analysis has failed.

We address this problem with Step (3) above: garbage-collecting elements of a machine state (such as its environment structure and bound values) permits the abstract interpretation to prune false branches from the state space's transition graph. To get a feel for the reduction in the state space, consider the following doubly nested loop, written in a direct-style Scheme:

```
(letrec ((lp1 (λ (i x)
              (if (= 0 i)  x
                  (letrec ((lp2 (λ (j f y) (if (= 0 j)
                                               (lp1 (- i 1) y)
                                               (lp2 (- j 1) f
                                                    (f y)))))))
                    (lp2 10 (λ (n) (+ n i)) x))))))
    (lp1 10 0))
```

Figure 1 shows the flow-sensitive, context-sensitive abstract transition graphs generated by this loop first without, and then with, abstract garbage collection. Garbage-collecting environment structure during the exploration of the abstract state space yields an order of magnitude improvement in the size of the state space—enough so that the doubly-nested structure of the loop is *visually* apparent from the second graph. (Besides the improvement in analytic precision, we also get a secondary benefit in that the processor time and memory space needed to explore the abstract state space are also greatly reduced.)

Abstract garbage collection sets the stage for another technique known as *abstract counting* [9]. With abstract counting, we track the "cardinality" of an abstract object; that is, we track whether an abstract object currently represents zero, one or more than one concrete values. Suppose we were to use sets of concrete values for our abstract values. Ordinarily, if abstract value A were equal to abstract value B, we could not infer that any concrete value $a \in A$ is equal to any concrete value $b \in B$, *except* for the case where A and B have size one. The ability to transfer abstract equality to concrete equality allows us to more precisely evaluate conditions, *e.g.* (= x y), in the abstract.

In previous work [9], we developed a higher-order flow-analysis framework, ΓCFA, which synergistically combines abstract counting and abstract garbage collection as we've just outlined above. The benefit of combining the two is that we can use abstract counts to reason more precisely about reachable values during abstract garbage collection. This, in turn, increases the chance that we can cut off even more branches from the abstract transition graph.

Our purpose in this paper is to show how ΓCFA technology can be applied to the problem of model-checking software written in higher-order languages. Our technical contributions are:

1. Enhancing abstract garbage collection by switching from *reachability* to *usability* as the criterion for liveness. That is, our garbage collector discards abstract values and environment structure which are "reachable," but whose use is dominated by conditions which have become unsatisfiable. We term this *conditional garbage collection*.

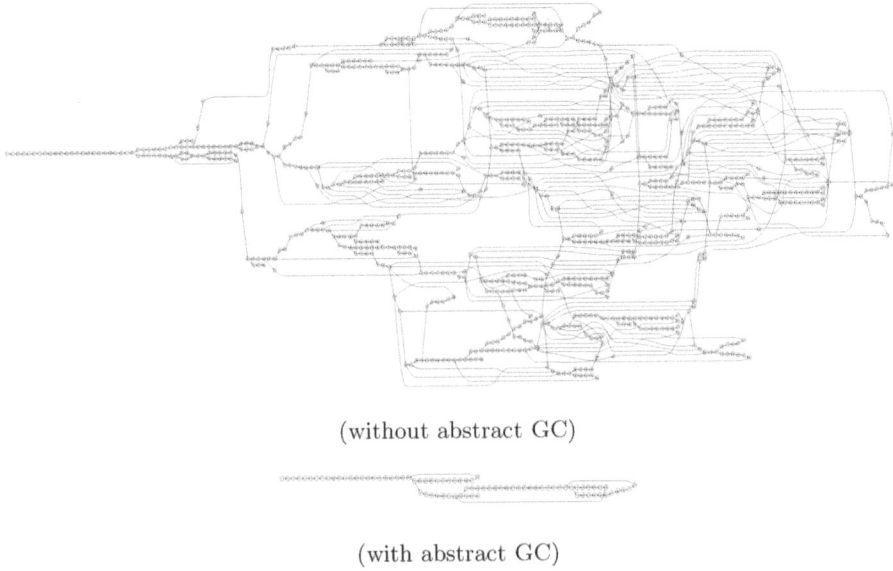

(without abstract GC)

(with abstract GC)

Fig. 1. These images are abstract state-to-state transition graphs generated from the same doubly nested loop. Construction of the top graph did not utilize abstract garbage collection. The bottom graph is the result of garbage collecting at each step.

2. Using abstract counting to more precisely evaluate conditionals during abstract garbage collection. We also improve the precision of abstract counting by accounting for objects that remain invariant across transitions.

2   CPS

Our first task in preparing a program for model checking is to put it into a continuation-passing style (CPS) representation [1,6,12]. In CPS, function calls do not return; they are one-way control transfers. Further, all control structures (call, return, loops, exceptions, and so forth) are encoded using this restricted mechanism. Among other benefits, CPS reifies implicit control context, thus rendering it into a form that can be handled by the abstract garbage-collection machinery we'll be using.

The grammar for our particular CPS representation is given in Figure 2. Note that our language has some syntactic structure more reminiscent of A-Normal Form (ANF) [10] than minimal CPS: it includes an explicit **if** conditional form, instead of encoding conditionals as primitive procedures that take multiple continuation arguments, and we also have a **let** form for binding variables to the results of "trivial" expressions, which can be trees of primop applications whose leaves are variables, constants and λ terms. We also provide a **letrec** form for defining mutually-recursive functions, and a **halt** form that terminates the computation, providing its final result. Note the signature syntactic distinction of

$$const \in CONST \; = \; \mathbb{Z} + \{\texttt{\#f}\}$$
$$prim \in PRIM \quad = \; \{\texttt{+}, \texttt{*}, \texttt{equal?}, \texttt{<}, \ldots\}$$

$$v \in VAR \quad ::= \text{a set of identifiers}$$

$$
\begin{aligned}
e, f \in EXP \quad &::= v \mid const \\
&\mid \; (\lambda \; (v_1 \cdots v_n) \; call) \\
&\mid \; (prim \; v_1 \cdots v_n)
\end{aligned}
$$

$$
\begin{aligned}
call \in CALL \quad &::= (f \; e_1 \cdots e_n) \\
&\mid \; (\texttt{if} \; e_c \; e_t \; e_f) \\
&\mid \; (\texttt{let} \; ((v \; e)) \; call) \\
&\mid \; (\texttt{letrec} \; ((v \; lam)^*) \; call) \\
&\mid \; (\texttt{halt} \; e)
\end{aligned}
$$

Fig. 2. A grammar for restricted CPS. Programs are alphatised terms with no free variables, *i.e.*, any two binding variables are distinct.

a CPS representation: the arguments e_i to a function call $(f \; e_1 \cdots e_n)$ cannot themselves be function calls—that would require function calls to return a value, which CPS does not permit.

3   Generating the Abstract State Graph with ΓCFA

Our objective in this section is to create a computable, *finite* abstract transition relation—that is, a small-step operational semantics for our CPS language whose set of possible machine states is finite. (We skip over the development of the corresponding concrete semantics. It is completely standard, and can, in any event, be inferred from the abstract semantics.) Figure 3 gives the state-space for ΓCFA.

The set $\widehat{State}$ is the set of possible abstract states—the nodes in the forthcoming abstract transition graph. We distinguish two kinds of states: $\widehat{Eval}$ states and $\widehat{Apply}$ states. In an $\widehat{Eval}$ state, execution has reached a call site, *e.g.* $(f \; e_1 \cdots e_n)$, where the function f and its arguments e_i need *evaluation*. In an $\widehat{Apply}$ state, execution has reached the *application* of a procedure to a vector of argument values.

In $\widehat{Eval}$ states, arguments are evaluated under the current environment, which is decomposed into a "local" variable-to-binding portion ($\widehat{BEnv}$) and a "global" binding-to-value portion ($\widehat{VEnv}$) [11]. Given a factored environment $(\hat{\beta}, \hat{ve})$, a variable maps to a value in two stages: (1) the time of its binding in the current environment $\hat{\beta}$ is found: $\hat{\beta}(v)$; and (2) the value attached to the variable at this time is looked up: $\hat{ve}(v, \hat{\beta}(v))$. Consequently, the binding $(v, \hat{t})$ acts as a reference to this value. (When using a binding in this referential sense, we refer to it as a member of $\widehat{Ref}$ to emphasize the distinction.) We also sometimes refer to the variable environment $\hat{ve}$ as the *abstract heap*.

$$\widehat{\varsigma} \in \widehat{State} \;\; = \widehat{Eval} + \widehat{Apply}$$
$$\widehat{Eval} \;\; = \widehat{CALL} \times \widehat{BEnv} \times \widehat{VEnv} \times \widehat{Count} \times \widehat{Time}$$
$$\widehat{Apply} = \widehat{Proc} \times \widehat{D}^* \times \widehat{Ref}^* \times \widehat{VEnv} \times \widehat{Count} \times \widehat{Time}$$
$$\widehat{\beta} \in \widehat{BEnv} = VAR \rightarrow \widehat{Time}$$
$$\widehat{b} \in \widehat{Bind} = VAR \times \widehat{Time}$$
$$\widehat{ve} \in \widehat{VEnv} = \widehat{Bind} \rightarrow \widehat{D}$$
$$\widehat{r} \in \widehat{Ref} \;\; = \widehat{Bind}$$
$$\widehat{d} \in \widehat{D} \;\;\;\; = \mathcal{P}(\widehat{Bas} + \widehat{Proc})$$
$$\widehat{proc} \in \widehat{Proc} = \widehat{Clo}$$
$$\widehat{clo} \in \widehat{Clo} \;\; = LAM \times \widehat{BEnv}$$
$$\widehat{bas} \in \widehat{Bas} \;\; = \cdots$$
$$\widehat{\mu} \in \widehat{Count} = \widehat{Bind} \rightarrow \{0, 1, \infty\}$$
$$\widehat{t} \in \widehat{Time} \;\; = \text{a } \textit{finite} \text{ set of abstract times}$$

Fig. 3. The abstract state-space

The set of abstract denotable values $(\widehat{D})$ is the power set of basic values $(\widehat{Bas})$ and procedures $(\widehat{Proc})$. The finite set $\widehat{Time}$ takes the place of Shivers' contour set [11]; consequently, the context-sensitivity of the analysis depends on the choice of the set $\widehat{Time}$ and the next-time function, $\widehat{succ} : \widehat{State} \times \widehat{Time} \rightarrow \widehat{Time}$.

Up to now, our semantic domains have been completely standard for a higher-order control-flow analysis; we now introduce the extra machinery that gives our ΓCFA abstract semantics the ability to engage in abstract garbage collection and counting. Every state features a counter map $\widehat{\mu}$. For a binding $\widehat{b}$ and counter $\widehat{\mu}$, the count $\widehat{\mu}(\widehat{b})$ approximates how many *concrete* bindings the abstract binding $\widehat{b}$ represents. The set of approximate counts is $\{0, 1, \infty\}$, where the symbol ∞ denotes any number greater than one, and the operator $\oplus$ is the natural abstraction of addition.

The argument-evaluation function $\widehat{\mathcal{A}} : EXP \times \widehat{BEnv} \times \widehat{VEnv} \rightarrow \widehat{D}$ is:

$$\widehat{\mathcal{A}}(const, \widehat{\beta}, \widehat{ve}) = \{const\}$$
$$\widehat{\mathcal{A}}(v, \widehat{\beta}, \widehat{ve}) = \widehat{ve}(v, \widehat{\beta}(v))$$
$$\widehat{\mathcal{A}}(lam, \widehat{\beta}, \widehat{ve}) = \{(lam, \widehat{\beta})\}$$
$$\widehat{\mathcal{A}}([\![(prim\; v_1 \cdots v_n)]\!], \widehat{\beta}, \widehat{ve}) = \widehat{\mathcal{O}}(prim)\langle\widehat{\mathcal{A}}(v_1, \widehat{\beta}, \widehat{ve}), \ldots, \widehat{\mathcal{A}}(v_n, \widehat{\beta}, \widehat{ve})\rangle$$

where the function $\widehat{\mathcal{O}} : PRIM \rightarrow (\widehat{D}^* \rightarrow \widehat{D})$ maps a primitive to a sound abstraction.

Figure 4 defines the transition $\widehat{\varsigma} \approx\!\!\!> \widehat{\varsigma}'$. The first transition rule (arg. eval.) looks up the procedure for the expression f, evaluates the arguments $e_1, \ldots, e_n$ and moves forward. The next rule (conditional) makes a best-effort attempt to avoid forking on conditional evaluation. The subsequent rule (let-binding) covers the $\widehat{Eval}$-to-$\widehat{Eval}$ transition for let constructs. The (letrec-binding) rule is similar, but it implements recursive environment structure by evaluating the λ

$$([\![(f\ e_1\cdots e_n)]\!],\widehat{\beta},\widehat{ve},\widehat{\mu},\widehat{t}) \approx (\widehat{proc},\widehat{\boldsymbol{d}},\widehat{\boldsymbol{r}},\widehat{ve},\widehat{\mu},\widehat{succ}(\widehat{\varsigma},\widehat{t}))$$

where $\begin{cases} \widehat{proc} \in \widehat{\mathcal{A}}(f,\widehat{\beta},\widehat{ve}) \\ \widehat{d_i} = \widehat{\mathcal{A}}(e_i,\widehat{\beta},\widehat{ve}) \\ \widehat{r_i} = \textbf{if } e_i \in VAR \textbf{ then } (e_i,\widehat{t}) \textbf{ else } \bot \end{cases}$ (arg. eval.)

$$([\![(\texttt{if}\ e_c\ e_t\ e_f)]\!],\widehat{\beta},\widehat{ve},\widehat{\mu},\widehat{t}) \approx (\widehat{proc},\langle\rangle,\widehat{ve},\widehat{\mu},\widehat{succ}(\widehat{\varsigma},\widehat{t}))$$

where $\widehat{proc} \in \begin{cases} \widehat{\mathcal{A}}(e_t,\widehat{\beta},\widehat{ve}) & \texttt{\#f} \notin \widehat{\mathcal{A}}(e_c,\widehat{\beta},\widehat{ve}) \\ \widehat{\mathcal{A}}(e_f,\widehat{\beta},\widehat{ve}) & \{\texttt{\#f}\} = \widehat{\mathcal{A}}(e_c,\widehat{\beta},\widehat{ve}) \\ \widehat{\mathcal{A}}(e_t,\widehat{\beta},\widehat{ve}) \sqcup \widehat{\mathcal{A}}(e_f,\widehat{\beta},\widehat{ve}) & \text{otherwise} \end{cases}$ (conditional)

$$([\![(\texttt{let}\ ((v\ e))\ call)]\!],\widehat{\beta},\widehat{ve},\widehat{\mu},\widehat{t}) \approx (call,\widehat{\beta}[v \mapsto \widehat{t}],\widehat{ve}',\widehat{\mu}',\widehat{succ}(\widehat{\varsigma},\widehat{t}))$$

where $\begin{cases} \widehat{ve}' = \widehat{ve} \sqcup [(v,\widehat{t}) \mapsto \widehat{\mathcal{A}}(e,\widehat{\beta},\widehat{ve})] \\ \widehat{\mu}' = \widehat{\mu} \oplus (\lambda\_.0)[(v,\widehat{t}) \mapsto 1] \end{cases}$ (let-binding)

$$([\![(\texttt{letrec}\ ((v\ e)^*)\ call)]\!],\widehat{\beta},\widehat{ve},\widehat{\mu},\widehat{t}) \approx (call,\widehat{\beta}',\widehat{ve}',\widehat{\mu}',\widehat{t}')$$

where $\begin{cases} \widehat{t}' = \widehat{succ}(\widehat{\varsigma},\widehat{t}) \\ \widehat{\beta}' = \widehat{\beta}[v_i \mapsto \widehat{t}'] \\ \widehat{ve}' = \widehat{ve} \sqcup [(v_i,\widehat{t}') \mapsto \widehat{\mathcal{A}}(lam_i,\widehat{\beta}',\widehat{ve})] \\ \widehat{\mu}' = \widehat{\mu} \oplus (\lambda\_.0)[(v_i,\widehat{t}') \mapsto 1] \end{cases}$ (letrec-binding)

$$(([\![(\lambda\ (v_1\cdots v_n)\ call)]\!],\widehat{\beta}),\widehat{\boldsymbol{d}},\widehat{\boldsymbol{r}},\widehat{ve},\widehat{\mu},\widehat{t}) \approx (call,\widehat{\beta}',\widehat{ve}',\widehat{\mu}',\widehat{succ}(\widehat{\varsigma},\widehat{t}))$$

where $\begin{cases} \widehat{\beta}' = \widehat{\beta}[v_i \mapsto \widehat{t}] \\ \widehat{ve}' = \widehat{ve} \sqcup [(v_i,\widehat{t}) \mapsto \widehat{d_i}] \\ \widehat{\mu}' = \widehat{\mu}[(v_i,\widehat{t}) \mapsto \widehat{\mu}(v_i,\widehat{t}) \oplus \textbf{if } (v_i,\widehat{t}) = \widehat{r_i} \textbf{ then } 0 \textbf{ else } 1]. \end{cases}$ (proc. app.)

Fig. 4. The abstract transition $\widehat{\varsigma} \approx \widehat{\varsigma}'$. (ΓCFA)

terms within the *next* environment $\widehat{\beta}'$. The final rule (proc. app.) covers $\widehat{Apply}$-to-$\widehat{Eval}$ transitions for the application of a procedure.

In an improvement upon previous work [9], we include machinery to detect when a binding remains invariant across a call. The sole purpose of passing a vector of references (*i.e.*, bindings) is to determine when a variable is being rebound to itself. In the (proc. app.) rule, when it's found that a binding is being rebound to itself, its abstract cardinality—the number of concrete bindings it represents—does not increase.

The root of the abstract graph for a program *call* is the initial machine state, an $\widehat{Eval}$ state with an empty environment and a counter that maps everything to 0: $(call,\bot,\bot,(\lambda\_.0),\widehat{t_0})$.

Note that using a CPS-based representation renders all the rules of our semantics axioms: none of the rules in Figure 4 are inference rules with antecedents. Thus, a CPS semantics really captures the notion of a "machine," where each transition depends on a local, bounded amount of computation and context.

Finally, note what happens when we cast our fairly standard higher-order control-flow analysis as an abstract small-step semantics: it maps a program into a finite state-graph... which is exactly what a model-checker needs. Before invoking a model checker, however, we'll first turn our attention to techniques to "sharpen" our abstract state graph, reducing the degree of approximation inherent in its finite structure.

4 Governors

Conditional abstract garbage collection attempts to discard even some "reachable" abstract objects by proving that an unsatisfiable condition guards their use. This requires a syntactic function that yields the sequence of the conditions that hold upon reaching an expression. For example, in the expression:

```
(let ((a 3))
  (if (= a b) e1 e2))
```

The *binding* ($\mapsto$ a 3) and the *condition* (= a b) govern the use of the expression e1, whereas ($\mapsto$ a 3) and (not (= a b)) govern the use of e2. Formally, given a term t and a subterm $s \in t$, the governors of s within t are the conditions in the vector $\mathcal{G}(t, s)$, where $\mathcal{G}$ is defined in Figure 5.

$$\mathcal{G}(v, s) = \langle\rangle$$

$$\mathcal{G}(const, s) = \langle\rangle$$

$$\mathcal{G}([\![(\lambda\ (v_1 \cdots v_n)\ call)]\!], s) = \mathcal{G}(call, s)$$

$$\mathcal{G}([\![(e_1 \cdots e_n)]\!], s) = \begin{cases} \mathcal{G}(e_i, s) & s \in e_i \\ \langle\rangle & \text{otherwise} \end{cases}$$

$$\mathcal{G}([\![(\texttt{let}\ ((v\ e))\ call)]\!], s) = \begin{cases} \mathcal{G}(e, s) & s \in e \\ \langle [\![(\mapsto\ v\ e)]\!]\rangle\ \S\ \mathcal{G}(call, s) & s \in call \\ \langle\rangle & \text{otherwise} \end{cases}$$

$$\mathcal{G}([\![(\texttt{letrec}\ ((v\ lam)^*)\ call)]\!], s) = \begin{cases} \langle [\![(\mapsto\ v_i\ lam_i)]\!]\rangle\ \S\ \mathcal{G}(lam_i, s) & s \in lam_i \\ \langle [\![(\mapsto\ v_i\ lam_i)]\!]\rangle\ \S\ \mathcal{G}(call, s) & s \in call \\ \langle\rangle & \text{otherwise} \end{cases}$$

$$\mathcal{G}([\![(\texttt{if}\ e_c\ e_t\ e_f)]\!], s) = \begin{cases} \langle e_c\rangle\ \S\ \mathcal{G}(e_t, s) & s \in e_t \\ \langle [\![(\texttt{not}\ e_c)]\!]\rangle\ \S\ \mathcal{G}(e_f, s) & s \in e_f \\ \langle\rangle & \text{otherwise} \end{cases}$$

Fig. 5. The governor function. (We write $v_1\ \S\ v_2$ to concatenate two vectors.)

5 Conditional Abstract Garbage Collection

In previous work [9], we based abstract garbage collection on the same notion as concrete garbage collection: *reachability*. That is, if object a is reachable, and a points to b, then object b is also considered reachable. Reachability, however, is overly conservative, as it might keep objects uncollected when they will never again be *used*.

Consider the following thunk-creating function, f:

```
(define (f a b c d)
  (λ () (if (equal? a b) c d)))
```

Analyzing the expression (f x x y z) produces an abstract closure containing entries for the variables a, b, c and d in its environment. So, all four bindings would be considered *reachable* from this closure. In reality, however, it is impossible to reach the binding to the variable d, since the predicate (not (equal? a b)) governs its use, and because the predicate is provably unsatisfiable from the information x = a = b. To lessen such problems, we annotate object-to-object links with governing conditions in the abstract heap $\widehat{ve}$; these conditions must be satisfiable for a binding to be potentially usable.

To build this stronger GC, we first need the concept of the set of bindings *touched* by a value. The touching function accepts an environment, a counter and a value, and it returns the bindings directly touched by that value:

$$\widehat{\mathcal{T}}_{\widehat{ve}}^{\widehat{\mu}}(lam, \widehat{\beta}) = \{(v, \widehat{\beta}(v)) : v \in \mathit{free}(lam) \text{ and } (\widehat{\beta}, \widehat{ve}, \widehat{\mu}, \langle\rangle) \; \mathit{MaySat} \; \mathcal{G}(lam, v)\},$$

where the *MaySat* (may satisfy) relation includes a binding only if all of its governors could be satisfiable.

The *MaySat* relation is a subset of $(\widehat{BEnv} \times \widehat{VEnv} \times \widehat{Count} \times \widehat{Gov}^*) \times \widehat{Gov}^*$. The notion that a compound environment $(\widehat{\beta}, \widehat{ve}, \widehat{\mu}, \boldsymbol{g})$ may satisfy a vector of governors $\boldsymbol{g}'$ is defined recursively:

$$\frac{(\widehat{\beta}, \widehat{ve}, \widehat{\mu}, \boldsymbol{g}) \; \mathit{MaySat} \; g_1' \qquad (\widehat{\beta}, \widehat{ve}, \widehat{\mu}, \boldsymbol{g} \S \langle g_1' \rangle) \; \mathit{MaySat} \; \langle g_2', \ldots, g_n' \rangle}{(\widehat{\beta}, \widehat{ve}, \widehat{\mu}, \boldsymbol{g}) \; \mathit{MaySat} \; \langle g_1', \ldots, g_n' \rangle}$$

The base case, $(\widehat{\beta}, \widehat{ve}, \widehat{\mu}, \boldsymbol{g}) \; \mathit{MaySat} \; \langle\rangle$, holds trivially.

Clearly, we can specify a number of rules to describe the *MaySat* relation on a single governor. The less obvious rules are below. For any case not covered, the *MaySat* relation can always conservatively report "yes," Were the relation *MaySat* to always report "yes," the GC would become reachability-based.

Binding governors are trivially satisfied, and they also yield an equivalence:

$$\frac{(\mapsto v\ e) \in \boldsymbol{g}}{(\widehat{\beta}, \widehat{ve}, \widehat{\mu}, \boldsymbol{g}) \; \mathit{MaySat} \; (\equiv v\ e)}$$

Surprisingly, with the use of abstract counting, we can also attempt to prove complete equality ($\equiv$) for function values by checking (efficiently) to see if two closures happen to describe the same function:

$$\frac{\widehat{\mathcal{A}}(v_1, \widehat{\beta}, \widehat{ve}) = \widehat{\mathcal{A}}(v_2, \widehat{\beta}, \widehat{ve}) = (lam, \widehat{\beta}') \qquad \forall v \in \mathit{free}(lam) : \widehat{\mu}(v, \widehat{\beta}'(v)) = 1}{(\widehat{\beta}, \widehat{ve}, \widehat{\mu}, \boldsymbol{g}) \; \mathit{MaySat} \; (\equiv v_1\ v_2)}$$

We may also choose to invoke an external theorem prover in an attempt to demonstrate the *MaySat* relation. In other work [8], we explored the sound integration of abstract interpretation and theorem proving. The issues and solutions encountered there are adaptable to this context as well.

At this point, we can define the remainder of the garbage-collection machinery. Basic values touch nothing; for denotables, we extend touching:

$$\widehat{\mathcal{T}}_{\widehat{ve}}^{\widehat{\mu}}\{\widehat{proc}_1,\ldots,\widehat{proc}_n\} = \widehat{\mathcal{T}}_{\widehat{ve}}^{\widehat{\mu}}(\widehat{proc}_1) \cup \cdots \cup \widehat{\mathcal{T}}_{\widehat{ve}}^{\widehat{\mu}}(\widehat{proc}_n).$$

We can then extend the notion of touching to states:

$$\widehat{\mathcal{T}}(call,\widehat{\beta},\widehat{ve},\widehat{\mu},\widehat{t}) = \left\{ (v,\widehat{\beta}(v)) : \begin{array}{l} v \in \mathit{free}(call), \text{ and} \\ (\widehat{\beta},\widehat{ve},\widehat{\mu},\langle\rangle) \; \mathit{MaySat} \; \mathcal{G}(call,v) \end{array} \right\}$$

$$\widehat{\mathcal{T}}(\widehat{proc},\widehat{d},\widehat{r},\widehat{ve},\widehat{\mu},\widehat{t}) = \widehat{\mathcal{T}}_{\widehat{ve}}^{\widehat{\mu}}(\widehat{proc}) \cup \widehat{\mathcal{T}}_{\widehat{ve}}^{\widehat{\mu}}(\widehat{d}_1) \cup \cdots \cup \widehat{\mathcal{T}}_{\widehat{ve}}^{\widehat{\mu}}(\widehat{d}_n).$$

These functions return the root set from which garbage collection begins. Note that the touching function does *not* return the references supplied, $\widehat{r}$. These references are never used to index into the abstract heap $\widehat{ve}$, and so do not constitute a reachable use.

The resource we care about is the set of reachable bindings (not values), so the following relation links binding to binding, skipping over intervening values:

$$\widehat{b}_{\text{toucher}} \leadsto_{\widehat{ve}}^{\widehat{\mu}} \widehat{b}_{\text{touched}} \text{ iff } \widehat{b}_{\text{touched}} \in \widehat{\mathcal{T}}_{\widehat{ve}}^{\widehat{\mu}}(\widehat{ve}(\widehat{b}_{\text{toucher}})).$$

The abstract reachable-bindings function, $\widehat{\mathcal{R}} : \widehat{State} \to \mathcal{P}(\widehat{Bind})$ computes the bindings reachable from a state:

$$\widehat{\mathcal{R}}(\widehat{\varsigma}) = \{\widehat{b} : \widehat{b}_{\text{root}} \in \widehat{\mathcal{T}}(\widehat{\varsigma}) \text{ and } \widehat{b}_{\text{root}} \leadsto_{\widehat{ve}_{\widehat{\varsigma}}}^{\widehat{\mu}_{\widehat{\varsigma}}}{}^{*} \widehat{b}\}.$$

Now we can define the abstract GC function, $\widehat{\Gamma} : \widehat{State} \to \widehat{State}$:

$$\widehat{\Gamma}(\widehat{\varsigma}) = \begin{cases} (\widehat{proc},\widehat{d},\widehat{r},\widehat{ve}|\widehat{\mathcal{R}}(\widehat{\varsigma}),\widehat{\mu}|\widehat{\mathcal{R}}(\widehat{\varsigma}),\widehat{t}) & \widehat{\varsigma} = (\widehat{proc},\widehat{d},\widehat{r},\widehat{ve},\widehat{\mu},\widehat{t}) \\ (call,\widehat{\beta},\widehat{ve}|\widehat{\mathcal{R}}(\widehat{\varsigma}),\widehat{\mu}|\widehat{\mathcal{R}}(\widehat{\varsigma}),\widehat{t}) & \widehat{\varsigma} = (call,\widehat{\beta},\widehat{ve},\widehat{\mu},\widehat{t}). \end{cases}$$

Less formally, abstract garbage collection restricts the global variable environment and the counter to those bindings which are reachable from that state.[1]

For any state, we can make a garbage-collecting transition instead of a regular transition:

$$\frac{\widehat{\Gamma}(\widehat{\varsigma}) \Rrightarrow \widehat{\varsigma}'}{\widehat{\varsigma} \Rrightarrow_{\widehat{\Gamma}} \widehat{\varsigma}'}.$$

Unlike the flow-analytic version of ΓCFA, there is no advantage for precision in delaying a collection, so every transition now collects.[2] Figure 6 provides a visual representation of the abstract heap both without governors (traditional ΓCFA) and with governors (our enhanced ΓCFA).

---

[1] When an entry in a counter $\widehat{\mu}$ is restricted, it maps to 0 rather than the value $\bot$.

[2] Some optimizations, such as Super-β copy propagation, require that the flow analysis preserves information about dead bindings as long as possible. If counting can prove a dead binding equivalent to a live binding, it is sometimes efficient to replace the live variable with the otherwise dead variable.

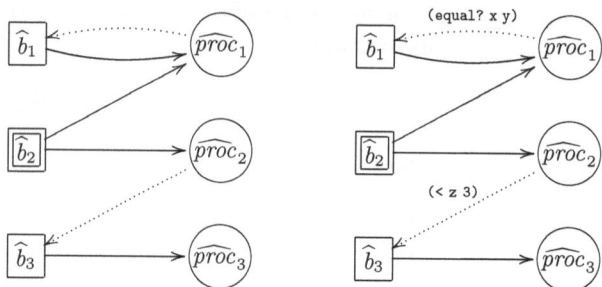

Fig. 6. Two illustrations of an abstract environment ($\widehat{ve}$). Abstract bindings (in boxes) behave like addresses. Abstract values are in circles. Solid arrows denote that a binding yields a particular value in this abstract machine state's total environment $\widehat{ve}$. Dotted arrows denote that a value touches ($\widehat{T}$) a particular binding. The labels on dotted arrows denote the guards which must be satisfiable in order for the binding to be semantically touchable. The image on the left denotes a heap without governors; the image on the right includes sample governors which must be satisfied for a value to touch a binding.

6   Termination

Naïvely exploring the entire abstract transition graph, while sound, is not the best approach to running the analysis. At the very least, the state-space should be explored in depth-first order; each time a new state $\widehat{\varsigma}$ is encountered, the analysis should check to see whether there exists previously-visited state $\widehat{\varsigma}'$ such that $\widehat{\varsigma} \sqsubseteq \widehat{\varsigma}'$. If so, this branch terminates soundly.

Even this approach, however, misses opportunties to cut off forking due to conditionals such as if. Instead, the search can use *two* work lists: a *normal* work list, and a *join-point* work list. In the normal phase, the search pulls from the normal work list. When queueing subsequent states, a state applying a join-point continuation[3] goes in the join-point work list. After exhausting the normal work list, the search runs garbage collection on all states in the join-point list. After this, the search is free to merge (through $\sqcup : Apply \times Apply \rightarrow Apply$) those states currently at the same continuation. Aggressive merging lowers precision in exchange for speed, whereas less enthusiastic merging leads to higher precision but more time. After this, the join-point and normal lists are swapped, and the exploration continues.

7   A Small Example

In this section, we will trace through a small example that very simply demonstrates how abstract garbage collection leads to increased flow-sensitivity even in a context-insensitive analysis. Flow-sensitivity, in turn, is important when

---

[3] Join-point continuations are easily annotated during CPS conversion.

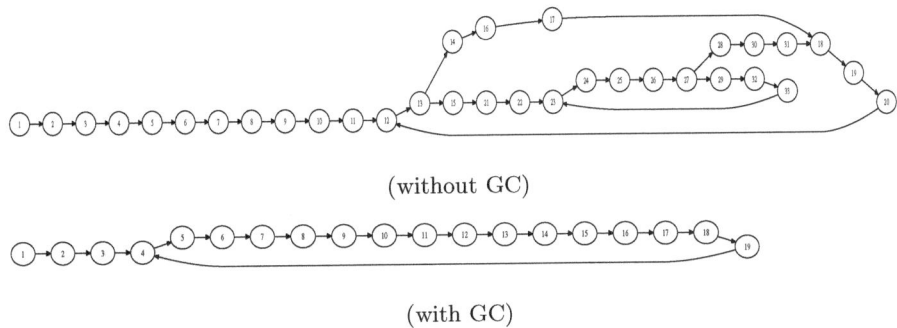

(without GC)

(with GC)

Fig. 7. Abstract state transition graphs without, and then with, abstract garbage collection for the infinite lock-unlock loop example

verifying the safety of programs that must obey an ordering in their use of an API. We opt for a very simple specification: that calls to `lock` and `unlock` are in the right order and never nested.

Take the following program:

```
(define (lockloop n)
   (if (= n 0) (begin (lock mutex) (lockloop 1))
               (begin (unlock mutex) (lockloop 0)))))
(lockloop 0)
```

Clearly, this program will forever alternate between locking and unlocking `mutex`. But can we model check the computation's abstract state space to verify that it correctly observes the lock/unlock protocol? Unfortunately, if we proceed with an ordinary 0CFA-level abstract interpretation, we're told that this code could potentially lock `mutex` twice. Here's what happens:

1. The flow set for n grows to $\{0\}$.
2. The true conditional arm is taken.
3. `mutex` is locked.
4. `lockloop` is called recursively.
5. The flow set for n grows to $\{0, 1\}$.
6. Both conditional arms are taken.
7. The analysis tries to re-lock `mutex`.
8. Lock-order-safety verification fails.

The problem we're encountering is that in a traditional abstract interpretation, the flow sets increase monotonically. With abstract garbage collection enabled, however, flow sets can contract, and we get the following scenario:

1. The flow set for n grows to $\{0\}$.
2. The true conditional arm is taken.
3. `mutex` is locked.
4. The flow set for n is GC'd.
5. `lockloop` is called recursively.
6. The flow set for n grows to $\{1\}$.
7. The false conditional arm is taken.
8. `mutex` is unlocked.
9. The flow set for n is GC'd.
10. `lockloop` is called recursively.
11. The flow set for n grows to $\{0\}$.
12. Lock-order verification succeeds.

With abstract garbage collection enabled, this small example is verified to be safe with respect to proper locking behavior even with 0CFA-level precision. Figure 7 depicts the abstract transition graphs generated both without, and then with, abstract garbage collection enabled. As before, the simplification makes it possible *visually* to reconstruct the control flow of the code from the garbage-collected graph.

Note that we have *not* verified the (enormous) state space produced by interleaving execution steps of the locking thread with execution steps of some other thread in some concurrent semantics, which, of course, is the context in which we usually care about locks. We have simply verified that a single sequential computation manipulates a resource such as a lock or a file descriptor according to the requirements of some prescribed use protocol.

8 A Higher-Order Example

Garbage collection also plays a critical role in taming higher-orderness during model checking. Consider the following code, which demonstrates this point:

```
(define mylock   (identity lock))
(define myunlock (identity unlock))
(mylock mutex)   (myunlock mutex)
```

Once again, running the 0CFA-level interpretation without garbage collection fails to verify. Running it again, but with garbage collection, succeeds.

As before, the problem is flow-set merging. Both `lock` and `unlock` are seen flowing out of the identity function `id` when `myunlock` is bound. Hence, the flow set for `myunlock` includes both `lock` and `unlock`. Thus, it appears to the program that "lock lock" is a possible sequence.

With garbage collection enabled, the flow set for the return value of `id` is collected before the second call, thereby keeping the flow set of `myunlock` to strictly `unlock`. Consequently, the only lock sequence exhibited is "lock unlock."

Figure 8 contains the abstract transition graphs both with and without garbage collection for a 0CFA-level contour set. Once again, the collected graph has exactly the linear progression of states we expect from this example. The uncollected graph is even more unwieldy than expected. This happens because continuations (unseen in the direct-style code) also merge in the abstract, and this leads to further losses in precision and speed. In the garbage-collected version, however, flow sets for continuations are also collected.

When a sequence of locks must be taken in order to use a resource, handling higher-orderness precisely is even more important, for then code patterns such as the following become commonplace and natural to the functional programmer:

```
(map lock lock-list)
...
(map unlock lock-list)
```

Fortunately, with ΓCFA, the flow sets for `f` don't merge between invocations of `map`, as they ordinarily would without garbage collection.

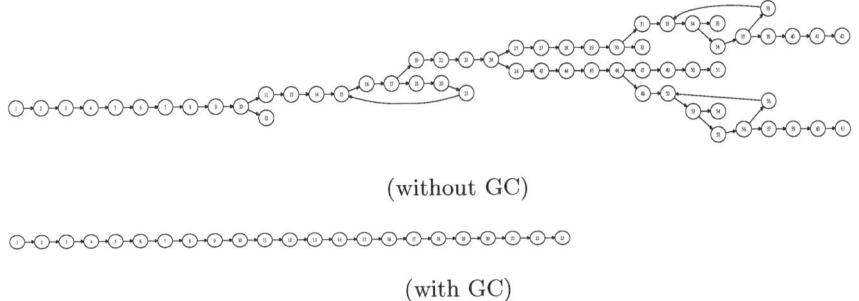

(without GC)

(with GC)

Fig. 8. Abstract state transition graphs without and then with abstract garbage collection for the higher-order lock-unlock example

9   Understanding Abstract Garbage Collection

It's worth exploring the subtle interaction between flow sensitivity, continuations and abstract GC with a quick case-wise analysis. Programmers hoping to have their programs validated by this technology should know when abstract GC wins, and when it loses.

Suppose the call site (f ... e) with continuation argument e invokes the function (λ (... k) ...) during abstract interpretation. Let's also assume a 0CFA contour set for now. We can divide this situation into three possible cases.

The first case is when this function is being called recursively as a self-tail call. That is, a frame for this λ term is live and topmost on the stack, the continuation e is the variable k, and the function f evaluates to this λ term. Because this is a tail call, the flow set for the variable k is going to merge with itself. In other words, no precision is lost for this continuation. As a result, no additional branching results when this function returns to the values that k represents. This is important, because iteration constructs such as for loops and while loops transform to this kind of tail recursion in CPS. The extra intelligence we have added about re-binding a variable to itself prevents counting precision from degrading in this case, too.

The second case is when this λ term is being called recursively (perhaps indirectly or mutually) but not as a tail-call. That is, a frame for this λ term is live on the stack. This liveness makes the binding for k uncollectable. As a result, the flow set for the return point e will merge into the flow set for the continuation k, which already contains return points for the external call to this λ term. Consequently, when interpretation returns from this λ term, it will return to external callers from internal or indirectly recursive call sites. If the precision loss is an issue, switching to a 1CFA contour set or to polymorphic-splitting [13] removes some of this kind of merging.

The third case is when this λ term is not live on the stack; that is, an external call to this λ term. In this case, the binding to the continuation variable k is collectable. Consequently, before merging the flow set for the return point e into the flow set for the continuation k, the flow set for the continuation k is reset to empty. So, in the abstract interpretation, this λ term returns only to the return points in the flow set for the return point e.

This behavior is a major departure from ordinary flow-sensitive 0CFA analyses, where a function spuriously returns to the return points of all previous callers. The net effect of this behavior is to augment the degree of polyvariance achieved for any given contour set. Perhaps most importantly, we can make promises to the programmer that if they use strict tail-recursion and imperative iteration constructs such as `while` and `for`, they will be rewarded during abstract interpretation.

10   Implementation

We have an implementation of ΓCFA for Scheme, written in Haskell. This is the implementation that we used to analyse the lock protocols of the examples in the previous two sections. The implementation also produces warnings for possible list-access violations, *e.g.* taking the `car` of the empty list. In addition, it performs shape analysis on linked lists, reporting back locations through which improper (*i.e.*, non-`nil`-terminated) lists may pass. At present, the implementation does not utilize an external theorem prover for the *MaySat* relation. We are currently working with our colleagues at Georgia Tech to integrate the ACL2 theorem prover into the system.

11   Related Work

The analysis of recursive, higher-order functions in the λ calculus has a rich history dating back to Church's original work. In recent years, software verification and model-checking have made strides with tools such as SLAM [2] and TERMINATOR [3]. TERMINATOR, in fact, can reason about function pointers, which are a strictly weaker, environmentless cousin to the higher-order closures we deal with here. Fusing Leuschel *et al.*'s recent work [7] on symbolic closures with our own presents a promising avenue for future research.

ΓCFA is embedded within the Cousots' framework of abstract interpretation [4,5]. It falls into the family of *sound, context-sensitive, flow-sensitive, non-monotonic* model checkers for higher-order programs. ΓCFA differs from other approaches in that it is geared specifically toward controlling spurious branches that result from control structures such as continuations and higher-order functions. We believe it is possible to adapt the notion of abstract garbage collection to abstract-interpretation-based checkers.

References

1. APPEL, A. W. *Compiling with Continuations.* Cambridge University Press, 1992.
2. BALL, T., AND RAJAMANI, S. K. The SLAM project: Debugging system software via static analysis. In *Proceedings of the 29th Annual ACM SIGPLAN Conference on the Principles of Programming Languages* (Portland, Oregon, January 2002), pp. 1–3.

3. COOK, B., PODELSKI, A., AND RYBALCHENKO, A. Termination proofs for systems code. In *Proceedings of the ACM SIGPLAN Conference on Programming Language Design and Implementation (PLDI 2006)* (Ottawa, Canada, June 2006).

4. COUSOT, P., AND COUSOT, R. Abstract interpretation: a unified lattice model for static analysis of programs by construction or approximation of fixpoints. In *ACM SIGPLAN Symposium on Principles of Programming Languages* (Los Angeles, California, Jan. 1977), vol. 4, pp. 238–252.

5. COUSOT, P., AND COUSOT, R. Systematic design of program analysis frameworks. In *ACM SIGPLAN Symposium on Principles of Programming Languages* (San Antonio, Texas, Jan. 1979), vol. 6, pp. 269–282.

6. DANVY, O. A first-order one-pass CPS transformation. *Theoretical Computer Science 308*, 1-3 (2003), 239–257.

7. LEUSCHEL, M., AND BENDISPOSTO, J. Animating and model checking b specifications with higher-order recursive functions. In *Rigorous Methods for Software Construction and Analysis* (2006), J.-R. Abrial and U. Glässer, Eds., no. 06191 in Dagstuhl Seminar Proceedings.

8. MIGHT, M. Logic-flow analysis of higher-order programs. In *Proceedings of the 34th Annual ACM SIGPLAN Conference on the Principles of Programming Languages* (Nice, France, January 2007).

9. MIGHT, M., AND SHIVERS, O. Improving Flow Analysis via ΓCFA: Abstract Garbage Collection and Counting. In *Proceedings of the 11th ACM SIGPLAN International Conference on Functional Programming (ICFP 2006)* (Portland, Oregon, September 2006).

10. SABRY, A., AND FELLEISEN, M. Reasoning about programs in continuation-passing style. *Lisp and Symbolic Computation 6*, 3/4 (1993), 289–360.

11. SHIVERS, O. Control-flow analysis in Scheme. In *Proceedings of the SIGPLAN '88 Conference on Programming Language Design and Implementation (PLDI)* (Atlanta, Georgia, June 1988), pp. 164–174.

12. STEELE JR., G. L. RABBIT: a compiler for SCHEME. Master's thesis, Artificial Intelligence Laboratory, Massachusetts Institute of Technology, Cambridge, Massachusetts, May 1978. Technical report AI-TR-474.

13. WRIGHT, A. K., AND JAGANNATHAN, S. Polymorphic splitting: An effective polyvariant flow analysis. *ACM Transactions on Programming Languages and Systems 20*, 1 (January 1998), 166–207.

Using First-Order Theorem Provers in the Jahob Data Structure Verification System

Charles Bouillaguet[1], Viktor Kuncak[2],
Thomas Wies[3], Karen Zee[2], and Martin Rinard[2]

[1] Ecole Normale Supérieure de Cachan, Cachan, France
charles.bouillaguet@ens.fr
[2] MIT Computer Science and Artificial Intelligence Lab, Cambridge, USA
{vkuncak,kkz,rinard}@csail.mit.edu
[3] Max-Planck-Institut für Informatik, Saarbrücken, Germany
wies@mpi-inf.mpg.de

Abstract. This paper presents our integration of efficient resolution-based theorem provers into the Jahob data structure verification system. Our experimental results show that this approach enables Jahob to automatically verify the correctness of a range of complex dynamically instantiable data structures, such as hash tables and search trees, without the need for interactive theorem proving or techniques tailored to individual data structures.

Our primary technical results include: (1) a translation from higher-order logic to first-order logic that enables the application of resolution-based theorem provers and (2) a proof that eliminating type (sort) information in formulas is both sound and complete, even in the presence of a generic equality operator. Our experimental results show that the elimination of type information often dramatically decreases the time required to prove the resulting formulas.

These techniques enabled us to verify complex correctness properties of Java programs such as a mutable set implemented as an imperative linked list, a finite map implemented as a functional ordered tree, a hash table with a mutable array, and a simple library system example that uses these container data structures. Our system verifies (in a matter of minutes) that data structure operations correctly update the finite map, that they preserve data structure invariants (such as ordering of elements, membership in appropriate hash table buckets, or relationships between sets and relations), and that there are no run-time errors such as null dereferences or array out of bounds accesses.

1 Introduction

One of the main challenges in the verification of software systems is the analysis of unbounded data structures with dynamically allocated linked data structures and arrays. Examples of such data structures are linked lists, trees, and hash tables. The goal of these data structures is to efficiently implement sets and relations, with operations such as lookup, insert, and removal. This paper explores

B. Cook and A. Podelski (Eds.): VMCAI 2007, LNCS 4349, pp. 74–88, 2007.

the verification of programs with such data structures using resolution-based theorem provers for first-order logic with equality. We only summarize the main ideas here; see [4] for details.

Initial goal and the effectiveness of the approach. The initial motivation for using first-order provers is the observation that quantifier-free constraints on sets and relations that represent data structures can be translated to first-order logic. This approach is suitable for verifying clients of data structures, because such verification need not deal with transitive closure present in the implementation of recursive data structures. The context of this work is the Jahob system for verifying data structure consistency properties [7]. Our initial goal was to incorporate first-order theorem provers into Jahob to verify data structure clients. While we have indeed successfully verified data structure clients, we also discovered that this approach has a wider range of applicability than we had initially anticipated, in several respects. 1) We were able to apply this technique not only to data structure clients, but also to data structure implementations, using recursion and ghost variables and, in some cases, confining data structure mutation to newly allocated objects only. 2) Theorem provers were effective at dealing with quantified invariants that often arise when reasoning about unbounded numbers of objects. 3) Using a simple partial axiomatization of linear arithmetic, we were able to verify not only linking properties traditionally addressed by shape analyses, but also ordering properties in a binary search tree, hash table invariants, and bounds for all array accesses.

The context of our results. We find our current results encouraging and attribute them to several factors. Our use of ghost variables eliminated the need for transitive closure in specifications for our examples. Our use of recursion in combination with Jahob's approach to handling procedure calls resulted in more tractable verification conditions. The semantics of procedure calls that we used in our examples is based on complete hiding of modifications to encapsulated objects. This semantics avoids the pessimistic assumption that every object is modified unless semantically proven otherwise, but currently prevents external references to encapsulated objects using simple syntactic checks. Finally, for those of our procedures that were written using loops instead of recursion, we manually supplied loop invariants.

Key ideas. The complexity of the properties we are checking makes verification non-trivial even under these assumptions, and we found it necessary to introduce the following techniques for proving the generated verification conditions.

1. We introduce a translation to first-order logic with equality that avoids the potential inefficiencies of a general encoding of higher-order logic into first-order logic by handling the common cases and soundly approximating the remaining cases.
2. We use a translation to first-order logic that ignores information about sorts that would distinguish integers from objects. The results are smaller proof obligations and substantially better performance of provers. Moreover, we

prove a somewhat surprising result: omitting such sort information is always sound and complete for disjoint sorts of the same cardinality. This avoids the need to separately check the generated proofs for soundness. Omitting sorts was essential for obtaining our results. Without it, difficult proof obligations are impossible to prove or take a substantially larger amount of time.

3. We use heuristics for filtering assumptions from first-order formulas that reduce the input problem size, speed up the theorem proving process, and improve the automation of the verification process.

The first two techniques are the main contribution of this paper; the use of the third technique confirms previous observations about the usefulness of assumption filtering in automatically generated first-order formulas [13].

Verified data structures and properties. Together, these techniques enabled us to verify, for example, that binary search trees and hash tables correctly implement their relational interfaces, including an accurate specification of removal operations. Such postconditions of operations in turn required verifying representation invariants: in binary search tree, they require proving sortedness of the tree; in hash table, they require proving that keys belong to the buckets given by their hash code. To summarize, our technique verifies that

1. representation invariants hold in the initial state;
2. each data structure operation
   a) establishes the postcondition specifying the change of a user-specified abstract variable such as a set or relation; for example, an operation that updates a key is given by the postcondition
      $$\text{content} = (\text{old content} \setminus \{(x, y) \mid x = \text{key}\}) \cup \{(\text{key}, \text{value})\};$$
   b) does not modify unintended parts of the state, for example, a mutable operation on an instantiable data structure preserves the values of all instances in the heap other than the receiver parameter;
   c) preserves the representation invariants; and
   d) never causes run-time errors such as null dereference or array bounds violation.

We were able to prove such properties for an implementation of a hash table, a mutable list, a functional implementation of an ordered binary search tree, and a functional association list. All these data structures are instantiable (as opposed to global), which means that data structure clients can create an unbounded number of their instances. Jahob verifies that changes to one instance do not cause changes to other instances. In addition, we verified a simple client, a library system, that instantiates several set and relation data structures and maintains object-model like constraints on them in the presence of changes to sets and relations.

What is remarkable is that we were able to establish these results using a general-purpose technique and standard logical formalisms, without specializing our system to particular classes of properties. The fact that we can use continuously improving resolution-based theorem provers with standardized interfaces suggests that this technique is likely to remain competitive in the future.

From the theorem proving perspective, we expect the techniques we identify in this paper to help make future theorem provers even more useful for program verification tasks. From the program verification perspective, our experience suggests that we will soon have a verified library of linked data structures that we can use to build and verify larger applications.

```
public ghost specvar content :: "(int * obj) set" = "{}";

public static FuncTree empty_set()
  ensures "result..content = {}"

public static FuncTree add(int k, Object v, FuncTree t)
  requires "v ~= null & (ALL y. (k,y) ~: t..content)"
  ensures "result..content = t..content + {(k,v)}"

public static FuncTree update(int k, Object v, FuncTree t)
  requires "v ~= null"
  ensures "result..content = t..content - {(x,y). x=k} + {(k,v)}"

public static Object lookup(int k, FuncTree t)
  ensures "(result ~= null & (k, result) : t..content)
        | (result = null & (ALL v. (k,v) ~: t..content))"

public static FuncTree remove(int k, FuncTree t)
  ensures "result..content = t..content - {(x,y). x=k}"
```

Fig. 1. Method contracts for a tree implementation of a map

2   Binary Tree Example

We illustrate our technique using an example of a binary search tree implementing a finite map. Our implementation is written in Java and is persistent, which means that the data structure operations do not mutate existing objects, only newly allocated objects. This makes the verification easier and provides a data structure which is useful in, for example, backtracking algorithms.

Figure 1 shows the public interface of our tree data structure. The interface introduces an abstract specification variable **content** as a set of (key,value)-pairs and specifies the contract of each procedure using a precondition (given by the **requires** keyword) and postcondition (given by the **ensures** keyword). The methods have no **modifies** clauses, indicating that they only mutate newly allocated objects. In Jahob, the developer specifies annotations such as procedure contracts in special comments /*: ... */ that begin with a colon. The formulas in annotations belong to an expressive subset of the language used by the Isabelle proof assistant [16]. This language supports set comprehensions and tuples, which makes the specification of procedure contracts in this example very natural. Single dot . informally means "such that", both for quantifiers and set comprehensions. The notation f x denotes function f applied to argument x. Jahob models instance fields as functions from objects to values (objects, integers, or booleans). The operator .. is a variant of function application given by x..f = f x. Operator : denotes set membership, ~= denotes disequality, Un (or, overloaded, +) denotes union and \<setminus> (or, overloaded, −) denotes set difference.

```
public static Object lookup(int k, FuncTree t)
/*: ensures "(result ~= null & (k, result) : t..content)
            | (result = null & (ALL v. (k,v) ~: t..content))" */
{
    if (t == null) return null;
    else
        if (k == t.key) return t.data;
        else if (k < t.key) return lookup(k, t.left);
        else return lookup(k, t.right);
}
```

Fig. 2. Lookup operation for retrieving the element associated with a given key

```
class FuncTree {
  private int key;
  private Object data;
  private FuncTree left, right;
/*:
public ghost specvar content :: "(int * obj) set" = "{}";

invariant nullEmpty: "this = null --> content = {}"

invariant contentDefinition: "this ~= null -->
            content = {(key, data)} + left..content + right..content"

invariant noNullData: "this ~= null --> data ~= null"

invariant leftSmaller: "ALL k v. (k,v) : left..content --> k < key"
invariant rightBigger: "ALL k v. (k,v) : right..content --> k > key" */
```

Fig. 3. Fields and representation invariants for the tree implementation

Figure 2 presents the tree lookup operation. The operation examines the tree and returns the appropriate element. Note that, to prove that lookup is correct, one needs to know the relationship between the abstract variable content and the data structure fields left, right, key, and data. In particular, it is necessary to conclude that if an element is not found, then it is not in the data structure. Such conditions refer to private fields, so they cannot be captured by the public precondition; they are instead given by *representation invariants*. Figure 3 presents the representation invariants for our tree data structure. Using these

```
public static FuncTree update(int k, Object v, FuncTree t)
/*: requires "v ~= null"
    ensures "result..content = t..content - {(x,y). x=k} + {(k,v)}"    */
{
    FuncTree new_left, new_right;    Object new_data;    int new_key;
    if (t==null) {
        new_data = v;   new_key = k;
        new_left = null;   new_right = null;
    } else {
        if (k < t.key) {
            new_left = update(k, v, t.left);
            new_right = t.right;
            new_key = t.key;   new_data = t.data;
        } else if (t.key < k) {
            new_left = t.left;
            new_right = update(k, v, t.right);
            new_key = t.key;   new_data = t.data;
        } else {
            new_data = v;   new_key = k;
            new_left = t.left;   new_right = t.right;
        }
    }
    FuncTree r = new FuncTree();
    r.left = new_left;   r.right = new_right;
    r.data = new_data;   r.key = new_key;
    //: "r..content" := "t..content - {(x,y). x=k} + {(k,v)}";
    return r;
}
```

Fig. 4. Map update implementation for functional tree

representation invariants and the precondition, Jahob proves (in 4 seconds) that
the postcondition of the lookup method holds and that the method never performs null dereferences. For example, when analyzing tree traversal in lookup,
Jahob uses the sortedness invariants (leftSmaller, rightBigger) and the definition of tree content contentDefinition to narrow down the search to one of
the subtrees.

Jahob also ensures that the operations preserve the representation invariants.
Jahob reduces the invariants in Figure 3 to global invariants by implicitly quan-
tifying them over all allocated objects of FuncTree type. This approach yields
simple semantics to constraints that involve multiple objects in the heap. When
a method allocates a new object, the set of all allocated objects is extended, so a
proof obligation will require that these newly allocated objects also satisfy their
representation invariants at the end of the method.

Figure 4 shows the map update operation in our implementation. The postcondition of update states that all previous bindings for the given key are absent
in the resulting tree. Note that proving this postcondition requires the sortedness

invariants `leftSmaller`, `rightBigger`. Moreover, it is necessary to establish all representation invariants for the newly allocated `FuncTree` object.

The specification field `content` is a *ghost* field, which means that its value changes only in response to specification assignment statements, such as the one in the penultimate line of Figure 4. The use of ghost variables is sound and can be explained using simulation relations [5]. For example, if the developer incorrectly specifies specification assignments, Jahob will detect the violation of the representation invariants such as `contentDefinition`. If the developer specifies incorrect representation invariants, Jahob will fail to prove postconditions of observer operations such as `lookup` in Figure 2.

Jahob verifies (in 10 seconds) that the update operation establishes the postcondition, correctly maintains all invariants, and performs no null dereferences. Jahob establishes such conditions by first converting the Java program into a loop-free guarded-command language using user-provided or automatically inferred loop invariants (the examples in this paper mostly use recursion instead of loops). A verification condition generator then computes a formula whose validity entails the correctness of the program with respect to its explicitly supplied specifications (such as invariants and procedure contracts) as well as the absence of run-time exceptions (such as null pointer dereferences, failing type casts, and array out of bounds accesses). The specification language and the generated verification conditions in Jahob are expressed in higher-order logic [16]. In the rest of this paper we show how we translate such verification conditions to first-order logic and prove them using theorem provers such as SPASS [22] and E [20].

3   Translation to First-Order Logic

This section presents our translation from an expressive subset of Isabelle formulas (the input language) to first-order unsorted logic with equality (the language accepted by first-order resolution-based theorem provers). The soundness of the translation is given by the condition that, if the output formula is valid, so is the input formula. The details of the translation are in [4].

Input language. The input language allows constructs such as lambda expressions, function update, sets, tuples, quantifiers, cardinality operators, and set comprehensions. The translation first performs type reconstruction. It uses the type information to disambiguate operations such as equality, whose translation depends on the type of the operands.

Splitting into sequents. Generated proof obligations can be represented as conjunctions of multiple statements, because they represent all possible paths in the verified procedure, the validity of multiple invariants and postcondition conjuncts, and the absence of run-time errors at multiple program points. The first step in the translation splits formulas into these individual conjuncts to prove each of them independently. This process does not lose completeness, yet it improves the effectiveness of the theorem proving process because the resulting formulas are smaller than the starting formula. Moreover, splitting enables Jahob to prove different conjuncts using different techniques, allowing the translation described in this paper to be combined with other translations [23, 8]. After splitting, the resulting formulas have the form of implications $A_1 \wedge \ldots \wedge A_n \Rightarrow G$, which we call *sequents*. We call $A_1, \ldots, A_n$ the *assumptions* and G the *goal* of the sequent. The assumptions typically encode a path in the procedure being verified, the precondition, class invariants that hold at procedure entry, as well as properties of our semantic model of memory and the relationships between sets representing Java types. During splitting, Jahob also performs syntactic checks that eliminate some simple valid sequents such as the ones where the goal G of the sequent is equal to one of the assumptions A_i.

Definition substitution and function unfolding. When one of the assumptions is a variable definition, the translation substitutes its content in the rest of the formula. This approach supports definitions of variables that have complex and higher-order types, but are used simply as shorthands, and avoids the full encoding of lambda abstraction in first-order logic. When the definitions of variables are lambda abstractions, the substitution enables beta reduction, which is done subsequently. In addition to beta reduction, this phase also expands the equality between functions using the extensionality rule ($f = g$ becomes $\forall x. f\, x = g\, x$).

Cardinality constraints. Constant cardinality constraints express natural generalizations of quantifiers. For example, the statement "there exists at most one element satisfying P" is given by $\mathsf{card}\,\{x.\ P\,x\} \leq 1$. Our translation reduces constant cardinality constraints to constructs in first-order logic with equality.

Set expressions. Our translation uses universal quantification to expand set operations into their set-theoretic definitions in terms of the set membership operator. This process also eliminates set comprehensions by replacing $x \in \{y \mid \varphi\}$ with $\varphi[y \mapsto x]$. These transformations ensure that the only set expressions in formulas are either set variables or set-valued fields occurring on the right-hand side of the membership operator.

Our translation maps set variables to unary predicates: $x \in S$ becomes $S(x)$, where S is a predicate in first-order logic. This translation is applicable when S is universally quantified at the top level of the sequent (so it can be skolemized), which is indeed the case for the proof obligations in this paper. Fields of type object or integer become uninterpreted function symbols: $\mathtt{y = x.f}$ translates as $y = f(x)$. Set-valued fields become binary predicates: $\mathtt{x} \in \mathtt{y.f}$ becomes $F(y, x)$ where F is a binary predicate.

Function update. Function update expressions (encoded as functions fieldWrite and arrayWrite in our input language) translate using case analysis. If applied to arbitrary expressions, such case analysis would duplicate complex subterms, potentially leading to an exponential expansion. To avoid this problem, the translation first flattens expressions by introducing fresh variables and then duplicates only variables and not complex expressions, keeping the size of the translated formula polynomial.

Flattening. Flattening introduces fresh quantified variables, which could in principle create additional quantifier alternations, making the proof process more difficult. However, each variable can be introduced using either existential or universal quantifier because $\exists x.x=a \land \varphi$ is equivalent to $\forall x.x=a \Rightarrow \varphi$. Our translation therefore chooses the quantifier kind that corresponds to the most recently bound variable in a given scope (taking into account the polarity), preserving the number of quantifier alternations. The starting quantifier kind at the top level of the formula is $\forall$, ensuring that freshly introduced variables for quantifier-free expressions become skolem constants.

Arithmetic. Resolution-based first-order provers do not have built-in arithmetic operations. Our translation therefore introduces axioms that provide a partial axiomatization of integer operations $+, <, \leq$. In addition, the translation supplies axioms for the ordering relation between all numeric constants appearing in the input formula. Although incomplete, these axioms are sufficient to verify our examples.

Tuples. Tuples in the input language are useful, for example, as elements of sets representing relations, such as the `content` ghost field in Figure 3. Our translation eliminates tuples by transforming them into individual components. The translation maps a variable x denoting an n-tuple into n individual variables $x_1, \ldots, x_n$ bound in the same way as x. A tuple equality becomes a conjunction of equalities of components. The arity of functions changes to accommodate all components, so a function taking an n-tuple and an m-tuple becomes a function symbol of arity $n + m$. The translation handles sets as functions from elements to booleans. For example, a relation-valued field `content` of type `obj => (int * obj) set` is viewed as a function `obj => int => obj => bool` and therefore becomes a ternary predicate symbol.

Approximation. Our translation maps higher-order formulas into first-order logic without encoding lambda calculus or set theory, so there are constructs that it cannot translate exactly. Examples include transitive closure (which other Jahob components can translate into monadic second-order logic [23]) and symbolic cardinality constraints (as in BAPA [8]). Our first-order translation approximates such subformulas in a sound way, by replacing them with `True` or `False` depending on the polarity of the subformula occurrence. The result of the approximation is a stronger formula whose validity implies the validity of the original formula.

4   From Multisorted to Unsorted Logic

This section discusses our approach for handling type and sort information in the translation to first-order logic with equality. This approach proved essential for making verification of our examples feasible. The key insight is that omitting sort information 1) improves the performance of the theorem proving effort, and 2) is guaranteed to be sound in our context.

To understand our setup, note that the verification condition generator in Jahob produces proof obligations in higher-order logic notation whose type system essentially corresponds to simply typed lambda calculus [2] (we allow some simple forms of parametric polymorphism but expect each occurrence of a symbol to have a ground type). The type system in our proof obligations therefore has no subtyping, so all Java objects have type obj. The verification-condition generator encodes Java classes as immutable sets of type obj set. It encodes primitive Java integers as mathematical integers of type int (which is disjoint from obj). The result of the translation in Section 3 is a formula in multisorted first-order logic with equality and two disjoint sorts, obj and int.[1] On the other side, the standardized input language for first-order theorem provers is untyped first-order logic with equality. The key question is the following: *How should we encode multisorted first-order logic into untyped first-order logic?*

The standard approach [11, Chapter 6, Section 8] is to introduce a unary predicate P_s for each sort s and replace $\exists x::s.F(x)$ with $\exists x.P_s(x) \land F(x)$ and replace $\forall x::s.F(x)$ with $\forall x.P_s(x) \Rightarrow F(x)$ (where $x :: s$ in multisorted logic denotes that the variable x has the sort s). In addition, for each function symbol f of sort $s_1 \times \ldots s_n \to s$, introduce a Horn clause $\forall x_1, \ldots, x_n. P_{s_1}(x_1) \land \ldots \land P_{s_n}(x_n) \Rightarrow P_s(f(x_1, \ldots, x_n))$.

The standard approach is sound and complete. However, it makes formulas larger, often substantially slowing down the automated theorem prover. What if we omitted the sort information given by unary sort predicates P_s, representing, for example, $\forall x::s.F(x)$ simply as $\forall x.F(x)$? For potentially overlapping sorts, this approach is unsound. As an example, take the conjunction of two formulas $\forall x::\mathsf{Node}.F(x)$ and $\exists x::\mathsf{Object}.\neg F(x)$ for distinct sorts Object and Node where Node is a subsort of Object. These assumptions are consistent in multisorted logic. However, their unsorted version $\forall x.F(x) \land \exists x.\neg F(x)$ is contradictory, and would allow a verification system to unsoundly prove arbitrary claims.

In our case, however, the two sorts considered (int and obj) are disjoint and have the same cardinality. Moreover, there is no overloading of predicate or function symbols other than equality. Under these assumptions, we have the following result. Let φ^* denote the result of omitting all sort information from a multisorted formula φ and representing the equality (regardless of the sort of arguments) using the built-in equality symbol.

Theorem 1. *There exists a function mapping each multisorted structure $\mathcal{I}$ into an unsorted structure $\mathcal{I}^*$ and each multisorted environment ρ to an unsorted environment ρ^*, such that the following holds: for each formula φ, structure $\mathcal{I}$, and a well-sorted environment ρ,*

$$\llbracket \varphi^* \rrbracket_{\rho^*}^{\mathcal{I}^*} \qquad \textit{if and only if} \qquad \llbracket \varphi \rrbracket_{\rho}^{\mathcal{I}}$$

The proof of Theorem 1 is in [4, Appendix F]. It constructs $\mathcal{I}^*$ by taking a new set S of same cardinality as the sort interpretations $S_1, \ldots, S_n$ in $\mathcal{I}$, and defining

---

[1] The resulting multisorted logic has no sort corresponding to booleans (as in [11, Chapter 6]). Instead, propositional operations are part of the logic itself.

the interpretation of symbols in $\mathcal{I}^*$ by composing the interpretation in $\mathcal{I}$ with bijections $f_i : S_i \to S$. Theorem 1 implies that if a formula $(\neg\psi)^*$ is unsatisfiable, then so is $\neg\psi$. Therefore, if ψ^* is valid, so is ψ.

A resolution theorem prover with paramodulation rules can derive ill-sorted clauses as consequences of φ^*. However, Theorem 1 implies that the existence of a refutation of φ^* implies that φ is also unsatisfiable, guaranteeing the soundness of the approach. This approach is also complete. Namely, notice that stripping sorts only *increases* the set of resolution steps that can be performed on a set of clauses. Therefore, we can show that if there exists a proof for φ, there exists a proof of φ^*. Moreover, *the shortest proof for the unsorted case is no longer than any proof in multisorted case.* As a result, any advantage of preserving sorts comes from the reduction of the branching factor in the search, as opposed to the reduction in proof length.

Impact of omitting sort information. Figure 5 shows the effect of omitting sorts on some of the most problematic formulas that arise in our benchmarks. They are the formulas that take more than one second to prove using SPASS with sorts, in the two hardest methods of our Tree implementation. The figure shows that omitting sorts usually yields a speed-up of one order of magnitude, and sometimes more. In our examples, the converse situation, where omitting sorts substantially slows down the theorem proving process, is rare.

Benchmark	Time (s)				Proof length		Generated clauses			
	SPASS		E		SPASS		SPASS		E	
	w/o	w.	w/o	w.	w/o	w.	w/o	w.	w/o	w.
FuncTree.Remove	1.1	5.3	30.0	349.0	155	799	9425	18376	122508	794860
	0.3	3.6	10.4	42.0	309	1781	1917	19601	73399	108910
	4.9	9.8	15.7	18.0	174	1781	27108	33868	100846	256550
	0.5	8.1	12.5	45.9	301	1611	3922	31892	85164	263104
	4.7	8.1	17.9	19.3	371	1773	28170	37244	109032	176597
	0.3	7.9	10.6	41.8	308	1391	3394	41354	65700	287253
FuncTree.RemoveMax	0.22	$+\infty$	59.0	76.5	97	-	1075	-	872566	953451
	6.8	78.9	14.9	297.6	1159	2655	19527	177755	137711	1512828
	0.8	34.8	38.1	0.7	597	4062	5305	115713	389334	7595

Fig. 5. Verification time, and proof data using the provers SPASS and E, on the hardest formulas from our examples

5   Experimental Results

We implemented our translation to first-order logic and the interfaces to the first-order provers E [20] (using the TPTP format for first-order formulas [21]) and SPASS [22] (using its native format). We also implemented filtering described in [4, Appendix A] to automate the selection of assumptions in proof obligations. We evaluated our approach by implementing several data structures, using the system during their development. In addition to the implementation of a relation as a functional tree presented in Section 2, we ran our system on dynamically instantiable sets and relations implemented as a functional singly-linked list, an imperative linked list, and a hash table. We also verified operations of a data structure client that instantiates a relation and two sets and maintains invariants between them.

Table 6 illustrates the benchmarks we ran through our system and shows their verification times. Lines of code and of specifications are counted without blank lines or comments.[2]

Our system accepts as command-line parameters timeouts, percentage of retained assumptions in filtering, and two flags that indicate desired sets of arithmetic axioms. For each module, we used a fixed set of command line options to verify all the procedures in that module. Some methods can be verified faster (in times shown in parentheses) by choosing a more fine-tuned set of options. Jahob allows specifying a cascade of provers to be tried in sequence; when we used multiple provers we give the time spent in each prover and the number of formulas proved by each of them.

The values in the "entire class" row for each module are not the sum of all the other rows, but the time actually spent in the verification of the entire class, including some methods not shown and the verification that the invariants hold initially. Running time of first-order provers dominates the verification time, the remaining time is mostly spent in our simple implementation of polymorphic type inference for higher-order logic formulas.

Verification experience. The time we spent to verify these benchmarks went down as we improved the system and gained experience using it. It took approximately one week to code and verify the ordered trees implementation. However, it took only half a day to write and verify a simple version of the hash table. It took another few days to verify an augmented version with a rehash function that can dynamically resize its array when its filling ratio is too high.

6   Related Work

We are not aware of any other system capable of verifying, without interactive theorem proving, such strong properties of operations on data structures that use arrays, recursive memory cells, and integer keys.

Verification systems. Boogie [3] is a sound verification system for the Spec# language, which extends C# with specification constructs and introduces a particular methodology for ensuring sound modular reasoning in the presence of aliasing and object-oriented features. Specification variables are present in Boogie [9] under the name *model fields*. We are not aware of any results on

---

[2] We ran the verification on a single-core 3.2 GHz Pentium 4 machine with 3GB of memory, running GNU/Linux. As first-order theorem provers we used SPASS and E in their automatic settings. The E version we used comes from the CASC-J3 (Summer 2006) system archive and calls itself v0.99pre2 "Singtom". We used SPASS v2.2, which comes from its official web page.

Benchmark	lines of code	lines of specification	number of methods
Relation as functional list	76	26	9
Relation as functional Tree	186	38	10
Set as imperative list	60	24	9
Library system	97	63	9
Relation as hash table	69	53	10

Benchmark	Prover	method	Verification time (sec)	decision procedures (sec)	formulas proved
AssocList	E	cons	0.9	0.8	9
		remove_all	1.7	1.1	5
		remove	3.9	2.6	7
		lookup	0.7	0.4	3
		image	1.3	0.6	4
		inverseImage	1.2	0.6	4
		domain	0.9	0.5	3
		entire class	**11.8**	**7.3**	**44**
FuncTree	SPASS + E	add	7.2	5.7	24
		update	9.0	7.4	28
		lookup	1.2	0.6	7
		min	7.2	6.6	21
		max	7.2	6.5	22
		removeMax	106.5 (12.7)	46.6+59.3	9+11
		remove	17.0	8.2	26
		entire class	**178.4**	**96.0+65.7**	**147+16**
Imperative List	SPASS	add	1.5	1.2	9
		member	0.6	0.3	7
		getOne	0.1	0.1	2
		remove	11.4	9.9	48
		entire class	**17.9**	**14.9**	**74**
Library	E	currentReader	1.0	0.9	5
		checkOutBook	2.3	1.7	6
		returnBook	2.7	2.1	7
		decommissionBook	3.0	2.2	7
		entire class	**20.0**	**17.6**	**73**
HashTable	SPASS	init	25.5 (3.8)	25.2 (3.4)	12
		add	2.7	1.6	7
		add1	22.7	22.7	14
		lookup	20.8	20.3	9
		remove	57.1	56.3	12
		update	1.4	0.8	2
		entire class	**119**	**113.8**	**75**

Fig. 6. Benchmarks Characteristics and Verification Times

non-interactive verification that data structures such as trees and hash tables meet their specifications expressed in terms of model fields.

Abstract interpretation. Shape analyses [19,18] typically verify weaker properties than in our examples. In [10] the authors use the TVLA system to verify insertion sort and bubble sort. In [17, Page 35], the author uses TVLA to verify implementations of insertion and removal operations on sets implemented as mutable lists and binary search trees. The approach [17] uses manually supplied predicates and transfer functions and axioms for the analysis, but is able to infer loop invariants in an imperative implementation of trees. Our implementation of trees is functional and uses recursion, which simplifies the verification and results in much smaller running times. The analysis we describe in this paper does not infer loop invariants, but does not require transfer functions to be specified either. The only information that the data structure user needs to trust is that procedure contracts correctly formalize the desired behavior of data structure operations; if the developer incorrectly specifies an invariant or an update to a specification variable, the system will detect an error.

Translation from higher-order to first-order logic. In [6, 12, 14] the authors also address the process of proving higher-order formulas using first-order theorem provers. Our work differs in that we do not aim to provide automation to a general-purpose higher-order interactive theorem prover. Therefore, we were able to avoid using general encoding of lambda calculus into first-order logic and we believe that this made our translation more effective. The authors in [6, 14] also observe that encoding the full type information slows down the proof process. The authors therefore omit type information and then check the resulting proofs for soundness. A similar approach was adopted to encoding multi-sorted logic in the Athena theorem proving framework [1]. In contrast, we were able to prove that omitting sort information preserves soundness and completeness when sorts are disjoint and have the same cardinality.

Type systems and separation logic. Recently, researchers have developed a promising approach [15] that can verify shape and content properties of imperative recursive data structures (although it has not been applied to hash tables yet). Our approach uses standard higher-order and first-order logic and seems conceptually simpler, but generates proof obligations that have potentially more quantifiers and case analyses.

References

1. K. Arkoudas, K. Zee, V. Kuncak, and M. Rinard. Verifying a file system implementation. In *Sixth International Conference on Formal Engineering Methods (ICFEM'04)*, volume 3308 of *LNCS*, Seattle, Nov 8-12, 2004 2004.
2. H. P. Barendregt. Lambda calculi with types. In *Handbook of Logic in Computer Science, Vol. II*. Oxford University Press, 2001.

3. M. Barnett, K. R. M. Leino, and W. Schulte. The Spec# programming system: An overview. In *CASSIS: Int. Workshop on Construction and Analysis of Safe, Secure and Interoperable Smart devices*, 2004.

4. C. Bouillaguet, V. Kuncak, T. Wies, K. Zee, and M. Rinard. On using first-order theorem provers in a data structure verification system. Technical Report MIT-CSAIL-TR-2006-072, MIT, November 2006. http://hdl.handle.net/1721.1/34874.

5. W.-P. de Roever and K. Engelhardt. *Data Refinement: Model-oriented proof methods and their comparison*. Cambridge University Press, 1998.

6. J. Hurd. An LCF-style interface between HOL and first-order logic. In *CADE-18*, 2002.

7. V. Kuncak. *Modular Data Structure Verification*. PhD thesis, EECS Department, Massachusetts Institute of Technology, February 2007.

8. V. Kuncak, H. H. Nguyen, and M. Rinard. Deciding Boolean Algebra with Presburger Arithmetic. *J. of Automated Reasoning*, 2006. http://dx.doi.org/10.1007/s10817-006-9042-1.

9. K. R. M. Leino and P. Müller. A verification methodology for model fields. In *ESOP'06*, 2006.

10. T. Lev-Ami, T. Reps, M. Sagiv, and R. Wilhelm. Putting static analysis to work for verification: A case study. In *Int. Symp. Software Testing and Analysis*, 2000.

11. M. Manzano. *Extensions of First-Order Logic*. Cambridge University Press, 1996.

12. J. Meng and L. C. Paulson. Experiments on supporting interactive proof using resolution. In *IJCAR*, 2004.

13. J. Meng and L. C. Paulson. Lightweight relevance filtering for machine-generated resolution problems. In *ESCoR: Empirically Successful Computerized Reasoning*, 2006.

14. J. Meng and L. C. Paulson. Translating higher-order problems to first-order clauses. In *ESCoR: Empir. Successful Comp. Reasoning*, pages 70–80, 2006.

15. H. H. Nguyen, C. David, S. Qin, and W.-N. Chin. Automated verification of shape, size and bag properties via separation logic. In *VMCAI*, 2007.

16. T. Nipkow, L. C. Paulson, and M. Wenzel. *Isabelle/HOL: A Proof Assistant for Higher-Order Logic*, volume 2283 of *LNCS*. Springer-Verlag, 2002.

17. J. Reineke. Shape analysis of sets. Master's thesis, Universität des Saarlandes, Germany, June 2005.

18. R. Rugina. Quantitative shape analysis. In *Static Analysis Symposium (SAS'04)*, 2004.

19. M. Sagiv, T. Reps, and R. Wilhelm. Parametric shape analysis via 3-valued logic. *ACM TOPLAS*, 24(3):217–298, 2002.

20. S. Schulz. E – A Brainiac Theorem Prover. *Journal of AI Communications*, 15(2/3):111–126, 2002.

21. G. Sutcliffe and C. B. Suttner. The tptp problem library: Cnf release v1.2.1. *Journal of Automated Reasoning*, 21(2):177–203, 1998.

22. C. Weidenbach. Combining superposition, sorts and splitting. In A. Robinson and A. Voronkov, editors, *Handbook of Automated Reasoning*, volume II, chapter 27, pages 1965–2013. Elsevier Science, 2001.

23. T. Wies, V. Kuncak, P. Lam, A. Podelski, and M. Rinard. Field constraint analysis. In *Proc. Int. Conf. Verification, Model Checking, and Abstract Interpratation*, 2006.

Interpolants and Symbolic Model Checking

K.L. McMillan

Cadence Berkeley Labs

Abstract. An interpolant for a mutually inconsistent pair of formulas (A, B) is a formula that is (1) implied by A, (2) inconsistent with B, and (3) expressed over the common variables of A and B. An interpolant can be efficiently derived from a refutation of $A \wedge B$, for certain theories and proof systems. In this tutorial we will cover methods of generating interpolants, and applications of interpolants, including invariant generation and abstraction refinement.

1 Introduction

An interpolant for a mutually inconsistent pair of formulas (A, B) is a formula that is (1) implied by A, (2) inconsistent with B, and (3) expressed over the common variables of A and B. Craig's interpolation lemma [1] states that every pair of inconsistent first-order formulas has an interpolant. For certain theories and proof systems, we can derive an interpolant for (A, B) from a refutation of $A \wedge B$. For example, interpolants can be derived from resolution proofs in propositional logic. We can also derive interpolants from refutation proofs in first-order logic, and in the quantifier-free fragment of first-order logic with various interpreted theories [5].

Interpolants derived from proofs have a variety of applications in model checking. In various contexts, interpolation can be used as a substitute for image computation, which involves quantifier elimination and is thus computationally expensive. The idea is to replace the image operation with a weaker approximation that is still strong enough to prove a given property.

For example, interpolation can be used to construct an inductive invariant of a sequential system, such as a hardware design or a program. This invariant contains only information actually deduced by a prover in refuting counterexamples a given property. Thus, in a certain sense, this method abstracts the invariant relative to a given property, exploiting the prover's ability to focus the proof on a small set of relevant facts. This avoids the complexity of computing the strongest inductive invariant (i.e., the reachable states) as is typically done in model checking, and works well in the the case where a relatively simple, localized invariant suffices to prove a property of a large system.

This approach gives us a complete procedure for model checking temporal properties of finite-state systems that allows us to exploit recent advances in SAT solvers for the proof generation phase. Experimentally, the method is found to be quite robust for industrial hardware verification problems, relative to other

B. Cook and A. Podelski (Eds.): VMCAI 2007, LNCS 4349, pp. 89–90, 2007.

model checking approaches [4]. The same approach can be applied to infinite-state systems, such as programs and parameterized protocols, using first-order provers, or proof-generating decision procedures. Using interpolants to avoid the expense of predicate image computations, we can obtain substantial efficiencies in software model checking [6]. Moreover, using appropriate techniques we can guarantee to find an inductive invariant proving a given property, if one exists in the prover's theory (though in general the verification problem is undecidable).

Interpolants can also be used for abstraction refinement in various contexts. For example, the Blast software model checker uses interpolants to derive predicates for use in predicate abstraction [2], and also to refine the predicate transition relation, to compensate for the inaccuracy of the Cartesian image approximation [3].

The tutorial will cover methods for generating interpolants from proofs, for both the propositional and first-order cases, and the various applications of these methods.

References

1. W. Craig. Three uses of the herbrand-gentzen theorem in relating model theory and proof theory. *J. Symbolic Logic*, 22(3):269285, 1957.
2. T. A. Henzinger, R. Jhala, Rupak Majumdar, and K. L. McMillan. Abstractions from proofs. In *Principles of Prog. Lang. (POPL 2004)*, pages 232244, 2004.
3. R. Jhala and K. L. McMillan. Interpolant-based transition relation approximation. In Kousha Etessami and Sriram K. Rajamani, editors, CAV, volume 3576 of *Lecture Notes in Computer Science*, pages 3951. Springer, 2005.
4. K. L. McMillan. Interpolation and sat-based model checking. In *Computer-Aided Verification (CAV 2003)*, pages 113, 2003.
5. Kenneth L. McMillan. An interpolating theorem prover. *Theor. Comput. Sci.*, 345(1):101121, 2005.
6. Kenneth L. McMillan. Lazy abstraction with interpolants. In Thomas Ball and Robert B. Jones, editors, *CAV*, volume 4144 of *Lecture Notes in Computer Science*, pages 123136. Springer, 2006.

Shape Analysis of Single-Parent Heaps[*]

Ittai Balaban[1], Amir Pnueli[1,2], and Lenore D. Zuck[3]

[1] New York University, New York
{balaban,amir}@cs.nyu.edu
[2] Weizmann Institute of Science
[3] University of Illinois at Chicago
lenore@cs.uic.edu

Abstract. We define the class of *single-parent heap systems*, which rely on a singly-linked heap in order to model destructive updates on tree structures. This encoding has the advantage of relying on a relatively simple theory of linked lists in order to support abstraction computation. To facilitate the application of this encoding, we provide a program transformation that, given a program operating on a multi-linked heap without sharing, transforms it into one over a single-parent heap. It is then possible to apply shape analysis by predicate and ranking abstraction as in [3]. The technique has been successfully applied on examples with trees of fixed arity (balancing of and insertion into a binary sort tree).

1 Introduction

In [3] we propose a framework for shape analysis of singly-linked graphs based on a small model property of a restricted class of first order assertions with transitive closure. Extending this framework to allow for heaps with multiple links per node entails extending the assertional language and proving a stronger small model property. At this point, it is not clear whether such a language extension is decidable (see [11,12] for relevant results).

This paper deals with verification of programs that perform destructive updates of heaps consisting only of trees of bounded or unbounded arity, to which we refer as *multi-linked* heaps. We bypass the need to handle trees directly by transforming heaps consisting of multiple trees into structures consisting of singly-linked lists (possibly with shared suffixes). This is accomplished by "reversing" the parent-to-child edges of the trees populating the heap, as well as associating scalar data with nodes. We refer to the transformed heap as a *single-parent* heap.

Verification of temporal properties of multi-linked heap systems can be performed as follows: Given a multi-linked system and a temporal property, the system and property are (automatically) transformed into their single-parent counterparts. Then, a counter-example-guided predicate- (and possibly ranking-) abstraction refinement method ([3,4]) is applied. If a counter-example (on the transformed system) is produced, it is automatically mapped into a counter-example of the original (multi-linked) system.

The rest of this paper is organized as follows: After we discuss related work, we present the formal model in Section 2 and define predicate abstraction thereof.

---

[*] This research was supported in part by ONR grant N00014-99-1-0131, and SRC grant 2004-TJ-1256.

Section 3 defines systems over single-parent heaps and Section 4 describes their model reduction. Section 5 defines systems over multi-linked heaps, and Section 6 shows how to transform them to single-parent heap systems. We conclude in Section 7.

Related Work

Numerous frameworks have been suggested for analyzing singly-linked heaps, e.g., [7,8,10,16,19], all assuming that programs access heap cells solely by reachability from variables. This effectively disallows backward traversal, a necessary feature when reducing trees to singly-linked structures.

The correspondence between tree structures and singly-linked structures is the basis of the proof of decidability of first-order logic with one function symbol in [9]. More generally, the observation that complex data structures with regular properties can be reduced to simpler structures has been utilized in [13,15,17,20]. However, it is not always straightforward to apply, and, to our knowledge, has not been applied in the context of predicate abstraction. Several assumptions that hold true in analysis of "conventional" programs over singly-linked heaps (e.g., C- or Pascal-programs), cannot be relied upon when reducing trees to lists. For example, the number of roots of the heap is no longer bounded by the number of program variables.

The use of path compression in heaps to prove small model properties of logics of linked structures, has been used before, e.g., in [6] and more recently in [3,21]. Our work on parameterized systems relies on a small model theorem for checking inductiveness of assertions. The small model property there is similar to the one here with respect to *stratified data*. However, with respect to unstratified data (such as graphs), the work on parameterized systems suggests using logical instantiation as a heuristic (see, e.g., [1]), whereas here completeness is achieved using graph-theoretic methods.

2   The Formal Framework

In this section we present our computational model, as well as the method of predicate abstraction.

2.1   Fair Discrete Systems

As our computational model, we take a *fair discrete system* (FDS) $\langle V, \Theta, \rho, \mathcal{J}, \mathcal{C} \rangle$, where

- V — A set of *system variables*. A *state* of $\mathcal{D}$ provides a type-consistent interpretation of the variables V. For a state s and a system variable $v \in V$, we denote by $s[v]$ the value assigned to v by the state s. Let Σ denote the set of all states over V.
- Θ — The *initial condition*: An assertion (state formula) characterizing the initial states.
- $\rho(V, V')$ — The *transition relation*: An assertion, relating the values V of the variables in state $s \in \Sigma$ to the values V' in a $\mathcal{D}$-successor state $s' \in \Sigma$. We assume that every state has a ρ-successor.
- $\mathcal{J}$ — A set of *justice* (*weak fairness*) requirements (assertions); A computation must include infinitely many states satisfying each of the justice requirements.

- $\mathcal{C}$ — A set of *compassion (strong fairness)* requirements: Each compassion require-ment is a pair $\langle p, q \rangle$ of state assertions; A computation should include either only finitely many p-states, or infinitely many q-states.

For an assertion ψ, we say that $s \in \Sigma$ is a ψ-state if $s \models \psi$.

A *run* of an FDS $\mathcal{D}$ is a possibly infinite sequence of states $\sigma : s_0, s_1, \ldots$ satisfying the requirements:

- *Initiality* — s_0 is initial, i.e., $s_0 \models \Theta$.
- *Consecution* — For each $\ell = 0, 1, \ldots$, the state $s_{\ell+1}$ is a $\mathcal{D}$-successor of s_ℓ. That is, $\langle s_\ell, s_{\ell+1} \rangle \models \rho(V, V')$ where, for each $v \in V$, we interpret v as $s_\ell[v]$ and v' as $s_{\ell+1}[v]$.

A *computation* of $\mathcal{D}$ is an infinite run that satisfies

- *Justice* — for every $J \in \mathcal{J}$, σ contains infinitely many occurrences of J-states.
- *Compassion* – for every $\langle p, q \rangle \in \mathcal{C}$, either σ contains only finitely many occurrences of p-states, or σ contains infinitely many occurrences of q-states.

We say that a temporal property φ is *valid over* $\mathcal{D}$, denoted by $\mathcal{D} \models \varphi$, if for every computation σ of $\mathcal{D}$, $\sigma \models \varphi$. We are interested in *safety* properties, of the form $\Box\, p$, and *progress* properties, of the form $\Box(p \to \Diamond q)$, where p and q are state assertions. Since our methodology for verifying safety properties can be easily extended to verification of progress properties (along the lines of [4]), we restrict here to the former. Yet, we include the fairness requirements here for sake of completeness, while they are only necessary when dealing with progress.

2.2   Predicate Abstraction

The material here is a summary of [14] and [3]. We fix an FDS $\mathcal{D} = \langle V, \Theta, \rho, \mathcal{J}, \mathcal{C} \rangle$ whose set of states is Σ. We consider a set of *abstract variables* $V_A = \{u_1, \ldots, u_n\}$ that range over finite domains. An *abstract state* is an interpretation that assigns to each variable u_i a value in the domain of u_i. We denote by Σ_A the (finite) set of all abstract states. An *abstraction mapping* is presented by a set of equalities

$$\alpha_\varepsilon : \quad u_1 = \mathcal{E}_1(V), \ \ldots, \ u_n = \mathcal{E}_n(V),$$

where each $\mathcal{E}_i$ is an expression over V ranging over the domain of u_i. The abstraction α_ε induces a semantic mapping $\alpha_\varepsilon : \Sigma \mapsto \Sigma_A$, from the states of $\mathcal{D}$ to the set of abstract states.

Usually, most of the abstract variables are boolean, and then the corresponding expressions $\mathcal{E}_i$ are predicates over V, which is why this type of abstraction is referred to as *predicate abstraction*. The abstraction mapping α_ε can be expressed succinctly by $V_A = \mathcal{E}(V)$.

Throughout the rest of the paper, when there is no ambiguity, we shall refer to α_ε simply as α. For an assertion $p(V)$, we define its α-abstraction (with some overloading of notation) by $\alpha(p)$: $\exists V.(V_A = \mathcal{E}(V) \land p(V))$.

The semantics of $\alpha(p)$ is $\|\alpha(p)\| : \{\alpha(s) \mid s \in \|p\|\}$. Note that $\|\alpha(p)\|$ is, in general, an over-approximation – an abstract state S is in $\|\alpha(p)\|$ iff *there exists* some concrete p-state that is abstracted into S. A bi-assertion $\beta(V, V')$ is abstracted by:

$$\alpha^2(p): \quad \exists V, V'.(V_A = \mathcal{E}(V) \wedge V_A' = \mathcal{E}(V') \wedge \beta(V, V'))$$

See [3] for a discussion justifying the use of over-approximating abstractions in this setting. The abstraction of $\mathcal{D}$ by α is the system

$$\mathcal{D}^\alpha = \langle V_A, \alpha(\Theta), \alpha^2(\rho), \bigcup_{J \in \mathcal{J}} \alpha(J), \bigcup_{(p,q) \in \mathcal{C}} \langle \alpha(p), \alpha(q) \rangle \rangle$$

The soundness of predicate abstraction is derived from [14]:

Theorem 1. *For a system $\mathcal{D}$, abstraction α, and a temporal formula ψ:*

$$\mathcal{D}^\alpha \models \psi^\alpha \quad \Longrightarrow \quad \mathcal{D} \models \psi$$

3 Single-Parent Heaps

A *single-parent heap system* is an extension of the model of *finite heap systems* (FHS) of [3] specialized for representing trees. Such a system is parameterized by a positive integer h, which is the heap size. Some auxiliary arrays may be used to specify more complex structures (e.g., ordered trees). However, each node u has a single link to which we refer as its "parent," and denote it by $parent(u)$.

For example, we present in Fig. 1 a program that inserts a node into a binary sort tree rooted at a node r. To allow for the presentation of a sorted binary tree, we use an array ct (child-type) such that $ct[u]$ equals *left* or *right* if node u is, respectively, the left or right child of its parent. We also require that any two children of the same parent must have different child-types. One may wish to show, for example, that program TREE-INSERT satisfies the following for every x:

$$no\text{-}loss : parent^*(x, r) \rightarrow \square \, parent^*(x, r)$$
$$no\text{-}gain : x \neq n \wedge \neg parent^*(x, r) \rightarrow \square \, \neg parent^*(x, r)$$

The ϵ-expressions, $\epsilon j.cond$ in lines 8 and 12 denote "choose any node j that satisfies *cond*." For both statements in this program, it is easy to see that there is exactly one node j that meets *cond*. However, this is not always the case, and then such an assignment is interpreted non-deterministically. We also allow for universal tests, as those in lines 5 and 9, that test for existence of a particular node's left or right child.

We now formally define the class of single-parent heap systems. Let $h > 0$ be the *heap size*. We allow the following data types:

bool Variables whose values are boolean. With no loss of generality, we assume that all *finite domain* (unparameterized) values are encoded as **bool**s;
index Variables whose value is in the range $[0..h]$;
index $\mapsto$ **bool** arrays (**bool** arrays) that map heap elements to some finite domain (such as ct above);

$$
\begin{array}{ll}
r, t & : [1..h] \textbf{ init } t = r \\
n & : [1..h] \\
parent & : \textbf{array } [0..h] \textbf{ of } [0..h] \textbf{ init } parent[n] = parent[r] = 0 \\
& \quad \textbf{and } parent[0] = 0 \wedge \forall u \,.\, parent[u] \neq n \\
ct & : \textbf{array } [0..h] \textbf{ of } \{left, right\} \\
& \quad \textbf{init } \forall i \neq j \,.\, parent[i] = parent[j] \neq 0 \rightarrow ct[i] \neq ct[j] \\
data & : \textbf{array } [0..h] \textbf{ of } [1..k] \\
done & : \textbf{bool init } \text{FALSE} \\
\end{array}
$$

```
┌ 1 :  while ¬done do
│     ┌ 2 : if data[n] = data[t] then
│     │      3 : done := TRUE
│     │  4 : elseif data[n] < data[t] then
│     │          ┌ 5 : if ∀j.parent[j] ≠ t ∨ ct[j] ≠ left then
│     │          │      6 : (parent[n], ct[n]) := (t, left)
│     │          │      7 : done := TRUE
│     │          │  else
│     │          └      8 : t := ε j . parent[j] = t ∧ ct[j] = left
│     │      9 : elseif ∀j.parent[j] ≠ t ∨ ct[j] ≠ right then
│     │             10 : (parent[n], ct[n]) := (t, right)
│     │             11 : done := TRUE
│     │          else
│     └             12 : t := ε j . parent[j] = t ∧ ct[j] = right
└ 13 :
```

Fig. 1. Program TREE-INSERT inserts a new node n into a binary sort tree rooted at node r

index $\mapsto$ index arrays (**index** arrays), that describe the heap structure. We allow at most two **index** arrays, which we usually denote by *parent* and *parent'*.

We assume a signature of variables of all of these types. Constants are introduced as variables with reserved names. Thus, we admit the boolean constants FALSE and TRUE, and the **index** constant 0. In order to have all functions in the model total, we define both **bool** and **index** arrays as having the domain **index**. A well-formed program should never assign a value to $Z[0]$ for any (**bool** or **index**) array Z. On the other hand, unless stated otherwise, all quantifications are taken over the range $[1..h]$.

We refer to **index** elements as *nodes*. If in state s, the **index** variable x has the value ℓ, then we say that in s, *x points to the node ℓ*. An **index** *term* is the constant 0, an **index** variable, or an expression $Z[y]$, where Z is an **index** array and y is an **index** variable. *Atomic formulae* are defined as follows:

- If x is a boolean variable, B is a **bool** array, and y is an **index** variable, then x and $B[y]$ are atomic formulae.
- If t_1 and t_2 are **index** terms, then $t_1 = t_2$ is an atomic formula.
- A *Transitive closure* formula (*tcf*) of the form $Z^*(x_1, x_2)$, denoting that x_2 is Z-reachable from x_1, where x_1 and x_2 are **index** variables and Z is an **index** array.

We find it convenient to include "preservation statements" for each transition, that describe the variables that are not changed by the transition. There are two types of such statements:

1. Assertions of the form $pres(\{v_1, \ldots, v_k\}) = \bigwedge_{i=1}^{k} v_i' = v_i$ where all v_i's are scalar (**bool** or **index**) variables;
2. Assertions of the form $pres_H(\{a_1, \ldots, a_k\}) = \bigwedge_{i=1}^{k} \forall h \notin H \,.\, a_i'[h] = a_i[h]$ where all a_i's are arrays and H is a (possible empty) set of **index** variables. Such

$$
\begin{aligned}
&error \wedge error' \wedge presEx(error)\\
&\quad \vee\\
&\neg error \wedge\\
&\Big[\ \ \pi = 1 \wedge \neg done \wedge \pi' = 2 \wedge presEx(\pi)\\
&\quad\vee\ \pi = 1 \wedge done \wedge \pi' = 13 \wedge presEx(\pi)\\
&\quad\vee\ \pi = 2 \wedge data[t] = data[n] \wedge \pi' = 3 \wedge presEx(\pi)\\
&\quad\vee\ \pi = 2 \wedge data[t] \neq data[n] \wedge \pi' = 4 \wedge presEx(\pi)\\
&\quad\vee\ \pi = 3 \wedge \pi' = 1 \wedge done' \wedge presEx(\pi, done)\\
&\quad\vee\ \pi = 4 \wedge data[n] < data[t] \wedge \pi' = 5 \wedge presEx(\pi)\\
&\quad\vee\ \pi = 4 \wedge data[t] \leq data[n] \wedge \pi' = 9 \wedge presEx(\pi)\\
&\quad\vee\ \pi = 5 \wedge \pi' = 6 \wedge (\forall j.parent[j] \neq t \vee ct[j] \neq \textit{left}) \wedge presEx(\pi)\\
&\quad\vee\ \pi = 5 \wedge \pi' = 8 \wedge (\exists j.parent[j] = t \wedge ct[j] = \textit{left}) \wedge presEx(\pi)\\
&\quad\vee\ \pi = 6 \wedge n = 0 \wedge error' \wedge presEx(error)\\
&\quad\vee\ \pi = 6 \wedge \pi' = 7 \wedge n \neq 0 \wedge parent'[n] = t \wedge ct'[n] = \textit{left} \wedge presEx(\pi, parent[n], ct[n])\\
&\quad\vee\ \pi = 7 \wedge \pi' = 1 \wedge done' \wedge presEx(\pi, done)\\
&\quad\vee\ \pi = 8 \wedge \pi' = 1 \wedge (\exists j . parent[j] = t \wedge ct[j] = \textit{left} \wedge t' = j) \wedge presEx(\pi, t)\\
&\quad\vee\ \pi = 9 \wedge \pi' = 10 \wedge (\forall j.parent[j] \neq t \vee ct[j] \neq \textit{right}) \wedge presEx(\pi)\\
&\quad\vee\ \pi = 9 \wedge \pi' = 12 \wedge (\exists j.parent[j] = t \wedge ct[j] = \textit{right}) \wedge presEx(\pi)\\
&\quad\vee\ \pi = 10 \wedge n = 0 \wedge error' \wedge presEx(error)\\
&\quad\vee\ \pi = 10 \wedge \pi' = 11 \wedge n \neq 0 \wedge parent'[n] = t \wedge ct'[n] = \textit{right} \wedge presEx(\pi, parent[n], ct[n])\\
&\quad\vee\ \pi = 11 \wedge \pi' = 1 \wedge done' \wedge presEx(\pi, done)\\
&\quad\vee\ \pi = 12 \wedge \pi' = 1 \wedge (\exists j . parent[j] = t \wedge ct[j] = \textit{right} \wedge t' = j) \wedge presEx(\pi, t)\\
&\quad\vee\ \pi = 13 \wedge \pi' = 13 \wedge presEx(\pi)\ \Big]
\end{aligned}
$$

Fig. 2. The transition relation of TREE-INSERT. The variable π represents the program counter.

an assertion denotes that all but finitely many (usually a none or a single) entries of arrays indexed by certain nodes remain intact.

Note that preservation formulae are at most universal. We abuse notation and use the expression $presEx(v_1, \ldots, v_k)$ to denote the preservation of all variables, excluding the terms $v_1, \ldots, v_k$, which are either variables or array terms of the form $A[x]$.

Fig. 2 presents the transition relation associated with the program of Fig. 1. The implied encoding introduces an additional **bool** variable $error$ which is set to TRUE whenever there is an attempt to assign a value to $A[0]$, for some array A. Consequently, the transitions corresponding to statements 6 and 10 set $error$ to TRUE if $n = 0$, which is tested before assigning values to $parent[n]$ and to $ct[n]$.

A *restricted A-assertion* is either one of the following forms: $\forall y . Z[y] \neq u$, $\forall y . Z[y] \neq u \vee B[y]$, $\forall y . Z[y] \neq u \vee \neg B[y]$, $pres_H(Z)$, and $pres_H(B)$, where Z is an **index** array and B is a **bool** array, and H is a (possibly empty) set of **index** variables. A *restricted EA-assertion* is a formula of the form $\exists \vec{x} . \psi(\vec{u}, \vec{x})$, where $\vec{x}$ is a list of **index** variables, and $\psi(\vec{u}, \vec{x})$ is a boolean combination of atomic formulae and restricted A-assertions, where restricted A-assertions appear under positive polarity. Note that in restricted EA-assertions, universally quantified variables may *not* occur in tcf's. As the initial condition Θ we allow restricted EA-assertions, and in the transition relation ρ and fairness requirements we only allow restricted EA-assertions without tcf's. Properties of systems are restricted EA-assertions, and abstraction predicates are boolean combinations of atomic formulae and non-preservation universal formulae. Note that restricted EA-assertions are more expressive than restricted A-assertions of [3] in that they allow, by means of existential and universal quantification, for traversal of trees in both directions.

4 Computing Symbolic Abstractions of Single-Parent Heaps

We show how to symbolically compute the abstraction of a single-parent heap system by extending the methodology of [3]. That methodology is based on a small model property establishing that satisfiability of a restricted assertion is checkable on a small instantiation of a system. The main effort here is dealing with the extensions to the assertional language introduced for single-parent heap systems. For simplicity, it is assumed that all scalar values are represented by multiple boolean values.

Assume a vocabulary $\mathcal{V}$ of typed variables, as well as the *primed* version of said variables. Furthermore, assume that there is a single unprimed **index** array in $\mathcal{V}$ as well as a single primed one. These will be denoted throughout the rest of this section by *parent* and *parent'*, respectively. A *model* M of *size* $h + 1$ for $\mathcal{V}$ consists of:

- A positive integer $h > 0$;
- For each boolean variable $b \in \mathcal{V}$, a boolean value $M[b] \in \{\text{FALSE}, \text{TRUE}\}$. It is required that $M[\text{FALSE}] = \text{FALSE}$ and $M[\text{TRUE}] = \text{TRUE}$;
- For each **index** variable $x \in \mathcal{V}$, a value $M[x] \in [0..h]$. It is required that $M[0] = 0$;
- For each **bool** array $B \in \mathcal{V}$, a function $M[B]\colon [0..h] \to \{\text{FALSE}, \text{TRUE}\}$;
- For each **index** array $Z \in \{parent, parent'\}$, a function $M[Z]\colon [0..h] \to [0..h]$.

Let φ be a restricted EA-assertion, which we fix for this section. We require that if a term of the form $parent'[u]$ occurs in φ where u is a free or existentially quantified variable in φ, then φ also contains the preservation formula associated with $parent$. Note that this requirement is satisfied by any reasonable φ — assertions that contain primed variables occur only in proofs for abstraction computation (rather than in properties of systems), and are generated automatically by the proof system. In such cases, the assertion generated includes also the transition relation, which includes all preservation formulae. We include this requirement explicitly since the proof of the small model theorem depends on it.

Given a model M, one can evaluate the formula φ over the model M. The model M is a *satisfying model* for φ, if φ evaluates to TRUE in M, i.e., if $M \models \varphi$. An **index** term $t \in \{u, Z[u]\}$ in φ, where u is an existentially quantified or a free variable, is called a *free term*. Let $\mathcal{T}_\varphi$ denote the minimal set consisting of the following:

- The term 0 and all free terms in φ;
- For every array $Z \in \mathcal{V}$, if $Z[u] \in \mathcal{T}_\varphi$ then $u \in \mathcal{T}_\varphi$;
- For every **bool** array $B \in \mathcal{V}$, if $B[u] \in \varphi$, then if B is unprimed, $parent[u] \in \mathcal{T}_\varphi$, and if B is primed, $parent'[u] \in \mathcal{T}_\varphi$;
- If $parent'[u] \in \mathcal{T}_\varphi$ then $parent[u] \in \mathcal{T}_\varphi$ (this is similar to *history closure* of [3]).

Let M be a model that satisfies φ with size greater then $|\mathcal{T}_\varphi| + 1$ as follows: Let N be the set of $[0..h]$ values that M assigns to free terms in $\mathcal{T}_\varphi$. Assume that $N = \{n_0, \ldots, n_m\}$ where $0 = n_0 < \cdots < n_m$. Obviously, $m \leq |\mathcal{T}_\varphi|$. Define a mapping $\gamma\colon N \to [0..m]$ such that $\gamma(u) = i$ iff $M[u] = n_i$ (Recall that $M[\mathcal{T}_\varphi] = N$, so that γ is onto).

We now define the model $\overline{M}$. We start with its size and the interpretation of the scalars: $\overline{M}[h] = m+1$; For each **bool** variable b, $\overline{M}[b] = M[b]$; For each term $u \in \mathcal{T}_\varphi$ $\overline{M}[u] = \gamma(u)$.

Let $Z \in \{parent, parent'\}$ be an **index** array, and let $j \in [0..m]$. Consider the Z-chain in M α: $n_j = u_0, \ldots$ such that for every $i \geq 1$, $M[Z](u_{i-1}) = M[u_i]$. If there is some $i \geq 1$ such that $u_i \in N$, then let k be the minimal such i. We then say that u_{k-1} is the M *representative of Z for j* and define $\overline{M}[Z](j) = \gamma(u_k)$. If no such i exists, then $\overline{M}[Z](j) = m+1$.

As for the interpretation of $\overline{M}$ over **bool** arrays, we distinguish between the case of unprimed and primed arrays. For an unprimed (resp. primed) **bool** array B, for every $j \in [0..m]$, if the M representative of $parent$ (resp. $parent'$) is defined and equals v, then let $\overline{M}[B](j) = \gamma(v)$. Otherwise, $\overline{M}[B](j) = M[B](n_j)$. As for $\overline{M}[B](m+1)$, let $d \in [0..h]$ be the minimal such that $M[d] \notin N$. Then $\overline{M}[B](m+1)$ is defined to be $M[B](d)$.

Example 1 (Model Reduction).

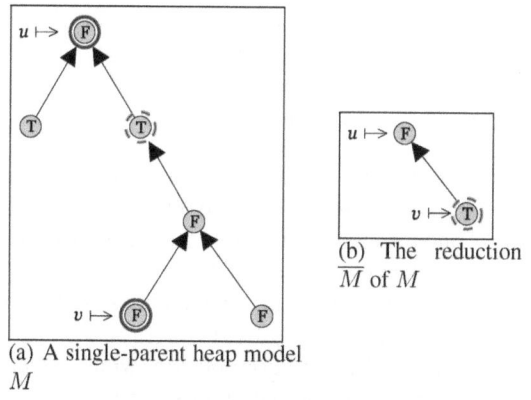

(a) A single-parent heap model M

(b) The reduction $\overline{M}$ of M

Fig. 3. Model Reduction

Let $parent$ and $data$ be **index** and **bool** arrays respectively, and let φ be the assertion:

$$\varphi: \quad \exists u, v \,.\, u \neq v \,\wedge\, \forall y \,.\, (parent[y] \neq u \,\vee\, data[y])$$

Since there are no free variables in φ, and since no array term refers to the uth or v^{th} element, it follows that $\mathcal{T}_\varphi$ consists only of the **index** terms u and v. Let M be a model of φ of size 7, as shown in Fig. 3(a). The interpretations by M of terms in $\mathcal{T}_\varphi$ are the highlighted nodes. Each node y is annotated with the value $M[data](y)$ (e.g., the node pointed to by u has data value of FALSE). $\overline{M}$, which is the reduction of M with respect to $\mathcal{T}_\varphi$, is given in Fig. 3(b). The M representative of $parent$ for $M[v]$ is given by the node highlighted by a dashed line in Fig. 3(a). As shown here, the node pointed to by v in $\overline{M}$ takes on the properties of this representative node.

In the full version of the paper [2] we prove:

Theorem 2. *If $M \models \varphi$ then φ is satisfiable by a model of size at most $|\mathcal{T}_\varphi| + 1$.*

The discussion below is similar to the one in [3]; see details there. For a restricted EA-assertion φ and a positive integer $h_0 > 0$, define the h_0-*bounded* version of φ, denoted by $\lfloor \varphi \rfloor_{h_0}$, to be the conjunction $\varphi \wedge \forall y . y \leq h_0$. Theorem 2 can be interpreted as stating that φ is satisfiable iff $\lfloor \varphi \rfloor_{|\mathcal{T}_\varphi|}$ is satisfiable.

We next extend the small model theorem to the computation of abstraction of systems. Consider an abstraction α, where the set of (finitely many combinations of) values of the abstract system variables V_A is $\{U_1, \ldots, U_k\}$. Let $sat(\varphi)$ be the subset of indices $i \in [1..k]$, such that $U_i = \mathcal{E}_\alpha(V) \wedge \varphi(V)$ is satisfiable. Then $\alpha(\varphi)(V_A) = \bigvee_{i \in sat(\varphi)} (V_A = U_i)$.

Consider the assertion $\psi_0 : U_i = \mathcal{E}_\alpha(V) \wedge \varphi(V)$. Let $h_0 = |\mathcal{T}_{\psi_0}|$. Our reinterpretation of Theorem 2 states that ψ_0 is satisfiable iff $\lfloor \psi_0 \rfloor_{h_0}$ is satisfiable. Therefore, $sat(\lfloor \varphi \rfloor_{h_0}) = sat(\varphi)$. Thus, $\alpha(\varphi)(V_A) \leftrightarrow \alpha(\lfloor \varphi \rfloor_{h_0})(V_A)$. This can be extended to abstraction of assertions that refer to primed variables. Recall that the abstraction of such an assertion involves a double application of the abstraction mapping, an unprimed version and a primed version. Assume that $\varphi(V, V')$ is such an assertion, and consider $\psi_1 : (U_i = \mathcal{E}_A(V)) \wedge (U_j = \mathcal{E}_A(V')) \wedge \varphi(V, V')$. Let $h_1 = |\mathcal{T}_{\psi_1}|$. By the same reasoning, we have $\alpha(\varphi)(V_A, V_A') \leftrightarrow \alpha(\lfloor \varphi \rfloor_{h_1}(V_A, V_A'))$.

Next we generalize these results to entire systems. For an FHS $S = \langle V, \Theta, \rho, \mathcal{J}, \mathcal{C} \rangle$ and positive integer h_0, we define the h_0-bounded version of S, denoted $\lfloor S \rfloor_{h_0}$, as $\langle V \cup \{H\}, \lfloor \rho \rfloor_{h_0}, \lfloor \mathcal{J} \rfloor_{h_0}, \lfloor \mathcal{C} \rfloor_{h_0} \rangle$, where $\lfloor \mathcal{J} \rfloor_{h_0} = \{\lfloor J \rfloor_{h_0} \mid J \in \mathcal{J}\}$ and $\lfloor \mathcal{C} \rfloor_{h_0} = \{(\lfloor p \rfloor_{h_0}, \lfloor q \rfloor_{h_0}) \mid (p, q) \in \mathcal{C}\}$. Let h_0 be the maximum size of the sets $\mathcal{T}_\psi$, for every abstraction formula ψ necessary for computing the abstraction of all the components of S. Then we have the following theorem:

Theorem 3. *Let S be an* FHS, *α be an abstraction mapping, and h_0 the maximal size of the relevant sets of free terms as described above. Then the abstract system S^α is equivalent to the abstract system $\lfloor S \rfloor_{h_0}^\alpha$.*

As a consequence, in order to compute the abstract system S^α, we can instantiate the system S to a heap of size h_0, and use propositional methods, e.g., BDD-techniques[1], to compute the abstract system $\lfloor S \rfloor_{h_0}^\alpha$. Note that h_0 is linear in the number of system variables. This process is fully automatic once the predicate base is given. The exact manner by which predicates themselves are derived (e.g., by user input or as part of a refinement loop) is orthogonal to the method presented here.

5 Multi-linked Heap Systems

In this section we define *multi-linked heap systems* with a bounded out-degree on nodes. A multi-linked heap is represented similar to a single-parent heap, only, instead of having a single **index** array, we allow for some $k > 1$ **index** arrays, each describing one of the links a node may have. We denote these arrays by $link_1, \ldots, link_k$. Thus, each $link_i$ is an array $[0..h] \mapsto [0..h]$. We are mainly interested in *non-sharing heaps*, which satisfy the following requirements:

---

[1] In our experiments we use TLV ([18]).

1. For every $i = 1, \ldots, k$, $link_i[0] = 0$.
2. No two distinct positive nodes may share a common positive child. This requirement can be formalized as

$$\forall j, \ell \in [1..h], i, r \in [1..k] . (j \neq \ell) \wedge (link_i[j] = link_r[\ell]) \rightarrow link_i[j] = 0$$

3. No two distinct links of a positive node may point to the same positive child. This can be formalized as

$$\forall j \in [1..h], s, t \in [1..k] . (s \neq t) \wedge (link_s[j] = link_t[j]) \rightarrow link_s[j] = 0$$

A state violating one of these three requirements is called a *sharing state*. We refer to the conjunction of these three requirements as the formula *no_sharing*. A multi-linked system is called *sharing-free* if none of its computations ever reaches a sharing state, nor does a computation ever attempt to assign a value to $A[0]$ for some array A.

Let $\mathcal{D}: \langle V, \Theta, \rho, \mathcal{J}, \mathcal{C} \rangle$ be a k-bounded multi-linked heap system. Fig. 4 describes a BNF-like syntax of the assertions used in describing $\mathcal{D}$. There, Ivar denotes an unprimed **index** variable, Iarr denotes an unprimed **index** array, Bvar denotes an unprimed **bool** variable, and Barr denotes an unprimed **bool** array. The expression $reach(x, y)$ abbreviates $(x, y) \in (\bigcup_{i=1}^{k} link_i)^*$, and the expression $cycle(x)$ abbreviates $(x, x) \in (\bigcup_{i=1}^{k} link_i)^+$. The **Preservation** assertion is just like in the single-parent case and we require that if Assign appears in τ, then the **Preservation** assertion that is conjoined with it includes preservation of all variables that don't appear in the left-hand-side of any clause of Assign.

```
MCond1 ::= TRUE | Bvar | Barr[Ivar] | Ivar = Ivar | Ivar = 0 |
           Iarr[Ivar] = Ivar | Iarr[Ivar] = 0 |
           MCond1 ∨ MCond1 | ¬MCond1

MCond2 ::= MCond1 | reach(Ivar,Ivar) | cycle(Ivar) |
           ¬MCond2 | MCond2 ∨ MCond2

Assign ::= ε | Bvar' | ¬Bvar' | Barr'[Ivar] | ¬Barr'[Ivar] |
           Bvar' = Bvar | Ivar' = 0 | Ivar' = Ivar |
           Iarr'[Ivar] = Ivar | Iarr'[Ivar] = 0 | Assign ∧ Assign

    Θ ::= MCond2 ∧ no_sharing

    ρ ::= TRUE | MCond1 ∧ Assign ∧ Preservation | ρ ∨ ρ

    𝒥 ::= ∅ | 𝒥 ∪ { MCond1 }

    𝒞 ::= ∅ | 𝒞 ∪ {(MCond1 , MCond1)}
```

Fig. 4. Grammar for Assertions for Multi-Linked Systems

For example, consider a binary tree, which is a multi-linked heap with bound 2 and no sharing. Each of *left* and *right* is a *link*. Program TREE-INSERT in Fig. 5 is the standard algorithm for inserting a new node, n, into a sorted binary tree rooted at r. In [2] we describe the transition relation of the algorithm.

```
r, t, n    : [1..h]                    init t = r ∧ ¬reach(r, n) ∧ ¬cycle(r)
left, right : array [0..h] of [0..h] init no_sharing
data       : array [0..h] of bool
done       : bool                      init done = FALSE
┌ 1 :  while ¬done do
│         ┌ 2 : if data[n] = data[t] then                                    ┐
│         │       3 : done := TRUE                                           │
│         │     4 : elseif data[n] < data[t] then                           │
│         │         ┌ 5 : if left[t] = 0 then                               ┐│
│         │         │       6 : left[t] := n                                ││
│         │         │       7 : done := TRUE                                ││
│         │         │     else                                              ││
│         │         └       8 : t := left[t]                                ┘│
│         │     9 : elseif right[t] = 0 then                                │
│         │       10 : right[t] := n                                        │
│         │       11 : done := TRUE                                         │
│         │     else                                                        │
│         └       12 : t := right[t]                                        ┘
└ 13 :
```

Fig. 5. Program TREE-INSERT of Fig. 1, adapted to the encoding of trees as multi-linked heaps

6   Reducing Multi-linked into Single-Parent Heaps

We now show how to transform multi-linked heap systems into single-parent heap systems.

6.1   The Transformation

Let $\mathcal{D}_m : \langle \mathcal{V}_m, \Theta_m, \rho_m, \mathcal{J}_m, \mathcal{C}_m \rangle$ be a k-bounded multi-linked heap system. Thus, $\mathcal{V}_m$ includes the **index** arrays $link_1, \ldots, link_k$. We transform $\mathcal{D}_m$ into a single-parent heap system $\mathcal{D}_s : \langle \mathcal{V}_s, \Theta_s, \rho_s, \mathcal{J}_s, \mathcal{C}_s \rangle$ as follows:

The set of variables $\mathcal{V}_s$ consists of the following:

1. $\mathcal{V}_m \setminus \{link_1, \ldots, link_k\}$, i.e., we remove from $\mathcal{V}_m$ all the $link$ arrays;
2. An **index** array $parent \colon [0..h] \mapsto [0..h]$ that does not appear in $\mathcal{V}_m$;
3. A **bool** array $ct \colon [0..h] \mapsto [0..k]$ that does not appear in $\mathcal{V}_m$ (recall our convention that "**bool**" can be any finite-domain type);
4. A new **bool** variable $error$; $error$ is set when $\mathcal{D}_m$ contains an erroneous transition such as one that introduces sharing in the heap, or attempts to assign values to $A[0]$ for some array A.

Intuitively, we replace the **index** $link$ arrays with a single **index** $parent$ array that reverses the direction of the links, and assign to $ct[i]$ (*child type*) the "birth order" of i in the heap. The variable $error$ is boolean and is set when $\mathcal{D}_m$ cannot be transformed into a singe-parent system. This is caused by either an assignment to $A[0]$ or by a violation of the non-sharing requirements. When such an error occurs, $error$ is raised, and remains so, i.e., ρ_s implies $error \to error'$.

A single-parent state is said to be *well formed* if the parent of 0 is itself, and no parent has two distinct children with the same birth order, i.e.,

$$\mathtt{wf} \colon parent[0] = 0 \ \wedge \ \forall i \neq j \, . \, (parent[i] = parent[j] \neq 0 \ \to \ ct[i] \neq ct[j])$$

To transform ρ_m, $\mathcal{J}_m$, and $\mathcal{C}_m$ into their $\mathcal{D}_s$ counterparts, it suffices to transform M-assertions over $\mathcal{V}_m \cup \mathcal{V}'_m$ into restricted EA-assertions over $\mathcal{V}_s \cup \mathcal{V}'_s$. To transform Θ_m, which is of the form $no\_sharing \wedge \varphi$, where φ is an MCond2, into Θ_s, we take the conjunction of wf and the transformation of φ. It thus remains to transform M-assertions. Recall that ρ_m is a disjunction of clauses (see Section 5), each one of the form

$$\varphi \wedge \tau \wedge presEx(\mathcal{V}_m - \{V\})$$

where $V \subseteq \mathcal{V}_m$, φ is an MCond over $\mathcal{V}_m$, and τ is an Assign statement of the form $\bigwedge_{v \in V} v' = E_v(\mathcal{V}_m)$ (where E_v is some expression). When we transform such a ρ_m-disjunct, we sometimes obtain several disjuncts. We assume that each has its obvious $presEx$ assertions over $\mathcal{V}_s$. At times, for simplicity of representation, we do not express the transformation directly in DNF. Yet, in those cases, the DNF form is straightforward.

It thus remains to show how to transform M-assertions into restricted EA-assertions. This is done by induction on the M-assertions, where we ignore the preservation part (which, as discussed above, is defined by the transition relation for both $\mathcal{D}_m$ and $\mathcal{D}_s$.)

Let ψ be an M-assertion. In the following cases, ψ remains unchanged in the transformation:

1. ψ contains no reference to **index** variables and arrays;
2. ψ is of the form $x_1 = x_2$ where x_1 and x_2 are both primed, or both unprimed, **index** variables;
3. ψ is of the form $x_1 = x_2$ where x_1 is a primed, and x_2 is an unprimed, **index** variable;
4. ψ is of the form $x = 0$ where x is a (either primed or unprimed) **index** variable;
5. ψ is of the form $B[x]$, where B is a **bool** array.

The other cases are treated below. We now denote primed variables explicitly, e.g., x_1 refers to an unprimed variable, and x'_1 refers to a primed variable:

1. An assertion of the form $link_j[x_2] = x_1$ is transformed into

$$\begin{aligned}
&(x_2 = 0 \wedge x_1 = 0) \\
\vee\ &(x_2 \neq 0 \wedge x_1 = 0 \wedge \forall . (parent[z] \neq x_2 \vee ct[z] \neq j)) \\
\vee\ &(x_2 \neq 0 \wedge x_1 \neq 0 \wedge parent[x_1] = x_2 \wedge ct[x_1] = j)
\end{aligned}$$

In the case that $x_2 \neq 0$ and $x_1 = 0$, x_2 should have no j^{th} child. If $x_2 \neq 0$ and $x_1 \neq 0$, then x_1 should have x_2 as a parent and the child type of x_1 should be j.
2. A transitive closure formula $reach(x_1, x_2)$ is transformed into

$$(x_1 \neq 0 \wedge x_2 \neq 0 \wedge parent^*(x_2, x_1)) \vee (x_2 = 0)$$

The first disjunct deals with the case where x_1 and x_2 are both non-0 nodes, and then the reachability direction is reversed, reflecting reversal of heap edges in the transformation to a single-parent heap. The second disjunct deals with the case that $x_2 = 0$, and then, since $k > 0$, there is a path from any node into 0.
3. A transitive closure formula $cycle(x)$, where x is an **index** variable, is transformed into $parent^*(parent[x], x)$.

4. An assertion of the form "$x_1' = link_j[x_2]$" is transformed into:

$$(x_2 = 0 \wedge x_1' = 0) \vee (x_2 \neq 0 \wedge x_1' = 0 \wedge \forall y . (parent[y] \neq x_2 \vee ct[y] \neq j))$$
$$\vee (x_2 \neq 0 \wedge \exists y . (parent[y] = x_2 \wedge ct[y] = j \wedge x_1' = y))$$

In case $x_2 = 0$, this transition sets x_1 to 0 since we assume that in non-sharing states $link_j[0] = 0$ for every $j = 1, \ldots, k$. Otherwise, if x_2 has no j^{th} child, then x_1 is set to 0. Otherwise, there exists a y which is the jth child of x_2, and then x_1 is set to y.

5. An assertion of the form "$link_j'[x_1] = x_2$" is transformed into:

$$Err \wedge error' \quad \vee$$
$$\neg Err$$
$$\wedge (x_2 = 0 \vee (x_2 \neq 0 \wedge parent'[x_2] = x_1 \wedge ct'[x_2] = j))$$
$$\wedge \left(\begin{array}{l} \forall z.(parent[z] \neq x_1 \vee ct[z] \neq j) \\ \vee \exists z.(parent[z] = x_1 \wedge ct[z] = j \wedge (z = x_2 \vee parent'[z] = 0)) \end{array} \right)$$

Where Err is defined by:

$$x_1 = 0 \vee (x_2 \neq 0 \wedge parent[x_2] \neq 0 \wedge (parent[x_2] \neq x_1 \vee ct[x_2] \neq j))$$

I.e., the assignment may cause an error by either attempting to assign a value to $link_j[0]$, or by introducing sharing (when x_2 either has a parent that is not x_1, or is x_1's i^{th} child for some $i \neq j$).

When there is no error, x_2 should become the jth child of x_1 unless it is 0, which is expressed by the first conjunct of the non-error case; in addition, any node that was the jth child of x_1 before the transition should become "orphaned," which is expressed by the second conjunct of the non-error case.

The following observation follows trivially from the construction above:

Observation 1. *The transformation of an* M-*assertion is a restricted EA-assertion.*

In [2] we show how to transform the multi-linked heap system defined by the program in Fig. 5 into a single-parent heap system. We also establish there:

6.2 Correctness of Transformation

In order for the above transformation to fit into the verification process proposed in Section 1, we have to show that the result of the verification, as carried out on the transformed system and property, holds with respect to the untransformed counterparts. Such a result is provided by Theorem 4 below. To show that the abstraction computation method of Section 4 is sound with respect to a transformed program and property, we use Observation (1) and Theorem 5 below.

Let $\mathcal{D}_m : \langle \mathcal{V}_m, \Theta_m, \rho_m, \mathcal{J}_m, \mathcal{C}_s \rangle$ be a k-bounded multi-linked heap system over the set of variables $\mathcal{V}_m$, with $k > 1$, and let $\mathcal{D}_s : \langle \mathcal{V}_s, \Theta_s, \rho_s, \mathcal{J}_s, \mathcal{C}_s \rangle$ be its transformation into a single-parent heap system. The transformation into a single-parent heap system induces a mapping $\mathcal{S} : \Sigma_m \to \Sigma_s$.

The following theorems are presented without proofs, which are found in the full version [2].

Theorem 4 (Soundness). *Assume that for every $s \in \Sigma_m$, $s \models no\_sharing$. Let φ_m be a temporal property over M-restricted A-assertions over $\mathcal{V}_m$, and let φ_s be φ_m, where every assertion over $\mathcal{V}_m$ is replaced with its transformation into a restricted EA-assertion over $\mathcal{V}_s$. Then: $\mathcal{D}_s \models \varphi_s \iff \mathcal{D}_m \models \varphi_m$*

While Theorem 4 shows that validity of temporal formulae carries from multi-linked systems into single-parent ones only when the former satisfy non-sharing, we prove that if the latter never reaches an error state, then the former never violates non-sharing:

Theorem 5 (Non-sharing). *If $\mathcal{D}_s \models \Box \neg error$ then $\mathcal{D}_m \models \Box no\_sharing$.*

Thus, to verify $\mathcal{D}_m \models \varphi_m$, one would initially perform a "sanity check" by verifying $\mathcal{D}_s \models \Box \neg error$. If this is successful, then the process outlined in Section 1 can be carried out. Theorem 4 guarantees not only that correctness of $\mathcal{D}_s$ implies correctness of $\mathcal{D}_m$, but also that a counterexample over $\mathcal{D}_s$ is mappable back into $\mathcal{D}_m$.

7   Conclusion

We describe a transformation from programs that perform destructive updates over multi-linked heaps without sharing into single-parent heaps that is based on the idea of simulating a tree (or forest) by a set of converging lists. We then apply an abstraction-based verification framework to automatically verify properties of systems over multi-linked heaps.

We applied our technique to verify properties of insertion into AVL trees. We are currently implementing more benchmarks, including an implementation of 2-3 trees. We are also extending the transformation to allow for unbounded out-degrees in the multi-linked heap, and to heaps whose "backbone" is single-parent, which would allow us to model algorithms that "flip" heap edges (a surprisingly useful feature). In the longer term, we would like to investigate how to use multi-linked heap systems as the basis for further structure simulation (e.g., as in [20,13]).

Acknowledgement. We would like to thank Viktor Kuncak and Greta Yorsh for their insight regarding structure simulation. We also would like to thank the anonymous reviewers for their constructive comments.

References

1. T. Arons, A. Pnueli, S. Ruah, J. Xu, and L. Zuck. Parameterized verification with automatically computed inductive assertions. In CAV'01, pages 221–234. LNCS 2102, 2001.
2. I. Balaban, A. Pnueli, and L. Zuck. Shape analysis of single-parent heaps. Research Report TR2006-885, Computer Science Department, New York University, Warren Weaver Hall, Room 405, 251 Mercer St., New York, NY 10012, November 2006.
3. I. Balaban, A. Pnueli, and L. D. Zuck. Shape analysis by predicate abstraction. In *VM-CAI'2005: Verification, Model Checking, and Abstraction Interpretation*, pages 164–180, 2005.

4. I. Balaban, A. Pnueli, and L. D. Zuck. Modular ranking abstraction. To appear in International Journal of Foundations of Computer Science (IJFCS), 2007. See http://www.cs.nyu.edu/acsys/pubs/permanent/ranking-companion-pre.pdf.
5. T. Ball and R. B. Jones, editors. *Computer Aided Verification, 18th International Conference, CAV 2006, Seattle, WA, USA, August 17-20, 2006, Proceedings*, volume 4144 of *Lecture Notes in Computer Science*. Springer, 2006.
6. M. Benedikt, T. W. Reps, and S. Sagiv. A decidable logic for describing linked data structures. In S. D. Swierstra, editor, *ESOP*, volume 1576 of *Lecture Notes in Computer Science*, pages 2–19. Springer, 1999.
7. J. Berdine, B. Cook, D. Distefano, and P. W. O'Hearn. Automatic termination proofs for programs with shape-shifting heaps. In Ball and Jones [5], pages 386–400.
8. J. D. Bingham and Z. Rakamaric. A logic and decision procedure for predicate abstraction of heap-manipulating programs. In E. A. Emerson and K. S. Namjoshi, editors, *VMCAI*, volume 3855 of *Lecture Notes in Computer Science*, pages 207–221. Springer, 2006.
9. E. Börger, E. Grädel, and Y. Gurevich. *The Classical Decision Problem*. Perspectives of Mathematical Logic. Springer-Verlag, 1997. Second printing (Universitext) 2001.
10. A. Bouajjani, M. Bozga, P. Habermehl, R. Iosif, P. Moro, and T. Vojnar. Programs with lists are counter automata. In Ball and Jones [5], pages 517–531.
11. E. Grädel, M. Otto, and E. Rosen. Undecidability results on two-variable logics. In R. Reischuk and M. Morvan, editors, *STACS*, volume 1200 of *Lecture Notes in Computer Science*, pages 249–260. Springer, 1997.
12. N. Immerman, A. M. Rabinovich, T. W. Reps, S. Sagiv, and G. Yorsh. The boundary between decidability and undecidability for transitive-closure logics. In J. Marcinkowski and A. Tarlecki, editors, *CSL*, volume 3210 of *Lecture Notes in Computer Science*, pages 160–174. Springer, 2004.
13. N. Immerman, A. M. Rabinovich, T. W. Reps, S. Sagiv, and G. Yorsh. Verification via structure simulation. In *Computer Aided Verification CAV*, pages 281–294. Springer Verlag, 2004.
14. Y. Kesten and A. Pnueli. Verification by augmented finitary abstraction. *Information and Computation*, 163(1):203–243, 2000.
15. N. Klarlund and M. I. Schwartzbach. Graph types. In *POPL '93: Proceedings of the 20th ACM SIGPLAN-SIGACT symposium on Principles of programming languages*, pages 196–205, New York, NY, USA, 1993. ACM Press.
16. R. Manevich, E. Yahav, G. Ramalingam, and S. Sagiv. Predicate abstraction and canonical abstraction for singly-linked lists. In R. Cousot, editor, *VMCAI*, volume 3385 of *Lecture Notes in Computer Science*, pages 181–198. Springer, 2005.
17. A. Møller and M. I. Schwartzbach. The Pointer Assertion Logic Engine. In *Programming Language Design and Implementation*, 2001.
18. A. Pnueli and E. Shahar. A platform combining deductive with algorithmic verification. In Rajeev Alur and Thomas A. Henzinger, editors, *Proceedings of the Eighth International Conference on Computer Aided Verification CAV*, volume 1102, page 184, New Brunswick, NJ, USA, / 1996. Springer Verlag.
19. J. C. Reynolds. Separation logic: A logic for shared mutable data structures. In *LICS*, pages 55–74. IEEE Computer Society, 2002.
20. T. Wies, V. Kuncak, P. Lam, A. Podelski, and M. Rinard. On field constraint analysis. In *Verification, Model Checking, and Abstract Interpretation*, 2006.
21. G. Yorsh, A. M. Rabinovich, M. Sagiv, A. Meyer, and A. Bouajjani. A logic of reachable patterns in linked data-structures. In L. Aceto and A. Ingólfsdóttir, editors, *FoSSaCS*, volume 3921 of *Lecture Notes in Computer Science*, pages 94–110. Springer, 2006.

An Inference-Rule-Based Decision Procedure for Verification of Heap-Manipulating Programs with Mutable Data and Cyclic Data Structures[*]

Zvonimir Rakamarić[1], Jesse Bingham[2], and Alan J. Hu[1]

[1] Department of Computer Science, University of British Columbia, Canada
{zrakamar,ajh}@cs.ubc.ca
[2] Intel Corporation, Hillsboro, Oregon, USA
jesse.d.bingham@intel.com

Abstract. Research on the automatic verification of heap-manipulating programs (HMPs) — programs that manipulate unbounded linked data structures via pointers — has blossomed recently, with many different approaches all showing leaps in performance and expressiveness. A year ago, we proposed a small logic for specifying predicates about HMPs and demonstrated that an inference-rule-based decision procedure could be performance-competitive, and in many cases superior to other methods known at the time. That work, however, was a proof-of-concept, with a logic fragment too small to verify most real programs. In this work, we generalize our previous results to be practically useful: we allow the data in heap nodes to be mutable, we allow more than a single pointer field, and we add new primitives needed to verify cyclic structures. Each of these extensions necessitates new or changed inference rules, with the concomitant changes to the proofs and decision procedure. Yet, our new decision procedure, with the more general logic, actually runs as fast as our previous results. With these generalizations, we can automatically verify many more HMP examples, including three small container functions from the Linux kernel.

1 Introduction

Heap-manipulating programs (HMPs) are programs that access and modify linked data structures consisting of an unbounded number of uniform *heap nodes*. They are a somewhat idealized model of programs with dynamic memory allocation, and given that most real software applications use dynamic memory allocation, they are an important frontier for software verification.

Research on verification of HMPs has blossomed recently, with over a dozen papers published in the past year alone, and many different approaches showing incredible progress. For example, automatically verifying the sortedness of applying bubble sort to a singly-linked list required well over 4 minutes of runtime for a state-of-the-art approach a year and a half ago [25], whereas by a year ago, we could verify sortedness (and no memory leaks or cycles) in less than 2 minutes [2]. Verifying no leaks

---

[*] This work was supported by a research grant from the Natural Sciences and Engineering Research Council of Canada and a University of British Columbia Graduate Fellowship.

B. Cook and A. Podelski (Eds.): VMCAI 2007, LNCS 4349, pp. 106–121, 2007.

or cycles (but not sortedness) took us only 11.4 seconds, but this verification could be done in a mere 0.08 seconds a half year later! [29] While one may quibble about details when comparing performance results in this research area (e.g., machine speeds vary slightly, many papers do not report exact run times or the precise property being verified, amount of human effort is hard to quantify, etc.), the overall trend of rapid advancement is clear. Numerous approaches are now efficient enough to be potentially practically relevant.

Given the large amount of related work, we provide here only a very crude sketch of the research milieu surrounding our work. We can roughly group most work on HMP verification into three broad categories: shape analysis based on abstract interpretation [13], deductive verification using classical Floyd-Hoare-style pre- and post-conditions [36] augmented with a specialized logic for heap structures, or model checking [37] using predicate abstraction [15] to deal with the infinite state space.

Perhaps most widely known is the shape analysis work, epitomized by the TVLA system [31]. As the name implies, a major strength of these approaches is in the analysis of the shape of heap structures, and they are able to handle shapes, like trees, that most other approaches cannot. Data, on the other hand, is commonly abstracted away, e.g., the impressively fast 0.08 second verification cited above ignores data in heap nodes. Earlier shape analysis work also required user assistance to specify "instrumentation predicates" and how they are affected by updates. More recent work has improved precision (e.g., [33]) and automation (e.g., [29]).

The deductive approach to verifying HMPs is the most venerable, dating back to Nelson's pioneering work [10]. Nelson was working with first-order logic, imposing a penalty in both performance and manual effort. Much more recently, PALE [18] is based on the weak, monadic, second-order logic of graph types, which is a decidable logic for which the MONA decision procedure [30] exists. Unfortunately, the complexity is non-elementary, so the decision procedure must be used with care. Separation logic [27] is apparently the key to much greater efficiency, with recent results reporting fast verification times (e.g., [6]) and interprocedural scalability [4]. A decidable fragment of separation logic is also known [5]. Deductive approaches typically require manual effort, particularly to specify loop invariants, but recent work is addressing that problem as well (e.g., [26,28]).

Model checking, on the other hand, has always emphasized full automation, including automatic computation of invariants via fixpoints, and great precision. Model checking has revolutionized hardware verification, and with the use of predicate abstraction, has started to impact software verification as well (e.g., [15,16,32,17]). Predicate abstraction conservatively abstracts a program into a Boolean program whose state space is the truth valuations of a finite set of predicates over the concrete program state. Once the predicates are specified, the method runs fully automatically. (In this paper, we do not consider heuristics for discovering predicates.) To verify HMPs, we therefore need a logic for specifying predicates about the heap state. Furthermore, to compute abstract pre- or post-images, the decision procedure for the logic must be extremely fast, since most predicate abstraction approaches make numerous queries to the decision procedure. Dams and Namjoshi were the first to explore this approach, but not having a decision procedure for their logic, they had to rely on manual guidance to assure termination [14]. Balaban et al. proposed a simple logic and small-model-theorem-based decision procedure, and demonstrated the feasibility and promise of this approach [7]. Alternatively, Lahiri and Qadeer proposed first-order axioms for their heap properties and used a first-order prover [23]. In both works, the decision procedure was a major bottleneck, and performance was substantially worse than the more established approaches. We were inspired by these pioneering works and created a simple logic and novel decision procedure that demonstrated that an approach based on model checking and predicate abstraction could be performance competitive, and often superior, to other methods available at the time [1,2].[1] (Other recent promising logics for the predicate-abstraction-based approach include [21] and [34], but no decision procedures are available yet.)

In addition to the fast run times and low memory usage, another feature of our approach was the architecture of the decision procedure. Rather than being based on a small model theorem, it fires inference rules until saturation, backtracking as needed. Such a decision procedure promises several potential benefits: it simplifies integration into a combined satisfiability-modulo-theories solver; it suggests the ability to generate proofs automatically, which could be checked for higher assurance; and proof-generation suggests the possibility of computing interpolants, which have demonstrated enormous potential for improving model-checking efficiency [35]. Accordingly, there is value in pursuing an inference-rule-based decision procedure for HMP verification, as long as the performance is adequate, which it is.

Unfortunately, our previous work was only a proof-of-concept. The logic we proposed is too simplistic: data in heap nodes was not allowed to change, we could not specify important properties about cyclic lists, and heap nodes had only a single pointer field. These restrictions eliminated the vast majority of real programs from consideration.

Contributions: This paper expands and generalizes our previous, preliminary results to be practically useful:

- The new logic and decision procedure allow data stored in heap nodes to be mutable. With this extension, our method can in principle model any operations on data to full bit-accuracy. (In practice, of course, data fields will be downsized as much as possible, as is typical in model checking.) Changing the logic to allow data updates necessitated discovering and adding four new inference rules to the decision procedure.
- We now allow a finite number of pointer fields per heap node. This is needed by all but the most simplistic data structures. This change required all inference rules to be parameterized over the pointer fields, and the proofs must consider interacting constraints arising from the different points-to relations.
- To support cyclic data structures (e.g., cyclic singly- and doubly-linked lists), we added a generalized, ternary transitive closure between operator $btwn_f(x, y, z)$, similar to Nelson's [10]. While the idea of such an operator is not new, how to support such an operator in an inference-rule-based decision procedure is completely new.

---

[1] The published paper has some minor errors, which are corrected in the technical report [2]. The technical report gives run times for the corrected algorithm, which are also much faster than in the paper, due to an improved implementation.

This was the most difficult change to our decision procedure, requiring the addition of 14 new inference rules, most of which are quite complicated.

- Despite the vastly increased complexity of the inference rule set, the essential structure of the decision procedure remained unchanged — the basic approach is still empirically very efficient. In fact, with continuing improvements to the implementation, performance actually improved slightly.
- The additional inference rules did greatly complicate the theoretical underpinnings of our approach. We report some theoretical results for our new logic and decision procedure: our decision procedure is sound and always terminates, and the decision procedure is complete for the fragment of the logic without updates. (In practice, completeness was not an issue, as we could verify all examples that we could specify.) The statements of the theorems are completely analogous to our previous work (e.g., "The decision procedure is sound."), but the proofs had to be completely reworked to account for the greater complexity of the expanded logic.

Overall, the contributions in this paper enable us to very efficiently verify a much larger variety of HMPs, including three small container functions from the Linux kernel.

2   Review of Our Previous Logic and Decision Procedure

To make this paper self-contained, we briefly review our original, simple logic and the proof-of-concept decision procedure. Details are in the published paper and technical report [1,2].

One of the most fundamental concepts for verifying HMPs is unbounded *reachability* (a.k.a. *transitive closure*) between nodes, i.e., can one follow pointers from node x to node y. Several papers have previously identified the importance of transitive closure for HMPs, e.g., [9,10,11,12,7,23,38]. Unfortunately, adding support for transitive closure to even simple logics often yields undecidability [12], hence our decision to start with a minimal logic and add features as needed to verify real examples.

In particular, the logic we originally proposed in [1] is as minimal as imaginable while usable to verify some non-trivial HMPs using predicate abstraction. Fig. 1 shows the logic. While there can be an arbitrary amount of data, allowing modeling with

$$
\begin{array}{rcl}
term & ::= & v \mid f(term) \\
atom & ::= & f^*(term, term) \mid term = term \mid d(term) \mid b \\
literal & ::= & atom \mid \neg atom
\end{array}
$$

Fig. 1. Our original, simple transitive closure logic [1]. v is any of a finite set of node variables that point to heap nodes. b is any of a finite set of Boolean variables that model data not contained in heap nodes. Each heap node has a finite set of data fields D, each able to hold a Boolean value, and $d \in D$. These model data contained in a heap node, with whatever precision is desired. There is a single pointer field f in each heap node, which points to another heap node. The term $f(x)$ denotes the heap node reached by following the f pointer from node x. Similarly, the atom $d(x)$ denotes the content of data field d in node x. Transitive closure is specified with $f^*(x, y)$, which denotes whether node x reaches node y by following 0 or more f pointers. The decision procedure decides satisfiability of conjunctions of literals.

$$\frac{f(x)=y \quad f^*(x,z)}{x=z \quad f^*(y,z)}\text{FUNC}$$

Fig. 2. Inference rule example. This is a typical inference rule from the decision procedure. Above the line are antecedents; below the line are consequents. This rule says that if we get to node y by following one f pointer from node x, and if we can get from x to z by following 0 or more f pointers, then we conclude that $x = z$ or that we can get from y to z by following 0 or more f pointers.

bit-accurate precision, there is only a single pointer field, with a single transitive closure operator, which greatly restricts the heap properties that could be specified.

To specify the effect of program assignments that modify pointers in the heap, i.e., modify f, we need to be able to specify a transition relation between the old and new values of f. Accordingly, for each assignment of the form $f(\tau_1) := \tau_2$, we allow the user to specify a pointer function symbol f' that represents the value of f after the assignment. The semantic relationship between f and f' is

$$f' = \text{update}(f, \tau_1, \tau_2) \tag{1}$$

Our decision procedure implicitly constrains f and f' appropriately, which is previous work. However, our original logic did not have the analogous constructs to allow heap data to be modified.

Conjunction and disjunction are conspicuous by their absence. The decision procedure decides satisfiability of a conjunction of literals. The satisfiability of a conjunction of predicates is the fundamental operation in computing the abstract pre- or post-image operators in predicate abstraction, potentially being called an exponential number of times per image, so we designed the decision procedure for that problem. We would handle a general formula with disjunctions by going to DNF and checking satisfiability of each disjunct separately.

The decision procedure is based on applying inference rules (IRs). Viewed from a high level, the decision procedure repeatedly searches for an applicable IR, applies it (i.e. adds one of its consequents to the set of literals), and recurses. The recursion is necessary for those IRs that branch, i.e. have multiple consequents. If the procedure ever infers a contradiction, it backtracks to the last branching IR with an unexplored consequent, or returns *unsatisfiable* if there is no such IR. If the procedure reaches a point where there are no applicable IRs and no contradictions, it returns that the set of literals is *satisfiable*. Fig. 2 shows one sample inference rule. The decision procedure for our original logic has 17 inference rules, some of which are parameterized.

3   New Extensions to Logic and Decision Procedure

Our previous work was proof-of-concept: HMP verification based on model-checking and predicate abstraction could be performance competitive with other approaches, thanks to our efficient, inference-rule-based decision procedure. But our simplistic logic was too inexpressive for all but a few examples.

This paper addresses that problem. In the following subsections, we describe three extensions to our original logic and decision procedure. These extensions are absolutely indispensable for verifying a wide range of real programs. For each extension, we give a short example illustrating typical program constructs that motivated the extension, and then present how we changed the logic and decision procedure. The BNF for the extended logic is provided in Fig. 3.

3.1   Mutable Data Fields

Fig. 4 presents a simple example of a procedure that mutates data fields. The procedure sets the values of the data field of all nodes in the non-empty acyclic singly-linked input list *head* to true. Necessary assumptions are formalized by the **assume** statement on line 2 of the program. The body of the procedure is simple; it traverses the list, and on line 5 assigns true to the data field d at each iteration. The specification is expressed by the **assert** statement on line 8, and indicates that whenever line 8 is reached, *head* must point to an acyclic singly-linked list with data field d of all nodes set to true.

Assignments that modify a data field $d \in D$ have the general form $d(\tau) := b$, where τ is a term, and b is a data variable. Line 5 of the HMP of Fig. 4 is an example of such assignment. In order to be able to handle data mutations, for each data assignment we allow the user to introduce a data function symbol d' that represents d after the assignment. The semantic relationship between d and d' is

$$d' = \mathsf{update}(d, \tau, b) \tag{2}$$

Our decision procedure implicitly enforces the constraint (2) when it encounters the symbols d and d'. We accomplished this through the additional set of inference rules that capture the effects of a data field update. Fig. 5 presents these rules, and for example PRESERVEVALUE ensures the data values of nodes that are not equal to τ are preserved.

3.2   Cyclicity

We illustrate the extension for supporting cyclic lists with an example called INIT-CYCLIC in Fig. 6. The procedure takes a node *head* that points to a cyclic list and sets the data fields of all nodes in the list to true. Necessary assumptions are again formalized by the **assume** statement on line 2 of the program. In the predicates required for the verification of this example, the subformulas of the form $\mathrm{btwn}_f(x, y, z)$ express that by following a sequence of f links from node x, we'll reach node y before we reach node z, i.e. node y comes between nodes x and z. The fact that *head* is reachable from $f(head)$

$$
\begin{aligned}
term &::= v \mid f(term) \\
atom &::= f^*(term, term) \mid term = term \mid d(term) \mid b \mid \mathrm{btwn}_f(term, term, term) \\
literal &::= atom \mid \neg atom
\end{aligned}
$$

Fig. 3. The syntax of our new logic. Aside from the addition of the important new btwn atom, the pointer function symbol f now ranges over a *set* of names F.

enforces the cyclicality assumption. The body of INIT-CYCLIC is straightforward. First, the data field of *head* is set to true on line 4. Then, the loop sets the data fields of all other nodes in the list to true. The specification is expressed by the **assert** statement on line 9, and indicates that whenever line 9 is reached, data fields of all nodes in the list have to be set to true.

Cyclic lists are commonly used data structures, and therefore supporting cyclicity is very important. In our experience and others' [10,24], expressing "betweenness" is often necessary to construct invariants to verify cyclic list HMPs. For example, in order to prove the assertion on line 9 of INIT-CYCLE, the predicate abstraction engine must be able to construct an appropriate loop invariant (i.e. at line 5). This invariant must be strong enough to imply that all nodes x lying between *head* and *curr* on the cyclic list have $d(x) = $ true. It is not hard to show that our base logic of Sect. 2 is not capable of expressing this.

To solve this deficiency, we have added a generalized, ternary transitive closure between predicate $\text{btwn}_f(x,y,z)$ to our logic, similar to Nelson's [10]. Formally, the interpretation of a between atom is defined as follows: a between atom $\text{btwn}_f(\tau_1, \tau_2, \tau_3)$ is interpreted as true iff there exist $n_0, m_0 \geq 0$ such that $\tau_2 = f^{n_0}(\tau_1)$, $\tau_3 = f^{m_0}(\tau_1)$, $n_0 \leq m_0$, and for all n,m such that $\tau_2 = f^n(\tau_1)$, $\tau_3 = f^m(\tau_1)$, we have $n_0 \leq n$ and $m_0 \leq m$.

While the idea of such a construct is not new, how to support it in an inference-rule-based decision procedure is completely new. This was also the most difficult extension of our decision procedure, requiring the addition of 14 new inference rules presented in Fig. 7, most of which are quite involved. For instance, BTW9 asserts that if x, y, z, and w are on the same chain, y is between x and w, and f (z)=w, then y is also between x and z, unless y=w. Furthermore, the introduction of the between atom broke our soundness and completeness results from the previous paper, and we had to completely redo all of our proofs. We give the intuition behind our new theoretical results in Sect. 4, while the complete proofs are presented in the technical report [3].

3.3 Multiple Pointer Fields

Fig. 8 shows a list container procedure LINUX-LIST-DEL from the Linux kernel. It illustrates the need for both multiple pointer fields and cyclic lists. The procedure takes

```
1: procedure INIT-LIST(head)
2:     assume  f*(head,t) ∧ f*(head, nil) ∧ f(nil) = nil
3:     curr := head;
4:     while ¬curr = nil do
5:         d(curr) := true;
6:         curr := f(curr);
7:     end while
8:     assert  d(t)
9: end procedure
```

Fig. 4. INIT-LIST initializes the data fields of an acyclic singly-linked list. In the **assume** and **assert** statements, variable t represents an arbitrary node (see Sect. 5).

a node *entry* and removes it from a cyclic doubly-linked list. Each node in the list has two pointer fields: a *prev* and a *next* pointer. The body of the procedure is simple; it connects the *prev* and *next* pointers of *entry*'s neighbors, thus removing *entry* from the list. The assumptions and specifications for this example are quite involved and are given in our technical report [3].

Cyclic doubly-linked lists are widely used data structures. For instance, they are commonly used in kernels, such as the Linux kernel from where this example was taken. Handling multiple pointer fields is theoretically hard; it is a well-known result that unrestricted use of reachability in the presence of only two pointer fields is undecidable [12]. We therefore had to take special care in defining our extension. It turns out that if each individual reachability operator only refers to a single pointer field and there are no quantifiers, the decidability results still hold. This restriction prevents us from, e.g., expressing transitive closure in a tree, since that would require formulas like $(left \lor right)^*(root, leaf)$. However, we can still handle doubly-linked lists and similar structures.

On the logic side, this extension is reflected in symbol f being an element of a set of pointer function symbols F, rather than a single pointer function symbol (see Sect. 2). Our extended decision procedure supports for multiple pointer fields by instantiating the inference rules for each pointer field. In a sense, the decision procedure processes each field as a separate theory, and interaction between these theories is limited to communication of deduced term equalities and disequalities.

4   Correctness of the Decision Procedure

In this section, we will give the soundness and completeness theorems that show the correctness of our decision procedure. The detailed proofs of all theorems and more formal presentation of the decision procedure can be found in the technical report [3].

We'll start with noting that the problem our decision procedure solves is NP-hard, hence a polytime algorithm is unlikely to exist.

Theorem 1. *Given a set of literals Φ, the problem of deciding if Φ is satisfiable is NP-hard.*

Theorem 1 still holds when Φ contains no pointer function updates, no btwn predicates, no data fields, and only mentions a single pointer function f; hence it even applies to our simplistic original logic [1].

$$\frac{d'(\tau) \qquad \neg d'(\tau)}{b \qquad \neg b}\text{EQDATA} \qquad \frac{\neg \tau = x}{\frac{d(x) \qquad \neg d(x)}{d'(x) \qquad \neg d'(x)}}\text{PRESERVEVALUE}$$

$$\frac{d(x) \qquad \neg d'(x)}{\tau = x}\text{EQNODES1} \qquad \frac{\neg d(x) \qquad d'(x)}{\tau = x}\text{EQNODES2}$$

Fig. 5. Data update inference rules. The rules are used to extend our logic to support a data function symbol d' with the implicit constraint $d' = \text{update}(d, \tau, b)$, where $\tau \in V$ and b is a boolean variable.

The following theorem tells us that if iterative application of the IRs in the decision procedure yields a contradiction, then we can conclude that the original set of literals is unsatisfiable.

Theorem 2. *The inference rules of Fig. 5, Fig. 7, Fig. 9, and Fig. 10 (see Appendix A) are sound.*

The proof proceeds by arguing in turn that each of the IRs given in the figures is sound.

To prove completeness we first reduce the problem to sets of literals in a certain normal form, then prove completeness for only normal sets:

Let $\mathsf{Vars}(\Phi)$ denote the subset of the node variables V appearing in Φ.

Definition 1 (normal). *A set of literals Φ is said to be* normal *if all terms appearing in Φ are variables, except that for each $f \in F$ and $v \in \mathsf{Vars}(\Phi)$ there may exist at most one equality literal of the form $f(v) = u$, where $u \in \mathsf{Vars}(\Phi)$.*

Theorem 3. *There exists a polynomial-time algorithm that transforms any set Φ into a normal set Φ' such that Φ' is satisfiable if and only if Φ is satisfiable.*

Thanks to Theorem 3, our decision procedure can without loss of generality assume that Φ is normal. Let us call a set of literals Φ *consistent* if it does not contain a contradiction, and call Φ *closed* if none of the IRs of Fig. 7 and Fig. 9 are applicable. Our completeness theorem may then be stated as follows.

Theorem 4. *If Φ is consistent, closed, and normal, then Φ is satisfiable.*

The proof of Theorem 4 is quite technical, and involves reasoning about the dependencies between digraphs of partial functions and the digraphs of their transitive closures.

If the procedure reaches a point where there are no applicable IRs and no contradictions, then the inferred set of literals is consistent, closed, and normal. Hence, by Theorem 4, it may correctly return *satisfiable*. We still don't have a proof that the procedure is complete when its input includes a data or pointer field update. Fortunately, not having such a theorem *does not* compromise the soundness of verification by predicate abstraction. In practice, in our experiments of Sect. 5, we never found any property

```
1: procedure INIT-CYCLIC(head)
2:     assume f*(head,t) ∧ f*(f(head),head) ∧ ¬head=nil
3:     curr := f(head);
4:     d(head) := true;
5:     while ¬curr=head do
6:         d(curr) := true;
7:         curr := f(curr);
8:     end while
9:     assert d(t)
10: end procedure
```

Fig. 6. INIT-CYCLIC sets data fields of all nodes in a cyclic list to true. Additional predicates required for the verification: $curr = head$, $curr = f(head)$, $\mathsf{btwn}_f(curr,t,head)$, $t = head$, $\mathsf{btwn}_f(head,t,curr)$, $f^*(t,curr)$.

$$\frac{}{\mathrm{btwn}_f(x,x,x)}\text{BTWReflex} \qquad \frac{f^*(x,y) \qquad f^*(y,z) \qquad f(z)=x}{\mathrm{btwn}_f(x,y,z)}\text{BTW1}$$

$$\frac{\mathrm{btwn}_f(x,y,z)}{\begin{array}{c}f^*(x,y)\\f^*(y,z)\end{array}}\text{BTW2} \qquad \frac{f(x)=w \qquad \mathrm{btwn}_f(x,y,z)}{\mathrm{btwn}_f(w,y,z) \qquad x=y}\text{BTW3}$$

$$\frac{\mathrm{btwn}_f(x,y,z) \qquad \mathrm{btwn}_f(x,z,y)}{y=z}\text{BTW4} \qquad \frac{f^*(x,y) \qquad f^*(x,z)}{\mathrm{btwn}_f(x,y,z) \qquad \mathrm{btwn}_f(x,z,y)}\text{BTW5}$$

$$\frac{f^*(x,y) \quad f^*(y,z) \quad f^*(z,x)}{\begin{array}{c}\mathrm{btwn}_f(x,y,z) \quad \mathrm{btwn}_f(x,z,y)\\\mathrm{btwn}_f(y,z,x) \quad \mathrm{btwn}_f(z,y,x) \quad x=y \quad x=z \quad y=z\\\mathrm{btwn}_f(z,x,y) \quad \mathrm{btwn}_f(y,x,z)\end{array}}\text{BTW6} \qquad \frac{f^*(x,y)}{\begin{array}{c}\mathrm{btwn}_f(x,x,y)\\\mathrm{btwn}_f(x,y,y)\end{array}}\text{BTW7}$$

$$\frac{\mathrm{btwn}_f(x,y,z) \qquad f(x)=z}{y=x \qquad y=z}\text{BTW8} \qquad \frac{f(z)=w \quad \mathrm{btwn}_f(x,y,w) \quad f^*(x,z)}{\mathrm{btwn}_f(x,y,z) \qquad y=w}\text{BTW9}$$

$$\frac{\mathrm{btwn}_f(x,y,z) \quad \mathrm{btwn}_f(w,z,y) \quad f^*(x,w)}{f^*(z,w) \qquad y=z}\text{BTW10} \qquad \frac{\mathrm{btwn}_f(w,x,y) \quad \mathrm{btwn}_f(w,y,z)}{\mathrm{btwn}_f(w,x,z)}\text{BTW11}$$

$$\frac{\mathrm{btwn}_f(v,u,x) \quad \mathrm{btwn}_f(v,u,y) \quad \mathrm{btwn}_f(u,x,y)}{\mathrm{btwn}_f(v,x,y)}\text{BTW12} \qquad \frac{\mathrm{btwn}_f(x,y,z) \qquad \neg x=z}{\mathrm{btwn}_{f'}(x,y,z) \qquad \begin{array}{c}\mathrm{btwn}_f(x,\tau_1,z)\\\neg \tau_1=z\end{array}}\text{UPDBTWN}$$

Fig. 7. Between inference rules. Here x, y, z, etc. range over variables V and $f \in F$ ranges over pointer fields. UPDBTWN enforces the implicit constraint $f' = \mathrm{update}(f, \tau_1, \tau_2)$, where τ_1 and τ_2 are variables (see Sect. 2).

violations caused by the extended decision procedure erroneously concluding that a set of literals was satisfiable.

Theorem 5. *The decision procedure always terminates.*

The theorem follows from the fact that none of the IRs create new terms, and there is only a finite number of possible literals that one could add given a fixed set of terms.

Our soundness, completeness, and termination results given in this section also ensure that the logic without pointer and data field updates is decidable. Furthermore, we believe that our logic with updates is subsumed by the slightly more general decidable logic presented in [7], and therefore also decidable.

5   Experimental Results

We ran our experiments using the new decision procedure[2] in the same verification setup as before [2]: a straightforward implementation of model checking with predicate abstraction. Once the predicates are specified, everything is fully automatic, including computation of most-precise abstract images and loop invariants.

Table 1 gives a baseline performance comparison on the same examples from our previously published work [2]. Table 2 gives results for the more than twice as many examples that we could not verify previously. We ran all experiments on a 2.6 Ghz Pentium 4 machine.

---

[2] The decision procedure is publicly available at http://www.cs.ubc.ca/~zrakamar

Table 1. Performance comparison against our previous work [2]. Although our extensions required adding several complex inference rules to the decision procedure, the running times stayed roughly the same: there was no practical performance penalty. "property" specifies the verified property; "CFG edges" is the number of edges in the control-flow graph of the program; "preds" is the number of predicates required for verification; "DP calls" is the number of decision procedure queries; "old time" is the total execution time from [2] (faster than [1]); "new time" is the total execution time using our new decision procedure.

program	property	CFG edges	preds	DP calls	old time (s)	new time (s)
LIST-REVERSE	NL	6	8	184	0.1	0.2
LIST-ADD	NL∧AC∧IN	7	8	66	0.1	0.1
ND-INSERT	NL∧AC∧IN	5	13	259	0.5	0.5
ND-REMOVE	NL∧AC∧RE	5	12	386	0.9	0.9
ZIP	NL∧AC	20	22	9153	17.8	17.3
SORTED-ZIP	NL∧AC∧SO∧IN	28	22	14251	23.4	22.8
SORTED-INSERT	NL∧AC∧SO∧IN	10	20	5990	14.2	13.8
BUBBLE-SORT	NL∧AC	21	18	3444	11.4	11.1
BUBBLE-SORT	NL∧AC∧SO	21	24	31446	119.5	114.9

The examples from Table 1 perform operations on acyclic singly linked lists — reverse, add elements, remove elements, sort, merge, etc. Therefore, we have been able to verify them without using the extensions described in this paper. The comparison supports our claim that although we greatly improved the expressiveness of the logic and therefore extended the decision procedure with a number of intricate inference rules, the practical running times haven't changed.

Table 2 presents results of the experiments using examples that involve data field updates, cyclic lists, and doubly-linked lists. We could not handle them using the old logic and decision procedure. However, we have been successful in verifying them using the described new features added to our logic and decision procedure. These example programs are the following:

REMOVE-ELEMENTS – removes from a cyclic list elements whose data field is false.
REMOVE-SEGMENT – removes the first contiguous segment of elements whose data field is true from a cyclic singly-linked list. This example is taken from a paper by Manevich et al. [24].

```
1: procedure LINUX-LIST-DEL(entry)
2:     p := prev(entry);
3:     n := next(entry);
4:     prev(n) := p;
5:     next(p) := n;
6:     next(entry) := nil;
7:     prev(entry) := nil;
8: end procedure
```

Fig. 8. LINUX-LIST-DEL is a standard function that removes a node from a cyclic doubly-linked list taken from a Linux kernel

Table 2. Results for HMPs that could not be handled in our previous work. "property" specifies the verified property; "CFG edges" denotes the number of edges in the control-flow graph of the program; "preds" is the number of predicates required for verification; "DP calls" is the number of decision procedure queries; "time" is the total execution time.

program	property	CFG edges	preds	DP calls	time(s)
REMOVE-ELEMENTS	NL∧CY∧RE	15	17	3062	8.8
REMOVE-SEGMENT	CY	17	15	902	2.2
SEARCH-AND-SET	NL∧CY∧DT	9	16	4892	5.3
SET-UNION	NL∧CY∧DT∧IN	9	21	374	1.4
CREATE-INSERT	NL∧AC∧IN	9	24	3020	14.8
CREATE-INSERT-DATA	NL∧AC∧IN	11	27	8710	39.7
CREATE-FREE	NL∧AC∧IN∧RE	19	31	52079	457.4
INIT-LIST	NL∧AC∧DT	4	9	81	0.1
INIT-LIST-VAR	NL∧AC∧DT	5	11	244	0.2
INIT-CYCLIC	NL∧CY∧DT	5	11	200	0.2
SORTED-INSERT-DNODES	NL∧AC∧SO∧IN	10	25	7918	77.9
REMOVE-DOUBLY	NL∧DL∧RE	10	34	3238	24.3
REMOVE-CYCLIC-DOUBLY	NL∧CD∧RE	4	27	1695	15.6
LINUX-LIST-ADD	NL∧CD∧IN	6	25	1240	6.4
LINUX-LIST-ADD-TAIL	NL∧CD∧IN	6	27	1598	7.3
LINUX-LIST-DEL	NL∧CD∧RE	6	29	2057	24.7

SEARCH-AND-SET – searches for an element with specified integer value in a cyclic singly-linked list, and initializes integer data fields of previous elements. Although this example uses merely 2-bit integers, it shows that our logic and decision procedure support any finite enumerated data type.

SET-UNION – joins two cyclic lists. This example is taken from a paper by Nelson [10].

CREATE-INSERT, CREATE-INSERT-DATA, CREATE-FREE – create new nodes (*malloc*), initialize their data fields, and insert them nondeterministically into a linked list. Also, remove nodes from a linked list and *free* them.[3]

INIT-LIST, INIT-LIST-VAR, INIT-CYCLIC – initialize data fields of acyclic and cyclic singly-linked lists, and set values of data variables.

SORTED-INSERT-DNODES – inserts an element into a sorted linked list so that sortedness is preserved. Every node in the linked list has an additional pointer to a node that contains a data field which is used for sorting.

REMOVE-DOUBLY – removes an element from an acyclic doubly-linked list.

REMOVE-CYCLIC-DOUBLY – removes an element from a cyclic doubly-linked list. This example is taken from a paper by Lahiri and Qadeer [23].

LINUX-LIST-ADD, LINUX-LIST-ADD-TAIL, LINUX-LIST-DEL – examples from Linux kernel list container that add and remove nodes from a cyclic doubly-linked list.

Our technical report [3] provides pseudocode and lists the required predicates for all examples.

---

[3] *malloc* and *free* are modelled as removing and adding nodes to an infinite cyclic list [20].

The safety properties we checked (when applicable) of the HMPs are roughly:

- *no leaks* (NL) – all nodes reachable from the head of the list at the beginning of the program are also reachable at the end of the program.
- *insertion* (IN) – a distinguished node that is to be inserted into a list is actually reachable from the head of the list, i.e. the insertion "worked".
- *acyclic* (AC) – the final list is acyclic, i.e. nil is reachable from the head of the list.
- *cyclic* (CY) – list is a cyclic singly-linked list, i.e. the head of the list is reachable from its successor.
- *doubly-linked* (DL) – the final list is a doubly-linked list.
- *cyclic doubly-linked* (CD) – the final list is a cyclic doubly-linked list.
- *sorted* (SO) – list is a sorted linked list, i.e. each node's data field is less than or equal to its successor's.
- *data* (DT) – data fields of selected (possibly all) nodes in a list are set to a value.
- *remove elements* (RE) – for examples that remove node(s), this states that the node(s) was (were) actually removed. For the program REMOVE-ELEMENTS, RE also asserts that the data field of all removed elements is false.

Often, the properties one is interested in verifying for HMPs involve universal quantification over the heap nodes. For example, to assert the property NL, we must express that for all nodes t, if t is reachable from *head* initially, then t is also reachable from *head* (or some other node) at the end of the program. Since our logic doesn't support quantification, we introduce a Skolem constant t to represent a universally quantified variable [8,7]. Here, t is a new node variable that is initially assumed to satisfy the antecedent of our property, and is otherwise unmodified by the program. For the program of Fig. 4, we express NL by conjoining $f^*(head, t)$ to the **assume** statement on line 2, and conjoining $f^*(head, t)$ to the assertion on line 8. Since (after the **assume**) t can be any node reachable from *head*, if the assertion is never violated, we have proven NL.

6   Future Work and Conclusions

We have introduced a logic for verifying HMPs that is expressive enough, and an inference-rule-based decision procedure for the logic that is efficient enough, to verify a wide range of small, but realistic programs. There are many directions for future research, some of which are outlined here.

We have found that even minimal support for universally quantified variables (as in the logic of Balaban et al. [7]) would allow expression of many common heap structure attributes. For example, the current logic cannot assert that two terms x and y point to disjoint linked lists; a single universally quantified variable would allow for this property (see Nelson [9, page 22]). We also found that capturing disjointedness is necessary for verifying that LIST-REVERSE always produces an acyclic list; hence we were unable to verify this property. We believe that our decision procedure can be enhanced to handle this case, either by introducing limited support for quantifiers, or by adding a new "disjoint predicate" with appropriate inference rules.

A broader expressiveness deficiency is the expression of more involved heap structure properties, such as for trees. Though our logic cannot capture "x points to a tree", we believe that it is possible that an extension could be used to verify simple properties of programs that manipulate trees, for example that there are no memory leaks. It may also be possible to use techniques like structure simulation [22] or field constraint analysis [19], which use decidable logics to verify data structures originally beyond the scope of such logics (e.g., skip lists). We have run our decision procedure on some queries for MONA generated by the field constraint analysis tool Bohne [19], where we appear to be faster than MONA, but the queries have run so quickly on both tools that the comparison is meaningless.

We also plan on investigating how existing techniques for predicate discovery and more advanced predicate abstraction algorithms mesh with our decision procedure.

We have initial results showing the possibility of incorporating our decision procedure into a combined satisfiability-modulo-theories decision procedure and have started exploring such integration. We believe that by doing so, it would be possible to improve the precision of heap abstraction used by the existing software verification tools that employ theorem provers. We also plan to look into extending our decision procedure to generate proofs and interpolants.[4]

References

1. J. Bingham and Z. Rakamarić. A Logic and Decision Procedure for Predicate Abstraction of Heap-Manipulating Programs. In *Conf. on Verification, Model Checking and Abstract Interpretation (VMCAI)*, 2006.
2. J. Bingham and Z. Rakamarić. A Logic and Decision Procedure for Predicate Abstraction of Heap-Manipulating Programs, 2005. UBC Dept. Comp. Sci. Tech Report TR-2005-19, http://www.cs.ubc.ca/cgi-bin/tr/2005/TR-2005-19.
3. Z. Rakamarić, J. Bingham, and A. J. Hu. A Better Logic and Decision Procedure for Predicate Abstraction of Heap-Manipulating Programs, 2006. UBC Dept. Comp. Sci. Tech Report TR-2006-02, http://www.cs.ubc.ca/cgi-bin/tr/2006/TR-2006-02.
4. A. Gotsman, J. Berdine, and B. Cook. Interprocedural Shape Analysis with Separated Heap Abstractions. In *Static Analysis Symposium (SAS)*, 2006.
5. J. Berdine, C. Calcagno, and P. W. O'Hearn. A Decidable Fragment of Separation Logic. In *Conf. on Foundations of Software Technology and Theoretical Computer Science (FSTTCS)*, 2004.
6. J. Berdine, C. Calcagno, and P. W. O'Hearn. Smallfoot: Modular Automatic Assertion Checking with Separation Logic. In *Intl. Symp. on Formal Methods for Components and Objects (FMCO)*, 2006.
7. I. Balaban, A. Pnueli, and L. Zuck. Shape Analysis by Predicate Abstraction. In *Conf. on Verification, Model Checking and Abstract Interpretation (VMCAI)*, 2005.
8. C. Flanagan and S. Qadeer. Predicate Abstraction for Software Verification. In *Symp. on Principles of Programming Languages (POPL)*, 2002.
9. G. Nelson. Techniques for Program Verification. PhD thesis, Stanford University, 1979.
10. G. Nelson. Verifying Reachability Invariants of Linked Structures. In *Symp. on Principles of Programming Languages (POPL)*, 1983.
11. M. Benedikt, T. Reps, and M. Sagiv. A Decidable Logic for Describing Linked Data Structures. In *European Symposium on Programming (ESOP)*, 1999.
12. N. Immerman, A. Rabinovich, T. Reps, M. Sagiv, and G. Yorsh. The Boundary Between Decidability and Undecidability for Transitive Closure Logics. In *Workshop on Computer Science Logic (CSL)*, 2004.

---

[4] Thanks to Ken McMillan for the proof-generation and interpolant suggestion.

13. P. Cousot and R. Cousot. Abstract Interpretation: A Unified Lattice Model for Static Analysis of Programs by Construction or Approximation of Fixpoints. In *Symp. on Principles of Programming Languages (POPL)*, 1977.
14. D. Dams and K. S. Namjoshi. Shape Analysis Through Predicate Abstraction and Model Checking. In *Conf. on Verification, Model Checking and Abstract Interpretation (VMCAI)*, 2003.
15. S. Graf and H. Saidi. Construction of Abstract State Graphs with PVS. In *Conf. on Computer Aided Verification (CAV)*, 1997.
16. S. Das, D. L. Dill, and S. Park. Experience with Predicate Abstraction. In *Conf. on Computer Aided Verification (CAV)*, 1999.
17. T. A. Henzinger, R. Jhala, R. Majumdar, and G. Sutre. Lazy Abstraction. In *Symp. on Principles of Programming Languages (POPL)*, 2002.
18. A. Møller and M. I. Schwartzbach. The Pointer Assertion Logic Engine. In *Conf. on Programming Language Design and Implementation (PLDI)*, 2001.
19. T. Wies, V. Kuncak, P. Lam, A. Podelski, and M. Rinard. Field Constraint Analysis. In *Conf. on Verification, Model Checking and Abstract Interpretation (VMCAI)*, 2006.
20. T. Reps, M. Sagiv, and A. Loginov. Finite Differencing of Logical Formulas for Static Analysis. In *European Symposium on Programming (ESOP)*, 2003.
21. G. Yorsh, A. Rabinovich, M. Sagiv, A. Meyer, and A. Bouajjani. A Logic of Reachable Patterns in Linked Data-Structures. In *Foundations of Software Science and Computation Structures (FOSSACS)*, 2006.
22. N. Immerman, A. Rabinovich, T. Reps, M. Sagiv, and G. Yorsh. Verification via Structure Simulation. In *Conf. on Computer Aided Verification (CAV)*, 2004.
23. S. K. Lahiri and S. Qadeer. Verifying Properties of Well-Founded Linked Lists. In *Symp. on Principles of Programming Languages (POPL)*, 2006.
24. R. Manevich, E. Yahav, G. Ramalingam, and M. Sagiv. Predicate Abstraction and Canonical Abstraction for Singly-Linked Lists. In *Conf. on Verification, Model Checking and Abstract Interpretation (VMCAI)*, 2005.
25. A. Loginov, T. W. Reps, and S. Sagiv. Abstraction Refinement via Inductive Learning. In *Conf. on Computer Aided Verification (CAV)*, 2005.
26. D. Distefano, P. W. O'Hearn, and H. Yang. A Local Shape Analysis Based on Separation Logic. In *Tools and Algorithms for the Construction and Analysis of Systems (TACAS)*, 2006.
27. S. Ishtiaq and P. W. O'Hearn. BI as an Assertion Language for Mutable Data Structures. In *Symp. on Principles of Programming Languages (POPL)*, 2001.
28. S. Magill, A. Nanevski, E. M. Clarke, and P. Lee. Inferring Invariants in Separation Logic for Imperative List-processing Programs. In *Workshop on Semantics, Program Analysis, and Computing Environments for Memory Management (SPACE)*, 2006.
29. T. Lev-Ami, N. Immerman, and M. Sagiv. Abstraction for Shape Analysis with Fast and Precise Transformers. In *Conf. on Computer Aided Verification (CAV)*, 2006.
30. N. Klarlund, A. Møller, and M. I. Schwartzbach. MONA Implementation Secrets. In *Conf. on Implementation and Application of Automata (CIAA)*, 2000.
31. T. Lev-Ami and M. Sagiv. TVLA: A System for Implementing Static Analyses. In *Static Analysis Symposium (SAS)*, 2000.
32. T. Ball, R. Majumdar, T. D. Millstein, and S. K. Rajamani. Automatic Predicate Abstraction of C Programs. In *Conf. on Programming Language Design and Implementation (PLDI)*, 2001.
33. G. Yorsh, T. Reps, and M. Sagiv. Symbolically Computing Most-Precise Abstract Operations for Shape Analysis. In *Tools and Algorithms for the Construction and Analysis of Systems (TACAS)*, 2004.
34. S. Ranise and C. G. Zarba. A Theory of Singly-Linked Lists and its Extensible Decision Procedure. In *IEEE Int. Conf. on Software Engineering and Formal Methods (SEFM)*, 2006.

35. K. L. McMillan. Applications of Craig Interpolants in Model Checking. In *Tools and Algorithms for the Construction and Analysis of Systems (TACAS)*, 2005.
36. C. A. R. Hoare. An Axiomatic Basis for Computer Programming. *Communications of the ACM*, 12(10):576–583, 1969.
37. E. M. Clarke, E. A. Emerson, and A. P. Sistla. Automatic Verification of Finite-State Concurrent Systems Using Temporal Logic Specifications. *ACM Transactions on Programming Languages and Systems (TOPLAS)*, 8(2):244–263, 1986.
38. T. Lev-Ami, N. Immerman, T. W. Reps, M. Sagiv, S. Srivastava, and G. Yorsh. Simulating Reachability using First-Order Logic with Applications to Verification of Linked Data Structures. In *Conf. on Automated Deduction (CADE)*, 2005.

A   Inference Rules from Previous Work [1,2]

$$\frac{}{x=x}\text{IDENT} \qquad \frac{}{f^*(x,x)}\text{REFLEX} \qquad \frac{f(x)=y}{f^*(x,y)}\text{TRANS1}$$

$$\frac{f^*(x,y) \quad f^*(y,z)}{f^*(x,z)}\text{TRANS2} \qquad \frac{f(x)=y \quad f^*(x,z)}{x=z \quad f^*(y,z)}\text{FUNC}$$

$$\frac{f(x_1)=x_2 \quad f(x_2)=x_3 \quad \cdots \quad f(x_k)=x_1 \quad f^*(x_1,y)}{y=x_1 \qquad y=x_2 \qquad \cdots \qquad y=x_k}\text{CYCLE}_k$$

$$\frac{f^*(x,y) \quad f^*(y,x) \quad f^*(x,z)}{x=y \qquad f^*(z,x)}\text{SCC} \qquad \frac{f^*(x,y) \quad f^*(x,z)}{f^*(y,z) \qquad f^*(z,y)}\text{TOTAL}$$

$$\frac{f(x)=z \quad f(y)=z \quad f^*(x,y) \quad f^*(y,x)}{x=y}\text{SHARE} \qquad \frac{d(x) \qquad \neg d(y)}{\neg x=y}\text{NOTEQNODES}$$

Fig. 9. Basic inference rules. Here x, y, z, etc. range over variables V and $d \in D$ ranges over data fields. Note that CYCLE_k actually defines a separate rule for each $k \geq 1$.

$$\frac{}{f'(\tau_1)=\tau_2}\text{UPDATE}$$

$$\frac{f(x)=y}{x=\tau_1 \quad f'(x)=y}\text{UPDFUNC1} \qquad \frac{f(\tau_1)=w}{\ } \quad \frac{f'(x)=y}{x=\tau_1 \quad f(x)=y}\text{UPDFUNC2}$$
$$\frac{}{y=w} \qquad\qquad \frac{}{y=\tau_2}$$

$$\frac{f^*(x,y)}{f'^*(x,\tau_1) \quad f'^*(x,y)}\text{UPDTRANS1} \qquad \frac{f'^*(x,y)}{f^*(x,\tau_1) \quad f^*(x,y)}\text{UPDTRANS2}$$
$$\frac{}{f'^*(w,y)} \qquad\qquad \frac{}{f^*(\tau_2,y)}$$

$$\frac{f^*(x,\tau_1) \quad f'^*(x,y)}{f^*(x,y) \quad f'^*(\tau_1,y)}\text{UPDTRANS3} \qquad \frac{f'^*(x,\tau_1) \quad f^*(x,y)}{f'^*(x,y) \quad f^*(\tau_1,y)}\text{UPDTRANS4}$$

Fig. 10. Pointer update inference rules. The rules are used to extend our logic to support a pointer function symbol f' with the implicit constraint $f' = \text{update}(f, \tau_1, \tau_2)$, where τ_1 and τ_2 are variables, and w is a fresh variable used to capture $f(\tau_1)$.

On Flat Programs with Lists

Marius Bozga and Radu Iosif

VERIMAG, 2 av. de Vignate, F-38610 Gières
{iosif,bozga}@imag.fr

Abstract. In this paper we analyze the complexity of checking safety and termination properties, for a very simple, yet non-trivial, class of programs with singly-linked list data structures. Since, in general, programs with lists are known to have the power of Turing machines, we restrict the control structure, by forbidding nested loops and destructive updates. Surprisingly, even with these simplifying conditions, verifying safety and termination for programs working on heaps with more than one cycle are undecidable, whereas decidability can be established when the input heap may have at most one loop. The proofs for both the undecidability and the decidability results rely on non-trivial number-theoretic results.

1 Introduction

The design of automatic verification methods for programs manipulating dynamic linked data structures is a challenging problem. Indeed, the analysis of the behavior of such programs requires reasoning about complex data structures that have general graph-like representations. There are several approaches for tackling this problem addressing different subclasses of programs and using different kinds of formalisms for representing and reasoning about infinite sets of heap structures, e.g., [21,17,24,10].

We consider in this paper the class of programs manipulating linked data structures with a single data-field selector. It corresponds to programs manipulating linked lists with the possibility of sharing and circularities. It is well-known that programs handling lists can simulate, for instance, 2-counter machines, when the control structure is unrestricted. A customary approach to finding decidable classes of counter automata is to consider flat control structures that is, no nested loops are allowed [14,15,7]. The decidability of the reachability and termination problems for counter automata is usually established by reduction to the validity problem of Presburger arithmetic [22].

We analyze the problems of deciding safety and termination for programs with lists, assuming the flatness condition on the control structure. Since this restriction is generally not enough, we assume moreover that the program does not perform assignments to selector fields (destructive updates). That is, a program can only traverse the input data structure, but not modify it. We found out that, surprisingly, even this restricted class of programs is undecidable. By further restricting the input heap to at most one cycle, we can establish the decidability of checking both safety and termination properties. The proof relies on the encoding of the set of configurations reachable by the program, as a formula in a decidable fragment of the theory of addition and divisibility [23], that is described in [11].

Let us present in more detail the results. We start with the observation that flat programs with lists can be used to encode the solutions of general Diophantine systems.

B. Cook and A. Podelski (Eds.): VMCAI 2007, LNCS 4349, pp. 122–136, 2007.

The existence of such solutions is a well-known undecidable problem, a.k.a *Hilbert's Tenth Problem* [20]. Our reduction uses simple flat programs to encode the $z = x + y$ and $z = [x, y]$ (least common multiple) relations, relying on the fact that multiplication can be defined using only addition and least common multiple.

The source of undecidability lies exactly in the complexity of the input data structure. We noticed that the least common multiple relation can only be encoded by programs running on input structures with at least two (separate) cycles. This observation leads to a decidability result, by imposing that the input heap has at most one cycle. We obtain decidability by first representing the program with lists as a counter automaton. The idea of modeling general programs with singly-linked lists as counter automata, originates in [8,3]. However, due to the restricted form of our programs, we define a different encoding than the one described in [8,3], that uses deterministic actions on counters, and preserves the flatness of the control structure. In consequence, we reduce the safety and termination problems from programs with lists to flat counter automata. Finally, we show that, for the latter we can effectively compute the exact loop invariants, using the decidable theory of [11]. In this way, we reduce the original problems of checking safety and termination to verifying validity of formulae in a known decidable logic.

1.1 Related Work

Programs manipulating singly-linked lists have gained a lot of attention within the past two years, as shown by the fairly large number of recent publications on the subject [2,5,19,1,10]. Interestingly, the idea of abstracting away all the list segments with no incoming edges is common to many of these works, even though they are independent and use different approaches and frameworks (e.g. static analysis [19], predicate abstraction [1], symbolic reachability analysis [2] and proof search [5]). The fact that the number of sharing points in abstract heap structures is bounded by the number of variables in the program is also behind the techniques proposed in [19,10].

The work that is probably closest to ours has been reported in [8] and [3]. However, the authors' concerns there were rather to develop a general framework for the analysis of programs with lists, than to assess the complexity of the verification problems. Their translation of programs into counter automata uses a generic scheme, which works in the presence of destructive updates. Our translation method concerns programs without destructive updates, the main reason for this being that of establishing decidability. Other closely related work is the one of Chakaravarthy [12], reporting on the undecidability of the points-to analysis in non-flat programs with scalar variables, for which the generated memory configurations are of the same type as in the case of singly-linked lists. Moreover, a reduction from Hilbert's Tenth Problem is also used to prove undecidability, however this result does not hold against the flatness condition on the control structure.

2 Preliminaries

2.1 Programs with Lists

We consider imperative programs working with a set of pointer variables *PVar*. The pointer variables refer to list cells. Pointers can be used in assignments such as u :=

$$l \in Lab; \quad u,v,i,j \in PVar$$
$$Program := \{l : Stmnt; \}^*$$
$$Stmnt := WhileStmnt \mid IfStmnt \mid AsgnStmnt \mid Assert$$
$$WhileStmnt := \text{while } Guard \text{ do } \{AsgnStmnt; \}^* \text{ od}$$
$$IfStmnt := \text{if } Guard \text{ then } \{Stmnt; \}^* \left[\text{else } \{Stmnt; \}^* \right] \text{ fi}$$
$$AsgnStmnt := u := \text{null} \mid u := \text{new} \mid u := v \mid u := v.next \mid u.next := \text{null} \mid u.next := v$$
$$Assert := \text{assert}(Guard)$$
$$Guard := u = v \mid u = \text{null} \mid \neg Guard \mid Guard \wedge Guard \mid Guard \vee Guard \mid \text{true}$$

Fig. 1. Abstract Syntax of Flat Programs with Lists

null, u:= v and u := v.next, u.next := v and u.next := null, and new cell creation u:= new. The control structure is composed of iteration (while) statements and conditionals (if-then-else), and is supposed to be *flat*, meaning that there are no further conditionals or iterations inside a while loop. This syntactic restriction is sufficient to ensure that the control flow graph of the program has no nested loops. The guards of the control constructs are pointer equality u = v, undefinedness u = null tests, and boolean combinations of the above. The assert statement has no effect if the condition is true, otherwise the program is sent to an error state.

An assignment statement is said to be a *destructive update* if it is of the form u := new, u.next := v or u.next := null. These are the only statements that can modify a heap structure. Programs without destructive updates can only traverse the heap, but not modify it.

The semantics of programs with lists is defined in terms of heap updates. For a detailed presentation, the reader is referred to [9]. Formally, a heap is a rooted graph in which each node has at most one successor. In the rest of the paper, for a set A we denote by $A_\perp$ the set $A \cup \{\perp\}$. The element $\perp$ is used to denote that a (partial) function is undefined at a given point, e.g. $f(x) = \perp$.

Definition 1. *Let PVar be a set of pointer variables. A* heap *is a tuple* $H = \langle N, S, V, Roots \rangle$, *where* N *is a finite set of nodes,* $S : N \to N_\perp$ *is a* successor function, $V : PVar \to N_\perp$ *is a function associating nodes to variables, and* $Roots \subseteq PVar$ *is a set of* root variables.

Intuitively, the nodes represent heap-allocated cells, the successor function describes the position of the next selectors, for each node, and the variable mapping keeps track of which nodes are directly pointed to by program variables. The set of roots denotes special points in the heap, which will be used mainly in Section 4 for technical purposes. For now, we consider the following conditions, that must be satisfied by any program P, operating on a heap $\langle N, S, V, Roots \rangle$:

- for all $r \in Roots$, $V(r)$ is defined,
- P does not change the values of the variables in *Roots*,
- all nodes in N are reachable via S, from a node pointed to by a variable in *Roots*,
- all nodes in N having two or more distinct predecessors via S are pointed by a variable in *Roots*.

Technically, the conditions above are not real limitations, since any program with lists can be transformed into a program that meets the requirements concerning *Roots*. In particular, the third point can be ensured by keeping a free list pointed to by a root variable, and linking all nodes that become unreachable from the other program variables (garbage nodes) into it.

A heap is said to be *n-cyclic* if it contains exactly n different cycles. Notice that, since each node in the heap can have at most one selector, each cycle must reside in a separate part of the heap. A *list segment* is a sequence of nodes $n_1, n_2, \ldots, n_k$ related by the successor function $(S(n_i) = n_{i+1}, 1 \le i < k)$, such that either (i) n_1 and n_k are the only roots in the sequence, or (ii) n_1 is the only root and $S(n_k) = \bot$. Obviously, the number of list segments is bounded by the number of roots. In the following, we will denote by $ls_H(n,m)$ the list segment that lies between the roots n and m in H, or $ls_H(n, \bot)$, if the last node of the list segment has a null successor. The subscript may be omitted when it is not needed or obvious from the context. If the two roots are distinct and not directly connected (either they are disconnected or there are other root in between) we consider that $ls(n,m) = \emptyset$. If $V(u) = n$ and $V(v) = m$, for some $u, v \in PVar$, we may also denote $ls(n,m)$ by $ls(u,v)$. The length of a list segment $ls(n,m)$, i.e. the number of nodes it contains, is denoted by $|ls(n,m)|$.

2.2 Arithmetic of Integers

The undecidability of first-order arithmetic of natural numbers occurs as a consequence of Gödel's Incompleteness Theorem [16], discovered by A. Church [13]. Consequences of this result are the undecidability of the theory of natural numbers with *multiplication and successor function* and with *divisibility and successor function*, both discovered by J. Robinson in [23]. To complete the picture, the existential fragment of the full arithmetic i.e., *Hilbert's Tenth Problem* was proved undecidable by Y. Matiyasevich [20]. The interested reader is further pointed to [6] for an excellent survey of the (un)decidability results in arithmetic.

On the positive side, the decidability of the arithmetic of natural numbers with addition and successor function $\langle \mathbb{N}, +, 0, 1 \rangle$ has been shown by M. Presburger [22], result which has found many applications in modern computer science, especially in the field of automated reasoning. Another important result is the decidability of the *existential* theory of addition and divisibility, proved independently by A. P. Beltyukov [4] and L. Lipshitz [18]. Namely, it is shown that formulas of the form $\exists x_1, \ldots \exists x_n \bigwedge_{i=1}^{K} f_i(\mathbf{x}) | g_i(\mathbf{x})$ are decidable, where f_i, g_i are linear functions over $x_1, \ldots x_n$ and the symbol | means that each f_i is an integer divisor of g_i when both are interpreted over $\mathbb{N}^n$. The decidability of formulas of the form $\exists x_1, \ldots \exists x_n \varphi(\mathbf{x})$, where φ is an open formula in the language $\langle +, |, 0, 1 \rangle$, is stated as a corollary in [18]. This theory will be denoted further by $\langle \mathbb{N}, +, |, 0, 1 \rangle^{\exists}$.

A related result has been presented in [11], involving the class of formulae of the form $Q z Q_1 x_1 \ldots Q_m x_m \varphi(\mathbf{x}, z)$, where $Q, Q_i \in \{ \forall, \exists \}$ and φ is a boolean combination of formulae of the form $f(z) | g(\mathbf{x}, z)$, and arbitrary Presburger formulae. In other words, the first variable occurring in the quantifier prefix is the only variable allowed to occur to the left of the divisibility sign. The decidability of this class of formulae, denoted by $\mathcal{L}^{(1)}$, has been established in [11] using quantifier elimination, by reduction to Presburger arithmetic.

However, the result on $\langle \mathbb{N}, +, |, 0, 1 \rangle^{\exists}$ remains one of the strongest decidability results in integer arithmetic. It can be shown that even formulae involving one universal quantifier, i.e. of the form $\exists x_1, \ldots \exists x_n \forall y\ \varphi(\mathbf{x}, y)$ are undecidable. This is done using the classical definition of the least common multiple relation $[x, y] = z : \forall t\ x | t \wedge y | t \leftrightarrow z | t$. The undecidability of this fragment is a direct consequence of the following[1]:

Theorem 1. *The satisfiability and validity problems for the quantifier-free fragment of the theory $\langle \mathbb{N}, +, [] \rangle$ of natural numbers with addition and the least common multiple relation are undecidable.*

2.3 Counter Automata

A counter automaton with n counters is a tuple $A = \langle \mathbf{x}, Q, \rightarrow \rangle$, where $\mathbf{x} = \{x_1, \ldots, x_n\}$ are the counter variables, Q is a finite set of control states, and $\rightarrow \in Q \times \Phi \times Q$ are the transitions, and Φ is the set of arithmetic formulae with free variables from $\{x_i, x_i' \mid 1 \leq i \leq n\}$. A configuration of a counter automata with n counters is a tuple $\langle q, v \rangle$, where v is a mapping from $\mathbf{x}$ to $\mathbb{N}$. The transition relation is defined by $(q, v) \rightarrow (q', v')$ iff there exists a transition $q \xrightarrow{\varphi} q'$ such that, if σ is an assignment of the free variables of φ (denoted in the following by $FV(\varphi)$), such that, for all $x \in \mathbf{x}$, $\sigma(x) = v(x)$ and $\sigma(x') = v'(x)$, we have that $\varphi\sigma$ holds and $v(x) = v'(x)$, for all variables x with $x' \notin FV(\varphi)$. A *run* of A is a sequence of configurations $(q_0, v_0), (q_1, v_1), \ldots$ such that $(q_i, v_i) \rightarrow (q_{i+1}, v_{i+1})$, for each $i \geq 0$.

The control graph of a counter automaton A is the graph having as vertices the set Q of control states, and, for any two states q and q', there is an edge between q and q' in the control graph if and only if there exists a transition $q \xrightarrow{\varphi} q'$ in A. A counter automaton is said to be *flat* if its control graph has no nested loops.

3 Undecidable Flat List Programs

In this section we define the safety and termination properties for various classes of flat list programs with possibly unbounded input, and prove their undecidability. A decidable subclass is defined in the next section. Before proceeding, we need to introduce several notions.

Definition 2. *A tuple of strictly positive natural numbers $\mathbf{n} \in \mathbb{N}^k$ is said to be encoded by a heap $H = \langle N, S, V, Roots \rangle$, denoted as $H(\mathbf{n})$, if and only if there exists two mappings $e : \{1, \ldots, k\} \rightarrow Roots$ and $f : \{1, \ldots, k\} \rightarrow Roots_\perp$ such that, for all $1 \leq i \leq k$, $n_i = |ls_H(e(i), f(i))|$.*

---

[1] Theorem 1 gives a simple proof of the undecidability of $\langle \mathbb{N}, +, |, 0, 1 \rangle$ that is different from the one published by J. Robinson in [23]. However, the undecidability of Hilbert's Tenth Problem, which is used here was not known in 1949.

In other words, each number is represented by a list segment in between two root variables, or between a root variable and $\perp$. Notice that the condition $n_i > 0$ for all $1 \leq i \leq k$ implies that $e(i)$ and $f(i)$ actually delineate a non-trivial list segment.

Definition 3. *Two heaps* $H = \langle N, S, V, Roots \rangle$ *and* $H' = \langle N', S', V', Roots \rangle$ *are said to share the same structure, denoted by* $H \simeq H'$ *if and only if for all* $r_1, r_2 \in Roots$ $ls_H(r_1, r_2) \neq \emptyset \iff ls_{H'}(r_1, r_2) \neq \emptyset$.

In other words, H and H' differ only by the lenghts of their list segments that are delineated by roots. Notice that $\simeq$ is an equivalence relation on heaps. This leads to a notion of *parametric heap* $H(\mathbf{x})$, defined as the infinite set of heaps that share the same structure, with respect to a set of variables $\mathbf{x} = \{x_1, \ldots, x_k\}$, ranging over natural numbers. Given any interpretation $\mathbf{x} \mapsto \mathbf{n}$, we have that $H(\mathbf{n}) \in H(\mathbf{x})$. In other words, $H(\mathbf{x})$ is the equivalence class of $H(\mathbf{n})$ with respect to $\simeq$. By $ls^{x_i}(u, v)$ we denote the set $\{ls(u, v) \mid n_i = |ls(u, v)| \text{ in some } H(n_1, \ldots, n_i, \ldots, n_k) \in H(x_1, \ldots, x_i, \ldots, x_k)\}$. For instance, in Figure 2 (a), $ls^x(u, v)$ in $H(x, y, z)$ denotes all list segments that encode the values of x, and $ls^y(v, \perp)$, $ls^z(w, \perp)$ encode all possible values of y and z, respectively.

We consider the following definition of *safety properties*:

Definition 4. *Let P be a flat list program,* $S = \{l_i : assert(\varphi_i)\}_{i=1}^k$ *a set of statements occurring in P, and* $H(\mathbf{x})$ *a parametric heap. P is said to be safe w.r.t* $H(\mathbf{x})$ *and S if and only if for all heaps* $G \in H(\mathbf{x})$, *and* $1 \leq i \leq k$, φ_i *is true whenever P, started on input G, reaches* l_i.

The above property is vacuously true if the given program never reaches any of the locations in S. In order to cover this case, we consider the following definition of *termination*, with respect to a parametric heap.

Definition 5. *Let P be a flat list program, and* $H(\mathbf{x})$ *a parametric heap. P is said to terminate w.r.t* $H(\mathbf{x})$ *if and only if for all heaps* $G \in H(\mathbf{x})$, *P started on input G, has a finite execution.*

Notice that Definition 4 corresponds to partial correctness, whereas the combination of Definitions 4 and 5 can express total correctness, as understood in the setting of program verification using Hoare logic.

In order to prove undecidability of safety and termination for flat list programs, with respect to parametric heaps, we shall use the undecidability of the *validity* problem for the quantifier-free fragment of the theory of addition and least common multiple $\langle \mathbb{N}, +, [] \rangle$, which is stated by Theorem 1. The reduction is as follows: given a quantifier-free formula φ of $\langle \mathbb{N}, +, [] \rangle$, we build a flat list program P and a parametric heap $H(\mathbf{x})$, such that φ is valid if and only if P is safe w.r.t $H(\mathbf{x})$. The same reasoning is done for termination. This leads to undecidability results for both the safety and termination problems, as defined in the previous.

The key of the reduction is to use three basic programs, $P_{x=y}$, $P_{x+y=z}$ and $P_{[x,y]=z}$ (Figure 2), that encode the atomic formulae $x = y$, $x + y = z$ and $[x, y] = z$, respectively. Each program works on a heap of a predefined shape, also shown in Figure 2. The program $P_{x=y}$, in Figure 2 (a) is guaranteed to terminate, since both the lists pointed to by u and v are acyclic. Moreover, if i and j are both null at the end, the lists have equal length.

The program in Figure 2 (b) is guaranteed to terminate because both lists pointed to by u and w are acyclic. Moreover, at the end line, both i and j are null if and only if both lists have equal length, which is only the case if and only if $x + y = z$. In this case the variable v plays the only role of splitting the list segment pointed to by u into $ls^x(u,v)$ and $ls^y(v, \perp)$.

The program in Figure 2 (c) terminates because eventually $i = u$ and $j = v$ at the same time. In fact this happens after a number of loop iterations equal to the least common multiple of x and y. Then k is null at the end if and only if the length of the list pointed by w equals this number, i.e. $[x,y] = z$.

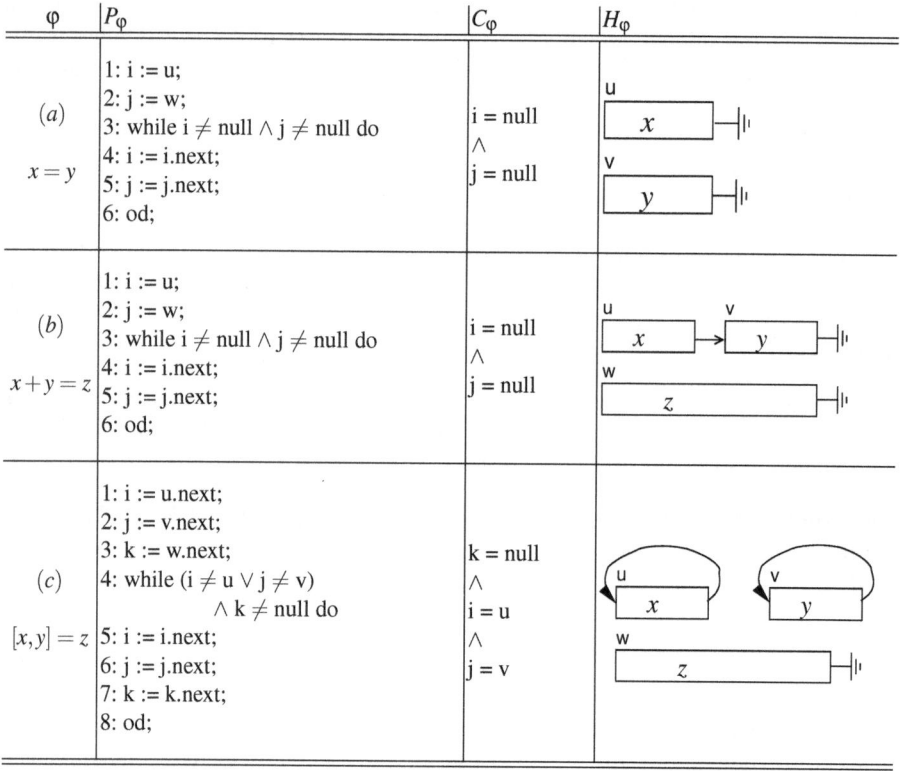

φ	P_φ	C_φ	H_φ
(a) $x = y$	1: i := u; 2: j := w; 3: while i ≠ null ∧ j ≠ null do 4: i := i.next; 5: j := j.next; 6: od;	i = null ∧ j = null	
(b) $x+y=z$	1: i := u; 2: j := w; 3: while i ≠ null ∧ j ≠ null do 4: i := i.next; 5: j := j.next; 6: od;	i = null ∧ j = null	
(c) $[x,y]=z$	1: i := u.next; 2: j := v.next; 3: k := w.next; 4: while (i ≠ u ∨ j ≠ v) ∧ k ≠ null do 5: i := i.next; 6: j := j.next; 7: k := k.next; 8: od;	k = null ∧ i = u ∧ j = v	

Fig. 2. Basic Programs

Let us consider now a quantifier-free formula $\varphi(\mathbf{x})$ in the language of $\langle \mathbb{N}, +, [] \rangle$. Since we are interested in reducing the validity problem, i.e $\forall \mathbf{x} . \varphi(\mathbf{x})$, it is sufficient to consider w.l.o.g. that φ is a disjunction of atomic formulae of the forms $x = y, x + y = z$ or $[x,y] = z$ and their negations. Let $\varphi = \bigvee_{i=1}^n \psi_i$, where ψ_i is either (1) $x_i = y_i$, (2) $x_i + y_i = z_i$, (3) $[x_i, y_i] = z_i$ or their negations, for $x_i, y_i, z_i \in \mathbf{x}$. For each condition of the form (2) or (3) the input heap contains a separate heap as in Figure 2 with roots u_i, v_i and w_i. Then the program encoding the validity of φ has the following structure:

P_{ψ_1};
if $C_{\neg\psi_1}$ then P_{ψ_2};
   if $C_{\neg\psi_2}$ then P_{ψ_3};

     ...

    assert(false);

     ...

  fi
fi

where, for all $1 \leq p \leq n$ we have:

- if ψ_p is a positive literal, P_{ψ_p} and C_{ψ_p} are as in Figure 2.
- if ψ_p is a negative literal, P_{ψ_p} is $P_{\neg\psi_p}$ and C_{ψ_p} is $\neg C_{\neg\psi_p}$.

Moreover, the program has to test that all list segments encoding occurrences of the same variable are of the same length. This can be done in the beginning, using a sequence of flat programs of the same kind as $P_{x=y}$, and is skipped for brevity reasons.

For any heap that corresponds to the parameterized input, the above program reaches the assert(false) statement if and only if the input encodes a tuple of numbers that falsifies all disjuncts of the original formula. Hence the program is safe if and only if for all instance $H(\mathbf{n})$ of the parametric input heap $H(\mathbf{x})$, $\mathbf{n}$ satisfies at least one clause ψ_i, hence φ is valid. This proves the undecidability of the safety problem.

To show undecidability of the termination problem, we use the same reduction, with the only difference that the assert(false) statement is replaced by a non-terminating loop while(true) do ... od. The program then terminates if and only if φ is valid.

Notice further that the least common multiple relation has been encoded using an input heap with at least two separate cycles. The above considerations lead to the following Theorem:

Theorem 2. *The classes of problems of verifying safety and termination properties, for flat list programs without destructive updates, running on n-cyclic inputs, with arbitrary $n > 1$, are undecidable.*

3.1 Extensions of the Undecidability Results

The properties of safety and termination for list programs parameterized by the shape of their input are universally quantified properties (see Definition 4 and 5). The following *reachability* property is existential:

Definition 6. *Let P be a flat list program, l a control location of P, and $H(\mathbf{x})$ a parametric heap. l is said to be* reachable *in P w.r.t. $H(\mathbf{x})$ if and only if there exists a heap $G \in H(\mathbf{x})$ such that P, started with input G, eventually reaches l.*

We can show undecidability of the reachability problem by reduction from the satisfiability problem for the quantifier-free fragment of $\langle \mathbb{N}, +, [] \rangle$ (Theorem 1). The reduction is similar to the one in the previous section.

Theorem 3. *The problem of verifying reachability for flat list programs without destructive updates, running on n-cyclic input, with arbitrary $n > 1$ is undecidable.*

Up to now, we have considered separately the problems of verifying safety and termination properties for programs parameterized by the shape of the input heap, and abstracting away the exact lengths of the list segments. We show now how these results can be extended to verifying properties of programs with either unknown shape, or empty input heap.

Definition 7. *Let P be a flat list program, and $S = \{l_i \ : \ assert(\varphi_i)\}_{i=1}^{k}$ a set of statements occurring in P. P is said to be* correct w.r.t *S if and only if for all heaps H, P started on input H, reaches location l_i, and φ_i is true whenever the control is at l_i, for all $1 \leq i \leq k$.*

The problem of correctness of a program P with unknown input can be shown undecidable by reducing the safety problem for programs on parameterized heaps to it. Namely, given $P, H(\mathbf{x})$ and $S = \{l_i \ : \ assert(\varphi_i)\}_{i=1}^{n}$ a set of the statements in P, we can build a program Q such that P is a subset of Q, and P is safe w.r.t. $H(\mathbf{x})$ and S if and only if Q is correct w.r.t. S. In order to obtain Q, we prefix P with a program T, i.e. $Q = T; P$. The role of T is to test that the input heap is an instance of $H(\mathbf{x})$. In case this test succeeds, the control is passed on to P, otherwise, T (and implicitly Q) does not terminate.

In order to build the tester program T, we remember that each list segment is marked by two root variables. For each $ls(u, v)$, with $u, v \in Roots$, T will test if v is the first root variable reachable starting from u:

```
i := u;
while ⋀_{w∈Roots} i ≠ w do
      i := i.next;
od
assert(i = v);
```

Note that this program might not terminate, in case when the given input heap is not an instance of $H(\mathbf{x})$, the list pointed to by u is cyclic, and the starting point of the loop is not properly marked by a root variable.

Corollary 1. *The correctness problem for flat list programs is undecidable.*

The other problem for which we show undecidability, based on the previous results, is the reachability problem for non-deterministic flat list programs, started on empty heap. A non-deterministic program uses undefined guards of the conditional statements, i.e. `while * do ... do` or `if * then ... else ... fi`.

Definition 8. *Let P be a non-deterministic flat list program, and l a control location of P. l is said to be* reachable on empty heap *if and only if P, started with the empty heap, has at least one execution path leading to l.*

We show undecidability of the reachability problem on empty heap, by reduction from the reachability problem on parametric input heap (Definition 6). Namely, given a program P and a parametric heap $H(\mathbf{x})$, we build a program Q as sequential composition of a (non-deterministic) constructor program C and P, i.e. $Q = C; P$, such that for a given location l of P, P reaches l w.r.t. $H(\mathbf{x})$ if and only if l is reachable on empty heap.

Intuitively, C is a flat non-deterministic program with dynamic creation and destructive updates, that will create an arbitrary instance of $H(\mathbf{x})$. For each list segment $ls^x(u,v)$ of $H(\mathbf{x})$, C will have a loop of the form:

```
i := u;
i.next := new; i := i.next;
while * do
        i.next := new; i := i.next;
od
if v = null then v := i;
else i.next := v;
fi
```

Note that each distinct path through the loop generates a list segment of a different length. Consequently, each path through C will generate a different instance of $H(\mathbf{x})$. Then there exists an instance $H(\mathbf{n})$ of $H(\mathbf{x})$, such that l is reachable in P started on $H(\mathbf{n})$ if and only if there exists a path through Q that reaches l and vice versa.

Corollary 2. *The problem of reachability on empty heap for non-deterministic flat list programs is undecidable.*

4   Decidability on Acyclic and 1-Cyclic Heaps

As pointed out before, the undecidability of the safety and termination problems for programs parameterized by the shape of the input heap relies on the fact that the input heap has at least two loops. In this section, we prove that, by restricting the input heap to have at most one loop, both problems become decidable. In practice, this result provides a precise and fully automated way of analyzing simple programs with list iterators, i.e. variables that can only traverse a list, but not modify it.

The tool for proving decidability is a sub-fragment of the arithmetic of addition and divisibility $\langle \mathbb{N}, +, |, 0, 1 \rangle$, namely the class of formulae of the form $Q z Q_1 x_1 \dots Q_m x_m \varphi(\mathbf{x}, z)$, where φ is a boolean combination of divisibility predicates of the form $f(z) | g(\mathbf{x}, z)$ and Presburger constraints. The restriction here is that z is the only variable occurring to the left of the divisibility sign. This fragment, called $\mathcal{L}_{|}^{(1)}$, has been shown decidable in [11].

4.1   From List Programs to Counter Automata

Let P be a flat list program without destructive updates, and $H(\mathbf{x})$, $\mathbf{x} = \{x_1, \dots, x_k\}$ be a parametric heap with at most one cycle. Since P is flat, its control structure has a finite number of branches, and each branch is a finite sequence of simple loops, connected via linear paths. Assume that, for each loop, one can describe the relation between the input and output heaps, after any number of iterations. Then the input-output relation of the whole program can be described as a finite composition of relations. In order to compute this relation, we simulate P by a counter automaton A, and reduce both the safety and termination problems for P to safety and termination problems for A.

Let $Roots = \{r_1, \ldots, r_p\}$ be the set of root variables of $H(\mathbf{x})$, and $H = \langle N, S, V, Roots \rangle$ be an instance of $H(\mathbf{x})$. We recall upon the fact that each node $n \in N$ must be reachable from a node pointed to by a variable from $Roots$. Moreover, each variable from $PVar$, that is not a root variable, can be assigned by P. Since the structure of the heap does not change during the execution of P, the current configuration of the program can be represented only by recording the position of the variables from $PVar \setminus Roots$ in the structure. Let u be such a variable. If $V(u)$ is defined, i.e. $V(u) = n \in N$, then n must be reachable from at least one root variable, call it r_i, for some $1 \leq i \leq p$. The number of steps on the path between $V(r_i)$ and $V(u)$ is denoted by δ_i. The pair of integers $\langle i, \delta_i \rangle$ gives the exact position of u in H, see e.g. Figure 3 (right). Obviously, this encoding of the position is not unique, since u may be reachable from more than one root variable, and there might be more than one path from r_i to u, due to the possible presence of a cycle. In the following, let $root(u)$ and $dist(u)$ denote the first and the second elements of the pair encoding the position of u.

The counter automaton corresponding to P is $A = \langle \mathbf{x} \cup \mathbf{y}, Q, \rightarrow \rangle$, where the set of counters consists of a set of parameters $\mathbf{x}$ and a set of working counters $\mathbf{y} = \{y_1, \ldots, y_r\}$, i.e. one working counter for each variable from $PVar \setminus Roots = \{u_1, \ldots, u_r\}$, and the set of control states $Q = Lab \times \{1, \ldots, p\}^r$. A configuration of A is a tuple $\langle q, \delta_1, \ldots, \delta_r \rangle \in Q \times \mathbb{N}^r$, where:

- $q = \langle l, \rho_1, \ldots, \rho_r \rangle$ represents the current program label, and the current roots of the iterator variables of P.
- δ_i is the distance of u_i from its root ρ_i, for each $1 \leq i \leq r$.

In principle, the counter y_i keeps track of $dist(u_i)$, w.r.t $root(u_i)$. A transition between two configurations $c = \langle \langle l, \rho \rangle, \delta \rangle$ and $c' = \langle \langle l', \rho' \rangle, \delta' \rangle$ is triggered by the execution of a program statement $l : s; l'$, and is denoted by $c \xrightarrow{s} c'$. The table in Figure 3 (left) summarizes the transition relation for all non-destructive assignment statements from Figure 2.1.

The most interesting case is $u_i := u_j.\text{next}$, which is depicted in Figure 3 (right). Notice that all assignment statements are encoded by deterministic transitions in the counter automaton. Since the program P is supposed to be flat, the resulting counter automaton will also have a flat control structure.

Assignment	Control change	Counter update
$u_i := \text{null}$	$\rho_i' = 0$	$y_i' = 0$
$u_i := u_j$	$\rho_i' = \rho_j$	$y_i' = y_j$
$u_i := u_j.\text{next}$	$\rho_i' = \rho_j$	$y_i' = y_j + 1$

Fig. 3. Semantics of Assignments

A guard condition of the form $u_i = \text{null}$ is encoded by an arithmetic constraint on the position of u. We distinguish between three situations:

- $root(u_i) = 0$, e.g. because of an assignment $u_i := $ null,
- $root(u_i) \neq 0$ is the origin of a path that ends in a cycle, in which case $u_i = $ null is false,
- the path starting with $root(u_i) \neq 0$ is finite, and let π_i denote the set of list segments on this path. In this case, we have: $y_i > \Sigma_{ls^x(n,m)\in\pi_i} x$, meaning that u_i has gone beyond the end of the path.

Due to the fact that the encoding of the variables is not unique, a pointer equality condition of the form $u_i = u_j$ has a more complex encoding, which is going to be detailed next. The fact that the parametric structure of $H(\mathbf{x})$ is known, is playing an important role. Suppose that $u_i = u_j$ is true for some arbitrary instance $H = \langle N, S, V, Roots \rangle$ of $H(\mathbf{x})$, i.e $V(u_i) = V(u_j) = n_0 \in N$. We distinguish two cases, as shown in Figure 4:

- n_0 does not belong to a cycle in H. In this case, there is a unique path from $V(root(u_i))$ to n_0, and a unique path from $V(root(u_j))$ to n_0. Let $ls^{x_0}(m_1,m_2)$ be the list segment on which n_0 resides, π_i be the set of list segments on the path from $V(root(u_i))$ to m_1, and π_j be the set of list segments on the path from $V(root(u_j))$ to m_1. Consequently, we have:

$$0 \leq y_i - \sum_{ls^x(n,m)\in\pi_i} x = y_j - \sum_{ls^x(n,m)\in\pi_j} x \leq x_0$$

For instance, the guard corresponding to the configuration in Figure 4 (a) is: $0 \leq y_i - x_1 = y_j - x_2 \leq x_3$.
- n_0 belongs to the only cycle in H. Let γ denote the set of list segments in the cycle, and $\pi_{i,j}$ denote the paths from $V(root(u_{i,j}))$ to the beginning of γ, respectively. Then we have:

$$\left(\sum_{ls^x(n,m)\in\gamma} x \right) \Big| \left((y_i - \sum_{ls^x(n,m)\in\pi_i} x) - (y_j - \sum_{ls^x(n,m)\in\pi_j} x) \right)$$

As an example, the guard corresponding to the configuration in Figure 4 (b) is: $x_3 + x_4 | (y_i - x_1) - (y_j - x_2)$

The semantics of a pointer equality condition in the program with lists can be written as a finite disjunction of all possible configurations, which will fall into one of the cases above. This formula denotes all possible values of $\mathbf{x}$ and $\mathbf{y}$ for which $u_i = u_j$ in $H(\mathbf{x})$. Therefore, a boolean condition on pointers, of the form $\neg Guard$ or $Guard \diamond Guard$, for $\diamond \in \{\wedge, \vee\}$ can be translated to a counter automaton guard, by replacing all atomic

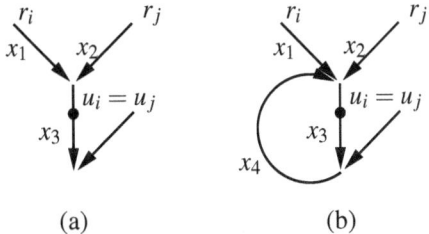

(a)   (b)

Fig. 4. Two Cases of Equality between Pointers

propositions with the corresponding formulae on counters. Notice that, since $H(\mathbf{x})$ has at most one cycle, all divisibility predicates will have the same expression on the left-hand side.

4.2 Reasoning About Counter Automata

Our translation scheme associates one program statement exactly one action on counters, therefore the resulting counter automaton A preserves the control structure of the original program P. In particular, if P was flat, A is also flat. The goal of this section is to compute, for a given control location q of A, the relation between the input values of the counters and the values at q. Since A is flat, it is sufficient to compute, for each loop, the input-output relation after n iterations of the loop, and define global input-output relations by composition. The safety and termination properties are decidable if this relation can be expressed in a decidable logic. We shall use here the $\mathcal{L}^{(1)}$ fragment of $\langle \mathbb{N}, +, |, 0, 1 \rangle$ [11], explained in Section 2.2.

By construction, all transitions of A are of the form $q \xrightarrow{\varphi(\mathbf{x},\mathbf{y},\mathbf{y}')} q'$ where φ is of the form:

$$\varphi(\mathbf{x},\mathbf{y},\mathbf{y}') \; : \; \psi(\mathbf{x},\mathbf{y}) \wedge \bigwedge_{1 \leq i,j \leq r} y'_i = b_i y_j + c_i \tag{1}$$

with ψ a boolean combination of divisibility predicates of the form $f(\mathbf{x})|g(\mathbf{x},\mathbf{y})$ (the same f occurs everywhere to the left of $|$) and Presburger constraints, $b_i \in \{0,1\}$ and $c_i \in \mathbb{Z}$, for all $1 \leq i \leq r$.

It can be easily shown that this class of relations is closed under composition, defined as:

$$(\varphi_1 \circ \varphi_2)(\mathbf{x},\mathbf{y},\mathbf{y}') = \exists \mathbf{y}'' \; \varphi_1(\mathbf{x},\mathbf{y},\mathbf{y}'') \wedge \varphi_2(\mathbf{x},\mathbf{y}'',\mathbf{y}')$$

In other words, the existential quantifiers above can be eliminated, the result being written as another relation of the same form. As a consequence, we can assume without losing generality, that each control path $q_1 \xrightarrow{\varphi_1} q_2 \ldots q_{n-1} \xrightarrow{\varphi_{n-1}} q_n$, with no incoming or outgoing transitions, is equivalent to a single transition $q_1 \xrightarrow{\varphi_1 \circ \ldots \circ \varphi_{n-1}} q_n$.

Without losing generality, we consider that A consists of only two transitions:

$$q \xrightarrow{\psi(\mathbf{x},\mathbf{y}) \wedge \bigwedge_{1 \leq i,j \leq r} y'_i = b_i y_j + c_i} q \text{ and } q \xrightarrow{\neg\psi(\mathbf{x},\mathbf{y})} q'$$

Here the variables $\mathbf{x}$ are meant as parameters, while $\mathbf{y}$ are the working counter variables. Let $I(n,\mathbf{x},\mathbf{y},\mathbf{y}')$ denote the relation between the input ($\mathbf{y}$) and the output ($\mathbf{y}'$) values of the counters after exactly n iterations of the loop, where $\mathbf{x}$ are the values of the parameters. For the moment, let us assume that $I(n,\mathbf{x},\mathbf{y},\mathbf{y}')$ is effectively computable and can be expressed in the quantifier-free fragment of $\mathcal{L}^{(1)}$.

A safety property for a counter automaton can be described by a pair $\langle q, \phi(\mathbf{x},\mathbf{y}) \rangle$, where $\phi(\mathbf{x},\mathbf{y})$ is a formula expressible in the quantifier-free fragment of $\mathcal{L}^{(1)}$, with the following meaning: for all valuations of the parameters, whenever the control reaches the location q, the values of the counters must satisfy ϕ. Moreover, let us assume that all atomic predicates in I and φ satisfy the condition that only variables from $\mathbf{x}$ may appear to the left of the divisibility sign, and moreover, that only one linear combination $f(\mathbf{x})$ can occur in this position. With the assumptions above, the safety problem reduces to checking the validity of the formula:

$$\sigma \stackrel{\Delta}{=} \forall \mathbf{x} \forall \mathbf{y} \forall \mathbf{y}' \forall n \ . \ I(n, \mathbf{x}, \mathbf{y}, \mathbf{y}') \rightarrow \phi(\mathbf{x}, \mathbf{y}')$$

Termination is the problem whether the counter automaton reaches its final control location, for every valuation of the parameters. In our case, this is equivalent to the validity of:

$$\theta \stackrel{\Delta}{=} \forall \mathbf{x} \exists n \exists \mathbf{y} \exists \mathbf{y}' \ . \ I(n, \mathbf{x}, \mathbf{y}, \mathbf{y}') \wedge \neg \phi(\mathbf{x}, \mathbf{y}')$$

We can prove the validity of σ and θ by proving that their negations are contradictions. For instance, $\neg \sigma$ is expressible in the decidable fragment of $\mathcal{L}_1^{(1)}$ [11], as: $\exists z \ . \ \neg \sigma[z/f(\mathbf{x})] \wedge z = f(\mathbf{x})$. Same is done for θ. In order to prove decidability of safety and termination for counter automata, it is sufficient to show how to express I as a quantifier-free formula of $\mathcal{L}_1^{(1)}$. This is achieved in the proof of the following Theorem:

Theorem 4. *The safety and termination problems for flat counter automata with transitions of the form (1) are decidable.*

The decidability of safety and termination for programs with lists is consequence of Theorem 4:

Corollary 3. *The problems of verifying safety and termination properties, for flat list programs without destructive updates, running on acyclic and 1-cyclic inputs, are decidable.*

5   Conclusions

We addressed the problems of verifying safety and termination properties for programs handling singly-linked lists, without destructive update assignments, and whose control structure is flat. We found out that, despite the strong syntactic restrictions, these programs, parameterized by the size of the input heap, have the expressive power of Turing machines. These undecidability results are a consequence of the complexity of the input data structures, even when the program does not change the structure. By further limiting the input heaps to at most one cycle, we obtain decidability of the safety and termination problems. All our results rely on non-trivial number-theoretic arguments.

References

1. I. Balaban, A. Pnueli, and L. Zuck. Shape Analysis by Predicate Abstraction. In *VMCAI*, volume 3385 of *LNCS*, 2005.
2. S. Bardin, A.Finkel, and D. Nowak. Toward Symbolic Verification of Programs Handling Pointers. In *AVIS*, Barcelona, Spain, 2004.
3. Sebastien Bardin, Alain Finkel, Etienne Lozes, and Arnaud Sangnier. From pointer systems to counter systems using shape analysis. In Springer Verlag, editor, *Proc. 5th International Workshop on Automated Verification of Infinite-State Systems (AVIS)*. LNCS, 2006.

4. A. P. Beltyukov. Decidability of the universal theory of natural numbers with addition and divisibility. *Zapiski Nauch. Sem. Leningrad Otdeleniya Mathematical Institute*, 60:15 – 28, 1976.
5. J. Berdine, C. Calcagno, and P. O'Hearn. A Decidable Fragment of Separation Logic. In *FSTTCS*, volume 3328 of *LNCS*, 2004.
6. Alexis Bés. A survey of arithmetical definability. *A Tribute to Maurice Boffa. Bulletin de la Société Mathématique de Belgique*, 1 - 54, 2002.
7. B. Boigelot. On iterating linear transformations over recognizable sets of integers. *TCS*, 309(2):413–468, 2003.
8. A. Bouajjani, M. Bozga, P. Habermehl, R. Iosif, P. Moro, and T. Vojnar. Programs with lists are counter automata. In Springer Verlag, editor, *Proc. Computer Aided Verification (CAV)*. LNCS, 2006.
9. A. Bouajjani, M. Bozga, P. Habermehl, R. Iosif, P. Moro, and T. Vojnar. Programs with lists are counter automata. Technical Report TR-2006-3, VERIMAG, 2006.
10. A. Bouajjani, P. Habermehl, P. Moro, and T. Vojnar. Verifying Programs with Dynamic 1-Selector-Linked Structures in Regular Model Checking. In *TACAS*, volume 3440 of *LNCS*, 2005.
11. M. Bozga and R. Iosif. On decidability within the arithmetic of addition and divisibility. In Springer Verlag, editor, *Proc. Foundations of Software Science and Computation Structures (FOSSACS)*, volume 3441, pages 425 – 439. LNCS, 2005.
12. Venkatesan T. Chakaravarthy. New results on the computability and complexity of points-to-analysis. In Springer Verlag, editor, *Proc. International Conference on Principles of Programming Languages (POPL)*. LNCS, 2003.
13. Alonzo Church. An unsolvable problem of elementary number theory. *American Journal of Mathematics*, 58:345 – 363, 1936.
14. Hubert Comon and Yan Jurski. Multiple Counters Automata, Safety Analysis and Presburger Arithmetic. In *Proc. CAV*, volume 1427 of *LNCS*, pages 268 – 279. Springer, 1998.
15. A. Finkel and J. Leroux. How to compose presburger-accelerations: Applications to broadcast protocols. In *Proc. FST&TCS*, volume 2556 of *LNCS*, pages 145–156. Springer, 2002.
16. Kurt Gödel. Über formal unentscheidbare Sätze der Principia Mathematica und verwandter Systeme I. *Monatshefte für Mathematik und Physik*, 38:173 – 198, 1931.
17. S. Ishtiaq and P. O'Hearn. BI as an assertion language for mutable data structures. In *POPL*, 2001.
18. Leonard Lipshitz. The diophantine problem for addition and divisibility. *Transaction of the American Mathematical Society*, 235:271 – 283, January 1976.
19. R. Manevich, E. Yahav, G. Ramalingam, and M. Sagiv. Predicate Abstraction and Canonical Abstraction for Singly-Linked Lists. In *VMCAI*, volume 3385 of *LNCS*, 2005.
20. Yuri Matiyasevich. Enumerable sets are diophantine. *Journal of Soviet Mathematics*, 11:354 – 358, 1970.
21. A. Møller and M.I. Schwartzbach. The Pointer Assertion Logic Engine. In *PLDI*, 2001.
22. Mojzesz Presburger. Über die Vollstandigkeit eines gewissen Systems der Arithmetik. *Comptes rendus du I Congrés des Pays Slaves*, Warsaw 1929.
23. Julia Robinson. Definability and decision problems in arithmetic. *The Journal of Symbolic Logic*, 14(2):98 – 114, June 1949.
24. S. Sagiv, T.W. Reps, and R. Wilhelm. Parametric Shape Analysis via 3-Valued Logic. *TOPLAS*, 2002.

Automata-Theoretic Model Checking Revisited*

Moshe Y. Vardi**

Rice University, Department of Computer Science, Houston, TX 77251-1892, USA
vardi@cs.rice.edu
http://www.cs.rice.edu/~vardi

Abstract. In automata-theoretic model checking we compose the design under verification with a Büchi automaton that accepts traces violating the specification. We then use graph algorithms to search for a counterexample trace. The basic theory of this approach was worked out in the 1980s, and the basic algorithms were developed during the 1990s. Both explicit and symbolic implementations, such as SPIN and and SMV, are widely used. It turns out, however, that there are still many gaps in our understanding of the algorithmic issues involved in automata-theoretic model checking. This paper covers the fundamentals of automata-theoretic model checking, review recent progress, and outlines areas that require further research.

1   Introduction

Formal verification is a process in which mathematical techniques are used to guarantee the correctness of a design with respect to some specified behavior. Automated formal-verification tools, such as COSPAN [47], SPIN [49] and SMV [16,59], based on *model-checking technology* [20,63], have enjoyed a substantial and growing use over the last few years, showing an ability to discover subtle flaws that result from extremely improbable events [22]. While until recently these tools were viewed as of academic interest only, they are now routinely used in industrial applications, resulting in decreased time to market and increased product integrity [23, 24, 56]. It is fair to say that automated verification is one of the most successful applications of automated reasoning in computer science.

As model-checking technology matured, the demand for specification language of increased expressiveness increased interest in linear-time formalisms [3]. The automata-theoretic approach offers a uniform algorithmic framework for model checking linear-time properties [55, 75, 77] It turns out, however, that there are still many gaps in our understanding of the algorithmic issues involved in automata-theoretic model checking. This paper covers the fundamentals of automata- theoretic model checking, review recent progress, and outline areas that require further research.

---

  * I am grateful to Orna Kupferman for her comments on an earlier draft of this article.
 ** Supported in part by NSF grants CCR-9988322, CCR-0124077, CCR-0311326, and ANI-0216467, by BSF grant 9800096, and by a grant from the Intel Corporation.

B. Cook and A. Podelski (Eds.): VMCAI 2007, LNCS 4349, pp. 137–150, 2007.

2   Basic Theory

The first step in formal verification is to come up with a *formal specification* of the design, consisting of a description of the desired behavior. One of the more widely used specification languages for designs is *temporal logic* [61]. In *linear* temporal logics, time is treated as if each moment in time has a unique possible future. Thus, linear temporal formulas are interpreted over linear sequences, and we regard them as describing the behavior of a single computation of a system. (An alternative approach is to use *branching* time. For a discussion of linear vs. branching time, see [76].)

In the linear temporal logic LTL, formulas are constructed from a set $Prop$ of atomic propositions using the usual Boolean connectives as well as the unary temporal connective X ("next"), F ("eventually"), G ("always"), and the binary temporal connective U ("until"). For example, the LTL formula $G(request \rightarrow F\ grant)$, which refers to the atomic propositions *request* and *grant*, is true in a computation precisely when every state in the computation in which *request* holds is followed by some state in the future in which *grant* holds. The LTL formula $G(request \rightarrow (request\ U\ grant))$ is true in a computation precisely if, whenever *request* holds in a state of the computation, it holds until a state in which *grant* holds is reached. In LTL model checking we assume that the specification in given in terms of properties expressed by LTL formulas.

LTL is interpreted over *computations*, which can be viewed as infinite sequences of truth assignments to the atomic propositions; i.e., a computation is a function $\pi : I\!N \rightarrow 2^{Prop}$ that assigns truth values to the elements of $Prop$ at each time instant (natural number). For a computation π and a point $i \in I\!N$, the notation $\pi, i \models \varphi$ indicates that a formula φ holds at the point i of the computation π. In particular, $\pi, i \models X\varphi$ iff $\pi, i+1 \models \varphi$, and and $\pi, i \models \varphi U \psi$ iff for some $j \geq i$, we have $\pi, j \models \psi$ and for all k, $i \leq k < j$, we have $\pi, k \models \varphi$. The connectives F and G can be defined in terms of the connective U: $F\varphi$ is defined as $\textbf{true}\ U\varphi$, and $G\varphi$ is defined as $\neg F\neg\varphi$. We say that π *satisfies* a formula φ, denoted $\pi \models \varphi$, iff $\pi, 0 \models \varphi$. We denote by models(φ) the set of computations satisfying φ.

Designs can be described in a variety of formal description formalisms. Regardless of the formalism used, a *finite-state design* can be abstractly viewed as a *labeled transition system*, i.e., as a structure of the form $M = (W, W_0, R, V)$, where W is the finite set of states that the system can be in, $W_0 \subseteq W$ is the set of initial states of the system, $R \subseteq W^2$ is a transition relation that indicates the allowable state transitions of the system, and $V : W \rightarrow 2^{Prop}$ assigns truth values to the atomic propositions in each state of the system. (A labeled transition system is essentially a Kripke structure.) A *path* in M that *starts at* u is a possible infinite behavior of the system starting at u, i.e., it is an infinite sequence $u_0, u_1 \ldots$ of states in W such that $u_0 = u$, and $u_i R u_{i+1}$ for all $i \geq 0$. The sequence $V(u_0), V(u_1) \ldots$ is a *computation* of M that *starts at* u. It is the sequence of truth assignments visited by the path, and can be viewed as a function from $I\!N$ to 2^{Prop}. The *language* of M, denoted $L(M)$, consists of all computations of M that start at a state in W_0. Note that $L(M)$ can be viewed as a language of infinite words over the alphabet 2^{Prop}. The language $L(M)$ can be viewed as an abstract description of the system M, describing all possible "traces". We say that M *satisfies* an LTL formula φ if all computations in $L(M)$ satisfy φ, that is, if $L(M) \subseteq$ models(φ). When M satisfies

φ we also say that M is a model of φ, which explains why the technique is known as *model checking* [22].

One of the major approaches to automated verification is the *automata-theoretic approach*, which underlies model checkers that can handle linear-time specifications. The key idea underlying the automata-theoretic approach is that, given an LTL formula φ, it is possible to construct a finite-state automaton A_φ on infinite words that accepts precisely all computations that satisfy φ. The type of finite automata on infinite words we consider is the one defined by Büchi [12]. A *Büchi automaton* is a tuple $A = (\Sigma, S, S_0, \rho, F)$, where Σ is a finite alphabet, S is a finite set of states, $S_0 \subseteq S$ is a set of initial states, $\rho : S \times \Sigma \to 2^S$ is a nondeterministic transition function, and $F \subseteq S$ is a set of accepting states. A *run* of A over an infinite word $w = a_1 a_2 \cdots$, is a sequence $s_0 s_1 \cdots$, where $s_0 \in S_0$ and $s_i \in \rho(s_{i-1}, a_i)$ for all $i \geq 1$. A run $s_0, s_1, \ldots$ is *accepting* if there is some accepting state that repeats infinitely often, i.e., for some $s \in F$ there are infinitely many i's such that $s_i = s$. The infinite word w is *accepted* by A if there is an accepting run of A over w. The *language* of infinite words accepted by A is denoted $L(A)$. The following fact establishes the correspondence between LTL and Büchi automata [78] (for a tutorial introduction for this correspondence, see [75]):

Theorem 1. *Given an LTL formula φ, one can build a Büchi automaton $A_\varphi = (\Sigma, S, S_0, \rho, F)$, where $\Sigma = 2^{Prop}$ and $|S| \leq 2^{O(|\varphi|)}$, such that $L(A_\varphi) = models(\varphi)$.*

This correspondence reduces the verification problem to an automata-theoretic problem as follows [77]. Suppose that we are given a system M and an LTL formula φ. We check whether $L(M) \subseteq models(\varphi)$ as follows: (1) construct the automaton $A_{\neg\varphi}$ that corresponds to the *negation* of the formula φ (this automaton is called the *complementary* automaton), (2) take the *cross product* of the system M and the automaton $A_{\neg\varphi}$ to obtain an automaton $A_{M,\varphi}$, such that $L(A_{M,\varphi}) = L(M) \cap L(A_{\neg\varphi})$, and (3) check whether the language $L(A_{M,\varphi})$ is empty, i.e., $A_{M,\varphi}$ accepts *no* input.

Theorem 2. *Let M be a labeled transition system and φ be an LTL formula. Then M satisfies φ iff $L(A_{M,\varphi}) = \emptyset$.*

If $L(A_{M,\varphi})$ is empty, then the design is correct. Otherwise, the design is incorrect and the word accepted by $L(A_{M,\varphi})$ is an incorrect computation.

The *emptiness* problem for an automaton is to decide, given an automaton A, whether $L(A) = \emptyset$, i.e., if the automaton accepts no word. Algorithms for emptiness are based on testing *fair reachability* in graphs: an automaton is *nonempty* if starting from some initial state we can reach an accepting state from where there is a cycle back to itself [15]. An algorithm for nonemptiness is the following: (i) decompose the transition graph of the automaton into *maximal strongly connected components (mscc)* (linear cost depth-first search [26]); (ii) verify that one of the mscc's intersects with F (linear cost). More sophisticated Büchi nonemptiness algorithms have been studied, e.g., [27, 33]. When the automaton is nonempty, nonemptiness algorithms return a witness in the shape of a "lasso": an initial finite prefix followed by a finite cycle. (If the accepting states are "sink" states, then the finite cycle following the initial prefix can be ignored.) Thus, once the automaton $A_{\neg\varphi}$ is constructed, the verification task is reduced to automata-theoretic problems, namely, intersecting automata and testing emptiness of automata, which have highly efficient solutions [75]. Furthermore, using data structures that enable compact representation of very large state spaces makes it possible to verify designs of significant complexity [8, 13].

The linear-time framework is not limited to using LTL as a specification language. ForSpec and PSL are recent extensions of LTL, designed to address the need of the semiconductor industry [1, 3]. There are also those who prefer to use automata on infinite words as a specification formalism [78]; in fact, this is the approach of COSPAN [47, 55]. In this approach, we are given a design represented as a finite transition system M and a property represented by a Büchi (or a related variant) automaton P. The design is correct if all computations in $L(M)$ are accepted by P, i.e., $L(M) \subseteq L(P)$. This approach is called the *language-containment* approach. To verify M with respect to P, we: (1) construct the automaton P^c that *complements* P, (2) take the product of the system M and the automaton P^c to obtain an automaton $A_{M,P}$, and (3) check that the automaton $A_{M,P}$ is nonempty. As before, the design is correct iff $A_{M,P}$ is empty. Thus, the verification task is again reduced to automata-theoretic problems, namely complementing and intersecting automata and testing emptiness of automata.

3   Automata-Theoretic Model Checking Revisited

By the late 1990s, the automata-theoretic approach to model checking seems to have stabilized. The algorithms developed can be classified as as *explicit*, based on explicit state enumeration, e.g., [27, 42], or *implicit/symbolic*, based on a symbolic encoding of the state space, using binary decision diagrams (BDDs) [13] or satisfiability solving [8]. These algorithms have been implemented in various model-checking tools [16, 49, 59].

In the last few years, further progress has been been on several aspects of automata-theoretic model checking. As a result of this progress, we know both more and both less. We now know that the simple picture that prevailed by the late 1990s is too simplistic, but we do not have a clear understanding of the space of relevant algorithms. In the rest of this section, we survey the progress made over the last few years and highlight the questions that have been opened by this progress.

3.1   Translating LTL Formulas to Büchi Automata

Translating LTL formulas to automata is a key building block in linear-time model checking. While the focus of the original translation [81, 78] was on mathematical simplicity, it was not appropriate for explicit model checking, since the automata constructed were always exponential in the size of the formula. Already in [80] it was shown that instead of starting with an exponentially large state pace, the translation can create states on a demand-driven basis. The optimized translation of [42] avoided the exponential blow-up in many cases of practical interest and was was used in the explicit model checker SPIN [49]. The original translation of [78], was appropriate for symbolic model checking and, after appropriate optimization [21], is used in symbolic model checkers such as NuSMV [16]. An approach to LTL translation via alternating automata was described in [74], again motivated by mathematical simplicity.

Two papers published in 1999 [28, 30] showed that [42] is not the last word on explicit LTL translation, which opened the door to many more papers [31, 34, 37, 38, 45,

43, 39, 70, 67, 73]. In fact, so many papers have been published over the last few years on this topic that it is difficult to say what is the best approach to translating LTL to automata. This is compounded by several issues:

- All the cited papers focus on optimizing automata generation (with respect to time and/or space), rather than optimizing model checking. It is not clear, however, that improving automata-generation performance yields an improvement in model-checking performance. One exception is [67], which aims at optimizing model checking by generating "more deterministic" automata, but again does not offer any evidence of improvement in model checking.
- There are reasons to believe that none of the existing LTL translators perform well on nontrivial formulas. For example, [68] reports not being able to translate a certain formula, expressing a conjunction of fairness conditions, by many of the available tools. A specialized tool generated an automaton with about 1200 states from this formula. Note that symbolic model checkers routinely handle BDDs with millions of nodes. It is not clear why LTL translators cannot handle automata with only thousands of states.
- A *generalized* Büchi automaton is a tuple $A = (\Sigma, S, S_0, \rho, \mathbf{F})$, where $\mathbf{F}$ is a set $\{F_1, \ldots, F_k\}$ of subsets of S, called *accepting* sets. A run of A is accepting if accepting set is visited infinitely often. It is known that a generalized Büchi automaton with k accepting sets can be *degeneralized*, that is, converted to an equivalent Büchi automaton, at the cost of multiplying the number of states by k [15]. As is shown in [42], it is natural to translate LTL to generalized Büchi automata. While symbolic model checkers support generalized Büchi automata, SPIN does not support them and requires degeneralization. There are, however, some who argue that it may be advantageous to avoid degeneralization [72]; see discussion of nonemptiness algorithms below.
- Industrial experience has shown that LTL is too weak expressively for industrial applications (see [79] for theoretical justification), resulting in more expressive industrial language such as ForSpec and PSL [1, 3]. So far there he been no report of an effort to develop an explicit translator for ForSpec or PSL. Some industrial symbolic implementations of ForSpec and PSL are known to exists; for example, Intel has a symbolic translator for ForSpec [4], but little is known about them. See [14, 17, 62] for recent descriptions of symbolic translations for certain fragments of PSL. None of these translations handle all features of PSL.

3.2 Deterministic vs. Nondeterministic Automata

For certain formulas, the very approach of translating temporal assertions to *nondeterministic* Büchi automata should be re-visited. The majority of the properties being verified are *safety* properties, whose violation can be witnessed by a finite counterexample. It is known that in such cases the complemented properties can be translated into automata on finite words [51]. Such automata can be determinized, though at a possibly exponential cost [64]. It may seem that such blow-up should be avoided, but symbolic model checking can be viewed as online determinization of the assertion automaton [51]. Thus, determinization is in some sense inherent to symbolic model checking.

Recent results point to the advantage of translation to deterministic automata in the context of SAT-based model checking [2]. Unlike the standard propositional encoding of LTL formulas [8, 18, 57], which is polynomial in the size of the formula, the encoding in [2] is exponential. It is shown in [2] that such encoding can nevertheless lead to improved model-checking performance. When the automaton is nondeterministic, the model checker has to find a bad behavior of the design under verification as well as an accepting run of the automaton on that behavior. When the automaton is deterministic, the search for an accepting run is avoided. This result raises the possibility that translation to deterministic automata would also be advantageous in the context of explicit and BDD-based model checking. (A theoretical advantage of translating to deterministic automata is described in [54], but it is not clear if this leads also to a practical advantage.)

3.3 Nonemptiness Algorithms

There are three types of nonemptiness algorithms for Büchi automata: explicit, BDD-based, and SAT-based.

Explicit Algorithms. As mentioned earlier, an obvious algorithm for nonemptiness of Büchi automata is the following: (i) decompose the transition graph of the input automaton into maximal strongly connected components using depth-first search, and (ii) verify that one of the component intersects with F (or with all members of $\mathbf{F}$ for generalized automata).

For large state spaces, maintaining the required data structures in main memory might be infeasible. An alternative algorithm, NDFS, was proposed in [27]. NDFS conducts two depth-first searches, but does not require a decomposition into maximal strongly connected components. This algorithm, with some modifications [44, 50], is the algorithm implemented in SPIN. NDFS was improved further in [66].

Other works [28, 40] developed optimized versions of the mscc-based algorithm and argued that it performs better than NDFS and its variants. The experimental evidence is limited, however, to automata with not too large state space, while NDFS was designed for large state spaces, where the mscc decomposition cannot be carried out in main memory. (NDFS can use state hashing, which underapproximates the set visited by the search [27].) The emerging picture is that mscc-based algorithms are appropriate for main-memory implementations, whereas NDFS algorithms are appropriate when the state space is too large for a main-memory implementation.

NDFS was extended to generalized Büchi automata in [72]; instead of conducting two depth-first searches, we may need to conduct $k + 1$ depth-first searches, where k is the number of accepting sets of the automaton. Thus, the blow-up in the size of the state space is replaced by a blow-up in the number of depth-first searches. It is not clear that this yields an improvement in performance.

A thorough discussion and experiments involving nonemptiness algorithms can be found in [29], which also introduces optimized versions of the mscc-based algorithm of [28] and the NDFS-based algorithm of [72]. At this point these two algorithms seem to be the best of their types. These algorithms are implemented in the model-checking library *Spot*, which is publicly available at `spot.lip6.fr`. For a survey of distributed algorithms for explicit model checking, see [6].

BDD-Based Algorithms. In the symbolic approach, we do not construct the state graphs of the system and property automaton explicitly. Rather, these graphs are described in a logical language, cf. [5]. The model-checking algorithms can then work directly on the symbolic representation. BDD-based model checkers such as SMV use propositional formulas as the user-level representation formalism. The tool then translates these formulas into Reduced Ordered Binary Decision Diagrams (BDDs) [11] and the nonemptiness algorithm works directly on these BDDs [13]. BDD-based algorithms are set based (the algorithms manipulates sets of states) and cannot directly implement depth-first search. In the symbolic approach, the property automaton also has to be represented symbolically [19,13]; in fact, that representation captures directly the structure of the automaton described in [78]. While the explicit representation of the automaton can be exponentially large with respect to the LTL formula it represents, the symbolic representation is linear in the size of the formula.

A set-based algorithm for fair reachability was described in [33], based on a fixpoint characterization of fair reachability [32]. The algorithm performs a nested fixpoint computation, which implies that it uses, in the worst case, a quadratic number of symbolic operations (with respect to the number of nodes in the state graph). This should be contrasted with explicit nonemptiness algorithms, which run in linear time.

The algorithm of [33], referred to as the *EL algorithm*, is the one implemented on available symbolic model checkers [16,59]. A heuristic optimization of the EL algorithm called *CTY*, was proposed in [48]. An improvement of CTY, called *OWCTY*, was proposed in [35], where it was argued that it is preferred to the standard EL algorithm, but this conclusion was disputed in [71].

Both CTY and OWCTY retain the structure of a nested fixpoint computation with a quadratic number of image operations. In contrast, the algorithm presented in [9] uses only $n \log n$ symbolic operations. Disappointingly, this algorithm does not perform better in practice than EL and its variants [71]. Further improvement was provided in [41], which described an algorithm with a *linear* number of symbolic steps. Unfortunately, there is no experimental information on the performance of that algorithm in practice.

Another approach to the fair-reachability problem is to reduce it to a simple reachability problem [7]. This replaces the nested fixpoint computation by a simple fixpoint computation, at the cost of doubling the number of BDD variables. Practical performance of this algorithm has been disappointing [7]. On the other hand, it was shown in [10] that for a certain class of LTL formulas the nested fixpoint algorithms can be replaced by a simple fixpoint algorithm with no increase in the number of variables, resulting in significant performance improvement. (A general characterization of LTL formulas for which model checking can be performed without nested fixpoints is provided in [54]. That characterization, however, does not yield a practical algorithm.)

A *hybrid* approach to LTL symbolic model checking, that is, an approach that uses explicit representations of the property automaton, whose state space is often quite manageable, and symbolic representations of the system, whose state space is typically exceedingly large, was studied in [68]. They compared the effects of using: (i) a purely symbolic representation of the property automaton, (ii) a symbolic representation, using binary encoding[1], of explicitly compiled property automaton, and (iii) a partitioning of the symbolic state space according to an explicitly translated property automaton. This comparison was applied to three model-checking algorithms: the nested fixpoint algorithm of [33], the reduction of fair reachability to reachability of [7], and the simple fixpoint algorithm of [10]. The emerging picture from this comparison is quite clear; the hybrid approach outperform pure symbolic model checking, while partitioning outperforms binary encoding. The conclusion is that the hybrid approaches benefits from state-of-the-art techniques in explicit compilation of LTL formulas. Also, partitioning gains from the fact that symbolic operations are applied to smaller sets of states.

SAT-Based Algorithms. In *bounded* model checking we check whether there exists a counterexample trace of bounded size (that is, both the prefix and the cycles have to be of bounded size). As is shown in [8], this can be expressed as a propositional formula whose satisfiability implies the existence of a counterexample. While propositional satisfiability is NP-complete, today's satisfiability-solving tools, known as *SAT solvers*, can solve instances with up to hundreds of thousands of variables [83]. It turned out that SAT-based bounded model checkers can handle designs that are order-of-magnitude larger than those handled by BDD-based model checkers, making this technology quite popular in the industry, cf. [25].

In spite of several papers on symbolic translation of LTL in the context of SAT-based model checking [8, 18, 57], we are far from having reached a solid understanding on the relative merits of the different approaches. These papers study various propositional encodings of LTL extended with past temporal connectives. These encodings compare favorably with what is referred to as "automata-theoretic encoding". The latter refers to a binary encoding of automata generated by some LTL translator. This encoding ignores the inner structure of automata states. In automata generated from LTL formulas, the states are sets of subformulas; a reasonable automata-theoretic encoding should then take the inner structure of states into account, rather than use an arbitrary binary encoding of states. Also, the reduction of fair reachability to reachability [7] has yet to be evaluated in the context of SAT-based model checking.

3.4   Büchi Properties

As mentioned earlier, in some cases it is desirable to specify properties directly in terms of Büchi automata, rather in terms of a temporal logic. In this case the automata-theoretic approach requires complementation of the property automaton. Note that while it is easy to complement properties given in terms of formulas in temporal logic, complementation of properties given in terms of nondeterministic automata is not simple. Indeed, a word w is rejected by a nondeterministic automaton A if all the runs of A on w rejects the word. Thus, the complementary automaton has to consider all possible runs, and complementation has the flavor of determinization.

For Büchi automata on infinite words, which are required for the modeling of liveness properties, optimal complementation constructions are quite complicated, as the subset construction is not sufficient. Due to the lack of a simple complementation

---

[1] That is, we encode n states by $\log n$ Boolean variables.

construction, the user is typically required to specify the property by a deterministic Büchi automaton [55] (it is easy to complement a deterministic Büchi automaton), or to supply the automaton for the negation of the property [49]. Thus, an effective algorithm for the complementation of Büchi automata would be of significant practical value.

Efforts to develop simple complementation constructions for nondeterministic automata started early in the 1960s, motivated by decision problems for second-order logics. Büchi suggested a complementation construction for nondeterministic Büchi automata that involved a complicated combinatorial argument and a doubly-exponential blow-up in the state space [12]. Thus, complementing an automaton with n states resulted in an automaton with $2^{2^{O(n)}}$ states. In [69], Sistla et al. suggested an improved implementation of Büchi's construction, with only $2^{O(n^2)}$ states, which is still, however, not optimal. Only in [65], Safra introduced a determinization construction, which also enabled a $2^{O(n \log n)}$ complementation construction, matching a lower bound described by Michel [60] (cf. [58]). Thus, from a theoretical point of view, some considered the problem solved since 1988.

A careful analysis, however, of the exact blow-up in Safra's and Michel's bounds reveals an exponential gap in the constants hiding in the $O()$ notations: while the upper bound on the number of states in the complementary automaton constructed by Safra is n^{2n}, Michel's lower bound involves only an $n!$ blow up, which is roughly $(n/e)^n$. Recent efforts focused on narrowing the gap between the upper and lower bounds. A new complementation construction, which avoids determinization, was introduced in [52], and then tightened in [36] to yield an upper bound of $(0.97n)^n$. On the other hand, Michel's bound was improved in [82] to yield a lower bound to $(0.76n)^n$. Thus, the gap between the lower and upper bound has narrowed, but it is still exponentially wide. (For a study of the relationship between complementation and the OWCTY fair-reachability algorithm, see [53].)

The construction if [52] has been implemented with many added optimizations [46]. This optimized construction proved to be highly effective on Büchi automata obtained from LTL formulas. It is shown in [46] that the automaton obtained by complementing A_φ, for a random LTL formula φ, is not much larger than the automaton $A_{\neg\varphi}$. This, however, does not imply that the construction is equally effective when applied to generic Büchi properties. So far no tool supports model checking Büchi properties.

4   Concluding Remarks

Since its introduction in 1981, model checking has proved to be a highly successful technology. The automata-theoretic approach offers a uniform algorithmic framework for model checking linear-time properties. As we saw, recent progress has increased our knowledge, but also opened many questions, regarding the translation of temporal properties to automata, algorithms for fair reachability, and complementation of Büchi properties. We hope to see many of these questions answered in the coming years. Equally important, we hope to see software tools implementing new algorithmic developments in this area.

References

1. K. Albin et al. Property specification language reference manual. Technical Report Version 1.1, Accellera, 2004.
2. R. Armoni, S. Egorov, R. Fraer, D. Korchemny, and M.Y. Vardi. Efficient LTL compilation for SAT-based model checking. In *Proc. Int'l Conf. on Computer-Aided Design*, pages 877–884, 2005.
3. R. Armoni, L. Fix, A. Flaisher, R. Gerth, B. Ginsburg, T. Kanza, A. Landver, S. Mador-Haim, E. Singerman, A. Tiemeyer, M.Y. Vardi, and Y. Zbar. The ForSpec temporal logic: A new temporal property-specification logic. In *Proc. 8th International Conference on Tools and Algorithms for the Construction and Analysis of Systems*, volume 2280 of *Lecture Notes in Computer Science*, pages 296–211, Grenoble, France, April 2002. Springer-Verlag.
4. R. Armoni, D. Korchemny, A. Tiemeyer, and M.Y. Vardi Y. Zbar. Deterministic dynamic monitors for linear-time assertions. In *Proc. Workshop on Formal Approaches to Testing and Runtime Verification*, volume 4262 of *Lecture Notes in Computer Science*. Springer, 2006.
5. J. L. Balcázar and A. Lozano. The complexity of graph problems for succinctly represented graphs. In *Proc. Graph-Theoretic Concepts in Computer Science*, Lecture Notes in Computer Science 411, pages 277–285. Springer, 1989.
6. J. Barnat, L. Brim, and I. Cerna. Cluster-based LTL model checking of large systems. In *Proc. 4th Int'l Symp. on Formal Methods for Components and Objects*, volume 4111 of *Lecture Notes in Computer Science*, pages 259–279. Springer, 2006.
7. A. Biere, C. Artho, and V. Schuppan. Liveness checking as safety checking. In *Proc. 7th Int'l Workshop on Formal Methods for Industrial Critical Systems*, volume 66:2 of *Electr. Notes Theor. Comput. Sci.*, 2002.
8. A. Biere, A. Cimatti, E.M. Clarke, and Y. Zhu. Symbolic model checking without BDDs. In *Tools and Algorithms for the Analysis and Construction of Systems*, volume 1579 of *Lecture Notes in Computer Science*. Springer-Verlag, 1999.
9. R. Bloem, H.N. Gabow, and F. Somenzi. An algorithm for strongly connected component analysis in $n \log n$ symbolic steps. In *Formal Methods in Computer Aided Design*, volume 1954 of *Lecture Notes in Computer Science*, pages 37–54. Springer-Verlag, 2000.
10. R. Bloem, K. Ravi, and F. Somenzi. Efficient decision procedures for model checking of linear time logic properties. In *Computer Aided Verification, Proc. 11th International Conference*, volume 1633 of *Lecture Notes in Computer Science*, pages 222–235. Springer-Verlag, 1999.
11. R.E. Bryant. Graph-based algorithms for boolean-function manipulation. *IEEE Trans. on Computers*, C-35(8), 1986.
12. J.R. Büchi. On a decision method in restricted second order arithmetic. In *Proc. International Congress on Logic, Method, and Philosophy of Science. 1960*, pages 1–12, Stanford, 1962. Stanford University Press.
13. J.R. Burch, E.M. Clarke, K.L. McMillan, D.L. Dill, and L.J. Hwang. Symbolic model checking: 10^{20} states and beyond. *Information and Computation*, 98(2):142–170, June 1992.
14. D. Bustan, D. Fisman, and John Havlicek. Automata construction for psl. Technical report, The Weizmann Institute of Science, May 2005. Technical Report MCS05-04.
15. Y. Choueka. Theories of automata on ω-tapes: A simplified approach. *Journal of Computer and System Sciences*, 8:117–141, 1974.
16. A. Cimatti, E.M. Clarke, E. Giunchiglia, F. Giunchiglia, M. Pistore, M. Roveri, R. Sebastiani, and A. Tacchella. Nusmv 2: An opensource tool for symbolic model checking. In *Proc. 14th Int'l Conf. on Computer Aided Verification*, Lecture Notes in Computer Science 2404, pages 359–364. Springer-Verlag, 2002.

17. A. Cimatti, M. Roveri, S. Semprini, and S. Tonetta. From psl to nba: A modular symbolic encoding. In *Proc. 6th Int'l Conf. on Formal Methods in Computer-Aided design*, 2006.
18. A. Cimatti, M. Roveri, and D. Sheridan. Bounded verification of past ltl. In *Proc. 5th Int'l Conf. on Formal Methods in Computer-Aided Design*, volume 3312 of *Lecture Notes in Computer Science*, pages 245–259. Springer, 2004.
19. E. M. Clarke, O. Grumberg, and K. Hamaguchi. Another look at ltl model checking. *Formal Methods in System Design*, 10(1):47–71, 1997.
20. E.M. Clarke, E.A. Emerson, and A.P. Sistla. Automatic verification of finite-state concurrent systems using temporal logic specifications. *ACM Transactions on Programming Languages and Systems*, 8(2):244–263, January 1986.
21. E.M. Clarke, O. Grumberg, and K. Hamaguchi. Another look at LTL model checking. In *Computer Aided Verification, Proc. 6th International Conference*, pages 415 – 427, Stanford, California, June 1994. Lecture Notes in Computer Science, Springer-Verlag.
22. E.M. Clarke, O. Grumberg, and D. Peled. *Model Checking*. MIT Press, 1999.
23. E.M. Clarke and R.P. Kurshan. Computer aided verification. *IEEE Spectrum*, 33:61–67, 1986.
24. E.M. Clarke and J.M. Wing. Formal methods: State of the art and future directions. *ACM Computing Surveys*, 28:626–643, 1996.
25. F. Copty, L. Fix, R. Fraer, E. Giunchiglia, G. Kamhi, A. Tacchella, and M.Y. Vardi. Benefits of bounded model checking at an industrial setting. In *Computer Aided Verification, Proc. 13th International Conference*, volume 2102 of *Lecture Notes in Computer Science*, pages 436–453. Springer-Verlag, 2001.
26. T.H. Cormen, C.E. Leiserson, and R.L. Rivest. *Introduction to Algorithms*. MIT Press and McGraw-Hill, 1990.
27. C. Courcoubetis, M.Y. Vardi, P. Wolper, and M. Yannakakis. Memory efficient algorithms for the verification of temporal properties. *Formal Methods in System Design*, 1:275–288, 1992.
28. J-M. Couvreur. On-the-fly verification of linear temporal logic. In *Proc. World Congress on Formal Methods*, pages 253–271, 1999.
29. J.M. Couvreur, A. Duret-Lutz, and D. Poitrenaud. On-the-fly emptiness checks for generalized Büchi automata. In *Proc. 12th Int'l SPIN Workshop on Model Checking of Software*, volume 3639 of *Lecture Notes in Computer Science*, pages 143–158. Springer, 2005.
30. N. Daniele, F. Guinchiglia, and M.Y. Vardi. Improved automata generation for linear temporal logic. In *Computer Aided Verification, Proc. 11th International Conference*, volume 1633 of *Lecture Notes in Computer Science*, pages 249–260. Springer-Verlag, 1999.
31. A. Duret-Lutz and Denis Poitrenaud. Spot: An extensible model checking library using transition-based generalized büchi automata. In *Proc. 12th Int'l Workshop on Modeling, Analysis, and Simulation of Computer and Telecommunication Systems*, pages 76–83. IEEE Computer Society, 2004.
32. E.A. Emerson and E.M. Clarke. Characterizing correctness properties of parallel programs using fixpoints. In *Proc. 7th InternationalColloq. on Automata, Languages and Programming*, pages 169–181, 1980.
33. E.A. Emerson and C.-L. Lei. Efficient model checking in fragments of the propositional μ-calculus. In *Proc. 1st Symp. on Logic in Computer Science*, pages 267–278, Cambridge, June 1986.
34. K. Etessami and G.J. Holzmann. Optimizing Büchi automata. In *Proc. 11th Int'l Conf. on Concurrency Theory*, Lecture Notes in Computer Science 1877, pages 153–167. Springer-Verlag, 2000.

35. K. Fisler, R. Fraer, G. Kamhi, M.Y. Vardi, and Z. Yang. Is there a best symbolic cycle-detection algorithm? In *7th International Conference on Tools and algorithms for the construction and analysis of systems*, number 2031 in Lecture Notes in Computer Science, pages 420–434. Springer-Verlag, 2001.
36. E. Friedgut, O. Kupferman, and M.Y. Vardi. Büchi complementation made tighter. *Int'l J. of Foundations of Computer Science*, 17(4):851–867, 2006.
37. C. Fritz. Constructing Büchi automata from linear temporal logic using simulation relations for alternating bchi automata. In *Proc. 8th Intl. Conference on Implementation and Application of Automata*, number 2759 in Lecture Notes in Computer Science, pages 35–48. Springer-Verlag, 2003.
38. C. Fritz. Concepts of automata construction from LTL. In *Proc. 12th Int'l Conf. on Logic for Programming, Artificial Intelligence, and Reasoning*, Lecture Notes in Computer Science 3835, pages 728–742. Springer-Verlag, 2005.
39. P. Gastin and D. Oddoux. Fast LTL to büchi automata translation. In *Computer Aided Verification, Proc. 13th International Conference*, volume 2102 of *Lecture Notes in Computer Science*, pages 53–65. Springer-Verlag, 2001.
40. J. Geldenhuys and A. Valmari. Tarjan's algorithm makes on-the-fly LTL verification more efficient. In *Proc. 10th International Conference on Tools and Algorithms for the Construction and Analysis of Systems*, Lecture Notes in Computer Science 2988, pages 205–219. Springer-Verlag, 2004.
41. R. Gentilini, C. Piazza, and A. Policriti. Computing strongly connected components in a linear number of symbolic steps. In *14th ACM-SIAM Symposium on Discrete Algorithms*, pages 573–582, Baltimore, Maryland, 2003.
42. R. Gerth, D. Peled, M.Y. Vardi, and P. Wolper. Simple on-the-fly automatic verification of linear temporal logic. In P. Dembiski and M. Sredniawa, editors, *Protocol Specification, Testing, and Verification*, pages 3–18. Chapman & Hall, August 1995.
43. D. Giannakopoulou and F. Lerda. From states to transitions: Improving translation of LTL formulae to büchi automata. In *Proc. 22nd IFIP Int'l Conf. on Formal Techniques for Networked and Distributed Systems*, pages 308–326, 2002.
44. P. Godefroid and G.J. Holzmann. On the verification of temporal properties. In *Proc. 13th Int. Conf on Protocol Specification Testing and Verification*, pages 109–124, 1993.
45. S. Gurumurthy, R. Bloem, and F. Somenzi. Fair simulation minimization. In *Computer Aided Verification, Proc. 14th International Conference*, volume 2404 of *Lecture Notes in Computer Science*, pages 610–623. Springer-Verlag, 2002.
46. S. Gurumurthy, O. Kupferman, F. Somenzi, and M.Y. Vardi. On complementing nondeterministic Büchi automata. In *12th Advanced Research Working Conference on Correct Hardware Design and Verification Methods*, volume 2860 of *Lecture Notes in Computer Science*, pages 96–110. Springer-Verlag, 2003.
47. R.H. Hardin, Z. Har'el, and R.P. Kurshan. COSPAN. In *Computer Aided Verification, Proc. 8th International Conference*, volume 1102 of *Lecture Notes in Computer Science*, pages 423–427. Springer-Verlag, 1996.
48. R.H. Hardin, R.P. Kurshan, S.K. Shukla, and M.Y. Vardi. A new heuristic for bad cycle detection using BDDs. *Formal Methods in System Design*, 18:131–140, 2001.
49. G.J. Holzmann. The model checker SPIN. *IEEE Trans. on Software Engineering*, 23(5):279–295, May 1997. Special issue on Formal Methods in Software Practice.
50. G.J. Holzmann, D. Peled, and M. Yannakakis. On nested depth-first search. In *Proc. 2nd Spin Workshop on The Spin Verification System*, pages 23–32. American Math. Soc., 1996.
51. O. Kupferman and M.Y. Vardi. Model checking of safety properties. *Formal methods in System Design*, 19(3):291–314, November 2001.
52. O. Kupferman and M.Y. Vardi. Weak alternating automata are not that weak. *ACM Trans. on Computational Logic*, 2(2):408–429, July 2001.

53. O. Kupferman and M.Y. Vardi. From complementation to certification. *Theoretical Computer Science*, 305:591–606, 2005.
54. O. Kupferman and M.Y. Vardi. From linear time to branching time. *ACM Trans. on Computational Logic*, 6(2):273–294, April 2005.
55. R.P. Kurshan. *Computer Aided Verification of Coordinating Processes*. Princeton Univ. Press, 1994.
56. R.P. Kurshan. Formal verification in a commercial setting. In *Proc. Conf. on Design Automation (DAC'97)*, volume 34, pages 258–262, 1997.
57. T. Latvala, A. Biere, K. Heljanko, and T. A. Junttila. Simple is better: Efficient bounded model checking for past ltl. In *Proc. 6th Int'l Conf. on Verification, Model Checking, and Abstract Interpretation*, volume 3385 of *Lecture Notes in Computer Science*, pages 380–395. Springer, 2005.
58. C. Löding. Optimal bounds for the transformation of omega-automata. In *Proc. 19th Conference on the Foundations of Software Technology and Theoretical Computer Science*, volume 1738 of *Lecture Notes in Computer Science*, pages 97–109, December 1999.
59. K.L. McMillan. *Symbolic Model Checking*. Kluwer Academic Publishers, 1993.
60. M. Michel. Complementation is more difficult with automata on infinite words. CNET, Paris, 1988.
61. A. Pnueli. The temporal logic of programs. In *Proc. 18th IEEE Symp. on Foundation of Computer Science*, pages 46–57, 1977.
62. A. Pnueli and A. Zaks. Psl model checking and run-time verification via testers. In *Proc. 14th Int'l Symp. on Formal Methods*, volume 4085 of *Lecture Notes in Computer Science*, pages 573–586. Springer, 2006.
63. J.P. Queille and J. Sifakis. Specification and verification of concurrent systems in Cesar. In *Proc. 5th International Symp. on Programming*, volume 137 of *Lecture Notes in Computer Science*, pages 337–351. Springer-Verlag, 1981.
64. M.O. Rabin and D. Scott. Finite automata and their decision problems. *IBM Journal of Research and Development*, 3:115–125, 1959.
65. S. Safra. On the complexity of ω-automata. In *Proc. 29th IEEE Symp. on Foundations of Computer Science*, pages 319–327, White Plains, October 1988.
66. S. Schwoon and J. Esparza. A note on on-the-fly verification algorithms. In *Proc. 11th International Conference on Tools and Algorithms for the Construction and Analysis of Systems*, Lecture Notes in Computer Science 3440, pages 174–190. Springer-Verlag, 2005.
67. R. Sebastiani and S. Tonetta. "more deterministic" vs. "smaller" büchi automata for efficient ltl model checking. In *12th Advanced Research Working Conference on Correct Hardware Design and Verification Methods*, volume 2860 of *Lecture Notes in Computer Science*, pages 126–140. Springer-Verlag, 2003.
68. R. Sebastiani, S. Tonetta, and M.Y. Vardi. Symbolic systems, explicit properties: on hybrid approaches for LTL symbolic model checking. In *Proc. 17th Int'l Conf. on Computer Aided Verification*, Lecture Notes in Computer Science 3576, pages 350–373. Springer-Verlag, 2005.
69. A.P. Sistla, M.Y. Vardi, and P. Wolper. The complementation problem for Büchi automata with applications to temporal logic. *Theoretical Computer Science*, 49:217–237, 1987.
70. F. Somenzi and R. Bloem. Efficient Büchi automata from LTL formulae. In *Computer Aided Verification, Proc. 12th International Conference*, volume 1855 of *Lecture Notes in Computer Science*, pages 248–263. Springer-Verlag, 2000.
71. F. Somenzi, K. Ravi, and R. Bloem. Analysis of symbolic scc hull algorithms. In *Proc. 4th Int'l Conf. on Formal Methods in Computer-Aided Design*, volume 2517 of *Lecture Notes in Computer Science*, pages 88–105. Springer, 2002.
72. Heikki Tauriainen. Nested emptiness search for generalized Büchi automata. *Fundamenta Informaticae*, 70(1–2):127–154, 2006.

73. X. Thirioux. Simple and efficient translation from LTL formulas to Büchi automata. *Electr. Notes Theor. Comput. Sci.*, 66(2), 2002.
74. M.Y. Vardi. Nontraditional applications of automata theory. In *Proc. International Symp. on Theoretical Aspects of Computer Software*, volume 789 of *Lecture Notes in Computer Science*, pages 575–597. Springer-Verlag, 1994.
75. M.Y. Vardi. An automata-theoretic approach to linear temporal logic. In F. Moller and G. Birtwistle, editors, *Logics for Concurrency: Structure versus Automata*, volume 1043 of *Lecture Notes in Computer Science*, pages 238–266. Springer-Verlag, Berlin, 1996.
76. M.Y. Vardi. Branching vs. linear time: Final showdown. In *Proc. 7th International Conference on Tools and algorithms for the construction and analysis of systems*, volume 2031 of *Lecture Notes in Computer Science*, pages 1–22. Springer-Verlag, 2001.
77. M.Y. Vardi and P. Wolper. An automata-theoretic approach to automatic program verification. In *Proc. 1st Symp. on Logic in Computer Science*, pages 332–344, Cambridge, June 1986.
78. M.Y. Vardi and P. Wolper. Reasoning about infinite computations. *Information and Computation*, 115(1):1–37, November 1994.
79. P. Wolper. Temporal logic can be more expressive. *Information and Control*, 56(1–2):72–99, 1983.
80. P. Wolper. The tableau method for temporal logic: An overview. *Logique et Analyse*, 110–111:119–136, 1985.
81. P. Wolper, M.Y. Vardi, and A.P. Sistla. Reasoning about infinite computation paths. In *Proc. 24th IEEE Symp. on Foundations of Computer Science*, pages 185–194, Tucson, 1983.
82. Q. Yan. Lower bounds for complementation of ω-automata via the full automata technique. In *Proc. 33rd Intl. Colloq. on Automata, Languages and Pr ogramming*, volume 4052 of *Lecture Notes in Computer Science*, pages 589–600. Springer-Verlag, 2006.
83. L. Zhang and S. Malik. The quest for efficient Boolean satisfiability solvers. In A. Voronkov, editor, *Proc. 18th Int'l Conf. on Automated Deduction (CADE'02)*, Lecture Notes in Computer Science 2392, pages 295–313. Springer-Verlag, 2002.

Language-Based Abstraction Refinement for Hybrid System Verification*

Felix Klaedtke[1], Stefan Ratschan[2], and Zhikun She[3]

[1] ETH Zurich, Computer Science Department, Zurich, Switzerland
[2] Institute of Computer Science, Czech Academy of Sciences, Prague, Czech Republic
[3] Max-Planck-Institut für Informatik, Saarbrücken, Germany

Abstract. The standard counterexample-guided abstraction-refinement (CEGAR) approach uses finite transition systems as abstractions of concrete systems. We present an approach to represent and refine abstractions of infinite-state systems that uses regular languages instead of finite transition systems. The advantage of using languages over transition systems is that we can store more fine-grained information in the abstraction and thus reduce the number of abstract states. Based on this language-based approach for CEGAR, we present new abstraction-refinement algorithms for hybrid system verification. Moreover, we evaluate our approach by verifying various non-linear hybrid systems.

1 Introduction

The verification of infinite-state systems is often done by abstracting the concrete system to an abstract finite state system. The abstract system over-approximates the concrete one, i.e., it includes all the behaviors of the concrete system. However, it can include behaviors that do not correspond to behaviors of the concrete system. Such behaviors are called *spurious*. In the *counterexample-guided abstraction-refinement* (CEGAR) paradigm [6] one usually starts with a very coarse abstraction and uses spurious counterexamples to iteratively refine the abstraction until verification reveals whether or not the property in question holds. CEGAR has been successfully used for verifying many different classes of infinite-state systems. For instance, CEGAR has been adopted and used for the verification of hybrid systems [5, 1, 17]. In this paper, we focus on the safety verification of hybrid systems. However, in principle, the presented method also applies to other infinite-state systems.

The standard CEGAR approach uses finite transition systems as abstractions of the concrete systems. The use of transition systems has the following disadvantages. Assume that we have abstract states a, b, c with transitions from a to b and from b to c (we write $a \to b$ and $b \to c$ with the obvious meaning). Even if $a \to b$ and $b \to c$ are not spurious, it is not necessarily the case that $a \to b \to c$ is not spurious. If $a \to b \to c$ is spurious, we can refine the abstraction by splitting

---

* This work was partly supported by the German Research Foundation (DFG) and the Swiss National Science Foundation (SNF).

B. Cook and A. Podelski (Eds.): VMCAI 2007, LNCS 4349, pp. 151–166, 2007.
© Springer-Verlag Berlin Heidelberg 2007

at least one of the abstract states such that the concrete system is reflected more closely. Splitting abstract states in such a way that the spurious sequence $a{\to}b{\to}c$ does not appear in the abstraction anymore can be difficult. Furthermore, the splitting of an abstract state introduces additional abstract states and it can introduce new spurious counterexamples. This can lead to a state space explosion of the abstract systems. For instance, in the worst case, the number of abstract states can double in each refinement step of the CEGAR algorithm for hybrid system [5]. One method [10] to address this problem splits abstract states based on graph-topological properties of the finite transition system.

As a means to reduce the number of abstract states we present an alternative to finite transition systems as abstractions in the CEGAR paradigm. Namely, we use languages to over-approximate the behaviors of concrete systems. In our approach, a language contains at least the sequences of abstract states that correspond to runs of the concrete system. The use of languages allows us to store more fine-grained information in the abstraction, and to refine the abstraction, we do not necessarily need to split abstract states. For instance, in the example above, if the sequence $a{\to}b{\to}c$ of abstract states is spurious, we can remove all sequences from the language that contain $a{\to}b{\to}c$ as a subsequence. For checking whether a sequence of abstract states is spurious, we present an extension of the method that is used in the hybrid system verifier HSOLVER [18, 19]. As in the standard CEGAR approach, we also allow to split abstract states to refine the abstraction. We use deterministic finite automata to represent the languages and present automata operations for refining the abstractions. We evaluate our language-based approach on various non-linear hybrid systems using a prototype implementation. Our experiments demonstrate that the use of languages often reduces the number of splittings significantly.

To our knowledge, the use of languages for representing and refining abstractions in the context of CEGAR for hybrid system verification is novel. The observation that regular languages/automata can be used to improve abstraction-refinement algorithms already appeared in [7]. However, [7] mainly focuses on the completeness of abstraction-refinement algorithms for infinite-state systems in general and does not provide concrete algorithms that beneficially make use of finite state automata in practice. Related to our work with respect to languages for representing the behavior of hybrid systems are [2] and [4,3]. Roughly speaking, Asarin et al. [2] use languages to show decidability of the reachability problem of a certain class of hybrid systems, and Brihaye et al. [4,3] use words of languages to construct bisimilar finite transition systems for so-called o-minimal hybrid systems. Other methods for verifying systems with continuous dynamics by over-approximating their behaviors, and automatically and incrementally refining the abstractions appeared recently in [9, 14]. In [9], rectangular hybrid automata [12] are used to over-approximate the behavior, and [14] uses finite transition systems. Both methods only apply to hybrid systems with restricted (linear, multi-affine) continuous dynamics.

We proceed as follows. In §2, we give the definition of hybrid systems that we use in this paper and the verification problem that we address. In §3, we describe our method for using languages as abstractions. In §4, we give details on how we manipulate the languages that represent our abstractions and in §5, we present methods to check if sequences of abstract states are spurious. In §6, we report on experimental results. Finally, in §7, we draw conclusions.

2   Verification of Hybrid Systems

Hybrid systems are systems with continuous and discrete state variables. In this paper, we use the mathematical model from [17, 19], which we briefly recall in this section. It captures many relevant classes of hybrid systems, and many other formalisms for hybrid systems in the literature are special cases of it.

We use a set S to denote the modes of a hybrid system, where S is finite and nonempty. $I_1, \ldots, I_k \subseteq \mathbb{R}$ are compact intervals over which the continuous variables of a hybrid system range. Φ denotes the state space of a hybrid system, i.e., $\Phi = S \times I_1 \times \cdots \times I_k$. Note that it is not a severe practical restriction that the continuous variables have to range over compact intervals because, in most applications, the variable ranges are bounded and engineers use their experience to choose reasonable values for the interval bounds.

Definition 1. *A hybrid system H is a tuple (Flow, Jump, Init, Unsafe), where Flow $\subseteq \Phi \times \mathbb{R}^k$, Jump $\subseteq \Phi \times \Phi$, Init $\subseteq \Phi$, and Unsafe $\subseteq \Phi$.*

Informally speaking, the predicate *Init* specifies the initial states of a hybrid system $H = (Flow, Jump, Init, Unsafe)$ and *Unsafe* the states that should not be reachable from an initial state. The relation *Flow* specifies how the system may develop continuously by relating each state to the corresponding derivative, and *Jump* specifies how H may change states discontinuously by relating each state to its successor states. Formally, the behavior of H is defined as follows:

Definition 2. *A flow of length $l \geq 0$ in a mode $s \in S$ is a function $r : [0, l] \to \Phi$ such that the projection of r to its continuous part is differentiable and for all $t \in [0, l]$, the mode of $r(t)$ is s. A trajectory of H is a sequence of flows $r_0, \ldots, r_p$ of lengths $l_0, \ldots, l_p$ such that for all $i \in \{0, \ldots, p\}$,*

(i) if $i > 0$ then $(r_{i-1}(l_{i-1}), r_i(0)) \in Jump$, and
(ii) if $l_i > 0$ then $(r_i(t), \dot{r}_i(t)) \in Flow$, for all $t \in [0, l_i]$, where $\dot{r}_i$ is the derivative of the projection of r_i to its continuous component.

In the following, we denote the length of a flow r by $|r|$. Moreover, we address the state $r_i(t)$ in a trajectory by the pair (i, t). This naturally gives us a (lexicographical) order $\preceq$ on the states in a trajectory.

Definition 3. *A (concrete) counterexample of H is a trajectory $r_0, \ldots, r_p$ of H such that $r_0(0) \in Init$ and $r_p(|r_p|) \in Unsafe$. H is safe if it does not have a counterexample.*

We use the following constraint language to describe hybrid systems. The variable s ranges over S and the variables $x_1, \ldots, x_k$ range over $I_1, \ldots, I_k$, respectively. In addition, to denote the derivatives of $x_1, \ldots, x_k$ we use the variables

$\dot{x}_1, \ldots, \dot{x}_k$ that range over $\mathbb{R}$,[1] and to denote the targets of jumps, we use the primed variables $s', x'_1, \ldots, x'_k$ that range over S and $I_1, \ldots, I_k$, respectively. Constraints are arbitrary Boolean combinations of equalities and inequalities over terms that may contain function symbols like $+$, $\times$, exp, sin, and cos.

We assume in the remainder of the text that a hybrid system is described by our constraint language. That means, the flows of a hybrid system are given by a constraint $flow(s, x_1, \ldots, x_k, \dot{x}_1, \ldots, \dot{x}_k)$, the jumps are given by a constraint $jump(s, x_1, \ldots, x_k, s', x'_1, \ldots, x'_k)$, the initial states are given by a constraint $init(s, x_1, \ldots, x_k)$, and a constraint $unsafe(s, x_1, \ldots, x_k)$ describes the unsafe states. To simplify notation, we do not distinguish between a constraint and the set it represents.

Example 1. For illustrating the above definitions, consider the following simple hybrid system. The hybrid system has two modes m_1, m_2 and the continuous variables x_1 and x_2, where x_1 ranges over the interval $[0, 2]$ and x_2 over $[0, 1]$, i.e, $\Phi = \{m_1, m_2\} \times [0, 2] \times [0, 1]$.

The set of initial states are given by the constraint $init(s, x_1, x_2) = (s = m_1 \wedge x_1 = 0 \wedge x_2 = 0)$ and $unsafe(s, x_1, x_2) = (x_1 > 1 \wedge x_2 = 1)$ describes the unsafe states. The hybrid system can switch modes from m_1 to m_2 if $x_2 = 1$, i.e.,

$$jump(s, x_1, x_2, s', x'_1, x'_2) = (s = m_1 \wedge x_2 = 1 \rightarrow s' = m_2 \wedge x'_1 = x_1 \wedge x'_2 = x_2).$$

The continuous behavior is quite simple: In mode m_1, the values of the variables x_1, x_2 change with slope 1; in mode m_2, the slope of x_1 is 1 and x_2 has slope -1. For a flow in mode m_1, the constraint $0 \le x_1 \le 1$ must hold and in mode m_2, $1 \le x_1 \le 2$ must hold. The corresponding flow constraint is

$$flow(s, x_1, x_2, \dot{x}_1, \dot{x}_2) = (s = m_1 \rightarrow \dot{x}_1 = 1 \wedge \dot{x}_2 = 1 \wedge 0 \le x_1 \le 1) \wedge$$
$$(s = m_2 \rightarrow \dot{x}_1 = 1 \wedge \dot{x}_2 = -1 \wedge 1 \le x_1 \le 2).$$

Note that the constraint $0 \le x_1 \le 1$ in *flow* forces a jump from mode m_1 to m_2 if x_1 becomes 1. Otherwise, the system makes no progress. In general, an invariant that has to hold in a mode can be modeled by formulating a flow constraint that does not allow a continuous behavior in certain parts of the state space.

A trajectory of the hybrid system starting from the initial state $(m_1, (0, 0))$ is r_0, r_1, where the flows $r_1, r_2 : [0, 1] \rightarrow \Phi$ are given by

$$r_0(t) = (m_1, (t, t)) \qquad \text{and} \qquad r_1(t) = (m_2, (t + 1, 1 - t)).$$

Obviously, this hybrid system is safe.

The verification problem we address in the following is to prove automatically that a hybrid system is safe. Note that the reachability problem for hybrid systems is undecidable [12]. So, it is only possible to give semi-algorithms for this problem that (hopefully) terminate on many relevant problem instances. In this paper, our focus is on verifying that a given hybrid system is safe and on

---

[1] The dot does not have any special meaning here; it is only used to distinguish dotted from undotted variables.

efficiency for instances of practical relevance. For the sake of readability, we use in the remainder of the paper the term "algorithm" liberally in the sense that we do not require that an algorithm terminates for every input instance.

3   Language-Based Abstractions

In this section, we present our language-based approach of abstracting hybrid systems and refining abstractions. For the remainder of the text, let $H = (Flow, Jump, Init, Unsafe)$ be a hybrid system.

As in many abstraction techniques we cover H's state space Φ by using finitely many subsets of Φ, which we call *regions*. We identify the regions by naming them with the symbols of an alphabet Ω and a function γ that assigns to every element of Ω a region and that *covers* Φ, i.e., $\Phi = \bigcup_{b \in \Omega} \gamma(b)$.

Intuitively speaking, we use a word $b_1 \ldots b_n \in \Omega^+$ to represent all the trajectories of H that pass in the order of the occurrences of the symbols through the regions $\gamma(b_1), \ldots, \gamma(b_n)$.

Definition 4. *Let* $w = b_1 \ldots b_n \in \Omega^+$ *with* $n \geq 1$. *A trajectory* $r_1, \ldots, r_p$ *of* H *follows* w *if there exists a non-decreasing sequence* $(i_1, t_1), \ldots, (i_{n+1}, t_{n+1})$ *with respect to the ordering* $\preceq$ *such that*
  (i) $i_1 = 1$ *and* $t_1 = 0$,
  (ii) $0 \leq t_j \leq |r_{i_j}|$, *for all* $j \in \{1, \ldots, n\}$,
  (iii) $i_{n+1} = p$, $t_{n+1} = |r_p|$, *and* $r_p(|r_p|) \in \gamma(b_n)$, *and*
  (iv) *for all* $j \in \{1, \ldots, n\}$ *and all* (i', t'), *if* $(i_j, t_j) \preceq (i', t') \prec (i_{j+1}, t_{j+1})$ *then* $r_{i'}(t') \in \gamma(b_j)$.

Note that different trajectories can follow the same word and a trajectory can follow different words.

Example 2. Consider again the hybrid system from Example 1. Assume that its state space is covered by $\gamma : \{a, b, c, d\} \rightarrow \Phi$ with $\gamma(a) = \{m_1\} \times [0, \frac{1}{2}] \times [0, 1]$, $\gamma(b) = \{m_1\} \times [\frac{1}{2}, 1] \times [0, 1]$, $\gamma(c) = \{m_2\} \times [1, \frac{3}{2}] \times [0, 1]$, and $\gamma(d) = \{m_2\} \times [\frac{3}{2}, 2] \times [0, 1]$. Let r_1, r_2 be the trajectory from $(m_1, (\frac{1}{4}, \frac{1}{4}))$ to $(m_2, (\frac{7}{4}, \frac{1}{4}))$ with

$$r_1(t) = (m_1, (\tfrac{1}{4} + t, \tfrac{1}{4} + t)) \qquad \text{and} \qquad r_2(t) = (m_2, (1 + t, 1 - t)),$$

for $t \in [0, \frac{3}{4}]$. The trajectory r_1, r_2 follows the word $abcd$, since the sequence $(1, 0), (1, \frac{1}{4}), (1, \frac{3}{4}), (2, \frac{1}{2}), (2, \frac{3}{4})$ is non-decreasing with respect to $\preceq$ and satisfies the conditions (i)–(iv) in Definition 4.

Definition 5. *We call a word* $w \in \Omega^+$ *prefix-spurious (suffix-spurious, respectively) if there is no trajectory* $r_1, \ldots, r_p$ *that follows* w *and starts in* Init, *i.e.,* $r_1(0) \in$ Init *(ends in* Unsafe, *i.e.,* $r_p(|r_p|) \in$ Unsafe, *respectively). Moreover, we call* w *midfix-spurious if there is no trajectory that follows* w. *For the sake of brevity, we use the following abbreviations: p-spurious for prefix-spurious, s-spurious for suffix-spurious, and m-spurious for midfix-spurious.*

Note that if a word is m-spurious then it is p-spurious and s-spurious. However, if a word is p-spurious or s-spurious, we cannot conclude that it is m-spurious.

Algorithm 1. Language-based abstraction-refinement algorithm

Input: hybrid system H
1: $\Omega \leftarrow \{b\}$, where b is some symbol
2: $L \leftarrow \Omega^+$
3: let $\gamma : \Omega \rightarrow 2^\Phi$ be the function with $\gamma(b) = \Phi$
4: **while** $L \neq \emptyset$ **do**
5:     **for all** $b \in \Omega$ with $L \cap \{bv \mid v \in \Omega^*\} \neq \emptyset$ and b is p-spurious **do**
6:         $L \leftarrow L \setminus \text{ext}(\{bv \mid v \in \Omega^*\})$
7:     **end for**
8:     **for all** $b \in \Omega$ with $L \cap \{ub \mid u \in \Omega^*\} \neq \emptyset$ and b is s-spurious **do**
9:         $L \leftarrow L \setminus \text{ext}(\{ub \mid u \in \Omega^*\})$
10:     **end for**
11:     **for all** $w \in C(\Omega)$ with $|w| = maxlen$ and $L \cap \{uwv \mid u, v \in \Omega^*\} \neq \emptyset$ **do**
12:         $L \leftarrow removeMidfixSpurious(H, L, w)$
13:     **end for**
14:     split region $\gamma(a)$ in regions U and V, for some $a \in \Omega$
15:     $\Omega \leftarrow \Omega \cup \{b\}$, where b is a fresh symbol
16:     $L \leftarrow L^{a \sim b}$
17:     update γ, i.e., $\gamma(a) = U$, $\gamma(b) = V$, and $\gamma(c)$ is not altered for $c \in \Omega \setminus \{a, b\}$
18: **end while**

We assume that we can check if a word is p-spurious, s-spurious, or m-spurious. Since the reachability problem for hybrid systems is undecidable [12] such a check has to be over-approximating, i.e., it returns either "spurious" or "don't know" (see §5 for more details on mechanizing such a check). Additionally, such a check may detect that a trajectory follows the given word, and returns "not spurious" in that case. This additional information can be used to further optimize the following algorithms. However, in order to keep the exposition simple, we do not consider this further.

To verify that the hybrid system H is safe, we use languages L such that every counterexample of H follows a word in L. We iteratively choose words $w \in L$ and check whether w is p-spurious, s-spurious, or m-spurious. Assume that $L \subseteq \Omega^+$, where Ω is some alphabet. If we can show that w is p-spurious, we remove the words of the form wv with $v \in \Omega^*$ from L, if we can show that w is s-spurious, we remove the words uw with $u \in \Omega^*$ from L, and if we can show that w is m-spurious, we remove the words uwv with $u, v \in \Omega^*$ from L. If the language becomes empty, we know that H is safe. In addition to the checks if a word is p-spurious, s-spurious, or m-spurious, we can split a region. For reflecting a split, we add a new symbol b to Ω, update γ, and add certain words to L.

Various details are left open in the description above. In the following, we provide the details by describing the language-based counterexample-abstraction-refinement algorithm in Alg. 1.

Note that the language L can be infinite. So, instead of checking all words in L in an iteration (lines 4–18 of Alg. 1), we only check the words up to a given maximal length $maxlen$, which we fix in advance. Moreover, we restrict ourselves to *contracted* words, i.e., words in which a subword of the form bb with $b \in \Omega$

Algorithm 2. removeMidfixSpurious

Input: hybrid system H, language L, word w

1: $N \leftarrow \emptyset$
2: **for** $l \leftarrow$ length of w **downto** 2 **do**
3:     **for all** subwords w' of w of length l and w' is not a subword of a word in N **do**
4:         **if** w' is m-spurious **then** $L \leftarrow L \setminus \text{ext}(\{uw'v \mid u, v \in \Omega^*\})$
5:                **else** $N \leftarrow N \cup \{w'\}$
6:     **end for**
7: **end for**
8: **return** L

---

does not occur. The reason for this is that if, e.g., $ubbv$ is m-spurious then ubv is also m-spurious. Let $C(\Omega)$ denote the set of contracted words in Ω^+. The *contraction* of a word w is the word w', where we remove repeated symbols, i.e., we replace the maximal subwords of the form $b \ldots b$ in w by b. For $K \subseteq \Omega^*$, we define $\text{ext}(K)$ as the language that contains a word $u \in \Omega^*$ iff there is some $v \in K$ such that the contractions of u and v are the same.

The decision in which order to check the words in $C(\Omega)$ of length at most *maxlen* is non-trivial. In particular, should we check short words or long words first? On the one hand, a longer word is more likely to be identified, e.g., as m-spurious since at most as many trajectories follow a word as any of its subwords. On the other hand, if we identify a short word w, e.g., as m-spurious then we do not need to check longer words in which w occurs. In each iteration (lines 4–18), Alg. 1 checks the words in the following order. First, we check words if they are p-spurious or s-spurious (lines 5–7 and 8–10, respectively). We only check words of length 1, i.e., for a region, we check if it contains initial and unsafe states. If we identify $b \in \Omega$ as p-spurious, we remove $\text{ext}(\{bu \mid u \in \Omega^*\})$ from L. Analogously, if we identify $b \in \Omega$ as s-spurious, we remove $\text{ext}(\{ub \mid u \in \Omega^*\})$. Then, for every word $w \in C(\Omega)$ of length *maxlen*, we use Alg. 2 to check if subwords w' of w are m-spurious. If we identify w' as m-spurious, we remove $\text{ext}(\{uw'v \mid u, v \in \Omega^*\})$ from L. Furthermore, Alg. 2 maintains a set N to avoid unnecessary checks whether a word w' is m-spurious. We do not check whether w' is m-spurious if w' is a subword of a word $\tilde{w}$ for which we could not prove in an earlier iteration (lines 2–7 of Alg. 2) that $\tilde{w}$ is m-spurious (i.e., the used solver has returned "don't know" for $\tilde{w}$). We assume here that the solver will then also return "don't know" for w'. Note that this is a reasonable assumption since intuitively it is easier·to show that a word is m-spurious than to show that one of its subwords is m-spurious.

After checking contracted words in L of length at most *maxlen*, Alg. 1 splits a region according to some heuristic, extends the alphabet Ω, and updates the language L and the function γ (lines 14–18). For reflecting a split of a region named by $a \in \Omega$, we need to specify that a fresh symbol behaves exactly like a.

Definition 6. *For $K \subseteq \Omega^*$ and symbols a, b, we define $K^{a \sim b}$ as the smallest set such that if $a_1 \ldots a_n \in K$ then $a'_1 \ldots a'_n \in K^{a \sim b}$, where $a'_i = a_i$ if $a_i \neq a$ and $a'_i \in \{a, b\}$ if $a_i = a$, for all $i \in \{1, \ldots, n\}$.*

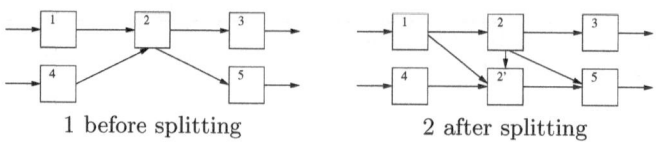

1 before splitting   2 after splitting

Fig. 1. Abstraction refinement

The correctness of Alg. 1 follows from the invariant that every trajectory from *Init* to *Unsafe* follows a word in L. Note that we only remove words from L that are p-spurious, s-spurious, or m-spurious.

Theorem 1. *If Alg. 1 terminates then H is safe.*

Before we describe how we represent and manipulate the languages L that describe the abstractions (§4) and how we check if a word is p-spurious, s-spurious, or m-spurious (§5), we relate our language-based approach to the standard approach of using finite transition systems in CEGAR to abstract the concrete system. Furthermore, we present optimizations of Alg. 1 (§3.1 and §3.2).

In the standard CEGAR approach one uses finite transition systems to overapproximate the behavior of a concrete system. From a finite transition system T we can obtain a language $L_T \subseteq S^+$, where S is the set of states of T. Assume that we associate to each state s of T a region $\eta(s)$ of H's state space. We define L_T as the language that consists of the words $s_0 \ldots s_n \in S^+$, where $s_0 \to \cdots \to s_n$ is a path in T with $\eta(s_0) \cap Init \neq \emptyset$ and $\eta(s_n) \cap Unsafe \neq \emptyset$. Note that T and L_T represent the same abstract counterexamples and deleting a transition $s \to s'$ in T corresponds to removing all words from L_T in which ss' occurs as a subword.

The other direction is as follows. Let $L \subseteq \Omega^+$ be a language in our language-based approach. The set of states of the finite transition system T_L is Ω. A state $b \in \Omega$ is initial iff $\gamma(b) \cap Init \neq \emptyset$ and b is an unsafe state in T_L iff $\gamma(b) \cap Unsafe \neq \emptyset$. We have a transition from state $b \in \Omega$ to $b' \in \Omega$ in T_L iff bb' is a subword of a word in L. Note that the abstraction L can be more accurate than T_L. In the case where $maxlen = 2$, the words that we check in line 11 of Alg. 1 are of the form ab, where $a, b \in \Omega$ and $a \neq b$. So, the elimination of words from the language L in line 12 corresponds to the elimination of edges between states in the transition system T_L.

We illustrate that choosing *maxlen* larger than 2 can be beneficial. Consider the abstraction in Figure 1(a) and assume that the abstract states 1 and 4 are reachable from an initial state in the abstraction, and the states 3 and 5 lead to an unsafe state in the abstraction. Assume further that the sequence $4 \to 2 \to 3$ is m-spurious because there is no trajectory from the abstract state 4 over 2 to 3. In our approach, we just remove $ext(\{u423v \mid u, v \in \Omega^*\})$ from the language. When using finite transition systems, we try to split the abstract state 2 into two new abstract states, which we name 2 and $2'$, in such a way that there is no trajectory from 4 to 2, no trajectory from $2'$ to 3, and no trajectory from $2'$ to 2 (see Figure 1(b)). The refined abstraction contains neither the sequence $4 \to 2 \to 3$ nor $4 \to 2' \to 3$. However, the splitting might introduce new fragments of spurious counterexamples, e.g., $1 \to 2' \to 5$. Moreover, to prove that $4 \to 2$,

$2' \to 3$, and $2' \to 2$ are m-spurious, it might be necessary to split the region of the original abstract state 2 into two parts of a very complex form. It might even be the case that our data structure for representing regions is not flexible enough to allow a split such that the edges $4 \to 2$, $2' \to 3$, and $2' \to 2$ can be removed. In this case, we have to split the regions 2 and $2'$ further. The experimental results in §6 demonstrate that such situations arise in practice and taking into account sequences of abstract states with more than two states can pay off.

3.1 Region Pruning

In Alg. 1, we only split regions and remove words from the language L to refine the abstraction. For instance, we remove a word if we can show that there is no trajectory that follows this word. In this subsection, we optimize our verification method by a complementary method: if we can prove that a part of a region is not reachable then we remove this part of the region, i.e., we prune certain states from regions. Observe that the regions may not cover the state space Φ anymore. However, since we only remove unreachable states, the regions still cover the part of Φ in which there might be a counterexample.

Definition 7. *A state $y \in \Phi$ is* reachable *from a state $x \in \Phi$ if there is a trajectory $r_0, \ldots, r_p$ with $r_0(0) = x$ and $r_p(|r_p|) = y$. For $w \in \Omega^+$, $y \in \Phi$ is w-reachable from $x \in \Phi$ if there is a trajectory $r_1, \ldots, r_p$ that follows w, $r_0(0) = x$, and $r_p(|r_p|) = y$.*

The following lemma allows us to remove states from regions that are neither w-reachable from an initial state, for all contracted words w of length less than *maxlen* nor w-reachable from some other state, for all contracted words w of length *maxlen*. Due to space limitations, we omit its proof.

Lemma 1. *Assume that γ covers the reachable states of Φ, i.e., for every $y \in \Phi$, if y is reachable from some initial state then $y \in \gamma(b)$, for some $b \in \Omega$. For every $l \geq 1$, if the state $y \in \Phi$ is reachable from an initial state then there is a word $w \in C(\Omega)$ such that*
- $|w| < l$ and y is w-reachable from some state $x \in$ Init, or
- $|w| = l$ and y is w-reachable from some state $x \in \Phi$.

In particular, for $l = 2$, it holds that if $y \in \gamma(b)$ is reachable from some initial state then y is either b-reachable from some $x \in Init$ or y is ab-reachable from some $x \in \gamma(a)$, where $a \neq b$. In [19], we already used the special case $l = 2$ to remove unreachable states from regions.

The optimized algorithm is Alg. 3, where $reach(H, b_1 \ldots b_n)$ computes a superset of the states in the region $\gamma(b_n)$ for which there is a trajectory of H that follows $b_1 \ldots b_n$, and, analogously, $reachInit(H, b_1 \ldots b_n)$ computes a superset of the states in the region $\gamma(b_n)$ for which there is a trajectory of H that starts in Init and follows $b_1 \ldots b_n$. Details on implementing $reach$ and $reachInit$ are in §5.

Algorithm 3. Optimized algorithm with region pruning

Input: hybrid system H

1: $\Omega \leftarrow \{b\}$, where b is some symbol
2: $L \leftarrow \Omega^+$
3: let $\gamma : \Omega \rightarrow 2^\Phi$ be the function with $\gamma(b) = \Phi$
4: **while** $L \neq \emptyset$ **do**
5:    **for all** $b \in \Omega$ **do**
6:      $R \leftarrow \emptyset$
7:      **for all** $wb \in C(\Omega)$ with $|wb| < maxlen$ and $L \cap \{wbv \,|\, v \in \Omega^*\} \neq \emptyset$ **do**
8:        **if** $reachInit(H, wb) \neq \emptyset$ **then** $R \leftarrow R \cup reachInit(H, wb)$
9:                  **else** $L \leftarrow L \setminus \mathrm{ext}(\{wbv \,|\, v \in \Omega^*\})$ // wb is p-spurious
10:      **end for**
11:      **if** $L \cap \{ub \,|\, u \in \Omega^*\} \neq \emptyset$ and b is s-spurious **then**
12:        $L \leftarrow L \setminus \mathrm{ext}(\{ub \,|\, u \in \Omega^*\})$
13:      **end if**
14:      **for all** $wb \in C(\Omega)$ with $|wb| = maxlen$ and $L \cap \{uwbv \,|\, u, v \in \Omega^*\} \neq \emptyset$ **do**
15:        $K \leftarrow removeMidfixSpurious(H, L, wb)$
16:        **if** $K = L$ **then** $R \leftarrow R \cup reach(H, wb)$
17:                **else** $L \leftarrow K$
18:      **end for**
19:      **if** $R = \emptyset$ **then** $\Omega \leftarrow \Omega \setminus \{b\}$ // no reachable states in region $\gamma(b)$
20:      update γ, i.e., restrict γ to the domain Ω, $\gamma(b) = R$ if $R \neq \emptyset$, and $\gamma(c)$ is not altered for $c \in \Omega \setminus \{b\}$
21:    **end for**
22:    split region $\gamma(a)$ in regions U and V, for some $a \in \Omega$
23:    $\Omega \leftarrow \Omega \cup \{b\}$, where b is a fresh symbol
24:    $L \leftarrow L^{a \sim b}$
25:    update γ, i.e., $\gamma(a) = U$, $\gamma(b) = V$, and $\gamma(c)$ is not altered for $c \in \Omega \setminus \{a, b\}$
26: **end while**

3.2   Incremental Computation

Our second optimization exploits the following fact: if we split a region then we only need to re-check the words in which a symbol b occurs such that $\gamma(b)$ was involved in this split. We do this by maintaining a set $Q \subseteq \Omega$: We only iterate the for-loops (lines 5–7, 8–10, and 11–13 of Alg. 1) for $b \in \Omega$ if it is in Q. After we have processed a symbol in Q, we remove it from Q. At the beginning of an iteration of the while-loop (lines 4–18 of Alg. 1) Q consists of the symbols for the regions that were involved in the split in the previous iteration, and if it is the first iteration, Q consists of the symbol chosen in line 1 of Alg. 1.

We can improve Alg. 3 in a similar way by iterating the for-loop (lines 5–21) for only the symbols in Q, and adding symbols b to Q for which the for-loop (lines 5–21) might be successful in changing the region $\gamma(b)$ or removing words from the language that contain b. Whenever a region $\gamma(b')$ has been changed, we add a symbol c to Q if there is a word w in which b' occurs, and either $|wc| = maxlen$ and $L \cap \{uwcv \,|\, u, v \in \Omega^*\} \neq \emptyset$, or $|wc| < maxlen$ and $L \cap \{wcv \,|\, v \in \Omega^*\} \neq \emptyset$. Note that pruning $\gamma(b')$ as well as splitting $\gamma(b')$ may add symbols to Q.

4   Language Representation and Manipulation

In this section, we discuss how we represent and manipulate the languages $L \subseteq \Omega^*$ in the algorithms presented in the previous section. First, observe that the algorithms satisfy the following invariants:

Lemma 2. *Throughout Alg. 1 and Alg. 3, L is regular and $L = \text{ext}(L)$.*

We use minimal DFAs to represent the languages L and our implementation uses the DFA library from the MONA tool [13]. All the DFA operations used in our algorithms are rather straightforward. For instance, for checking the non-emptiness of $L \cap \{wv \,|\, v \in \Omega^*\}$ for a word $w \in \Omega^+$ in line 7 of Alg. 3, it suffices to check whether we reach a non-rejecting sink state in the minimal DFA that represents L when reading w. For the operation $L^{a \sim b}$, we define the DFA $A^{a \sim b} = (Q, \Omega \cup \{b\}, \delta', q_0, F)$ with $\delta'(q, b) = \delta(q, a)$ and $\delta'(q, x) = \delta(q, x)$, for all $q \in Q$ and $x \in \Omega$, where the DFA $A = (Q, \Omega, \delta, q_0, F)$ accepts L. Obviously, $A^{a \sim b}$ accepts the language $L^{a \sim b}$ when b is fresh, i.e., $b \notin \Omega$.

Although the used automata operations are all fairly simple, it turned out that they dominate the running times. To reduce the number of performed automata operations, we maintain a list in which we store words that we have identified as m-spurious. We update the DFA and empty the list before we split a region because otherwise the list would become too long. Moreover, we remove words w from the list if there is another word w' in the list such that w' is a subword of w. Whenever we have a query about a word, we search in this list before we query the DFA.

5   Counterexample Checking

The presented language-based approach is independent of the method for checking if a word is spurious and for pruning unreachable states from the region of the last symbol of a word. In this section, we present a method that accomplishes these two tasks. It extends a method that is used in the verification tool HSOLVER [18, 19, 17] and it has advantages over other methods: pruning is inherent to the method and it handles non-linear differential equations so that the correctness of the results are not interfered with rounding errors due to floating-point arithmetic.

As in other approaches (e.g. [14]), we use hyper-rectangles (*boxes*) for decomposing the state-space. That is, we require that the regions that cover the reachable states in Φ of the hybrid system H are of the form (s, B), where $s \in S$ is a mode and $B \subseteq \mathbb{R}^k$ is a box, i.e. $B = [\ell_1, u_1] \times \cdots \times [\ell_k, u_k]$. Recall that k is the number of the continuous variables of H. In principle, regions can be represented by more complex geometrical shapes. However, since we utilize a constraint solver that uses boxes, we restrict ourselves in the following to boxes.

We need the following definitions. Let B be the box $[\ell_1, u_1] \times \cdots \times [\ell_k, u_k]$. The *ith lower face* of B is the box $[\ell_1, u_1] \times \cdots \times [\ell_{i-1}, u_{i-1}] \times [\ell_i, \ell_i] \times [\ell_{i+1}, u_{i+1}] \times \cdots \times [\ell_k, u_k]$ and the *ith upper face* of B is the box $[\ell_1, u_1] \times \cdots \times [\ell_{i-1}, u_{i-1}] \times [u_i, u_i] \times [\ell_{i+1}, u_{i+1}] \times \cdots \times [\ell_k, u_k]$. Assume that $flow_{(s,B)}(x, y)$ denotes a constraint that models the fact that there is a flow from $x \in \mathbb{R}^k$ to $y \in \mathbb{R}^k$ in mode $s \in S$ and box $B \subseteq \mathbb{R}^k$. Furthermore, to make the solving of such a constraint easier, we assume that $flow_{(s,B)}(x,y)$ does not contain differentiation symbols and the bound variables are existentially quantified. There are various possibilities to achieve these assumptions, e.g., by using linearization [20]. We use $flow_{(s,B)}(x,y)$ to define the following constraints. Let $s, s' \in S$ be modes and $B, B' \subseteq \mathbb{R}^k$ boxes.

- The constraint $reach^{J}_{(s,B),(s',B')}(x,y)$ models the fact that there is a jump from $x \in B$ and mode s to $y \in B'$ and mode s', i.e.,

$$x \in B \wedge y \in B' \wedge \exists x' \in B'.\ Jump(s,x,s',x') \wedge flow_{(s',B')}(x',y).$$

- The constraint $reach^{F}_{(s,B),(s',B')}(x,y)$ models the fact that there is a continuous flow in mode s from $x \in B \cap B'$ to $y \in B'$, i.e.,

$$s = s' \wedge x \in B \cap B' \wedge y \in B' \wedge flow_{(s',B')}(x,y) \wedge$$
$$\bigwedge_{F \text{ face of } B'} \left[x \in F \rightarrow incoming_{(s,B'),F}(x) \right],$$

where $incoming_{(s,B'),F}(x) = \exists \dot{x}_1, \ldots, \dot{x}_k \in \mathbb{R}.\ Flow(s, x, (\dot{x}_1, \ldots, \dot{x}_k)) \wedge \dot{x}_j \geq 0$ if F is the jth lower face of B', and if F is the jth upper face of B', $incoming_{(s,B'),F}(x) = \exists \dot{x}_1, \ldots, \dot{x}_k \in \mathbb{R}.\ Flow(s, x, (\dot{x}_1, \ldots, \dot{x}_k)) \wedge \dot{x}_j \leq 0$. Note that we need the conjuncts $[x \in F \rightarrow incoming_{(s,B'),F}(x)]$, for the faces F of B' to ensure that a flow starting in $x \in F$ stays in box B', i.e., the derivative in $x \in F$ does not point out of box B'.

A word $w \in \Omega^+$ has a *self-jump* if there are $(s,x), (s,x') \in \gamma(b)$ such that $(s,x,s,x') \in Jump$, for some symbol b in w.

In the following, let $w = b_0 \ldots b_n \in C(\Omega)$ with $\gamma(b_i) = (s_i, B_i)$, for $i \in \{0, \ldots, n\}$. The following theorem extends an earlier result [19, 17]. Its proof is similar and we omit it.

Theorem 2. *Assume that w does not have self-jumps. If a state $(s_n, y_n) \in \gamma(b_n)$ is w-reachable from some state in Φ then the constraint $\exists y_0 \in \mathbb{R}^k.\ reach_w(y_0, y_n)$ is satisfiable, where the constraint $reach_w(y_0, y_n)$ is defined as*

$$\exists y_1, \ldots, y_{n-1} \in \mathbb{R}^k.\ \bigwedge_{1 \leq i \leq n} \left[reach^{J}_{\gamma(b_{i-1}),\gamma(b_i)}(y_{i-1}, y_i) \vee reach^{F}_{\gamma(b_{i-1}),\gamma(b_i)}(y_{i-1}, y_i) \right].$$

So, if we can disprove the constraint $\exists y_0 \in \mathbb{R}^k.\ reach_w(y_0, y_n)$ and w does not have self-jumps, then w is m-spurious. We use the solver RSOLVER [15, 16], which is based on interval-constraint-propagation techniques [8]. Constraints as, e.g., the constraint in Thm. 2 can be solved efficiently by RSOLVER, where the correctness is not affected by rounding errors. We use the following feature of RSOLVER: take as input a constraint ϕ and a box B and output a box B' such that $B' \subseteq B$, where B' contains the solutions of ϕ in B. We denote this algorithm by $Prune(\phi, B)$. Note that if B' is empty, we know that ϕ has no solution in B.

If the constraint of Thm. 2 does have a solution, we are interested in a sub-box of B_n that contains all its solutions. However, RSOLVER would spend time to compute such sub-boxes not only for B_n but for the boxes $B_1, \ldots, B_n$. To

---

Algorithm 4. Counterexample checking without self-jumps

Input: word $b_0 \ldots b_n$ without self-jumps, where $\gamma(b_i) = (s_i, B_i)$, for $i \in \{0, \ldots, n\}$
Output: sub-box of $\gamma(b_n)$ containing the states in $\gamma(b_n)$ that are reachable via a trajectory following $b_0 \ldots b_n$

1: $B' \leftarrow B_0$
2: $F' \leftarrow B_0 \cap B_1$
3: **for** $1 \leq i \leq n-1$ **do**
4:      $B'_F \leftarrow proj_2(Prune(reach^F_{(s_{i-1}, F'),(s_i, B_i)}, F' \times B_i))$
5:      $B'_J \leftarrow proj_2(Prune(reach^J_{(s_{i-1}, B'),(s_i, B_i)}, B' \times B_i))$
6:      **if** $B'_F = \emptyset$ and $B'_J = \emptyset$ **then return** $\emptyset$
7:      $F' \leftarrow proj_2(Prune(reach^F_{(s_{i-1}, F'),(s_i, B'_F)}, F' \times (B'_F \cap B_{i+1}))) \cup$
            $proj_2(Prune(reach^J_{(s_{i-1}, B'),(s_i, B'_J)}, B' \times (B'_J \cap B_{i+1})))$
8:      $B' \leftarrow B'_F \cup B'_J$
9: **end for**
10: **return** $proj_2(Prune(reach^F_{(s_{n-1}, F'),(s_n, B_n)}, F' \times B_n)) \cup$
        $proj_2(Prune(reach^J_{(s_{n-1}, B'),(s_n, B_n)}, B' \times B_n))$

---

avoid this superfluous work and to deal later with words that have self-jumps, we apply RSOLVER not to the whole constraint but only to constituent pieces. We compute an over-approximation of the reachable states starting from (s_0, B_0) and in each iteration, we propagate the over-approximation to the box of the next symbol in the word. The details are in Alg. 4, where $proj_2$ denotes the function $proj_2(B) = \{y \in \mathbb{R}^k \mid (x, y) \in B, \text{ for some } x \in \mathbb{R}^k\}$, for a box $B \subseteq \mathbb{R}^{2k}$. Note that in each iteration we first compute an over-approximation B' of the set of reachable elements in the box (this is needed for following jumps) and then an over-approximation F' of the set of reachable elements in the intersection of this box and the next box (this is needed for following flows).

Corollary 1. *Assume that w does not have self-jumps. If $(s_n, y_n) \in \gamma(b_n)$ is w-reachable from an initial state in $\gamma(b_0)$ then the following constraint is satisfiable*

$$\exists y, y_0 \in B_0 . Init(s_0, y) \wedge flow_{\gamma(b_0)}(y, y_0) \wedge reach_w(y_0, y_n) .$$

So, if we can disprove the constraint in Cor. 1 for w and w does not have self-jumps, then w is p-spurious. Analogously, we can check if w is s-spurious. The corresponding adaptions of Alg. 4 are straightforward.

Now, we are left with the question of how to deal with self-jumps. The problem is that such a jump might occur arbitrarily often within a box. Note that splitting eventually removes all self-jumps that do not occur between the same point. Hence, we solve the problem by using the whole box to over-approximate the reachable information in such an abstract state. We adapt the loop in Alg. 4 in such a way that we check whether there is a jump from B_i to B_i before assigning new values to F' and B'. If such a jump exists, then we use the assignments $B' \leftarrow B$ and $F' \leftarrow B_i \cap B_{i+1}$ instead of the current assignments to F' and B'. Similarly, we deal with contracted words that might have self-jumps and where the region of the first letter contains an initial state.

Table 1. Experimental results

hybrid system	maxlen = 2			maxlen = 3			maxlen = 4		
	time	splits	size	time	splits	size	time	splits	size
2-tanks	0.40	34	20	**0.08**	6	5	0.13	6	5
car	**0.31**	0	1	0.39		1	0.50	0	1
clock	1.16	44	32	**0.68**	27	12	3.47	27	15
convoi-1	0.70	0	1	0.69	0	1	0.69	0	1
convoi	281.37	362	357	**79.27**	89	87	∞		
eco	**0.97**	45	48	8.45	43	66	127.58	43	71
focus	1.04	66	59	**0.15**	6	8	0.16	5	7
mixing	**31.57**	269	145	58.14	59	134	∞		
real-eigen	**0.11**	2	3	0.15	5	3	0.16	5	3
s-focus	**0.07**	2	4	0.13	2	4	0.19	2	4
trivial-hard	∞			**0.04**	5	6	0.06	5	6
van-der-pole	51.66	687	156	**0.77**	12	12	1.83	15	10

6   Experimental Results

We used our problem database[2] of hybrid systems from the literature as well as some new hybrid systems to evaluate our approach. Our implementation uses the following heuristic to split regions (see line 22 of Alg. 3). We choose a box with maximal side length. We split this box by bisecting one of its sides, where we use a round-robin strategy to choose the box side.

The experimental results are summarized in Tab. 1 for different values of $maxlen$ (the running times are in seconds; the symbol ∞ means "more than 600 seconds"; the columns "size" show the peak automata sizes). We used a computer with an Intel Pentium 2.60 GHz CPU with 512 Mbytes of main memory running Linux. Four hybrid system in our database (1-flow, circuit, heating, navigation) could not be verified within the time limit with any of the values of $maxlen$. They are not listed in the table.

First, recall that for $maxlen = 2$ the language-based approach is closely related to the standard approach of using transition systems (see discussion after Thm. 1 in §3). In particular, when applying the same heuristics, the number of splittings is identical for transition systems and $maxlen = 2$. Second, observe that for almost all test cases, the number of splittings decreases considerably when choosing $maxlen = 3$ instead of $maxlen = 2$. That means, (i) checking the existence of trajectories between two and three regions and (ii) exploiting this information when there are no trajectories is effective in reducing the number of region splittings. Third, observe that the number of splittings is approx. the same for $maxlen = 3$ and $maxlen = 4$. This is somewhat surprising. Fourth, observe that a smaller number of splittings does not necessarily result in better running times. For instance, for the test case mixing, the version with $maxlen = 2$ is faster than the version with $maxlen = 3$ by a factor of nearly 2 although approx. 4.5 times more splittings are needed. This can be explained as follows: For larger values of

---

[2] See http://hsolver.sourceforge.net/benchmarks for details and references.

maxlen, significantly more words are analyzed in an iteration of the algorithm. Profiling of our prototype implementation revealed that the time consumed by the solver for checking if a word is spurious remains rather small in comparison to the time consumed by the operations that maintain and refine the abstractions. Finally, we remark that the sizes of the DFAs remain rather small.

In summary, the experimental results suggest that $maxlen = 4$ is not a good choice, since the version with $maxlen = 4$ is always outperformed by one of the versions with $maxlen = 2$ or $maxlen = 3$. For larger values of $maxlen$, we expect that the running times increase further. Between $maxlen = 2$ and $maxlen = 3$ there is no clear winner. However, the version with $maxlen = 3$ seems to be more robust: for some test cases, the running times for $maxlen = 3$ are significantly faster than for $maxlen = 2$ and in the cases where $maxlen = 2$ is faster, the running times for $maxlen = 3$ increase only moderately (except the test case eco, where the number of splittings varies only slightly and the version with $maxlen = 2$ outperforms the version with $maxlen = 3$ by a factor of approx. 8).

We see mainly two reasons why our algorithm fails on the four examples 1-flow, circuit, heating, and navigation. First, since the used solver wraps the solutions for a given constraint into boxes, we obtain an over-approximation when solving a constraint. Sometimes these over-approximations are too coarse such that many splits are needed before we are able to identify a word as spurious. Second, some of the examples are not robustly safe, i.e., they become unsafe under some small perturbation [11]. Sometimes we can succeed by using another splitting heuristic. For example, our algorithm would verify 1-flow easily (for all values of *maxlen*) if we bisect in the first iteration the box on the third side and not on the first.

7   Conclusion

We presented a language-based approach to represent and refine abstractions for hybrid system verification. The advantage of using languages as abstractions instead of finite transition systems is that languages can over-approximate the behaviors of hybrid systems more accurately. On the one hand, the costs to maintain and refine these abstractions increase. On the other hand, our experiments show that the number of abstract states often reduces significantly. Moreover, we generalized the method that is used in the verification tool HSOLVER [18, 19, 17] to analyze non-empty sequences of abstract states of arbitrary finite length.

Future work includes the design of more sophisticated data structures to maintain such language-based abstractions and to investigate termination issues of this approach. It is also future work to incorporate better heuristics (e.g., for splitting regions and the words that are analyzed in an iteration). It is open if the techniques in [10] can be used for the language-based approach. Finally, we want to investigate the use of ω-languages and Büchi automata as abstractions for hybrid systems for verifying progress properties, like stability of hybrid systems.

References

1. R. Alur, T. Dang, and F. Ivančić. Predicate abstraction for reachability analysis of hybrid systems. *ACM Trans. Embedded Comput. Syst.*, 5(1):152–199, 2006.
2. E. Asarin, G. Schneider, and S. Yovine. On the decidability of the reachability problem for planar differential inclusions. In *Hybrid Systems: Computation and Control (HSCC'01)*, volume 2034 of *Lect. Notes Comput. Sci.*, pages 89–104, 2001.
3. T. Brihaye and C. Michaux. On the expressiveness and decidability of o-minimal hybrid systems. *J. Complexity*, 21(4):447–478, 2005.
4. T. Brihaye, C. Michaux, C. Rivière, and C. Troestler. On o-minimal hybrid systems. In *Hybrid Systems: Computation and Control (HSCC'04)*, volume 2993 of *Lect. Notes Comput. Sci.*, pages 219–233, 2004.
5. E. Clarke, A. Fehnker, Z. Han, B. Krogh, J. Ouaknine, O. Stursberg, and M. Theobald. Abstraction and counterexample-guided refinement in model checking of hybrid systems. *Internat. J. Found. Comput. Sci.*, 14(4):583–604, 2003.
6. E. Clarke, O. Grumberg, S. Jha, Y. Lu, and H. Veith. Counterexample-guided abstraction refinement for symbolic model checking. *J. ACM*, 50(5):752–794, 2003.
7. D. Dams. Comparing abstraction refinement algorithms. In *Proc. of 2nd Workshop on Software Model Checking (SoftMC'03)*, volume 89(3) of *Electr. Notes Theor. Comput. Sci.*, pages 405–416, 2003.
8. E. Davis. Constraint propagation with interval labels. *Artif. Intell.*, 32(3):281–331, 1987.
9. L. Doyen, T. A. Henzinger, and J.-F. Raskin. Automatic rectangular refinement of affine hybrid systems. In *Formal Modeling and Analysis of Timed Systems (FORMATS'05)*, volume 3829 of *Lect. Notes Comput. Sci.*, pages 144–161, 2005.
10. A. Fehnker, E. Clarke, S. Jha, and B. Krogh. Refining abstractions of hybrid systems using counterexample fragments. In *Hybrid Systems: Computation and Control (HSCC'05)*, volume 3414 of *Lect. Notes Comput. Sci.*, pages 242–257, 2005.
11. M. Fränzle. Analysis of hybrid systems: An ounce of realism can save an infinity of states. In *Computer Science Logic (CSL'99)*, volume 1683 of *Lect. Notes Comput. Sci.*, pages 126–140, 1999.
12. T. A. Henzinger, P. W. Kopke, A. Puri, and P. Varaiya. What's decidable about hybrid automata. *J. Comput. System Sci.*, 57:94–124, 1998.
13. N. Klarlund, A. Møller, and M. I. Schwartzbach. MONA implementation secrets. *Internat. J. Found. Comput. Sci.*, 13(4):571–586, 2002.
14. M. Kloetzer and C. Belta. Reachability analysis of multi-affine systems. In *Hybrid Systems: Computation and Control (HSCC'06)*, volume 3927 of *Lect. Notes Comput. Sci.*, pages 348–362, 2006.
15. S. Ratschan. RSOLVER. http://rsolver.sourceforge.net. Software package.
16. S. Ratschan. Continuous first-order constraint satisfaction. In *Artificial Intelligence, Automated Reasoning, and Symbolic Computation (AISC'02)*, volume 2385 of *Lect. Notes Comput. Sci.*, pages 181–195, 2002.
17. S. Ratschan and Z. She. Safety verification of hybrid systems by constraint propagation based abstraction refinement. *ACM Trans. Embedded Comput. Syst.* To appear.
18. S. Ratschan and Z. She. HSOLVER. http://hsolver.sourceforge.net. Software package.
19. S. Ratschan and Z. She. Safety verification of hybrid systems by constraint propagation based abstraction refinement. In *Hybrid Systems: Computation and Control (HSCC'05)*, volume 3414 of *Lect. Notes Comput. Sci.*, pages 573–589, 2005.
20. S. Ratschan and Z. She. Constraints for continuous reachability in the verification of hybrid systems. In *Artificial Intelligence and Symbolic Computation (AISC'06)*, volume 4120 of *Lect. Notes Comput. Sci.*, pages 196–210, 2006.

More Precise Partition Abstractions

Harald Fecher[1] and Michael Huth[2]

[1] Christian-Albrechts-University Kiel, Germany
hf@informatik.uni-kiel.de
[2] Imperial College London, United Kingdom
M.Huth@doc.imperial.ac.uk

Abstract. We define, for any partition of a state space and for formulas of the modal μ-calculus, two variants of precision for abstractions that have that partition set as state space. These variants are defined via satisfaction parity games in which the Refuter can replace a concrete state with any state in the same partition before, respectively after, a quantifier move. These games are independent of the kind of abstraction. Our first variant makes the abstraction games of de Alfaro et al. model-independent, captures the definition of precision given by Shoham & Grumberg, and corresponds to generalized Kripke modal transition systems. Our second variant is then shown, for a fixed abstraction function, to render more precise abstractions through μ-automata without fairness. We discuss tradeoffs of both variants in terms of the size of abstractions, the perceived cost of their synthesis via theorem provers, and the preservation of equations that are valid over concrete models. Finally, we sketch a combination of both abstraction methods.

1 Introduction

Model checking [4,20] provides a framework for verifying properties of systems: a system is represented by a mathematical model M, a property of interest is coded within a formal language (in this paper the modal μ-calculus [18]) as some ϕ, and satisfaction is a formally defined predicate $M \models \phi$. Since the size of M is often exponential or even infinite in its description, alternatives to the direct computation of $M \models \phi$ are needed. Predicate abstraction [14] addresses this by constructing an abstract model M^α from a partition of the state space of M such that certain properties of M^α also hold in M.

Dams [7] develops techniques that produce an abstract model M^α of M, with an abstraction relation between states of M and states of M^α, that is as precise as possible with respect to that abstraction relation: no other abstraction of M with the *same* abstraction relation as M^α will satisfy more properties that hold for M. This links "precision" to "completeness" as used in abstract interpretation [6]. Such notions of precision have then been studied further in the literature as, e.g., in [5,8,21,23,15]. De Alfaro et al. [1] define precision for the (alternating-time) μ-calculus for may- and must-transitions via a parity game in which the Refuter can replace a concrete state with any state in the same partition. In order to obtain a model-independent definition of precision (which cannot speak of must- and may-transitions) we transform their games into a satisfaction game, restricting our attention to the modal μ-calculus and to partition-based abstraction. We call the resulting approach *pre-abstraction*.

B. Cook and A. Podelski (Eds.): VMCAI 2007, LNCS 4349, pp. 167–181, 2007.

Main contribution. In this paper, we present a new variant of precision for abstractions over an underlying state space partition. It is similar to the definition of pre-abstraction except that the Refuter can replace a concrete state with any state in the same partition *after* a quantifier move (and not before, as is the case for pre-abstraction). We show that our variant of precision renders more precise abstractions in the form of μ-automata without fairness, whereas generalized Kripke modal transition systems are obtained from pre-abstraction. Both notions are incremental and sound for abstraction-based verification, and so suitable enhancements for algorithms based on counter-example-guided abstraction-refinement (CEGAR). Our discussion shows that both notions have their relative merits, so tools may benefit from having both notions at their disposal. Since we work with state space partitions, e.g. as derived in a predicate abstraction, we limit our attention to functional abstraction relations throughout.

Further related work. In [10] a kind of model is developed for which precise, finite-state abstractions can be computed by a generalization of predicate abstraction. Shoham & Grumberg [22] define precision also independent of the abstract models and in terms of properties of algebraic operators, instead of coinduction in terms of games. Their approach coincides with pre-abstraction for partition based abstractions, a fact we show in this paper, but also considers arbitrary abstraction relations, which render abstract models with may-hypertransitions. An alternative to studying the precision of abstract models is the analysis of precision of model checking algorithms: Bruns & Godefroid develop generalized model checking in [3] as an improvement of the compositional model checking semantics in [2], and Jagadeesan & Godefroid apply this in the context of abstraction refinement in [12]. Semantically self-minimizing formulas [13] enjoy the property that the compositional check of [2] yields the same result as the expensive one based on the thorough semantics of generalized model checking in [3].

Outline. In Section 2 we review Kripke structures, alternating tree automata, and their standard satisfaction game. For an abstraction function "pre-abstraction", and our new variant "post-abstraction", are presented in Section 3, shown to be sound approximations of standard satisfaction games, and our new variant is proved to be more precise than pre-abstraction. In Sections 4 and 5, these variant games — which operate on the concrete state space — are proven to have equivalent versions on abstract models: pre-abstraction corresponds to using generalized Kripke modal transition systems, and post-abstraction to using μ-automata without fairness. In Section 6 we sketch how both kinds of abstract models can be (approximatively) synthesized with the help of a theorem prover. Both abstraction methods are compared in Section 7 in terms of abstraction sizes and the existence of abstract models that witness a property. The incremental nature of both abstraction techniques is established in Section 8. A combination of both abstraction techniques is discussed in Section 9 and conclusions are stated in Section 10.

2   Preliminaries

Throughout, $\mathbb{P}(S)$ denotes the power set of a set S. Functional composition is denoted by $\circ$. For a relation $\rho \subseteq B \times C$ with subset $X \subseteq B$ we write $X.\rho$ for $\{c \in C \mid \exists b \in$

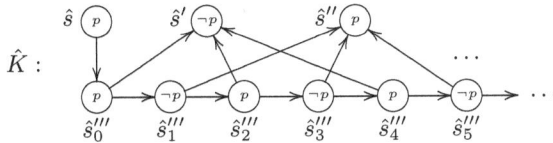

$\hat{K}$:

Fig. 1. A Kripke structure. The propositions true (resp. false) at a state are depicted (resp. depicted in negated form) within state borders. Arrows $s \rightarrow s'$ denote $(s, s') \in R$. State names are depicted close to the corresponding state.

$X \colon (b, c) \in \rho\}$. For a sequence of tuples Φ we write $\Phi[i]$ for the sequence obtained from Φ through projection into the i-th coordinate. Let $\mathrm{map}(f, \Phi)$ be the sequence obtained from Φ by applying function f to all elements of Φ in situ.

Kripke structures. Without loss of generality, we won't consider action labels on models in this paper. Thus the concrete models, e.g. discrete dynamical systems or the semantical models of programs, considered here are Kripke structures over a finite set of propositions AP, the building blocks for properties one wants to model check.

Definition 1 (Kripke structure). *A Kripke structure K over AP is a tuple (S, R, L) such that S is a set of states, $R \subseteq S \times S$ its state transition relation, and $L \colon S \rightarrow \mathbb{P}(\mathrm{AP})$ its labeling function.*

A Kripke structure is illustrated in Figure 1.

Alternating tree automata. We present the modal μ-calculus in its equivalent form of alternating tree automata [24].

Definition 2 (Tree automata). *An alternating tree automaton $A = (Q_A, \delta_A, \Theta_A)$ has*

- *a finite, nonempty set of states $(q \in) Q_A$*
- *a transition relation δ_A mapping automaton states to one of the following forms, where q', q'' are automaton states and p propositions from AP: $p \mid \neg p \mid q' \mid q' \tilde{\wedge} q'' \mid q' \tilde{\vee} q'' \mid \mathsf{EX}\, q' \mid \mathsf{AX} q'$ and*
- *an acceptance condition $\Theta_A \colon Q_A \rightarrow \mathbb{N}$ with finite image, where an infinite sequence of automata states is accepted iff the maximal acceptance number of those that occur infinitely often is even.*

An alternating tree automaton is depicted in Figure 2. For any infinite but bounded sequence n of elements in $\mathbb{N}$ we write $\sup(n)$ for the largest m that occurs in n infinitely often. The satisfaction relation of Kripke structures is defined via 2-person games over configurations with players Verifier and Refuter. In such games, only one player may move in a given configuration and a strategy for a player is a partial function that, given a finite word of configurations that ends in a configuration of that player, determines the new configuration whose choice is consistent with the rules of the game.

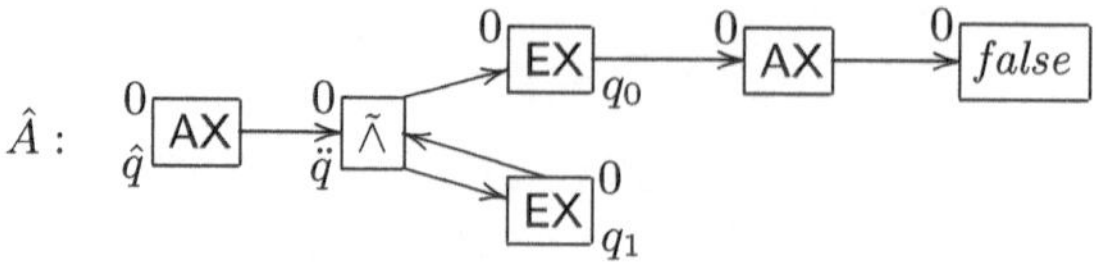

$$\hat{A}:$$

Fig. 2. An alternating tree automaton. Accepting values are depicted next to states. At state $\hat{q}$, it expresses that, after any transition, (i) there is a transition (to q_0) such that no further transition is possible; and (ii) there is a transition (to q_1) such that $\ddot{q}$ holds again.

Definition 3 (Satisfaction game).

- *Finite satisfaction plays for Kripke structure K and alternating tree automaton A have the rules and winning conditions given in Table 1. An infinite play Φ is a win for Verifier iff $\sup(\mathrm{map}(\Theta, \Phi[2]))$ is even; otherwise it is won by Refuter.*
- *Kripke structure K satisfies automaton A in $(s, q) \in S \times Q$, written $(K, s) \models (A, q)$, iff Verifier has a strategy for the corresponding satisfaction game between K and A with which he wins all satisfaction plays started at (s, q).*

Table 1. Rules for satisfaction game at configuration $(s, q) \in S \times Q$, specified through a case analysis on the value of $\delta(q)$. Satisfaction plays are sequences of configurations generated thus.

p: Verifier wins if $p \in L(s)$; Refuter wins if $p \notin L(s)$
$\neg p$: Verifier wins if $p \notin L(s)$; Refuter wins if $p \in L(s)$
q': the next configuration is (s, q')
$q_1 \tilde{\wedge} q_2$: Refuter picks a q' from $\{q_1, q_2\}$; the next configuration is (s, q')
$q_1 \tilde{\vee} q_2$: Verifier picks a q' from $\{q_1, q_2\}$; the next configuration is (s, q')
$\mathsf{EX}\, q'$: Verifier picks $s' \in \{s\}.R$; the next configuration is (s', q')
$\mathsf{AX}\, q'$: Refuter picks $s' \in \{s\}.R$; the next configuration is (s', q').

Example 1. For the Kripke structure $\hat{K}$ in Figure 1 and the alternating tree automaton $\hat{A}$ in Figure 2 we have $(\hat{K}, \hat{s}) \models (\hat{A}, \hat{q})$: at the EX-state q_0 Verifier chooses the transition pointing to $\hat{s}'$ or $\hat{s}''$, respectively; at the EX-state q_1 Verifier chooses the transition along the lower line of states in $\hat{K}$.

3 Partition-Induced Satisfaction Games

We introduce two variants of the satisfaction game between a Kripke structure K with state set S and an alternating tree automaton A: a pre-game and a post-game, referring to the pre- and post-image of the state transition relation of the Kripke structure, respectively. These games are derived from a surjective abstraction function $\alpha: S \to I$ that maps concrete states $s \in S$ into designated abstract ones $\alpha(s) \in I$. States s and s' are compatible iff $\alpha(s) = \alpha(s')$.

Intuitively, the imprecision residing in the state space partition is captured by Refuter's ability to exchange compatible states. If such exchanges happen only prior to quantifier moves, Verifier can only verify properties that hold for all compatible states of the current configuration (which therefore will correspond to must-hypertransitions). If such exchanges happen only after quantifier moves, Verifier has more freedom and is expected to be able to verify more properties (captured by transitions in μ-automata).

Technically, configurations of the pre-game are pairs $(i, q) \in I \times Q_A$, but Verifier will always be forced to move with respect to a concrete configuration (s, q) with $\alpha(s) = i$ where s is chosen by the Refuter, and these moves for Verifier are as for the ordinary satisfaction game. Configurations of the post-game are pairs $(s, q) \in S \times Q_A$. The difference between the pre- and the post-game resides in the capabilities of Refuter. In the pre-game he can switch between compatible states *before* a quantifier or literal move by either player is being made; in the post-game he may switch to a compatible state *after* a quantifier move by either player has been made. We formalize this:

Definition 4 (Pre-games and post-games). *Let $K = (S, R, L)$ be a Kripke structure and $\alpha \colon S \to I$ a surjective abstraction function. Pre-games:*

- *Finite pre-satisfaction plays for K, α, and alternating tree automaton A have the rules and winning conditions given in Table 2. An infinite play Φ is won by Verifier iff* $\sup(\mathrm{map}(\Theta, \Phi[2]))$ *is even; otherwise it is won by Refuter.*
- *Model K pre-satisfies automaton A for α in $(s, q) \in S \times Q$, written $(K, s) \models_{-}^{\alpha} (A, q)$, iff Verifier has a strategy for the corresponding pre-satisfaction game between K and A such that Verifier wins all pre-satisfaction plays started at $(\alpha(s), q)$ with that strategy.*

Post-games:

- *Finite post-satisfaction plays for K, α, and alternating tree automaton A have the rules and winning conditions given in Table 3. An infinite play Φ is won by Verifier iff* $\sup(\mathrm{map}(\Theta, \Phi[2]))$ *is even; otherwise it is won by Refuter.*
- *Model K post-satisfies automaton A for α in $(s, q) \in S \times Q$, written $(K, s) \models_{+}^{\alpha} (A, q)$, iff Verifier has a strategy for the corresponding post-satisfaction game between K and A such that Verifier wins all post-satisfaction plays started at (s, q) with that strategy.*

Example 2. Consider the Kripke structure $\hat{K}$ from Figure 1 and the alternating tree automaton $\hat{A}$ from Figure 2. Let $\hat{\alpha}$ be the function that maps $\hat{s}$ to $\hat{i}$, $\hat{s}'$ to $\hat{i}'$, $\hat{s}''$ to $\hat{i}''$, and $\hat{s}'''_n$ to $\hat{i}'''$ for $n \in \mathbb{N}$. Then $(\hat{K}, \hat{s}) \models_{-}^{\hat{\alpha}} (\hat{A}, \hat{q})$: at the EX-state q_0 Verifier chooses $\hat{s}'$ or $\hat{s}''$, depending on which one is possible; at the EX-state q_1 Verifier chooses an element from $\{\hat{s}'''_n \mid n \in \mathbb{N}\}$, depending on which one is possible. Furthermore, $(\hat{K}, \hat{s}) \models_{+}^{\hat{\alpha}} (\hat{A}, \hat{q})$ holds, reasoned similarly as before.

Both pre-satisfaction and post-satisfaction are sound, their satisfaction instances imply satisfaction instances of the underlying Kripke structure. Moreover, post-satisfaction is more precise than pre-satisfaction. Formally:

Theorem 1 (Soundness of abstract satisfaction games). *Let $K = (S, R, L)$ be a Kripke structure and $\alpha \colon S \to I$ a surjective function. Then pre-satisfaction implies* *post-satisfaction, which in turn implies satisfaction: for all states s and all rooted alternating tree automata (A, q):*

$$(K, s) \models_{-}^{\alpha} (A, q) \Rightarrow (K, s) \models_{+}^{\alpha} (A, q)$$
$$(K, s) \models_{+}^{\alpha} (A, q) \Rightarrow (K, s) \models (A, q) .$$

Moreover, the above implications are strict in general.

Table 2. Rules for pre-satisfaction game for $\alpha \colon S \to I$ at configuration $(i, q) \in I \times Q$, based on a case analysis of $\delta(q)$. Pre-satisfaction plays are sequences of configurations generated thus.

p: Refuter picks $s \in S$ with $\alpha(s) = i$; Verifier wins if $p \in L(s)$; Refuter wins if $p \notin L(s)$
$\neg p$: Refuter picks $s \in S$ with $\alpha(s) = i$; Verifier wins if $p \notin L(s)$; Refuter wins if $p \in L(s)$
q': the next configuration is (i, q')
$q_1 \tilde{\wedge} q_2$: Refuter picks a q' from $\{q_1, q_2\}$; the next configuration is (i, q')
$q_1 \tilde{\vee} q_2$: Verifier picks a q' from $\{q_1, q_2\}$; the next configuration is (i, q')
$\mathsf{EX}\, q'$: Refuter picks $s \in S$ with $\alpha(s) = i$; Verifier picks $s' \in \{s\}.R$; the next configuration is
    $(\alpha(s'), q')$
$\mathsf{AX}\, q'$: Refuter picks $s \in S$ with $\alpha(s) = i$ and then picks $s' \in \{s\}.R$; the next configuration is
    $(\alpha(s'), q')$.

Table 3. Rules for post-satisfaction game at configuration $(s, q) \in S \times Q$, specified through a case analysis of $\delta(q)$. Omitted rules are as for the standard satisfaction game in Table 1. Post-satisfaction plays are sequences of configurations generated thus.

$\mathsf{EX}\, q'$: Verifier picks $s' \in \{s\}.R$; Refuter picks $s'' \in S$ with $\alpha(s') = \alpha(s'')$; the next configu-
    ration is (s'', q')
$\mathsf{AX}\, q'$: Refuter picks $s' \in \{s\}.R$ and then some $s'' \in S$ with $\alpha(s') = \alpha(s'')$; the next configu-
    ration is (s', q').

Example 3. The strictness of the inclusions in Theorem 1 can be seen as follows: For the Kripke structure $\hat{K}$ from Figure 1 and $\hat{\alpha}$ from Example 2 we have $(\hat{K}, \hat{s}) \models \mathsf{EX}\, p$, but $(\hat{K}, \hat{s}) \not\models_{+}^{\hat{\alpha}} \mathsf{EX}\, p$; and $(\hat{K}, \hat{s}) \models_{+}^{\hat{\alpha}} \mathsf{EX}\, (p \,\tilde{\vee}\, \mathsf{EX}\, p)$, but $(\hat{K}, \hat{s}) \not\models_{-}^{\hat{\alpha}} \mathsf{EX}\, (p \,\tilde{\vee}\, \mathsf{EX}\, p)$.

The notions of pre- and post-satisfaction, and their soundness with respect to satisfaction, make them suitable for abstraction-based model checking. Their operational make-up appeals to information that resides only in the concrete model to begin with. Therefore a method for abstracting concrete models, such that the satisfaction game over abstract models precisely captures the pre- (resp. post-)game for the concrete model, is needed. We carry out this programme in the next two sections and show, as perhaps expected, that the generalized Kripke modal transition systems of [22] and their satisfaction game capture pre-satisfaction. For post-satisfaction, we suggest to work with μ-automata [16,9] without fairness and show a precise correspondence as well.

4   Precise Abstractions for Pre-satisfaction

Our models for abstraction of pre-satisfaction are taken from [22], and are a variant of disjunctive modal transition systems [19].

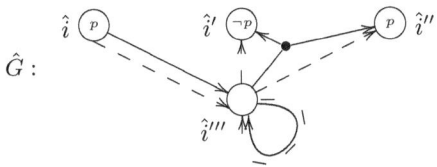

$\hat{G}$:

Fig. 3. A generalized Kripke modal transition system. Propositional labelings and state names are used as in Figure 1. Dashed arrows model may-transitions and solid arrows model must-transitions. The self-loop at state $\hat{i}'''$ is a must-transition with $\{\hat{i}'''\}$ as target. The must-hypertransition from $\hat{i}'''$ has set $\{\hat{i}', \hat{i}''\}$ as target.

Definition 5 (Generalized Kripke modal transition systems). *A generalized Kripke modal transition system M over* AP *is a tuple (S, R^-, R^+, L) with S as set of states, $R^- \subseteq S \times \mathbb{P}(S)$ as set of* must-*transitions,[1] $R^+ \subseteq S \times S$ as set of* may-*transitions, and $L\colon S \to \mathbb{P}(\mathrm{AP} \cup \{\neg p \mid p \in \mathrm{AP}\})$ as labeling function. To highlight that a must-transition (s, D) has a non-singleton target set D we speak of must-hypertransitions. This generalized Kripke modal transition system M is* finite *if S is finite.*

A generalized Kripke modal transition system is illustrated in Figure 3. We now define satisfaction over generalized Kripke modal transition systems:

Definition 6 (Satisfaction for generalized Kripke modal transition systems).

- *Finite satisfaction plays for a generalized Kripke modal transition system G and an alternating tree automaton A have the rules and winning conditions as stated in Table 4. An infinite play Φ is a* win *for Verifier iff $\sup(\mathrm{map}(\Theta, \Phi[2]))$ is even; otherwise it is won by the Refuter.*
- *The generalized Kripke modal transition system G* satisfies *the alternating tree automaton A in configuration $(s, q) \in S \times Q$, written $(G, s) \models (A, q)$, iff Verifier has a strategy for the corresponding satisfaction game between G and A such that Verifier wins all satisfaction plays started at (s, q) with that strategy.*

The satisfaction game in Table 4 amounts to playing a parity game, so the decidability of such satisfaction instances is in UP $\cap$ coUP [17].

Example 4. For the generalized Kripke modal transition system $\hat{G}$ from Figure 3 and the alternating tree automaton $\hat{A}$ from Figure 2 we have $(\hat{G}, \hat{i}) \models (\hat{A}, \hat{q})$: at the EX-state q_0 Verifier chooses the must-transition $(\hat{i}''', \{\hat{i}', \hat{i}''\})$; at the EX-state q_1 Verifier chooses the self-loop $(\hat{i}''', \{\hat{i}'''\})$. Note that $(\hat{G}, \hat{i})$ neither satisfies EX $(p \tilde{\vee} \mathrm{EX}\, p)$ nor its "negation" AX $(\neg p \tilde{\wedge} \mathrm{AX}\, \neg p)$.

Every Kripke structure K has a natural representation as a generalized Kripke modal transition system $G[K]$ where $L_{G[K]}(s) = L_K(s) \cup \{\neg p \mid p \notin L_K(s)\}$, $R^+_{G[K]} = R$, and $R^-_{G[K]}$ is R embedded from $S \times S$ into $S \times \mathbb{P}(S)$. Since $(K, s) \models (A, q)$ iff $(G[K], s) \models (A, q)$ the overloading of "satisfaction" and its symbol $\models$ are justified.

---

[1] We adhere to the convention of using $-$ for must-transitions and $+$ for may-transitions and note that the paper [22] uses $+$ for must-transitions and $-$ for may-transitions.

Table 4. Rules for satisfaction game between a generalized Kripke modal transition system and an alternating tree automaton at configuration $(s, q) \in S \times Q$, based on a case analysis of $\delta(q)$. Omitted rules are as in Table 1. Satisfaction plays are sequences of configurations generated thus.

$\neg p$: Verifier wins if $\neg p \in L(s)$; Refuter wins if $\neg p \notin L(S)$
$\mathsf{EX}\, q'$: Verifier picks $D' \in \{s\}.R^-$; Refuter picks $s' \in D'$; the next configuration is (s', q')
$\mathsf{AX}\, q'$: Refuter picks $s' \in \{s\}.R^+$; the next configuration is (s', q')

For a surjective function $\alpha: S \to I$ and Kripke structure $K = (S, R, L)$ we follow [22]: I is the abstract state set, a may-transition between two abstract states exists iff there is a transition in the Kripke structure such that the source and target are abstracted to the corresponding abstract states, and a must-transition from i to $I'(\subseteq I)$ exists iff every Kripke state s abstracted to i has a transition to an element that is abstracted to an element from I'. Abstract labelings have a similar interpretation. Formally:

Definition 7 (Pre-abstractions). *Let* $K = (S, R, L)$ *be a Kripke structure and* $\alpha: S \to I$ *a surjective function. Then the pre-abstraction of K for α is the generalized Kripke modal transition system* $G_\alpha^K = (I, R_{K,\alpha}^-, R_{K,\alpha}^+, L_{K,\alpha})$ *where*

$$R_{K,\alpha}^- = \{(i, D) \mid \forall s \in S: [\alpha(s) = i \Rightarrow \exists s' \in \{s\}.R : \alpha(s') \in D]\}$$
$$R_{K,\alpha}^+ = \{(i, i') \mid \exists (s, s') \in R: [\alpha(s) = i \,\&\, \alpha(s') = i']\}$$
$$L_{K,\alpha}(i) = \{p \mid p \in \mathrm{AP} \,\&\, \forall s \in S: [\alpha(s) = i \Rightarrow p \in L(s)]\} \cup$$
$$\{\neg p \mid p \in \mathrm{AP} \,\&\, \forall s \in S: [\alpha(s) = i \Rightarrow p \notin L(s)]\}$$

The pre-abstraction is finite whenever I is finite.

Example 5. The pre-abstraction of $\hat{K}$ from Figure 1 for $\hat{\alpha}$ from Example 3 is the generalized Kripke modal transition system from Figure 3, where must-transitions (s, D) are omitted if they have a must-transition (s, D') with $D' \subseteq D$ — those omissions won't impact the satisfaction relation and can speed up the synthesis of abstractions.

Possible occurrences of must-hypertransitions make the complexity of the abstraction exponential in I in the worst case. Pre-abstraction is precise and sound for pre-satisfaction, as already illustrated via Examples 2, 3, 4 and 5:

Theorem 2 (Correspondence of pre-game and pre-abstraction). *Let* $K = (S, R, L)$ *be a Kripke structure, A an alternating tree automaton, $q \in Q_A$, $s \in S$, and $\alpha: S \to I$ a surjective function. Then*

$$(K, s) \models_-^\alpha (A, q) \iff (G_\alpha^K, \alpha(s)) \models (A, q)$$

5   Precise Abstractions for Post-satisfaction

The models we propose for post-abstractions are μ-automata [16] without fairness. We use the notation of [9]. All μ-automata in this paper are without fairness.

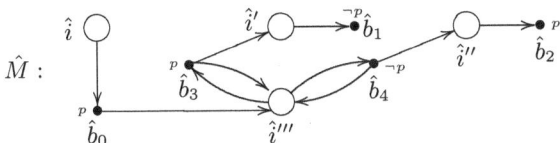

Fig. 4. A μ-automaton. OR-states are depicted as unfilled circles and BRANCH-states as filled circles. Literals (shown in smaller font) that are true at a BRANCH-state are depicted next to it. The name of a state is also shown close to it.

Definition 8 (μ-automata). *A μ-automaton M over AP is a tuple $(O, B, \Rightarrow, \rightarrow, L)$ such that $(o \in) O$ is the set of OR-states, $(b \in) B$ the set of BRANCH-states (disjoint from O), $\Rightarrow \subseteq O \times B$ the OR-transition relation, $\rightarrow \subseteq B \times O$ the BRANCH-transition relation, and $L \colon B \rightarrow \mathbb{P}(AP)$ the labeling function. M is* finite *if both O and B are.*

A μ-automaton is given in Figure 4. We define satisfaction over μ-automata next:

Definition 9 (Satisfaction for μ-automata).

- *Finite satisfaction plays for a μ-automaton M and alternating tree automaton A have the rules and winning conditions stated in Table 5. An infinite play Φ is a win for Verifier iff $\sup(\mathrm{map}(\Theta, \Phi[2]))$ is even; otherwise it is won by Refuter.*
- *The μ-automaton M satisfies the alternating tree automaton A in $(\beta, q) \in (O \cup B) \times Q$, written $(M, \beta) \models (A, q)$, iff Verifier has a strategy for the corresponding satisfaction game between M and A such that Verifier wins all satisfaction plays started at (β, q) with her strategy.*

Table 5. Rules for satisfaction game between a μ-automaton M and an alternating tree automaton A at configuration $(\beta, q) \in (O \cup B) \times Q$, based on the given case analysis. Satisfaction plays are sequences of configurations generated thus.

$\beta \in O$: Refuter picks $b \in \{\beta\}.\Rightarrow$; the next configuration is (b, q)
$\beta \in B$ and $q = p$: Verifier wins if $p \in L(\beta)$; Refuter wins if $p \notin L(\beta)$
$\beta \in B$ and $q = \neg p$: Verifier wins if $p \notin L(\beta)$; Refuter wins if $p \in L(\beta)$
$\beta \in B$ and $q = q'$: the next configuration is (β, q')
$\beta \in B$ and $q = q_1 \tilde{\wedge} q_2$: Refuter picks a q' from $\{q_1, q_2\}$; the next configuration is (β, q')
$\beta \in B$ and $q = q_1 \tilde{\vee} q_2$: Verifier picks a q' from $\{q_1, q_2\}$; the next configuration is (β, q')
$\beta \in B$ and $q = \mathsf{EX}\, q'$: Verifier picks $o \in \{\beta\}.\rightarrow$; the next configuration is (o, q')
$\beta \in B$ and $q = \mathsf{AX}\, q'$: Refuter picks $o \in \{\beta\}.\rightarrow$; the next configuration is (o, q').

Similar to the satisfaction game for generalized Kripke modal transition systems, the satisfaction game for μ-automata corresponds to a parity game. So deciding such satisfaction instances is in UP $\cap$ coUP.

Example 6. For the μ-automaton $\hat{M}$ in Figure 4 and the alternating tree automaton $\hat{A}$ in Figure 2 we have $(\hat{M}, \hat{i}) \models (\hat{A}, \hat{q})$: at $(\hat{b}_3, q_1)$ and at $(\hat{b}_4, q_1)$ Verifier chooses the transition to $\hat{i}'''$; at $(\hat{b}_3, q_0)$ and at $(\hat{b}_4, q_0)$ he chooses the transition to $\hat{i}'$, resp. $\hat{i}''$. Also, it is easily seen that $\hat{G}$ satisfies neither $\mathsf{EX}\, p$ nor its "negation" $\mathsf{AX}\, \neg p$ at $\hat{q}$.

Given a surjective function $\alpha\colon S \to I$ and a Kripke structure $K = (S, R, L)$ we now show that μ-automata yield precise abstractions for post-satisfaction. We consider two states of K to be post-equivalent iff (i) they satisfy the same propositions and (ii) the same elements of the partition induced by α are reachable by their one-step transitions. The equivalence classes obtained by the post-equivalences, called post-equivalence classes, are encoded as elements from $\mathbb{P}(I \cup \mathrm{AP})$, where (i) a proposition p is valid at $b \in \mathbb{P}(I \cup \mathrm{AP})$ iff $p \in b$; and (ii) exactly those elements of the partition induced by α that are contained in b are reachable. The expression $\mathrm{BR}_\alpha^K(s)$, formally defined below, determines the post-equivalence class of s. Post-equivalence classes become BRANCH-states. The ability of Refuter to switch to an element compatible with the target of a transition is modeled in the abstraction by OR-states, elements of I. The OR-state $i \in I$ has a transition to a post-equivalence class E iff a concrete state s exists that is abstracted to i by α and yields the post-equivalence class E. Formally:

Definition 10 (Post-abstractions). *For Kripke structure $K = (S, R, L)$ and surjective function $\alpha\colon S \to I$, its* post-abstraction *is the μ-automaton M_α^K over $\mathbb{P}(I \cup \mathrm{AP})$ where*

$$O_\alpha^K = I \qquad\qquad B_\alpha^K = \mathbb{P}(I \cup \mathrm{AP})$$
$$\Rightarrow_\alpha^K = \{(i, \mathrm{BR}_\alpha^K(s)) \mid \alpha(s) = i\} \qquad \text{with } \mathrm{BR}_\alpha^K(s) = L(s) \cup \alpha(\{s\}.R)$$
$$\to_\alpha^K = \{(b, i) \mid i \in b\}$$
$$L_\alpha^K(b) = b \cap \mathrm{AP}$$

The post-abstraction is finite whenever I is finite.

Example 7. The five post-equivalence classes of $\hat{K}$ from Figure 1 for $\hat{\alpha}$ from Example 3 are $\{\hat{s}\}$, $\{\hat{s}'\}$, $\{\hat{s}''\}$, $\{\hat{s}_{2n}''' \mid n \in \mathbb{N}\}$, and $\{\hat{s}_{2n+1}''' \mid n \in \mathbb{N}\}$, having the representatives (via function BR_α^K) $\hat{b}_0 = \{p, \hat{i}'''\}$, $\hat{b}_1 = \{\}$, $\hat{b}_2 = \{p\}$, $\hat{b}_3 = \{p, \hat{i}', \hat{i}'''\}$, and $\hat{b}_4 = \{\hat{i}'', \hat{i}'''\}$. The post-abstraction of $\hat{K}$ from Figure 1 for $\hat{\alpha}$ from Example 3 is the μ-automaton from Figure 4, where non-reachable BRANCH-states from $\hat{i}$ are omitted.

The size of this abstraction can be exponential in I and in AP. The post-abstraction is precise and sound for post-satisfaction, illustrated via Examples 2, 3, 6 and 7:

Theorem 3 (Correspondence of post-game and post-abstraction). *Let $K = (S, R, L)$ be a Kripke structure, A an alternating tree automaton, $q \in Q_A$, $s \in S$, and $\alpha\colon S \to I$ a surjective function. Then*

$$(K, s) \models_+^\alpha (A, q) \iff (M_\alpha^K, \mathrm{BR}_\alpha^K(s)) \models (A, q)$$

6   Automated Synthesis of Precise Abstractions

We discuss how the pre- and post-abstraction of a program can be automatically synthesized with the use of theorem provers for a Kripke structure $K = (S, R, L)$ and surjective abstraction function $\alpha\colon S \to I$, along the lines of [14,11]. Suppose $\mathcal{L}$ is a logic that contains at least all operators of propositional logic and all $p \in \mathrm{AP}$ as predicates with a closed interpretation $[\![p]\!] \subseteq S$ such that:

(i) The interpretation of atomic propositions matches that implicit in the labeling function; for all $p \in \mathrm{AP}$ we have $\llbracket p \rrbracket = \{s \in S \mid p \in L(s)\}$.

(ii) Satisfiability and validity of $\mathcal{L}$ are decidable.

(iii) The logic $\mathcal{L}$ is effectively closed under exact successor and predecessor operations in Kripke structures; that is, for every formula $\psi \in \mathcal{L}$ and every $R \subseteq S \times S$ we can compute $\mathrm{pre}(\psi), \mathrm{post}(\psi) \in \mathcal{L}$ such that

$$\llbracket \mathrm{pre}(\psi) \rrbracket = \{s' \in S \mid \exists s \in \llbracket \psi \rrbracket : (s', s) \in R\}$$
$$\llbracket \mathrm{post}(\psi) \rrbracket = \{s' \in S \mid \exists s \in \llbracket \psi \rrbracket : (s, s') \in R\}\,.$$

(iv) The surjective abstraction function $\alpha \colon S \to I$ is representable by a set of formulas $\{\psi_i \in \mathcal{L} \mid i \in I\}$ such that, for all $i \in I$, we have $\llbracket \psi_i \rrbracket = \{s \in S \mid \alpha(s) = i\}$. (This is, for example, the case in predicate abstraction.)

The first three conditions may be relaxed, as familiar in the judicious over- and under-approximation of precise abstract models for undecidable logics.

Pre-abstraction. A may-transition from i to i' exists iff $\psi_i \wedge \mathrm{pre}(\psi_{i'})$ is satisfiable. If satisfiability is undecidable, we ensure soundness but may lose precision by adding such a may-transition whenever the satisfiability of $\psi_i \wedge \mathrm{pre}(\psi_{i'})$ is unknown. A must-transition from i to D exists iff $\psi_i \Rightarrow (\bigvee_{i' \in D} \mathrm{pre}(\psi_{i'}))$ is valid. In case of the undecidability of validity, we add a must-transition only if the validity of $\psi_i \Rightarrow (\bigvee_{i' \in D} \mathrm{pre}(\psi_{i'}))$ is known. A predicate literal l (either some p or some $\neg p$) is in $L(i)$ iff $\psi_i \Rightarrow l$ is valid. As in the treatment of must-transitions, l is ruled to be a member of $L(i)$ only if the validity of $\psi_i \Rightarrow l$ can be established.

Post-abstraction. The transitions from BRANCH-states and the labeling function rely on an implementation of set membership, as specified in Definition 10. A transition from the OR-state $i \in I$ to the BRANCH-state $b \in \mathbb{P}(I \cup \mathrm{AP})$ exists iff

$$\psi_i \wedge \bigwedge_{i' \in b \cap I} \mathrm{pre}(\psi_{i'}) \wedge \bigwedge_{i' \in I \backslash b} \neg\mathrm{pre}(\psi_{i'}) \wedge \bigwedge_{p \in b \cap \mathrm{AP}} p \wedge \bigwedge_{p \in \mathrm{AP} \backslash b} \neg p \qquad (1)$$

is satisfiable. If satisfiability is undecidable, we over-approximate by adding a transition as described above.

7   Expressiveness of Pre- and Post-abstractions

In order to obtain a fair comparison between pre- and post-abstraction, we take into account the removal of hypertransitions whose targets are supersets of other hypertransition targets, as well as the sharing of identical hypertransition targets for different hypertransition sources through, what we refer to below as, *"division points"*. Pre-abstraction can be less complex than post-abstraction for the *same* abstraction function:

Example 8. Consider the Kripke structure with state set $(\mathbb{P}(X) \setminus \{\{\}\}) \cup X$ where $X = \{x_1, ..x_n\}$, transition relation $\{(X', x) \mid X' \in \mathbb{P}(X) \setminus \{\{\}\} \,\&\, x \in X'\}$, and arbitrary labeling function. The partition, which determines α, is given by $\{\mathbb{P}(X) \setminus \{\{\}\}, \{x_1\}, ..., \{x_n\}\}$. Then the post-abstraction yields the μ-automaton with the same structure as the considered Kripke structure, except that an additional OR-state per partition element is being used. In particular, that μ-automaton has at least 2^n BRANCH-states (depending on the labeling function, up to $n - 1$ further BRANCH-states can exist), $n + 1$ OR-states (of which n are trivial, i.e., have exactly one outgoing transition), at least 2^n transitions leading to OR-states, and $n2^{n-1}$ transitions leading to BRANCH-states.

On the other hand, the corresponding pre-abstraction yields the generalized Kripke modal transition system , which has $n + 1$ states, one division point, and $n + 1$ transitions to and from that division point, and n may-transitions.

Post-abstractions, in turn, can be less complex than pre-abstractions.

Example 9. Consider the Kripke structure with state set $X \cup X'$ with $X = \{x_1, \ldots, x_n\}$ and $X' = \{x'_1, \ldots, x'_n\}$, transition relation $\{(x_i, X' \setminus \{x'_i\}) \mid i \in \{1, ..., n\}\}$, and arbitrary labeling function. The partition, determining α, is given by $\{X, \{x'_1\}, ..., \{x'_n\}\}$. Then the post-abstraction yields the μ-automaton with the same structure as the considered Kripke structure, except that an additional OR-state per partition element is being used. In particular, that μ-automaton has $2n$ BRANCH-states, $n + 1$ OR-states (where n of them are trivial in the sense aforementioned), and $n^2 + n$ transitions (of which n result from trivial OR-states).

On the other hand, the corresponding pre-abstraction yields a generalized Kripke modal transition system with $n + 1$ states, $(n^2 - n)/2$ division points (all must-hyper-transitions having a target set consisting of two elements exist), $(3n^2 - 3n)/2$ transitions to and from division points, and n may-transitions.

Examples 8 and 9 illustrate that either pre- or post-abstractions can yield smaller abstractions. Taking the size of such abstractions and cost issues of their synthesis aside, both notions can verify the same properties of the concrete models they abstract but at the potential cost of using different abstraction functions.

Theorem 4 (Equal expressiveness). *Let $K = (S, R, L)$ be a Kripke structure, $\alpha \colon S \to I$ a surjective function, and (A, q) a rooted alternating tree automaton with $(K, s) \models^\alpha_+ (A, q)$. Then the pre-abstraction of K with respect to α' satisfies (A, q) where $\alpha' \colon S \to \{\mathrm{BR}^K_\alpha(s) \mid s \in S\}$ is defined by $\alpha'(s) = \mathrm{BR}^K_\alpha(s)$.*

Note that the converse of the expressiveness stated in Theorem 4 follows from Theorem 1. Theorem 4 may suggest that post-abstraction is a redundant notion. But in terms of efficiency, pre-abstractions with respect to the derived abstraction α' are more complex than post-abstractions with respect to the original abstraction α, since the calculation of must-hypertransitions leads to an additional exponential blow up (the number of configurations for the model-checking game is exponentially larger). Must-hypertransitions are essential: Theorem 4 won't hold if only must-transitions that point to singletons are allowed.

There is a curious difference between generalized Kripke modal transition systems and μ-automata with respect to their "equational theories". We write $\phi = \psi$ for formulas ϕ and ψ of the modal μ-calculus if, for a given notion of model and satisfaction game, all states in all models have the same satisfaction instances for A_ϕ and for A_ψ — the alternating tree automata encoding the respective formulas.[2] For example, we have $p \tilde{\vee} \neg p = true$ and $\mathsf{EX}\, p \tilde{\vee} \mathsf{AX}\, \neg p = true$ for all μ-automata and $p \in \mathrm{AP}$, but these equations won't hold in generalized Kripke modal transition systems: neither $p \tilde{\vee} \neg p$ nor $\mathsf{EX}\, p \tilde{\vee} \mathsf{AX}\, \neg p$ holds in state $\hat{i}'''$ of the generalized Kripke modal transition system from Figure 3. There are equations familiar from basic modal logic that hold neither for μ-automata nor for generalized Kripke modal transition systems, e.g. $\mathsf{EX}\, q_1 \tilde{\vee} \mathsf{EX}\, q_2 = \mathsf{EX}\, (q_1 \tilde{\vee} q_2)$ which is valid over Kripke structures. It is of interest to note that these equations seem to relate to the comparison of the thorough semantics of [3] and the compositional one of [2] for model checking partial Kripke structures, e.g. $p \vee \neg p$ is valid for the thorough but not for the compositional semantics.

8   Abstraction Refinement

The precise abstractions proposed in this paper are suitable for counter-example-guided abstraction-refinement since already checked properties can be reused. For both pre- and post-satisfaction, all previously valid satisfaction instances remain to be valid if abstract states are refined by further splitting:

Theorem 5 (Incremental analysis). *Let $K = (S, R, L)$ be a Kripke structure and both $\alpha_1 \colon S \to I_1$, $f_2 \colon I_1 \to I_2$ surjective functions. Then for all s and all (A, q) we have*

$$(K, s) \models_-^{f_2 \circ \alpha_1} (A, q) \Rightarrow (K, s) \models_-^{\alpha_1} (A, q)$$
$$(K, s) \models_+^{f_2 \circ \alpha_1} (A, q) \Rightarrow (K, s) \models_+^{\alpha_1} (A, q).$$

The above theorem also guarantees confluence of abstractions. Finite-state abstractions, if they exist, can always be found in principle, regardless of the particular history of incremental refinements of an initially chosen abstraction:

Theorem 6 (Confluence). *Let $K = (S, R, L)$ be a Kripke structure and both $\alpha_1 \colon S \to I_1$, $\alpha_2 \colon S \to I_2$ surjective functions. Then there exist surjective functions $\alpha_3 \colon S \to I_3$ and $f \colon I_3 \to I_2$ such that $\alpha_2 = f \circ \alpha_3$ and, for all s and (A, q), we have*

$$(K, s) \models_-^{\alpha_1} (A, q) \Rightarrow (K, s) \models_-^{\alpha_3} (A, q)$$
$$(K, s) \models_+^{\alpha_1} (A, q) \Rightarrow (K, s) \models_+^{\alpha_3} (A, q).$$

9   Discussion

The calculation of pre-abstractions may well be more efficient than the calculation of post-abstractions, even if the resulting state space is larger as it is, e.g., the case in

---

[2] We did not define $true$ or A_{true} but they hold in all states of all (kinds of) models.

Example 9. The reason being that more complex formulas have to be checked by a theorem prover in the synthesis of the post-abstraction, as seen in Section 6. Nevertheless, whether pre- or post-abstractions work better heavily depends on the Kripke structure and the alternating tree automata one wishes to check. We now sketch how a combination of pre- and post-abstraction may result in a more precise abstraction without increasing the cost of the abstraction synthesis too much. First an approximation of the pre-abstraction, which computes only must-transitions with singletons as targets, avoids the expensive calculation of must-hypertransitions. Then, *before* the abstraction function is being refined, a post-abstraction on the just computed approximation of a pre-abstraction is calculated where the information encoded in said approximative pre-abstraction is being reused. More precisely, the post-abstraction is calculated, locally, at those abstract states where the currently existing must-transition information is insufficient to verify or falsify the property. This needs only to consider those subsets of $\mathbb{P}(I)$ that are supersets of the local must-transition targets and subsets of the local may-transition targets, speeding up the synthesis of the abstraction. This on-demand calculation of structure has already been done in [22] for pre-abstraction.

In order to obtain precise models for this abstraction process, a new kind of model has to be developed: μ-automata in which there are also may-transitions and must-transitions between OR-states. In order to reduce the post-abstraction calculation with respect to predicates in a similar way as described above, there should be a predicate labeling function, as in generalized Kripke modal transition systems, over OR-states. Note that this kind of model is really different from that of the modal automata in [9], where may-transitions are allowed from BRANCH-states to OR-states only, and the labeling function is over BRANCH-states and not over OR-states.

10   Conclusions

Using parity games and avoiding any appeal to particular kinds of models, we presented two notions of precision for partition-based abstractions. We proved that our new notion of post-abstraction is generally more precise than the already established one based on pre-abstraction, and corresponds to the use of μ-automata as abstractions. For functional abstractions, pre-abstraction is shown to be an adaptation of the abstraction games of de Alfaro et al., and to coincide with the algebraic notion of precision given recently by Shoham & Grumberg. The relative tradeoffs of these two notions have been investigated along a number of dimensions: model size, cost of synthesis, and equational theories of abstractions. A combination of both approaches has been discussed informally as planned future work. For non-functional abstraction functions, subject of future work, variant games allow Refuter to switch more than once between related states. Precision then requires more complex models in pre/post-games [22].

Acknowledgments. This work is in part financially supported by the DFG project *Refism* (FE 942/1-1) and by UK Engineering and Physical Sciences Research Council (EP/D50595X/1). We thank the anonymous referees whose comments helped to improve the presentation of this paper.

References

1. L. de Alfaro, P. Godefroid, and R. Jagadeesan. Three-valued abstractions of games: Uncertainty, but with precision. In *Proc. of LICS'04*, pages 170–179. IEEE Comp. Soc. Press, 2004.
2. G. Bruns and P. Godefroid. Model Checking Partial State Spaces with 3-Valued Temporal Logics. In *Proc. of CAV'99*, LNCS 1633, pp. 274–287, Springer, 1999.
3. G. Bruns and P. Godefroid. Generalized model checking: Reasoning about partial state spaces. In *Proc. of CONCUR'00*, LNCS 1877, pp. 168–182. Springer, 2000.
4. E. M. Clarke and E. A. Emerson. Synthesis of synchronization skeletons for branching time temporal logic. In *Logic of Programs Workshop*, LNCS 131, pp. 244–263. Springer, 1981.
5. R. Cleaveland, S. P. Iyer, and D. Yankelevich. Optimality in abstractions of model checking. In *Proc. of SAS'95*, LNCS 983, pp. 51–63. Springer, 1995.
6. P. Cousot and R. Cousot. Abstract interpretation: a unified lattice model for static analysis of programs. In *Proc. of POPL'77*, pp. 238–252, ACM Press, 1977.
7. D. Dams. *Abstract interpretation and partition refinement for model checking*. PhD thesis, Technische Universiteit Eindhoven, The Netherlands, 1996.
8. D. Dams, R. Gerth, and O. Grumberg. Abstract interpretation of reactive systems. *ACM TOPLAS*, 19(2):253–291, 1997.
9. D. Dams and K. S. Namjoshi. Automata as abstractions. In *Proc. of VMCAI'05*, LNCS 3385, pp. 216–232. Springer, 2005.
10. H. Fecher and M. Huth. Ranked Predicate Abstraction for Branching Time: Complete, Incremental, and Precise. In *Proc. of ATVA'06*, LNCS 4218, pp. 322–336. Springer, 2006.
11. P. Godefroid, M. Huth, and R. Jagadeesan. Abstraction-based Model Checking using Modal Transition Systems. In *Proc. of CONCUR'01*, LNCS 2154, pp. 426–440, Springer, 2001.
12. P. Godefroid and R. Jagadeesan. Automatic abstraction using generalized model checking. In *Proc. of CAV'04*, LNCS 2404, pp. 137–150. Springer, 2002.
13. P. Godefroid and M. Huth. Model checking vs. generalized model checking: semantic minimization for temporal logics. In *Proc. of LICS'05*, pp. 158–167, IEEE Comp. Soc. Press, 2005.
14. S. Graf and H. Saidi. Construction of abstract state graphs with PVS. In *Proc. of CAV'97*, LNCS 1254, pp. 72–83, Springer, 1997.
15. A. Gurfinkel, O. Wei, and M. Chechik. Systematic construction of abstractions for model-checking. In *Proc. of VMCAI'06*, LNCS 3855, pp. 381–397. Springer, 2006.
16. D. Janin and I. Walukiewicz. Automata for the modal mu-calculus and related results. In *Proc. of MFCS'95*, LNCS 969, pp. 552–562. Springer, 1995.
17. M. Jurdziński. Deciding the winner in parity games is in UP∩co-UP. *Information Processing Letters*, 68(3):119–124, 1998.
18. D. Kozen. Results on the propositional μ-calculus. *TCS* 27:333–354, 1983.
19. K. G. Larsen and L. Xinxin. Equation solving using modal transition systems. In *Proc. of LICS'90*, pp. 108–117. IEEE Comp. Soc. Press, 1990.
20. J. P. Queille and J. Sifakis. Specification and verification of concurrent systems in CESAR. In *Proc. of the 5th International Symposium on Programming*, pp. 337–351, 1981.
21. D. A. Schmidt. Closed and logical relations for over- and under-approximation of powersets. In *Proc. of SAS'04*, LNCS 3148, pp. 22–37, Springer, 2004.
22. S. Shoham and O. Grumberg. 3-valued abstraction: More precision at less cost. In *Proc. of LICS'06*, pp. 399–410. IEEE Comp. Soc. Press, 2006.
23. S. Shoham and O. Grumberg. Monotonic abstraction-refinement for CTL. In *Proc. of TACAS'04*, LNCS 2988, pp. 546–560. Springer, 2004.
24. Th. Wilke. Alternating tree automata, parity games, and modal μ-calculus. *Bull. Soc. Math. Belg.*, 8(2):359–391, May 2001.

The Spotlight Principle⋆
On Combining Process-Summarizing State Abstractions

Björn Wachter[1] and Bernd Westphal[2]

[1] Universität des Saarlandes, Im Stadtwald, 66041 Saarbrücken, Germany
bwachter@cs.uni-sb.de
[2] Carl von Ossietzky Universität Oldenburg, 26111 Oldenburg, Germany
westphal@informatik.uni-oldenburg.de

Abstract. Formal verification of safety and liveness properties of systems with a dynamically changing, unbounded number of interlinked processes and infinite-domain local data is challenging due to the two sources of infiniteness. The existing state abstraction-based approaches Data Type Reduction and Environment Abstraction each address one aspect, but the former doesn't support infinite-domain local data and the latter doesn't support links and is restricted to particular properties.

The contribution of this paper is a combination of both which is obtained by first stating them in the framework of Canonical Abstraction. This new use of Canonical Abstraction, originally designed and used for the analysis of programs with heap-allocated data structures, furthermore unveils a formal connection between the two rather ad-hoc techniques.

1 Introduction

A good example for the systems we consider is car platooning as studied in the PATH project [1]. Its objective is to improve highway capacity and fuel consumption by having cars dynamically negotiate, via radio-based communication, the formation of platoons in which cars drive with reduced safety distance. A platoon consists of one or more followers and a leader, which is in particular responsible for notifying its followers in advance about braking manoeuvres. Roadside controllers announce the maximum platoon length for a certain highway segment and keep track of highway utilisation (cf. Figure 1(a)).

A formal model of the snapshot of car-platooning shown in Figure 1(a) is depicted in Figure 1(b). There, each car has a local state, like being a follower ('flw') or leader ('ldr'), and a finite-domain variable d indicating the destination, one of finitely many highway exits. A roadside controller also has a state pc, some finite-domain highway parameter x, for instance a maximum platoon length, and some infinite-domain ones, like a real-valued current utilisation of the highway y. Cars and roadside controllers do not have a global view on the entire highway,

---

⋆ This work was partly supported by the German Research Council (DFG) as part of the Transregional Collaborative Research Center SFB/TR 14 AVACS.

B. Cook and A. Podelski (Eds.): VMCAI 2007, LNCS 4349, pp. 182–198, 2007.

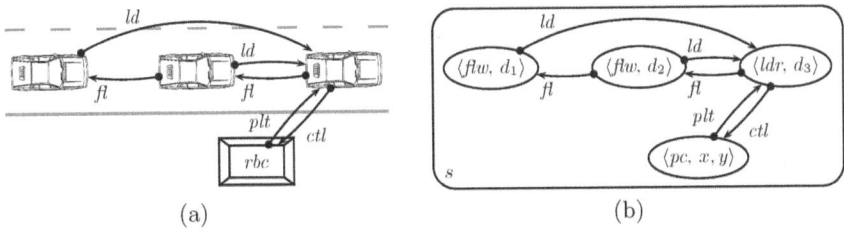

(a)   (b)

Fig. 1. Car Platooning. A three-car platoon and a roadside controller.

i.e. there is no shared memory, however cars have *links* to particular other cars. Followers have a *link* to their leader, a leader knows a list of followers, and there are links between roadside controllers and leaders. Links are used like pointers, that is, a follower can query (or even modify) the state of its leader. In addition, an inherent requirement on a model of car-platooning is that it provides for cars dynamically entering and leaving the highway, that is, there is no finite upper bound on the number of cars present at a certain point in time.

Thus the class of systems we consider is characterised by (i) dynamic creation and destruction of processes of different kinds, (ii) local state with finite-domain and other variables, and (iii) local and global links. The considered properties are general LTL formulae with outermost quantification over processes.

A well-established approach to the formal verification of safety ("two different cars never consider each other to be leader") or liveness ("a merge request is finally answered") properties of transition systems with large or infinite state-space are so-called finitary abstractions [2]. A finitary abstraction is defined by a finite abstract domain and a state abstraction mapping states (like the one shown in Figure 1(b)) to abstract representations of states. The set of initial abstract states and the transition relation are then induced by the state abstraction; abstract states are initial (or in transition relation) if they are the abstraction of initial states (or states in transition relation).

One of the oldest finitary abstractions is *Counter Abstraction* [3,4,5,2]. The basic idea is to map states with many processes, each in one of finitely many local states, to an abstract state, which only counts how many processes are in each local state. Processes are considered equivalent if they share the same local state. To obtain a finite abstract domain,

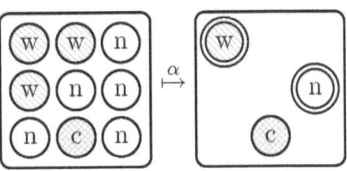

Fig. 2. Counter Abstraction

counters are typically cut off at two, i.e. distinguish only between 0, 1, and "many" processes. Such a state abstraction function α maps, for example, the concrete state on the left-hand side of Figure 2 to the one shown on the right where "many" processes are indicated by double-lines.

Classical Counter Abstraction seems inappropriate to verify car platooning as it does not support links, only admits finite-domain variables, and suffers from the problem that processes *migrate* freely between equivalence classes such that we cannot tell whether *a particular* process has made a particular transition. For example, if one process changes state from c to n and one from w to c in Figure 2, then the abstract state remains the same.

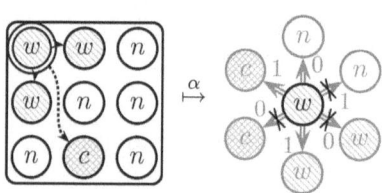

Fig. 3. Environment Abstraction

Recently, Counter Abstraction was combined with a particular instance of Predicate Abstraction to a technique called *Environment Abstraction* (EA) [6], admitting infinite-domain local variables, like unbounded counters. EA derives its name from the way it addresses the migration problem: by representing one process precisely and preserving information about the rest from the perspective of this process in terms of binary so called inter-predicates on the unbounded variables. In Figure 3, dashed lines indicate whether the single inter-predicate holds between another and the reference process (indicated by double-line). An abstract state consists of the reference process' local state and a vector of bits indicating whether there is at least one other process in a particular local state and in inter-predicate relation to the reference process, i.e. counters are already cut off at 1. For example, in Figure 3 there are no processes in local state n and in inter-predicate relation to the reference process, thus in the abstract state the north-east arrow is crossed out. The north-arrow is not crossed out as there are n-processes *not* in inter-relation. *Not supporting links*, EA seems inappropriate for platooning as well. Furthermore, EA cannot verify manoeuvres involving more than two cars, because it is restricted to two-process safety and one-process liveness properties.

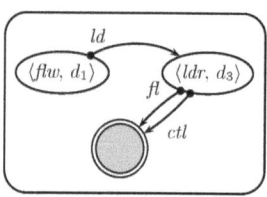

Fig. 4. Data-Type Red

The finitary abstraction *Data-Type Reduction* (DTR) supports links and the desired properties, however, it does not admit infinite-domain variables like counters. DTR was introduced as part of a compositional verification methodology for parameterised systems [7]. The underlying idea is to represent the local state of finitely many processes exactly, like links between reference processes, remember whether there are links into their environment, and dismiss any other information about their environment. For example, the state in Figure 1(b) maps to the abstract state shown in Figure 4 if the leader and the last follower are reference processes. One gray summary node represents all other cars and all roadside controllers.

EA and DTR come close to a good abstraction technique for platooning. They have complementary strengths: DTR supporting links and manoeuvres with more than two cars, and EA supporting infinite-domain local state. They share the common idea of keeping some distinguished processes exact, intuitively putting a "spotlight" on them, while abstracting from the rest. Therefore, we aim for a combination of EA and DTR in order to treat systems like the car-platooning example. As they are formalised in rather different manners and have some undesired restrictions, we use the general and powerful framework of canonical abstraction (CA) [8] to re-formulate in a common language and, ultimately, combine the concepts behind EA and DTR.

Canonical abstraction provides a general framework for concise and clear definition of state abstractions. It is widely used in the context of heap-manipulating programs. For example, the simplest instance of CA discussed in [8] maps a state with the linked list shown in Figure 5 to the abstract state at the bottom where nodes indistinguishable via links x and y collapse. Links into and between the summary become indefinite as,

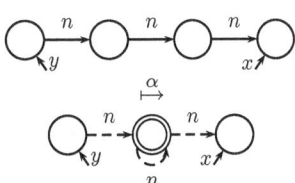

Fig. 5. Singly Linked List

for example, some summarised nodes point to the last one and some do not (cf. [8] for details). Thus CA provides natural means to handle structures with links, and, as it turns out, for the principle to represent the environment from the perspective of reference individuals. We obtain an alternative elegant soundness proof of EA and DTR via the framework of CA. This has practical relevance since, in practice, abstractions often need to be refined in order to be precise enough. As a consequence of the CA framework and contrary to the original formalizations of EA and DTR, abstraction refinement becomes a natural process with guaranteed soundness.

Other Abstractions and Related Work. The static analysis-based approach of Yahav [9] first demonstrated suitability of the CA framework for the verification of concurrent Java programs with unbounded creation of processes on the heap. The idea underlying the employed abstraction is similar to EA and DTR, but the approach is limited to safety properties (or state invariants). This approach is refined in [10] by demonstrating that splitting a given task into cases and treating each case separately with a specially tailored abstraction gains efficiency, and that keeping neighbours of reference processes precise gains precision.

Yahav, Reps, Sagiv, and Wilhelm [11] address the same class of systems but use significantly stronger *Evolutional Temporal Logic* (ETL) properties, which are basically LTL with arbitrary quantification over processes (not only outermost) and transitive closure. Their approach is different to finitary abstraction in that they construct a set of abstract sequences of abstract states via static analysis. ETL formulae are then checked on this set of abstract traces, where consecutive similar states collapse to summary states and where evolution of processes is explicitly traced between (abstract) states of an abstract trace. Our method implicitly preserves relevant evolution information since distinguished processes are singled out by the abstraction, however, in their work, process evolution is prone to imprecision due to abstraction.

Distefano, Katoen, and Rensink [12] propose automata-based model checking of evolution properties. Their method is restricted to link-based structures with single outgoing links, which would disallow follower links, and, further, their method does not support data such as counters.

Building on the compositional model checking approach of [7] which introduced DTR, McMillan, Qadeer, and Saxe [13] developed an induction-based
verfication technique that admits counters ranging over the natural numbers.
The underlying abstraction technique can be expressed in our framework. The
proposed induction-based verification scheme is orthogonal to our work. Yet, the
systems considered here do not exhibit totally ordered process identities and are
thus not amenable to their technique.

A thorough discussion why approaches, from instances of Predicate Abstraction to indexed predicates, are also insufficient appears in [6].

Most closely related to the aspect of our work, that we compare two independently developed and described state abstractions in the CA framework is
Manevich et al. [14] who compare particular state abstractions for linked lists
given via CA to equivalent Predicate Abstractions. Thus they compare single
state abstractions in different frameworks.

Outline. We proceed as follows. In Section 2 we formally define the class of
systems and properties we consider. Section 3 introduces state abstractions with
respect to reference processes and briefly provides the Canonical Abstraction
framework. In Section 4, we give native and CA-based definitions of DTR and
EA and propose a combination in Section 5. Section 6 concludes.

2   Computational Model and Property Specification

In order to represent the car-platooning example from the introduction we consider transition systems over signatures. A signature S consists of process types
T (like cars and roadside controllers), global links G and links local to processes
L (like cars' link to the leader ld), and finite- and infinite-domain variables X and
Y local to processes (like cars' current destination d and the controllers' highway utilisation y), all five sets disjoint, and a domain $\mathcal{D}$ assigning each variable
$v \in X \cup Y$ a domain $\mathcal{D}(v)$, which is finite if $v \in X$. That is, $S = (T, G, L, X, Y, \mathcal{D})$.

A transition system is a triple (S, S_0, R) of a set of states S, initial states
$S_0 \subseteq S$, and a transition relation $R \subseteq S \times S$. It is called transition system over S
iff each state $s \in S$ is a structure of S, that is, a pair (U, σ) of a set of individuals
U, called universe, which is partitioned into one (possibly empty) partition per
type in T and σ is a valuation of G, L, X and Y, that is,

- global links $g \in G$ are assigned individuals, i.e. $\sigma|_G : G \to U$,
- local links $l \in L$ and variables $v \in X \cup Y$ are assigned functions mapping
  individuals to other individuals or values, i.e. $\sigma|_L : L \to (U \to U)$ and
  $\sigma|_{X \cup Y} : L \to (U \to \mathcal{D})$.

2.1   Parameterised Systems

DTR and EA originally address *parameterised systems*, that is, systems where
$K \in \mathbb{N}$ processes execute a single program in parallel, so we also introduce a
rather general notion of parameterised systems over signatures. As we do not

aim at exploiting a particular description language, we do not specify one but consider $\mathcal{M}$ to be a finite behavioural description over a signature $\mathcal{S}$ with n process types which, given a tuple $(K_1, \ldots, K_n) \in \mathbb{N}^n$, determines a transition system over $\mathcal{S}$ whose state-set consists of all structures (U, σ) of $\mathcal{S}$ over a fixed universe U with K_i individuals of type τ_i, $1 \leq i \leq n$.

The set of all such instances of $\mathcal{M}$ is called $\mathcal{M}(\mathbb{N})$. Note that each instance has only finitely many processes, the challenge of parameterised system verification is to verify all instances at once.

In addition to common practice we use $\mathcal{M}(\infty)$ to denote the set of instances with countably infinitely many processes of some type because systems with a dynamically changing number of processes, like car platooning, can be encoded therein [15]. For the Canonical Abstraction versions of DTR and EA in Section 4, it is more suitable to consider the single transition system obtained by taking the union of all instances, denoted by $\mathcal{M}^{\mathbb{N}}$ etc., instead of a set of transition systems.

2.2   Properties

As Canonical Abstraction operates on logical structures (cf. Section 3.2), it is useful to only consider properties in form of formulae over a finite set of predicate symbols $\mathcal{P}$. Given a signature $\mathcal{S}$, we consider the set $\mathcal{P}_{\mathcal{S}}$ consisting of the predicate symbols given by Table 1. Note that the predicate symbols in $\mathcal{P}_{\mathcal{S}}$ distinguish the complete information about links and processes' finite variables in a state, thus together with quantification over processes we do not lose generality on these aspects by considering only $\mathcal{P}_{\mathcal{S}}$.

Table 1. Signature Predicates. Symbol p being of arity k is indicated by p/k.

$type[\tau]/1$	the given individual is of type $\tau \in T$
$ref[g]/1$	the global link $g \in G$ points to the given individual
$val[x, d]/1$	the local variable $x \in X$ has value $d \in \mathcal{D}$
$ref[l]/2$	the local link $l \in L$ of the given individual points to the other one
$eq/2$	the two given individuals are equal

For EA, we in addition need a set of binary predicate symbols that typically relate the non-finite aspects of two processes. In the car-platooning example it could compare the real-valued utilisation of two roadside controllers. We assume that a parameterised system $\mathcal{M}$ defines a finite set $\mathcal{P}_{\mathcal{M}}$ of these *inter-predicates*.

A structure $s = (U, \sigma)$ induces an interpretation ι_s of the predicate symbols in $\mathcal{P}_{\mathcal{S}}$. For example, $\iota_s(val[x, d])$ holds for $u \in U$ iff $\sigma(u)(x) = d$. For each inter-predicate $p \in \mathcal{P}_{\mathcal{M}}$ we assume an interpretation $\iota_s(p) : U^2 \to \{0, 1\}$ to be given. In general, a pair (U, ι) of a universe U and an interpretation ι of a set of predicate symbols $\mathcal{P}$ is called two-valued logical structure of $\mathcal{P}$. The set of all two-valued logical structures of $\mathcal{P}$ is denoted by *2-Struct[$\mathcal{P}$]*.

The language of *evolution properties* consists of formulae of the form

$$\forall z_1, \ldots z_n . \phi, \ n \in \mathbb{N}_0 \tag{1}$$

where $z_1, \ldots, z_n$ are logical variables (without loss of generality denoting *different* processes) and ϕ is an LTL formula with **X** (Next), **U** (Until), **G** (Globally), and **F** (Finally) and logical connectives over non-temporal state invariants

$$\psi \in SF ::= z_1 = z_2 \mid p(z_1, \ldots, z_n) \mid \neg\psi_1 \mid \psi_1 \vee \psi_2 \mid \exists z_1 . \psi_1 \tag{2}$$

where p is a predicate symbol from $\mathcal{P}_\mathcal{S} \cup \mathcal{P}_\mathcal{M}$. DTR supports all *evolution properties*, while EA is restricted to properties of the forms

$$\forall z_1, z_2 . \mathbf{G} \, \psi(z_1, z_2) \quad \text{and} \quad \forall z_1 . \mathbf{G} \, (\psi_1(z_1) \rightarrow \mathbf{F} \, \psi_2(z_1)) \tag{3}$$

over the predicate symbols $val[x, d]$. The former are called called *two-indexed safety properties*, the latter *one-indexed properties*. The semantics of a state invariant ψ in a state s, denoted by $[\![\psi]\!]_s$, and satisfaction of an evolution property by a sequence of states $\pi = (U_n, \sigma_n)_{n \in \mathbb{N}}$, denoted $\pi \models \Phi$, is inductively defined based on the logical structure $(U, \iota_s) \in 2\text{-}Struct[\mathcal{P}_\mathcal{S} \cup \mathcal{P}_\mathcal{M}]$ induced by state s.

2.3   Augmentation

As outlined in the introduction, both, DTR and EA, depend on a set of designated reference processes. To provide both uniformly with reference processes, we'll employ a simple, technical procedure that has similarly been applied, e.g. by [2] in the context of safety and liveness properties of parameterised systems and by [16] in the context of shape analysis for list insertion.

Given a transition system M over a signature $\mathcal{S}$ with global links G, let $G_a = \{g_{a_1}, \ldots, g_{a_n}\}$ be a set of fresh global *augmentation links*. Then the G_a-*augmentation* of M is a transition system $\widehat{M}$ over $\widehat{\mathcal{S}}$ with global links $G \cup G_a$ where the augmentation links consistently trace n different individuals. Consistency means that the valuation of G_a is constant over transitions, i.e.

$$((U, \widehat{\sigma}_1), (U, \widehat{\sigma}_2)) \in \widehat{R} \implies \widehat{\sigma}_1|_{G_a} = \widehat{\sigma}_1|_{G_a}. \tag{4}$$

States of $\widehat{M}$ are initial (in transition relation), if the projection onto $\mathcal{S}$ is initial (in transition relation). Among others, Figure 6 illustrates augmentation.

Then, for example, a formula $\forall z_1, z_2 . \mathbf{G} \, p(z_1, z_2)$ holds in M iff

$$\mathbf{G} \, (\forall z_1, z_2 . (ref[g_{a_1}](z_1) \wedge ref[g_{a_2}](z_2)) \rightarrow p(z_1, z_2)) \tag{5}$$

holds in $\widehat{M}$, the $\{g_{a_1}, g_{a_2}\}$-augmentation of M. The example easily extends into an inductive definition of the transformation of evolution properties Φ into $\widehat{\Phi}$.

3   Defining and Comparing State Abstractions

A state abstraction of a transition system $M = (S, S_0, R)$ consists of an abstract domain $S^\sharp$ and a state abstraction function α mapping concrete to abstract states, i.e. $\alpha : S \to S^\sharp$. It is called finite if $S^\sharp$ is finite. The function α induces an abstract transition system M_α with state-set $S^\sharp$ by considering an abstract state initial iff it is the abstraction of an initial concrete state, and two abstract states in transition relation if they are the abstractions of two concrete states in transition relation. This construction is known as *finitary abstraction* [17]. Together with α, we always consider its concretisation function γ mapping abstract states to the concrete states they represent, i.e. $\gamma(s^\sharp) = \{s \in S \mid \alpha(s) = s^\sharp\}$.

In order to establish properties of the original system on the abstract one, a state abstraction is complemented by a conservative, three-valued interpretation of the predicate symbols from $\mathcal{P}_S \cup \mathcal{P}_M$ in each abstract state. An interpretation is called three-valued iff predicates map to $\{0, 1, 1/2\}$ instead of $\{0, 1\}$; by *3-Struct*[$\mathcal{P}$] we denote the set of all pairs (U, ι) of universes and three-valued interpretations of the predicate symbols in $\mathcal{P}$.

An interpretation of predicate symbols $\mathcal{P}$ is called conservative with respect to another iff it doesn't introduce contradictions; in our case this spells out as

$$\forall p \in \mathcal{P} \; \forall s^\sharp \in S^\sharp \; \forall s \in \gamma(s^\sharp) : [\![p]\!]_s \sqsubseteq [\![p]\!]_{s^\sharp}^\sharp \tag{6}$$

where "$\sqsubseteq$" is the information order on $\{0, 1, 1/2\}$, defined as $\{b \sqsubseteq b, b \sqsubseteq 1/2 \mid b \in \{0, 1, 1/2\}\}$. Thus the third truth-value $1/2$ can be read as "don't know". Using the well-established three-valued semantics of state formulae [8] and temporal formulae [9], a conservative abstract semantics for temporal formulae is obtained. Thus if a property Φ holds in M_α, then it also holds in M.

3.1   Comparing State Abstractions

Recall that our overall aim is to provide alternative definitions of EA and DTR in the framework of Canonical Abstraction. In order to prove that the new definition is equivalent to the original one, we first introduce notions of equivalence and being coarser for state abstractions. The following Lemma provides more easily checkable, sufficient criteria that imply equivalence or being coarser.

A state abstractions $\alpha_1 : S \to S_1^\sharp$ is called coarser than $\alpha_2 : S \to S_2^\sharp$, denoted by $\alpha_1 \succeq \alpha_2$, iff the induced abstract transition system satisfies fewer evolution formulae, i.e. iff

$$M_{\alpha_1} \models \phi \implies M_{\alpha_2} \models \phi \tag{7}$$

for all evolution formulae Φ. Both are called equivalent, denoted $\alpha_1 \equiv \alpha_2$, iff $\alpha_2 \succeq \alpha_1$ and $\alpha_1 \succeq \alpha_2$, that is, if both satisfy the same properties.

If there is a simulation relation between the induced abstract models, (7) and thus the coarser-than relation follow. For existence of a simulation relation it is sufficient to find a relation ϱ between the two abstract domains such that related states do not interpret predicates contradictingly[1] and the states of the coarser state abstraction concretise to more concrete states.

Lemma 1 (State Abstraction Comparison). *Let $\alpha_1 : S \to S_1^\sharp$ and $\alpha_2 : S \to S_2^\sharp$ be two state abstractions. Let $\varrho : S_1^\sharp \times S_2^\sharp$ be a relation such that*

1. $\forall s \in S : (\alpha_1(s), \alpha_2(s)) \in \varrho$
2. $\forall (s_1^\sharp, s_2^\sharp) \in \varrho \; \forall p \in \mathcal{P} : [\![p]\!]_{s_2^\sharp}^\sharp \sqsubseteq [\![p]\!]_{s_1^\sharp}^\sharp$
3. $\forall (s_1^\sharp, s_2^\sharp) \in \varrho : \gamma_1(s_1^\sharp) \subseteq \gamma_2(s_2^\sharp)$

Then $\alpha_1 \succeq \alpha_2$. With "$=$" instead of "$\sqsubseteq$" and "$\subseteq$", $\alpha_1 \equiv \alpha_2$ is obtained.

3.2   Canonical Abstraction

Canonical Abstraction provides a framework for the definition of state abstraction functions if concrete states are three-valued structures of a finite set of predicate symbols $\mathcal{P}$. Following the framework, a choice of a set of unary, so-called abstraction predicates

$$\mathcal{A} = \{p_{a_1}, \ldots, p_{a_n}\} \subseteq \mathcal{P} \tag{8}$$

determines the abstract domain as the set of three-valued structures (U, ι) where U comprises only the canonical names with respect to $\mathcal{A}$, thus it is finite.

The canonical name $\kappa_\mathcal{A}(u)$ of an individual u is simply the valuation of the abstraction predicates on u, i.e., the vector $(p_{a_1}(u), \ldots, p_{a_n}(u))$. The abstract domain is finite as there are only finitely many such vectors.

The other predicates from $\mathcal{P}$, which are not used as abstraction predicates, are principally only required to evaluate conservatively in the abstract state. A best abstraction with respect to $\mathcal{A}$ evaluates them as precisely as possible, that is, to a definite value from $\{0, 1\}$ if all summarised individuals agree on the definite value and to $1/2$ only otherwise.

The state abstraction function $\alpha_\mathcal{A} : \textit{3-Struct} \to \textit{3-Struct}$ is such a best abstraction. That is, as it merges individuals indistinguishable by the abstraction predicates, it preserves information about the abstraction predicates precisely, all other information may be blurred to $1/2$.

If defined by $\mathcal{A} \subseteq \mathcal{P}_\mathcal{S} \cup \mathcal{P}_\mathcal{M}$, it naturally extends to states that are pairs $s = (U, \sigma)$ of a universe and a valuation of signature $\mathcal{S}$ by applying it to the induced structure (U, ι_s), that is, by setting $\alpha_\mathcal{A}(s) := \alpha_\mathcal{A}(U, \iota_s)$. The concretisation function is still defined as on page 189.

Formally, Canonical Abstraction is based on the notion of (tight) embedding of three-valued structures. A surjection $h : U \to U'$ between two universes is said to embed the logical structure $s = (U, \iota)$ of $\mathcal{P}$ into $s' = (U', \iota')$ iff

$$\forall p \in \mathcal{P}^k : \iota(p)(u_1, \ldots, u_{k(p)}) \sqsubseteq \iota'(p)(h(u_1), \ldots, h(u_{k(p)})). \tag{9}$$

---

[1] Assuming that the interpretation of formulae is inductively defined as discussed in the previous paragraph.

The embedding is called tight, if the stronger condition

$$\forall\, p \in \mathcal{P}^k : \iota'(p)(u'_1, \ldots, u'_{k(p)}) = \bigsqcup_{h(u_i)=u'_i, 1 \leq i \leq k(p)} \iota(p)(u_1, \ldots, u_{k(p)}), \qquad (10)$$

using the least upper bound with respect to information order, holds. A structure s *can* (tightly) be embedded into s' iff a (tight) embedding function exists.

Given the three-valued interpretation $[\![\psi]\!]^3_{s'}$ of state invariants in abstract states s' via the monotone Kleene semantics[2] the following theorem holds

Theorem 1 (Embedding Theorem [8]). *Let $s = (U, \iota)$ and $s' = (U', \iota')$ be logical structures, let h embed s in s', and let Z be a complete assignment of the free variables in ψ. Then $[\![\psi]\!]^3_s(Z) \sqsubseteq [\![\psi]\!]^3_{s'}(h \circ Z)$.*

4   The Spotlight Principle

Intuitively, both EA and DTR focus, or put a spotlight, on one or more processes and abstract from the rest, the ones in the shadows. Information about the latter is kept from the perspective of the spotlight individuals.

We say that a state abstraction α *follows the spotlight principle* if it is definable via Canonical Abstraction and there are abstraction predicates p_a in $\mathcal{A}$ that concretise to at most one individual in each abstract state, i.e.

$$\forall\, (U, \iota) \in S^\sharp : |\{u \mid \iota(p_a)(u)\}| \leq 1. \qquad (11)$$

A direct consequence is that all other unary predicates in $\mathcal{P}_\mathcal{S}$ are evaluated to definite values for a spotlight individual (or reference process); binary predicates may evaluate to $1/2$ if evaluated for non-spotlight individuals.

We call α disjoint, if spotlight predicates $p_{a_1}, \ldots, p_{a_n}$ mutually exclude each other on individuals. Given a transition system M over a signature, an evolution formula $\Phi = \forall\, z_1, \ldots, z_n \,.\, \phi$, and a corresponding G_a-augmentation $\widehat{M}$ of M with $G_a = \{g_{a_1}, \ldots, g_{a_n}\}$, each state abstraction

$$\mathcal{A} \supseteq \{ref[g_a] \mid g_a \in G_a\} \qquad (12)$$

is a disjoint spotlight abstraction.

In the following, we present the two abstractions EA and DTR in their original definition and give an equivalent Canonical Abstraction definition for each. Thereby, both can be identified as successful applications of the spotlight principle. In Section 5, we can then use the insights gained in the following sections to combine both abstractions into one which allows to treat the example from the introduction, which is neither in the scope of DTR nor in the scope of EA. For completeness, we additionally compare both to a typical example of the abstractions that are usually given via Canonical Abstraction, namely Shape Analysis of programs manipulating linked lists.

---

[2] Comparison of the summary node with itself then yields $1/2$ if there is more than one individual represented by a summary node, which is always the case in Section 4.

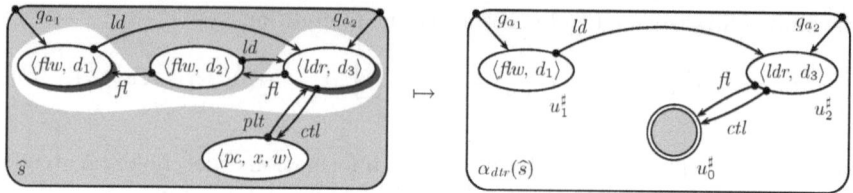

Fig. 6. Data-Type Reduction

4.1   Data-Type Reduction

Data-Type Reduction [7] (DTR) has been introduced for parameterised systems over signatures without infinite domain variables, i.e. $Y = \emptyset$, thus the considered systems are only infinite by the number of instantiations in $\mathcal{M}(\mathbb{N})$, or the number of processes in $\mathcal{M}(\infty)$.

In the following, let $\mathcal{M}$ be a parameterised system over signature $\mathcal{S}$ with $Y = \emptyset$ and, as DTR depends on the property, let $\Phi = \forall z_1, \ldots, z_n . \phi(z_1, \ldots, z_n)$ be an evolution property. Let $M \in \mathcal{M}(\infty)$ be the transition system with infinitely many processes of each type and $\widehat{M}$ a G_a-augmentation corresponding to Φ.

Native Definition. The finite state abstraction function $\alpha_{dtr} : \mathcal{S} \to \mathcal{S}^\sharp$ maps states $(U, \sigma) \in \mathcal{S}$ to abstract states $(U^\sharp, \sigma^\sharp)$ where $\sigma^\sharp$ maps global links from G_a to the corresponding abstract individuals, i.e.

$$\sigma^\sharp(g_{a_i}) = u_i^\sharp, \; g_{a_i} \in G_a, \tag{13}$$

and local and other global links, $g \notin G_a$, to the corresponding abstract individual or the summary individual $u_0^\sharp$, i.e.

$$\sigma^\sharp(g) = \begin{cases} u_i^\sharp & , \sigma(g_{a_i}) = \sigma(g) \\ u_0^\sharp & , \text{otherwise} \end{cases} \qquad \sigma^\sharp(l)(u_i^\sharp) = \begin{cases} u_j^\sharp & , \sigma(l)(\sigma(g_{a_i})) = \sigma(g_{a_j}) \\ u_0^\sharp & , \text{otherwise} \end{cases} \tag{14}$$

and keeps the values of local variables, i.e. $\sigma^\sharp(x)(u_i^\sharp) = \sigma(x)(\sigma(g_{a_i}))$.

Figure 6 illustrates the effect of α_{dtr} on a state of the car platooning system from Section 2 (assuming $w \in X$, instead of $y \in Y$). The abstract state preserves the state of the last follower and the leader. Links to individuals in the shadows change to links to the summary individual, links from them are lost.

The interpretation of a predicate $p \in \mathcal{P}_\mathcal{S} \cup \mathcal{P}_\mathcal{M}$ of arity k in $s^\sharp$ is defined as

$$[\![p]\!]_{s^\sharp}^\sharp(w_1^\sharp, \ldots, w_k^\sharp) = 1/2 \tag{15}$$

if one of the individuals is the summary individual, i.e. $w_i^\sharp = u_0^\sharp$ for some $1 \le i \le n$, and the value obtained using the regular definition from Section 2.2 otherwise. We immediately have $[\![p]\!]_s(u_1, \ldots, u_n) \sqsubseteq [\![p]\!]_{\alpha s}^\sharp(w_1^\sharp, \ldots, w_n^\sharp)$ if u_i and $w_i^\sharp$ are indistinguishable on the reference link predicates $ref[g_a]$, $g_a \in G_a$.

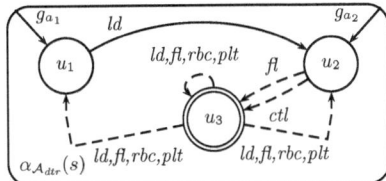

	ga_1	ga_2	car	ctl	flw	...		fl	u_1	u_2	u_3
u_1	1	0	1	0	1	...		0	0	0
u_2	0	1	1	0	0	...		0	1/2	0
u_3	0	0	1/2	1/2	1/2	1/2		1/2	1/2	1/2

Fig. 7. DTR via Canonical Abstraction. The tables exemplary show the valuation of some predicates, the unary reference individual predicates, the type predicates, and $val[st, flw]$ on the left and the binary predicate $ref[fl]$ on the right.

Data-Type Abstraction Via Canonical Abstraction is obtained by choosing the reference individual predicates as abstraction predicates, i.e.

$$\mathcal{A}_{dtr} = \{ref[g] \mid g_a \in G\} \subseteq \mathcal{P}_{\mathcal{S}}. \qquad (16)$$

Figure 7 illustrates, following the conventions of [8], the effect of $\alpha_{\mathcal{A}_{dtr}}$ on the concrete state from Figure 6. Dashed (indefinite) edges indicate the loss of precision that shows in the original definition only in the evaluation of expressions.

Note that $\alpha_{\mathcal{A}_{dtr}}$ is already too precise as it preserves information about the shadow individuals if predicates happen to agree on all of them. An equivalent state abstraction can be obtained by explicitly blurring the truth-value of all predicates, except for the spotlight predicates $ref[g_a]$, when evaluated for at least one non-reference individual, i.e. we set $\alpha'_{\mathcal{A}_{dtr}} := blur \circ \alpha_{\mathcal{A}_{dtr}}$ where $blur(U, \iota) := (U, blur(\iota))$ with

$$blur(\iota)(p)(u_1, \ldots, u_n) = \begin{cases} 1/2 & \text{, if } p \neq ref[g_a], g_a \in G_a, \text{ and} \\ & \bigwedge_{\substack{g_a \in G_a \\ 1 \leq i \leq n}} \neg\iota(ref[g_a])(u_i) \qquad (17) \\ \iota(p)(u_1, \ldots, u_n) & \text{, otherwise} \end{cases}$$

Theorem 2. *The native definition of DTR α_{dtr} is equivalent to $\alpha'_{\mathcal{A}_{dtr}}$.*

Proof. By Lemma 1, letting abstract DTR-states $s^{\sharp}_{dtr}$ and $s^{\sharp}_{\mathcal{A}_{dtr}}$ be ϱ-related iff

$$\forall p \in \mathcal{P}_{\mathcal{S}} \cup \mathcal{P}_{\mathcal{M}} : [\![p]\!]^{\sharp}_{s^{\sharp}_{\mathcal{A}_{dtr}}} (u_1, \ldots, u_n) = [\![p]\!]^{\sharp}_{s^{\sharp}_{dtr}} (u^{\sharp}_1, \ldots, u^{\sharp}_n) \qquad (18)$$

for u_i and $u^{\sharp}_i$ indistinguishable under $ref[g_a]$, $g_a \in G_a$. $\qquad \square$

4.2 Environment Abstraction

Environment Abstraction [6] (EA) has been introduced for parameterised systems over signatures with exactly one process type and no links. Thus the considered systems are infinite by the number of instantiations $\mathcal{M}(\mathbb{N})$, or the number of processes in $\mathcal{M}(\infty)$, and in addition possibly by the domain of variables in Y.

In the following, let $\mathcal{M}$ be a parameterised system over signature $\mathcal{S}$ without links and one process type. to simplify the presentation, we follow [6] in assuming that X comprises only the single, finite-domain variable pc.

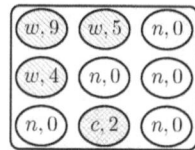

Fig. 8. Bakery State

The car-platooning example from the introduction is clearly out of scope for EA as it depends on links between processes. So we employ one (of the two) examples that have successfully been verified with EA [6], namely the parameterised system employing the bakery algorithm [18] for mutual exclusion. Assume, the program counter pc has a domain of three locations like n (non-critical), w (wait), c (critical) and there is one (unbounded) integer variable t for the ticket.

Figure 8 shows one state of bakery with $K = 9$ processes. Oval nodes represent processes, giving their state (also indicated by different hatch fillings) and ticket value, assuming idle processes reset the ticket to 0.

In the following, let $M \in \mathcal{M}(\infty)$ be the transition system with infinitely many processes (of the only type) and $\widehat{M}$ an augmentation with a single link g_a.

Native Definition. In [6], a set of predicates $env[i, j]$ is constructed in two steps. Let $\mathcal{P}_M = \{p_1, \ldots, p_n\}$ be the inter-predicates of M. Then firstly there are 2^n formulae R_i with two free variables characterise all (mutually exclusive) combinations of the inter-predicates holding or not for two individuals, i.e.

$$R_i(z_1, z_2) := \pm p_1(z_1, z_2) \wedge \cdots \wedge \pm p_n(z_1, z_2) \tag{19}$$

The R_i secondly induce $T := 2^n \cdot |\mathcal{D}(pc)|$ so-called *environment formulae* holding in state (U, σ) if at least one individual different from the reference individual has pc value j and is related to the reference individual as described by R_i, i.e.

$$env[i, j] := \exists z, z' . z \neq z' \wedge ref[g_a](z) \wedge R_i(z, z') \wedge val[pc, j](z') \tag{20}$$

The abstract domain $S^\sharp$ of the EA of M is the set of vectors

$$\langle d, \epsilon_{1,1}, \ldots, \epsilon_{2^n, |\mathcal{D}(pc)|} \rangle \in \mathcal{D}(pc) \times \{0, 1\}^T \tag{21}$$

comprising a pc-value $d \in \mathcal{D}(pc)$ and one boolean $\epsilon_{i,j}$ for each of the T environment formulae $env[i, j]$. It is finite as $\mathcal{D}(pc)$ is finite.

The finite state abstraction function $\alpha_{ea} : \widehat{S} \to S^\sharp$ maps states $\widehat{s} = (U, \sigma) \in \widehat{S}$ to the vector $\langle \sigma(pc)(\sigma(g_a)), [\![env[1, 1]]\!]_{\widehat{s}}, \ldots, [\![env[2^n, |\mathcal{D}(pc)|]]\!]_{\widehat{s}} \rangle$.

Figure 3 illustrates the effect of α_{ea} on an augmented state. Note that the valuation of inter-predicates is only shown with respect to the reference individual. The abstraction function α_{ea} keeps the value of pc for the reference process and one bit for each combination of program counter and inter-predicate being 0 iff there is no other process with a corresponding pc in the concrete state such that the inter-predicate holds. In other words, each $\epsilon_{i,j}$ encodes presence or absence of at least one individual that is in $env[i, j]$ relation to the reference individual.

The interpretation of a unary predicate $val[pc, d] \in \mathcal{P}_S$ is defined using a structure (U, ι) with an arbitrary, two-individual universe $\{u_1, u_2\}$ and

$$\iota(val[pc, d]) = \{u_1 \mapsto (pc = d), u_2 \mapsto \bigvee_{1 \leq i \leq 2^n} \epsilon_{i,d}\} \tag{22}$$

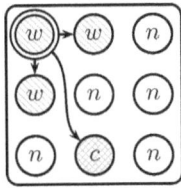
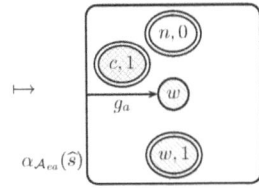

	g_a	n	w	c	$env[p_1]$	sm
u_1	1	0	1	0	0	0
u_2	0	0	1	0	1	$1/2$
u_3	0	1	0	0	0	$1/2$
u_4	0	0	0	1	1	$1/2$

Fig. 9. EA via Canonical Abstraction. The table shows the valuation of all predicates considered in the Bakery example and the summary predicate sm.

for an abstract state $s^\sharp = \langle pc, \epsilon_{1,1}, \dots, \epsilon_{2^n,|\mathcal{D}pc|} \rangle$. Then $[\![val[pc,d]]\!]^\sharp_{s^\sharp} = \iota(val[pc,d])$. Intuitively, $val[pc,d]$ holds in $s^\sharp$ if either the first component of the vector is equal to d or at least one $\epsilon_{i,d}$, $1 \le i \le 2^n$, is true.

Environment Abstraction Via Canonical Abstraction is based on a slightly different set of environment predicates. Let $env[p]$, $p \in \mathcal{P}_\mathcal{M}$ be unary predicate symbols that indicate whether an individual is *not* the reference individual and in p-relation to the reference individual, i.e.

$$[\![env[p]]\!]_{(U,\sigma)}(u) := (u \neq \sigma(g_a) \wedge [\![p]\!]_{(U,\sigma)}(\sigma(g_a), u)) \tag{23}$$

Then as abstraction predicates we choose the one for the reference individual, for finite-domain variable valuation, and the new environment predicates, i.e.

$$\mathcal{A}_{ea} = \{ ref[g_a] \} \cup \{ val[pc,d] \mid d \in \mathcal{D}pc \} \cup \{ env[p] \mid p \in \mathcal{P}_\mathcal{M} \} \tag{24}$$

Figure 9 illustrates the effect of CA with $\mathcal{A}_{ea}$ on the concrete state from Figure 3. Note that there are no edges between nodes as we do not have binary predicates in $\mathcal{P}$ and as all predicates in $\mathcal{P}$ are abstraction predicates. Loss of precision takes place in the choice of predicates which, in contrast to DTR, doesn't preserve all information of concrete states.

Similar to DTR, the more natural choice of abstraction predicates, namely

$$\mathcal{A}'_{ea} = \{ ref[g_a] \} \cup \{ val[pc,d] \mid d \in \mathcal{D}pc \} \tag{25}$$

is already more precise than the original definition of EA as it would preserve information on the relation *between* the individuals in the shadows.

Theorem 3. *The native definition of EA α_{ea} is equivalent to $\alpha_{\mathcal{A}_{dtr}}$.*

Proof. By Lemma 1, letting abstract states $s^\sharp_{ea} = \langle d, \epsilon_{1,1}, \dots, \epsilon_{2^n,|\mathcal{D}(pc)|} \rangle$ and $s^\sharp_{\mathcal{A}_{ea}} = (U, \iota)$ be ϱ-related iff $\epsilon_{i,j} = [\ \wedge ref[g](u)]\!]_{s^\sharp}$ and $\bigvee_{j \in \mathcal{D}}(d = j \Leftrightarrow [\ \wedge val[pc,j](u)]\!])$.   □

4.3   Shape Analysis

A natural question is how EA and DTR relate to the abstractions for which Canonical Abstraction is typically used (cf. Section 1). The abstraction predicates of the coarsest abstraction for linked lists in [8] are $\mathcal{A} = \{ ref[x], ref[y] \}$. As program variables refer to at most one individual at a time, the abstractions for singly linked lists also follow the spotlight principle (although not disjointly).

This observation doesn't contradict the intuition that program variables *change* on update, while augmentation is constant. The abstraction used for linked lists is on such a high level of abstraction that it concretises as well to topologies of interlinked processes where x denotes a fixed process; the expectation that the value of x necessarily changes, exists only in the eye of the beholder.

5   Combining DTR and EA

As discussed in the introduction, both DTR and EA alone are not sufficient to establish properties like liveness of the merge procedure of car-platooning as DTR excludes infinite-domain variables and EA doesn't handle links between cars and is restricted to properties over at most two processes.

Furthermore, DTR doesn't preserve invariants about individuals outside the spotlight. In practice, this tends to give rise to spurious counter-examples, which have to be excluded by user-supplied non-interference lemmata [7,15].

Given the formulation of both, DTR and EA, in the Canonical Abstraction framework a sound abstraction that combines the strengths of both is obtained by simply taking the union of their abstraction predicates, i.e. $\mathcal{A} := \mathcal{A}_{dtr} \cup \mathcal{A}_{ea}$. As adding abstraction predicates makes abstractions more precise, the state abstraction defined by $\mathcal{A}$ is more precise than both, DTR and EA. From EA it inherits support of unbounded local state variables and from DTR support for links and multiple process types in general evolution logic formulae.

Practically, stating a state abstraction is only one aspect, the other one is finding an implementation, which computes the abstract finite-state transition system directly without the need to explicitly enumerate the concrete, infinite state space. Specialised implementations for DTR and EA proposed in [7] and [6]. In contrast, the Canonical Abstraction framework is *generally* supported by tools like *TVLA* [19] and *bohne* [20] for the verification of state invariants. Due to their generality, a non-optimised application of, e.g., TVLA to DTR or EA may not be as efficient as the procedures of [7,6], but they provide for easy prototyping when refining abstractions. One of the authors successfully implemented the variant of DTR given in Section 4.1 in TVLA to verify mutual exclusion for the bakery algorithm [21]. There the unbounded counter domain is modeled and abstracted by the list-like abstraction described in [9] admitting only increment and decrement operations. The ability of CA to preserve information about individuals in the shadow proved crucial to verify mutual exclusion.

6   Conclusion

There is a need for state abstractions suitable to treat systems with dynamic links between processes and infinite-domain variables and general temporal properties. From the literature, DTR and EA come closest but neither one is sufficient.

In order to obtain a combination with the strengths of both, we stated them uniformly in the Canonical Abstraction framework, which is a new application of the framework. By comparison of the employed abstraction predicates it turns out that both DTR and EA share a common principle which we call the spotlight principle. Individuals in the spotlight are kept precise while information about the others is represented from the perspective of those in the spotlight.

Stating other abstractions like [9,10] in this framework in order to dissect the ideas employed there remains for the full version of the paper. Further work comprises an investigation of the effect of cutting off counters at 2, as it is done for Shape Analysis, instead of at 1. Another question concerns the other direction, i.e. whether particular abstractions stated via Canonical Abstraction may profit from the efficient implementations of DTR or EA. And we would like to gain a deeper insight into the consequences of the spotlight principle, i.e. whether a set of preserved properties (possibly along segments of computation paths) can be characterised.

Acknowledgements. The authors want to express their gratitude to Andreas Podelski and Reinhard Wilhelm for their valuable comments on early versions of this work.

References

1. Hsu, A., Eskafi, F., Sachs, S., Varaiya, P.: The Design of Platoon Maneuver Protocols for IVHS. PATH Research Report UCB-ITS-PRR-91-6, Institute of Transportation Studies, University of California at Berkeley (1991) ISSN 1055-1425.
2. Pnueli, A., Xu, J., Zuck, L.: Liveness with (0,1,infty)-counter abstraction. In Hunt, Jr., W.A., Somenzi, F., eds.: Computer Aided Verification, 15th International Conference, CAV 2003, Boulder, CO, USA, July 8-12, 2003, Proceedings. Volume 2725 of Lecture Notes in Computer Science., Springer (2003) 107–133
3. Lubachevsky, B.D.: An Approach to Automating the Verification of Compact Parallel Coordination Programs. Acta Informatica **21** (1984) 125–169
4. Pong, F., Dubois, M.: Formal verification of complex coherence protocols using symbolic state models. J. ACM **45** (1998) 557–587
5. German, S.M., Sistla, A.P.: Reasoning about systems with many processes. J. ACM **39** (1992) 675–735
6. Clarke, E.M., Talupur, M., Veith, H.: Environment abstraction for parameterized verification. In Emerson, E.A., Namjoshi, K.S., eds.: Verification, Model Checking, and Abstract Interpretation, 7th International Conference, VMCAI 2006, Charleston, SC, USA, January 8-10, 2006, Proceedings. Volume 3855 of Lecture Notes in Computer Science., Springer (2006) 126–141
7. McMillan, K.L.: Verification of infinite state systems by compositional model checking (charme). In Pierre, L., Kropf, T., eds.: Correct Hardware Design and Verification Methods, 10th IFIP WG 10.5 Advanced Research Working Conference, CHARME '99, Bad Herrenalb, Germany, September 27-29, 1999, Proceedings. Volume 1703 of Lecture Notes in Computer Science., Springer (1999) 219–234
8. Sagiv, S., Reps, T.W., Wilhelm, R.: Parametric shape analysis via 3-valued logic. ACM Transactions on Programming Languages and Systems **22** (2001)

9. Yahav, E.: Verifying safety properties of concurrent Java programs using 3-valued logic. ACM SIGPLAN Notices **36** (2001) 27–40
10. Yahav, E., Ramalingam, G.: Verifying safety properties using separation and heterogeneous abstractions. In: Proceedings of the ACM SIGPLAN 2004 conference on Programming language design and implementation, ACM Press (2004) 25–34
11. Yahav, E., Reps, T., Sagiv, S., Wilhelm, R.: Verifying Temporal Heap Properties Specified via Evolution Logic. In Degano, P., ed.: Programming Languages and Systems, 12th European Symposium on Programming, ESOP 2003, Held as Part of the Joint European Conferences on Theory and Practice of Software, ETAPS 2003, Warsaw, Poland, April 7-11, 2003, Proceedings. Number 2618 in Lecture Notes in Computer Science, Springer-Verlag (2003) 204–222
12. Distefano, D., Katoen, J.P., Rensink, A.: Who is Pointing When to Whom? In: Proceedings of the 24th International Conference On Foundations of Software Technology and Theoretical Computer Science. (2004) 250–262
13. McMillan, K.L., Qadeer, S., Saxe, J.B.: Induction in Compositional Model Checking. In: Proceedings of the 12th International Conference on Computer-Aided Verification, CAV 2000, Chicago, IL, USA, July 15-19, 2000. (2000) 312–327
14. Manevich, R., Yahav, E., Ramalingam, G., Sagiv, M.: Predicate abstraction and canonical abstraction for singly-linked lists. In Cousot, R., ed.: Verification, Model Checking, and Abstract Interpretation, 6th International Conference, VM-CAI 2005, Paris, France, January 17-19, 2005, Proceedings. Volume 3385 of Lecture Notes in Computer Science., Springer (2005) 181–198
15. Damm, W., Westphal, B.: Live and Let Die: LSC-based Verification of UML-Models. In Boer, F., Bonsangue, M., Graf, S., de Roever, W.P., eds.: Formal Methods for Components and Objects First International Symposium, FMCO 2002, Leiden, The Netherlands, November 5-8, 2002, Revised Lectures. Number 2852 in Lecture Notes in Computer Science, Springer-Verlag (2003) 99–135
16. Dams, D., Namjoshi, K.S.: Shape Analysis through Predicate Abstraction and Model Checking. In: VMCAI 2003: Proceedings of the 4th International Conference on Verification, Model Checking, and Abstract Interpretation, London, UK, Springer-Verlag (2003) 310–324
17. Kesten, Y., Pnueli, A.: Control and Data Abstraction: The Cornerstones of Practical Formal Verification. International Journal on Software Tools for Technology Transfer **2** (2000) 328–342
18. Lamport, L.: A New Solution of Dijkstra's Concurrent Programming Problem. Communications of the ACM **17** (1974) 453–455
19. Lev-Ami, T., Sagiv, M.: TVLA: A System for Implementing Static Analyses. In Palsberg, J., ed.: Static Analysis, 7th International Symposium, SAS 2000, Santa Barbara, CA, USA, June 29 - July 1, 2000, Proceedings. Number 1824 in Lecture Notes in Computer Science, Springer-Verlag (2000) 280–301
20. Podelski, A., Wies, T.: Boolean Heaps. In Hankin, C., Siveroni, I., eds.: Static Analysis, 12th International Symposium, SAS 2005, London, UK, September 7-9, 2005, Proceedings. Volume 3672 of Lecture Notes in Computer Science., Springer (2005) 268–283
21. Wachter, B.: Checking universally quantified temporal properties with three-valued analysis. Master's thesis, Universität des Saarlandes (2005)

Lattice Automata

Orna Kupferman and Yoad Lustig

Hebrew University, School of Engineering and Computer Science, Jerusalem 91904, Israel
{orna,yoadl}@cs.huji.ac.il

Abstract. Several verification methods involve reasoning about multi-valued systems, in which an atomic proposition is interpreted at a state as a lattice element, rather than a Boolean value. The automata-theoretic approach for reasoning about Boolean-valued systems has proven to be very useful and powerful. We develop an automata-theoretic framework for reasoning about multi-valued objects, and describe its application. The basis to our framework are *lattice automata* on finite and infinite words, which assign to each input word a lattice element. We study the expressive power of lattice automata, their closure properties, the blow-up involved in related constructions, and decision problems for them. Our framework and results are different and stronger then those known for semi-ring and weighted automata. Lattice automata exhibit interesting features from a theoretical point of view. In particular, we study the complexity of constructions and decision problems for lattice automata in terms of the size of both the automaton and the underlying lattice. For example, we show that while determinization of lattice automata involves a blow up that depends on the size of the lattice, such a blow up can be avoided when we complement lattice automata. Thus, complementation is easier than determinization. In addition to studying the theoretical aspects of lattice automata, we describe how they can be used for an efficient reasoning about a multi-valued extension of LTL.

1 Introduction

Several recent verification methods involve reasoning about *multi-valued Kripke structures* in which an atomic proposition is interpreted at a state as a *lattice* element[1], rather than a Boolean value. The multi-valued setting arises directly in systems in which the designer can give to the atomic propositions rich values like "uninitialized", "unknown", "high impedance", "don't care", "logic 1", "logic 0", and more (c.f., the IEEE Standard Multivalue Logic System for VHDL Model Interoperability [IEEE93]), and arise indirectly in applications like abstraction methods, in which it is useful to allow the abstract system to have unknown assignments to atomic propositions and transitions [GS97, BG99], query checking [Cha00], which can be reduced to model checking over multi-valued Kripke structures, and verification of systems from inconsistent viewpoints [HH04], in which the value of the atomic propositions is the composition of their values in the different viewpoints. The various applications use various types of lattices (see Figure 1). For example, in the abstraction application, researchers have used three

---

[1] A lattice $\langle A, \leq \rangle$ is a partially ordered set in which every two elements $a, b \in A$ have a least upper bound (a join b) and a greatest lower bound (a meet b).

B. Cook and A. Podelski (Eds.): VMCAI 2007, LNCS 4349, pp. 199–213, 2007.
© Springer-Verlag Berlin Heidelberg 2007

values ordered as in $\mathcal{L}_3$ [BG99], as well as its generalization to linear orders [CDG01]. In query checking, the lattice elements are sets of formulas, ordered by the inclusion order [BG01]. When reasoning about inconsistent viewpoints, each viewpoint is Boolean, and their composition gives rise to products of the Boolean lattice, as in $\mathcal{L}_{2,2}$ [EC01]. Finally, in systems with rich values of the atomic propositions, several orders may be used with respect to the various values, which in fact do not always induce a lattice.

The *automata-theoretic* approach uses the theory of automata as a unifying paradigm for system specification, verification, and synthesis [Kur94, VW94, KVW00]. Automata enable the separation of the logical and the algorithmic aspects of reasoning about systems, yielding clean and asymptotically optimal algorithms. The automata-theoretic framework for reasoning about Boolean-valued systems has proven to be very versatile. Automata are the key to techniques such as on-the-fly verification, and they are useful also for modular verification, partial-order verification, verification of real-time and hybrid systems, open systems, and infinite-state systems. Many decision and synthesis problems have automata-based solutions and no other solution for them is known. Automata-based methods have been implemented in both academic and industrial automated-verification tools (c.f., COSPAN and SPIN).

In this work, we describe an automata-theoretic framework for reasoning about multi-valued objects. Consider a lattice $\mathcal{L}$. For a set X of elements, an *$\mathcal{L}$-set over X* is a function $S : X \to \mathcal{L}$ assigning to each element of X a value in $\mathcal{L}$. For an alphabet Σ, an *$\mathcal{L}$-language* is a function $L : \Sigma^* \to \mathcal{L}$ that gives a value in $\mathcal{L}$ to each word over Σ. A *nondeterministic lattice automaton on finite words (LNFW, for short)* gets as input words over Σ and assigns to each word a value in $\mathcal{L}$. Thus, each LNFW defines an $\mathcal{L}$-language. Technically, in an LNFW $\mathcal{A} = \langle \mathcal{L}, \Sigma, Q, Q_0, \delta, F \rangle$, the sets of initial and final states are $\mathcal{L}$-sets over Q (i.e., $Q_0, F \in \mathcal{L}^Q$ describe the "initial value" and the "acceptance value" of each state), and δ is an $\mathcal{L}$-set over $Q \times \Sigma \times Q$ (i.e., $\delta \in \mathcal{L}^{Q \times \Sigma \times Q}$ describes the "traversal value" of each labeled transition). Then, the value of a run of $\mathcal{A}$ is the *meet* of values of the components of the run (that is, the initial value of the first state, the traversal values of the transitions that have been taken, and the acceptance value of the last state), and the value that $\mathcal{A}$ assigns to a word is the *join* of the values of the runs of $\mathcal{A}$ on w.

The definition of LNFW is not too surprising, and, as we mention in the sequel, it is similar to previous definitions of "weighted automata". Things, however, become very interesting when one starts to study properties of LNFWs. Essentially, in the Boolean setting, the only important piece of information about a run is the membership of its last state in the set of accepting states. In the lattice setting, on the other hand, all the components of the run are important. To see the computational challenges that the lattice setting involves, consider for example the simple property of closure under join for deterministic lattice automata (LDFW, for short, where only a single initial/successor state is possible (has a value different from $\bot$)). Stating that LDFW are closed under join, one has to construct, given two LDFWs $\mathcal{A}_1$ and $\mathcal{A}_2$, an LDFW $\mathcal{A}$ such that for every word w, the value of $\mathcal{A}$ on w is the join of the values of $\mathcal{A}_1$ and $\mathcal{A}_2$ on w. In the traditional Boolean setting, join corresponds to union, and it is easy to construct $\mathcal{A}$ as the product of $\mathcal{A}_1$ and $\mathcal{A}_2$. In the lattice setting, however, it is not clear how to define the traversal value of the transitions of $\mathcal{A}$ based on the traversal value of the transitions of $\mathcal{A}_1$ and $\mathcal{A}_2$. We show that, indeed, the product construction cannot work, and the LDFW $\mathcal{A}$ must contain in its state space a component that depends on $\mathcal{L}$. Dependency in $\mathcal{L}$ cannot be avoided also when we determinize LNFWs: every LNFW $\mathcal{A}$ has an equivalent LDFW $\mathcal{A}'$. Nevertheless, while in the traditional Boolean case the construction of $\mathcal{A}'$ involves the subset construction [RS59] and for $\mathcal{A}$ with n states we get $\mathcal{A}'$ with 2^n states, here the subset construction looses information such as the traversal value with which each state in the set has been reached, and we show a tight m^n bound on the size of $\mathcal{A}'$, where $m = |\mathcal{L}|$.

Of special interest is the complementation problem[2] for LNFW. In the Boolean setting, it is easy to complement deterministic automata, and complementation of nondeterministic automata involves determinization. In the lattice setting, determinization involves an m^n blow up, and moreover, complementation involves an nm blow up even if we start with a deterministic automaton. Interestingly, by adopting ideas from the theory of automata on infinite words [KV01][3], we are able to avoid determinization, avoid the dependency in m, and complement LNFW with a 2^n blow up only. For this purpose we define universal lattice automata (LUFW, for short), which dualize LNFW, show that complementation can be done by dualization, and that LUFW can be translated to LNFW with a 2^n blow up[4].

Once we prove closure properties, we proceed to study the fundamental decision problems for the new framework: the *emptiness-value* and the *universality-value* problems, which corresponds to the emptiness and universality problems in the Boolean setting and decide, given $\mathcal{A}$, how likely it is (formalized by means of values in $\mathcal{L}$) for $\mathcal{A}$ to accept some word or all words; and the *implication-value problem*, which corresponds to the language-inclusion problem and decides, given two LNFWs $\mathcal{A}_1$ and $\mathcal{A}_2$, how likely it is that membership in the language of $\mathcal{A}_1$ implies membership in the language of $\mathcal{A}_2$. We show that, using the tight constructions described earlier, the problems have the same complexities as the corresponding problems in the Boolean setting.

We then turn to applications of LNFW for reasoning about multi-valued temporal logics and systems. We define the logic *Lattice LTL* (*LLTL*, for short), where the constants can take lattice values, and whose semantics is defined with respect to multivalued Kripke-structures. We extend LNFW to the framework of automata on infinite words, define *nondeterministic lattice Büchi word automata* (*LNBW*, for short), and show that known translations of LTL to nondeterministic Büchi word automata [VW94] can be lifted to the lattice setting. Then, we use LNBW to solve the satisfiability and model-checking problems for LLTL, and show that both problems are PSPACE–complete — not harder than in the Boolean setting. In addition, we study some basic theory of lattice automata on infinite words. In particular, we show that the comple-

---

[2] Discussing complementation, we restrict attention to *De Morgan lattices*, where complementation inside the lattice is well defined (See Section 2.1).

[3] As we discuss in the paper, there are several common computational aspects of LNFW and automata on infinite words, as reasoning in both theories has to cope with the fact that the outcome of a run depends on its on-going behavior, rather than its last state only.

[4] We note that the latter construction is not trivial; it has the flavor of the construction in [MH84] for the case of infinite words, but unlike [MH84] (or the much simpler Boolean case), the result LNFW is nondeterministic; if one seeks an equivalent LDFW, a dependency in m cannot be avoided.

mentation construction of [KV01] can be combined with the ideas we use in the case of LNFW complementation, thus LNBW complementation involves a $2^{O(n \log n)}$ blow up and is independent of m.

Related Work. We are aware of two previous definitions of automata over lattices and their applications in verification. Our framework, however, is the first to study the theoretical aspects of lattice automata, rather than only use them. Also, the applications we suggest go beyond these that are known. Below we discuss the two known definitions and compare them with our contribution. In [BG01], Bruns and Godefroid introduce *Extended Alternating Automata* (EAA, for short). EAA extend the automata-theoretic approach to branching-time model checking [KVW00], they run on trees, and map each input tree to a lattice value. EAA have been used for query checking [BG01] and model checking multi-valued μ-calculus [BG04]. EAA are incomparable with the model we study here. On the one hand, EAA are more general, as they run on trees and are alternating. On the other hand, they are not making full use of the lattice framework, as their "lattice aspect" is limited to the transition function having lattice values in its range.

Also, the application of reasoning about LLTL properties, which we describe here, cannot be achieved with EAA, as it involves a doubly-exponential translation of LLTL to μ-calculus, which we avoid. In [CDG01], Chechik, Devereux, and Gurfinkel define *multiple-valued Büchi automata* ($\mathcal{X}$Büchi automata, for short) and use them for model checking multiple-valued LTL. Like LNFW, each transition in a $\mathcal{X}$Büchi automata has a traversal value and the automata define $\mathcal{L}$-languages. Unlike LNFW, $\mathcal{X}$Büchi automata (and the multiple-valued LTL that correspond to them) are restricted to lattices that are finite linear orders. Thus, the setting and its potential applications is weaker.

In addition to lattice-based multi-valued logics, other related concepts were investigated. Lattice-based automata (for distributive lattices) can be seen as a special case of *weighted automata* [Moh97], which are in turn a special case of *semiring automata* [KS86]. Semiring automata is a very general algebraic notion of automata in which computations get values from some semiring. However, the model of semiring automata is algebraic in nature and is relatively far from the standard notion of finite automata. Weighted automata is another notion in which computations get values from a semiring, one that closely resembles the standard model of finite automata. In fact, since a distributive lattice is a semiring in which $\oplus$ is a join and $\otimes$ is a meet, the definitions of lattice automata are a special case of the definitions of weighted automata. However, while (distributive) lattices are semirings, lattices share some properties that general semirings do not. Specifically, the idempotent laws (i.e., $a \vee a = a$ and $a \wedge a = a$) as well as the absorption laws (i.e., $a \vee (a \wedge b) = a$ and $a \wedge (a \vee b) = a$), which are very intuitive in a logical context, do not hold in a general semiring, and do hold for lattices. Furthermore, the complementation operand that is essential for choosing lattices as a framework for multi-valued reasoning, has no natural interpretation in a general semiring. Finally, our results here go beyond these that are known for semiring automata. In particular, we consider also automata on infinite words, both nondeterministic and universal automata, and we study the computational aspects of constructions and decision problems.

Due to space limitations, proofs are omitted and can be found in the full version at the authors web pages.

2 Preliminaries

2.1 Lattices

Let $\langle A, \leq \rangle$ be a partially ordered set, and let P be a subset of A. An element $a \in A$ is an *upper bound* on P if $a \geq b$ for all $b \in P$. Dually, a is a *lower bound* on P if $a \leq b$ for all $b \in P$. An element $a \in A$ is the *least element of P* if $a \in P$ and a is a lower bound on P. Dually, $a \in A$ is the *greatest element of P* if $a \in P$ and a is an upper bound on P. A partially ordered set $\langle A, \leq \rangle$ is a *lattice* if for every two elements $a, b \in A$ both the least upper bound and the greatest lower bound of $\{a, b\}$ exist, in which case they are denoted $a \vee b$ (*a join b*) and $a \wedge b$ (*a meet b*), respectively. A lattice is *complete* if for every subset $P \subseteq A$ both the least upper bound and the greatest lower bound of P exist, in which case they are denoted $\bigvee P$ and $\bigwedge P$, respectively. In particular, $\bigvee A$ and $\bigwedge A$ are denoted $\top$ (*top*) and $\bot$ (*bottom*), respectively. A lattice $\langle A, \leq \rangle$ is finite if A is finite. Note that every finite lattice is complete. A lattice is *distributive* if for every $a, b, c \in A$, we have $a \wedge (b \vee c) = (a \wedge b) \vee (a \wedge c)$ and $a \vee (b \wedge c) = (a \vee b) \wedge (a \vee c)$.

The traditional disjunction and conjunction logic operators correspond to the join and meet lattice operators. In a general lattice, however, there is no natural counterpart to negation. A *De Morgan* (or *quasi-Boolean*) lattice is a lattice in which every element a has a unique complement element $\neg a$ such that $\neg\neg a = a$, De Morgan rules hold, and $a \leq b$ implies $\neg b \leq \neg a$. In the rest of the paper we consider only finite[5] distributive De Morgan lattices.

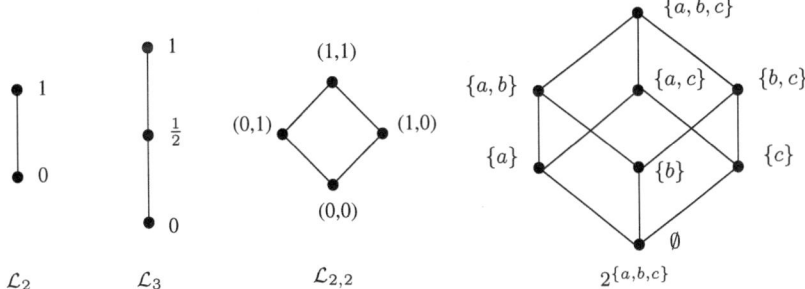

Fig. 1. Some lattices

In Figure 1 we describe some (finite distributive De Morgan) lattices. The elements of the lattice $\mathcal{L}_2$ are the usual truth values 1 (**true**) and 0 (**false**) with the order $0 \leq 1$. The lattice $\mathcal{L}_3$ contains in addition the value $\frac{1}{2}$, with the order $0 \leq \frac{1}{2} \leq 1$, and with negation defined by $\neg 0 = 1$ and $\neg \frac{1}{2} = \frac{1}{2}$. The lattice $\mathcal{L}_{2,2}$ is the Cartesian product of two $\mathcal{L}_2$ lattices, thus $(a, b) \leq (a', b')$ if both $a \leq a'$ and $b \leq b'$. Also, $\neg(a, b) = (\neg a, \neg b)$. Finally, the lattice $2^{\{a,b,c\}}$ is the power set of $\{a, b, c\}$ with the set-inclusion

---

[5] Note that focusing on finite lattices is not as restrictive as may first seem. Indeed, even when the lattice is infinite, the problems we consider involve only finite Kripke structures, formulas, and automata. Therefore, only a finite number of lattice elements appear in a problem, and since the lattice is distributive, the logical operations closure of these values is still finite.

order. Complementation is interpreted as set complementation relative to $\{a, b, c\}$. In this lattice, for example, $\{a\} \vee \{b\} = \{a, b\}$, $\{a\} \wedge \{b\} = \bot$, $\{a, c\} \vee \{b\} = \top$, and $\{a, c\} \wedge \{b\} = \bot$.

A *join irreducible* element $l \in \mathcal{L}$ is a value, other then $\bot$, for which if $l_1 \vee l_2 \geq l$ then either $l_1 \geq l$ or $l_2 \geq l$. By Birkhoff's representation theorem for finite distributive lattices in order to prove that $l_1 = l_2$ it is sufficient if to prove that for every join irreducible element l it holds that $l_1 \geq l$ iff $l_2 \geq l$. We denote the set of join irreducible elements of $\mathcal{L}$ by $JI(\mathcal{L})$. A *meet irreducible* element $l \in \mathcal{L}$ is a value for which if $l_1 \wedge l_2 \leq l$ then either $l_1 \leq l$ or $l_2 \leq l$. Note that in a De Morgan lattice an element is meet irreducible iff its complement is join irreducible. We denote the set of meet irreducible elements of $\mathcal{L}$ by $MI(\mathcal{L})$.

Consider a lattice $\mathcal{L}$ (we abuse notation and refer to $\mathcal{L}$ also as a set of elements, rather than a pair of a set with an order on it). For a set X of elements, an $\mathcal{L}$-*set over* X is a function $S : X \to \mathcal{L}$ assigning to each element of X a value in $\mathcal{L}$. It is convenient to think about $S(x)$ as the truth value of the statement "x is in S". We say that an $\mathcal{L}$-set S is *Boolean* if $S(x) \in \{\top, \bot\}$ for all $x \in X$. The usual set operators can be lifted to $\mathcal{L}$-sets as expected. Given two $\mathcal{L}$-sets S_1 and S_2 over X, we define join, meet, and complementation so that for every element $x \in X$, we have [6] $S_1 \vee S_2(x) = S_1(x) \vee S_2(x)$, $S_1 \wedge S_2(x) = S_1(x) \wedge S_2(x)$, and $comp(S_1)(x) = \neg S_1(x)$.

2.2 Lattice Automata

Consider a lattice $\mathcal{L}$ and an alphabet Σ. An $\mathcal{L}$-*language* is an $\mathcal{L}$-set over Σ^*. Thus an $\mathcal{L}$-language $L : \Sigma^* \to \mathcal{L}$ assigns a value in $\mathcal{L}$ to each word over Σ. A *nondeterministic lattice automaton* on finite words (LNFW, for short) is a six-tuple $\mathcal{A} = \langle \mathcal{L}, \Sigma, Q, Q_0, \delta, F \rangle$, where $\mathcal{L}$ is a lattice, Σ is an alphabet, Q is a finite set of states, $Q_0 \in \mathcal{L}^Q$ is an $\mathcal{L}$-set of initial states, $\delta \in \mathcal{L}^{Q \times \Sigma \times Q}$ is an $\mathcal{L}$-transition-relation, and $F \in \mathcal{L}^Q$ is an $\mathcal{L}$-set of accepting states.

A *run* of an LNFW on a word $w = \sigma_1 \cdot \sigma_2 \cdots \sigma_n$ is a sequence $r = q_0, \ldots, q_n$ of $n+1$ states. The *value* of r on w is $val(r, w) = Q_0(q_0) \wedge \wedge_{i=0}^{n-1} \delta(q_i, \sigma_{i+1}, q_{i+1}) \wedge F(q_n)$. Intuitively, $Q_0(q_0)$ is the value of q_0 being initial, $\delta((q_i, \sigma_{i+1}, q_{i+1}))$ is the value of q_{i+1} being a successor of q_i when σ_{i+1} is the input letter, $F(q_n)$ is the value of q_n being accepting, and the value of r is the meet of all these values, with $0 \leq i \leq n - 1$. We refer to $Q_0(q_0) \wedge \wedge_{i=0}^{n-1} \delta(q_i, \sigma_{i+1}, q_{i+1})$ as the *traversal value* of r and refer to $F(q_n)$ as its *acceptance value*. For a word w, the value of $\mathcal{A}$ on w, denoted $\mathcal{A}(w)$ is the join of the values of all the possible runs of $\mathcal{A}$ on w. That is, $val(\mathcal{A}, w) = \vee \{val(r, w) : r$ is a run of $\mathcal{A}$ on $w\}$. The $\mathcal{L}$-language of $\mathcal{A}$, denoted $L(\mathcal{A})$, maps each word w to its value in $\mathcal{A}$. That is, $L(\mathcal{A})(w) = val(\mathcal{A}, w)$.

An LNFW is a *deterministic* lattice automaton on finite words (LDFW, for short) if there is exactly one state $q \in Q$ such that $Q_0(q) \neq \bot$, and for every state $q \in Q$ and letter $\sigma \in \Sigma$, there is exactly one state $q' \in Q$ such that $\delta(q, \sigma, q') \neq \bot$. An LNFW is *simple* if Q_0 and δ are Boolean. Note that the traversal value of a run r of a simple LNFW is either $\bot$ or $\top$, thus the value of r is induced by F.

---

[6] If S_1 and S_2 are over different domains X_1 and X_2, we can view them as having the same domain $X_1 \cup X_2$ and let $S_1(x) = \bot$ for $x \in X_2 \setminus X_1$ and $S_2(x) = \bot$ for $x \in X_1 \setminus X_2$.

Traditional nondeterministic automata over finite words (NFW, for short) correspond to LNFW over the lattice $\mathcal{L}_2$. Indeed, over $\mathcal{L}_2$, the value of a run r on a word w is either $\top$, in case the run uses only transitions with value $\top$ and its final state has value $\top$, or $\bot$ otherwise. Also, the value of $\mathcal{A}$ on w is $\top$ iff the value of some run on it is $\top$. This reflects the fact that a word w is accepted by an NFW if some legal run on w is accepting.

Example 1. Figure 2 depicts three LNFWs. When we draw an LNFW, we denote the fact that $\delta(q, \sigma, q') = l$ by an edge attributed by (σ, l) from q to q'. For simplicity, we sometimes label an edge with a set $S \subseteq \Sigma \times L$. In particular, when $\Sigma = \mathcal{L}$, we use $(l, \top)$ to denote the set $\{(l, \top) : l \in \mathcal{L}\}$ and we use (l, l) to denote the set $\{(l, l) : l \in \mathcal{L}\}$. For states q with $Q_0(q) = l \neq \bot$, we draw into q an edge labeled l, and for states q with $F(q) = l \neq \bot$, we draw q as a double circle labeled l. For example, the LNFW $\mathcal{A}_2 = \langle \mathcal{L}, \mathcal{L}, \{q_1, q_2\}, Q_0, \delta, F \rangle$ is such that $Q_0(q_1) = \top$ and $Q_0(q_2) = \bot$. Also, for every $l \in \mathcal{L}$, we have $\delta(q_1, l, q_1) = \delta(q_2, l, q_2) = \top$, and $\delta(q_1, l, q_2) = l$. All other triplets $\langle q, l, q \rangle \in Q \times \mathcal{L} \times Q$ are mapped by δ to $\bot$. Finally, $F(q_1) = \bot$ and $F(q_2) = \top$.

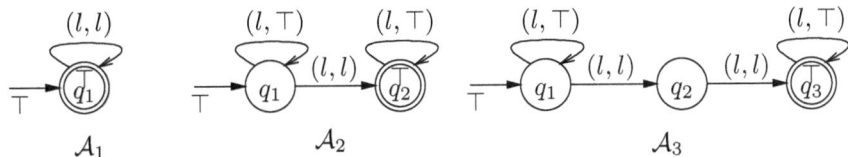

Fig. 2. Three LNFWs

Let us consider the $\mathcal{L}$-languages of the LNFWs in Figure 2. The LNFW $\mathcal{A}_1$ is deterministic. Its single run r a word $w = l_1 \cdot l_2 \cdots l_n$ starts in q_1 with value $\top$ and whenever the letter l_i is read, the traversal value so far is met with l_i. The acceptance value of r is $\top$, thus the value of r on w is $\bigwedge_{i=1}^{n} l_i$. Hence, the language L_1 of $\mathcal{A}_1$ is such that $L_1(l_1 \cdot l_2 \cdots l_n) = \bigwedge_{i=1}^{n} l_i$. The LNFW $\mathcal{A}_2$ is nondeterministic. Reading a word $w = l_1 \cdot l_2 \cdots l_n$, it guesses a letter l_i with which the transition from q_1 to q_2 is made. Since the values of the self loops in q_1 and q_2 are $\top$ and so are the initial and acceptance values, the value of such a run on w is l_i. Taking the join on all runs, we get that the language L_2 of $\mathcal{A}_2$ is such that $L_2(l_1 \cdot l_2 \cdots l_n) = \bigvee_{i=1}^{n} l_i$. Finally, the LNFW $\mathcal{A}_3$ is also nondeterministic. Here, going from q_1 to q_3 two successive letters are read, each contributing its value to the traversal value of the run. Hence the language L_3 of $\mathcal{A}_3$ is such that $L_3(l_1 \cdot l_2 \cdots l_n) = \bigvee_{i=1}^{n-1} (l_i \wedge l_{i+1})$. □

In the traditional Boolean setting, a *universal* automaton (UFW, for short) accepts a word w if all its runs on w are accepting. Lifting this definition to the lattice framework, a universal lattice automaton (LUFW, for short) has the same components as an LNFW, only that the value of a run $r = q_0 \ldots q_n$ on a word $w = \sigma_1 \cdot \sigma_2 \cdots \sigma_n$ is $val(r, w) = comp(Q_0(q_0)) \vee \bigvee_{i=0}^{n-1} comp(\delta(q_i, \sigma_{i+1}, q_{i+1})) \vee comp(F(q_n))$, and the value of $\mathcal{A}$ on w is $val(\mathcal{A}, w) = \bigwedge\{val(r, w) : r \text{ is a run of } \mathcal{A} \text{ on } w\}$. Thus, LUFW dualize LNFW in the three elements that determine the value of an automaton on a run:

first, the way we refer to the components of a single run is disjunctive (rather than conjunctive). Second, the way we refer to the collection of runs is conjunctive (rather than disjunctive). Finally, the initial values, transition values, and acceptance values are all complemented.

Example 2. Consider the three LNFWs discussed in Example 1. When we view them as LUFW, their languages $\tilde{L}_1$, $\tilde{L}_2$, and $\tilde{L}_3$ are such that $\tilde{L}_1(l_1 \cdot l_2 \cdots l_n) = \bigvee_{i=1}^{n} comp(l_i)$, $\tilde{L}_2(l_1 \cdot l_2 \cdots l_n) = \bigwedge_{i=1}^{n} comp(l_i)$, and $\tilde{L}_3(l_1 \cdot l_2 \cdots l_n) = \bigwedge_{i=1}^{n-1} (comp(l_i) \vee comp(l_{i+1}))$. □

Remark 3. In many applications, the input words to the LNFW are generated by a graph in which each vertex is labeled by a letter in Σ. In some applications, the transition relation of the graph is an $\mathcal{L}$-set, thus each edge has a value in $\mathcal{L}$. Accordingly, in a more general framework, each letter in Σ has a weight — a value in $\mathcal{L}$ that corresponds to the value of the edge between the current and next vertices. Then, the value of a run of the automaton over a weighted word $w = \langle \sigma_1, l_1 \rangle \cdot \langle \sigma_2, l_2 \rangle \cdots \langle \sigma_n, l_n \rangle$ takes the weights of the letters into account: when we are in state q_i, read a letter $\langle \sigma_{i+1}, l_{i+1} \rangle$, and move to state q_{i+1}, the contribution to the value of the run is $l_{i+1} \wedge \delta(q_i, \sigma_{i+1}, q_{i+1})$ (rather than $\delta(q_i, \sigma_{i+1}, q_{i+1})$ only). Since the lattice is distributive, it is easy to see that the value of such an LNFW over the word w is equal to the meet of its value on $\langle \sigma_1, \top \rangle \cdot \langle \sigma_2, \top \rangle \cdots \langle \sigma_n, \top \rangle$ with $\bigwedge_{1 \leq i \leq n} l_i$. Thanks to this decompositionality, it is easy to adjust our framework to automata that read words with weighted letters. For technical simplicity, we assume no weights. □

Remark 4. It is interesting to compare LNFW's to EAA's as defined in [BG04]. (Formally, EAA are defined only for infinite trees but it is easy to accommodate them to finite words). In EAA, there is no explicit concept of transition value. Since, however, EAA are alternating, it is possible to model a transition into state q with value l by the formula $q \wedge l$. By taking the meet of a transition with a lattice value, it is possible to ensure that in all runs, the value attached to the *source* vertex of the transition is at most l. Intuitively, the value of an EAA run flows "upwards" while the value of an LNFW run flows "downwards". An interesting outcome of this observation is that while it is natural to define the value of a prefix of a run of an LNFW, an LNFW run, it does not seem possible to define the value of a prefix of an EAA run. We find the ability to refer to this value helpful both in understanding the intuition behind the runs of automata and in reasoning about them — as we will demonstrate in Section 3. □

3   Closure Properties

In this section we study closure properties of LNFW and LDFW. We show that LNFW and LDFW are closed under join, meet, and complementation, show that LNFW can be determinized and simplified, and analyze the blow-up that the various constructions operators involve. In addition to the dependency in the size n of the original automaton (or automata, in case of the join and meet operators), our analysis refers to the size m of the lattice over which the automata are defined. The dependence on both n and m is tight and the proofs in full version provide both upper bounds and lower bounds.

3.1 Nondeterministic Automata on Finite Words

Theorem 5 [closure under join and meet]. *Let $\mathcal{A}_1$ and $\mathcal{A}_2$ be LNFW over $\mathcal{L}$, with n_1 and n_2 states, respectively. There are LNFW $\mathcal{A}_\vee$ and $\mathcal{A}_\wedge$, with $n_1 + n_2$ and $n_1 \cdot n_2$ states, respectively, such that $L(\mathcal{A}_\vee) = L(\mathcal{A}_1) \vee L(\mathcal{A}_2)$ and $L(\mathcal{A}_\wedge) = L(\mathcal{A}_1) \wedge L(\mathcal{A}_2)$.*

The constructions are slight variants of the standard Boolean case constructions.

Theorem 6 [simplification]. *Let $\mathcal{A}$ be an LNFW (LDFW) with n states, over a lattice $\mathcal{L}$ with m elements. There is a simple LNFW (resp. LDFW) $\mathcal{A}'$, with $n \cdot m$ states, such that $L(\mathcal{A}') = L(\mathcal{A})$.*

Intuitively, the state space of $\mathcal{A}'$ is $Q \times \mathcal{L}$, where $\langle q, l \rangle$ stands for state q with value l.

We now turn to consider determinization of LNFW. For simple LNFW, determinization can proceed using the subset construction as in the Boolean case [RS59]. If we start with a general LNFW $\mathcal{A}$ with state space Q, this results in an LDFW $\mathcal{A}'$ with state space $2^{Q \times \mathcal{L}}$. As Theorem 7 below shows, LNFW determinization does depend on $\mathcal{L}$, but we can do better than maintaining subsets of $Q \times \mathcal{L}$. The idea is to maintain, instead, functions in $\mathcal{L}^Q$, where each state q of $\mathcal{A}$ is mapped to the join of the values with which $\mathcal{A}$ might have reached q. Note that the resulting automaton is a simple LDFW.

Theorem 7 [determinization]. *Let $\mathcal{A}$ be an LNFW with n states, over a lattice $\mathcal{L}$ with m elements. There is a simple LDFW $\mathcal{A}'$, with m^n states, such that $L(\mathcal{A}') = L(\mathcal{A})$.*

We now turn to study complementation on LNFW. As with traditional automata, it is possible to complement an automaton through determinization. Starting with an LNFW with n states over a lattice with m elements, we can construct, by Theorem 7, a simple LDFW which can be easily complemented to LNFW with m^n states. We now show that by using universal automata, it is possible to circumvent determinization and avoid the dependency on m. We first observe that viewing an LNFW as an LUFW complements its language. The proof is easy and is based on applying De Morgan rules on $val(\mathcal{A}, w)$.

Lemma 1. *Let $\mathcal{A}$ be an LNFW and let $\tilde{\mathcal{A}}$ be $\mathcal{A}$ when viewed as an LUFW. Then, $L(\tilde{\mathcal{A}}) = comp(L(\mathcal{A}))$.*

Theorem 8. *Let $\mathcal{A}$ be an LUFW, with n states. There is an LNFW $\mathcal{A}'$, with 2^n states, such that $L(\mathcal{A}') = L(\mathcal{A})$.*

The intuition being the proof of Theorem 8 is as follows. Let $\mathcal{A} = \langle \mathcal{L}, \Sigma, Q, Q_0, \delta, F \rangle$. Consider a word $w = \sigma_1 \cdots \sigma_n$. The runs of $\mathcal{A}$ on w can be arranged in a directed acyclic graph $G = \langle Q \times \{0, \ldots, n\}, E \rangle$, where $E(\langle q, i-1 \rangle, \langle q', i \rangle)$ for all $q, q' \in Q$ and $1 \leq i \leq n$. Each edge $\langle \langle q, i-1 \rangle, \langle q', i \rangle \rangle$ in G has a value in $\mathcal{L}$, namely $comp(\delta(q, \sigma_i, q'))$. Also, vertices in $Q \times \{0\}$ and $Q \times \{n\}$ have an initial and an acceptance value, respectively, induced by $comp(Q_0)$ and $comp(F)$. The value of $\mathcal{A}$ on w is the meet of the values of the paths of G, where a value of a path is the join of the values of its components. In order for $\mathcal{A}'$ to map w to this value, we let $\mathcal{A}'$ keep track of paths that still have to contribute to a component value, and let the traversal value of the runs of $\mathcal{A}'$ maintain the value contributed so far. Thus, as in the subset construction,

$\mathcal{A}'$ follows all runs of $\mathcal{A}$ (that is, all the paths of G). However, at any time during the run, $\mathcal{A}'$ may decide nondeterministically to take into account the current component value of some of the paths. Two things happen in a transition in which $\mathcal{A}'$ decides to take into account paths that go through a vertex whose state component belongs to a set $P \subseteq Q$. First, the traversal value of the transition is the meet of the traversal value of transitions that enter P. Second, in its subset construction, $\mathcal{A}'$ release the set P, as there is no further need to follow paths that visit P.

In Section 3.3, we present a general paradigm for decomposing lattice automata to Boolean automata, each associated with a join-irreducible element of the lattice. The paradigm can be used for proving Theorem 8 too. In the full version we describe a direct construction, which applies the paradigm, but hides the intermediate Boolean automata.

We can now complement an LNFW $\mathcal{A}$ by transforming the LUFW with the same structure as $\mathcal{A}$ to an LNFW. Hence, by Lemma 1 and Theorem 8, we have the following:

Theorem 9 [closure under complementation]. *Let $\mathcal{A}$ be an LNFW with n states. There is an LNFW $\mathcal{A}'$, with 2^n states, such that $L(\mathcal{A}') = comp(L(\mathcal{A}))$.*

3.2 Deterministic Automata on Finite Words

Theorem 10 [closure under join and meet]. *Let $\mathcal{A}_1$ and $\mathcal{A}_2$ be LDFW over $\mathcal{L}$. There are LDFW $\mathcal{A}_\vee$ and $\mathcal{A}_\wedge$ such that $L(\mathcal{A}_\vee) = L(\mathcal{A}_1) \vee L(\mathcal{A}_2)$ and $L(\mathcal{A}_\wedge) = L(\mathcal{A}_1) \wedge L(\mathcal{A}_2)$. If $\mathcal{A}_1$ has n_1 states, $\mathcal{A}_2$ has n_2 states, and $\mathcal{L}$ has m elements, then $\mathcal{A}_\vee$ has at most $n_1 \cdot n_2 \cdot m^2$ and at least $n_1 \cdot n_2 \cdot m$ states, and $\mathcal{A}_\wedge$ has $n_1 \cdot n_2$ states.*

The meet construction coincides with the one for LNFW. For the join construction, we first simplify $\mathcal{A}_1$ and $\mathcal{A}_2$ using Theorem 6 and only then apply the construction for LNFW[7].

We now turn to study complementation of LDFW. In the Boolean setting, complementation of deterministic automata is easy, and involves dualization. In the lattice setting dualization does not work, and should be combined with simplification. Therefore, we have the following.

Theorem 11 [closure under complementation]. *Let $\mathcal{A}$ be an LDFW, with n states, over $\mathcal{L}$. There is an LDFW $\mathcal{A}'$, with $n \cdot m$ states, such that $L(\mathcal{A}') = comp(L(\mathcal{A}))$.*

3.3 Lattice Automata on Infinite Words

Lattice automata can run on infinite words and define $\mathcal{L}$-languages of words in Σ^ω. A *nondeterministic Büchi lattice automaton* on infinite words (LNBW, for short) has the

---

[7] The gap between the upper and the lower bound in Theorem 10 follows from the fact that the exact dependency in m depends on the type of the lattice $\mathcal{L}$. For all types, the join construction requires at most an m^2 blow-up, and at least an m blow-up. By considering the types individually, it is possible to tighten the bound. In particular, for a lattice that is a full order, the tight bound is $n_1 \cdot n_2 \cdot m$, and for the powerset lattice, the tight bound is $n_1 \cdot n_2 \cdot m^{\log_2 3}$. Essentially, the different types of lattices induce different ways to partition the m^2 pairs of lattice values between the state space of the joint automaton and the value accumulated by the run in the form of traversal value.

same components as an LNFW, thus $\mathcal{A} = \langle \mathcal{L}, \Sigma, Q, Q_0, \delta, F \rangle$, only that it runs on infinite words. A *run* of $\mathcal{A}$ on a word $w = \sigma_1 \cdot \sigma_2 \cdots$ is an infinite sequence $r = q_0, q_1, \ldots$ of states. The *traversal value* of r on w is $trval(r, w) = Q_0(q_0) \wedge \bigwedge_{i \geq 0} \delta(q_i, \sigma_{i+1}, q_{i+1})$. The *acceptance value* of r on w is $acval(r, w) = \bigwedge_{i \geq 0} \bigvee_{j \geq i} F(q_j)$. The *value* of r on w is $val(r, w) = trval(r, w) \wedge acval(r, w)$.

Note that the acceptance value of a run corresponds to the Büchi condition in the Boolean case. There, F should be visited infinitely often, thus all suffixes should visit F. Accordingly, here, the meet of all suffixes is taken, where each suffix contribute the join of its members.

Theorem 12 [LNBW closure properties]. *Let $\mathcal{A}_1$ and $\mathcal{A}_2$ be LNBWs with n_1 and n_2 states, respectively.*

1. *There is an LNBW $\mathcal{A}_\vee$ with $n_1 + n_2$ states such that $L(\mathcal{A}_\vee) = L(\mathcal{A}_1) \vee L(\mathcal{A}_2)$.*
2. *There is an LNBW $\mathcal{A}_\wedge$ with $3 \cdot n_1 \cdot n_2$ states such that $L(\mathcal{A}_\wedge) = L(\mathcal{A}_1) \wedge L(\mathcal{A}_2)$.*
3. *There is an LNBW $\tilde{\mathcal{A}}_1$ with $2^{O(n_1 \log(n_1))}$ states such that $L(\tilde{\mathcal{A}}_1) = comp(L(\mathcal{A}_1))$.*

The proof of Theorem 12 follows from a general paradigm for transformation between lattice automata. The key observation is that a lattice-automaton over lattice $\mathcal{L}$ can be decomposed to a family Boolean automata where each Boolean automaton in the family corresponds to a join-irreducible (or meet irreducible) element of $\mathcal{L}$. A transformation on the lattice automaton can then be obtained by applying the transformation on the underlying Boolean automata, which can then be composed back to a lattice automaton. For the paradigm to work, we need to ensure some consistency requirements that have to do with maintaining the order of the lattice. In the following NBW stands for Nondeterministic Büchi automata on Words. We proceed with the details.

For an underlying set of states Q, we introduce an ordering on NBWs whose state space is Q. For $i \in \{1, 2\}$, let $\mathcal{A}_i = \langle \Sigma, Q, Q_i^0, \delta_i, F_i \rangle$ be an NBW. Let $\mathcal{A}_1 \leq \mathcal{A}_2$ when $Q_2^0 \subseteq Q_1^0$, $\delta_2 \subseteq \delta_1$, and $F_2 \subseteq F_1$. Intuitively, "smaller automata have more accepting runs". Formally, it is easy to see that $\mathcal{A}_1 \leq \mathcal{A}_2$ implies $L(\mathcal{A}_2) \subseteq L(\mathcal{A}_1)$.

A family $\{\mathcal{A}_l\}_{l \in \mathcal{L}}$ of NBWs that share a state space and are indexed by lattice elements is $\mathcal{L}$-*consistent* if $l_1 \leq l_2$ implies $\mathcal{A}_{l_1} \leq \mathcal{A}_{l_2}$. Similarly, a family is $\mathcal{L}$-*reverse-consistent* if $l_1 \leq l_2$ implies $\mathcal{A}_{l_1} \geq \mathcal{A}_{l_2}$.

Lemma 2 [decomposition]. *For an LNBW $\mathcal{A}$ it is possible to construct, in logarithmic space, the following $\mathcal{L}$-consistent families:*

1. *A family $\{\mathcal{A}_l\}_{l \in JI(\mathcal{L})}$ of NBWs such that for all $w \in \Sigma^\omega$, we have $w \in L(\mathcal{A}_l)$ iff $\mathcal{A}(w) \geq l$.*
2. *A family $\{\mathcal{A}_l\}_{l \in MI(\mathcal{L})}$ of NBWs such that for all $w \in \Sigma^\omega$, we have $w \notin L(\mathcal{A}_l)$ iff $\mathcal{A}(w) \leq l$.*

The proof for the join irreducible case is based on a construction of the NBWs $\mathcal{A}_l$ according to criteria like $Q_l^0 = \{q \in Q \mid Q_0(q) \geq l\}$. The proof of the meet irreducible case is based on a construction according to criteria like $Q_l^0 = \{q \in Q \mid Q_0(q) \not\leq l\}$.

For tuples of NBWs, we say that $\langle \mathcal{A}_1, \ldots, \mathcal{A}_k \rangle \leq \langle \mathcal{B}_1, \ldots, \mathcal{B}_k \rangle$ iff $\mathcal{A}_i \leq \mathcal{B}_i$ for every $i \in \{1, \ldots, k\}$. We say that a construction $\varphi : \text{NBW}^k \to \text{NBW}$ is *monotone* if

$\langle \mathcal{A}_1, \ldots, \mathcal{A}_k \rangle \leq \langle \mathcal{B}_1, \ldots, \mathcal{B}_k \rangle$ implies $\varphi(\langle \mathcal{A}_1, \ldots, \mathcal{A}_k \rangle) \leq \varphi(\langle \mathcal{B}_1, \ldots, \mathcal{B}_k \rangle)$. A construction is *antitone* if $\langle \mathcal{A}_1, \ldots, \mathcal{A}_k \rangle \leq \langle \mathcal{B}_1, \ldots, \mathcal{B}_k \rangle$ implies $\varphi(\langle \mathcal{A}_1, \ldots, \mathcal{A}_k \rangle) \geq \varphi(\langle \mathcal{B}_1, \ldots, \mathcal{B}_k \rangle)$.

Lemma 3. *Let $k \geq 0$ be an integer. For every $i \leq k$, let $\{\mathcal{A}_l^i\}_{l \in \mathcal{L}}$ be an $\mathcal{L}$-consistent family. If $\varphi : \mathrm{NBW}^k \to \mathrm{NBW}$ is a monotone construction, then $\{\varphi(\mathcal{A}_l^1, \ldots \mathcal{A}_l^k)\}_{l \in \mathcal{L}}$ is an $\mathcal{L}$-consistent family. Similarly, if φ is antitone then $\{\varphi(\mathcal{A}_l^1, \ldots \mathcal{A}_l^k)\}_{l \in \mathcal{L}}$ is an $\mathcal{L}$-reverse-consistent family.*

Lemma 4 [composition]. *Let $\{\mathcal{A}_l\}_{l \in JI(\mathcal{L})}$ be an $\mathcal{L}$-consistent family of NBWs, parameterized by the join irreducible elements of $\mathcal{L}$. There is an LNBW $\mathcal{A}$, sharing the state space of the family, such that for every $w \in \Sigma^\omega$ and $l \in JI(\mathcal{L})$, it holds that $w \in L(\mathcal{A}_l)$ iff $L(\mathcal{A})(w) \geq l$. Furthermore, the construction of $\mathcal{A}$ can be made in logarithmic space.*

The proof is based on the construction of $\mathcal{A}$ from $\{\mathcal{A}_l\}_{l \in JI(\mathcal{L})}$ according to criteria like $Q_0(q) = \bigvee\{l \in JI(\mathcal{L}) \mid q \in Q_l^0\}$.

We now have the basic building blocks needed to apply the paradigm of reducing lattice automata constructions to Boolean ones. Below we show how to apply this paradigm in the case of LNBW complementation. The other cases are simpler and are left to the reader. As a first step, we need a Boolean construction for NBW complementation that is an antitone.

Lemma 5. *There exists an antitone construction $\varphi : \mathrm{NBW} \to \mathrm{NBW}$ such that for every NBW $\mathcal{A}$, we have $L(\varphi(\mathcal{A})) = comp(L(\mathcal{A}))$. Furthermore, if $\mathcal{A}$ has n states, then $\varphi(\mathcal{A})$ has at most $2^{O(n \log(n))}$ states, and the construction can be made using space polynomial in n.*

In the full version, we prove the lemma by proving that (a small variant of) the [KV01] construction for NBW complementation is antitone. To prove the results for join and meet of languages, we need similar constructions of monotone (rather than antitone) constructions of union and intersection. The standard construction for union is already monotone. For the meet case, a small variant of the usual [Cho74] construction for intersection is needed, and is discussed in the full version.

We can now complete the construction for LNBW complementation. Given an LNBW $\mathcal{A}$, we use the decomposition lemma to construct a consistent family $\{\mathcal{A}_l\}_{l \in MI(\mathcal{L})}$ of NBWs such that $\mathcal{A}(w) \leq l$ iff $w \notin L(\mathcal{A}_l)$ for all $w \in \Sigma$. By applying the construction from Lemma 5, we get a reverse-consistent family $\{\mathcal{A}_l'\}_{l \in MI(\mathcal{L})}$ of NBWs such that $\mathcal{A}(w) \leq l$ iff $w \in L(\mathcal{A}_l')$ for all $w \in \Sigma$.

Next, we re-index the family by identifying $\mathcal{A}_l'$ with $\mathcal{A}_{comp(l)}''$. Since an element is meet irreducible iff its complement is join irreducible, the resulting family $\{\mathcal{A}_{comp(l)}''\}_{l \in MI(\mathcal{L})}$ is indexed by the join irreducible elements of $\mathcal{L}$ and can be seen as $\{\mathcal{A}_l''\}_{l \in JI(\mathcal{L})}$. Furthermore, for $l_1, l_2 \in JI(\mathcal{L})$, if $l_1 \leq l_2$, then $comp(l_2) \geq comp(l_1)$. Therefore, since $\{\mathcal{A}_l'\}$ is a reverse-consistent family, we get that $\mathcal{A}_{comp(l_1)}' \leq \mathcal{A}_{comp(l_2)}'$; i.e., $\mathcal{A}_{l_1}'' \leq \mathcal{A}_{l_2}''$. Thus, $\{\mathcal{A}_l''\}_{l \in JI(\mathcal{L})}$ is a consistent family.

Finally, we apply the composition lemma on $\{\mathcal{A}_l''\}_{l \in JI(\mathcal{L})}$ to get a single LNBW $\tilde{\mathcal{A}}$. To prove that $\tilde{\mathcal{A}}$ is indeed $comp(\mathcal{A})$ fix a word $w \in \Sigma^\omega$ and a join irreducible element $l \in JI(\mathcal{L})$. The following equivalences hold: $\tilde{\mathcal{A}}(w) \geq l$ iff $w \in L(\mathcal{A}_l'')$ iff

$w \in L(\mathcal{A}'_{comp(l)})$ iff $w \notin L(\mathcal{A}_{comp(l)})$ iff $\mathcal{A}(w) \leq comp(l)$ iff $comp(\mathcal{A}(w)) \geq l$. The result follows from Birkhoff's representation theorem.

4 Applications

In this section we apply our framework to the satisfiability and model-checking problems of multi-valued LTL. We first discuss decision problems for LNFW and LNBW.

4.1 Decision Problems

Consider an LNFW (or LNBW) $\mathcal{A}$ over a lattice $\mathcal{L}$. The *range* of $\mathcal{A}$ is the set of lattice values l for which there is a word w that $\mathcal{A}$ accepts with value l. Thus, $range(\mathcal{A}) = \bigcup_{w \in \Sigma^*} val(\mathcal{A}, w)$. The *emptiness value* of $\mathcal{A}$, denoted $e\_val(\mathcal{A})$, is then the join of all the values in its range; i.e., $e\_val(\mathcal{A}) = \bigvee range(\mathcal{A})$. Intuitively, $e\_val(\mathcal{A})$ describes how likely it is for $\mathcal{A}$ to accept a word. In particular, if $e\_val(\mathcal{A}) = \bot$, then $\mathcal{A}$ gives value $\bot$ to all the words in Σ^*. Over Boolean lattice, $e\_val(\mathcal{A}) = \bot$ if $\mathcal{A}$ is empty and $e\_val(\mathcal{A}) = \top$ if $\mathcal{A}$ is not empty. Note, however, that for a general (finite distributive De Morgan) lattice, $e\_val(\mathcal{A}) \neq \bot$ does not imply that there is a word that is accepted with value $e\_val(\mathcal{A})$. The *emptiness-value problem* is to decide, given an LNFW (or LNBW) $\mathcal{A}$, a value $l \in \mathcal{L}$, and an order relation $\sim \in \{<, \leq, =, \geq, >\}$, whether $e\_val(\mathcal{A}) \sim l$.

Theorem 13. *The emptiness-value problem for LNFW (or LNBW) is NLOGSPACE-complete.*

In the full version we discuss the *universality-value* and the *implication-value* problems, which corresponds to the universality and the language inclusion problems in the Boolean setting.

4.2 LLTL Model Checking and Satisfiability

As discussed in Section 1, the multi-valued setting appears in practice either directly, with multi-valued systems and specifications, or indirectly, as various methods are reduced to reasoning in a multi-valued setting. In this section we show how lattice automata provide a unifying automata-theoretic framework for reasoning about multi-valued systems and specifications,

A *multi-valued Kripke structure* is a six-tuple $K = \langle AP, \mathcal{L}, W, W_0, R, L \rangle$, where AP is a set of atomic propositions, $\mathcal{L}$ is a lattice, W is a finite set of states, $W_0 \in \mathcal{L}^W$ is an $\mathcal{L}$-set of initial states, $R \in L^{W \times W}$ is an $\mathcal{L}$-transitions relation, and $L : W \to \mathcal{L}^{AP}$ maps each state to an $\mathcal{L}$-set of atomic propositions. We require R to be total in its first element, thus for every $w \in W$ there is at least one $w' \in w$ such that $R(w, w') \neq \bot$. A path of K is an infinite sequence $w_1, w_2, \ldots$ of states. For technical simplicity, we assume that W_0 and R are Boolean. As discussed in Remark 3, it is easy to adjust our framework to handle weighted input letters, and hence, weighted initial states and transitions. In the Boolean setting, a path of K is one that has value $\top$, thus $w_1 \in w_0$ and $R(w_i, w_{i+1})$ for all $i \geq 1$.

The logic *LTL* is a linear temporal logic. Formulas of LTL are constructed from a set AP of atomic propositions using the usual Boolean operators and the temporal operators X ("next time") and U ("until"). The semantics of LTL is traditionally defined with respect to computations of Kripke structures in which each state is labeled by a set of atomic propositions true in this state and each two states are either connected or not connected by an edge. Note that traditional Kripke structures correspond to multi-valued Kripke structures over the lattice $\mathcal{L}_2$. We define the logic *Latticed-LTL* (LLTL, for short), which is the expected extension of LTL to multi-valued Kripke structures. The syntax of LLTL is similar to the one of LTL, except that the logic is parameterized by a lattice $\mathcal{L}$ and its constants are elements of $\mathcal{L}$. Let $\pi = w_1, w_2, \ldots$ be a path of a multi-valued Kripke structure. The value of an LLTL formula ψ on the path π in position i, denoted $val(\pi, i, \psi)$ is inductively defined as follows:

- For a lattice element $l \in L$, we have $val(\pi, i, l) = l$ for all π and i.
- For an atomic proposition $p \in AP$, we have $val(\pi, i, p) = w_i(p)$ for all π and i.
- $val(\pi, i, \neg\psi) = \neg val(\pi, i, \psi)$.
- $val(\pi, i, \psi \wedge \theta) = val(\pi, i, \psi) \wedge val(\pi, i, \theta)$.
- $val(\pi, i, X\psi) = val(\pi, i+1, \psi)$.
- $val(\pi, i, \psi U \theta) = \bigvee_{k \geq i}(val(\pi, k, \theta) \wedge \bigwedge_{i \leq j < k} val(\pi, j, \psi))$.

For an LLTL formula ψ, the *satisfiability value* of ψ, denoted $sat(\psi)$, is $\bigvee\{val(\pi, 1, \psi) : \pi \in (\mathcal{L}^{AP})^\omega\}$. Thus, the satisfiability value describes how likely it is for some path to satisfy ψ. The LLTL satisfiability problem is to determine, given an LLTL formula ψ, a value $l \in \mathcal{L}$, and an order relation $\sim \in \{<, \leq, =, \geq, >\}$, whether $sat(\psi) \sim l$. For a multi-valued Kripke structure K and an LLTL formula ψ, the *satisfaction value* of ψ in K, denoted $sat(K, \psi)$, is $\bigwedge\{val(\pi, 1, \psi) : \pi$ is a path of $K\}$. Thus, the satisfaction value describes how likely it is for all paths of K to satisfy ψ. The LLTL model-checking problem is to determine, given a multi-valued Kripke structure K, an LLTL formula ψ, a value $l \in \mathcal{L}$, and an order relation $\sim \in \{<, \leq, =, \geq, >\}$, whether $sat(K, \psi) \sim l$.

Theorem 14. *Given an LLTL formula ψ, there is an LNBW $\mathcal{A}_\psi$ such that for every word $w \in (\mathcal{L}^{AP})^\omega$, we have $\mathcal{A}_\psi(w) = val(w, 1, \psi)$.*

We can now use the automata-theoretic approach in order to solve the satisfiability and model checking problems for LLTL.

Theorem 15 [LLTL satisfiability and model checking]. *The LLTL satisfiability-value and satisfaction-value problems are PSPACE-complete.*

The proof is similar to the standard automata-theoretic approach to verification proofs. The full proof can be found in the full version.

Note that Theorem 15 also follows from reduction to several Boolean problems as presented in [BG04]. The advantage of the approach presented here, is solving LLTL model checking and satisfiability using direct lattice methods. The advantages of such direct methods were argued in [BG04], which solved the model checking for μL (the lattice extension of μ-calculus) directly, using EAA. Theorem 15, however, does not follow from the latter due to the doubly-exponential blow up of translating LTL formulas to mu-calculus.

References

[BG99]   G. Bruns and P. Godefroid. Model checking partial state spaces with 3-valued temporal logics. In *Proc. 11th CAV*, LNCS 1633, pages 274–287, 1999.

[BG01]   G. Bruns and P. Godefroid. Temporal logic query checking. In *Proc. 16th LICS*, pages 409–420, 2001.

[BG04]   G. Bruns and P. Godefroid. Model checking with 3-valued temporal logics. In *31st ICALP*, LNCS 3142, pages 281–293, 2004.

[CDG01]   M. Chechik, B. Devereux, and A. Gurfinkel. Model-checking infinite state-space systems with fine-grained abstractions using SPIN. In *SPIN Workshop in model-checking software*, LNCS 2057, pages 16-36, 2001.

[Cha00]   W. Chan. Temporal-logic queries. In *Proc. 12th CAV*, LNCS 1855, pages 450–463, 2000.

[Cho74]   Y. Choueka. Theories of automata on ω-tapes: A simplified approach. *Journal of Computer and System Sciences*, 8:117–141, 1974.

[EC01]   S. Easterbrook and M. Chechik. A framework for multi-valued reasoning over inconsistent viewpoints. In *Proc. 23rd ICSE*, pages 411–420, 2001.

[GS97]   S. Graf and H. Saidi. Construction of abstract state graphs with PVS. In *Proc. 9th CAV*, LNCS 1254, pages 72–83, 1997.

[HH04]   A. Hussain and M. Huth. On model checking multiple hybrid views. Technical Report TR-2004-6, University of Cyprus, 2004.

[IEEE93]   IEEE standard multivalue logic system for VHDL model interoperability (std_logic_1164), 1993.

[Imm88]   N. Immerman. Nondeterministic space is closed under complement. *SIAM Journal on Computing*, 17:935–938, 1988.

[KS86]   W. Kuich and A. Salomaa. *Semirings, Automata, Languages*. EATCS Monographs on Theoretical Computer Science. Springer-Verlag, 1986.

[Kur94]   R.P. Kurshan. *Computer Aided Verification of Coordinating Processes*. Princeton Univ. Press, 1994.

[KV01]   O. Kupferman and M.Y. Vardi. Weak alternating automata are not that weak. *ACM TOCL*, 2(2):408–429, July 2001.

[KVW00]   O. Kupferman, M.Y. Vardi, and P. Wolper. An automata-theoretic approach to branching-time model checking. *Journal of the ACM*, 47(2):312–360, March 2000.

[MH84]   S. Miyano and T. Hayashi. Alternating finite automata on ω-words. *Theoretical Computer Science*, 32:321–330, 1984.

[Moh97]   Mehryar Mohri. Finite-state transducers in language and speech processing. *Computational Linguistics*, 23(2):269–311, 1997.

[RS59]   M.O. Rabin and D. Scott. Finite automata and their decision problems. *IBM Journal of Research and Development*, 3:115–125, 1959.

[Saf88]   S. Safra. On the complexity of ω-automata. In *Proc. 29th FOCS*, pages 319–327, 1988.

[VW94]   M.Y. Vardi and P. Wolper. Reasoning about infinite computations. *Information and Computation*, 115(1):1–37, November 1994.

Learning Algorithms and Formal Verification
(Invited Tutorial)

P. Madhusudan

University of Illinois at Urbana-Champaign
Dept. of Computer Science
Urbana, Illinois, USA

Abstract. This tutorial is on applications of computational learning theory to verification of systems. Computational learning theory deals with algorithmic models for learning formally representable concepts using either positive and negative samples or by access to an oracle that can answer certain queries about the concept.

The problem of learning formal languages has been particularly useful in verification applications. We will introduce Angluin's algorithm, a learning algorithm that learns *regular languages* efficiently using an oracle that can answer membership and equivalence queries. We will also survey results on learning regular languages in other learning models.

We will give an account of how learning has been used to solve a variety of problems in verification, spanning compositional verification, parameterized model-checking, synthesis of interfaces, machines with unbounded queues, and program testing. In all these examples, a crucial property that is exploited is the *simplicity* of certain concepts that underlie real-world systems, the learning of which yields a a simple mechanism to prove the correctness of the system. We will also lay out general arguments on why learning algorithms can play a crucial role in the design of verification algorithms, and list some open research directions that work towards this goal.

Constructing Specialized Shape Analyses for Uniform Change

Tal Lev-Ami[1,*], Mooly Sagiv[1], Neil Immerman[2,**], and Thomas Reps[3,***]

[1] School of Computer Science, Tel Aviv University
`{tla,msagiv}@post.tau.ac.il`
[2] Department of Computer Science, UMass, Amherst
`immerman@cs.umass.edu`
[3] Computer Science Department, University of Wisconsin, Madison
`reps@cs.wisc.edu`

Abstract. This paper is concerned with one of the basic problems in abstract interpretation, namely, for a given abstraction and a given set of concrete transformers (that express the concrete semantics of a program), how does one create the associated abstract transformers? We develop a new methodology for addressing this problem, based on a syntactically restricted language for expressing concrete transformers. We use this methodology to produce best abstract transformers for abstractions of many important data structures.

1 Introduction

Abstraction and abstract interpretation [1] are key tools for automatically verifying both hardware and software systems. This paper is concerned with one of the basic problems in abstract interpretation, namely, for a given abstraction and a given set of concrete transformers (that express the concrete semantics of a program), how does one create the associated abstract transformers? We develop a new methodology for addressing this problem, based on a syntactically restricted language for expressing concrete transformers. Of particular interest is that—by employing previous results from dynamic algorithms and dynamic descriptive complexity [2]—our methods allow precise reachability information to be maintained for abstractions of data structures. We use this methodology to produce best abstract transformers for abstractions of many important data structures.

Shape Analysis, Canonical Abstraction, and Dynamic Descriptive Complexity.
While our approach is quite general, the main application is to shape analysis (i.e., analysis of linked data structures) and to analyses based on canonical abstraction—the family of abstractions introduced by Sagiv, Reps, and Wilhelm [3] for analyzing programs that use dynamic data structures, including allocation and deallocation of memory cells and destructive updates of pointer-valued fields. In this approach, data

---

* Supported by an Adams Fellowship through the Israel Academy of Sciences and Humanities.
** Supported by NSF grants CCF-0514621 and CCF-0541018.
*** Supported by NSF grants CCF-0540955 and CCF-0524051.

B. Cook and A. Podelski (Eds.): VMCAI 2007, LNCS 4349, pp. 215–233, 2007.

structures are modeled using (3-valued) logical structures. Each element of the universe of the structure represents either a single memory cell, or, if the element is a *summary element*, it represents a set of memory cells.

The analysis simulates the program step-by-step, updating the structures appropriately, mimicking (i.e., approximating soundly) the semantics of program statements. When a fixpoint is reached, the resulting set of structures is a finite summary of relevant properties of the data structures built by the program. Note that any resulting properties of the set of structures are thus proven to hold: they necessarily hold on all runs of the program. This analysis framework has been implemented in the TVLA system. (The acronym stands for **T**hree-**V**alued **L**ogic **A**nalyzer.)

A key technical difficulty concerns the summary elements. They are needed so that the unbounded-size set of unbounded-size concrete data structures that can arise are always abstracted to a finite set of finite-size logical structures, which guarantees that the analysis always reaches a fixpoint. The problem caused by summary nodes is that some relations between cells in memory can be true for some elements represented by a summary node and false for others. Hence a truth value of "$\frac{1}{2}$" is introduced, and the framework is based on 3-valued logic [3]. As the analysis propagates 3-valued structures, however, there is a tendency for logical values of $\frac{1}{2}$, i.e., "don't know", to increase, which limits the quality of information that the analysis can provide.

A good way to combat this problem is to maintain extra, auxiliary relations in the logical structures [3,4]. The same approach is used in dynamic descriptive complexity, although the motivation is completely different:

- In dynamic descriptive complexity, we work with objects that undergo a series of inserts, deletes, changes, and queries; with each query, the goal is to return the answer with respect to the current object. The fundamental issue in dynamic descriptive complexity is one of *efficiency*: "What auxiliary information should be maintained to answer the query *quickly*?" The goal of maintaining extra information is to avoid recomputing each answer from scratch.
- In static analysis based on 3-valued logic, the issue is not so much to save computation time, but instead to preserve high-quality information, i.e., definite truth values—"0"s and "1"s, rather than "$\frac{1}{2}$"s—whenever possible.

A second key technical difficulty concerns reachability information, which is needed to express connectivity and separation properties of data structures. There has been extensive work in dynamic descriptive complexity on how to efficiently maintain reachability information. For example, Dong and Su showed that for acyclic graphs reachability may be maintained by first-order formulas [5]. Of particular interest to us is the result of Hesse that reachability for (not-necessarily acyclic) functional graphs can be maintained by quantifier-free formulas [6].

Our New Methodology. As explained above, TVLA maintains abstract (3-valued) structures, $\mathcal{A}$, that represent sets of concrete (2-valued) structures, $\gamma(\mathcal{A})$. We say that an abstract structure, $\mathcal{A}$, is **feasible** iff $\gamma(\mathcal{A}) \neq \emptyset$. Let β be the abstraction operator on individual concrete structures, i.e., $\beta(\mathcal{C})$ is the abstract representation of $\mathcal{C}$, so β and γ are (approximate) inverse operations (adjoined functions).

For each program statement, st, TVLA has an update formula τ_{st} so that on any concrete structure, C, $\tau_{st}(C)$ is the concrete structure produced by executing statement st. Furthermore, the update formula is always **safe** on abstract structures, meaning that $\tau_{st}(\gamma(\mathcal{A})) \subseteq \gamma(\tau_{st}(\mathcal{A}))$.

Given an abstraction, the gold standard of abstract transformers is called the **best transformer** [1], and satisfies the property, $bt_{st}(\mathcal{A}) = \{\beta(\tau_{st}(C)) \mid C \in \gamma(\mathcal{A})\}$. However, because $\gamma(\mathcal{A})$ may be infinite, the equation above does not provide an <u>algorithm</u> for computing the best transformer.

TVLA employs heuristics to efficiently compute a safe transformer that is not necessarily the best transformer. In this paper, we introduce a syntactic condition called **monadic uniform** with the following property (see also Thm. 11):

Main Theorem: *If the update formulas for a data structure are monadic uniform and we have an algorithm that given an abstract structure, $\mathcal{A}$, decides whether $\mathcal{A}$ is feasible, then we can automatically compute the best transformers for the operations on the data structure.*

We then show that our main theorem applies to many important situations:

- We use and modify known results from dynamic descriptive complexity to create monadic-uniform update formulas for many important classes of data structures, including linked lists, cyclic linked lists, doubly-linked lists, cyclic doubly-linked lists, trees, shared trees, directed graphs with no undirected cycles, and also some of the above data structures when arbitrary unary relations and an ordering relation are included.
- We also present efficient feasibility algorithms for most of the above. Thus, for these data structures we can implement best abstract transformers automatically.

Our vision is to build specialized shape analyses for many of the available programs and observed properties. This paper is an important step in this direction because it shows that it is possible to build — in a systematic manner — specialized shape analyses with good theoretical properties for many important data structures.

Predicate Abstraction. Our results are not limited to the TVLA context; in particular, they provide a way to improve the predicate-abstraction method given by Rakamaric et al. [7]. Their linked-list abstraction uses the relation $between(x, y, z)$ to capture whether there is a path from x to z through y. Rakamaric et al. give a complete decision procedure for checking feasibility of a given abstract state, but left open the question of how to handle transformers in the most-precise way. Our methodology solves this problem: we can use the quantifier-free update formulas given by Hesse [6] to build best transformers for this abstraction. For example, to compute the abstract transformer for the addition/removal of an edge we would: (1) extend the vocabulary with a constant capturing the current target of the edge; (2) replace each abstract state with the set of states that provide all possible interpretations to the predicates involving the new constant; (3) use the Rakamaric et al. decision procedure to remove the infeasible abstract states; (4) for the remaining states, evaluate Hesse's update formulas to get the successor states.

2 Overview

This section is an informal overview of the methodology presented in the paper. We use a simple Java procedure that reverses a singly-linked list specified in Fig. 1 as a running example. We will run reverse on a cyclic singly-linked list. We use a graphical representation of logical structures to depict a store as a graph.

```
Node reverse(Node x){
[0]  Node y = null;
[1]  while (x != null){
[2]    Node t = x.next;
[3]    x.next = y;
[4]    y = x; x = t; }
[5]  return y;  }
```

Fig. 1. The running example

Fig. 2(a) is an example of a singly linked list with a cycle. Memory cells are represented by the individuals of the structures (the nodes in the graph). Program variables are represented by constants (the text inside the nodes). Pointer fields in a memory cell are represented by binary relations (the edges of the graph, annotated with the relation name). In this case, the next field of the list nodes is represented by the n relation, which is a total function. We can add to the structure auxiliary relations defined using FO(TC) (First Order Logic with Transitive Closure) formulas over the core relations. For example, in Fig. 2(b) we use a unary relation $r_{x,n}$ (written below the nodes) to indicate the existence of a path from the node pointed to by x (defined by $r_{x,n}(v) \stackrel{\text{def}}{=} n^*(x, v)$). The unary relation c_n states that the node is on a cycle of next fields (defined by $c_n(v) \stackrel{\text{def}}{=} n^+(v, v)$).

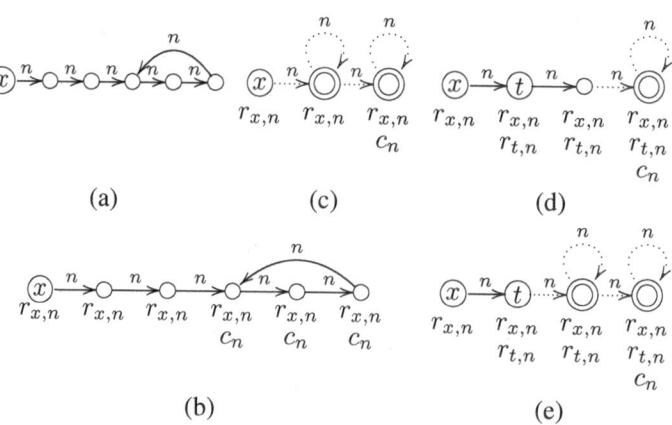

(a)   (c)   (d)

(b)   (e)

Fig. 2. (a) A concrete structure that represents a singly-linked list with a loop, which is pointed to by x and consists of 6 nodes. (b) The same singly-linked list, this time with auxiliary information. (c) Abstraction of singly-linked lists with loops. (d) & (e) The result of computing the best abstract transformer for the operation t=x.next on (c). Note there is also always a concrete node, **null**, with a self-loop (for n) and no other edges. We do not draw this to save space.

In abstract interpretation, we wish to represent a large (possibly infinite) set of stores using a finite set of structures; here this is done by collapsing nodes together into "summary nodes" (drawn as double circles). We use three-valued logic with an additional $\frac{1}{2}$ truth value (for binary relations, this is depicted as a dotted edge) to capture the case in which for some of the nodes represented by the summary node the value is true (1) while for others the value is false (0).[1] Fig. 2(c) shows an abstract structure in which constants are untouched and all the nodes with the same values for unary relations are collapsed together. This type of abstraction is called **canonical abstraction** and is guaranteed to result in structures of bounded size for a given vocabulary. The Embedding Theorem of [3] guarantees that if evaluating formulas (using Kleene semantics) on the abstract structure results in a definite value (i.e., 1 or 0), evaluating the formula on any concrete structure it represents will yield the same value. Kleene semantics can be understood as considering $\frac{1}{2}$ to be $\{0, 1\}$, 0 to be $\{0\}$, and 1 to be $\{1\}$ and evaluating pointwise, e.g., $1 \wedge \frac{1}{2} = \frac{1}{2}$, but $0 \wedge \frac{1}{2} = 0$.

Transformers are given for each operation according to the program's operational semantics. Transformers are specified using **guarded commands** with formulas in FO(TC) called update formulas. For example, for the operation t=x.next used in line 2 of Fig. 1, we can use a guard $x \neq null \wedge n(x, x_n)$ to (a) ensure that there is no null-dereference, and (b) bind the value of the next field of x to a new (temporary) constant x_n. The update formulas are: $t' := x_n$, $x' := x$, $n'(v_1, v_2) := n(v_1, v_2)$, $c'_n(v) = c_n(v)$, $r'_{x,n}(v) := r_{x,n}(v)$, $r'_{t,n}(v) := n^*(t', v)$. The most precise abstract transformer would return a set of abstract structures that captures as tightly as possible (for the abstraction in use) the result of applying the transformer on all the concrete structures represented by the original abstract structure. This kind of abstract transformer is called the best abstract transformer [1] and can be theoretically computed by finding all concrete structures represented by an abstract structure (a.k.a. concretization), computing the transformer on each of them, and abstracting the results. However, because the number of concrete structures represented by an abstract structure is unbounded (and potentially infinite), this is not an algorithm. Fig. 2(d) and Fig. 2(e) show the result for t=x.next on the structure in Fig. 2(c). The structure in Fig. 2(d) represents the case in which the list before the cycle is of length 2, and the structure in Fig. 2(e) represents the case it is of length 3 or more. Note that simply evaluating the update formulas on the structure in Fig. 2(c) would not have given us this precise result.

We seek a way to compute the same result as the best transformer without resorting to full concretization. One of the key principles of our methodology is to find a **partial concretization** that 1) is computable, 2) returns a finite set of abstract structures that represents the same concrete structures, and 3) for each of these structures the best abstract transformer can be computed by simply evaluating the update formulas. We call the operation of finding such a partial concretization **Focus** after a similar operation in [3]. Focus replaces each structure with a set of structures, representing the same concrete structures, in which the partitioning of the concrete nodes into summary nodes is more fine-grained. This can be achieved by bifurcating summary nodes into two groups: nodes for which an atomic formula holds, and nodes for which it does not hold. We call such a formula a **focus formula**. For example, Fig. 3(a) and (b) show the result of Focus for the focus formula $n(x, v)$ on the structure in Fig. 2(c). The second and third nodes in the lists of Fig. 3(a) and (b) are the result of bifurcating the second node in Fig. 2(c) according to the focus formula. For the second node, the formula holds,

---

[1] For readers familiar with [3], we use tight embedding in this paper. Thus, each summary node represents at least two nodes.

and for the third node the formula does not hold. As we can see, this process can result in multiple structures; Fig. 3(a) corresponds to the case in which the original summary node represents two concrete nodes and in Fig. 3(b) the case in which the summary node represents three or more concrete nodes. We can see that in both cases, the second node has been materialized out of the original summary node.

To automate the Focus operation, we propose an algorithm that can compute the partial concretization for a set of focus formulas: the first phase does not understand the intended meaning of the relations; the second phase applies a "feasibility check" supplied by the developer of the abstraction. An algorithm for feasibility checking should return true iff an abstract structure represents at least one concrete structure. Fig. 3(c) and (d) show structures arising in the Focus process that are infeasible. Structure 3(c) is infeasible because the second node must represent at least two nodes and the first node must have a direct edge to both of them, which contradicts that n is a function. Structure 3(d) is infeasible because the self-loop on the second node means that it must both have a self-loop and not have a self-loop. In §5, we provide algorithms for checking feasibility for several abstractions of commonly used data structures. Note that even if we cannot check feasibility for some abstraction (or have only a sound approximation), the resulting transformer is a sound approximation of the best transformer.

The problem with finding the right focus formulas and using Focus for the transformer given for t=x.next is that for the computation of $r'_{t,n}$ we require that the evaluation of $n^*(t', v)$ return precise results — in particular; for any element in the cycle, it should return 1. However, this means that all the edges until the cycle must be 1, which means we need to consider all possible lengths for the segment of the list before the cycle. This is not possible. To solve this problem, we need to somehow limit the update formulas. This leads to our second principle, **monadic-uniform update formulas**.

The update formula for $r'_{t,n}$ can be rewritten as $r'_{t,n}(v) := r_{x,n}(v) \wedge (c_n(x) \vee x \neq v)$. If x is on a cycle, t must be on the same cycle; thus, whatever was reachable from x is now also reachable from t. Otherwise, the only node that was reachable from x and is not reachable from t is x itself. Evaluating this updated transformer on the structures in Fig. 3(a) and (b) results in the structures in Fig. 2(d) and Fig. 2(e). Thus, focusing on $n(x, v)$ was enough. This is not a coincidence. We show that if we limit the update formulas to a certain syntactic class (which we call monadic-uniform), we can automatically find the focus formulas needed for the Focus operation, and the result of Focus is guaranteed to be bounded (a function of the size of the original structure).

The process of finding monadic-uniform update formulas is not trivial, especially when trying to update reachability. Fortunately, we can use existing results from the dynamic descriptive complexity [2,6] and database [5] communities on maintaining reachability when edges are added or removed. A key step in finding such monadic-uniform update formulas is the addition of auxiliary relations, which together with the other relations can be maintained by monadic-uniform update formulas. In §5, we provide monadic-uniform transformers for the abstractions used for many of the analyses done successfully with TVLA.

Our methodology can be summarized as follows:

1. Find an abstraction that captures the properties you want to verify. Describe it within the framework of parameterized shape analysis of [3].

2. Insure that all update formulas are monadic-uniform, adding extra auxiliary relations as needed.
3. Optionally, develop a feasibility check for abstract structures of this (possibly augmented) vocabulary; or, settle for a sound approximation of the best transformer.

The paper presents the necessary algorithms for binding these ingredients together to compute best abstract transformers.

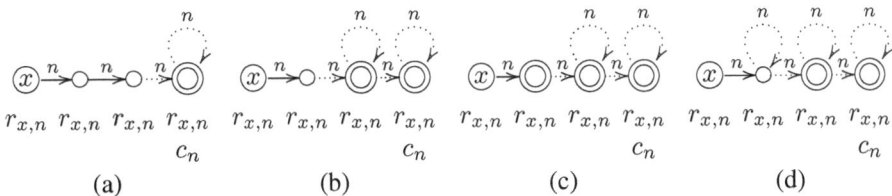

Fig. 3. Some of the structures arising in the process of Focus for the operation t=x.next on the structure in Fig. 2(c)

3 Preliminaries

We represent stores as logical structures. This allows us to use logical formulas to define the semantics of statements and abstractions of stores. To simplify the presentation, we describe everything in the context of a specific vocabulary. It should be clear from the description that the formulas are schematic and can be instantiated to the specific program fields and variables.

See [8] for a formal definition of the syntax of FO(TC) formulas. We use the short-hand (when $\varphi_1 \Rightarrow \psi_1, \ldots,$ when $\varphi_k \Rightarrow \psi_k$, default $\Rightarrow \psi$) for a sequential case split; i.e., formally it is: $\ldots \vee (\neg \varphi_1 \wedge \ldots \wedge \neg \varphi_{i-1} \wedge \varphi_i \wedge \psi_i) \vee \ldots \vee (\neg \varphi_1 \wedge \ldots \wedge \neg \varphi_k \wedge \psi)$

A 2-valued logical structure is a triple $S = \langle U^S, R^S, C^S \rangle$ of a universe U^S of individuals, a map R^S of relation symbols to truth-valued functions, and a map C^S of constant symbols to individuals. See [8] for a formal definition.

3.1 Programming-Language Statements

Formulas are used to update the store in a standard way as follows:

Definition 1. (Store Updates) *An **update formula** of a relation r of arity k has the form: $r'(v_1, \ldots, v_k) := \varphi_r(v_1, \ldots, v_k)$, where $\varphi_r(v_1, \ldots, v_k)$ is a formula with free variables $v_1, v_2, \ldots v_k$. An **update formula** of a constant c has the form:*
$c' := (\text{when } \varphi_1 \Rightarrow s_1, \ldots, \text{when } \varphi_k \Rightarrow s_k, \text{default} \Rightarrow s_{k+1})$, *where the φ_i are closed formulas and the s_i are constant symbols. This is a shorthand for the following formula with one free variable: $\varphi_c(v) \overset{\text{def}}{=} (\ldots, \text{when } \varphi_i \Rightarrow v = s_i, \ldots, \text{default} \Rightarrow v = s_{k+1})$ For the special case in which k=0 we simply write $c' := s_1$.*

*Every statement st in the programming language is associated with **transformer** τ_{st}, which consists of a **guard formula**, $\text{guard}_{\tau_{st}}$, and a set of update formulas for each relation and constant symbol in the vocabulary. If the guard formula has free variables, the update formulas can refer to them as constants.*

*Given a 2-valued logical structure, $S = \langle U, R, C \rangle$, the **expansion** of S for τ is the set $expand_\tau(S)$ of all the structures $S' = \langle U, R, C' \rangle$ s.t., C' is identical to C except it gives an interpretation to all the free variables of $guard_\tau$. We say S' is **expanded** for τ.*

*The application of the transformer τ on a structure $S' \in expand_\tau(S)$ is the 2-valued structure $\tau(S') \stackrel{\text{def}}{=} \langle U, R'', C'' \rangle$, where for every relation symbol r, $R''(r)(\vec{u}) = [\![\varphi_r(\vec{u})]\!]^{S'}$, and for every constant symbol c, let $u_c \in U$ be the unique element for which $S', u_c \models \varphi_c$, we have $C''(c) = u_c$. Note that C'' gives an interpretation only to the original constants and not to the free variables of $guard_\tau$. The **meaning** of the transformer τ on S is the set $[\![\tau]\!](S) \stackrel{\text{def}}{=} \{ \tau(S') \mid S' \in expand(S) \wedge S' \models guard_\tau \}$.*   □

The free variables in the guard formula allow for the introduction of nondeterminism. These free variables are considered as additional constants by the update formulas. The syntactic form of the update formulas for constants guarantees that for each constant symbol c there is only one u_c for which $S', u_c \models \varphi_c$. Thus, once the free variables have been assigned, the computation of the transformer is deterministic.

For simplicity, we do not support operations that change the universe. However, because we allow infinite universes, we can easily model the allocation and deallocation of individuals using a designated relation that holds only for allocated individuals (or, if the operational semantics allows, by using a free list).

Table 1 lists the transformers that define the operational semantics of the five kinds of Java-like statements. Here x, t, and y are constants that denote the target of pointer variables x, t, and y, respectively. *sel* is a binary relation that models the pointer field sel. We do not specify update-formulas for relations and constants with unchanged values. The guard formulas for statements that access sel ensure that no null-dereference has occurred. In case of a field traversal, the

Table 1. Relation-update formulas that define the semantics of statements that manipulate pointers and pointer-valued fields

st	$guard_{st}$	update formulas
x = null	1	$x' := null$
x = t	1	$x' := t$
x = t.sel	$t \neq null \wedge$ $sel(t, t_{sel})$	$x' := t_{sel}$
x.sel = y	$x \neq null$	$sel'(v_1, v_2) :=$ $(v_1 = x \wedge v_2 = y) \vee$ $(v_1 \neq x \wedge sel(v_1, v_2))$
x == y	$x = y$	

guard formula also selects the target of the field using the free variable t_{sel}. Note that program conditions are simply modeled by guard formulas.

Integrity Constraints. We allow restriction of the potential stores that may arise in the program by a finite set of closed formulas called **integrity constraints** and denoted by Σ. We assume that the meaning of every transformer τ **maintains the integrity constraints**, i.e., if $S \models \Sigma$, $S' \in [\![\tau]\!]^S$ a 2-valued structure, then $S' \models \Sigma$.

In the case of pointer fields, we require that every field be a total function. Thus, in particular, the pointer field(s) of *null* points to *null*.

Auxiliary Information. The most interesting integrity constraints occur as a result of extra relations whose values are derived from other relations. Formally, an **auxiliary** relation r of arity k is defined via a defining formula φ_r with k free variables. This results in the integrity constraint $\forall v_1, \ldots, v_k : r(v_1, \ldots, v_k) \iff \varphi_r$. Thus, every statement must maintain this invariant. Auxiliary information allows us to reduce the complexity of update formulas. Furthermore, it is often the information maintained by auxiliary relations that enables us to compute best abstract transformers.

§2 introduced two types of auxiliary relations, $r_{x,n}$ for reachability from a program variable, and c_n for cyclicity. The interaction between them is used to define a monadic-uniform update formula for traversal of an edge.

3.2 Monadic-Uniform Updates

In this section, we restrict the way the semantics of statements are allowed to be defined to use only formulas of a certain syntactic class. The new stores can differ from the original store in many values but the change should be uniform in the sense defined below. We begin by defining atomic formulas that are essentially unary.

Definition 2. *An atomic formula is **monadic** if it is of the form $r(c_1, \ldots, c_i, v, c_{i+1}, \ldots, c_{k-1})$ where r is k-ary relation and $c_1, \ldots, c_{k-1}$ are constant symbols. An FO(TC) formula φ is **monadic** if all of the atomic formulas appearing in φ are monadic or ground.* □

The following formulas are monadic: $r(v, c)$, $v = c$, $r(v)$, $\forall v.r(v, c)$. The following formulas have variables in more than one position, and thus are not monadic: $r(v, v)$, $r(v_1, v_2)$, $v_1 = v_2$. Note that although $r(v, v)$ uses a single variable, it is not monadic.

Next, we define monadic update formulas, which are a restricted case of update formulas in which a tuple is classified by monadic formulas, and for each class, the value of an existing relation is copied.

Definition 3. (Monadic-Uniform Updates) *A **monadic-uniform formula** $\varphi(v_1, \ldots, v_k)$ is syntactically equivalent to $(\ldots, \text{when } \varphi_i \Rightarrow \psi_i, \ldots, \text{default} \Rightarrow \psi_l)$ where the φ_i are monadic FO(TC) formulas with free variables $v_1, v_2, \ldots v_k$, and the ψ_i are restricted to either **1**, **0**, or a literal with distinct variables.*

*A **monadic-uniform transformer** is a transformer in which all the update formulas and the guard formula are monadic uniform.* □

All the transformers of Table 1 are constructed to be monadic-uniform transformers (see §5). Monadic-uniform formulas disallow direct interaction between non-monadic relations, e.g., $r(v_1, v_2) \wedge q(v_1, v_2)$ is not monadic-uniform. $r(v, v)$ is not monadic-uniform because it is equivalent to $r(v_1, v_2) \wedge v_1 = v_2$ and captures the interaction between r and equality.

3.3 Canonical Abstraction

In this section, we use 3-valued logic to conservatively represent sets of stores. Formally, we define a lattice of static information where lattice elements are sets of 3-valued structures. A 3-valued structure is similar to a 2-valued structure, except R^S maps to 3-valued truth functions, i.e., whose range is $\{0, 1, \frac{1}{2}\}$. See [8] for a formal definition. We say that the values 0 and 1 are definite values and that $\frac{1}{2}$ is an indefinite value, and define a partial (information) order on truth values as follows $l_1 \sqsubseteq l_2$ if $l_1 = l_2$ or $l_2 = \frac{1}{2}$. The symbol $\sqcup$ denotes the least-upper-bound operation with respect to $\sqsubseteq$.

Definition 4. *A tight embedding function is a surjective function* $f: U^S \rightarrow U^{S'}$ *such that, for every* $c \in C$, $C^{S'}(c) = f(C^S(c))$ *and for every relation* $r \in R$ *of arity* k, $R^{S'}(r)(u'_1, \ldots, u'_k) = \bigsqcup_{f(u_i)=u'_i, 1 \leq i \leq k} R^S(r)(u_1, \ldots, u_k)$. *We say that* $S' = f(S)$ *and that* S' *is a* **tight embedding** *of* S. [2]

When the embedding function maps more than one node to some node u, we say that u is a **summary node**. Otherwise, we call the node a **concrete node**. For summary nodes, $[\![u = u]\!]^{S'} = \frac{1}{2}$. Note that if $C^{S'}(c) = u$ and u is a summary node, only one of the nodes mapped to u equals c, not all of them.

Canonical embedding, denoted by β, is the embedding obtained by using unary relation symbols to distinguish between individuals, i.e., two concrete individuals $u_1, u_2 \in U^S$ are mapped to the same individual if and only if they agree on the values of unary relation symbols. For each constant, c, there is an implied unary relation, P_c, true just of c. □

According to the **embedding theorem** [3], every formula with a definite value in a structure has the same value in all of the embedded concrete structures.

Canonical abstraction allows us to define the set of stores represented by a 3-valued structure.

Definition 5. *For a 3-valued structure* S, $\gamma(S)$ *denotes the set of 2-valued structures that* S *represents, i.e.,* $\gamma(S) = \{S^\natural \models \Sigma \mid \beta(S^\natural) = S\}$. *We say that a structure* S *is* **feasible** *if* $\gamma(S) \neq \emptyset$. □

The complexity of checking feasibility of a structure comes from the need to satisfy the integrity constraints and because of interactions between auxiliary relations and core relations.

4   Methodology for Developing Computable Transformers

A shape-analysis problem is characterized by a triple of the class of allowed structures, the initial abstraction, and the set of possible atomic operations.

The running example (see Fig. 1) is an instance of the following shape-analysis problem: The class of allowed structures is (possibly cyclic) singly-linked lists. The initial abstraction tracks: pointed to by a program variable (by representing program variables as logical constants), the next field (by maintaining a binary relation n), reachability from program variables (by unary relations of the form $r_{x,n}(v)$, which indicate that v is reachable from program variable x using the next field), and cyclicity (by a unary relation $c_n(v)$, which indicates that v is part of a cycle).

The first step in developing computable best transformers for a shape-analysis problem is to find monadic-uniform transformers for all the operations required. A key step in finding such update formulas is the introduction of additional auxiliary relations that, together with the original relations, can be maintained in a monadic-uniform way.

The main difficulty in maintaining the relations used in the shape-analysis problem for the running example is the maintenance of reachability. Fortunately, we can use (with

---

[2] From now on, whenever we refer to embedding, we mean tight embedding and use the term tight embedding only for emphasis.

a small modification to make it monadic-uniform) the DynQF update formulas for transitive closure given by Hesse in [6]. We introduce three auxiliary binary relations. The relation $p_n(v_1, v_2)$ maintains the reflexive transitive closure of the n relation (i.e., existence of a path between v_1 and v_2 using the next field). The relation $cut_n(v_1, v_2)$ holds for exactly one edge in each cycle (enforced using appropriate integrity constraints). The relation $pc_n(v_1, v_2)$ (called PathCut by Hesse) maintains the reflexive transitive closure of the un-cut edges. Together, these relations allow us to create monadic-uniform transformers for all the needed operations (see [6] and §5 for more details).

Imperative programs lead to monadic-uniform transformers because they can only change information directly pointed to by variables. The difficulty comes from relations such as reachability in which a local update can cause widespread change. We take advantage of the specific structure of the graphs in each case to build a monadic-uniform transformer for them.

The final step in our methodology is to develop an algorithm for checking the feasibility of an abstract structure of the chosen vocabulary. Here we need to take into account the integrity constraints, including the set of allowed structures and the meaning for all the auxiliary relations.

In §5, we show that, to check feasibility of an abstract structure that can arise in the shape-analysis problem defined above, we can compute a candidate concrete structure s.t. the abstract structure is feasible iff the concrete structure is consistent (i.e., satisfies the integrity constraints) and its β is the original structure. The size of the candidate structure is linear in the size of the original abstract structure. Thus, we can check its feasibility in time polynomial in the size of the original abstract structure.

The rest of the section describes how to compute best transformers for a given shape-analysis problem that has monadic-uniform transformers and a decidable feasibility-checking problem. Proofs can be found in [8].

First, we define the concept of a **focused** structure for a monadic-uniform transformer. For such structures and transformers, the transformer preserves embedding (see Lem. 7).

Definition 6. *We say that S is **focused** for a τ (denoted by $focused_\tau(S)$) when (1) S is expanded for τ, (2) all the monadic atomic formulas that appear in any update formula of τ or in guard$_\tau$, evaluate to definite truth values in S, and (3) all the constants interpreted by C^S are mapped to concrete nodes.*

We define β_τ to be a canonical embedding function that honors all new constants and monadic atomic formulas appearing in transformer τ. γ_τ is defined analogously to γ but in relation to β_τ. ☐

The structures in Fig. 3(a) and (b) are focused for t = x.next if we map x_n to any concrete node (only when x_n is mapped to the second node of the list will the guard formula hold). For Fig. 2(c), when trying to interpret x_n in a way that will satisfy the guard formula, the only node worth considering is the second node of the list. There are two reasons why such a structure is not focused. First, the second node is a summary node, thus a constant cannot be mapped to it. Second, $n(x, x_n)$, which appears in the guard formula, evaluates to $\frac{1}{2}$. Note that the fact that the structures in Fig. 3(a) and (b) are focused does not mean that all the update formulas evaluate to definite values for all the nodes, e.g., the n relation has several indefinite tuples in resulting structure Fig. 2(e).

For structures that are focused for a transformer τ, we use the canonical embedding function β_τ, and when referring to the feasibility of a focused structure, we mean non-emptiness of γ_τ.

Lemma 7. *Let τ be a monadic-uniform transformer, S be a structure s.t. $focused_\tau(S)$ holds, C be a concrete structure, and f be an embedding function s.t. $f(C) = S$. The following properties hold: (1) $f(\tau(C)) = \tau(S)$, (2) $[\![guard_\tau]\!]^C = [\![guard_\tau]\!]^S$, (3) for every unary relation r and node u we have $[\![r(u)]\!]^{\tau(C)} = [\![r(f(u))]\!]^{\tau(S)}$, and (4) for every constant c, $\tau(S)$ maps c to a concrete node.*

When embedding is preserved, all unary relations are definite, and all the constants are mapped to non-summary nodes, β will return the same value for both updated structures. Cor. 8 entails that a monadic-uniform transformer is actually the best transformer for focused abstract structures.

Corollary 8. *Let τ be a monadic-uniform transformer. If $focused_\tau(S)$ and $f(C) = S$ then $\beta(\tau(C)) = \beta(\tau(S))$*

Cor. 8 suggests a way to compute the best abstract transformer: Given an abstract structure, find a set of feasible focused structures that represent the same concrete structures. Def. 9 makes this notion formal.

Definition 9. *$focus_\tau$ is an operation that given a feasible structure S returns a finite set of structures FS s.t. $\bigcup_{S' \in \gamma(S)} expand_\tau(S') = \bigcup_{F \in FS} \gamma_\tau(F)$ and for every $F \in FS$, F is feasible and $focused_\tau(F)$.* ☐

We now sketch the algorithm that computes $focus_\tau$. The algorithm systematically replaces each $\frac{1}{2}$ value for monadic formulas by 0 or 1, duplicating structures as necessary. There may be a large but bounded number of such structures. Each candidate structure is checked for feasibility and discarded if infeasible.

Algorithm 10. Given τ, S, compute $focus_\tau(S)$.

0. $FS = FS_{orig} = expand_\tau(S)$ *// the current set of structures*
       $MA = $ *the monadic atomic formulas of τ, including the new constants*
1.   **for** *each $A(v)$ from MA and F from FS* **do** {
2.   **for** *each node $b \in U^F$ s.t. $[\![A(b)]\!]^F = \frac{1}{2}$* **do** { *// b must be a summary node*
3.   *Remove F from FS and replace by $F_{u_1 u_2} : u_j \in \{s, c\}$*
               s.t. b is split into $b_0, b_1, [\![A(b_i)]\!]^{F_{u_1 u_2}} = i$, and,
               b_i is a summary node in $F_{u_1 u_2}$ iff $u_j = s$. } }
4.   **for** *each structure F, new tuple created, $\bar{t}$, and relation R s.t. $[\![R(\bar{t})]\!]^F = \frac{1}{2}$,*
       add structures $F_i : i \in \{0, 1\}$ s.t. $[\![R(\bar{t})]\!]^{F_i} = i$ and $\beta(F_i) \in FS_{orig}$
5.   **for** *each structure F, if $\gamma_t(F) = \emptyset$, remove F from FS*
6.   **return**(FS)

Focus can yield a double-exponential number of structures. The maximum number of individuals in a single structure can be exponential in the number of predicates and the number of possible structures is exponential in the number of nodes. From our experience with TVLA, the first blowup — the maximal number of individuals — rarely happens in practice. However, in contrast to TVLA, the use of tight embedding suggests that the second blowup may indeed occur in practice. We are working on ways to remedy the situation, e.g., by moving to non-tight embedding (see [3]).

From the correctness of Alg. 10, our main theorem follows:

Theorem 11. *If S is feasible then we can automatically compute the best transformer:*
$$bt_\tau(S) \equiv \left\{ \beta(\tau(S')) \mid S' \in focus_\tau(S) \land [\![guard_\tau]\!]^{S'} = 1 \right\}$$

Note that if there is no feasibility check, the methodology still guarantees that we obtain a best transformer, but with respect to a γ that does not force the concrete structures to adhere to the integrity constraints. However, when using this γ, the abstraction is not likely to be strong enough to establish the properties that we desire.

5   Applications

This section describes several applications of the methodology described in §4 for computing transformers for different shape-analysis problems. For each problem, we specify the class of allowed structures, the relations we maintain, and, when known, an algorithm for checking feasibility. Further details can be found in [8].

Table 2. Summary of the shape-analysis problems and their feasibility-check status

Structures	Vocabulary	Feasibility
Acyclic SLL	p_n, n, PVar	Direct
Acyclic SLL	$r_{x,n}$, n, PVar, Colors	Direct
Cyclic SLL	p_n, pc_n, n, PVar	Direct
Cyclic SLL	$r_{x,n}$, $rc_{x,n}$, n, PVar, Colors	Direct
DLL	p_f, p_b, $c_{f,b}$, $c_{b,f}$, PVar, Colors	Direct/Open
Ordered SLL	$r_{x,n}$, $rc_{x,n}$, n, dle, PVar, $inOrd_{n,dle}$, $inROrd_{n,dle}$	Open
Trees	p, l, r, PVar	Direct
Trees	p, l, r, PVar, Colors	MSO
NUC	p, l, r, $s_{x,y}$, PVar	Direct
NUC	p, l, r, $s_{x,y}$, PVar, Colors	MSO
Shared Trees	p, l, r, PVar	Open

Table 2 summarizes the different shape-analysis problems described in this section and the type of feasibility checks we have for them. For all of these problems, we show monadic-uniform transformers for field manipulations. SLL/DLL stands for Singly/Doubly Linked Lists, and NUC for No Undirected Cycles. PVar stands for Program Variables. A description of each class of structures and the meaning of each relation is given in the appropriate subsection below. Note that for every vocabulary we require a new feasibility-checking algorithm.

Dong and Su [5] show how to update reachability in a general acyclic graph using first-order logic. However, their formulas are not monadic-uniform and it is unclear whether it is possible to make them monadic-uniform.

Table 3. Monadic-uniform transformers for acyclic singly-linked lists

Relation	Update Formula
x = y.next	
guard	$n(y, y_n) \wedge y \neq null \wedge (x = null \vee \bigvee_{z \neq x} r_{z,n}(x))$
x'	y_n
$r'_{x,n}(v)$	$r_{y,n}(v) \wedge y \neq v$
x.next = null	
guard	$n(x, x_n) \wedge x \neq null \wedge (x_n = null \vee \bigvee_z (r_{z,n}(x_n) \wedge \neg r_{z,n}(x)))$
$n'(v_1, v_2)$	(when $v_1 = x \Rightarrow v_2 = null$, default $\Rightarrow n(v_1, v_2)$)
$p'_n(v_1, v_2)$	$p_n(v_1, v_2) \wedge \neg(p_n(v_1, x) \wedge p_n(x_n, v_2))$
$r'_{z,n}(v)$	$r_{z,n}(v) \wedge \neg(r_{z,n}(x) \wedge r_{x,n}(v) \wedge x \neq v)$
x.next = y	
guard	$x \neq null \wedge \neg r_{y,n}(x) \wedge n(x, null)$
$n'(v_1, v_2)$	(when $v_1 = x \Rightarrow v_2 = y$, default $\Rightarrow n(v_1, v_2)$)
$p'_n(v_1, v_2)$	$p_n(v_1, v_2) \vee (p_n(v_1, x) \wedge p_n(y, v_2))$
$r'_{z,n}(v)$	$r_{z,n}(v) \vee (r_{z,n}(x) \wedge r_{y,n}(v))$

Direct means there is a direct algorithm to check feasibility of an abstract structure. MSO means we can reduce the feasibility check to a satisfiability check of an MSO formula on trees. Open means we are still working on checking feasibility for this problem. We believe that checking feasibility is decidable for all of these problems.

Singly-Linked Lists. The first class of allowed structures we examine is acyclic singly linked lists. The vocabulary includes constants that represent program variables, a functional binary relation n that represents the next field, a unary relation $r_{x,n}$ for each program variable x that represents reachability from x (a.k.a., unary reachability), and a binary relation p_n (path of n) that represents reachability between any two elements. The guard formulas are used to detect null dereferences or the formation of garbage or cycles. Monadic-uniform update formulas can be easily written for all the needed operations.

Table 3 lists the transformers for the field-manipulating operations. Update formulas for unchanged relations are omitted. The update formulas for reachability follow the ones described in [6]. For traversal of a field, we use the free variable y_n of the guard formula to capture the target of the next field for y (x_n is used similarly in the removal of an edge).

To check feasibility of a focused abstract structure, we build a single candidate concrete structure s.t. the original structure is feasible iff it is the result of applying β on the candidate structure and the candidate structure satisfies the integrity constraints.

Algorithm 12. *(Checking Feasibility)*
Replace every summary node with two concrete nodes connected by an edge, all incoming edges to the summary node go to the first concrete node, all outgoing edges from the summary nodes start from the second node. Each edge in the abstract structure is translated into a single edge in the concrete structure. We then simply compute β on

this structure and return true if it equals the original structure and satisfies the integrity constraints (i.e., n is a total function).

Cyclicity. To handle cyclicity, we use the ideas from [6], which allow for quantifier-free update of reachability in singly-linked lists. The update of [6] is based on the addition of a binary relation, called PathCut, as an auxiliary relation. For every cycle, we call the last edge added to the cycle (i.e., the edge that closed the cycle) a **cut edge**. PathCut indicates reachability over n minus the cut edges. When the cycle is broken, its cut edge is readded to PathCut. The update formula suggested by [6] for removal of an edge is not monadic-uniform. Fortunately, we can easily rewrite that formula to be monadic-uniform.

To analyze programs that manipulate cyclic singly-linked lists, we use a vocabulary similar to that of acyclic singly-linked lists. The additional relations needed to allow updates to be monadic-uniform (and ease feasibility checking) are: cut_n is a binary relation representing the cut edges, pc_n is a binary relation representing PathCut, $rc_{x,n}(v)$ is a unary relation indicating v is reachable from program variable x using pc_n, and $c_n(v)$ is unary relation indicating that v is on a cycle. The resulting abstraction is similar in the distinctions it makes to that of [9]. Because cut_n is needed only to update itself, and the feasibility check can recover the cut edges from pc_n, we can remove cut_n and still compute the best transformer.

We use the DynQF updates by [6] as a basis for monadic-uniform update formulas.

Feasibility checking can be done using the same ideas as for acyclic lists with the necessary changes to support the cut edges.

Trees. To analyze trees using monadic-uniform transformers, we use the following vocabulary: constants represent program variables; two functional binary relations l and r represent the `left` and `right` fields respectively; two new constants x_l and x_r for each program variable x indicate the target of its left and right fields, respectively; a binary relation p represents reachability (existence of a path) between any two elements (using any fields); unary relation $r_{x,sel}$ for each program variable x represents reachability from the sel field of x. The guard formulas verify that each operation maintains treeness.

The key to updating reachability in this case is the observation that between every two nodes there is at most one path. Thus, the paths that should be removed when removing an edge from x to x_l are exactly the ones that would have been added if this edge had been added.

We can either check feasibility by reduction to satisfiability of an MSO formula (similar to the $\hat{\gamma}$ of [10]) on trees or we can check it directly (with lower complexity) by building a single candidate concrete structure in a way similar to singly-linked lists.

No Undirected Cycles. In [11], we introduced a class of structures whose underlying undirected graphs are acyclic (a.k.a. No Undirected Cycles). There we show an abstraction for handling this class of structures and algorithms for computing best abstract transformers for this abstraction. Structures with No Undirected Cycles are acyclic and have the interesting property that each pair of program variables can meet only once (i.e., there is a single shared node reachable from both variables s.t. none of the nodes pointing to that node are reachable from both variables). Furthermore, between any two nodes there is at most one path.

We now define an abstraction similar to [11] and apply our methodology. The vocabulary used for trees in extended with the following constants: For each pair of distinct program variables x and y, we add $s_{x,y}$, which is the unique node in which x and y meet and create sharing (or *null* if no such node exists).These are used in the guard formulas to detect formation of undirected cycles. We also maintain unary reachability from these constants. We can write a monadic-uniform guard formula using transitive closure that detects the formation of undirected cycles. We can check feasibility of such structures using methods similar to the ones using for trees.

Shared Trees. Shared trees are graphs in which between any two nodes there is at most one (possibly empty) path. A way to visualize shared trees is that from every node looking down the graph you see a tree. Shared trees arise in applicative data structures (e.g., see [12,13]) and in operating systems and databases performing shadow paging (e.g., see [14]).

We use the same vocabulary as in the case of trees. Updating reachability for this class of structures is done in the same way as in trees, because between any two nodes there is at most one path. Detecting when the shared-trees property has been violated is done by a guard formula when adding an edge. Again, the formula is monadic-uniform but not quantifier-free.

We are working on checking feasibility for shared trees in this vocabulary and believe it is decidable. Because shared trees have unbounded tree width, a direct translation into satisfiability of an MSO formula will not yield decidability.

Uninterpreted Unary Relations. Sets and boolean fields can be added to any of the above shape-analysis problems by introducing uninterpreted unary relations (a.k.a. colors). We allow addition and removal of an element from a set, query for existence of an element in a set, and selection of an arbitrary element from a set. The additional update formulas needed are trivial. Selection is done by using a guard formula with a free variable. The difficulty in checking feasibility when adding colors to a vocabulary, in contrast to the original feasibility-checking problem, comes from the fact that the colors can make distinctions that the original abstraction could not. The binary relations between the now-separate nodes need to be taken into account.

Checking feasibility for singly-linked lists can be done by first checking feasibility ignoring the colors, and then reducing the feasibility for each segment of the list to the Directed Chinese Postman Problem [15], which can be solved in polynomial time. Checking feasibility for trees and structures with No Undirected Cycles, can be done by reduction to MSO.

Other cases. The relations required for analyzing doubly linked lists and ordered lists can also be maintained using monadic-uniform transformers.

We do not have a general feasibility check for any structure over the vocabulary of doubly-linked lists. However, we do know how to check feasibility for all the structures arising in most programs that manipulate doubly-linked lists (e.g., all the example programs of TVLA) because all such structures are only ever small perturbations of well-formed doubly linked lists.

6 Related Work

Specialized Shape Analyzers. Developing specialized shape analysis for commonly used data structures is an active line of research [16,9,11,17]. We are encouraged by the fact that we are able to express all of the above-cited work using our methodology. Moreover, our methodology supports shared trees and the addition of arbitrary colors, which are beyond the scope of existing methods. It should be noted that our current algorithms are more costly. In particular, the ad-hoc algorithm in [11] runs in time essentially linear in the output, which is hard to beat. In the future, we plan to reduce the costs of creating the transformers by: (i) focusing only the necessary parts, (ii) developing more efficient focus algorithms, and (iii) using incrementality to reduce the cost of feasibility checks.

The TVLA System. The results in this paper are inspired by the TVLA system. The TVLA system does not require that update formulas be monadic-uniform. It also allows arbitrary classes of graphs to be used. Also, [18] includes an algorithm for automatically generating update formulae for auxiliary information, which is fully integrated into the system. (§5.4.1 of [19] describes the application of that machinery for an abstraction similar to the one described for cyclic singly-linked lists.) However, the TVLA system does not guarantee that the transformers are the best. Moreover, the system can issue a runtime exception in certain cases when an operation may lead to an infinite number of structures. In this paper, we build specialized shape analyses that can handle many of cases for which TVLA was used. For most of these cases, we can now compute the best abstract transformer. In the future, it may be possible to combine methods like the ones in [18] with our method. For example, there may be a way to generate monadic-uniform update formulas in certain cases.

The focus operation in TVLA differs from the one in this paper in several key aspects including: (i) it requires the user to specify which formulas to focus on, and (ii) it may yield an infinite number of structures. In contrast, in this paper we show that for every monadic-uniform update, there is a computable set of focused structures that lead to best transformers. Our results also shed light on the cases when the updates in TVLA are precise.

Procedures and Libraries. In this paper, we focused on handling programs without procedures and libraries. It is possible to handle procedures and libraries by tabulation of input/output relations between abstract values (e.g., see [20,21]). It may be also possible to handle specific libraries by allowing monadic-uniform specifications of auxiliary relations that describe an abstraction of the effect on the client module.

Employing Theorem Provers and Decision Procedures. Theorem provers and decision procedures can be employed to prove properties of programs that manipulate the heap (e.g., see [22,23,24,25,7]). Moreover, they can be used to fully automate the process of generating transformers (e.g., see [26,27,28,10]).

Results from dynamic descriptive complexity and the methodology of this paper improve the aforementioned results in various ways. For instance, in contrast to the method of Lahiri and Qadeer [24], which requires user intervention, our method handles programs that manipulate cyclic lists in a totally automatic way.

In essence, the introduction of transformers that use only monadic-uniform update formulas can be seen as a way to replace a characterization of *mutations* of data structures with a characterization in terms of *invariants*. That is, two-vocabulary structures (which describe the state before and after the transition) are a natural way to express mutations, whereas standard one-vocabulary structures express invariants. In some cases, the switch from two-vocabulary to one-vocabulary structures results in an order-of-magnitude complexity improvement. In other cases, where decision procedures are not known for—or known not to exist for—two-vocabulary structures, the reduction to one-vocabulary structures restores the possibility of employing decision procedures:

– With two-vocabulary structures, it is easy to see that monadic second-order logic is undecidable even on linked lists. (The intuitive reason is that two functions, plus a few unary relations, can be used to encode a grid.) However, monadic second-order logic on trees is decidable [29], and thus can be used to perform the feasibility checks on one-vocabulary structures that are needed when our method is employed.
– Rakamaric et al. [7] gave a complete decision procedure for checking feasibility of a given (one-vocabulary) abstract state, but left open the question of how to handle transformers in the most-precise way. Our methodology solves this problem: the DynQF updates for singly linked lists of Hesse [6] can be used to recast the problematic transformers using only one-vocabulary formulas, and hence the best transformer is computable as explained in §1.

References

1. Cousot, P., Cousot, R.: Systematic design of program analysis frameworks. In: POPL. (1979)
2. Immerman, N.: Descriptive Complexity. Springer-Verlag (1999)
3. Sagiv, M., Reps, T., Wilhelm, R.: Parametric shape analysis via 3-valued logic. Trans. on Prog. Lang. and Syst. (2002)
4. Loginov, A., Reps, T., Sagiv, M.: Abstraction refinement via inductive learning. In: Proc. Computer-Aided Verif. (2005)
5. Dong, G., Su, J.: Incremental and decremental evaluation of transitive closure by first-order queries. Inf. & Comput. **120** (1995) 101–106
6. Hesse, W.: Dynamic Computational Complexity. PhD thesis, Department of Computer Science, UMass, Amherst (2003)
7. Rakamaric, Z., Bingham, J., Hu, A.: A better logic and decision procedure for predicate abstraction of heap-manipulating programs. Tech. Rep. TR-2006-02, Dept. of Comp. Sci., Univ. of BC, Canada (2006)
8. Lev-Ami, T., Sagiv, M., Immerman, N., Reps, T.: Constructing specialized shape analyses for uniform change. Technical Report TR-2006-11-01, Tel-Aviv Univ. (2006) http://www.cs.tau.ac.il/~tla/2006/papers/TR-2006-11-01.pdf.
9. Manevich, R., Yahav, E., Ramalingam, G., Sagiv, M.: Predicate abstraction and canonical abstraction for singly-linked lists. In: VMCAI. (2005) 181–198
10. Yorsh, G., Reps, T., Sagiv, M.: Symbolically computing most-precise abstract operations for shape analysis. In: TACAS. (2004) 530–545
11. Lev-Ami, T., Immerman, N., Sagiv, M.: Abstraction for shape analysis with fast and precise transformers. In: CAV. (2006) 533–546
12. Myers, E.: Efficient applicative data types. In: POPL. (1984) 66–75
13. Okasaki, C.: Purely Functional Data Structures. Cambridge University Press (1998)

14. Brown, A.L.: Persistent Object Stores. Univ. of St Andrews (1989)
15. Edmonds, J., Johnson, E.L.: Matching, Euler tours and the chinese postman. Mathematical Programming **5** (1973) 88–124
16. Hendren, L.: Parallelizing Programs with Recursive Data Structures. PhD thesis, Cornell Univ., Ithaca, NY (1990)
17. Distefano, D., O'Hearn, P.W., Yang, H.: A local shape analysis based on separation logic. In: TACAS. (2006) 287–302
18. Reps, T., Sagiv, M., Loginov, A.: Finite differencing of logical formulas for static analysis. In: ESOP. (2003)
19. Loginov, A.: Refinement-based program verification via three-valued-logic analysis. PhD thesis, Comp. Sci. Dept., Univ. of Wisconsin, Madison (2006)
20. Cousot, P., Cousot, R.: Static determination of dynamic properties of recursive procedures. In: Formal Descriptions of Programming Concepts. (1978) 237–277
21. Rinetzky, N., Sagiv, M., Yahav, E.: Interprocedural shape analysis for cutpoint-free programs. In: SAS. (2005) 284–302
22. Nelson, G.: Verifying reachability invariants of linked structures. In: POPL. (1983) 38–47
23. Møller, A., Schwartzbach, M.I.: The pointer assertion logic engine. In: PLDI. (2001) 221–231
24. Lahiri, S.K., Qadeer, S.: Verifying properties of well-founded linked lists. In: POPL. (2006)
25. Lev-Ami, T., Immerman, N., Reps, T.W., Sagiv, M., Srivastava, S., Yorsh, G.: Simulating reachability using first-order logic with applications to verification of linked data structures. In: CADE. (2005) 99–115
26. Ball, T., Rajamani, S.K.: Automatically validating temporal safety properties of interfaces. In: SPIN. (2001) 103–122
27. Henzinger, T.A., Jhala, R., Majumdar, R., Sutre, G.: Software verification with BLAST. In: SPIN. (2003) 235–239
28. Reps, T., Sagiv, M., Yorsh, G.: Symbolic implementation of the best transformer. In: Proc. VMCAI. (2004)
29. Rabin, M.: Decidability of second-order theories and automata on infinite trees. Trans. Amer. Math. Soc. **141** (1969) 1–35

Maintaining Doubly-Linked List Invariants in Shape Analysis with Local Reasoning*

Sigmund Cherem and Radu Rugina

Computer Science Department
Cornell University
Ithaca, NY 14853
{siggi,rugina}@cs.cornell.edu

Abstract. This paper presents a novel shape analysis algorithm with local reasoning that is designed to analyze heap structures with structural invariants, such as doubly-linked lists. The algorithm abstracts and analyzes one single heap cell at a time. In order to maintain the structural invariants, the analysis uses a local heap abstraction that models the sub-heap consisting of one cell and its immediate neighbors. The proposed algorithm can successfully analyze standard doubly-linked list manipulations.

1 Introduction

Shape analyses are aimed at extracting heap invariants that describe the "shape" of recursive data structures [1]. For instance, heap reference count invariants allow a program analyzer to distinguish acyclic and unshared data structures, such as acyclic lists or trees, from structures with sharing or cycles. Shape information has many potential applications such as: verification of heap manipulations [2]; automatic parallelization [3]; static detection of memory leaks and other heap errors [4]; and compile-time memory management [5]. Statically computing reference count invariants is challenging because destructive heap mutations temporarily break these invariants. A shape analysis must determine that the invariants are restored as the destructive operations finish.

In recent work, we have developed a novel shape analysis framework that uses local reasoning about single heap cells [4]. In this framework, the analysis uses a local abstraction to describe the state of a single heap cell. Using the local abstraction, the analysis tracks the state of the single cell through the program, from the point where the cell is allocated, and up to the point where it becomes unreachable. The single cell is referred to as the tracked cell. As shown in [4], this approach makes it possible to build efficient intra-procedural and inter-procedural analysis algorithms. However, a shortcoming of the current formulation is that it cannot accurately compute shape information for data structures with local invariants, such as doubly-linked lists.

In this paper we present a shape analysis with local reasoning about single heap cells that is capable of identifying and maintaining information about doubly-linked list invariants. We propose a new local abstraction capable of expressing such invariants. Then, we develop an analysis algorithm that computes shape information using this abstraction. The local abstraction for a heap cell describes the local heap around the

---

* This work was supported in part by NSF grants CCF-0541217 and CNS-0406345.

B. Cook and A. Podelski (Eds.): VMCAI 2007, LNCS 4349, pp. 234–250, 2007.

cell, consisting of the cell itself and its immediate neighboring cells. Points-to relations between the cell and its neighbors allow the analysis to express local structural invariants. The paper shows that maintaining structural invariants for the tracked cell requires knowledge about its neighbors' reference counts. Our abstraction can also express other forms of local invariants, in particular the parent-child relationship in trees with parent pointers. However, this paper mainly focuses on studying doubly-linked lists.

When a distant cell gets closer to the tracked cell and becomes one of its neighbors (for instance, when removing the element next to the tracked cell), a local analysis has no knowledge about the reference counts of the new neighbor. To address this issue, we propose an *assume-and-check* approach: when the analysis of a single cell reaches an assumption point in the program, it assumes facts about the neighbors' reference counts; at the same time, the analysis checks the reference counts of all tracked cells at that point, to ensure that the assumptions were correct.

The rest of the paper is organized as follows. Section 2 gives the background. Section 3 shows an example and discusses the issues that the analysis must overcome. Next, Section 4 presents the local abstraction and Section 5 shows the analysis algorithm. Finally, related work is discussed in Section 6 and we conclude in Section 7.

2 Background: Local Analysis of Single Heap Cells

This section discusses the key concepts behind heap analysis with local reasoning about single heap cells. The main idea is that the analysis uses a local abstraction to model one single heap cell at a time. Hence, the analysis has only local information about the one cell, but knows nothing about the rest of the heap. In contrast, traditional shape analyses that use shape graphs [6] or 3-valued logic [7] have a global view of the heap. Recent work has explored formulations using procedure-local sub-heaps [8], or using separation logic [9, 10]. Although these approaches restrict themselves to sub-heaps, their abstractions still describe entire structures (e.g., entire lists), not single cells.

Roughly speaking, an analysis that reasons about single cells is concerned with questions of the form "if property X holds for *one* heap cell before an operation, does X hold for that cell afterwards?". In contrast, global analyses answer questions of the form "if property X holds for *all* the cells before an operation, does X hold for all cells afterwards?". A local analysis is more efficient due to the finer granularity of the abstraction. However, it is more restricted because less information is available when analyzing a single cell.

The local abstraction of a heap cell is referred to as a *configuration*. The cell described by the configuration is referred to as *the tracked cell*. Each configuration contains reference counts for the tracked cell, plus additional information for accurately maintaining these reference counts. Reference counts are expressed relative to a *region partitioning* of the program's memory (both stack and heap) into a finite set of disjoint regions, so that each configuration keeps track of one reference count per region. To ensure a finite abstraction, reference counts are bound to a fixed value k per region (and a top value is used for larger counts). Usually, $k = 2$ suffices. In this paper, we assume a type-safe Java-like language, where a simple region partitioning can be constructed by using one region per variable and one region per heap field. In the rest of the paper,

```
class DLList {                    void insert(DLList x, int d) {
    DLList n, p;                      DLList t;
    int data;                         t = x.p;
                                      y = new DLList(d);
    DLList(int d) {                   y.n = x;
        data = d;                     y.p = t;
    }                                 t.n = y;
}                                     x.p = y;
                                  }
```

Fig. 1. Doubly-linked list insertion

we refer to regions using their variable or field names. The entire heap abstraction at a program point is the finite set of possible configurations at that point. However, configurations are independent, so they can be analyzed separately. The analysis uses efficient, fine-grained worklist algorithms to process individual configurations, not entire heap abstractions (in a fashion similar to attribute-independent analyses).

For a given program, the analysis generates a configuration after each allocation site, to model a *representative cell* created at that site. Then, the analysis tracks this configuration through the program using a dataflow analysis.

In our previous work [4, 5], each local abstraction is a triple (r, h, m), where r indicates the reference counts per region, h is a set of expressions that reference the tracked cell (or *hit* expressions); and m is a set of expressions that do not reference the cell (*miss* expressions). The h and m sets need not be complete; the richer these sets are, the more precise the analysis is. In general, redundant information is avoided, i.e., h and m exclude expressions e for which r already indicates whether e hits or misses.

For example, consider an acyclic singly-linked list, where next fields are named n. Assume that the first two list elements are pointed by variables x and y, respectively. This heap can be described using three local abstractions: $(x^1, \varnothing, \varnothing)$ describes the first list element; $(y^1 n^1, \{x.n\}, \varnothing)$ describes the second list element; and $(n^1, \varnothing, \{x.n\})$ describes one list element other than the first two, that is, it describes a representative among the cells in the tail of the list. Here, reference counts are described using superscripts, and missing regions have zero reference counts by default. The analysis can analyze each of these pieces separately, reasoning locally about each of them.

However, the triples (r, h, m) cannot express local structural invariants, such as doubly-linked list invariants. In this paper we propose a new local abstraction for describing and maintaining structural invariants.

3   Example

Consider the program in Figure 1. The program is written using a Java-like syntax and is used as a running example. The program inserts a new element y in a doubly-linked list, right before element x. Each list element has a field n that points to the next element, and a field p that points to the previous element. A correct manipulation of the list must maintain the doubly-linked list (DLL) invariant:

$$\forall h \ . \ (h.p \neq \mathsf{null} \Rightarrow h.p.n = h) \wedge (h.n \neq \mathsf{null} \Rightarrow h.n.p = h)$$

a) Before insert(x)   b) After insert(x)

Fig. 2. Counterexample: the property rc for the shaded cell holds before insert(x), but not after. The shaded box denotes the tracked cell. Solid lines are next links n, and dashed lines are previous links p.

3.1   Reference Counts and DLL Invariants

First, we show that maintaining precise heap reference counts requires knowledge about the DLL invariant. Consider the two predicates below for a heap cell h in a list:

- $rc(h)$ is true if it has reference counts of at most 1 from each of the fields n and p;
- $dll(h)$ indicates that the DLL invariant holds for h.

We ask the following question: given a cell h such that $rc(h)$ holds, but $dll(h)$ might not hold before insert, does $rc(h)$ hold after the insertion? The answer is negative:

$$rc(h) \not\Rightarrow rc'(h)$$

where $rc(h)$ and $rc'(h)$ are the values of the reference counting predicate in the states before and after insert, respectively. This is shown by the counterexample in Figure 2. A concrete heap before insert(x) is shown on the left of the figure, and the resulting heap after the insertion is shown on the right. The cell in question h (i.e., the tracked cell) is shown using the shaded box. Next links are shown using solid lines, and previous links are shown using dashed lines. The property $rc(h)$ holds before insert, but not after, because the cell pointed to by x has two references from n fields in the result heap.

Hence, the analysis must have knowledge about the DLL invariant in order to preserve accurate reference counts during destructive doubly-linked list operations. This is the case for both local and global analyses.

3.2   Maintaining the DLL Invariant Using Local Reasoning

Next we want to determine the amount of local information needed so that a local analysis can conclude that the DLL invariant is restored. We ask the following question: if one cell h is such that both $rc(h)$ and $dll(h)$ hold before insert, is it the case that $dll(h)$ also holds after insert? Note that nothing is known about the rc and dll properties of elements other than h. The answer to this question is again negative:

$$rc(h) \wedge dll(h) \not\Rightarrow dll'(h)$$

This is shown by the counterexample in Figure 3. The cell in question h is the shaded cell. In the heap before insert both $rc(h)$ and $dll(h)$ hold. However, the neighboring

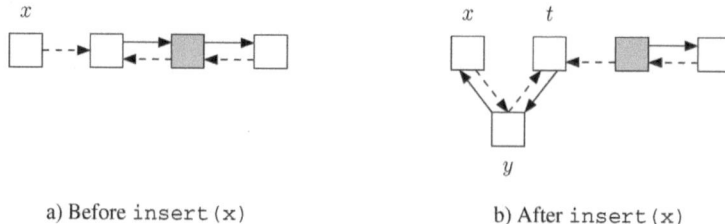

a) Before insert (x)   b) After insert (x)

Fig. 3. Counterexample: a) before insert (x), both the rc and dll properties hold for the shaded cell; b) after insertion, property dll doesn't hold for the shaded cell

cell to the left of h is malformed because it is referenced by two p fields, one from the tracked cell and one from x. Inserting a new element before x "steals" a reference from h and breaks its DLL property: after insertion, $h.p.n \neq h$.

Still, it is possible to determine that insert maintains the DLL invariant using local reasoning. The required piece of information is that the neighbors $h.n$ and $h.p$ of the tracked cell h also satisfy the reference count property rc before insertion [1]. The analysis can then prove that if the tracked cell satisfies rc and dll before insert, and its neighbors satisfy rc, then rc and dll hold for the tracked cell after insert:

$$rc(h) \wedge dll(h) \wedge rc(h.p) \wedge rc(h.n) \ \Rightarrow \ rc'(h) \wedge dll'(h)$$

The goal of our analysis is to build an appropriate local abstraction and prove this property using that abstraction.

4   The Local Abstraction

Based on the above observations, the local abstraction must capture: a) local invariants, such as the dll property, and b) reference counts for both the tracked cell and its neighbors. We build the abstraction as follows. The configuration of the tracked cell models the local heap consisting of itself and its immediate neighbors, i.e., those cells that are pointed by, or point to the tracked cell. The configuration models the following:

– Points-to relations between the tracked cell and its neighbors;
– Precise reference counts for the tracked cell, from each variable and each field; and
– Partial reference counts for the neighbors, from some variables and fields.

Graphically, a configuration can be thought as being a "circle" whose center is the tracked cell, and whose heap neighbors at distance 1 lie on this circle.

For instance, the local abstraction shown in Figure 4 arises during the analysis of insert. The tracked cell is the shaded node in the center. The points-to relations between the center node and its neighbors allow the analysis to express the local structural invariants. The reference counts from variables (x, y, or t) and fields (n or p) are shown

---
[1] A slightly weaker condition is actually sufficient: that $h.n$ has only one n reference, and $h.p$ has only one p reference, each of them from h.

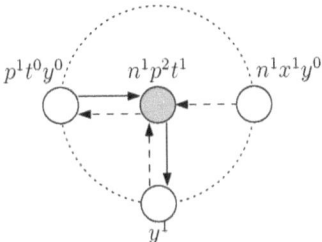

Fig. 4. Example local abstraction

using superscripts, for each node. Reference counts from variables can only be 0 or 1. For the tracked cell, the reference counts not shown (from x and y) are zero, by default. For the neighboring cells, the missing reference counts are unknown by default. Hence, reference counts are fully known for the tracked cell, but partially known for the neighbors. To explain the examples in this paper, we will refer to each local abstraction using the reference counts of the tracked cell. For instance, the above abstraction is $n^1 p^2 t^1$.

Note that the local abstraction does not contain summary nodes. In particular, nothing is known about the heap beyond the circle. This is the key aspect that distinguishes it from traditional global abstractions such as shape graphs.

4.1   Analysis of the Example

Figure 5 shows the analysis result for `insert` using this local abstraction. The possible local abstractions are shown at each point. In each abstraction, the tracked cell is shown as the shaded node. For simplicity, we consider only two input configurations at the entry of the function, $n^1 p^1$ and $n^1 p^1 x^1$. The former describes a list cell that is not referenced by x; the latter is the cell that x references. Both cases assume that the cell in question is in the middle of the list. Four other configurations describe cases where the tracked cell is the first or the last element: n^1, $n^1 x^1$, p^1, and $p^1 x^1$. The analysis of those cases are similar and we omit them.

Consider the initial abstraction $n^1 p^1$ and the first assignment t = x.p. The analysis tries to determine whether x.p is the tracked cell. Since there is not enough information to figure this out, the analysis bifurcates into two possible cases. These correspond to the first two columns in the figure. In the first case, x.p is not the tracked cell, so t will not reference the cell after the assignment. The resulting abstraction is $n^1 p^1$. In the second case, x.p is the tracked cell, so t will reference it after the assignment. The resulting abstraction is $n^1 p^1 t^1$.

The analysis of t = x.p also infers that x does not reference the right neighbor in the first case (otherwise, x.p references the tracked cell); and that x references the right neighbor in the second case (because the only other cell that has a p field pointing to the tracked cell is the right neighbor). This information about x is needed later, when analyzing the assignment x.p = y.

Furthermore, in both cases the analysis of t = x.p infers that t doesn't reference the left neighbor, as shown by the reference count t^0. This is because the left neighbor

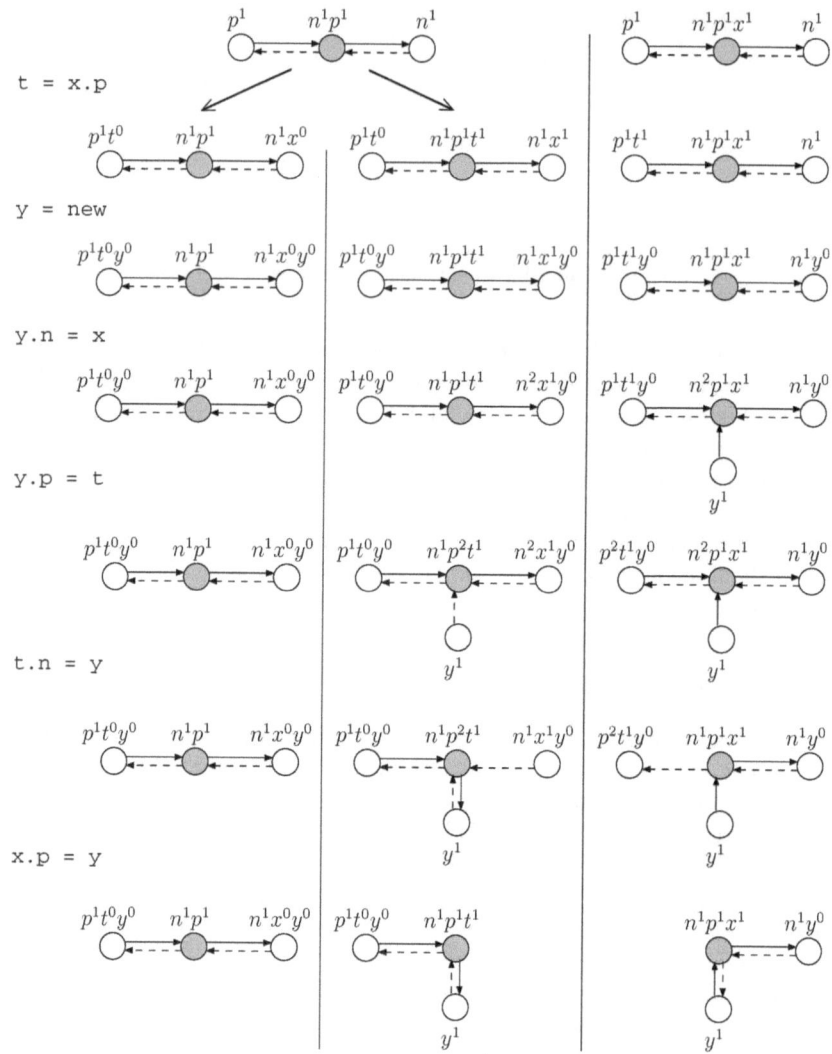

Fig. 5. Analysis of the example program

has exactly one p reference, from the tracked cell. If t would point to the left neighbor, then x would reference the tracked cell, which is known to be false. Hence, the p^1 knowledge for the left neighbor allows the analysis to infer that t doesn't reference that neighbor. As a result, situations such as the one in Figure 3 are not possible.

The analysis of the other statements and local abstractions is similar. The configurations at the end of the function indicate that the rc and dll properties hold for all heap cells at that point.

$$mayAlias(S, v_i, v_j) \Leftrightarrow (v_i \neq v_o \neq v_j \ \wedge$$
$$(\forall r \,.\, ||v_i||_r = ||v_j||_r \ \vee \ ||v_i||_r = \top \ \vee \ ||v_j||_r = \top))$$

$$hit(S, e, v) \quad \Leftrightarrow \begin{cases} e = x \quad \wedge \ ||v||_x = 1 \text{ or} \\ e = x.f \ \wedge \ ||v||_f \neq 0 \ \wedge \ (\exists v' \,.\, hit(S, x, v') \ \wedge \ v' \rightarrow_f v) \text{ or} \\ e = \text{null} \ \wedge \ v = v_{\text{null}} \end{cases}$$

$$contains(S, e) \quad \Leftrightarrow (\exists v \in V \,.\, hit(S, e, v))$$

$$miss(S, e, v) \quad \Leftrightarrow \begin{cases} e = x \quad \wedge \ ||v||_x = 0 \text{ or} \\ e = x.f \ \wedge \ ||v||_f = 0 \text{ or} \\ e = x \quad \wedge \ (\exists v' \,.\, ||v'||_x = 1 \ \wedge \ \neg mayAlias(S, v, v')) \text{ or} \\ e = x.f \ \wedge \ ||v||_f = 1 \ \wedge \ (\exists v' \,.\, v' \rightarrow_f v \ \wedge \ miss(S, x, v')) \text{ or} \\ e = \text{null} \ \wedge \ v \neq v_{\text{null}} \text{ or} \\ e = x.f \ \wedge \ hit(S, x, v_o) \ \wedge \ v_o \rightarrow_f v_{\text{null}} \ \wedge \ \neg mayAlias(S, v, v_{\text{null}}) \end{cases}$$

Fig. 6. Queries on configurations

Abstraction Model. The local abstraction is modeled as a star graph S:

$$S = (V, v_o, v_{\text{null}}, O, I, || \cdot ||) \qquad \text{where,}$$

$$v_o, v_{\text{null}} \in V \qquad O \subseteq \text{Field} \times V \qquad I \subseteq V \times \text{Field} \qquad || \cdot || : V \rightarrow (\text{Field} \cup \text{Var}) \rightarrow \mathbb{N}_\top$$

The set V contains all nodes in the graph, where $v_o \in V$ is a distinguished center node representing the tracked cell. The node $v_{\text{null}} \in V$ is a special node to represent null values. The set O contains outgoing edges from v_o. A pair $(f, v) \in O$ denotes the edge $v_o \rightarrow_f v$. The special edge $v_o \rightarrow_f v_{\text{null}}$ indicates that the field f of the tracked cell is null. Similarly, an incoming edge $v \rightarrow_f v_o$ is denoted by a pair $(v, f) \in I$. The cardinality function $|| \cdot ||$ models the reference counts for each node in V, both from variables (Var) and fields (Field). The set $\mathbb{N}_\top$ extends natural numbers with a special top value $\top$, such that $\top + 1 = \top - 1 = \top$. The heap reference count from a field f is denoted $||v||_f$. The reference counts from a variable x is denoted as $||v||_x$. If this value is not $\top$, it can only be 1 or 0, indicating whether the cell v is referenced by variable x or not. The special value $\top$ represents unknown information. As mentioned in Section 2, we use an upper bound k (e.g., $k = 2$) for the number of reference counts per field. In addition, the analysis uses a top configuration $S_\top$ to model cases where the analysis has lost precision about the tracked cell.

Given a configuration S, the analysis can derive the queries presented Figure 6:

- *Alias information.* Two nodes are unaliased if any of their reference counts is inconsistent, i.e. they have different numeric values.
- *Hit expressions.* The function $hit(S, e, v)$ indicates that expression e references the cell represented by the node v. This is defined recursively using the reference counts and points-to relations.
- *Miss expressions.* The function $miss(S, e, v)$ indicates that e doesn't reference the cell represented by v.

$$V = \{v_o, v_{\text{null}}\} \cup \text{range}(O) \cup \{v \mid v \in \text{dom}(I) \wedge \exists x . \|v\|_x = 1\} \quad (1)$$
$$v_{\text{null}} \notin \text{dom}(I) \quad (2)$$
$$\forall r \in \text{Var} \cup \text{Field} . \|v_o\|_r \neq \top \quad (3)$$
$$\forall v \in V, f \in \text{Field} . |\{v \rightarrow_f v' \mid v' \in V\}| = 1 \quad (4)$$
$$\forall v . \|v\|_f = 1 \Rightarrow |\{v' \mid v' \rightarrow_f v\}| \leq 1 \quad (5)$$
$$\forall v_1, v_2, e . \, hit(S, e, v_1) \wedge hit(S, e, v_2) \Rightarrow v_1 = v_2 \quad (6)$$

Fig. 7. Consistency invariants maintained by the algorithm

We will use these queries to formalize the analysis algorithm in the next Section. Figure 7 presents several invariants that our analysis maintains at all times:

1. All nodes other than v_{null} must be directly connected to v_o. Moreover, a node v pointing into v_o ($v \rightarrow_f v_o$) must also be pointed by v_o ($v_o \rightarrow_g v$) or by some variable ($\|v\|_x = 1$). This invariant ensures that the number of nodes and edges in the graph is bounded by the number of variables and fields in the program.
2. Since v_{null} represents null values, it can't have outgoing edges.
3. All references to the tracked cell are precisely known.
4. A node can have at most one outgoing edge with the same field.
5. If a node v has a single incoming reference from some field f, a configuration can only have one node to represent this predecessor.
6. Each expression references at most one node.

5   Analysis Algorithm

We now proceed to present the dataflow algorithm that computes a heap abstraction at each program point. For each configuration that models the state of the tracked cell before a statement, the analysis computes a set of configurations that describes the possible states of the cell after the statement.

We assume a simple program representation consisting of a control-flow graph whose nodes are simple assignment. Assignments and expressions have the form:

Statements $s ::= x = \text{new} \mid x = \text{null} \mid x = y \mid x = y.f \mid x.f = y \mid x.f = \text{null}$
Expressions $e ::= \text{null} \mid x \mid x.f$

where $x \in \text{Var}$ ranges over variables, and $f \in \text{Field}$ ranges over fields.

Initialization. As discussed in Section 2, for each allocation site $x = \text{new}$, the analysis builds a configuration $S = (\{v_o, v_{\text{null}}\}, v_o, v_{\text{null}}, \varnothing, \{v_o \rightarrow_f v_{\text{null}} \mid f \in \text{Field}\}, \| \cdot \|)$ at the program point after the allocation, where $\|v_o\|_x = 1$ and $\|v_o\|_r = 0$ for any $r \neq x$. The configuration describes a representative heap cell allocated at this site. Then, the analysis tracks this configuration through the program.

Alternatively, if a code fragment is to be analyzed separately, the set of all possible configurations at the beginning of that fragment must be supplied.

$$focusH(S, x.f) = (V', v'_o, v'_{null}, O', I'', || \cdot ||') \quad \text{where,}$$

$$S' = \begin{cases} unify(addNode(S, v_x, x, 1), v_x, v) & \neg contains(S, x) \land ||v_o||_f = 1 \land v \to_f v_o \\ addNode(S, v_x, x, 1) & \neg contains(S, x) \quad v_x \text{ fresh} \\ unify(S, v_x, v) & ||v_o||_f = 1 \land v \to_f v_o \\ S & \text{otherwise} \end{cases}$$

$$I'' = I' \cup \{v_x \to_f v_o\}$$

$$focusM(S, x.f) = (V', v'_o, v'_{null}, O', I'', || \cdot ||') \quad \text{where,}$$

$$S' = \begin{cases} unify(addNode(S, v', x, 0), v', v) & ||v_o||_f = 1 \land v \to_f v_o \quad v' \text{ fresh} \\ addNode(S, v', x, 0) & ||v_o||_f = 1 \quad v' \text{ fresh} \\ S_\top & \text{otherwise} \end{cases}$$

$$I'' = I' \cup \{v' \to_f v_o\}$$

Fig. 8. Focus operations. The helper functions *addNode* and *unify* are defined in Figure 11. We use S' as a shorthand notation for $(V', v'_o, v'_{null}, O', I', || \cdot ||')$.

Focus Operations. Given an input configuration describing the state of the tracked cell before an assignment statement $e_1 = e_2$, the analysis tries to determine whether e_1 and e_2 reference the tracked cell. Whenever the analysis cannot determine if e_i ($i \in \{1, 2\}$) hits or misses the tracked cell (i.e. $\neg hit(S, e_i, v_o) \land \neg miss(S, e_i, v_o)$), the analysis bifurcates and creates two new configurations that are focused with respect to e_i.

Figure 8 shows the focus operations. Since exact reference counts are known for v_o, it is known whether variables hit or miss v_o. Therefore, the analysis only focuses expressions of the form $x.f$. To make an expression $x.f$ hit v_o, the analysis simply unifies the predecesor of v_o via field f (v) and the node referenced by x (v_x). The operation will also add the node v_x or the incoming field f if they didn't exist before focusing. A similar algorithm is used to make an expression $x.f$ miss v_o. Although, if $||v_o||_f \geq 2$, it is not possible to express the fact that $x.f$ misses the object. If this situation occurs, the focus operation returns an imprecise configuration $S_\top$ indicating that the analysis no longer tracks the state of the tracked cell.

Transfer Function. The analysis then applies the transfer function to each focused configuration. Figure 9 presents the transfer function for an assignment $e_1 = e_2$. First, the analysis nullifies e_1 using the helper function *kill*. For store assignments $x.f = y$, the analysis also creates the node for y in case it didn't exist, as this node might become a neighbor after the store. The reference counts are then updated. The appropriate reference count of each node v is increased when e_2 hits v, it remains unchanged when e_2 misses, and it is set to $\top$ when the analysis cannot determine whether e_2 hits or misses. The points-to edges are added in the case of store statements. Finally, the *clean* helper function removes nodes that are not neighbors of the tracked cell.

Merge Operation. At join points, the analysis uses the merge operation from Figure 10 to combine configurations from different branches. Two configurations are combined only if they have identical reference counts and the same set of self-edges on the tracked cell. The merge operation defines one node for each pair of nodes in the input configurations. The reference counts are combined using the join in the flat lattice $(\mathbb{N}_\top, \sqsubseteq)$. Thus, if $i \neq j$: $i \sqcup i = i$, $i \sqcup j = \top$, and $i \sqcup \top = \top \sqcup i = \top$. The *clean*

$$transfer(S, e_1 = e_2) = clean(V', v'_o, v'_{null}, O'', I'', || \cdot ||'') \quad \text{where,}$$

$$S' = \begin{cases} addNode(kill(S, e_1), v', y, 1) & e_1 = x.f \ \wedge \ e_2 = y \ \wedge \ \neg contains(S, y) \\ kill(S, e_1) & \text{otherwise} \end{cases}$$

$$||v||''_r = \begin{cases} ||v||'_r + 1 & hit(S, e_2, v) \ \wedge [(e_1 = x \wedge r = x) \ \vee \ (e_1 = x.f \wedge r = f)], \text{ or} \\ ||v||'_r & miss(S, e_2, v) \vee (e_1 = x \wedge r \neq x) \ \vee \ (r \neq f \wedge e_1 = x.f), \text{ or} \\ \top & \text{otherwise} \end{cases}$$

$$O'' = O' \cup \{v_o \rightarrow_f v \mid e_1 = x.f \ \wedge \ hit(S', x, v_o) \ \wedge \ hit(S', e_2, v)\}$$

$$I'' = I' \cup \{v \rightarrow_f v_o \mid e_1 = x.f \ \wedge \ hit(S', x, v) \ \wedge \ hit(S', e_2, v_o)\}$$

Fig. 9. Transfer function. The helper functions *addNode*, *kill* and *clean* are defined in Figure 11. We use S' as a shorthand notation for $(V', v'_o, v'_{null}, O', I', || \cdot ||')$.

$$merge(S^1, S^2) = clean(V', v'_o, v'_{null}, O', I', || \cdot ||') \quad \text{where,}$$

$$V' = \{v_{i,j} \mid v_i \in V^1 \wedge v_j \in V^2\}$$
$$v'_o = v_{o,o}$$
$$v'_{null} = v_{null,null}$$
$$O' = \{v'_o \rightarrow_f v_{i,j} \mid v'_o \rightarrow^1_f v_i \ \wedge \ v^2_o \rightarrow^2_f v_j\}$$
$$I' = \{v_{i,j} \rightarrow_f v'_o \mid v_i \rightarrow^1_f v'_o \ \wedge \ v_j \rightarrow^2_f v^2_o\}$$
$$||v_{i,j}||'_r = ||v_i||^1_r \ \sqcup \ ||v_j||^2_r$$

Fig. 10. Merge operation. Precondition: $||v^1_o|| = ||v^2_o||$ and $(v^1_o \rightarrow^1_f v^1_o \Leftrightarrow v^2_o \rightarrow^2_f v^2_o)$.

operation guarantess that the number of nodes and edges in the resulting configuration is bounded by the number of variables and fields in the program.

Auxiliary Functions. The auxiliary operations used by the analysis are fairly straightforward. They are shown in Figure 11 and are summarized below:

- The *addNode* operation adds a neighboring node, without connecting it to v_o. The reference count of the added node from variable x is set according to $i \in \{0, 1\}$. This function is used both when focusing and when applying the transfer function.
- The *kill* operation removes an expression and updates the reference counts accordingly. The operation supports strong updates when field expressions are killed.
- The *clean* operation removes unnecessary nodes from a configuration. This operation is used by the end of the transfer functions and merge operation.
- The *unify* operation combines two nodes that may alias into one single node. This is done by transferring all information from one node to the other. Moreover, the result has the most precise reference counts from the input nodes.

5.1 Assume-and-Check Approach

Although the analysis can successfully determine that the reference count property rc and the doubly-linked list invariant are preserved for the tracked cell during destructive operations, in many cases it cannot determine that the reference count property of the neighbors is restored. For instance, in the `insert` example from Figure 5 the heap reference counts are not known for the neighboring cell pointed by y, because y "came from the outside" to join the local heap. A similar situation occurs when removing an

$$addNode(S, v', x, i) = (V \cup \{v'\}, v_o, v_{\text{null}}, O, I, || \cdot ||') \quad \text{where,}$$

$$||v||'_r = \begin{cases} i & r = x \wedge v = v' \\ \top & r \neq x \wedge v = v' \\ ||v||_r & \text{otherwise} \end{cases}$$

$$kill(S, e) = (V, v_o, v_{\text{null}}, O - K, I - K, || \cdot ||') \text{ where,}$$

$$||v||'_r = \begin{cases} 0 & e = r = x \\ ||v||_r - 1 & e = x.f \wedge r = f \wedge hit(S, e, v) \\ ||v||_r & \text{otherwise} \end{cases}$$

$$K = \{v \rightarrow_f v' \mid e = x.f \wedge \neg miss(S, x, v)\}$$

$$clean(S) = (V', v_o, v_{\text{null}}, O, V' \lhd I, V' \lhd || \cdot ||) \text{ where,}$$
$$V' = \{v_o, v_{\text{null}}\} \cup range(O) \cup \{v \mid v \in \text{dom}(I) \wedge \exists x . ||v||_x = 1\}$$
$$\text{where } V' \lhd f \text{ restricts the domain of } f \text{ to } V'$$

$$unify(S, v_i, v_j) = (V', v_o, v_{\text{null}}, O', I', || \cdot ||') \text{ where,}$$
$$V' = V - \{v_j\}$$
$$O' = O - \{v_o \rightarrow_f v_j\} \cup \{v_o \rightarrow'_f v_i \mid v_o \rightarrow_f v_j \in O\}$$
$$I' = I - \{v_j \rightarrow_f v_o\} \cup \{v_i \rightarrow'_f v_o \mid v_j \rightarrow_f v_o \in I\}$$
$$||v||'_r = \begin{cases} ||v_i||_r \sqcap ||v_j||_r & v = v_i \\ ||v||_r & \text{otherwise} \end{cases}$$

Fig. 11. Helper operations. The function *unify* assumes $mayAlias(S, v_i, v_j)$ holds, and $v_j \neq v_{\text{null}}$.

element from a list: a cell two levels of indirection away from the tracked cell gets closer and becomes one of its neighbors. As discussed, the neighbor's reference count information is, however, needed before `insert`.

We address this issue using an assume-and-check approach. This approach is based on defining *assumption points* in the program. We consider that such points are manually marked by the user using a special `assume-and-check` instruction. The assumption points are program points where the analysis can safely restore the reference count information for the neighbors. As implied by the name, the analysis performs two tasks when it reaches such points:

- **Assume:** Whenever the analysis of a tracked cell reaches an assumption point, it assumes that the reference count property rc holds for all of its neighbors. More precisely, all neighbors are assumed to have at most one reference from each field. This enables the analysis to restore their reference counts: if the current configuration is such that the tracked cell points to neighbor v via some field f, i.e., $v_o \rightarrow_f v$, then the analysis restores v's reference count from f: $||v||_f = 1$.
- **Check:** Whenever the analysis of a tracked cell reaches an assumption point, it checks if the tracked cell itself satisfies the reference count property rc, i.e., if it has at most one reference per field. When the assumption is violated, the analysis reports an error and all of the analysis results are invalidated. Otherwise, if all checks succeed, then all assumptions were correct.

Essentially, restoring the reference counts of the neighbors requires knowledge about all cells. The assume-and-check approach provides a simple mechanism for gathering such global information without breaking the local analysis methodology.

Standard heap operations typically require one single assumption point, after the operation finishes. In the example from Section 3, an assume-and-check instruction is added at the end of the function. This suggests that default assumption at such points could be used to reduce the amount of annotations. In addition, assume-and-check instructions can be refined to indicate the specific field for which the reference count must be assumed and checked.

The assumptions presented here are specifically formulated for doubly-linked lists. Other shapes might require different assumptions. For instance, in the case of trees with parent pointers, the analysis must assume and check that the sum of the reference counts from left and right fields is at most one, i.e., no cell is pointed by both a left and a right link.

5.2   Soundness

This section summarizes the formal framework and the soundness result for our analysis. We refer the reader to a technical report [11] for a detailed presentation of the formal model and the complete proofs.

Each concrete program state $\sigma = (\varphi, h) \in$ State consists of a variable environment φ that maps variables to values, and a heap h that maps the fields of each location to their values. Values are either heap locations (Loc) or the constant null. By abuse of notation, we write $l \in \sigma$ to indicate that l is an allocated heap cell, i.e. in the range or domain of φ or h. The execution of the program is modeled using denotational semantics via a function $[\![s]\!]$: State $\rightarrow$ State that maps the state σ before a statement s, to the state $[\![s]\!](\sigma)$ after the statement. An abstraction function $\alpha_\sigma(l)$ maps each heap cell l in a concrete heap to a local abstraction $S = (V, v_o, v_{\text{null}}, O, I, \|\cdot\|)$. The relation $\sqsubseteq$ is the partial order over local abstractions. An entire heap abstraction A consists of a finite set of local abstractions S. The main result is as follows.

Theorem 1. *Given a program P, program point p, a concrete state σ that can arise at point p during the execution of the program, and an abstraction A that the analysis computes at that program point, then each concrete heap cell in σ is modeled by at least one local abstraction in A: $\forall l \in \sigma . \exists S \in A . \alpha_\sigma(l) \sqsubseteq S$.*

The correctness proof is divided into four lemmas regarding the correctness of each of the following: the generating function at allocation sites; the transfer functions; the focus operation; and the assume-and-check coercions. The correctness of transfer functions forms the bulk of the proof.

5.3   Evaluation

We have developed a prototype implementation of the local analysis presented in this paper in Java, and used it to analyze the doubly-linked list programs shown in Table 1. Our local analysis has successfully verified that all of these programs maintain the

Table 1. Analysis Evaluation

Program	Local Abs.				Global Abs. (TVLA)		
	Configs. In Avg.	Avg. Nodes per Config.	Time (sec)		Avg. Structures	Avg. Nodes per Struct.	Time (sec)
insertBefore	7	6.5	2.2	0.07	2.7	3.9	0.59
appendLast	4	4.5	2.1	0.06	4.6	3.7	0.77
concat	4	4.5	2.3	0.07	4.8	3.7	0.88
copy	4	4.5	2.1	0.09	4.8	3.5	1.24
insertNth	4	6.2	2.3	0.09	7.0	3.2	1.38
removeData	3	8.2	2.3	0.13	10.1	3.0	1.86
filter	3	26.3	2.0	0.37	24.7	2.2	4.19

doubly-linked list shape. All of the experiments were run on a 2GHz Pentium machine with 1GB of memory, running Linux.

The input to each program is described using at least 3 configurations (one for the middle, and one for each end of the list). Additional configurations are needed to indicate where the arguments point in the list. Programs that allocate new heap cells also include one configuration for the allocation site. The number of input configurations is shown in the first column of the table.

Each program, except `filter`, has been annotated with one single assume-and-check instruction, inserted at the end of the program. The `filter` program uses a loop to remove several elements from the input list. For this program, and additional assume annotation has been added at the beginning of the loop body. This ensures that the rc property holds on the neighboring cells after every removal from the list. The analysis successfully verifies the checks at all of the assumption points.

The data in Table 1 shows several statistics about our analysis: the average number of configurations per program point; the average number of nodes per configuration (excluding the null node); and the analysis running time. These results show that the analysis is fast, with an average running time of about 0.1 seconds per program.

To compare our implementation to a global analysis, we have also tested an implementation in TVLA [12]. We have added an instrumentation predicate to describe the DLL invariant. However, no global predicates, such as reachability, were included in this implementation. The right part of Table 1 shows the results obtained with TVLA. We observe that the number of 3-valued structures per program point is roughly equal to the number of configurations per program point in our analysis, but the number of nodes in those structures is larger than the number of nodes per configuration. Furthermore, the running time of the TVLA implementation is about 10 times slower. We attribute this in part to the fact that TVLA uses of a global abstraction, and in part to the fact that the TVLA engine is generic, while ours is specialized.

6   Related Work

The work on shape analysis dates back to Jones and Muchnick [13]. They developed a dataflow analysis for identifying (the lack of) cyclicity and sharing in heap structures using k-limited abstract heaps. Since then, many different approaches based on dataflow analysis and abstract interpretation have been proposed to address this problem [14, 15, 16, 17, 18, 6, 7, 19, 20, 8, 9]. Existing techniques include analyses that use path matrices and or matrices that describe reachability [15, 18], reference counting analyses [14], analyses that use shape graphs [21, 19, 6], shape analyses and abstractions expressed using three-valued logic [22, 23, 7, 8]. In addition, heap verification techniques using model-checking or Hoare logic has also been explored [24, 25, 26]. Unlike abstract interpretation, logic-based tools rely on theorem provers and typically require heavyweight loop annotations. Alternatively, it is possible to synthesize loop invariants via predicate abstraction [26, 27, 28, 29, 30]. The common aspect of all of the above techniques is that the analyzer or verifier requires a global view of the entire heap in order to analyze a particular piece of computation. In contrast, the analysis in this paper and our earlier analysis [4] are fundamentally different, as the analysis has knowledge about the local properties of one single heap cell, but is oblivious to the way the rest of the heap is structured. This fine-grained abstraction leads to efficient algorithms. This is achieved at the expense of giving up on global properties (such as reachability) that involve reasoning about unbounded sets of cells.

This paper follows our initial work on shape analysis with tracked heap cells [4]. The contribution of this work is a new local heap abstraction that expresses local structural invariants, and the development of an analysis that uses this abstraction to maintain these invariants. This algorithm makes shape analysis with local reasoning about single cells applicable to an important class of heap structures.

A related direction of research is the recent work on separation logic [31, 32]. This line of research has explored extensions of Hoare logic for reasoning about mutable heap structures, by providing features such as the separating conjunction and the frame rule, that makes it easier to write correctness proof for heap-manipulating programs. Recently, separation logic has also been applied to the shape analysis problem [10, 9]. Although the state transformers modify local portions of the abstract heap, their abstractions still describe entire linked structures. For instance, operations such as inserting or removing elements from a list require knowing that the entire list is well-formed, using a "listness" predicate ls. This predicate behaves similarly to the summary node in standard shape analyses; it describes a global invariant for the entire list, not a local property of a single cell.

7   Conclusions

We have presented an abstraction and analysis algorithm that makes it possible to apply shape analysis with local reasoning to data structures that maintain structural invariants, such as doubly-linked lists. The local abstraction of a cell describes the local heap around that cell, and is therefore able to express local structural invariants. The algorithm can successfully show that standard operations such as doubly-linked list insertions or removals maintain the doubly-linked list invariant.

References

1. Wilhelm, R., Sagiv, M., Reps, T.: Shape analysis. In: Proceedings of the 2000 International Conference on Compiler Construction, Berlin, Germany (2000)
2. Lev-ami, T., Reps, T., Sagiv, M., Wilhelm, R.: Putting static analysis to work for verification: A case study. In: Proceedings of the 2000 International Symposium on Software Testing and Analysis. (2000)
3. Ghiya, R., Hendren, L., Zhu, Y.: Detecting parallelism in C programs with recursive data structures. In: Proceedings of the 1998 International Conference on Compiler Construction, Lisbon, Portugal (1998)
4. Hackett, B., Rugina, R.: Region-based shape analysis with tracked locations. In: Proceedings of the 32th Annual ACM Symposium on the Principles of Programming Languages, Long Beach, CA (2005)
5. Cherem, S., Rugina, R.: Compile-time deallocation of individual objects. In: Proceedings of the International Symposium on Memory Management, Ottawa, Canada (2006)
6. Sagiv, M., Reps, T., Wilhelm, R.: Solving shape-analysis problems in languages with destructive updating. ACM Transactions on Programming Languages and Systems **20**(1) (1998) 1–50
7. Sagiv, M., Reps, T., Wilhelm, R.: Parametric shape analysis via 3-valued logic. ACM Transactions on Programming Languages and Systems **24**(3) (2002)
8. Rinetzky, N., Sagiv, M., Yahav, E.: Interprocedural shape analysis for cutpoint-free programs. In: Proceedings of the 12th International Static Analysis Symposium, London, UK (2005)
9. Distefano, D., O'Hearn, P., Yang, H.: A local shape analysis based on separation logic. In: Proceedings of the 12th International Conference on Tools and Algorithms for the Construction and Analysis of Systems, Vienna, Austria (2006)
10. Gotsman, A., Berdine, J., Cook, B.: Interprocedural shape analysis with separated heap abstractions. In: The 13th International Static Analysis Symposium, Seoul, Korea (2006)
11. Cherem, S., Rugina, R.: Maintaining structural invariants in shape analysis with local reasoning. TR CS TR2006-2048, Cornell University (2006)
12. Lev-Ami, T., Sagiv, M.: TVLA: A system for implementing static analyses. In: Proceedings of the 7th International Static Analysis Symposium, Santa Barbara, CA (2000)
13. Jones, N., Muchnick, S.: Flow analysis and optimization of Lisp-like structures. In: Conference Record of the 6th Annual ACM Symposium on the Principles of Programming Languages, San Antonio, TX (1979)
14. Chase, D., Wegman, M., Zadek, F.: Analysis of pointers and structures. In: Proceedings of the SIGPLAN '91 Conference on Program Language Design and Implementation, White Plains, NY (1990)
15. Hendren, L., Nicolau, A.: Parallelizing programs with recursive data structures. IEEE Transactions on Parallel and Distributed Systems **1**(1) (1990) 35–47
16. Hendren, L., Hummel, J., Nicolau, A.: A general data dependence test for dynamic, pointer-based data structures. In: Proceedings of the SIGPLAN '94 Conference on Program Language Design and Implementation, Orlando, FL (1994)
17. Deutsch, A.: Interprocedural may-alias analysis for pointers: Beyond k-limiting. In: Proceedings of the SIGPLAN '94 Conference on Program Language Design and Implementation, Orlando, FL (1994)
18. Ghiya, R., Hendren, L.: Is is a tree, a DAG or a cyclic graph? A shape analysis for heap-directed pointers in C. In: Proceedings of the 23rd Annual ACM Symposium on the Principles of Programming Languages, St. Petersburg Beach, FL (1996)
19. Chong, S., Rugina, R.: Static analysis of accessed regions in recursive data structures. In: Proceedings of the 10th International Static Analysis Symposium, San Diego, CA (2003)

20. Rugina, R.: Quantitative shape analysis. In: Proceedings of the 11th International Static Analysis Symposium, Verona, Italy (2004)
21. Sagiv, M., Reps, T., Wilhelm, R.: Solving shape-analysis problems in languages with destructive updating. In: Proceedings of the 23rd Annual ACM Symposium on the Principles of Programming Languages, St. Petersburg Beach, FL (1996)
22. Sagiv, M., Reps, T., Wilhelm, R.: Parametric shape analysis via 3-valued logic. In: Proceedings of the 26th Annual ACM Symposium on the Principles of Programming Languages, San Antonio, TX (1999)
23. Rinetzky, N., Sagiv, M.: Interprocedural shape analysis for recursive programs. In: Proceedings of the 2001 International Conference on Compiler Construction, Genova, Italy (2001)
24. Moller, A., Schwartzbach, M.: The pointer assertion logic engine. In: Proceedings of the SIGPLAN '01 Conference on Program Language Design and Implementation, Snowbird, UT (2001)
25. McPeak, S., Necula, G.: Data structure specification via local equality axioms. In: Proceedings of the 2005 Conference on Computer-Aided Verification, Seattle, WA (2005)
26. Lahiri, S., Qadeer, S.: Verifying properties of well-founded linked lists. In: Proceedings of the 33th Annual ACM Symposium on the Principles of Programming Languages, Charleston, SC (2006)
27. Ball, T., Majumdar, R., Millstein, T., Rajamani, S.: Automatic predicate abstraction of C programs. In: Proceedings of the SIGPLAN '01 Conference on Program Language Design and Implementation, Snowbird, UT (2001)
28. Balaban, I., Pnueli, A., Zuck, L.D.: Shape analysis by predicate abstraction. In Cousot, R., ed.: VMCAI. Volume 3385 of Lecture Notes in Computer Science., Springer (2005) 164–180
29. Dams, D., Namjoshi, K.S.: Shape analysis through predicate abstraction and model checking. In Zuck, L.D., Attie, P.C., Cortesi, A., Mukhopadhyay, S., eds.: VMCAI. Volume 2575 of Lecture Notes in Computer Science., Springer (2003) 310–324
30. Bingham, J.D., Rakamaric, Z.: A logic and decision procedure for predicate abstraction of heap-manipulating programs. In Emerson, E.A., Namjoshi, K.S., eds.: VMCAI. Volume 3855 of Lecture Notes in Computer Science., Springer (2006) 207–221
31. Reynolds, J.: Separation logic: A logic for shared mutable data structures. In: Proceedings of the Seventeenth Annual IEEE Symposium on Logic in Computer Science, Copenhagen, Denmark (2002)
32. Ishtiaq, S., O'Hearn, P.: BI as an assertion language for mutable data structures. In: Proceedings of the 28th Annual ACM Symposium on the Principles of Programming Languages, London, UK (2001)

Automated Verification of Shape and Size Properties Via Separation Logic

Huu Hai Nguyen[1], Cristina David[2], Shengchao Qin[3], and Wei-Ngan Chin[1,2]

[1] Computer Science Programme, Singapore-MIT Alliance
[2] Department of Computer Science, National University of Singapore
[3] Department of Computer Science, Durham University
{nguyenh2,davidcri,chinwn}@comp.nus.edu.sg, shengchao.qin@durham.ac.uk

Abstract. Despite their popularity and importance, pointer-based programs remain a major challenge for program verification. In this paper, we propose an automated verification system that is concise, precise and expressive for ensuring the safety of pointer-based programs. Our approach uses *user-definable* shape predicates to allow programmers to describe a wide range of data structures with their associated size properties. To support automatic verification, we design a new entailment checking procedure that can handle *well-founded* inductive predicates using *unfold/fold* reasoning. We have proven the soundness and termination of our verification system, and have built a prototype system.

1 Introduction

In recent years, separation logic has emerged as a contender for formal reasoning about heap-manipulating imperative programs. While the foundations of separation logic have been laid in seminal papers by Reynolds [17] and Isthiaq and O'Hearn [10], new automated reasoning tools based on separation logic, such as [2,8], are beginning to appear. Several major challenges are faced by the designers of such reasoning systems, including key issues on *automation* and *expressivity*. This paper's main goal is to raise the level of expressivity and verifiability that is possible with an automated verification system based on separation logic. We make the following technical contributions towards this overall goal :

- We provide a *shape predicate specification* mechanism that can capture a wide range of data structures together with size properties, such as various height-balanced trees, priority heap, sorted list, etc. We provide a mechanism to soundly approximate each shape predicate by a heap-independent *invariant* which plays an important role in entailment checking (Secs 2 and 4.1).
- We design a new procedure to check entailment of separation heap constraints. This procedure uses *unfold/fold* reasoning to deal with shape definitions. While the unfold/fold mechanism is not new, we have identified sufficient conditions for soundness and termination of the procedure in the presence of recursive user-defined shape predicates. (Secs 3.1, 4 and 5)
- We have implemented a prototype verification system with the above features and have also proven both its soundness and termination (Secs 6 and 7).

B. Cook and A. Podelski (Eds.): VMCAI 2007, LNCS 4349, pp. 251–266, 2007.
© Springer-Verlag Berlin Heidelberg 2007

2   User-Definable Shape Predicates

Separation logic [17,10] extends Hoare logic to support reasoning about shared mutable data structures. It adds two more connectives to classical logic : separating conjunction $*$, and separating implication $-\!*$. $h_1 * h_2$ asserts that two heaps described by h_1 and h_2 are domain-disjoint. $h_1-\!*h_2$ asserts that if the current heap is extended with a disjoint heap described by h_1, then h_2 holds in the extended heap. In this paper we use only separating conjunction.

We propose an intuitive mechanism based on inductive predicates (or relations) to allow user specification of shapely data structures with size properties. Our shape specification is based on separation logic with support for disjunctive heap states. Furthermore, each shape predicate may have pointer or integer parameters to capture relevant properties of data structures. We use the following data node declarations for the examples in the paper. They are recursive data declarations with different number of fields.

```
data node { int val; node next }
data node2 { int val; node2 prev; node2 next }
data node3 { int val; node3 left; node3 right; node3 parent }
```

We use $\text{p::c}\langle v^*\rangle$ to denote two things in our system. When c is a data name, $\text{p::c}\langle v^*\rangle$ stands for singleton heap $\text{p}\mapsto[(\text{f}:\text{v})^*]$ where f^* are fields of data declaration c. When c is a predicate name, $\text{p::c}\langle v^*\rangle$ stands for the formula $\text{c}(\text{p},\text{v}^*)$. The reason we distinguish the first parameter from the rest is that each predicate has an implicit parameter self as the first one. Effectively, self is a "root" pointer to the specified data structure that guides data traversal and facilitates the definition of *well-founded* predicates (Sec 3.1). As an example, a singly linked list with length n is described by :

$$\text{ll}\langle \text{n}\rangle \equiv (\text{self=null}\wedge \text{n=0})\vee(\exists \text{i,m,q}\cdot \text{self::node}\langle \text{i,q}\rangle *\text{q::ll}\langle \text{m}\rangle \wedge \text{n=m+1})\,\mathbf{inv}\,\text{n}\geq 0$$

Note that the parameter n captures a *derived* value. The above definition asserts that an ll list can be empty (the base case self=null) or consists of a head data node (specified by $\text{self::node}\langle \text{i,q}\rangle$) and a separate tail data structure which is also an ll list ($\text{q::ll}\langle \text{m}\rangle$). The $*$ connector ensures that the head node and the tail reside in disjoint heaps. We also specify a default invariant $\text{n}\geq 0$ that holds for all ll lists. Our predicate uses existential quantifiers for local values and pointers, such as i,m,q.

A more complex shape, doubly linked-list with length n, is described by :

$$\text{dll}\langle \text{p,n}\rangle \equiv (\text{self=null}\wedge \text{n=0})\vee(\text{self::node2}\langle \_,\text{p,q}\rangle *\text{q::dll}\langle \text{self,n}-1\rangle)\,\mathbf{inv}\,\text{n}\geq 0$$

The dll shape predicate has a parameter p that represents the prev field of the first node of the doubly linked-list. It captures a chain of nodes that are to be traversed via the next field starting from the current node self. The nodes accessible via the prev field of the self node are not part of the dll list. This example also highlights some shortcuts we may use to make shape specification shorter. We use underscore _ to denote an anonymous variable. Non-parameter variables in the RHS of the shape definition, such as q, are considered existentially quantified. Furthermore, terms may be directly written as arguments of shape predicate or data node.

User-definable shape predicates provide us with more flexibility than some recent automated reasoning systems [1,3] that are designed to work with only a small set of fixed predicates. Furthermore, our shape predicates can describe not only the *shape* of data structures, but also their *size* properties. This capability enables many applications, especially to support data structures with sophisticated invariants. For example, we may define a non-empty sorted list as below. The predicate also tracks the length, the minimum and maximum elements of the list.

$$\text{sortl}\langle n, \min, \max \rangle \equiv (\text{self::node}\langle \min, \text{null} \rangle \wedge \min = \max \wedge n = 1)$$
$$\vee\ (\text{self::node}\langle \min, q \rangle * q\text{::sortl}\langle n-1, k, \max \rangle \wedge \min \leq k)\ \mathbf{inv}\ \min \leq \max \wedge n \geq 1$$

The constraint $\min \leq k$ guarantees that sortedness property is adhered between any two adjacent nodes in the list. We may now specify (and then verify) the following insertion sort algorithm :

```
node insert(node x, node vn) where
   x::sortl⟨n, sm, lg⟩ * vn::node⟨v, _⟩ *↦ res::sortl⟨n+1, min(v, sm), max(v, lg)⟩
{ if (vn.val≤x.val) then { vn.next:=x; vn }
  else if (x.next=null) then { x.next:=vn; vn.next:=null; x }
  else { x.next:=insert(x.next, vn); x }}


node insertion_sort(node y) where y::ll⟨n⟩ ∧ n>0 *↦ res::sortl⟨n, _, _⟩
{ if (y.next=null) then y
  else { y.next:=insertion_sort(y.next); insert(y.next, y) }}
```

We use the notation $\Phi_{pr} *\!\!\mapsto \Phi_{po}$ to capture a precondition Φ_{pr} and a postcondition Φ_{po} of a method. We also use an expression-oriented language where the last subexpression (e.g. e_2 from $e_1;e_2$) denotes the result of an expression. A special identifier res is also used in the postcondition to denote the result of a method. The postcondition of insertion_sort shows that the output list is sorted and has the same number of nodes as the input list.

3   Automated Verification

In this section, we first introduce a core object-based imperative language and then propose a set of forward verification rules to systematically check that preconditions are satisfied at call sites, and that the declared postcondition is successfully verified (assuming the precondition) for each method definition.

3.1   Language

We provide a simple imperative language in Figure 1. Our language is strongly typed and we assume programs and constraints are well-typed. The language supports data type declaration via *datat*, and shape predicate definition via *spred*. For each shape definition *spred*, we also declare a heap-independent invariant π_0 over the parameters $\{\texttt{self}, v^*\}$ that holds for each instance of the predicate.

$$
\begin{array}{lll}
P & ::= tdecl^* \; meth^* & tdecl ::= datat \mid spred \\
datat & ::= \textbf{data} \; c \; \{ \; field^* \; \} & field ::= t \; v \qquad t ::= c \mid \tau \\
\tau & ::= \textbf{int} \mid \textbf{bool} \mid \textbf{float} \mid \textbf{void} \\
spred & ::= c\langle v^* \rangle \equiv \Phi \; \textbf{inv} \; \pi_0 \\
meth & ::= t \; mn \; ((t \; v)^*) \; \textbf{where} \; \Phi_{pr} \ast\!\!\rightarrow \Phi_{po} \; \{e\} \\
e & ::= \textbf{null} \mid k^\tau \mid v \mid v.f \mid v{:=}e \mid v_1.f{:=}v_2 \mid \textbf{new} \; c(v^*) \\
& \quad \mid e_1; e_2 \mid t \; v; \; e \mid mn(v^*) \mid \textbf{if} \; v \; \textbf{then} \; e_1 \; \textbf{else} \; e_2 \\
& \quad \mid \textbf{while} \; v \; \textbf{where} \; \Phi_{pr} \ast\!\!\rightarrow \Phi_{po} \; \textbf{do} \; e \\
\Phi & ::= \bigvee (\exists v^* \cdot \kappa \wedge \pi)^* & \pi ::= \gamma \wedge \phi \\
\gamma & ::= v_1{=}v_2 \mid v{=}\textbf{null} \mid v_1 {\neq} v_2 \mid v {\neq} \textbf{null} \mid \gamma_1 \wedge \gamma_2 \\
\kappa & ::= \textbf{emp} \mid v{::}c\langle v^* \rangle \mid \kappa_1 \ast \kappa_2 \\
\Delta & ::= \Phi \mid \Delta_1 \vee \Delta_2 \mid \Delta \wedge \pi \mid \Delta_1 \ast \Delta_2 \mid \exists v \cdot \Delta \\
\phi & ::= b \mid a \mid \phi_1 \wedge \phi_2 \mid \phi_1 \vee \phi_2 \mid \neg\phi \mid \exists v \cdot \phi \mid \forall v \cdot \phi \\
b & ::= \textbf{true} \mid \textbf{false} \mid v \mid b_1{=}b_2 \qquad a ::= s_1{=}s_2 \mid s_1 {\leq} s_2 \\
s & ::= k^{\text{int}} \mid v \mid k^{\text{int}} {\times} s \mid s_1{+}s_2 \mid -s \mid max(s_1, s_2) \mid min(s_1, s_2)
\end{array}
$$

Fig. 1. A Core Imperative Language

Each method *meth* and $\texttt{while}$ loop is declared with pre- and post-conditions of the form $\Phi_{pr} \ast\!\!\rightarrow \Phi_{po}$. For simplicity, we assume that variable names declared in each method are all distinct and that parameters are passed by-value. Primed notation is used to denote the latest value of variables and may appear in the postcondition of loops. For example, a simple loop with pre/post conditions is shown below :

$$\texttt{while x<0 where true} \ast\!\!\rightarrow (x{>}0 \wedge x'{=}x) \vee (x{\leq}0 \wedge x'{=}0) \;\texttt{do} \; \{ \; \texttt{x:=x+1} \; \}$$

Here x and x' denote the values of variable x at the entry and exit of the loop, respectively.

The separation constraints we use are in a disjunctive normal form Φ. Each disjunct consists of a $\ast$-separated heap constraint κ, referred to as *heap part*, and a heap-independent formula π, referred to as *pure part*. The pure part does not contain any heap nodes and is presently restricted to pointer equality/inequality γ and Presburger arithmetic ϕ. Furthermore, Δ denotes a composite formula that could always be normalised into the Φ form (see Figure 3). The semantic model for the separation constraints is left in the technical report [15].

Separation constraints are used in pre/post conditions and shape definitions. In order to handle them correctly without running into unmatched residual heap nodes, we require each separation constraint to be well-formed, as given by the following definitions:

Definition 3.1 (Accessible). *A variable is said to be* accessible *w.r.t. a shape predicate if it is a parameter or it is a special variable, either* $\texttt{self}$ *or* $\texttt{res}$.

Definition 3.2 (Reachable). *Given a heap constraint* $\kappa = \text{p::c}\langle v^* \rangle * \kappa_1$, *node* $\text{p::c}\langle v^* \rangle$ *is reachable from a variable* q *if and only if the following relation holds:*

$$\text{reach}(\kappa, \text{q}, \text{p::c}\langle v^* \rangle) =_{df} (\text{p=q}) \vee (\kappa_1 = \text{q::c}_\text{q}\langle .., \text{r}, .. \rangle * \kappa_2 \wedge \text{reach}(\kappa_2, \text{r}, \text{p::c}\langle v^* \rangle))$$

Definition 3.3 (Well-Formed Constraint). *A separation constraint* Φ *is well-formed if (i) every data node and shape predicate are reachable from their accessible variables, (ii) it is in a disjunctive normal form* $\bigvee (\exists v^* \cdot \kappa \wedge \gamma \wedge \phi)^*$ *where* κ *is for heap nodes,* γ *is for pointer constraint, and* ϕ *is for arithmetic formula.*

The primary significance of the *well-formed* condition is that all heap nodes of a heap constraint are reachable from accessible variables. This allows the entailment checking procedure to correctly match nodes from the consequent with nodes from the antecedent of an entailment relation.

Arbitrary recursive shape relation can lead to non-termination in unfold/fold reasoning. To avoid that problem, we propose to use only *well-founded* shape predicates in our framework.

Definition 3.4 (Well-Founded Predicate). *A shape predicate is said to be well-founded if it satisfies four conditions, namely: (i) it is a well-formed constraint, (ii) the parameter* self *may only be bound to a data node and not a predicate, (iii) only* self *is allowed to be bound to a data node and (iv) every predicate is reachable from* self.

Note that the definitions above are syntactic and can easily be enforced. Two examples of well-founded shape predicates are treep – binary tree with parent pointer, and avl – binary tree with near balanced heights, as follows :

$$\text{treep}\langle p \rangle \equiv (\text{self=null}) \vee (\text{self::node3}\langle \_, \text{l}, \text{r}, \text{p} \rangle * \text{l::treep}\langle \text{self} \rangle$$
$$*\text{r::treep}\langle \text{self} \rangle) \text{ inv true}$$
$$\text{avl}\langle \text{n}, \text{h} \rangle \equiv (\text{self=null} \wedge \text{n=0} \wedge \text{h=0}) \vee (\text{self::node2}\langle \_, \text{p}, \text{q} \rangle * \text{p::avl}\langle \text{n}_1, \text{h}_1 \rangle$$
$$*\text{q::avl}\langle \text{n}_2, \text{h}_2 \rangle \wedge \text{n=1+n}_1\text{+n}_2 \wedge \text{h=1+max}(\text{h}_1, \text{h}_2) \wedge -1 \leq \text{h}_1 - \text{h}_2 \leq 1) \text{ inv n}, \text{h} \geq 0$$

In contrast, the following three shape definitions are <u>not</u> well-founded.

$$\text{foo}\langle \text{n} \rangle \equiv \text{self::foo}\langle \text{m} \rangle \wedge \text{n=m+1}$$
$$\text{goo}\langle \rangle \equiv \text{self::node}\langle \_, \_ \rangle * \text{q::goo}\langle \rangle$$
$$\text{too}\langle \rangle \equiv \text{self::node}\langle \_, \text{q} \rangle * \text{q::node}\langle \_, \_ \rangle$$

For foo, the self identifier is bound to a shape predicate. For goo, the heap node pointed by q is *not* reachable from variable self. For too, an extra data node is bound to a non-self variable. The first example may cause infinite unfolding, while the second example captures an unreachable (junk) heap that cannot be located by our entailment procedure. The last example is just a syntactic restriction to facilitate termination proof reasoning, and can be easily overcome by introducing intermediate predicates.

$$\begin{array}{ccc}
\boxed{\text{FV-PRED}} & \boxed{\text{FV-VAR}} & \boxed{\text{FV-NEW}} \\[4pt]
\dfrac{XPure_0(\Phi) \Longrightarrow [0/\texttt{null}]\pi_0}{\vdash c\langle v^*\rangle \equiv \Phi \text{ inv } \pi_0} & \dfrac{\Delta_1=(\Delta\wedge res=v')}{\vdash \{\Delta\}\, v \,\{\Delta_1\}} & \dfrac{\Delta_1=(\Delta * res::c\langle v_1',..,v_n'\rangle)}{\vdash \{\Delta\}\, \texttt{new } c(v_1,..,v_n)\,\{\Delta_1\}}
\end{array}$$

$$\begin{array}{cc}
\boxed{\text{FV-ASSIGN}} & \boxed{\text{FV-CALL}} \\[4pt]
\dfrac{\begin{array}{c}\vdash \{\Delta\}\, e\, \{\Delta_1\} \\ \Delta_2=\exists res\cdot(\Delta_1\wedge_{\{v\}} v'=res)\end{array}}{\vdash \{\Delta\}\, v:=e\, \{\Delta_2\}} & \dfrac{\begin{array}{c}t\ mn((t_i\ v_i)_{i=1}^n) \text{ where } \Phi_{pr} \;\ast\!\!\!\rightarrowtail\; \Phi_{po}\ \{..\} \in P \\ \rho=[v_i'/v_i] \quad \Delta\vdash\rho\Phi_{pr} * \Delta_1 \quad \Delta_2=(\Delta_1 * \Phi_{po})\end{array}}{\vdash \{\Delta\}\, mn(v_1..v_n)\, \{\Delta_2\}}
\end{array}$$

$$\boxed{\text{FV-METH}}$$

$$\dfrac{V=\{v_1..v_n\} \quad W=prime(V) \quad \Delta=\Phi_{pr}\wedge nochange(V) \quad \vdash \{\Delta\}\, e\, \{\Delta_1\} \quad (\exists W\cdot\Delta_1)\vdash\Phi_{po} * \Delta_2}{\vdash t_0\ mn(t_1\ v_1,..,t_n\ v_n) \text{ where } \Phi_{pr} \;\ast\!\!\!\rightarrowtail\; \Phi_{po}\ \{e\}}$$

Fig. 2. Some Forward Verification Rules

3.2 Forward Verification

We use P to denote the program being checked. With pre/post conditions declared for each method in P, we can now apply modular verification to its body using Hoare-style triples $\vdash \{\Delta_1\}\, e\, \{\Delta_2\}$. These are *forward verification* rules as we expect Δ_1 to be given before computing Δ_2. Some rules given in Fig 2 while others are left in the technical report [15]. They are used to track heap states as accurately as possible with path-, flow-, and context-sensitivity. For each call site, [**FV-CALL**] ensures that its method's precondition is satisfied. For each method definition, [**FV-METH**] checks that its postcondition holds for the method body assuming its precondition. A method postcondition may capture only part of the heap at the end of the method, leaving the residue heap nodes in Δ_2. For each shape definition, [**FV-PRED**] checks that its given invariant is a consequence of the well-founded heap formula. The soundness of the forward verification is also left in the technical report.

We now explain the operators/functions used in our verification rules. The operator $\wedge_{\{v\}}$ in assignment rule is an instance of *composition with update* operators. Given a state Δ_1, a state change Δ_2, and a set of variables to be updated $X=\{x_1,\ldots,x_n\}$, the composition operator $\oplus_X$ is defined as :

$$\Delta_1 \oplus_X \Delta_2 =_{df} \exists\, r_1..r_n \cdot \rho_1\, \Delta_1 \oplus \rho_2\, \Delta_2$$
where $r_1,\ldots,r_n$ are fresh variables; $\rho_1 = [r_i/x_i']_{i=1}^n$; $\rho_2 = [r_i/x_i]_{i=1}^n$

Note that ρ_1 and ρ_2 are substitutions that link each latest value of x_i' in Δ_1 with the corresponding initial value x_i in Δ_2 via a fresh variable r_i. The binary operator $\oplus$ is either $\wedge$ or $*$. Function $nochange(V)$ returns a formula asserting that the unprimed and primed versions of each variable in V are equal; $prime(V)$ returns the primed form of all variables in V. $[e^*/v^*]$ represents substitutions of v^* by e^*. A special case is $[0/\texttt{null}]$, which denotes replacement of $\texttt{null}$ by 0. Normalization rules for separation constraints are given in Figure 3. *XPure* is described in the next section.

$$
\begin{array}{ll}
(\Delta_1 \vee \Delta_2) \wedge \pi & \rightsquigarrow (\Delta_1 \wedge \pi) \vee (\Delta_2 \wedge \pi) \\
(\Delta_1 \vee \Delta_2) * \Delta & \rightsquigarrow (\Delta_1 * \Delta) \vee (\Delta_2 * \Delta) \\
(\kappa_1 \wedge \pi_1) * (\kappa_2 \wedge \pi_2) \rightsquigarrow (\kappa_1 * \kappa_2) \wedge (\pi_1 \wedge \pi_2) \\
(\kappa_1 \wedge \pi_1) \wedge (\pi_2) & \rightsquigarrow \kappa_1 \wedge (\pi_1 \wedge \pi_2)
\end{array}
\qquad
\begin{array}{ll}
(\gamma_1 \wedge \phi_1) \wedge (\gamma_2 \wedge \phi_2) \rightsquigarrow (\gamma_1 \wedge \gamma_2) \wedge (\phi_1 \wedge \phi_2) \\
(\exists x \cdot \Delta) \wedge \pi & \rightsquigarrow \exists y \cdot ([y/x]\Delta \wedge \pi) \\
(\exists x \cdot \Delta_1) * \Delta_2 & \rightsquigarrow \exists y \cdot ([y/x]\Delta_1 * \Delta_2)
\end{array}
$$

Fig. 3. Normalization Rules

3.3 Forward Verification Example

We present the detailed verification of the first branch of the `insert` function from Sec 2. Note that program variables appear primed in formulae whereas logical variables unprimed. The proof is straightforward, except for the last step where a disjunctive heap state is folded to form a shape predicate. The procedure to perform the folding step is presented in Sec 4.

```
{x'::sortl⟨n, mi, ma⟩ * vn'::node⟨v, _⟩} // precondition
     if (vn.val ≤ x.val) then {
{(x'::node⟨mi, null⟩ * vn'::node⟨v, _⟩ ∧ mi=ma ∧ n=1 ∧ v≤mi)
  ∨ (∃q, k · x'::node⟨mi, q⟩ * q::sortl⟨n−1, k, ma⟩ * vn'::node⟨v, _⟩
     ∧ mi≤k ∧ mi≤ma ∧ n≥2 ∧ v≤mi)} // unfold and conditional
          vn.next := x;
{(x'::node⟨mi, null⟩ * vn'::node⟨v, x'⟩ ∧ mi=ma ∧ n=1 ∧ v≤mi)
  ∨ (∃q, k · x'::node⟨mi, q⟩ * q::sortl⟨n−1, k, ma⟩ * vn'::node⟨v, x'⟩
     ∧ mi≤k ∧ mi≤ma ∧ n≥2 ∧ v≤mi)} // field update
          vn
{(x'::node⟨mi, null⟩ * vn'::node⟨v, x'⟩ ∧ mi=ma ∧ n=1 ∧ v≤mi ∧ res=vn')
  ∨ (∃q, k · x'::node⟨mi, q⟩ * q::sortl⟨n−1, k, ma⟩ * vn'::node⟨v, x'⟩
     ∧ mi≤k ∧ mi≤ma ∧ n≥2 ∧ v≤mi ∧ res=vn')} // returned value
     }
{res::sortl⟨n+1, min(v, mi), max(v, ma)⟩} // fold to postcondition
```

4 Entailment

We present in this section the entailment checking rules for the class of constraints used by our verification system.

4.1 Separation Constraint Approximation

Entailment between separation formulae (detailed in section 4.2) is reduced to entailment between pure formulae by successively removing heap nodes from the consequent until only a pure formula remains. When the consequent is pure, the heap formula in the antecedent is soundly approximated by function $XPure_n$. The function $XPure_n(\Phi)$, whose definition is given in Fig 4, returns a sound approximation of Φ as formula $\textbf{ex } i^* \cdot \bigvee (\exists v^* \cdot \pi)^*$ where i^* are (non-null) distinct symbolic addresses of heap nodes of Φ. The function $IsData(c)$ returns `true` if c is a data node, while $IsPred(c)$ returns `true` if c is a shape predicate.

We illustrate how this function works by the following example :

$$XPure_n(p_1::\mathbf{node}\langle \_, \_\rangle * p_2::\mathbf{node}\langle \_, \_\rangle)$$
$$= (\mathbf{ex}\ i_1 \cdot (p_1{=}i_1 \wedge i_1{>}0)) \wedge (\mathbf{ex}\ i_2 \cdot (p_2{=}i_2 \wedge i_2{>}0))$$
$$= \mathbf{ex}\ i_1, i_2 \cdot (p_1{=}i_1 \wedge i_1{>}0 \wedge p_2{=}i_2 \wedge i_2{>}0 \wedge i_1{\neq}i_2)$$

The following normalization rules are also used :

$$(\mathbf{ex}\ I \cdot \phi_1) \vee (\mathbf{ex}\ J \cdot \phi_2) \rightsquigarrow \mathbf{ex}\ I{\cup}J \cdot (\phi_1 \vee \phi_2)$$
$$\exists\ v \cdot (\mathbf{ex}\ I \cdot \phi) \qquad \rightsquigarrow \mathbf{ex}\ I \cdot (\exists\ v \cdot \phi)$$
$$(\mathbf{ex}\ I \cdot \phi_1) \wedge (\mathbf{ex}\ J \cdot \phi_2) \rightsquigarrow \mathbf{ex}\ I{\cup}J \cdot \phi_1 {\wedge} \phi_2 {\wedge} \bigwedge_{i \in I, j \in J} i{\neq}j$$

The $\mathbf{ex}\ i^*$ construct is converted to $\exists i^*$ when the formula is used as a pure formula. The soundness of $XPure_n$ is formalized by :

Lemma 4.1 (Sound Invariant). *Given a shape predicate $c\langle v^*\rangle \equiv \Phi$ inv π_0, we have $\Phi \models Inv_n(\mathtt{self}::c\langle v^*\rangle)$ if $XPure_0(\Phi) \Longrightarrow [0/\mathtt{null}]\pi_0$. π_0 is said to be sound.*

Proof: *By structural induction on Φ.*

Lemma 4.2 (Sound Abstraction). *Given a separation constraint Φ where the invariants of the predicates appearing in Φ are sound, we have $\Phi \models XPure_n(\Phi)$.*

Proof: *By structural induction on Φ.*

Lemma 4.1 ensures that a supplied invariant that passes [FV-PRED] is a semantic consequence of the predicate. Lemma 4.2 asserts that it is safe to approximate an antecedent by using $XPure$ if all the predicate invariants are sound. They also allow the possibility of obtaining a more precise invariant by applying $XPure$ one or more times. For example, when given

$$\frac{(c\langle v^*\rangle \equiv \Phi\ \mathbf{inv}\ \pi_0) \in P}{Inv_0(p::c\langle v^*\rangle) = [p/\mathtt{self}, 0/\mathtt{null}]\pi_0}$$

$$\frac{(c\langle v^*\rangle \equiv \Phi\ \mathbf{inv}\ \pi_0) \in P}{Inv_n(p::c\langle v^*\rangle) = [p/\mathtt{self}, 0/\mathtt{null}]XPure_{n-1}(\Phi)}$$

$$XPure_n(\bigvee(\exists v^* \cdot \kappa \wedge \pi)^*) =_{df} \bigvee(\exists v^* \cdot XPure_n(\kappa) \wedge [0/\mathtt{null}]\pi)^*$$

$$XPure_n(\mathbf{emp}) =_{df} \mathbf{true}$$

$$\frac{IsData(c) \quad fresh\ i}{XPure_n(p::c\langle v^*\rangle) =_{df} \mathbf{ex}\ i \cdot (p{=}i \wedge i{>}0)}$$

$$\frac{IsPred(c) \quad fresh\ i^* \quad Inv_n(p::c\langle v^*\rangle) = \mathbf{ex}\ j^* \cdot \bigvee(\exists u^* \cdot \pi)^*}{XPure_n(p::c\langle v^*\rangle) =_{df} \mathbf{ex}\ i^* \cdot [i^*/j^*]\bigvee(\exists u^* \cdot \pi)^*}$$

$$XPure_n(\kappa_1 * \kappa_2) =_{df} XPure_n(\kappa_1) \wedge XPure_n(\kappa_2)$$

Fig. 4. $XPure$: Translating to Pure Form

a pure invariant $n{\geq}0$ for the predicate $\mathtt{ll}\langle n\rangle$, a single application returns $\mathbf{ex}\ i \cdot (\mathtt{self}{=}0 \wedge n{=}0 \vee \mathtt{self}{=}i \wedge i{>}0 \wedge n{>}0)$ which is sound and more precise, as it relates the nullness of the $\mathtt{self}$ pointer with the size $\mathtt{n}$ of the list.

The invariants associated with shape predicates play an important role in our system. Without the knowledge $m \geq 0$, the entailment $x::node\langle \_, y\rangle * y::ll\langle m\rangle \vdash x::ll\langle n\rangle \wedge n \geq 1$ would not have succeeded due to $n \geq 1$. Without the more precise derived invariant using *XPure* for predicate ll, the entailment $x::ll\langle n\rangle \wedge n > 0 \vdash x \neq null$ would not have succeeded either.

4.2 Separation Constraint Entailment

We express the main procedure for heap entailment by the relation

$$\Delta_A \vdash_V^\kappa \Delta_C * \Delta_R$$

which denotes $\kappa * \Delta_A \vdash \exists V \cdot (\kappa * \Delta_C) * \Delta_R$.

$$
\boxed{
\begin{array}{c}
\text{[ENT–EMP]} \\
\rho = [0/\texttt{null}] \\
\hline
XPure_n(\kappa_1 * \kappa) \wedge \rho \pi_1 \Longrightarrow \rho \exists V \cdot \pi_2 \\
\hline
\kappa_1 \wedge \pi_1 \vdash_V^\kappa \pi_2 * (\kappa_1 \wedge \pi_1)
\end{array}
}
\quad
\boxed{
\begin{array}{c}
\text{[ENT–MATCH]} \\
XPure_n(p_1::c\langle v_1^*\rangle * \kappa_1 * \pi_1) \Longrightarrow p_1 = p_2 \quad \rho = [v_1^*/v_2^*] \\
\hline
\kappa_1 \wedge \pi_1 \wedge freeEqn(\rho, V) \vdash_{V - \{v_2^*\}}^{\kappa * p_1::c\langle v_1^*\rangle} \rho(\kappa_2 \wedge \pi_2) * \Delta \\
\hline
p_1::c\langle v_1^*\rangle * \kappa_1 \wedge \pi_1 \vdash_V^\kappa (p_2::c\langle v_2^*\rangle * \kappa_2 \wedge \pi_2) * \Delta
\end{array}
}
$$

$$
\boxed{
\begin{array}{c}
\text{[ENT–FOLD]} \\
IsPred(c_2) \wedge IsData(c_1) \quad (\Delta^r, \kappa^r, \pi^r) \in fold^\kappa(p_1::c_1\langle v_1^*\rangle * \kappa_1 \wedge \pi_1, p_2::c_2\langle v_2^*\rangle) \\
XPure_n(p_1::c_1\langle v_1^*\rangle * \kappa_1 * \pi_1) \Longrightarrow p_1 = p_2 \quad (\pi^a, \pi^c) = split_V^{\{v_2^*\}}(\pi^r) \quad \Delta^r \wedge \pi^a \vdash_V^{\kappa^r} (\kappa_2 \wedge \pi_2 \wedge \pi^c) * \Delta \\
\hline
p_1::c_1\langle v_1^*\rangle * \kappa_1 \wedge \pi_1 \vdash_V^\kappa (p_2::c_2\langle v_2^*\rangle * \kappa_2 \wedge \pi_2) * \Delta
\end{array}
}
$$

$$
\boxed{
\begin{array}{c}
\text{[ENT–UNFOLD]} \\
XPure_n(p_1::c_1\langle v_1^*\rangle * \kappa_1 * \pi_1) \Longrightarrow p_1 = p_2 \quad IsPred(c_1) \wedge IsData(c_2) \\
unfold(p_1::c_1\langle v_1^*\rangle) * \kappa_1 \wedge \pi_1 \vdash_V^\kappa (p_2::c_2\langle v_2^*\rangle * \kappa_2 \wedge \pi_2) * \Delta \\
\hline
p_1::c_1\langle v_1^*\rangle * \kappa_1 \wedge \pi_1 \vdash_V^\kappa (p_2::c_2\langle v_2^*\rangle * \kappa_2 \wedge \pi_2) * \Delta
\end{array}
}
\quad
\boxed{
\begin{array}{c}
\text{[ENT–LHS–OR]} \\
\Delta_1 \vdash_V^\kappa \Delta_3 * \Delta_4 \\
\Delta_2 \vdash_V^\kappa \Delta_3 * \Delta_5 \\
\hline
\Delta_1 \vee \Delta_2 \vdash_V^\kappa \Delta_3 * (\Delta_4 \vee \Delta_5)
\end{array}
}
$$

$$
\boxed{
\begin{array}{c}
\text{[ENT–RHS–OR]} \\
\Delta_1 \vdash_V^\kappa \Delta_i * \Delta_i^R \\
\hline
\Delta_1 \vdash_V^\kappa (\Delta_2 \vee \Delta_3) * \Delta_i^R
\end{array} i \in \{2, 3\}
}
\quad
\boxed{
\begin{array}{c}
\text{[ENT–RHS–EX]} \\
\Delta_1 \vdash_{V \cup \{w\}}^\kappa ([w/v]\Delta_2) * \Delta_3 \\
fresh \ w \quad \Delta = \exists \ w \cdot \Delta_3 \\
\hline
\Delta_1 \vdash_V^\kappa (\exists \ v \cdot \Delta_2) * \Delta_3
\end{array}
}
\quad
\boxed{
\begin{array}{c}
\text{[ENT–LHS–EX]} \\
[w/v]\Delta_1 \vdash_V^\kappa \Delta_2 * \Delta \\
fresh \ w \\
\hline
\exists v \cdot \Delta_1 \vdash_V^\kappa \Delta_2 * \Delta
\end{array}
}
$$

Fig. 5. Separation Constraint Entailment

The purpose of heap entailment is to check that heap nodes in the antecedent Δ_A are sufficiently precise to cover all nodes from the consequent Δ_C, and to compute a residual heap state Δ_R. κ is the history of nodes from the antecedent that have been used to match nodes from the consequent, V is the list of existentially quantified variables from the consequent. Note that k and V are derived. The entailment checking procedure is invoked with $\kappa = \texttt{emp}$ and $V = \emptyset$. The entailment checking rules are given in Fig 5. We discuss the matching rule in what follows, and leave unfold/fold rules to Sec 5.

The procedure works by successively matching up heap nodes that can be proven aliased. As the matching process is incremental, we keep the successfully matched nodes from antecedent in κ for better precision. For example, consider the following (valid) proof:

$$\frac{\dfrac{(((\texttt{p=null} \wedge \texttt{n=0}) \vee (\texttt{p}{\neq}\texttt{null} \wedge \texttt{n>0})) \wedge \texttt{n>0} \wedge \texttt{m=n}) \implies \texttt{p}{\neq}\texttt{null}}{\Delta_{\mathsf{R}} = (\texttt{n>0} \wedge \texttt{m=n})}}{\dfrac{\texttt{n>0} \wedge \texttt{m=n} \vdash_{\texttt{p::ll}\langle\texttt{n}\rangle} \texttt{p}{\neq}\texttt{null} * \Delta_{\mathsf{R}}}{\texttt{p::ll}\langle\texttt{n}\rangle \wedge \texttt{n>0} \vdash \texttt{p::ll}\langle\texttt{m}\rangle \wedge \texttt{p}{\neq}\texttt{null} * \Delta_{\mathsf{R}}}}$$

Had the predicate $\texttt{p::ll}\langle\texttt{n}\rangle$ not been kept and used, the proof would not have succeeded. Such an entailment would be useful when, for example, a list with positive length $\texttt{n}$ is used as input for a function that requires a non-empty list.

Another feature of the entailment procedure is exemplified by the transfer of $\texttt{m=n}$ to the antecedent (and subsequently to the residue). In general, when a match occurs (rule [**ENT–MATCH**]) and an argument of the heap node coming from the consequent is free, the entailment procedure binds the argument to the corresponding variable from the antecedent and moves the equality to the antecedent. In our system, free variables in consequent are variables from method preconditions. Hence these bindings act as substitutions that have to be kept in antecedent to allow subsequent program state (from residual heap) to be aware of their values. This process is formalized by the function *freeEqn* below, where V is the set of existentially quantified variables :

$$\mathit{freeEqn}([u_i/v_i]_{i=1}^n, V) =_{\mathit{df}} \texttt{let } \pi_i = (\texttt{if } v_i{\in}V \texttt{ then true else } v_i{=}u_i) \texttt{ in} \bigwedge_{i=1}^n \pi_i$$

For soundness, we perform a preprocessing step to ensure that variables appearing as arguments of heap nodes and predicates are i) distinct and ii) if they are free, they do not appear in the antecedent by adding (existentially quantified) fresh variables and equalities. This guarantees that the generated substitutions are well-defined. It also guarantees that the formula generated by *freeEqn* does not introduce any additional constraints over existing variables in the antecedent, as one side of each equation does not appear anywhere else in the antecedent. An additional outcome is that the order of picking nodes from the consequent for matching does not matter.

5   Unfold/Fold Mechanism

Unfold/fold operations can be used to handle well-founded inductive predicates in a deductive manner. In particular, we can unfold a predicate that appears in the antecedent that matches with a data node in the consequent. Correspondingly, we fold a predicate that appears in the consequent if it matches with a data node in the antecedent. The well-founded condition is sufficient to ensure termination.

5.1   Unfolding a Shape Predicate in the Antecedent

We apply an unfold operation on a predicate in the antecedent that matches with a data node in the consequent. Consider :

$$x\text{::}\mathtt{ll}\langle n\rangle \wedge n{>}3 \ \vdash \ (\exists r\cdot x\text{::}\mathtt{node}\langle\_,r\rangle * r\text{::}\mathtt{node}\langle\_,y\rangle \wedge y{\neq}\mathtt{null}) * \Delta_R$$

where Δ_R captures the residual of entailment. For the entailment to succeed, we would unfold the $\mathtt{ll}\langle n\rangle$ predicate in the antecedent twice to allow the two data nodes on the consequent to be matched up. This would result in the following reduction towards a residual state :

$$\exists q_1 \cdot x\text{::}\mathtt{node}\langle\_,q_1\rangle * q_1\text{::}\mathtt{ll}\langle n{-}1\rangle \wedge n{>}3 \ \vdash \ (\exists r\cdot x\text{::}\mathtt{node}\langle\_,r\rangle * r\text{::}\mathtt{node}\langle\_,y\rangle \wedge y{\neq}\mathtt{null}) * \Delta_R$$
$$q_1\text{::}\mathtt{ll}\langle n{-}1\rangle \wedge n{>}3 \ \vdash \ (q_1\text{::}\mathtt{node}\langle\_,y\rangle \wedge y{\neq}\mathtt{null}) * \Delta_R$$
$$\exists q_2 \cdot q_1\text{::}\mathtt{node}\langle\_,q_2\rangle * q_2\text{::}\mathtt{ll}\langle n{-}2\rangle \wedge n{>}3 \vdash q_1\text{::}\mathtt{node}\langle\_,y\rangle \wedge y{\neq}\mathtt{null} * \Delta_R$$
$$q_2\text{::}\mathtt{ll}\langle n{-}2\rangle \wedge n{>}3 \wedge q_2{=}y \ \vdash \ y{\neq}\mathtt{null} * \Delta_R$$

Note that due to the well-founded condition, each unfolding exposes a data node that matches the data node in the consequent. Thus a reduction of the consequent imme-

$$\boxed{\text{UNFOLDING}}$$
$$c\langle v^*\rangle \equiv \Phi \in P$$
$$\overline{unfold(p\text{::}c\langle v^*\rangle) \ =_{df} \ [p/\mathtt{self}]\Phi}$$

diately follows, which contributes to the termination of the entailment check. A formal definition of unfolding is given by the rule [UNFOLDING].

5.2 Folding a Shape Predicate in the Consequent

We apply a fold operation when a data node in the antecedent matches with a predicate in the consequent. An example is :

$$x\text{::}\mathtt{node}\langle 1,q_1\rangle * q_1\text{::}\mathtt{node}\langle 2,\mathtt{null}\rangle * y\text{::}\mathtt{node}\langle 3,\mathtt{null}\rangle \ \vdash \ x\text{::}\mathtt{ll}\langle n\rangle \wedge n{>}1 * \Delta_R$$

The fold step may be recursively applied but is guaranteed to terminate for well-founded predicate as it will reduce a data node in the antecedent for each recursive invocation. This reduction in the antecedent cannot go on forever. Furthermore, the fold operation may introduce bindings for the parameters of the folded predicate. In the above, we obtain $n{=}2$ which may be transferred to the antecedent if n is free, but kept in the consequent otherwise. Since n is indeed free, our folding step would finally derive :

$$y\text{::}\mathtt{node}\langle 3,\mathtt{null}\rangle \wedge n{=}2 \ \vdash \ n{>}1 * \Delta_R$$

The effects of folding may seem similar to unfolding the predicate in the consequent. However, there is a subtle difference in their handling of bindings for free derived variables. If we choose to use unfolding on the consequent instead, these bindings may not be transferred to the antecedent. Consider the example below where n is free :

$$z{=}\mathtt{null} \ \vdash \ z\text{::}\mathtt{ll}\langle n\rangle \wedge n{>}{-}1 * \Delta_R$$

By unfolding the predicate $\mathtt{ll}\langle n\rangle$ in the consequent, we obtain :

$$z{=}\mathtt{null} \vdash (z{=}\mathtt{null} \wedge n{=}0 \wedge n{>}{-}1) \vee (\exists q\cdot z\text{::}\mathtt{node}\langle\_,q\rangle * q\text{::}\mathtt{ll}\langle n{-}1\rangle \wedge n{>}{-}1) * \Delta_R$$

There are now two disjuncts in the consequent. The second one fails because it mismatches. The first one matches but still fails as the derived binding $n{=}0$ was not transferred to the antecedent.

When a fold to a predicate $p_2::c_2\langle v_2^* \rangle$ is performed, the constraints related to variables v_2^* are important. The *split* function projects these constraints out and differentiates those constraints based on free variables.

$$split_V^{\{v_2^*\}}(\bigwedge_{i=1}^n \pi_i^r) =$$
$$\texttt{let } \pi_i^a, \pi_i^c = \texttt{if } FV(\pi_i^r) \cap v_2^* = \emptyset \texttt{ then } (true, true)$$
$$\texttt{else if } FV(\pi_i^r) \cap V = \emptyset \texttt{ then } (\pi_i^r, true) \texttt{ else } (true, \pi_i^r)$$
$$\texttt{in } (\bigwedge_{i=1}^n \pi_i^a, \bigwedge_{i=1}^n \pi_i^c)$$

A formal definition of folding is specified by rule [FOLDING]. Some heap nodes from κ are removed by the entailment procedure so as to match with the heap

$$\text{[FOLDING]}$$
$$\frac{c\langle v^* \rangle \equiv \Phi \in P \quad W_i = V_i - \{v^*, p\}}{\kappa \wedge \pi \vdash_{\{p,v^*\}}^{\kappa'} [p/\texttt{self}]\Phi * \{(\Delta_i, \kappa_i, V_i, \pi_i)\}_{i=1}^n}$$
$$fold^{\kappa'}(\kappa \wedge \pi, p::c\langle v^* \rangle) =_{df} \{(\Delta_i, \kappa_i, \exists W_i \cdot \pi_i)\}_{i=1}^n$$

formula of predicate $p::c\langle v^* \rangle$. This requires a special version of entailment that returns three extra things: (i) consumed heap nodes, (ii) existential variables used, and (iii) final consequent. The final consequent is used to return a constraint for $\{v^*\}$ via $\exists W_i \cdot \pi_i$. A set of answers is returned by the fold step as we allow it to explore multiple ways of matching up with its disjunctive heap state. Our entailment also handles empty predicates correctly.

6   Soundness of Entailment

The following theorems state that our entailment check procedure(given in Fig. 5) is sound and terminating. Proofs are given in the technical report [15].

Theorem 6.1 (Soundness). *If entailment check* $\Delta_1 \vdash \Delta_2 * \Delta$ *succeeds, we have: for all* s, h, *if* $s, h \models \Delta_1$ *then* $s, h \models \Delta_2 * \Delta$.

Theorem 6.2 (Termination). *The entailment check* $\Delta_1 \vdash \Delta_2 * \Delta$ *always terminates.*

7   Implementation

We have built a prototype system using Objective Caml. The proof obligations generated by our verification are discharged by our entailment checking procedure with the help of Omega Calculator [16].

Fig 6 summarizes a suite of programs tested. These examples use complicated recursion and data structures with sophisticated shape and size properties. They help show that our approach is general enough to handle interesting data structures such as sorted lists, sorted trees, priority queues, various balanced trees, etc. in a uniform way. Verification time of a function includes time to verify all functions that it calls. The time required for shape and size verification is mostly within a couple of seconds. The average annotation cost (number of annotations/LOC ratio) for our examples is around 7%.

Programs	Verification Time (sec)	Programs	Verification Time (sec)
Linked List (size/length)		Binary Search Tree (min, max, sortedness)	
delete	0.09	insert	0.20
reverse	0.07	delete	0.38
Circular List (size, cyclic structure)		Priority Queue (size, height, max-heap)	
delete	0.09	insert	0.45
count	0.16	delete_max	7.17
Doubly Linked List (size, double links)		AVL Tree (size, height-balanced)	
append	0.16	insert	5.06
flatten (from tree)	0.30	Red-Black Tree (size, black-height-balanced)	
Sorted List (size, min, max, sortedness)		insert	1.53
delete	0.13	2-3 Tree (height-balanced)	
insertion_sort	0.27	insert	24.41
selection_sort	0.41	Perfect Tree (perfectness)	
bubble_sort	0.64	insert	0.26
merge_sort	0.61	Complete Tree (completeness)	
quick_sort	0.59	insert	1.50

Fig. 6. Verifying Data Structures with Arithmetic Properties

We have also investigated the precision/cost tradeoff of using $XPure_n$ and settled on $n = 1$ as the default. $XPure_0$ fails for many examples, while $XPure_2$ incurs substantial overheads without increasing precision for our examples.

8   Related Work

Separation Logic. The general framework of separation logic [17,10] is highly expressive but undecidable. Likewise, [13] formalised the proof rules for handling abstract predicates (with scopes on visibility of predicates) but provided no automated procedure for checking the user supplied specifications. In the search for a decidable fragment of separation logic for automated verification, Berdine *et al.* [1] supports only a limited set of predicates *without* size properties, disjunctions and existential quantifiers. Similarly, Jia and Walker [11] postponed the handling of recursive predicates in their recent work on automated reasoning of pointer programs. Our approach is more pragmatic as we aim for a sound and terminating formulation of automated verification via separation logic but do not aim for completeness in the expressive fragment that we handle. On the inference front, Lee et al. [12] has conducted an intraprocedural analysis for loop invariants using grammar approximation under separation logic. Their analysis can handle a wide range of shape predicates with local sharing but is restricted to predicates with two parameters and without size properties. A recent work [8] has also formulated interprocedural shape inference but is restricted to just the list segment shape predicate. Sims [20] extends separation logic with fixpoint connectives and postponed substitution to express recursively defined formulae to model the analysis of while-loops. However, it is unclear how to check for entailment in their extended separation logic. While our work does not address the inference/analysis challenge, we have succeeded in providing direct support for automated verification via an expressive shape and size specification mechanism.

Shape Checking/Analysis. Many formalisms for shape analysis have been proposed for checking user programs' intricate manipulations of shapely data structures. One well-known work is Pointer Assertion Logic [14] by Moeller and Schwartzbach where shape specifications in monadic second-order logic are given by programmers for loop invariants and method pre/post conditions, and checked by their MONA tool. For shape inference, Sagiv et al. [19] presented a parameterised framework, called TVLA, using 3-valued logic formulae and abstract interpretation. Based on the properties expected of data structures, programmers must supply a set of predicates to the framework which are then used to analyse that certain shape invariants are maintained. However, most of these techniques were focused on analysing shape invariants, and did not attempt to track the size properties of complex data structures. An exception is the quantitative shape analysis of Rugina [18] where a data flow analysis was proposed to compute quantitative information for programs with destructive updates. By tracking unique points-to reference and its height property, their algorithm is able to handle AVL-like tree structures. Even then, the author acknowledged the lack of a general specification mechanism for handling arbitrary shape/size properties.

Size Properties. In another direction of research, size properties have been most explored for declarative languages [9,22,6] as the immutability property makes their data structures easier to analyse statically. Size analysis was later extended to object-based programs [7] but was restricted to tracking either size-immutable objects that can be aliased and size-mutable objects that are unaliased, with no support for complex shapes. The Applied Type System (ATS) [5] was proposed for combining programs with proofs. In ATS, dependent types for capturing program invariants are extremely expressive and can capture many program properties with the help of accompanying proofs. Using linear logic, ATS may also handle mutable data structures with sharing. However, users must supply all expected properties, and precisely state where they are to be applied, with ATS playing the role of a proof-checker. Comparatively, we use a more limited class of constraint for shape and size analysis but supports automated modular verification.

Unfold/Fold Mechanism. Unfold/fold techniques were originally used for program transformation [4] on purely functional programs. A similar technique called unroll/roll was later used in alias types [21] to *manually* witness the isomorphism between a recursive type and its unfolding. Here, each unroll/roll step must be manually specified by programmer, in contrast to our approach which applies these steps automatically during entailment checking. In [1], an automated procedure that uses unroll/roll was given but it was hardwired to work for only `lseg` and `tree` predicates. Furthermore, it performs rolling by unfolding a predicate in the consequent which would miss bindings on free variables. Our unfold/fold mechanism is general, automatic and terminates for heap entailment checking.

9   Conclusion

We have presented a new approach to verifying pointer-based programs that can precisely track shape and size properties. Our approach is built on well-founded shape relations and well-formed separation constraints from which we have designed a sound procedure for heap entailment. We have implemented a verification system that is both precise and expressive. Our automated deduction mechanism is based on the unfold/fold reasoning of user-definable predicates that has been proven to be sound and terminating.

Acknowledgement

We thank the reviewers for their insightful comments. This work is supported by the Singapore-MIT Alliance and NUS research grant R-252-000-213-112.

References

1. J. Berdine, C. Calcagno, and P. W. O'Hearn. Symbolic Execution with Separation Logic. In *APLAS*. Springer-Verlag, November 2005.
2. J. Berdine, C. Calcagno, and P. W. O'Hearn. Smallfoot: Modular automatic assertion checking with separation logic. In *FMCO*, Springer LNCS 4111, 2006.
3. J. Bingham and Z. Rakamaric. A Logic and Decision Procedure for Predicate Abstraction of Heap-Manipulating Programs. In *VMCAI*, Springer LNCS 3855, pages 207–221, Charleston, U.S.A, January 2006.
4. R.M. Burstall and J. Darlington. A transformation system for developing recursive programs. *Journal of ACM*, 24(1):44–67, January 1977.
5. C. Chen and H. Xi. Combining Programming with Theorem Proving. In *ACM SIGPLAN ICFP*, Tallinn, Estonia, September 2005.
6. W.N. Chin and S.C. Khoo. Calculating sized types. In *ACM SIGPLAN PEPM*, pages 62–72, Boston, United States, January 2000.
7. W.N. Chin, S.C. Khoo, S.C. Qin, C. Popeea, and H.H. Nguyen. Verifying Safety Policies with Size Properties and Alias Controls. In *ACM SIGSOFT ICSE*, St. Louis, Missouri, May 2005.
8. A. Gotsman, J. Berdine, and B. Cook. Interprocedural Shape Analysis with Separated Heap Abstractions. In *SAS*, Springer LNCS, Seoul, Korea, August 2006.
9. J. Hughes, L. Pareto, and A. Sabry. Proving the correctness of reactive systems using sized types. In *ACM POPL*, pages 410–423. ACM Press, January 1996.
10. S. Isthiaq and P.W. O'Hearn. BI as an assertion language for mutable data structures. In *ACM POPL*, London, January 2001.
11. L. Jia and D. Walker. ILC: A foundation for automated reasoning about pointer programs. In *15th ESOP*, March 2006.
12. O. Lee, H. Yang, and K. Yi. Automatic verification of pointer programs using grammar-based shape analysis. In *ESOP*. Springer Verlag, April 2005.
13. M.J.Parkinson and G.M.Bierman. Separation logic and abstraction. In *ACM POPL*, pages 247–258, 2005.
14. A. Moeller and M. I. Schwartzbach. The Pointer Assertion Logic Engine. In *ACM PLDI*, June 2001.

15. H.H. Nguyen, C. David, S.C. Qin, and W.N. Chin. Automated Verification of Shape and Size Properties via Separation Logic. Technical report, SoC, Natl Univ. of Singapore, July 2006. avail. at http://www.comp.nus.edu.sg/~nguyenh2/papers/vmcai07-report.pdf.
16. W. Pugh. The Omega Test: A fast practical integer programming algorithm for dependence analysis. *Communications of the ACM*, 8:102–114, 1992.
17. J. Reynolds. Separation Logic: A Logic for Shared Mutable Data Structures. In *IEEE LICS*, Copenhagen, Denmark, July 2002.
18. R. Rugina. Quantitative Shape Analysis. In *SAS*, Springer LNCS, Verona, Italy, August 2004.
19. S. Sagiv, T. Reps, and R. Wilhelm. Parametric shape analysis via 3-valued logic. *ACM TOPLAS*, 24(3), May 2002.
20. É-J. Sims. Extending separation logic with fixpoints and postponed substitution. *Theoretical Computer Science*, 351(2):258–275, 2006.
21. D. Walker and G. Morrisett. Alias Types for Recursive Data Structures. In *TIC*, Springer LNCS 2071, pages 177–206, 2000.
22. H. Xi. *Dependent Types in Practical Programming*. PhD thesis, Carnegie Mellon University, 1998.

Towards Shape Analysis for Device Drivers

Hongseok Yang

Queen Mary, University of London, UK

Abstract. Shape analysis algorithms statically infer deep properties of the runtime heap, such as whether a variable points to a cyclic or acyclic linked list. Unfortunately, there are unsolved problems that make it difficult for shape analyses being to be used for real-world programs. The problems include: performance of the analysis; dealing with low-level language features; and supporting complex data-structures used in real-world programs, without sacrificing precision or performance of the analysis.

In this talk, I will present work on shape analysis for Windows device drivers based on separation logic formulae. Device drivers basically use linked lists, but complex varieties of linked list unlike those usually studied in shape analysis. I will explain the nature of those structures, which open problems matter most for our analysis, and how we approach some of those problems. In particular, I will describe how higher-order predicates let us succinctly describe a variety of data structures, and how discovery of parameters to higher-order predicates allows an analysis that is not tied to specific structures.

B. Cook and A. Podelski (Eds.): VMCAI 2007, LNCS 4349, p. 267, 2007.
© Springer-Verlag Berlin Heidelberg 2007

An Abstract Domain
Extending Difference-Bound Matrices
with Disequality Constraints*

Mathias Péron and Nicolas Halbwachs

Vérimag**, Grenoble – France
{Mathias.Peron,Nicolas.Halbwachs}@imag.fr

Abstract. Knowing that two numerical variables always hold different values, at some point of a program, can be very useful, especially for analyzing aliases: if $i \neq j$, then $A[i]$ and $A[j]$ are not aliased, and this knowledge is of great help for many other program analyses. Surprisingly, disequalities are seldom considered in abstract interpretation, most of the proposed numerical domains being restricted to convex sets. In this paper, we propose to combine simple ordering properties with disequalities. "Difference-bound matrices" (or DBMs) is a domain proposed by David Dill, for expressing relations of the form "$x - y \leq c$" or "$c_1 \leq x \leq c_2$". We define dDBMs ("*disequalities* DBMs") as conjunctions of DBMs with simple disequalities of the form "$x \neq y$" or "$x \neq 0$". We give algorithms on dDBMs, for deciding the emptiness, computing a normal form, and performing the usual operations of an abstract domain. These algorithms have the same complexity ($O(n^3)$, where n is the number of variables) than those for classical DBMs, if the variables are considered to be valued in a dense set ($\mathbb{R}$ or $\mathbb{Q}$). In the arithmetic case, the emptiness decision is NP-complete, and other operations run in $O(n^5)$.

Keywords: abstract domains, alias analysis, difference-bound matrices, disequalities, static analysis.

1   Introduction

In many situations, integer variables are used to address objects: it is the case with array indexes, memory addresses and pointers in languages like C, and — this last case being the initial motivation of this work — with the addressing of devices (memories, processors, sensors,...) in systems-on-chips.

It is well-known that this kind of addressing mechanism raises *aliasing* phenomena: these aliasing problems are error-prone, can make the programs obscure, and tremendously complicate their analysis: if $i = j$, then $A[i]$ and $A[j]$ are aliased, meaning that any change to $A[i]$ implicitly changes $A[j]$. Knowing

---

* This work has been partially supported by the APRON project of the "ACI Sécurité et Informatique" of the French Ministry of Research.
** Verimag is a joint laboratory of Université Joseph Fourier, CNRS and INPG associated with IMAG.

B. Cook and A. Podelski (Eds.): VMCAI 2007, LNCS 4349, pp. 268–282, 2007.

that $i = j$ allows this fact to be precisely captured; knowing that $i \neq j$ allows to keep $A[j]$ unaffected by the changes to $A[i]$; ignoring whether $i = j$ or not forces any change to $A[i]$ or $A[j]$ to potentially affect (i.e., lose information about) the other. So, determining whether two addresses may or must be equal is an important goal.

Most abstract domains classically used to analyze the behavior of numerical variables (like affine equations [Kar76], intervals [CC76], octagons [Min01], octahedra [CC04], polyhedra [CH78]), take equalities into account, but cannot be used for determining disequalities, because they are *convex*. On the other hand, equality and disequality relations, considered alone, are too poor to permit an interesting analysis: the only new relations that one can deduce from a set of equalities/disequalities come from the transitivity of '=' $((x = y \land y = z) \Rightarrow x = z)$ and the obvious rule $(x = y \land x \neq z) \Rightarrow y \neq z$. This is why it is interesting to combine this kind of relations with other properties, which enrich the deduction power: in this paper, we intend to combine equalities/disequalities with ordering relations. For instance the obvious rule $(x \leq y \leq z \land x \neq y) \Rightarrow x \neq z$ may allow non completely trivial deductions.

Our goal is to extend an existing domain with disequalities, without increasing the complexity of the representation and operations. In this paper, we study such an extension of the domain of *difference-bound matrices* [Dil89, ACD93], used for expressing relations of the form $(c_1 \leq x \leq c_2)$ and $(c_1 \leq x - y \leq c_2)$. The simplest kind of disequalities that we can add to these inequalities, are of the form $(x - y \neq 0)$. It is enough for our initial goal, and, coupled with difference-bound matrices, they allow strict inequalities to be expressed. Now, if we consider also disequalities of the form $(x - y \neq c)$, we get systems of constraints of arbitrary size (e.g., $x - y \neq 0 \land x - y \neq 2 \land x - y \neq 4 \ldots$) which contradicts our goal of not increasing the complexity. So, we will limit ourselves to inequalities of the form $(x - y \neq 0)$ or $(x \neq 0)$.

The content of the paper is the following: Section 2 is a rapid review of the related works. In Section 3, we recall the definition of difference-bound matrices and the main algorithms used for their manipulation, in particular the use of potential graphs. In Section 4 we define "*disequalities* DBMs" (or dDBMs), which are a simple extension of DBMs with simple disequality relations of the form $(x \neq y)$. The notion of potential graph is extended into "disequal potential graph". Section 5 is devoted to the central problem of deciding emptiness of the domain of solutions of a dDBM, and of normalizing dDBMs. Two cases are distinguished, according to whether the solutions are searched in a dense numerical set (like $\mathbb{R}$ or $\mathbb{Q}$) or in the set of integers. In the dense case, we exhibit algorithms for emptiness check and normal form computation, with the same theoretical complexity as in the case of classical DBMs. In the arithmetic case, unfortunately, the emptiness problem is NP-complete, and the complexity of the computation of a normal form increases from n^3 to n^5 (n being the number of variables). However, notice that the dense domain is a correct approximation of the discrete one. Section 6 describes other classical operators on dDBMs, and Section 7 gives some simple examples of application to program analysis.

2   Related Works

Several structures for representing finite unions of convex sets have been proposed in the model-checking community. In particular, "difference decision diagrams" [MLAH99] and "clock difference diagrams" [LPWY99] are more general than the domain we consider, but with an exponential complexity.

Another way of dealing with finite unions of convex set is by using "dynamic partitioning" in abstract interpretation [Bou93, JHR99, MR05, SISG06]. This could be used, for our problem, by separating the cases $i < j$ and $i > j$. However, here also, this can involve an exponential partitioning.

Of course, some non convex abstract domains have also been proposed, like congruences [Gra91, Mas93], but their expressiveness is not comparable to our present proposal. The weakly relational domains proposed by [Min02] are a family of numerical domains, not necessarily convex, based on representation and algorithmic similar to those of DBMs. However, strict conditions on expressible constraints do not allow disequations.

In constraint logic programming, algorithms were proposed to deal with constraints on finite domains. Constraints propagation is expensive, in particular because of representation problems [HS03]. [HS97] considers a restricted class of constraints ($\pm x \pm y \leq c$), corresponding to octagons [Min01], for which they propose a polynomial solver. Disequalities are not considered, because of the NP-completeness of the satisfiability problem. However, [Pug98] notices that, if all variables are pairwise different, the satisfiability can be checked in $O(n \log n)$.

In dependence analysis (which concerns alias analysis among array elements), many approaches are based on the resolution of linear constraints (e.g., [PW98] use the Omega library). Among these works, [SW02] addresses constraints of the form ($\pm x \pm y \leq c$) and disequalities. However, they use algorithmic devoted to more general constraints (Omega Test), and they don't have the same concerns, since they don't need to compute a normal form.

About normal forms of systems of linear inequalities and disequalities, we will use Lassez's works [LM92]. Imbert [Imb93] addresses the problem of eliminating variables from such systems. All these results are too general with respect to the constraints we consider, and only apply when solutions belong to dense sets.

3   Difference-Bound Matrices [Dil89]

Difference-Bound Matrices (DBMs) are a practical representation of potential constraints ($x - y \leq c$) introduced by D. Dill [Dil89].

Let $Var = \{v_1, ..., v_{n-1}\}$ be a finite set of variables, $\mathcal{V}$ ($= \mathbb{Z}$, $\mathbb{Q}$ or $\mathbb{R}$) be the numerical set in which variables and constants take their values, and $\overline{\mathcal{V}}$ be the extension of $\mathcal{V}$ with $+\infty$, ordered as usual. Let C be a set of potential constraints ($v_i - v_j \leq c$) where $c \in \mathcal{V}$ and $v_i, v_j \in Var$. The DBM representing C is a $n \times n$ matrix M defined by (cf. Figure 2(a)):

$$M_{ij} = \inf\{c \mid (v_j - v_i \leq c) \in C\}$$

where $\inf(\emptyset) = +\infty$. In other words, if there is some constraint $v_j - v_i \leq c$ in C, then M_{ij} equals (the tightest) c, otherwise it is $+\infty$.

A special variable $v_0 \in Var$, always valued to zero is used to express bounds on variables: $(v_i \leq c)$ is written $(v_i - v_0 \leq c)$. The set of all possible valuations of the variables represented by a DBM M will be called its domain, and will be noted $\mathcal{D}(M)$.

Potential Graph. DBMs enjoy a useful graphical representation, called potential graphs, interpreting a DBM M as the adjacency matrix of a weighted directed graph (Figure 2(b)). In the potential graph, the variable v_0 corresponds to the node labelled by 0.

Emptiness Test and Closure. Using the potential graph representation, we understand that unfeasible sets of constrains are only those which form a circuit with a strictly negative weight in the graph. As a consequence, in order to test whether the domain of a DBM is empty, we simply have to check for the existence of such a circuit: this could be achieved in polynomial time ($O(n^3)$, e.g., with Bellman-Ford algorithm).

Because any potential graph including a strictly negative cycle is one possible representation of an empty domain, we are interested in finding a normal form for *non-empty* DBMs. Then, the shortest-path closure of their potential graph is well-defined and can be computed by the Floyd-Warshall algorithm that runs in $O(n^3)$ time (Figure 1).

for $i \leftarrow 0$ *to* $n - 1$ **do**
  $\quad\quad M_{ii} \leftarrow 0$
for $k \leftarrow 0$ *to* $n - 1$ **do**
  $\quad$**for** $i \leftarrow 0$ *to* $n - 1$ **do**
    $\quad\quad$**for** $j \leftarrow 0$ *to* $n - 1$ **do**
      $\quad\quad\quad M_{ij} \leftarrow \min(M_{ij}, M_{ik} + M_{kj})$;

Fig. 1. The Floyd Warshall algorithm [CLRS90] computes the shortest-path closure of a weighted digraph represented by a matrix M

Through the potential graph, the algorithm computes, for each pair of variables, the implicit constraints obtained by summation over paths of the graph, and uses the tightest one for replacement. The resulting graph represents a DBM with the same domain as the initial one, and minimal bounds for representing this domain: it is indeed a normal form. Figure 2 is an illustration of the execution of the closure algorithm of DBMs.

Notice that, after applying the shortest-path closure, testing for strictly negative cycles can be reduced to check if there is a variable i such that $M_{ii}^{\leq} < 0$, an emptiness test running in linear time.

Classical DBMs can be ordered according to the pointwise extension of the $\leq$ order on $\mathcal{V}$: $M \trianglelefteq M' \iff \forall i, j\ M_{ij} \leq M'_{ij}$. This order has the nice property to

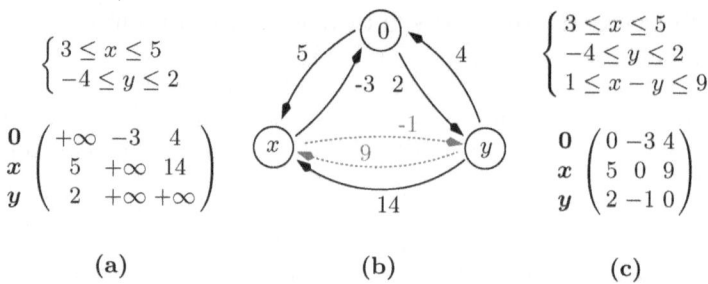

$$\begin{cases} 3 \leq x \leq 5 \\ -4 \leq y \leq 2 \end{cases}$$

$$\begin{matrix} \mathbf{0} \\ x \\ y \end{matrix} \begin{pmatrix} +\infty & -3 & 4 \\ 5 & +\infty & 14 \\ 2 & +\infty & +\infty \end{pmatrix}$$

$$\begin{cases} 3 \leq x \leq 5 \\ -4 \leq y \leq 2 \\ 1 \leq x - y \leq 9 \end{cases}$$

$$\begin{matrix} \mathbf{0} \\ x \\ y \end{matrix} \begin{pmatrix} 0 & -3 & 4 \\ 5 & 0 & 9 \\ 2 & -1 & 0 \end{pmatrix}$$

(a)   (b)   (c)

Fig. 2. Application of the closure algorithm on the DBM (a): (b) its potential graph where dashed edges are the implicit constraints computed (null-loops on each variable have been omitted) and (c) the resulting closed DBM

imply inclusion on domains: $M \trianglelefteq M' \Rightarrow \mathcal{D}(M) \subseteq \mathcal{D}(M')$. Moreover, the normal form $\overline{M}$ of a non-empty DBM M is the minimal DBM, with respect to $\trianglelefteq$, with the same domain as M: $\overline{M} = \inf_\trianglelefteq \{M' \mid \mathcal{D}(M') = \mathcal{D}(M)\}$.

4   Extending DBMs

Let C be a set of constraints obeying the following grammar, where $c \in \mathcal{V}$ and $v_i, v_j \in Var$.

$$constraint ::= v_i \leq c \mid v_i - v_j \leq c \mid v_i \neq 0 \mid v_i - v_j \neq 0$$

We propose to represent C by means of a pair of matrices $(M^\leq, M^{\neq})$, called a dDBM (for *disequalities* DBM): A dDBM is made of a classical DBM $M^\leq$ with values in $\overline{\mathcal{V}}$, together with a symmetric boolean matrix $M^{\neq}$ where $M_{ij}^{\neq} = true$ iff $(v_i \neq v_j) \in C$. We use the special variable $v_0 \in Var$ in order to represent also non-nullity constraints $(v_i \neq 0)$.

Representing disequality constraints by a matrix may seem costly in space, $M^{\neq}$ being a symmetric matrix and mostly sparse. However this representation has a trivial map with $M^\leq$ allowing easier reasoning later.

Domain and Order. All the possible valuations of the variables of a dDBM M will be called its domain, denoted by $\mathcal{D}(M)$. Its definition is straightforward:

$$\mathcal{D}(M) = \{(s_1, ..., s_{n-1}) \in \mathcal{V}^{n-1} \mid \exists s_0 \text{ such that } \forall i, j \in [0..n-1]$$
$$s_j - s_i \leq M_{ij}^{\leq} \wedge M_{ij}^{\neq} \Rightarrow s_j - s_i \neq 0 \wedge s_0 = 0\}$$

Similarly to DBMs, dDBMs can be provided with an order $\trianglelefteq$:

$$M \trianglelefteq M' \iff \forall i, j \quad M_{ij}^{\leq} \leq M_{ij}'^{\leq} \wedge M_{ij}'^{\neq} \Rightarrow M_{ij}^{\neq}$$

which enjoys the same connection with domain inclusion: $M \trianglelefteq M' \Rightarrow \mathcal{D}(M) \subseteq \mathcal{D}(M')$. Of course, as for DBMs, the converse implication is not true, because of possible redundant constraints.

Disequal Potential Graph. The disequal potential graph of a dDBM $(M^\leq, M^\neq)$ is obtained by juxtaposing to the potential graph of $M^\leq$, the non-directed graph obtained by interpreting $M^\neq$ as an adjacency matrix (Figure 3). This mixed graph $\mathcal{G}(M) = (Var, E^\leq, E^\neq, w)$ is defined by:

$$E^\leq \subseteq Var \times Var \qquad\qquad E^\neq \subseteq Var \times Var$$
$$E^\leq = \{(v_i, v_j) \mid M^\leq_{ij} < +\infty\} \qquad E^\neq = \{(v_i, v_j) \mid M^\neq_{ij}\}$$
$$w \in E^\leq \to \mathcal{V} \qquad\qquad \forall e = (v_i, v_j) \in E^\leq \quad w(e) = M^\leq_{ij}$$

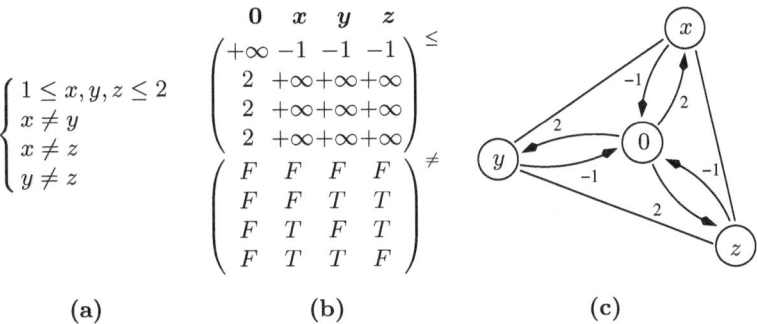

      (a)   (b)   (c)

Fig. 3. (a) A set of constraints, (b) its associated dDBM and (c) its disequal potential graph

5   Emptiness Test and Normal Form

As for DBMs, we need to define a normal form, which will work for non-empty dDBMs, in order to decide equivalence of domains by a simple syntactic check, and to easily get all the consequences of given set of constraints. In this section, we provide closure algorithms to compute the normal form of a dDBM, separating the dense case ($\mathcal{V} = \mathbb{Q}$ or $\mathbb{R}$) and the arithmetic case ($\mathcal{V} = \mathbb{Z}$).

By analogy with classical DBMs, we define the normal form $\overline{M}$ of a dDBM M by:

$$\overline{M} = inf_\unlhd \{M' \mid \mathcal{D}(M) = \mathcal{D}(M')\}$$

In the arithmetic case, such normalization will narrow some bounds for arithmetic reasons: for instance the set of constraints $\{x \neq 0, x \leq 0\}$ must be replaced by $\{x \neq 0, x \leq -1\}$. Unfortunately, this is not the only difficulties brought by arithmetic: the emptiness test problem will be in the NP-complete class [RH80].

5.1   The Dense Case

Testing Emptiness. dDBMs are extensions of DBMs by disequality constraints. Of course, the domain of a dDBM $(M^\leq, M^\neq)$ can be empty because of the emptiness of the domain of $M^\leq$ (which we know how to check), but it can also be empty because of the disequalities.

In the case where variables take values in a dense set, the following result due to Lassez and McAloon [LM92] solves the problem, thanks to the independence of disequalities. The constraints concerned by the theorem are more general than ours, but in our special case, the result is the following:

Theorem 1 (independence of disequalities (Lassez _et al._, 1992)). _Let I be a system of linear inequalities, and D be a finite set of linear disequalities. Then the conjunction of I and D is feasible if and only if, for each single disequality $d \in D$, the conjunction of I and $\{d\}$ is feasible._

In other words, for a dDBM $(M^{\leq}, M^{\neq})$, if no single disequality eliminates all the solutions of $M^{\leq}$, there is no way for a _finite_ number of disequalities constraints to make together the system unsatisfiable.

As a consequence, in dDBMs, the only way for a disequality constraint to make the system unsatisfiable is to contradict an equality between the corresponding variables. Thus the emptiness test boils down to check, for each disequality constraint between variables, that these variables are not forced equal by the DBM component of the dDBM (Figure 4).

$empty \leftarrow false$;
for $i \leftarrow 0$ _to_ $n-2$ _as long as_ $\neg empty$ **do**
$\quad$ **for** $j \leftarrow i+1$ _to_ $n-1$ _as long as_ $\neg empty$ **do**
$\quad\quad$ **if** $M_{ij}^{\neq}$ **then**
$\quad\quad\quad$ $empty \leftarrow M_{ij}^{\leq} = 0 \wedge M_{ji}^{\leq} = 0$

Fig. 4. The algorithm testing dDBM emptiness in the dense case. Runs in $O(n^2)$ time.

This test is correct when $M^{\leq}$ is in normal form: all equalities must have been expressed to perform this syntactic check.

Normal Form and Closure Algorithm. In order to compute the normal form of a dDBM $(M^{\leq}, M^{\neq})$, we can first apply the closure of DBMs to $M^{\leq}$. This makes sense because, in the dense case, disequality constraints will not involve any narrowing of the bounds in $M^{\leq}$.

Now, $M^{\neq}$ must be completed with all the disequalities resulting from the conjunction of $M^{\leq}$ and $M^{\neq}$. These inequalities are deduced according to 3 rules:

1. $v_i - v_j \leq c, \; c < 0 \; \Rightarrow \; v_i \neq v_j$
2. $v_i = v_j \wedge v_j \neq v_k \; \Rightarrow \; v_i \neq v_k$
3. $v_i \leq v_j \leq v_k \wedge v_j \neq v_k \; \Rightarrow \; v_i \neq v_k$

Rules (1) and (2) can easily be applied, in $O(n^3)$, using the disequal potential graph: rule (1) says that any arc with negative weight must be doubled by a disequality edge, rule (2) says that two equal variables are concerned with the same disequalities. The following algorithm (Figure 5) takes these rules into account ($M_{i*}^{\neq}$ and $M_{*j}^{\neq}$ respectively denote the ith row and the jth column of $M^{\neq}$):

for $i \leftarrow 0$ *to* $n - 2$ **do**
    for $j \leftarrow i + 1$ *to* $n - 1$ **do**
        if $M_{ij}^{\leq} < 0 \vee M_{ji}^{\leq} < 0$ **then**
            $M_{ij}^{\neq} \leftarrow true$; $M_{ji}^{\neq} \leftarrow true$
        if $M_{ij}^{\leq} = 0 \wedge M_{ji}^{\leq} = 0$ **then**
            $v \leftarrow M_{i*}^{\neq} \vee M_{j*}^{\neq}$;
            $M_{i*}^{\neq} \leftarrow v$; $M_{*i}^{\neq} \leftarrow v$; $M_{j*}^{\neq} \leftarrow v$; $M_{*j}^{\neq} \leftarrow v$

Fig. 5. Algorithm applying rules (1) and (2) for deducing disequality constraints. Runs in $O(n^3)$ time.

Concerning rule (3), let's first notice that this rule only concerns inequalities of the form $x \leq y$, that it, zero-weighted arcs in the disequal potential graph. Thus, the propagation of rule (3) can be done on a restriction of the disequal potential graph to zero-weighted arcs, and where nodes corresponding to equal variables are merged: let us note $G^{\bullet} = (V^{\bullet}, A^{\bullet}, E^{\bullet})$ this reduced graph, where $(V^{\bullet}, A^{\bullet})$ is the directed acyclic graph of zero-weighted arcs, and $(V^{\bullet}, E^{\bullet})$ is the non-directed graph of disequalities. Let $n^{\bullet}$ be its number of nodes. Now, taking rule (3) into account boils down to propagating an irreflexive and symmetric relation along an order relation. This propagation can be written on $G^{\bullet}$ as follows:

$$\left. \begin{array}{l} (v_1, v_2) \in A^{\bullet}, (v_2, v_3) \in A^{\bullet} \\ (v_1, v_2) \in E^{\bullet} \vee (v_2, v_3) \in E^{\bullet} \end{array} \right\} \implies (v_1, v_3) \in E^{\bullet}$$

and is a kind of transitive closure. Among the numerous algorithms for transitive closure, Koubeck's algorithm [GK79] is particularly interesting, since its worst-case complexity is $O((n^{\bullet})^2 n_r^{\bullet})$ (where $n_r^{\bullet}$ is the number of arcs of the transitive reduction of the graph) and its average complexity is $O((n^{\bullet})^2 \log n^{\bullet})$ [Sim88]. A more recent paper evaluate it to $O((n^{\bullet})^2)$ [SCC93].

Figure 6(a) shows an example of mixed graph, and Figure 7 gives our version of Koubeck's algorithm, adapted to solve our closure problem. The only change is that the result $\Phi(v)$ of the algorithm is no longer the set of nodes reachable from v, but its partitioning into 2 sets: the set $\Phi_1(v)$ of nodes which are reachable from v by some path traversing an arc doubled by a disequality edge, and the set $\Phi_2(v)$ of other reachable nodes. The application of the algorithm is illustrated in Figure 6(b). Notice the importance of considering successors of v in increasing topological order: if, when dealing with node 0, we start with node 3 instead of node 1, node 3 and 4 would finally belong to both $\Phi_1(0)$ and $\Phi_2(0)$.

Finally, the new disequalities resulting from rule (3) are all the pairs (v, w) with $w \in \Phi_1(v)$ and must be symmetrically reported in the initial dDBM. Notice that these new disequalities are not subject to rule (1) and take into account rule (2). The phases of complete algorithm for computing the normal form of a dDBM are given in Figure 8.

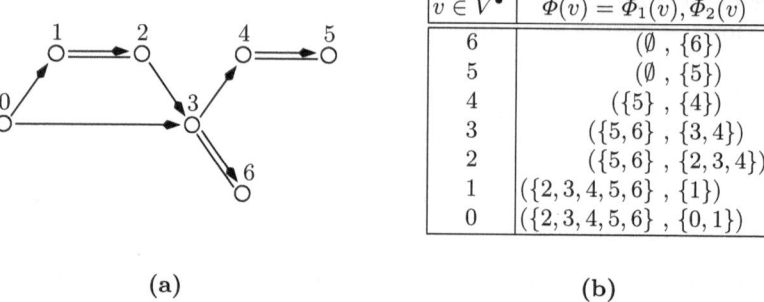

$v \in V^\bullet$	$\Phi(v) = \Phi_1(v), \Phi_2(v)$
6	$(\emptyset , \{6\})$
5	$(\emptyset , \{5\})$
4	$(\{5\} , \{4\})$
3	$(\{5,6\} , \{3,4\})$
2	$(\{5,6\} , \{2,3,4\})$
1	$(\{2,3,4,5,6\} , \{1\})$
0	$(\{2,3,4,5,6\} , \{0,1\})$

(a)   (b)

Fig. 6. (a) A mixed graph $G^\bullet = (V^\bullet, A^\bullet, E^\bullet)$, labelled in topological order, and (b) the edges to propagate with respect to the order described by arcs, for each node v in $\Phi_1(v)$

> **for** *each $v \in V^\bullet$ in decreasing topological order* **do**
> $\Phi(v) \leftarrow (\emptyset, \{v\})$;
>   **for** *each successor w of v in increasing topological order* **do**
>   **if** $w \notin \Phi(v)$ **then**
>   **if** $(M^\bullet)^{\neq}_{vw}$ **then**
> | $\Phi_1(v) \leftarrow \Phi_1(v) \cup \Phi_1(w) \cup \Phi_2(w)$
>   **else**
> $\llcorner$ $\Phi_1(v) \leftarrow \Phi_1(v) \cup \Phi_1(w)$; $\Phi_2(v) \leftarrow \Phi_2(v) \cup \Phi_2(w)$

Fig. 7. Algorithm computing the propagation of disequality constraints, derived from Koubeck's transitive closure algorithm. Worst-case complexity is $O((n^\bullet)^3)$ time and expected complexity is $O((n^\bullet)^2 \log n^\bullet)$ time [Sim88].

5.2   The Arithmetic Case

Testing Emptiness. Checking constraints satisfiability in $\mathbb{Z}^n$ is classically more difficult than in dense sets. Arithmetic satisfiability of DBMs and octagons is polynomial, but it is no longer the case when combined with disequalities. The dDBM of Figure 3 illustrates the problem: it has solutions in $\mathbb{R}^3$ or $\mathbb{Q}^3$, but not in $\mathbb{Z}^3$, since we can't find three distinct integers between 1 and 2. The complexity of the emptiness problem in arithmetic was studied by [RH80], who showed its NP-completeness by a reduction of the 3-coloration of graphs problem.

A brute force technique consists in considering separately, for each disequality $x - y \neq 0$, the cases $x - y \leq -1$ and $x - y \geq 1$. This leads, for d disequalities, to 2^d problems of emptiness for classical DBMs.

[SW02] suggests an improvement, allowing to decrease the number d of considered disequalities: they define an "inert" disequality, as a disequality which either eliminates *alone* all solutions of the system of inequalities or cannot participate in the absence of such solutions. Lassez theorem states that, in the dense case, all disequalities are inert. For our restricted disequalities, some inert disequalities can be easily detected in the arithmetic case: if some variable v_i involved in a disequal-

1 Apply the shortest-path closure on $M^{\leq}$ *(Figure 1)* ;
2 Add implicit disequality constraints (rules (1) and (2)) to $M^{\neq}$ *(Figure 5)* ;
3 Consider G the disequal potential graph of M where the set of arcs is restricted to those with null weight ;
4 Compute $\mathcal{SCC}$, the set of strongly connected components of the directed graph of G ;
5 Consider $G^{\bullet}$ the mixed reduced graph of G constructed on $\mathcal{SCC}$;
6 Compute $\mathcal{O}$, a topological order on the directed acyclic graph of $G^{\bullet}$;
7 Apply the disequality propagation algorithm (rule (3)) on $G^{\bullet}$ with respect to $\mathcal{O}$ *(Figure 7)* ;
8 Add induced disequality constraints into $M^{\neq}$

Fig. 8. Abstract algorithm of the closure of a dDBM M in the dense case. Runs in $O(n^3)$ time.

ity is not bounded by the system of inequalities (which can be checked in constant time, by checking if either $\overline{M_{i0}^{\leq}}$ or $\overline{M_{0i}^{\leq}}$ is $+\infty$), then the disequality is inert: either it contradicts an equation, or it can be discarded in the emptiness check.

Normal Form. The key novelty, in the arithmetic case, is that disequalities may involve a narrowing of the bounds in inequalities: $(x - y \leq 0 \ \wedge \ x \neq y) \Rightarrow (x - y \leq -1)$. Since narrowed inequalities may in turn involve new narrowings, making explicit all the consequences of a dDBM is clearly an iterative process. Figure 9 shows an example of such an iterative computation: each rewriting consists of a narrowing followed by an update of weights by Floyd-Warshall; the first rewriting corresponds to the narrowing $(y - x \leq 0 \wedge x \neq y) \Rightarrow (y - x \leq -1)$, which involves an update of $z - x \leq 1$ into $z - x \leq 0$; this new inequality is narrowed in turn into $z - x \leq -1$, which involves an update of $y - x \leq -1$ into $y - x \leq -2$ (2nd rewriting).

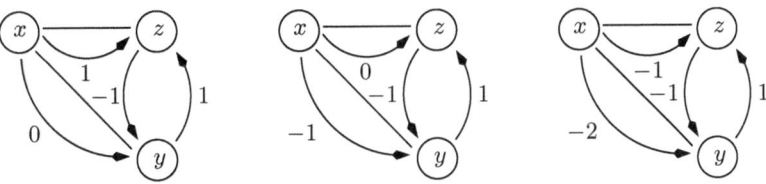

Fig. 9. Propagation of disequality constraints in the arithmetic case

A brute force algorithm, shown in Figure 10 performs the computation in $O(n^5)$. In this algorithm, *Dense-Closure* stands for the computation of the normal form in the dense case, or, more efficiently, only steps 1 (Floyd-Warshall on inequality matrix) and 2 (propagation of rules (1) and (2)) of the algorithm of Figure 8. As a matter of fact, in the arithmetic case, rule (3) is taken into account by iterative applications of narrowing of inequalities and application of Floyd-Warshall.

repeat

$\quad M \leftarrow Dense\text{-}Closure(M)$;

$\quad to\_narrow \leftarrow \{(i,j) \mid M_{ij}^{\leq} = 0 \wedge M_{ij}^{\neq}\}$;

$\quad$**forall** $(i,j) \in to\_narrow$ **do**

$\qquad M_{ij}^{\leq} \leftarrow -1$

until $to\_narrow = \emptyset$;

Fig. 10. Closure algorithm of a dDBM M in the arithmetic case. Runs in $O(n^5)$ time.

Nevertheless, this algorithm can be improved by performing weight changes from 0 to -1 on the fly, during the application of Floyd-Warshall.

Remark. The opposite disequal potential graph is the closure of the one of Figure 3(c). Although it does not contain any negative cycle, it represents an empty domain in arithmetic. It shows that testing the emptiness of the domain described by a dDBM defined in $\mathbb{Z}$ is harder than computing its normal form.

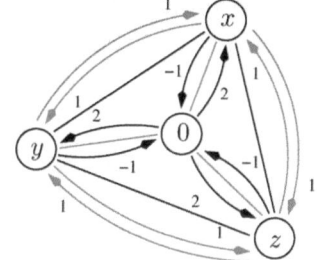

6   Operators on dDBMs

6.1   The Lattice of dDBMs

We note $\mathcal{M}$ the set of dDBMs, with a least element $\perp$ added (representing the empty set, $\mathcal{D}(\perp) = \emptyset$). $\mathcal{M}$ is partially ordered as follows:

$$M \sqsubseteq M' \Leftrightarrow \begin{cases} \text{either } M = \perp \\ \text{or} \quad M, M' \neq \perp, \ M \trianglelefteq M' \end{cases}$$

The greatest dDBM, denoted $\top$ is such that, $\forall i,j = 0\ldots n-1$, $\top_{ij}^{\leq} =$ if $i = j$ then 0 else $+\infty$, and $\top_{ij}^{\neq} = false$.

Lattice Operators. Let M, M' be two dDBMs in normal form. Let us note:

$$\check{M} = \begin{bmatrix} \check{M}_{ij}^{\leq} = \max(M_{ij}^{\leq}, M'_{ij}^{\leq}) \\ \check{M}_{ij}^{\neq} = M_{ij}^{\neq} \vee M'_{ij}^{\neq} \end{bmatrix} \quad , \quad \hat{M} = \begin{bmatrix} \hat{M}_{ij}^{\leq} = \min(M_{ij}^{\leq}, M'_{ij}^{\leq}) \\ \hat{M}_{ij}^{\neq} = M_{ij}^{\neq} \wedge M'_{ij}^{\neq} \end{bmatrix}$$

Then the least upper bound $M \sqcup M'$ and the greatest lower bound $M \sqcap M'$ are defined by:

$$M \sqcup M' = \begin{cases} M \text{ if } M' = \perp \\ M' \text{ if } M = \perp \\ \check{M} \text{ otherwise} \end{cases} , \quad M \sqcap M' = \begin{cases} \perp \text{ if } M = \perp \text{ or } M' = \perp \text{ or } \mathcal{D}(\hat{M}) = \emptyset \\ \hat{M} \text{ otherwise} \end{cases}$$

6.2   Other Operators

Existential quantification and projection. Both operations consist in losing all information, in a dDBM M, about a variable x, while keeping the remaining information about other variables. In the quantification $\exists x, M$, the variable x is eliminated, while in the projection $M\downarrow_x$, x is left as a non-constrained variable. Both operations need first a normalization of M, to gather all the consequences on other variables, then $\exists x, M$ is obtained by suppressing in $\overline{M}^{\leq}$ and $\overline{M}^{\neq}$ all the rows and columns corresponding to x, while for $M\downarrow_x$, the rows and columns corresponding to x in $\overline{M}^{\leq}$ (resp., in $\overline{M}^{\neq}$) must be filled with '+∞' (resp., with 'false').

Post-condition of an assignment. As usual, the abstract post-condition of an assignment $x \leftarrow e$ can be computed using existential quantification (z is a fresh variable) and projection:

$$[x \leftarrow e](M) = \exists z \left((M \wedge (z = e)) \downarrow_x \wedge (x = z) \right)$$

It will be precise when the expression e is of the form $y + c$ or c; otherwise, the term $(z = e)$ cannot be expressed in a dDBM, and all information about x is lost, unless some ad-hoc treatment is applied: for instance, if M includes the constraints $(x = y), (w \neq 0)$ then the precision of $[x \leftarrow x + w](M)$ can be improved with $(y \neq x)$.

Conditions. In order to propagate dDBMs over conditional statements, we must define the abstraction of conditions. Obviously, only conditions expressible in dDBMs can be precisely taken into account, i.e., conjunctions of conditions of the form $x - y \leq c$, $\pm x \leq c$, $x \neq y$, $x \neq 0$. The lattice operator $\sqcup$ can be used to approximate disjunctions of such conditions. Ad-hoc interpretations can be defined for some other kinds of conditions, but otherwise the abstraction will be $\top$.

Widening operator. The lattice of classical DBMs being of infinite depth, so is the lattice of dDBMs; so we must define a widening operator. However, there is no infinite chain of disequality matrices.

Consider $M, M' \in \mathcal{M}$, with $M \sqsubseteq M'$ and M' in normal form (this always improves the precision of the operator). The widening $M \nabla M'$ will remove, as usual, the inequalities of M which are not satisfied in M', but all the disequalities in M' can be kept in the result. In fact, our exact definition depends of $\mathcal{V}$: of course, we want to specialize the bounds 0 and -1 in the arithmetic case in order to preserve the constraint $(x \leq y)$ when we widen $(x < y)$ by this constraint. When $\mathcal{V} = \mathbb{Z}$, without this specialization, the inequality $(x - y \leq 0)$ would get lost in $(x - y \leq -1, x - y \neq 0) \nabla (x - y \leq 0)$.

As usual, $M \nabla M'$ is M', if $M = \bot$. Otherwise, $M \nabla M' = (M^{\nabla \leq}, M'^{\neq})$, where $\forall i, j = 0 \ldots n - 1$,

$$M_{ij}^{\nabla \leq} = \begin{cases} M_{ij}^{\leq} & \text{if } M'_{ij}^{\leq} \leq M_{ij}^{\leq} \\ M'_{ij}^{\leq} & \text{if } M_{ij}^{\leq} = -1, M'_{ij}^{\leq} = 0 \text{ and } \mathcal{V} = \mathbb{Z} \\ +\infty & \text{otherwise} \end{cases}$$

7 Application to Program Analysis

A prototype analyzer has been implemented, using the general fixpoint computation engine developed by Bertrand Jeannet for NBAC [Jea].

Figure 11 gives the results of the analysis of a very simple, ad-hoc program. The goal was to show that $(x \neq y)$ at point (3).

```
(1) read(x) ; read(y) ;
if (x = y) then (2) OK
else
    while true do
        (3) if (x = y) then ERR ;
        read(z) ;
        (4) if (x <= y) then
        |   (5) if (y <= z) then y ← z; (6)
        else
        └  (7) if (x <= z) then x ← z; (8)
```

	Results
(1)	$\top$
(2)	$x = y$
(3)	$x \neq y$
(4)	$x \neq y$
(5)	$x < y$
(6)	$y = z,\ x < y,\ x < z$
(7)	$x > y$
(8)	$x = z,\ x > y,\ z > y$
ERR	$\bot$

Fig. 11. Example of a toy program and the obtained results

Other simple programs have been successfully analyzed, e.g.: a circular buffer, where we show that, when the buffer is neither full nor empty, the indexes of the first and last elements are always different; the bakery algorithm, which is proved, by means of invariants of the form $p_i \neq 0$, to properly synchronize two processes p_1 and p_2.

Beyond these simple examples, our abstract domain of dDBMs can be used in other kinds of analyzes: for instance, in Deutsch's pointer analysis [Deu94], dDBMs could be used instead of other classical abstract domains, to represent the possible aliases between two linked lists.

8 Conclusion

We have proposed a new numerical domain dealing with both potential constraints and disequalities between variables. The complexity is $O(n^3)$ when variables take their values in a dense set. In the arithmetic case, apart from the emptiness problem which is well-known to be exponential, other operations are in $O(n^5)$.

Our very rough prototype did not allow large examples to be dealt with, so our next task will be to integrate the new domain in an existing analyzer, in particular to check its effectiveness for alias analysis.

Another short-term perspective is to extend this work to octagons [Min01], where disequalities of the form $(x \neq -y)$ could also be expressed. Moreover, in this paper, we wanted, as far as possible, not to increase the complexity of the DBM domain, but if this constraint is released, we could consider more general disequalities.

References

[ACD93]   R. Alur, C. Courcoubetis, and D.L. Dill. Model-checking in dense real-time. *Information and Computation*, 104(1):2–34, 1993.

[Bou93]   F. Bourdoncle. Abstract debugging of higher-order imperative languages. In *PLDI'93*, pages 46–55, New York, 1993.

[CC76]   P. Cousot and R. Cousot. Static determination of dynamic properties of programs. In *2nd Int. Symp. on Programming*, pages 106–130. Dunod, Paris, 1976.

[CC04]   R. C. Clarisó and J. Cortadella. Verification of parametric timed circuits using octahedra. In *Designing correct circuits, DCC'04*, Barcelona, 2004.

[CH78]   P. Cousot and N. Halbwachs. Automatic discovery of linear restraints among variables of a program. In *POPL'78*, pages 84–96, January 1978.

[CLRS90]   T. H. Cormen, C. E. Leiserson, R. L. Rivest, and C. Stein. *Introduction to Algorithms*. The MIT Press, Cambridge, Massachusetts, 1990.

[Deu94]   A. Deutsch. Interprocedural may-alias analysis for pointers: beyond k-limiting. In *PLDI'94*, pages 230–241, 1994.

[Dil89]   D. L. Dill. Timing assumptions and verification of finite-state concurrent systems. In *Automatic Verification Methods for Finite State Systems*, pages 197–212. LNCS 407, Springer-Verlag, 1989.

[GK79]   A. Goralciková and V. Koubek. A reduct-and-closure algorithm for graphs. In *MFCS*, pages 301–307, 1979.

[Gra91]   P. Granger. Static analysis of linear congruence equalities among variables of a program. In *CAAP'91*, pages 169–192, 1991.

[HS97]   W. Harvey and P. J. Stuckey. A unit two variable per inequality integer constraint solver for constraint logic programming. In *Twentieth Australasian Computer Science Conference, ACSC'97*, pages 102–111, February 1997.

[HS03]   W. Harvey and P. J. Stuckey. Improving linear constraint propagation by changing constraint representation. *Constraints*, 8(2):173–207, 2003.

[Imb93]   J.-L. Imbert. Variable elimination for generalized linear constraints. In *ICLP'93*, pages 499–516, 1993.

[Jea]   B. Jeannet. The NBAC verification/slicing tool. http://www.inrialpes.fr/pop-art/people/bjeannet/nbac/.

[JHR99]   B. Jeannet, N. Halbwachs, and P. Raymond. Dynamic partitioning in analyses of numerical properties. In *SAS'99*, Venezia, September 1999.

[Kar76]   M. Karr. Affine relationships among variables of a program. *Acta Informatica*, 6:133–151, 1976.

[LM92]   J.-L. Lassez and K. McAloon. A canonical form for generalized linear constraints. *J. Symb. Comput.*, 13(1):1–24, 1992.

[LPWY99]   K. G. Larsen, J. Pearson, C. Weise, and W. Yi. Clock difference diagrams. *Nordic J. of Computing*, 6(3):271–298, 1999.

[Mas93]   F. Masdupuy. Semantic analysis of interval congruences. In *International Conference on Formal Methods in Programming and Their Applications*, pages 142–155, 1993.

[Min01]   A. Miné. The octagon abstract domain. In *AST 2001 in WCRE 2001*, IEEE, pages 310–319. IEEE CS Press, October 2001.

[Min02]   A. Miné. A few graph-based relational numerical abstract domains. In *SAS'02*, pages 117–132, London, UK, 2002. Springer-Verlag.

[MLAH99]   J. B. Møller, J. Lichtenberg, H. R. Andersen, and H. Hulgaard. Difference decision diagrams. In *CSL'99*, pages 111–125. Springer-Verlag, 1999.

[MR05]   L. Mauborgne and X. Rival. Trace partitioning in abstract interpretation based static analyzers. In *ESOP'05*, Edinburgh, April 2005.

[Pug98]   J.-F. Puget. A fast algorithm for the bound consistency of alldiff constraints. In *AAAI'98/IAAI'98: Proceedings of the fifteenth national/tenth conference on Artificial intelligence/Innovative applications of artificial intelligence*, pages 359–366, Menlo Park, CA, USA, 1998. American Association for Artificial Intelligence.

[PW98]   W. Pugh and D. Wonnacott. Constraint-based array dependence analysis. *TOPLAS*, 20(3):635–678, 1998.

[RH80]   D. J. Rosenkrantz and H. B. Hunt III. Processing conjunctive predicates and queries. In *VLDB*, pages 64–72, 1980.

[SCC93]   K. Simon, D. Crippa, and F. Collenberg. On the distribution of the transitive closure in a random acyclic digraph. In *ESA'93*, pages 345–356. Springer-Verlag, 1993.

[Sim88]   K. Simon. An improved algorithm for transitive closure on acyclic digraphs. *TCS*, 58(1-3):325–346, 1988.

[SISG06]   S. Sankaranarayanan, F. Ivančić, I. Shlyakhter, and A. Gupta. Static analysis in disjunctive numerical domains. In *SAS'06*, Seoul, Korea, August 2006.

[SW02]   R. Seater and D. Wonnacott. Efficient Manipulation of Disequalities During Dependence Analysis. In *LCPC'02: Proceedings of the 15th international workshop on Languages and Compilers for Parallel Computing*, volume 2481, pages 295–308, December 2002.

Cibai: An Abstract Interpretation-Based Static Analyzer for Modular Analysis and Verification of Java Classes

Francesco Logozzo

École Normale Supérieure
45, rue d'Ulm, Paris, France
Francesco.Logozzo@Polytechnique.edu

Abstract. We introduce Cibai a generic static analyzer based on abstract interpretation for the modular analysis and verification of Java classes. We present the abstract semantics and the underlying abstract domain, a combination of an aliasing analysis and octagons. We discuss some implementation issues, and we compare Cibai with similar tools, showing how Cibai achieves a higher level of automation and precision while having comparable performances.

1 Introduction

Object-oriented programming emphasizes the development by components. Components are written once and used in many, different contexts. Component reliability is a main issue in object-oriented development.

Testing has been for long time the main approach for assuring component's reliability. A popular approach is that of unit testing, *e.g.* JUnit [1], which allows to write test cases for single components, and then to "*validate*" the tests through the use of assertions. The problems of the approach are that: (i) it requires the programmers to write test cases (ii) it is not sound as just finitely many execution paths and inputs can be considered; and (iii) it does not scale up very well as, if one wants full code coverage, the complexity of the test cases grows up very quickly with the size of the program. As a consequence, the need for formal methods arises.

Most of the verification tools that have been developed so far heavily relies on program annotations, *e.g.* [5,17,3]. Following the Design by Contract approach [18], such tools allow the programmer to express class invariants, pre-condition, post-conditions for the class. From the annotated program they derive the verification conditions, which are passed to a theorem prover. This approach has two main problems: (i) it has an inherent exponential behavior, as the checking of verification conditions by the theorem prover roughly corresponds to the exploration of all the possible paths in the program; and (ii) it requires the developer to provide inductive arguments, *e.g.* loop invariants, either as further annotations to the source code, or during the interactive proof.

B. Cook and A. Podelski (Eds.): VMCAI 2007, LNCS 4349, pp. 283–298, 2007.

We believe that in order to have a practical interest, a tool for the verification of object-oriented programs must be automatic, or it must require the least possible amount of interaction with the user. We have developed a tool, Cibai, based on abstract interpretation [6], for the analysis of Java classes. The tool analyzes *"pure"* Java classes, *i.e.* it does not require any annotation. It infers class invariants, loop invariants and method postconditions. The inferred properties are then used for verifying the absence of run-time errors in the class. Currently we can verify (i) the absence of divisions by zero; (ii) the absence of accesses out of the bounds of arrays; (iii) the absence of null dereferences; and (iv) simple user-provided assertions.

As an example consider the class `MiniBag` in Fig. 1. Cibai can discover in few milliseconds the class invariant $0 \leq$ `top` $\leq$ `elements.length`. It discovers that the array creation at line (∗) may launch an exception when `initial` is negative. It uses the inferred class invariant to prove that all the array accesses in the body of the methods are correct, *i.e.* no exception is thrown. Unlike existing tools, as ESC/Java or Spec#, it does require no annotation nor interaction with the user.

Paper organization. Section 2 recalls some notation and results from [15]. Section 3 describes the abstract domains designed for and implemented in Cibai. Section 4 presents the structure of the analyzer and the description of the most interesting transfer functions. Section 5 reports some experience with the tool. Section 6 compares Cibai with related tools and Section 7 conclude the paper.

2   Preliminaries

Syntax. In order to simplify the presentation, we perform some simplifying assumptions on the syntax of programs. We assume that a class has a unique constructor and that all the fields are protected. We also omit access modifiers in the definition of fields and methods. Nevertheless, in our implementation we handle those cases. We assume that all the fields are typed (as it is the case in mainstream object-oriented languages as Java or C#) and we also assume the basic types to be just `int` and `boolean`. We omit here the details of the statements that constitute the body of the class constructor and of the methods, too.

A class C is a tuple ⟨`init`, F, M⟩ where `init` is the class constructor, F is a set of field declarations and M is a set of methods.

Concrete Semantic Domains. We model an execution state of a Java program with a pair made up of an environment and a state An environment is a map from variables to memory addresses. A store is a map from addresses to values. Values are either basic values (`ints`, `booleans`), the `void` value Φ or references. A reference is a pair made up of a type and an environment.

The internal environment of an object is stored at a given memory location. The address corresponding to such a location is the *identity* of the object. In the following, we will denote the set of all the concrete states by Σ.

```
class BoundError extends Throwable { }
class MiniBag {
    private int[] elements;
    private int top;

    MiniBag(int initial) {
(*)  top = 0; elements = new int[initial]; }

    int remove() throws BoundError {
    int r;
    if(top > 0 ) {
        top--; r = elements[top];
    } else throw new BoundError();
    return r; }

    void add(int i) {
      if(top < elements.length) {
        elements[top] = i; top++;
      } else throw new BoundError(); }

    void removeMinimum() {
      if(top > 0) {
        int min = 0, i;
        for(i = 1; i < top; i++)
          if(elements[min] > elements[i])
            min = i;
        elements[min] = elements[i-1]; top--; } } }
```

Fig. 1. A bag of `int`. Cibai emits a warning at (∗) as `initial` may be negative. It proves correct all the other array accesses. Unlike ESC/Java 2 or Spec# it does not require the user to provide annotations for the class invariant and for the loop invariant of `removeMinimum`.

Abstract Semantics. Let $\bar{D}$ be an abstract domain $\bar{D}$ related to $\mathcal{P}(\Sigma)$ by a monotonic concretization function γ such that $\langle \mathcal{P}(\Sigma), \subseteq, \emptyset, \Sigma, \cup, \cap \rangle \xleftarrow{\gamma} \langle \bar{D}, \bar{\sqsubseteq}, \bar{\bot}, \bar{\top}, \bar{\sqcup}, \bar{\sqcap} \rangle$. As a consequence, we drop the need for the best possible abstraction of concrete elements, putting ourselves in a relaxed abstract interpretation framework, [7].

We recall from [15, §5] the fixpoint formulation of class invariants:

Proposition 1 (Abstract class invariant). *Let* C *be a class. Let* $\mathbb{I}[\![init]\!] \in \mathcal{P}(\Sigma)$ *be the collecting semantics of the constructor, let* $\mathbb{M}[\![\cdot]\!] \in [\mathbb{M} \to \mathcal{P}(\Sigma) \to \mathcal{P}(\Sigma)]$ *be the collecting semantics of the methods, and let* $\mathrm{Context}(C) \in \mathcal{P}(\Sigma)$ *be the collecting semantics for the behavior of the context, [15].*

Let $\bar{\mathbb{I}}[\![init]\!] \in \bar{D}$ *be a sound approximation for the constructor's semantics:* $\mathbb{I}[\![init]\!] \subseteq \gamma(\bar{\mathbb{I}}[\![init]\!])$. *For each* $m \in M$ *let* $\bar{\mathbb{M}}[\![m]\!] \in [\bar{D} \to \bar{D}]$ *be a sound approximation of its semantics:*

$$\forall S \in \mathcal{P}(\varSigma). \ \forall \bar{S} \in \bar{\mathsf{D}}. \ S \subseteq \gamma(\bar{S}) \implies \mathbb{M}[\![\mathtt{m}]\!](S) \subseteq \gamma(\bar{\mathbb{M}}[\![\mathtt{m}]\!](\bar{S})).$$

Finally, let $\overline{\mathrm{Context}} \in [\bar{\mathsf{D}} \to \bar{\mathsf{D}}]$ *be a sound approximation of the context behavior:*
$\forall S \in \mathcal{P}(\varSigma). \ \forall \bar{S} \in \bar{\mathsf{D}}. \ S \subseteq \gamma(\bar{S}) \implies \mathrm{Context}(S) \subseteq \gamma(\overline{\mathrm{Context}}(\bar{S})).$ *Then*

$$\bar{\mathbb{C}}[\![\mathtt{C}]\!] = \mathrm{lfp}_{\bar{\perp}}^{\bar{\sqsubseteq}} \lambda X. \ \bar{\mathbb{I}}[\![\mathtt{init}]\!] \bar{\sqcup} \bigsqcup_{\mathtt{m} \in \mathtt{M}} \bar{\mathbb{M}}[\![\mathtt{m}]\!](X) \bar{\sqcup} \mathrm{Context}(X) \qquad (1)$$

is such that $\mathbb{C}[\![\mathtt{C}]\!] \subseteq \gamma(\bar{\mathbb{C}}[\![\mathtt{C}]\!])$.

Please note that, as we do not restrict ourselves to abstract domains that respect the ascending chain condition (ACC) we need of a widening operator to upper approximate the fixpoint in (1).

3   Abstract Domains

In Cibai we chose $\bar{\mathsf{D}}$ to be the abstract domain $\overline{\mathsf{Env}} \times \overline{\mathsf{Store}} \times \mathcal{P}(\overline{\mathsf{Addr}})$. $\overline{\mathsf{Env}}$ is a map between variables and sets of abstract addresses. $\overline{\mathsf{Store}}$ is the (reduced) Cartesian product of the abstraction for integers, basic values and references. Finally, $\mathcal{P}(\overline{\mathsf{Addr}})$ is the set of the abstract addresses, corresponding to class fields, which may escape from the class context.

3.1   Abstract Environment

Intuitively, an abstract address stands for one of the two: a single address or a possibly infinite set of addresses. We require that it exists a partition of $\overline{\mathsf{Addr}}$ into two disjoint sets such that in the concrete the elements of one does not overlap with those of the other set. More formally:

Definition 1 (Abstract addresses, $\overline{\mathsf{Addr}}$). *Let* $\mathcal{P}(\mathsf{Addr})$ *be a set of addresses. Let* $\overline{\mathsf{Addr}}$ *be a set, and* $\gamma_{\mathsf{a}} \in [\mathcal{P}(\overline{\mathsf{Addr}}) \to \mathcal{P}(\mathsf{Addr})]$ *a monotonic concretization function. Then, we say that* $\mathcal{P}(\overline{\mathsf{Addr}})$ *is a set of abstract addresses if it can be partitioned into two disjoint subsets* $\mathcal{P}(\overline{\mathsf{Addr}_e})$ *(exact addresses) and* $\mathcal{P}(\overline{\mathsf{Addr}_s})$ *(summary addresses) such that:*

- $\forall \bar{\mathsf{a}} \in \mathcal{P}(\overline{\mathsf{Addr}_e}). \ \exists \mathsf{a} \in \mathcal{P}(\mathsf{Addr}). \ \gamma_{\mathsf{a}}(\bar{\mathsf{a}}) = \{\mathsf{a}\}$
- $\forall \bar{\mathsf{a}} \in \mathcal{P}(\overline{\mathsf{Addr}_s}). \ \gamma_{\mathsf{a}}(\bar{\mathsf{a}}) = A \implies \forall A'. A \neq A' \wedge (\exists \bar{\mathsf{a}}' \in \mathcal{P}(\overline{\mathsf{Addr}_s}). \ \gamma_{\mathsf{a}}(\bar{\mathsf{a}}') = A') \implies A \cap A' = \emptyset.$

Please note that we do not require to have the *best* approximation for a set of concrete addresses, so that once again we use a relaxed abstraction interpretation framework.

An abstract environment tracks, for each variable the set of addresses it may point to. We define it as a map from variables to sets of abstract addresses. The abstract operations on such an abstract domain are defined as the point-wise and functional extension of those on $\mathcal{P}(\overline{\mathsf{Addr}})$.

Definition 2 (Abstract environment, $\overline{\text{Env}}$). *The domain of abstract environments is* $\langle[\text{Vars} \to \mathcal{P}(\overline{\text{Addr}})], \sqsubseteq_e, \bar{\bot}_e, \bar{\top}_e, \sqcup_e, \sqcap_e\rangle$. *The relation with the concrete is given by a monotonic map* $\gamma_e \in [\overline{\text{Env}} \to \mathcal{P}(\text{Env})]$ *defined as*

$$\gamma_e = \lambda\bar{e}.\ \{e \in \mathcal{P}(\text{Env}) \mid \forall x.\ e(x) \in \gamma_a(\bar{e}(x))\}.$$

3.2   Abstract Store

The abstract store must approximate (i) basic values as booleans or integers; and (ii) reference values.

Abstraction of basic values. We approximate all the basic values but integers using a non-relational abstraction.

We chose booleans as representative for the abstraction of non-integer basic values. Booleans are approximated by an abstract domain $\bar{B} = [\text{Addr} \to \{\bar{\top}, \text{true}, \text{false}, \bar{\bot}\}]$. The abstract operations (join, meet, widening, etc.) are defined point-wise. The concretization function, $\gamma_b \in [\bar{B} \to \mathcal{P}(\text{Store})]$ is straightforward.

For integers, we have implemented two different abstract domains. The first one is that of Intervals [6], in which we abstract each location corresponding to an integer value (int-location) with the lower and the upper bounds for the values that can be stored in such location. This one gives excellent performances, but in practice we found it to be too imprecise for the purposes of our analysis. The second one is the abstract domain of octagons [19]. We recall that the Octagon abstract domain captures relations in the form of $\pm x \pm y \leq k$, where x and y are identifiers and k is a numeric constant. As a consequence, the Octagon abstract domain allow us to keep relations between different int-locations, so to achieve a greater precision yet keeping good performances. We do not recall here the order, the join, the meet and the widening on octagons. However, as we use it later, we recall the concretization function:

Definition 3 (Octagon concretization, γ_o). *Let* Id *be a set of identifiers. We denote by* $\text{Octagon}_{\text{Id}}$ *the set of octagons constraints built on the top of* Id. *Then* $\gamma_o \in [\text{Octagon}_{\text{Id}} \to (\text{Id} \to \mathbb{N})]$ *is defined as*

$$\gamma_o = \lambda\text{oct}.\ \{\sigma \mid \forall \text{id}_1, \text{id}_2 \in \text{Id}.\forall s_1, s_2 \in \{0, +, -\}.$$
$$s_1 * \text{id}_1 + s_2 * \text{id}_2 \leq k \in \text{oct} \implies s_1 \cdot \sigma(\text{id}_1) + s_2 \cdot \sigma(\text{id}_2) \leq k\}.$$

In the following, we will often write Octagon_n to denote an octagon with n distinct identifiers or simply Octagon when neither the identifiers nor the dimensions of the octagon are relevant to the context.

In the context of our analyzer we have to pay attention to (i) the fact that not all the addresses correspond to a dimension in the octagon; and (ii) the size of the octagons may dynamically change, because of dynamic memory allocation. As a consequence, we map each address corresponding to an int-location to a dimension in the octagon. We lift the usual operations on octagons so to handle, *e.g.* the join of two octagons of different sizes. We postpone the detailed description of such operations to the Section 4.2, as they involve several implementation details. The concretization of a dynamic octagon is the set of all the concrete stores where the octagon constraints are satisfied by the int-locations.

Definition 4 (Dynamic octagons, DynOctagon). *Let* Id *be a set of identifiers. The abstract domain of dynamic octagons is*

$$\mathsf{DynOctagon_{Id}} = \langle [\overline{\mathsf{Addr}} \to \mathsf{Id}] \times \mathsf{Octagon_{Id}}, \sqsubseteq_{\mathsf{do}}, \bar{\bot}_{\mathsf{do}}, \bar{\top}_{\mathsf{do}}, \sqcup_{\mathsf{do}}, \sqcap_{\mathsf{do}} \rangle.$$

The meaning of a dynamic octagon is given by the monotonic function $\gamma_{\mathsf{do}} \in [\mathsf{DynOctagon_{Id}} \to \mathcal{P}(\mathsf{Store})]$ *defined as*

$$\tilde{\gamma} = \lambda \langle f, \mathsf{oct} \rangle. \{\sigma \in [\overline{\mathsf{Addr}} \to \mathbb{N}] \mid \sigma' \in \gamma_o(\mathsf{oct}), \ \sigma = \sigma' \circ f\},$$
$$\gamma_{\mathsf{do}} = \lambda \langle f, \mathsf{oct} \rangle. \{\mathsf{s} \in \mathsf{Store} \mid \forall \bar{\mathsf{a}} \in \mathrm{dom}(f). \ \sigma \in \tilde{\gamma}(\langle f, \mathsf{oct} \rangle)$$
$$\implies \exists \mathsf{a} \in \gamma_\mathsf{a}(\bar{\mathsf{a}}). \ \mathsf{s}(\mathsf{a}) = \sigma(\bar{\mathsf{a}})\}.$$

Abstraction of reference values. We chose to approximate reference values with a pair made up of a set of reference types, *i.e.* the possible dynamic types of the reference, and an abstract environment. We *"squeeze"* together all the references that can be stored at a given address. In particular if we have o_B instance of a class Base and o_S instance of a class Sub, with Sub subclass of Base, and both o_B and o_S may be stored at the same address, then (i) the dynamic type of the abstract reference is {Base, Sub}; and (ii) the abstract environment is an over-approximation of the union of the two environments.

The domain of abstract references is defined below, where the domain operations are the functional and point-wise extension on operations on sets and abstract environments.

Definition 5 (Abstract references, $\overline{\mathsf{Ref}}$). *Let* RType *be the set of reference types. The abstract domain of abstract references is*

$$\overline{\mathsf{Ref}} = \langle [\overline{\mathsf{Addr}} \to (\mathcal{P}(\mathsf{RType}) \times \overline{\mathsf{Env}})], \bar{\sqsubseteq}_\mathsf{r}, \bar{\bot}_\mathsf{r}, \bar{\top}_\mathsf{r}, \bar{\sqcup}_\mathsf{r}, \bar{\sqcap}_\mathsf{r} \rangle.$$

The meaning is given by the monotonic function $\gamma_\mathsf{r} \in [\overline{\mathsf{Ref}} \to \mathcal{P}(\mathsf{Store})]$ *defined as*

$$\gamma_\mathsf{r} = \lambda f. \{\mathsf{s} \in \mathsf{Store} \mid \forall \bar{\mathsf{a}} \in \mathrm{dom}(f). \ f(\bar{\mathsf{a}}) = \langle \mathsf{T}, \bar{\mathsf{e}} \rangle \wedge \mathsf{a} \in \gamma_\mathsf{a}(\bar{\mathsf{a}}) \wedge \mathsf{s}(\mathsf{a}) = \langle \mathsf{t}, \bar{\mathsf{e}} \rangle$$
$$\implies \mathsf{t} \in \mathsf{T} \wedge \mathsf{e} \in \gamma_\mathsf{e}(\bar{\mathsf{e}})\}.$$

Abstract Store. To recapitulate, an abstract store is a non-relational abstraction of basic values and references. We use a relational abstraction for integers, and a non-relation for all the other basic values. Furthermore as Java is a strongly typed language, we can partition the (abstract) addresses depending to the type of the locations they refer to. So if $\langle \bar{\mathsf{b}}, \langle f_o, \mathsf{oct} \rangle, \bar{\mathsf{r}} \rangle$ is an element of $\bar{\mathsf{B}} \times \mathsf{DynOctagon} \times \overline{\mathsf{Ref}}$, then

$$\mathrm{dom}(\bar{\mathsf{b}}) \cap \mathrm{dom}(f_o) = \emptyset \wedge \mathrm{dom}(\bar{\mathsf{b}}) \cap \mathrm{dom}(\bar{\mathsf{r}}) = \emptyset \wedge \mathrm{dom}(f_o) \cap \mathrm{dom}(\bar{\mathsf{r}}) = \emptyset. \quad (2)$$

The definition of the operations on the domain of abstract stores are as usual the point-wise extension of the operations of the components.

Definition 6 (Abstrace store, $\overline{\mathsf{Store}}$). *The domain of abstract stores is*

$$\overline{\mathsf{Store}} = \langle \bar{\mathsf{B}} \times \mathsf{DynOctagon} \times \overline{\mathsf{Ref}}, \bar{\sqsubseteq}_{\mathsf{s}}, \bar{\bot}_{\mathsf{s}}, \bar{\top}_{\mathsf{s}}, \bar{\sqcup}_{\mathsf{s}}, \bar{\sqcap}_{\mathsf{s}} \rangle$$

whose elements satisfy (2). The concretization $\gamma_{\mathsf{s}} \in [\overline{\mathsf{Store}} \to \mathcal{P}(\mathsf{Store})]$ is defined as $\gamma_{\mathsf{s}} = \lambda \langle \bar{\mathsf{b}}, \bar{\mathsf{d}}, \bar{\mathsf{r}} \rangle . \gamma_{\mathsf{b}}(\bar{\mathsf{b}}) \cap \gamma_{\mathsf{do}}(\bar{\mathsf{d}}) \cap \gamma_{\mathsf{r}}(\bar{\mathsf{r}}).$

3.3   Abstract State

An abstract state is a non-relational abstraction of a set of interaction states. It is a triple made up of an abstract environment, and abstract store and an abstraction of the addresses which escapes from a class. We refer the interested reader to [16] for an extensive description of escaping addresses.

Proposition 2 (Abstract state, $\bar{\varSigma}$). *The domain of abstract states is*

$$\bar{\varSigma} = \langle \overline{\mathsf{Env}} \times \overline{\mathsf{Store}} \times \mathcal{P}(\overline{\mathsf{Addr}}), \bar{\sqsubseteq}_{\bar{\varSigma}}, \bar{\bot}_{\bar{\varSigma}}, \bar{\top}_{\bar{\varSigma}}, \bar{\sqcup}_{\bar{\varSigma}}, \bar{\sqcap}_{\bar{\varSigma}} \rangle.$$

The concretization function is the monotonic function $\gamma_{\bar{\varSigma}} \in [\bar{\varSigma} \to (\mathcal{P}(\varSigma) \times \mathcal{P}(\mathsf{Addr}))]$ defined as

$$\gamma_{\bar{\varSigma}} = \lambda \langle \bar{\mathsf{e}}, \bar{\mathsf{s}}, \overline{\mathsf{Esc}} \rangle . \langle \{ \langle \mathsf{e}, \mathsf{s} \rangle \mid \mathsf{e} \in \gamma_{\mathsf{e}}(\bar{\mathsf{e}}), \ \mathsf{s} \in \gamma_{\mathsf{s}}(\bar{\mathsf{s}}) \}, \cup_{\bar{\mathsf{a}} \in \overline{\mathsf{Esc}}} \ \gamma_{\mathsf{a}}(\bar{\mathsf{a}}) \rangle .$$

As a consequence, $\bar{\varSigma}$ is a sound abstraction of $\mathcal{P}(\varSigma)$.

4   The Analyzer

4.1   Overall Structure

Our analyzer takes as input a Java compilation unit, [10]. A compilation unit is a bunch of interface and class definitions.

First, Cibai parses the compilation unit, determines the dependencies between the different classes and interfaces. A class/interface A depends on a class/interface B if it extends (or implements) B or it has a field, a local declaration, a parameter of type B or it contains a cast expression to B or it depends on a class/interface C which depends on B.

Second, Cibai performs some syntactic transformations on the abstract syntax tree. We can divide those transformations into two classes. The first one rewrites some constructs so to reduce the number of syntactic constructs the analysis must handle. For instance in this phase Cibai rewrites `for` loops and `do...while` loops in terms of `while` loops. The second syntactic transformation instruments the code with assertions. For instance, for each array access `a[E]` we emit the two assertions `assert 0 ≤ E` and `assert E < a.length`.

Third, it analyzes the compilation unit according to such dependencies: if a class A depends on a class B, then B is analyzed before A. It may be the case that two or more classes are mutually dependent. In its current version, Cibai breaks the dependencies by assuming the worst case. For instance, suppose that A depends on B and B depends on A. Then, when analyzing A we assume B to be unknown (*i.e.* we assume its semantics to be "top") and *vice versa*. This is quite a rough approximation. We may solve it by using a global fixpoint computation involving both A and B. Nevertheless, we plan to do it another way, namely by using the technique that we introduced in [14], which allows to split the analyses of both A and B yet preserving a good precision.

Finally, the analysis of a class boils down to the computation of (1), when instantiated with the abstract domain of Proposition 2. More precisely, as the abstract domain $\bar{\Sigma}$ does not respect the ACC, we use a widening operator to ensure the convergence of the analysis, so that we actually compute a post-fixpoint of (1). In order to improve the precision, we also use a narrowing operator. To sum up, first we apply the iteration schema

$$I^0 = \bar{\mathbb{I}}[\![\mathtt{init}]\!]$$

$$I^{k+1} = I^k \bar{\sqcup} \bigsqcup_{\mathtt{m} \in M} \bar{\mathbb{M}}[\![\mathtt{m}]\!](I^k) \,\bar{\sqcup}\, \overline{\mathrm{Context}}(I^k) \qquad 0 \le k \le w$$

$$I^{k+1} = I^k \bar{\nabla} \left(\bigsqcup_{\mathtt{m} \in M} \bar{\mathbb{M}}[\![\mathtt{m}]\!](I^k) \,\bar{\sqcup}\, \overline{\mathrm{Context}}(I^k) \right) \qquad w < k,$$

to get a post-fixpoint $I^{\bar{\nabla}}$. Finite convergence to $I^{\bar{\nabla}}$ follows by the properties of the widening $\bar{\nabla}$, [6]. Next, we refine $I^{\bar{\nabla}}$ by a downward iteration:

$$I^\omega = I^0 \bar{\sqcup} \left(I^{\bar{\nabla}} \bar{\sqcap} \left(\bigsqcup_{\mathtt{m} \in M} \bar{\mathbb{M}}[\![\mathtt{m}]\!](I^{\bar{\nabla}}) \bar{\sqcup}\, \overline{\mathrm{Context}}(I^{\bar{\nabla}}) \right) \right). \tag{3}$$

Proposition 3 (Soundness of Cibai). *Under the hypotheses of Proposition 1, let I^{lfp} be the solution of (1) and I^ω be as in (3). Then $I^{\mathsf{lfp}} \bar{\sqsubseteq}_{\bar{\Sigma}} I^\omega$.*

4.2 Dynamic Octagon Operations

We were left by previous sections to the definition of the abstract operations on dynamic octagons.

Without loss of generality from now on we assume that for all the dynamic octagons, the same address corresponds to the same identifier in the octagon. Formally, we assume that

$$\forall \langle f_1, \mathsf{o}_1 \rangle, \langle f_2, \mathsf{o}_2 \rangle \in \mathsf{DynOctagon}.\ \forall \bar{\mathsf{a}} \in \mathrm{dom}(f_1) \cap \mathrm{dom}(f_2).\ f_1(\bar{\mathsf{a}}) = f_2(\bar{\mathsf{a}}).$$

Our implementation satisfies the such an assumption.

Join. The join of the dynamic octagons, as well as the other operations, must take into account the fact that the dynamic octagons to join may have different dimensions. This is the case when we have the allocation of an object containing integer fields in one of the branches of a conditional.

Let $\langle f_1, o_1 \rangle$ and $\langle f_2, o_2 \rangle$ be in DynOctagon. The *kernel* is defined as $\mathrm{dom}(f_1) \cap \mathrm{dom}(f_2)$. Let $\bar{d}_1$ and $\bar{d}_2$ be two dynamic octagons of size n and m. If $n == m$, then we can apply the standard join on octagons. If $n < m$, we construct the dynamic octagon $\bar{d}_1 \sqcup_{do} \bar{d}_2$ by first joining the octagon constraints corresponding to their kernel. Then we add the constraints involving the abstract addresses not in the kernel, *i.e.* the addresses that correspond to fresh allocated memory. In fact, if an address is in the dynamic octagon $\bar{d}_1$ but not in the kernel, it means that its value in $\bar{d}_2$ is bottom. As a consequence joining a constraint with the bottom value is equivalent to the constraint itself. In our case, this is equivalent to just adding the constraint to the result.

Example 1. Let $\langle f_1, o_1 \rangle$ and $\langle f_2, o_2 \rangle$ be two dynamic octagons such that $f_1 = \langle \bar{a}_1 \mapsto d_1, \bar{a}_2 \mapsto d_2, \bar{a}_3 \mapsto d_3 \rangle$, $o_1 = \{d_1 = 5, d_1 - d_2 \le 0, d_3 = 99\}$, $f_2 = \langle \bar{a}_1 \mapsto d_1, \bar{a}_2 \mapsto d_2 \rangle$ and $o_2 = \{d_1 = -6\}$.

The kernel is $\{\bar{a}_1, \bar{a}_2\}$. The address $\bar{a}_2$, corresponding to the dimension d_2 is unconstrained in o_2. As a consequence it can assume any value, so that the join of the octagons projected on the kernel is $-6 \le d_1 \le 5$.

On the other hand, the address $\bar{a}_3$ is not in the kernel, *i.e.* it is not defined for the first octagon. Intuitively, it is as its value is $\bot$, so that the join is simply the constraint $d_3 = 99$.

Finally, the join of the two dynamic octagons is $\langle \{\bar{a}_1 \mapsto d_1, \bar{a}_2 \mapsto d_2, \bar{a}_3 \mapsto d_3\}, \{-6 \le d_1 \le 5, d_3 = 99\} \rangle$.   □

Definition 7 (Join of dynamic octagons, $\sqcup_{do}$). *Let $\bar{d}_1 \in$ DynOctagon$_n$ and $\bar{d}_2 \in$ DynOctagon$_m$ be dynamic octagons different from $\bot_{do}$ and $\top_{do}$. Let k be the size of the kernel of $\bar{d}_1$ and $\bar{d}_2$. Then their join $\sqcup_{do} \in$ [DynOctagon$_n \times$ DynOctagon$_m \to$ DynOctagon$_{n+m-k}$] is defined as in Fig. 2.*

Please note that in the definition of $\sqcup_{do}$ we pay attention that for the constraints involving addresses not in the kernel we apply a renaming so to avoid (potential erroneous) overlapping of identifiers.

Meet. The meet of dynamic octagon is similar in spirit to the join. We identify the common constraints to both the dynamic octagons, and we "meet" them by using the standard meet operation on octagons, $\sqcap_o$. We discard all the addresses (and the corresponding constraints) not in the kernel. This is equivalent to setting the value of the addresses not in the kernel to bottom.

Definition 8 (Meet of dynamic octagons, $\sqcap_{do}$). *Let $\bar{d}_1 \in$ DynOctagon$_n$ and $\bar{d}_2 \in$ DynOctagon$_m$ be two dynamic octagons different from top and bottom. Let r the size of the kernel of $\bar{d}_1$ and $\bar{d}_2$. Their meet $\sqcap_{do} \in$ [DynOctagon$_n \times$ DynOctagon$_m \to$ DynOctagon$_r$] is defined in Fig. 3.*

Please note that the result of the meet of two dynamic octagons is, in general, a dynamic octagon with fewer dimensions than the operands.

$$\bar{d}_1 \sqcup_{do} \bar{d}_2 = \text{let } \bar{d}_1 = \langle f_1, o_1 \rangle, \bar{d}_2 = \langle f_2, o_2 \rangle$$
$$\text{in let } \iota = \text{dom}(f_1) \cap \text{dom}(f_2)$$
$$\text{in let } \kappa_1 = \pi_{f_1(\iota)}(o_1), \kappa_2 = \pi_{f_2(\iota)}(o_2)$$
$$\text{in let } \eta_1 = \text{dom}(f_1) - \iota, \eta_2 = \text{dom}(f_2) - \iota$$
$$\text{in let } \theta \text{ be a renaming from } f_1(\eta_1) \cup f_2(\eta_2) \text{ to fresh identifiers}$$
$$\text{in let } \rho_1 = \theta(\pi_{f_1(\eta_1)}(o_1)), \rho_2 = \theta(\pi_{f_2(\eta_2)}(o_2))$$
$$\text{in let } g = \{\bar{a} \mapsto i \mid \bar{a} \in \iota, i = f_1(\bar{a})\} \cup \{\bar{a} \mapsto i \mid \bar{a} \in \eta_1, i = \theta(f_1(\bar{a}))\}$$
$$\cup \{\bar{a} \mapsto i \mid \bar{a} \in \eta_2, i = \theta(f_2(\bar{a}))\}$$
$$\text{in} \langle (\kappa_1 \sqcup_o \kappa_2) \cup \rho_1 \cup \rho_2, g \rangle$$

Fig. 2. The definition of the join of dynamic octagons. $\pi_{Id}(o)$ is the projection of the octagon o on the identifiers Id. With an abuse of notation we lift function application to sets.

$$\bar{d}_1 \sqcap_{do} \bar{d}_2 = \text{let } \bar{d}_1 = \langle f_1, o_1 \rangle, \bar{d}_2 = \langle f_2, o_2 \rangle$$
$$\text{in let } \iota = \text{dom}(f_1) \cap \text{dom}(f_2)$$
$$\text{in let } \kappa_1 = \pi_{f_1(\iota)}(o_1), \kappa_2 = \pi_{f_2(\iota)}(o_2)$$
$$\text{in} \langle \kappa_1 \sqcap_o \kappa_2, f_1 \cap f_2 \rangle.$$

Fig. 3. The definition of the meet of two dynamic octagons. $\pi_{Id}(o)$ is the projection of the octagon o on the identifiers Id. The intersection of functions is defined as the intersection of the domains and the co-domains.

Widening. When performing the widening of two dynamic octagons, we identify the addresses that are common to the two. Then we perform the widening of just the constraints involving addresses in the kernel. For all the addresses not in the kernel, we keep them in the resulting dynamic octagon unconstrained. This is equivalent to setting their value to top.

Proposition 4 (Widening of dynamic octagons, $\bar{\nabla}_{do}$). *Let $\bar{d}_1 \in$ DynOctagon$_n$ and $\bar{d}_2 \in$ DynOctagon$_m$ be two dynamic octagons different from top and bottom. Let k be the size of the kernel of $\bar{d}_1$ and $\bar{d}_2$. Let us consider the operator $\bar{\nabla}_{do}$ in Fig. 4. If the set of abstract addresses is bounded, then $\bar{\nabla}_{do}$ is a widening operator such that $[\text{DynOctagon}_n \times \text{DynOctagon}_m \to \text{DynOctagon}_{n+m-k}]$.*

The proposition above requires that the set of abstract addresses to be bounded in order to have a widening operator on dynamic octagons. In our implementation we pay attention to generate finitely many abstract addresses during the analysis.

$$\bar{d}_1 \bar{\nabla}_{do} \bar{d}_2 = \text{let } \bar{d}_1 = \langle f_1, o_1 \rangle, \bar{d}_2 = \langle f_2, o_2 \rangle$$
$$\text{in let } \iota = \text{dom}(f_1) \cap \text{dom}(f_2)$$
$$\text{in let } \kappa_1 = \pi_{f_1(\iota)}(o_1), \kappa_2 = \pi_{f_2(\iota)}(o_2)$$
$$\text{in} \langle \kappa_1 \bar{\nabla}_o \kappa_2, f_1 \cup f_2 \rangle.$$

Fig. 4. The definition of the widening of two dynamic octagons. $\pi_{Id}(o)$ is the projection of the octagon o on the identifiers Id. The union of functions is defined as the union of the domains and of the co-domains.

4.3 Transfer Functions

The analysis of the bodies of the constructors and the methods is by induction on the syntax of the program. The analyzer provides transfer functions for most of the constructors of sequential Java. It does not support reflection. Here we describe the implementation of the most interesting transfer functions, the others being quite standard.

Parameters. Before analyzing the body of a constructor or of a method we have to set up the initial state considering the input parameters. We describe the parameter initialization just for methods, the constructor's case being easier. We distinguish two cases, whether the parameters are of basic type or of a reference type.

If the method input parameters are of a basic type, we know that no aliasing may be created thanks to the semantics of parameter passing in Java. We extend the abstract environment with the new variable and assume the value to be unknown.

Example 2. Let $\langle \bar{e}, \langle \bar{b}, \langle f, o \rangle, \bar{r} \rangle, S \rangle$ be an abstract state. Let void m(bool b, int i) $\{\dots\}$ be a public method. Let $\bar{a}_1$ and $\bar{a}_2$ be fresh addresses, id be a fresh identifier, and o′ be the octagon o extended with a new dimension corresponding to the identifier id. Then the initial abstract state for the analysis of the body of m is $\langle \bar{e}[b \mapsto \{\bar{a}_1\}, i \mapsto \{\bar{a}_2\}], \langle \bar{b}[\bar{a}_2 \mapsto \bar{\top}], \langle f[\bar{a}_1 \mapsto \text{id}], o′ \rangle, \bar{r} \rangle, S \rangle.$ □

If the parameters are of reference type we have to pay attention to possible aliasing. We assume that parameters of the same type (or subtype) may alias. For instance if we have

```
class A { B bRef; }
class B { int i; }
class ToAnalyze {
//...
public void m(A a, B b) { ... } }
```

Then a.bRef and b may alias. Our choice is to use summary locations for objects of a type that appears at least twice in the method's parameters.

Example 3. Referring to the classes A, B and ToAnalyze above, let us consider an input abstract state $\langle \bar{e}, \langle \bar{b}, \langle f, o \rangle, \bar{r} \rangle, S \rangle$ for the analysis of m. Let $\bar{a}_1$, be an abstract address, $\bar{a}_2^*, \bar{a}_3^*$ be summary abstract addresses, id a fresh identifier and o$'$ the octagon o extended with the new identifier id. Furthermore let $\bar{e}' = \bar{e}[a \mapsto \{\bar{a}_1\}, b \mapsto \{\bar{a}_2^*\}], f' = f[\bar{a}_2^* \mapsto id], \bar{r}' = \bar{r}[\bar{a} \mapsto \langle \{A\}, [bRef \mapsto \bar{a}_1^*]\rangle, \bar{a}_1^* \mapsto \langle \{B\}, [i \mapsto \bar{a}_2^*]\rangle]$, then the initial state for the analysis of the body of m is $\langle \bar{e}[a \mapsto \{\bar{a}_1\}, b \mapsto \{\bar{a}_1^*\}], \langle \bar{b}, \langle f', o' \rangle, \bar{r}' \rangle, S \rangle$. □

Assignments. When performing an assignment $e_1 = e_2$ we distinguish between two cases depending whether the static type of e_1 is a basic type or a reference type. Furthermore, there is the orthogonal issue of considering if we are assigning to a location corresponding to a summary address. We skip here the technical details of our implementation, but the intuition behind is that (i) the update of a location corresponding to an *exact* abstract address is destructive, in that the old value is replaced by the new one; and (ii) the update of a location corresponding to a *summary* abstract address is *weak*, in that the new value is joined with the old one.

The assignment to a boolean consists in (i) the evaluation of e_2; and (ii) the update of the abstract location corresponding to e_1.

The assignment to an integer is more complicated as e_1 and e_2 may evaluate to several addresses, and we want to keep a relational information between the int-locations.

Example 4. Suppose to have the assignment $a.x = b.c.y + 2$ in an abstract state $\langle \bar{e}, \langle \bar{b}, \langle f, o \rangle, \bar{r} \rangle, S \rangle$ where, for some classes C, D, E:

$$\bar{e} = [a \mapsto \{\bar{a}_1, \bar{a}_2\}, b \mapsto \{\bar{a}_3\}]$$
$$f = [\bar{a}_4 \mapsto id_0, \bar{a}_5 \mapsto id_1, \bar{a}_7 \mapsto id_2]$$
$$\bar{r} = [\bar{a}_1 \mapsto \langle \{C\}, x \mapsto \{\bar{a}_4\}\rangle, \bar{a}_2 \mapsto \langle \{C\}, x \mapsto \{\bar{a}_5\}\rangle,$$
$$\bar{a}_3 \mapsto \langle \{D\}, c \mapsto \{\bar{a}_6\}\rangle, \bar{a}_6 \mapsto \langle \{E\}, y \mapsto \{\bar{a}_7\}\rangle].$$

Resolving the variable addresses using this abstract state, we get the possible assignments $\bar{a}_4 = \bar{a}_7 + 2$ and $\bar{a}_5 = \bar{a}_7 + 2$. The corresponding octagon constraints are $id_0 = id_2 + 2$ and $id_1 = id_2 + 2$. We use the assignment on octagons to get two new octagons $o_1 = o.assign(id_0 = id_2 + 2)$ and $o_2 = o.assign(id_1 = id_2 + 2)$. The octagon after the assignment is the join of the two cases : $o' = o_1 \sqcup_o o_2$. □

To sum up, when analyzing an assignment to an int-location, we first consider all the octagons constraints that are enabled by the incoming abstract state, then we create enough copies of the incoming octagon, perform the assignments independently, *i.e.* a constraint for each duplicated octagon, and we join all the octagons together.

Finally, if in the assignment $e_1 = e_2$ the static type of e_1 is of a reference type, then the effect of the assignment is to create an alias for e_2. Therefore, we update the abstract environment (and the abstract store if needed) to reflect the fact that e_1 points to the same abstract addresses e_2 points to.

Assertions. We have two kinds of assertions: (i) those explicitly written by the programmer; and (ii) those generated by the program-transformation phase. The last ones include array access bounds-checking and division by zero. Our choice is to handle the two kind of assertions in the same way: During the analysis, when we reach an assertion (i) we check whether the assertion does hold, does not hold, or *"we do not know"* in the incoming abstract state; and (ii) we meet the incoming state with the asserted expression so to produce the outgoing abstract state.

Object Instantiations. Objects are created through the **new** statement. In the concrete, the invocation of **new** returns an address to a freshly allocated memory location where to store the object. Such an address is the identity of the object. In the abstract, in order to guarantee the convergence of the analysis we limit, for each **new** statement in the source code, the allocation of just k fresh objects. k is a command line parameter of the analyzer. After k exact instantiations, we create a summary location that collects the behavior of all the other objects that can be instantiated in such particular statement.

Return statements. We join together all the abstract states that reach a **return** statement in the body of a method. Let $\langle \bar{e}, \langle \bar{b}, \langle f, o \rangle, \bar{r} \rangle, S \rangle$ the abstract state at the method's exit point. We assume that the returned value is stored into a special variable #ret.

If #ret is of a basic type, then no address reachable from one of the fields of the class we are analyzing is exposed to the context, [15]. Then we do not need to add any new address to S, the set of exposed abstract addresses. Please note that the statements that constitute the body of the method do not affect either S, too.

If #ret is of a reference type, then it is possible that the returned object may contain, in its fields, references to memory locations that are reachable also from the fields of the class we are analyzing. Therefore, we determine the sets of abstract addresses reachable from the fields of the class under analysis, F, and then of addresses reachable from the returned reference, R. The abstract addresses in $F \cap R$ may be exposed to the context, so we update S to be $S \cup (F \cap R)$. In Cibai, we perform a similar reasoning also for parameters.

Abstract context. The abstract context over-approximate the behavior of a worst-context, *i.e.* a context that once is aware of an address it changes its value arbitrarily. The input to the $\overline{\text{Context}}$ is an abstract state $\langle \bar{e}, \langle \bar{b}, \langle f, o \rangle, \bar{r} \rangle, S \rangle$. Then, for each abstract address in S, it sets the corresponding value to top.

5   Experiments

We have compared Cibai and ESC/Java 2 on a class library consisting of 2800 lines of sequential Java code. We did not annotated nor modified the code. The library is quite representative in that its code contains dynamic memory allocation, non-trivial loops, method calls and aliasing issues. Because of its nature, it also allows the testing of the modular aspects of the tools.

The testing platform is a 1.40 GHz Pentium M laptop, with 632MB of RAM, running Windows XP Service Pack 2 and the Sun JVM version 1.6 beta 2. Cibai analyzed the 40 files of the library in 28.6 seconds, whereas ESC/Java took 50.2 seconds. Cibai was able to verify the library except for two assertions involving non-octogonal arithmetic relations. ESC/Java 2 emitted 107 warnings, mainly about null dereferences and out of bound array accesses.

In order to understand the reasons of the difference in precision, let us consider the initial example (cf. Fig. 1). ESC/Java is not able to infer that (i) the field `elements` is always non-null, as it is allocated in the constructor and never modified; (ii) the field `top` is always positive and smaller or equal to the length of the array. As a consequence, it cannot check the array accesses and dereferences in the body of the methods of `BagOfInts`, so it emits the warnings. To overcome this problem, the tool requires the user to modify the code by adding annotations. On the other hand, Cibai can infer the right class invariants for `BagOfInts`, so that without any user interaction it can verify the class to be correct.

We have tuned the performances by using a profiler to find the bottlenecks. For instance, in one of the test cases, written on purpose to stress the allocation of many objects containing integer fields, we experienced very bad performances. The profiler showed that the problem was because of the closure operation on octagons. Closure is used everywhere: for emptiness checks, for the order, etc. In a first version, octagons were represented as a square matrix of `IExtendedInt`. `IExtendedInt` is an interface implemented by three classes `AnInt`, `PlusInf` and `MinusInf`. We replaced the representation of octagons with a square matrix of `int`, `maxint` and `minint` standing respectively for $+\infty$ and $-\infty$. We also implemented a form of sharing of octagons. With the optimized representation, we obtained an improvement of the 900% of the performances in the stress test. We conjecture that such a dramatic speedup is obtained because the matrix of integers can be stored inside the processor cache, so that each access is internal to the processor.

6   Related Work

There are several tools for the static analysis and verification of object-oriented languages. Most of them are based on the Java Modeling Language (JML), [13]. JML is a Hoare-like logic for the specification of Java program.

ESC/Java 2 tries to check that a JML-annotated program satisfies its specification. It is neither sound nor complete, [5]. Other tools as Jack [23], LOOP [12], Krakatoa [17] are sound, but they present a low level of automation. In fact, they need the programmer to supply, among the other others, loop invariants. Furthermore, as they are based on interactive theorem provers, they also need the user assistance for conducting the proof.

Spec# adds the support for design-by-contract to C#, [3]. Contracts are checked either dynamically or statically. The Spec# static program verifier,

Boogie, integrates an inference engine for reduce the burden of program annotations when dealing with loops. Nevertheless, the inference engine inside Boogie is quite limited and it is not able to infer class invariants.

Daikon is a tool for discovering class invariants-like in Java, [8]. It monitors the execution of a program trying to determine if some simple properties hold or not. Being based on testing, it is inherently unsound. Axiom Meister is a step forward w.r.t. Daikon as it tries to infer preconditions in .net programs using symbolic execution, [24]. The discover of algebraic specifications for Java classes is also the goal of the tool introduced in [11].

Julia is generic static analyzer that works on the bytecode level, [22], and it focuses mainly on non-numeric and non-relational properties. Jail is a static analyzer specialized for the verification of applet isolation in JavaCard, [9]. Other static analyses for object-oriented languages infer particular properties as escape analysis [4], shape analysis [20], data structures cyclicity [21] or the inference of very simple properties on class fields [2].

7   Conclusions and Future Work

We described Cibai, an automatic tool for the analysis of Java programs. The tool can analyze classes in isolation, can infer class invariants and method post-conditions. It uses such information to prove the absence of some runtime errors, as the violation of user-defined assertions, the access out of the bounds of arrays or the dereference of null objects. The abstract domain underlying Cibai is a composition of an alias analysis, so to precisely track the identity of objects, and several other domains to approximate the values of Java values, as ints, booleans or references. The structure of the analyzer is modular, so that is possible to change the approximation for one class of values, without having to modify the others.

The next step in the development of Cibai is the generation of method summaries: we plan to apply Cibai on the Java API so to generate stubs, and then to reuse these stubs when analyzing large programs. We want also to improve the handling of mutually recursive classes, using the technique we introduced in [14]; and we want to provide a translation of the inferred invariants in JML, so to automatically produce code annotations.

References

1. JUnit. http://junit.sourceforge.net/.
2. A. Aggarwal and K. H. Randall. Related field analysis. In *PLDI '01*.
3. M. Barnett, K.R.M. Leino, and W. Schulte. The Spec# programming system: An overview. In *CASSIS 2004*.
4. B. Blanchet. Escape Analysis: Correctness proof, implementation and experimental results. In *POPL'98*.
5. D. R. Cok and J. Kiniry. ESC/Java 2: Uniting ESC/Java and JML. In *CASSIS 2004*.

6. P. Cousot and R. Cousot. Abstract interpretation: a unified lattice model for static analysis of programs by construction or approximation of fixpoints. In *POPL'77*.
7. P. Cousot and R. Cousot. Abstract interpretation frameworks. *Journal of Logic and Computation*, 2(4), August 1992.
8. M. D. Ernst. *Dynamically Discovering Likely Program Invariants*. PhD thesis, University of Washington, 2000.
9. P. Ferrara. JAIL: Firewall analysis of JavaCard by Abstract Interpretation. In *EAAI 2006*.
10. J. Gosling, B. Joy, G. Steele, and G. Bracha. *The Java Language Specification - 2nd Edition*. Sun Microsystems, 2001.
11. J. Henkel and A. Diwan. Discovering algebraic specifications from java classes. In *ECOOP'03*.
12. B. Jacobs, J. van den Berg, H. Huismann, M. van Berkum, U. Hensel, and Tews H. Reasoning about Java classes (preliminary report). In *OOPSLA'98*.
13. G. T. Leavens, A. L. Baker, and C. Ruby. *Preliminary Design of JML: A Behavioral Interface Specification Language for Java*, November 2003.
14. F. Logozzo. Separate compositional analysis of class-based object-oriented languages. In *AMAST'2004*.
15. F. Logozzo. *Modular Static Analysis of Object-oriented languges*. PhD thesis, École Polytecnique, 2004.
16. F. Logozzo. Class invariants as abstract interpretation of trace semantics. *Computer Languages, Systems and Structures*, 2007.
17. C. Marché, C. Paulin-Mohring, and X. Urbain. The Krakatoa tool for certificationof Java/Javacard programs annotated in JML. *J. Log. Algebr. Program*, 58(1–2), 2004.
18. B. Meyer. *Object-Oriented Software Construction (2nd Edition)*. Professional Technical Reference. Prentice Hall, 1997.
19. A. Miné. The octagon abstract domain. In *AST 2001*.
20. I. Pollet, B. Le Charlier, and A. Cortesi. Distinctness and sharing domains for static analysis of Java programs. In *ECOOP '01*.
21. S. Rossignoli and F. Spoto. Detecting Non-Cyclicity by Abstract Compilation into Boolean Functions. In *VMCAI'06*.
22. F. Spoto. Julia: A generic static analyser for the java bytecode. In *FTfJP'05*.
23. Everest Team. Jack, Java Applet Correctness Kit.
    http://www-sop.inria.fr/everest/soft/Jack/jack.html.
24. N. Tillmann, F. Chen, and Schulte. W. Discovering likely method specifications. Technical report, Microsoft Research, 2006.

Symmetry and Completeness in the Analysis of Parameterized Systems

Kedar S. Namjoshi

Bell Labs
kedar@research.bell-labs.com

Abstract. It is shown that the *cutoff* method—which summarizes a parameterized system by a finite set of its instances—is complete for proving safety properties. This implies completeness of other, less stringent, proof methods for parameterized verification. It is shown that the cutoff method is equivalent to determining a (parameterized) inductive invariant. The second part of the paper describes a new algorithm to construct universally quantified, parameterized inductive invariants. This algorithm is shown to compute the *strongest* invariant of a given shape, and is complete under certain conditions. A key observation is a previously unnoticed connection between inductiveness, small model theorems, and compositional analysis.

1 Introduction

Parameterization is ubiquitous in programming: most programs are parameterized in some manner (e.g., the size of buffers, or the number of threads). A particularly fascinating case is that of network protocols which are composed of a variable number of finite-state, isomorphic processes. Any particular instance of this parameterized system is finite-state, and its correctness can be determined automatically through model checking. But the real goal is to verify *all*—i.e., an infinite number of—instances.

In this regard, a common experience is that the correctness argument for small instances includes all the case analysis required for full correctness. It is tempting to conjecture that there is a small bound such that the correctness of instances up to that bound suffices to establish correctness in general. Unfortunately, this conjecture is incorrect. Apt and Kozen [2] showed that the parameterized verification question—showing correctness of all instances—is undecidable, even if the component processes are finite-state and isomorphic (cf. [42]). This negative result has led naturally to two forms of analyses: (i) showing decidability for restricted classes of protocols (cf. [21,17,15]), and (ii) generally applicable, semi-automated proof principles based on induction and abstraction.

This article focuses on the general, type (ii) methods, which exploit the symmetry of the problem to reduce or to simplify proof obligations. Let P^n represent the parameterized system $P_0||P_1||...||P_{n-1}$, produced by asynchronous composition of n isomorphic copies of a process P. A central concept is that the behavior

B. Cook and A. Podelski (Eds.): VMCAI 2007, LNCS 4349, pp. 299–313, 2007.

of arbitrary instances of a protocol can be summarized by a finite-state process. The *closure process*, introduced in [9,7], is precisely such a summary. The *process invariant* method, introduced in [32,43], requires that the summarizing process, I, is also invariant, in the sense that the behavior of both P and $P||I$ is simulated by I — the stronger requirement makes it easier to show that I is a closure. The *cutoff method*, implicit in [32,21] and made explicit in [17], goes further and requires that the process invariant be a union of instances up to a (typically small) cutoff bound K. (i.e., $I = P^1 + P^2 + \ldots + P^K$). The cutoff method formalizes the verifier's intuition that all interesting patterns of behavior are already present in instances of a small size.

These proof methods have been applied successfully to several protocols, but it is not immediately apparent whether they are universally applicable. Does every correct protocol have a cutoff proof? If so, is the cutoff proportional to the individual process size?

1.1   Contributions

The first part of the paper analyzes completeness for safety (invariance) properties. It shows that an invariance property (e.g., "the protocol ensures mutual exclusion") which holds of the protocol can always be shown using a cutoff of 1 — I.e., by showing that the smallest instance simulates instances of arbitrary size, and is itself correct. This implies completeness for the two other methods. Known bounds for cutoffs[1] are either property-dependent (cf. [32,17,15]), or are exponentially large in the process description [21,16]. The cutoff of 1 holds also for arbitrary linear-time properties, and for multi-parameter systems. These results provide formal justification to the intuition regarding small instances. The proof also shows that a cutoff-based proof is equivalent to the construction of an *inductive* parameterized invariant.

The second part of the paper, therefore, focuses on automatic methods of computing inductive parameterized invariants. The starting point is a method of "invisible invariants", proposed by Pnueli, Ruah, and Zuck in [39]. The central idea is to generalize from the reachable states of small instances into an assertion of the shape $(\forall i : \varphi(i))$. Remarkably, this simple heuristic suffices to construct inductive assertion proofs of safety for several protocols. On the other hand, it is known to be incomplete: for some protocols, it fails to construct a quantified inductive invariant, even though one is known to exist.

This paper demonstrates a previously unnoticed connection between the inductiveness of quantified assertions and compositional reasoning. The key observation is that the *only* assertions of the shape $(\forall i : \varphi(i))$ which are inductive are those where actions of process $P(j)$ do not "interfere" with the inductiveness of $\varphi(i)$. This connection gives rise to an algorithm, called the *"split-invariant method"*, for the generation of quantified inductive invariants. The algorithm constructs the strongest assertion φ (in a restricted logic) such that $(\forall i : \varphi(i))$

---

[1] These are cutoffs for decidability, so they apply also to showing that a protocol incorrect, whereas the cutoff of 1 applies only to a correctness proof.

is inductive for all instances. This fact, combined with a small model theorem from [39], ensures completeness. As pleasing side-effects, non-interference explains the incompleteness of the inductive invariant method (reachable states do not always form non-interfering assertions), and also explains the occasional need to introduce auxiliary variables—it is known from work by Owicki and Gries [38] and Lamport [35] that this is necessary for non-interference. The method has been implemented with TLV [40]. Initial results show that completeness is not achieved at the cost of efficiency.

2   Completeness of the Cutoff Method

Programs are given meaning through transition systems. A transition system over a set of atomic propositions AP is a tuple (I, S, R, L), where S is a set of states, I is a subset of S, the initial states, R is a subset of $S \times S$, the transition relation, and $L : S \times 2^{AP}$ is a labeling function that assigns a subset of propositions to each state. If (s, s') is a tuple in R, s' is a *successor* of s, and there is a *transition* from s to s'. A state s is *reachable* if there is a finite sequence $s_0, s_1, \ldots s_k$ where s_0 is in I, s_{i+1} (where defined) is a successor of s_i for each i, and $s_k = s$. Transition systems are assumed to be *left-total*, i.e., every state has a successor. A *state predicate* is a Boolean combination of atomic propositions. The satisfaction of a predicate p at a state, written $s \models p$ or $p(s)$, is defined in the usual way by induction on formula structure. A state predicate φ is *invariant* of M if it holds at all reachable states of M.

Definition 0. *For transition systems M and N, and a set of state predicates SP, a relation $X : X \subseteq S_M \times S_N$ is a simulation respecting SP if:*

- *(initiality) for every initial state s of M, there is an initial state t of N such that (s, t) is in X,*
- *(step) for every (s, t) in X, and every successor s' of s, there is a successor t' of t such that (s', t') is in X,*
- *(label) for every pair (s, t) in X, and every predicate p in SP, $p_M(s) \equiv p_N(t)$*

Definition 1. *For transition systems M and N, and state predicates SP, a relation $X : S_M \times S_N$ is a bisimulation respecting SP if both X and its inverse are simulations respecting SP.*

Two transition systems are "(bi)simular *upto SP*" if there exists a (bi)simulation relation respecting SP between the transition systems. The usual definition of bisimulation between Kripke structures can be recovered by setting $SP = AP$.

Inductiveness, Invariance, and Fixpoints. A state assertion ξ is *inductive* for M if it is implied by the initial condition for M and it is preserved by every transition of M. This is formalized by the conditions (1) (initiality) and (2) (inductiveness) below. Here, *wlp* is the weakest liberal precondition transformer introduced by Dijkstra [13]. The notation $[\psi]$, from Dijkstra and Scholten [14], indicates that ψ is valid.

$$[I_M \Rightarrow \xi] \tag{1}$$
$$[\xi \Rightarrow wlp(M,\xi)] \tag{2}$$

An inductive assertion is *adequate* to show the invariance of a state property φ if it implies φ (condition (3)).

$$[\xi \Rightarrow \varphi] \tag{3}$$

Applying the duality (the Galois connection) between *wlp* and the strongest post-condition operator, *sp*, condition (2) is equivalent to

$$[sp(M,\xi) \Rightarrow \xi] \tag{4}$$

Theorem 0. *(Knaster-Tarski) A monotonic function f on a complete lattice has a least fixpoint, which is also the strongest solution to $X : [f(X) \Rightarrow X]$, and a greatest fixpoint, which is the weakest solution to $X : [X \Rightarrow f(X)]$.*

For *finite* lattices, the least fixpoint can be computed as the limit of the sequence $X_0 = \bot; X_{i+1} = f(X_i)$. The greatest fixpoint can be computed as the limit of the sequence $X_0 = \top; X_{i+1} = f(X_i)$, where $\top$ and $\bot$ are, respectively, the top and bottom elements of the lattice.

Taken together, conditions (1) and (4) give $[(I_M \vee sp(M,\xi)) \Rightarrow \xi]$. As function $f(\xi) = I_M \vee sp(M,\xi)$ is monotonic, by the Knaster-Tarski theorem, it has a least fixpoint, which is the set of reachable states of M. Taken together, conditions (2) and (3) give $[\xi \Rightarrow (\varphi \wedge wlp(M,\xi))]$. The function $g(\xi) = \varphi \wedge wlp(M,\xi)$ is monotonic, hence there is a greatest solution in ξ. This is expressed in CTL as $\mathsf{AG}(\varphi)$. If φ is invariant for M, the reachable states of M additionally satisfies (3), and $\mathsf{AG}(\varphi)$ additionally satisfies (1).

2.1   Completeness

Lemma 0. *Any pair of transition systems M, N which satisfy the invariance property $\mathsf{AG}(\varphi)$ are bisimular upto $\{\varphi\}$.*

Proof. Define the relation X between states of M and N by $(s,t) \in X$ iff $M, s \models \mathsf{AG}(\varphi)$ and $N, t \models \mathsf{AG}(\varphi)$. We have to show that X and its inverse are simulation relations respecting $\{\varphi\}$.

(initiality) consider initial states s and t of M and N respectively. By the assumption, both s and t satisfy $\mathsf{AG}(\varphi)$, and are therefore related by X.

(step) Let s, t be such that $(s,t) \in X$, and let s' be a successor of s. As s satisfies $\mathsf{AG}(\varphi)$, by the fixpoint formulation, all of its successors also satisfy $\mathsf{AG}(\varphi)$. For the same reason, all successors of t satisfy $\mathsf{AG}(\varphi)$, and t has at least one successor, say t', as N is left-total. Thus, (s',t') is a pair in X. A symmetric argument establishes the step property for the inverse of X.

(label) Let s, t be such that $(s, t) \in X$. As s and t satisfy $\mathsf{AG}(\varphi)$, by the fixpoint formulation, they satisfy φ. As φ is a state predicate, $\varphi_M(s) \equiv \varphi_N(t)$. $\square$

The cutoff method is defined below for arbitrary parameterized programs—not just those arising from a composition of processes. A parameterized program is a family of transition systems $\{M(n)\}$, indexed by a parameter n. The property is also parameterized by n; for instance, mutual exclusion between critical sections, identified by C, can be specified by $\varphi(n) = (\forall i, j : i, j \in [0..n-1] \wedge i \neq j : \neg(C_i \wedge C_j))$.

Definition 2. *[**Cutoff Method**] To show that a parameterized program $M(n)$ satisfies a similarly parameterized invariance property $\mathsf{AG}(\varphi(n))$ for all n, find a cutoff bound K such that:*

- *For every $n : n > K$, there is $j : j \leq K$ such that $M(n)$ is simulated upto φ by $M(j)$, and*
- *For every $j : j \leq K$, $M(j)$ satisfies $\mathsf{AG}(\varphi(j))$.*

Theorem 1. *The cutoff method is complete for invariance properties: i.e., if $M(n)$ satisfies $\mathsf{AG}(\varphi(n))$ for all n, there is a cutoff bound K such that the conditions are met. In particular, $K = 1$ suffices.*

Proof. Let $K = 1$. As $M(n)$ satisfies $\mathsf{AG}(\varphi(n))$ for all n, the second condition is met: $M(1)$ satisfies $\mathsf{AG}(\varphi(1))$.

Consider $M(n)$, for any $n : n > 1$. As $M(n)$ satisfies $\mathsf{AG}(\varphi(n))$, and $M(1)$ satisfies $\mathsf{AG}(\varphi(1))$, a proof on the lines of that for Lemma 0 shows that $M(1)$ and $M(n)$ are bisimular upto φ. The only modification to the previous proof is in the definition of X. A pair (s, t) is in X (where s is a state of $M(1)$ and t is a state of $M(n)$) if $M(1), s$ satisfies $\mathsf{AG}(\varphi(1))$ and $M(n), t$ satisfies $\mathsf{AG}(\varphi(n))$. This proves the first condition. $\square$

To illustrate the workings of this theorem by an example, consider the simple mutual exclusion protocol[2] described in Figure 1. The desired invariant predicate $\varphi(n)$ is $(\forall i, j : i, j \in [n] \wedge i \neq j : \neg(C_i \wedge C_j))$, where C_i is shorthand for $(st(i) = C)$. It is easily checked that this predicate is **not** inductive. The completeness proof works with any predicate that is inductive and is stronger than φ. One such predicate is $\xi(n) = (\forall i, j : i, j \in [n] \wedge i \neq j : (C_i \vee E_i) \Rightarrow (x \wedge \neg(C_j \vee E_j)))$. The bisimulation relation defined in the completeness proof relates state s of P^n with t of P^1 if they agree on ξ. As $\xi(1) = true$, every state of P^n is bisimular (in the new sense) to any state of P^1!

The completeness proof constructs a bisimulation from $\mathsf{AG}(\varphi(n))$. In fact, any inductive invariant stronger than φ will do: $\mathsf{AG}(\varphi)$ is simply the weakest such assertion. Determining an appropriate simulation relation, and finding a proof of a candidate relation, are both difficult questions, which are undecidable in general. Similarly, determining whether a protocol has a particular cutoff bound is also undecidable, in general. The following theorem establishes the converse.

---

[2] This protocol is taken from [39] but with a change of notation.

```
var x: boolean /* semaphore */
initially x=true

process P(i) ::
  var st: {I,T,C,E}
  initially st=I
  do
  | (st=I) -> st := T
  | (st=T) and x -> st,x := C,false
  | (st=C) -> st := E
  | (st=E) -> st,x := I,true
  od
```

Fig. 1. Mutual Exclusion Protocol

Theorem 2. *A cutoff proof of invariance for program $M(n)$ and property $\varphi(n)$ induces an assertion $\xi(n)$ that is inductive for $M(n)$, and implies $\varphi(n)$.*

3   Parameterized Invariants and Non-interference

The discussion in Section 2 showed that the existence of cutoffs for invariance properties is equivalent to the existence of parameterized inductive invariants. The "invisible invariant" method of [39] computes inductive predicates of the shape $(\forall i : \theta(i))$, where θ is a limited assertion. It consists of two steps: in the first step, a candidate for θ is constructed by generalizing the set of reachable states of small instances up to a cutoff size N_0; in the second step, the generated candidate, $(\forall i : \theta(i))$, is checked for inductiveness and adequacy for arbitrary N. The second step can be automated based on a *small model theorem*, which shows that these properties need to be checked only up to a second cutoff N_1.

In a series of papers [3,4] the authors showed that this simple heuristic suffices to show correctness of a number of parameterized protocols. On the other hand, the authors also point out that this method is not guaranteed to succeed—even if a suitable invariant exists, generalization from the reachable states may fail for some protocols [4].

To understand the source of incompleteness, it is helpful to reason in reverse from the goal: how does an assumption of inductive invariance for $(\forall i : \theta(i))$ constrain θ? A first consequence is that $\theta(0)$ must be inductive for process 0 in an instance of size 1. Thus, it suffices to enumerate every inductive invariant for process 0 in $M(1)$, and check inductiveness for all N by applying the small model theorem. (The set of inductive assertions forms a lattice with top element $\mathsf{AG}(\varphi(1))$ and bottom element the reachable states.) While complete, the procedure is extremely inefficient, as there could be exponentially many inductive invariants for process 0. (If a process state is described by k Boolean variables, there are 2^{2^k} distinct Boolean expressions to consider.) While this line of reasoning does not lead to a useful algorithm, it does suggest that generalizing the set of reachable states — just one out of many candidates — need not give rise to a parameterized invariant.

Let us continue by analyzing the case $N = 2$. Parameterized inductiveness of $(\forall i : \theta(i))$ implies the following inductiveness conditions for $N = 2$. (The notation $P_0(2)$ represents process 0 in a 2-process composition $M(2) = P_0 \| P_1$. The symmetric condition for $P_1(2)$ is not shown.)

$$[I_{M(2)} \Rightarrow (\theta(0) \wedge \theta(1))] \tag{5}$$
$$[(\theta(0) \wedge \theta(1)) \Rightarrow wlp(P_0(2), \theta(0) \wedge \theta(1))] \tag{6}$$

As wlp distributes over conjunction, (6) is equivalent to

$$[(\theta(0) \wedge \theta(1)) \Rightarrow wlp(P_0(2), \theta(0))] \tag{7}$$
$$[(\theta(0) \wedge \theta(1)) \Rightarrow wlp(P_0(2), \theta(1))] \tag{8}$$

The first is expected: it says (roughly) that $\theta(0)$ is preserved by transitions of process P_0. The second is quite different in nature: it says that $\theta(1)$ is *also* preserved by transitions of process P_0—i.e., process P_0 *does not interfere* with the invariance of $\theta(1)$. The notion of non-interference was introduced by Owicki and Gries in their seminal work on compositional reasoning [38]. The rest of this section explores this connection in detail.

3.1   Background

The class of parameterized programs to which the invisible invariant method is applied is called *bounded-data discrete systems* (BDS's) [39,3]. Program variables can be Boolean and finite-domain variables (type $\mathbf{T}_0$), variables with ranges $[0..N_i - 1]$, for a parameter N_i (types $\mathbf{T}_i$), and arrays with domain $\mathbf{T}_i$ and elements from $\mathbf{T}_j$ for some i, j (types $\mathbf{T}_i \mapsto \mathbf{T}_j$).

Atomic formulas can only compare for inequality basic expressions of the same type. Basic expressions are limited to variables x, or 1-level indexed entries $Z[x]$ (not $Z[Z[x]]$). Formulas are built up from atomic formulas by Boolean combination, and quantification. The transition relation of a parameterized system is constrained to the shape $(\exists h_1, h_2, \ldots, h_k : (\forall t_1, t_2, \ldots, t_m : R(h, t)))$, where h_i, t_i are vectors of variables of $\mathbf{T}_i$, for all i. Intuitively, the h-variables identify the process that makes a transition, the t-variables are used to express the constraint that a transition by one process leaves the local state of all other processes unchanged. The expression defining the initial condition is assumed to be symmetric (i.e., left unchanged by permutations of indices). For example, the protocol from Figure 1 has types $x : \mathbf{T}_0$ and $state : \mathbf{T}_1 \mapsto \mathbf{T}_0$; its initial condition is $x \wedge (\forall i : state(i) = I)$.

Candidate invariance assertions have the shape $(\forall i_1, i_2, \ldots, i_k : \theta(i_1, i_2, \ldots, i_k))$, where i_m is a vector of variables of type $\mathbf{T}_m$, for each m, and the variables of any given type are given distinct values. An example is the mutual exclusion property: $(\forall i, j : i \neq j : \neg(C_i \wedge C_j))$, where $i, j : \mathbf{T}_1$.

3.2   Non-interference and Split Invariants

Consider a program, $A\|B$, formed by the *asynchronous* composition of processes A and B, and a correctness property φ. Let A (B) have state defined by sets of variables V_A (V_B). A *local* assertion (for A; symmetrically for B) is an assertion formed from V_A. Variables local to A are denoted by $L_A = V_A \setminus V_B$, while the global (shared) variables are those in $V_A \cap V_B$.

A pair of assertions (θ_A, θ_B), which are local over A and B, respectively, is called a *split assertion*. A split assertion (θ_A, θ_B) is a *split invariant* if $\theta_A \wedge \theta_B$ is an inductive invariant for $A\|B$. For asynchronous composition, the invariance conditions obtained from (1)-(3) simplify to the following.

$$[I_{A\|B} \Rightarrow (\theta_A \wedge \theta_B)] \tag{9}$$
$$[(\theta_A \wedge \theta_B) \Rightarrow wlp(A, (\theta_A \wedge \theta_B))] \tag{10}$$
$$[(\theta_A \wedge \theta_B) \Rightarrow wlp(B, (\theta_A \wedge \theta_B))] \tag{11}$$

A split invariant satisfies a property φ if

$$[(\theta_A \wedge \theta_B) \Rightarrow \varphi] \tag{12}$$

A k-split assertion over k processes $P_0\|P_1 \ldots \|P_{k-1}$ (these are not necessarily isomorphic) is a k-vector of the form $(\theta_0, \ldots, \theta_{k-1})$ where each θ_i is defined over the variables of P_i. It is a k-split invariant if $(\forall i : \theta_i)$ is an inductive invariant of the k-process system.

Computing the strongest split invariant. Applying the Galois connection between wlp and sp to (10) and (11), combining with (9), and re-arranging results in the following equivalent formulation. The existential quantification encodes locality: e.g., variables quantified out in (13) are irrelevant to θ_A by locality.

$$[(\exists L_B : sp(A, \theta_A \wedge \theta_B) \vee sp(B, \theta_A \wedge \theta_B) \vee I) \Rightarrow \theta_A] \tag{13}$$
$$[(\exists L_A : sp(A, \theta_A \wedge \theta_B) \vee sp(B, \theta_A \wedge \theta_B) \vee I) \Rightarrow \theta_B] \tag{14}$$

Implications (13) and (14), in turn, can be written as the pre-fixpoint formulation: $[\mathcal{F}(\theta_A, \theta_B) \preceq (\theta_A, \theta_B)]$, where $\mathcal{F}$ is the pair function formed by the left-hand expressions in the implication, and $\preceq$ denotes pair-wise implication. Since $\mathcal{F}$ is monotone over (θ_A, θ_B) according to $\preceq$ (sp is a monotone function), by the Knaster-Tarski theorem, $\mathcal{F}$ has a *least* fixpoint, which, by construction, is also the least solution to conditions (9)-(11).

The Knaster-Tarski algorithm applied to $\mathcal{F}$ results in the least fixpoint (θ_A^*, θ_B^*), which is the *strongest* inductive split assertion. The operations required to evaluate $\mathcal{F}$ (the computation of sp, existential quantification) can be carried out with BDD's for finite variable domains.

Theorem 3. *(Completeness of the procedure) There exists an inductive split-invariant that is adequate for φ if, and only if, $[(\theta_A^* \wedge \theta_B^*) \Rightarrow \varphi]$.*

This method is easily extended to compute the strongest k-split invariant over a k-process instance. The general form of $\mathcal{F}$ is represented as $\mathcal{F}^k$, which is a vector of functions over a k-split assertion $\theta = (\theta_0, \ldots, \theta_{k-1})$. For each $i \in [k]$, the ith component of $\mathcal{F}^k(\theta)$ is given below, where $L = (\cup i : L_i)$ is the set of local variables.

$$\mathcal{F}_i^k(\theta) = (\exists L \setminus L_i : init(k) \vee (\exists j : sp(P_j(k), (\forall m : \theta_m)))) \tag{15}$$

For a parameterized system, the symmetry in its definition ensures that, during the fixpoint calculation, it is necessary only to compute the new value for a single component, say $\theta(0)$; $\theta(i)$ is constructed by applying the substitution $0 \mapsto i$.

Theorem 4. *(Symmetric split invariant) For a parameterized instance, P^k, with a symmetric initial condition, there is an assertion $\theta^*(V_i)$ such that the least fixpoint of $\mathcal{F}^k$ is given by $(\forall i : \theta^*(V_i))$.*

3.3 Quantified Inductive Invariants

The previous discussion showed that, for a parameterized system, (i) for any *inductive* quantified assertion $(\forall i : \theta(i))$, the vector $(\theta(0), \ldots, \theta(k-1))$ is a symmetric k-split invariant for all k; and (ii) for any k, the *strongest* k-split invariant can be computed through a least fixpoint procedure, and this is symmetric. In this section, we close the loop by showing that, given a small model property for an assertion logic $\mathcal{L}$ with bound K, the assertion $(\forall i : \theta^*(i))$ induced by the strongest K-split invariant is an inductive parameterized invariant.

Definition 3. *("Near-inductive" invariant) A quantified assertion (e.g., $(\forall i : \theta(i)))$ is K-inductive if it is inductive for all instances of size at least K. An assertion is near-inductive if it is K-inductive for some K.*

Definition 4. *(Small Model Property) For any θ in $\mathcal{L}$, checks of the form (9)-(12) for an assertion $(\forall i : \theta(i))$ are valid for all N if, and only if, there exists K such that they are valid for all instances of size up to K. The bound K may depend on the quantification over i, but should be independent of θ.*

A *strong* small model property holds if validity need be checked only for the instance of size K. In [3], the small model property is shown for BDS's with variables of type $\mathbf{T}_0, \mathbf{T}_1$, and $\mathbf{T}_1 \mapsto \mathbf{T}_2$. The proof can be strengthened to show the stronger form of this property.

Let V_i be the set of variables accessed by process i (local as well as global). The computation of K-split invariants on general BDS's does not necessarily produce assertions that are expressible in the logic $\mathcal{L}$. In order to ensure this, let α_i be the closure operator, defined as follows: $\alpha_i^K(S)$, for an index $i \in [K]$ and a set of states S in $M(K)$, is the smallest superset of S that is expressible in the logic $\mathcal{L}$ together with the assertion $y = i$ for each $\mathbf{T}_1$ variable y (this is well-defined if $\mathcal{L}$ is closed under arbitrary intersection). The closure operator can be computed using BDD's if $\mathcal{L}$ is based on a finite set of predicates[3].

The condition $[\alpha_i^K(\theta(V_i)) \Rightarrow \theta(V_i)]$ is added to the fixpoint formulation for $\mathcal{F}$. This defines a new monotonic operator, written $\mathcal{F}_{\alpha,i}^K(\theta) = \alpha_i^K(\theta(V_i)) \vee \mathcal{F}_i^K(\theta)$. Not only is any pre-fixpoint $\theta(V_i)$ of this operator a pre-fixpoint of $\mathcal{F}_i^K$ (which is desired for inductiveness), it is also a pre-fixpoint of α_i^K, which ensures that (as α is a closure) $[\alpha_i^K(\theta(V_i)) \equiv \theta(V_i)]$; i.e., $\theta(V_i)$ is expressible in $\mathcal{L}$.

Theorem 5. *(Completeness) For a BDS with a strong small model property and bound K, and assertions of the type $(\forall i : \theta(V_i))$, let $\theta^*(V_i)$ describe the symmetric K-split invariant computed as the strongest fixpoint of $\mathcal{F}_\alpha^K$. Then, $(\forall i : \theta^*(V_i))$ is K-inductive, and this is the strongest such assertion.*

Proof. By the preceding discussion, any fixpoint of $\mathcal{F}_\alpha^K$ is expressible in the logic $\mathcal{L}$ and is a K-split invariant.

We need to show K-inductiveness, i.e., that $(\forall i : \theta^*(V_i))$ is inductive for all $N : N \geq K$. The proof is by contradiction. If the assertion is non-inductive for some N, the strong form of the small model property implies that it is non-inductive for the instance of size K, which contradicts the assumption that it is a K-split invariant. Note that it is important that the bound K is independent of the particular θ^*.

Any K-inductive assertion of the shape $(\forall i : \theta(V_i))$ that is expressible in $\mathcal{L}$ is a K-split invariant. This implies that θ is a pre-fixpoint of $\mathcal{F}_\alpha^K$. As θ^* is the strongest pre-fixpoint, $[\theta^*(V_i) \Rightarrow \theta(V_i)]$; hence, $[(\forall i : \theta^*(V_i)) \Rightarrow (\forall i : \theta(V_i))]$.
□

The strong form of the small model property can be dispensed with, at the cost of computing a weaker inductive assertion. For a simpler notation, this is explained for $\mathcal{F}^K$, not $\mathcal{F}_\alpha^K$. The computation of θ^* is set up so that it is a k-split invariant, for *every* $k : k \leq K$. Recall, from the discussion following Theorem 4, that the computation of a k-split invariant can be carried out by computing $\theta(V_0)$ using $\mathcal{F}_0^k(\theta)$, deriving the others by substitution. Thus, consider the assertion that $[(\mathcal{F}_0^k(\theta))(V_0) \Rightarrow \theta(V_0)]$ for all $k : k \leq K$. This is equivalent to

$$[(\exists k : k \leq K : (\mathcal{F}_0^k(\theta))(V_0)) \Rightarrow \theta(V_0)] \tag{16}$$

The left-hand side of the implication defines a new monotonic operator: $\mathcal{G}_0^K(\theta) = (\exists k : k \leq K : \mathcal{F}_0^k(\theta))$. This is used in place of $\mathcal{F}_\alpha^K$ in Theorem 5. While this substitution ensures inductiveness for all N, the additional $\mathcal{F}$ computations that are required could cause computational difficulty in practice. Moreover, as $\mathcal{G}^K$ is weaker than $\mathcal{F}^K$, the fixpoint that is produced is also a weaker assertion. This makes it less likely to satisfy the correctness condition. From these considerations, it appears that the weaker K-inductiveness requirement is preferable to inductiveness for all N.

---

[3] For a set of predicates $\{P_i\}$, $\alpha(S)(x) = (\exists y : (\bigwedge i : P_i(x) \equiv P_i(y)) \wedge S(y))$.

3.4 Simple BDS's

The simplest case of a BDS is one where all global variables are of type $\mathbf{T}_0$, and the local variables are expressed by an array of type $\mathbf{T}_1 \mapsto \mathbf{T}_0$. This simple case is important, as it describes, for instance, the mutual exclusion protocol from Figure 1, and many multi-threaded programs, where the data structures that the threads operate on have a structure that is independent of the number of threads. For a simple BDS, the small model bounds are very small: 2 processes for a singly-quantified assertion $(\forall i : \theta(i))$, and 3 processes for a doubly-quantified assertion $(\forall i, j : i < j : \theta(i, j))$.

4 Experiments

This method has been implemented with TLV [40]. This implementation succeeds on several of the examples from [4]. Preliminary results are shown in Figure 2; details are at http://www.cs.bell-labs.com/who/kedar/split-invariance. The implementation generates quantified inductive assertions of the shape $(\forall i : \theta(i))$ and $(\forall i, j : i \neq j : \theta(i, j))$, denoted by 1-$\forall$ and 2-$\forall$, respectively.

The completeness of the split invariant calculation, especially the fact that it computes the *strongest* assertion, can be used to advantage. If the strongest split invariant θ_K^* calculated for an instance of size K fails the adequacy test, there can be no other θ' for which $(\forall i : \theta'(i))$ is inductive for all N. Thus, a failure indicates that there is no inductive invariant of the particular shape.

It is possible to dualize the theory presented here to compute "best" existential invariants, i.e., assertions of the form $(\exists i : \theta(i))$ where θ is the weakest formula for which the assertion is inductive and implies the correctness property. (This corresponds to the least/greatest fixpoint duality in the computation of the reachable states and $\mathsf{AG}(\phi)$.)

Some of the more difficult properties proved by the IIV tool require inductive assertions that are combinations of universal and existential properties. (The fact that something more than pure universal or existential invariants are required can be inferred by the failure to compute such a split invariant, as discussed above.) IIV uses a heuristic method (which may fail) to construct a Boolean combination of universal and existential assertions. It is not clear whether there is a complete and efficient method to construct such mixed invariants—our current implementation fails to prove these properties automatically. It is possible to replace (Skolemize) the existential quantifications with auxiliary program

Program	Invariant Type	Time(sec)	Bound	BDD size $\theta(1)$ or $\theta(1,2)$	Max. BDD
mutex	2-$\forall$	0.01	4	9	1327
mutex+	1-$\forall$	0.01	3	8	1007
szymanski	2-$\forall$	0.03	4	18	9956
token-ring	2-$\forall$	0.01	4	177	18341

Fig. 2. Results on the IIV examples (+ indicates introduction of auxiliary variables)

variables, leaving purely universal quantification that can be handled by the split-invariant method, but this requires a guess at the definition of the auxiliary variable. Devising a systematic procedure for introducing such variables is an important open question; ideas from the "environment abstraction" work [10] might be of help.

5 Related Work

There is a large body of work on parameterized verification and compositional analysis, the two subjects most closely connected with the topic of this paper.

The parameterized verification question is decidable for some classes: [21,17,15] are representative. These results are based on small model theorems for *temporal* properties. General methods for parameterized verification include those discussed in the introduction and others based on process summaries (cf. [36,31,41]) and acceleration methods based on automata-theory (cf. [30,1]). This earlier work does not consider completeness: the results on cutoffs, and the connection to inductive invariance are new contributions.

Compositional reasoning about concurrency goes back to the seminal work on non-interference by Owicki and Gries [38], extended to assume-guarantee reasoning by Chandy and Misra, and Jones [8,27,28]. (The book [12] has the history and technical relationships.) Flanagan and Qadeer apply the assume-guarantee approach to the verification of fixed instances of multi-threaded programs [20,18]. Assume-guarantee reasoning is combined with program abstraction in the BLAST tool [24]. These verification procedures are formulated for fixed-size instances, and do not, in general, lead to a correctness proof of a full parameterized system. The relationship between parameterized invariance, small model theorems, and compositional reasoning that forms the basis of the split-invariant method is also a new contribution.

Predicate abstraction [22] has been quite successful in deriving inductive invariants for non-parameterized programs [5,23]. Predicate abstraction is extended to derive quantified indexed predicates (typically for parameterized data structures) in [19,33]. This method is analyzed, and shown to be complete in [34], provided an appropriate indexed predicate set is given. The papers [19,33] give heuristics to determine this set, but the heuristics are not known to be complete.

It is worthwhile to compare the approaches based on predicate abstraction with indexed predicates and invisible/split invariants in a little more detail. Both have a common goal: to construct universally quantified invariants for parameterized programs. The indexed predicate method approaches this problem from "above", exploring a succession of abstract transition systems, all of which over-approximate the entire parameterized system. On the other hand, the invisible/split invariant method approaches this from "below", exploring successively larger instances of the parameterized system. Thus, split invariants always define states that are necessarily part of any inductive invariant, while indexed predicate exploration requires removal of non-inductive states. It is unclear which method performs better in practice; but there may be fruitful ways of combining these different approximation approaches — this is the subject of ongoing work. Another interesting question for future work is whether the small model theorems in the BDS framework can be extended to apply to two examples identified in [33] that are outside the current class of BDS's; new results in [6] on array properties, and completeness results for (non-parameterized) predicate abstraction from [37,25,26] may apply here.

Acknowledgements. Thanks to the authors of the IIV tool [4], especially Ittai Balaban, for making their examples accessible. Thanks also to Ariel Cohen for discussions on split invariants, and for help with TLV. This research is supported, in part, by NSF grant CCR-0341658.

References

1. Parosh Aziz Abdulla, Ahmed Bouajjani, Bengt Jonsson, and Marcus Nilsson. Handling global conditions in parameterized system verification. In *CAV*, volume 1633 of *LNCS*, pages 134–145, 1999.
2. Krzysztof R. Apt and Dexter Kozen. Limits for automatic verification of finite-state concurrent systems. *Inf. Process. Lett.*, 22(6):307–309, 1986.
3. Tamarah Arons, Amir Pnueli, Sitvanit Ruah, Jiazhao Xu, and Lenore D. Zuck. Parameterized verification with automatically computed inductive assertions. In *CAV*, volume 2102 of *LNCS*, pages 221–234, 2001.
4. Ittai Balaban, Yi Fang, Amir Pnueli, and Lenore D. Zuck. IIV: An invisible invariant verifier. In *CAV*, volume 3576 of *LNCS*, pages 408–412, 2005.
5. T. Ball and S. K. Rajamani. The SLAM toolkit. In *CAV*, volume 2102 of *LNCS*. Springer Verlag, 2001.
6. Aaron R. Bradley, Zohar Manna, and Henny B. Sipma. What's decidable about arrays? In *VMCAI*, volume 3855 of *LNCS*, pages 427–442, 2006.
7. Michael C. Browne, Edmund M. Clarke, and Orna Grumberg. Reasoning about networks with many identical finite state processes. *Inf. Comput.*, 81(1):13–31, 1989.
8. K.M. Chandy and J. Misra. Proofs of networks of processes. *IEEE Transactions on Software Engineering*, 7(4), 1981.
9. Edmund M. Clarke and Orna Grumberg. Avoiding the state explosion problem in temporal logic model checking. In *PODC*, pages 294–303, 1987.
10. Edmund M. Clarke, Muralidhar Talupur, and Helmut Veith. Environment abstraction for parameterized verification. In *VMCAI*, volume 3855 of *LNCS*, pages 126–141, 2006.
11. D. Dams and K.S. Namjoshi. The existence of finite abstractions for branching time model checking. In *LICS*, 2004.
12. W-P. de Roever, F. de Boer, U. Hannemann, J. Hooman, Y. Lakhnech, M. Poel, and J. Zwiers. *Concurrency Verification: Introduction to Compositional and Noncompositional Proof Methods.* Cambridge University Press, 2001.
13. E.W. Dijkstra. Guarded commands, nondeterminacy, and formal derivation of programs. *CACM*, 18(8), 1975.
14. E.W. Dijkstra and C.S. Scholten. *Predicate Calculus and Program Semantics.* Springer Verlag, 1990.

15. E. Allen Emerson and Vineet Kahlon. Reducing model checking of the many to the few. In *CADE*, volume 1831 of *LNCS*, pages 236–254, 2000.
16. E. Allen Emerson and Kedar S. Namjoshi. Automatic verification of parameterized synchronous systems (extended abstract). In *CAV*, volume 1102 of *LNCS*, pages 87–98, 1996.
17. E.A. Emerson and K.S. Namjoshi. Reasoning about rings. In *ACM Symposium on Principles of Programming Languages*, 1995.
18. Cormac Flanagan, Stephen N. Freund, Shaz Qadeer, and Sanjit A. Seshia. Modular verification of multithreaded programs. *Theor. Comput. Sci.*, 338(1-3):153–183, 2005.
19. Cormac Flanagan and Shaz Qadeer. Predicate abstraction for software verification. In *POPL*, pages 191–202, 2002.
20. Cormac Flanagan and Shaz Qadeer. Thread-modular model checking. In *SPIN*, volume 2648 of *LNCS*, pages 213–224, 2003.
21. S. German and A.P. Sistla. Reasoning about systems with many processes. *Journal of the ACM*, 1992.
22. S. Graf and H. Saïdi. Construction of abstract state graphs with PVS. In *CAV*, volume 1254 of *LNCS*, 1997.
23. T. A. Henzinger, R. Jhala, R. Majumdar, G. C. Necula, G. Sutre, and W. Weimer. Temporal-safety proofs for systems code. In *CAV*, volume 2404 of *LNCS*, 2002.
24. Thomas A. Henzinger, Ranjit Jhala, Rupak Majumdar, and Shaz Qadeer. Thread-modular abstraction refinement. In *CAV*, volume 2725 of *LNCS*, pages 262–274, 2003.
25. Thomas A. Henzinger, Ranjit Jhala, Rupak Majumdar, and Grégoire Sutre. Lazy abstraction. In *POPL*, pages 58–70, 2002.
26. Ranjit Jhala and Kenneth L. McMillan. A practical and complete approach to predicate refinement. In *TACAS*, volume 3920 of *LNCS*, pages 459–473, 2006.
27. C.B. Jones. *Development methods for computer programs including a notion of interference*. PhD thesis, Oxford University, 1981.
28. C.B. Jones. Tentative steps toward a development method for interfering programs. *ACM Trans. on Programming Languages and Systems (TOPLAS)*, 1983.
29. Y. Kesten and A. Pnueli. Verification by augmented finitary abstraction. *Information and Computation*, 163(1), 2000.
30. Yonit Kesten, Oded Maler, Monica Marcus, Amir Pnueli, and Elad Shahar. Symbolic model checking with rich ssertional languages. In *CAV*, volume 1254 of *LNCS*, pages 424–435, 1997.
31. Yonit Kesten and Amir Pnueli. Control and data abstraction: The cornerstones of practical formal verification. *STTT*, 2(4):328–342, 2000.
32. Robert P. Kurshan and Kenneth L. McMillan. A structural induction theorem for processes. In *PODC*, pages 239–247, 1989.
33. Shuvendu K. Lahiri and Randal E. Bryant. Constructing quantified invariants via predicate abstraction. In *VMCAI*, volume 2937 of *LNCS*, pages 267–281, 2004.
34. Shuvendu K. Lahiri and Randal E. Bryant. Indexed predicate discovery for unbounded system verification. In *CAV*, volume 3114 of *LNCS*, pages 135–147, 2004.
35. Leslie Lamport. Proving the correctness of multiprocess programs. *IEEE Trans. Software Eng.*, 3(2), 1977.
36. Ranko Lazic and David Nowak. A unifying approach to data-independence. In *CONCUR*, volume 1877 of *LNCS*, pages 581–595, 2000.
37. K. S. Namjoshi and R. P. Kurshan. Syntactic program transformations for automatic abstraction. In *CAV*, volume 1855 of *LNCS*. Springer Verlag, 2000.

38. Susan S. Owicki and David Gries. Verifying properties of parallel programs: An axiomatic approach. *Commun. ACM*, 19(5):279–285, 1976.
39. Amir Pnueli, Sitvanit Ruah, and Lenore D. Zuck. Automatic deductive verification with invisible invariants. In *TACAS*, volume 2031 of *LNCS*, pages 82–97, 2001.
40. Amir Pnueli and Elad Shahar. A platform for combining deductive with algorithmic verification. In *CAV*, volume 1102 of *LNCS*, pages 184–195, 1996. web: www.cs.nyu.edu/acsys/tlv.
41. Amir Pnueli, Elad Shahar, and Lenore D. Zuck. Network invariants in action. In *CONCUR*, volume 2421 of *LNCS*, pages 101–115, 2002.
42. Ichiro Suzuki. Proving properties of a ring of finite-state machines. *Inf. Process. Lett.*, 28(4):213–214, 1988.
43. Pierre Wolper and Vinciane Lovinfosse. Verifying properties of large sets of processes with network invariants. In *Automatic Verification Methods for Finite State Systems*, volume 407 of *LNCS*, pages 68–80, 1989.

Better Under-Approximation of Programs
by Hiding Variables

Thomas Ball[1] and Orna Kupferman[2]

[1] Microsoft Research, One Microsoft way, Redmond, WA, 98052, USA
tball@microsoft.com
research.microsoft.com/~tball
[2] Hebrew University, School of Eng. and Comp. Sci., Jerusalem 91904, Israel
orna@cs.huji.ac.il
www.cs.huji.ac.il/~orna

Abstract. Abstraction frameworks use under-approximating transitions in order to prove existential properties of concrete systems. Under-approximating transitions refer to the concrete states that correspond to a particular abstract state in a universal manner. For example, there is a *must* transition from abstract state a to abstract state a' only if all the concrete states in a have successors in a'.

The universal nature of under-approximating transitions makes them closed under transitivity. Consequently, reachability queries about the concrete system, which have applications in falsification and testing, can be answered by reasoning about its abstraction. On the negative side, the universal nature of under-approximating transitions makes them dependent on all the variables of the program. The abstraction, on the other hand, often hides some of the variables. Since the universal quantification in must transitions ranges over all variables, this often prevents the abstraction from associating a must transition with statements that refer to hidden variables.

We introduce and study *partitioned-must* transitions. The idea is to partition the program variables to relevant and irrelevant ones, and restrict the universal quantification inside must transitions to the relevant variables. Usual must transitions are a special case of partitioned-must transitions in which all variables are relevant. Partitioned-must transitions exist in many realistic settings in which usual must transitions do not exist. As we show, they retain the advantages of must transitions: they are closed under transitivity, their calculation can be automated, and the three-valued semantics induced by usual must transitions is refined to a multi-valued semantics that takes into an account the set of relevant variables.

1   Introduction

Abstraction frameworks [CC77] generally use *over-approximation* to check safety properties. If a safety property holds in the abstract (over-approximate) system then it holds in the concrete system that it abstracts. However, if the safety property does not hold in the abstract system, we do not know if the concrete system violates the safety property.

Since the ideal goal of proving a system correct involves many obstacles, the primary use of formal methods nowadays is *falsification*. There, as in *testing*, the goal is to detect errors, rather than to prove correctness. In the falsification setting, we are interested

B. Cook and A. Podelski (Eds.): VMCAI 2007, LNCS 4349, pp. 314–328, 2007.

in using abstractions based on *under-approximation*. This allows us to prove that if a safety property does not hold in the abstract system then it does not hold in the concrete system. Our investigations are based on modal transition systems (MTS) [LT88], which combine both overapproximation and under-approximation. Traditional MTSs have two types of transitions: *may* (over-approximating transitions) and *must* (under-approximating transitions).

A must transition from an abstract state a to an abstract state a' implies that for all concrete states c that correspond to a there is a successor concrete state c' that corresponds to a'. The importance of must transitions comes from the fact they are closed under transitivity: if there is a sequence of must transitions from a to a', we can conclude that all concrete states c that correspond to a can reach some concrete state c' that corresponds to a'.

Unfortunately, must transitions are very fragile with respect to updates of *irrelevant variables*. To see this, consider, for example, two abstract states $(x > 6)$ and $(x > 8)$. Assume that the statement if y=0 then {x:=x+4;read(y)} is executed at $(x > 6)$. Since the abstraction ignores the variable y, and not all the concrete states in $(x > 6)$ have $y = 0$, there is no must transition from $(x > 6)$ to $(x > 8)$. For example, the concrete state $\langle 7, 1 \rangle$ has no successor state in $(x > 8)$. Current abstraction frameworks would therefore include a may transition from $(x > 6)$ to $(x > 8)$, and are likely to end up refining these states with predicates that refer to y.

This is needlessly too weak. A may transition only guarantees reachability for existentially quantified values of x and y: there exist values of x and y satisfying $(x > 6)$ for which there exist successor values satisfying $(x > 8)$. The actual situation, however, has a richer type of reachability, in which we can quantify the value of x universally and quantify only the value of y existentially. In this work we introduce and study *partitioned must* transitions, which enable us to capture situations as above.

In order to understand our partitioned-must transitions, let us first recall earlier efforts to extend the usefulness of must transitions. Consider again the abstract states $(x > 8)$ and $(x > 6)$, and assume that the statement x:=x-4 is executed at $(x > 8)$. Since there are concrete states satisfying $x > 8$ (namely $x = 9$ and $x = 10$) for which the assignment statement results in a successor state that does not satisfy $x > 6$, the abstract transition from $(x > 8)$ to $(x > 6)$ is not a must transition. Augmenting MTSs with hyper-must transitions [LX90, SG04] does not help in this setting either (and is orthogonal to the contribution we describe here).

Such cases motivated the introduction of $must^-$ transitions [Bal04]. A $must^-$ transition from a to a' implies that for all concrete states c' that correspond to a' there is a concrete predecessor state c that corresponds to a. In the above example, there is a $must^-$ transition from $(x > 8)$ to $(x > 6)$. Like must transitions (let us refer to them in the sequel as $must^+$ transitions), $must^-$ transitions are closed under transitivity, and as argued in [Bal04, BKY05], they are often useful in cases $must^+$ transitions do not exist.

While $must^-$ transitions are helpful in scenarios as above, they do not address the fragility of must transitions with respect to updates of irrelevant variables. In particular, in our earlier example, of $(x > 6)$ if y=0 then {x:=x+4;read(y)} $(x > 8)$, there is no $must^-$ transition from $(x > 6)$ to $(x > 8)$, as there are concrete states

(i) *a must* $^+_{\{x\}}$ *transition:*   **(ii)** *a must* $^-_{\{x\}}$ *transition:*

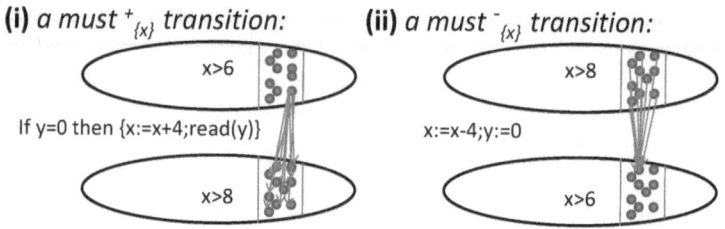

Fig. 1. Partitioned-must transitions

satisfying $x > 8$ (namely $\langle 9, 0 \rangle$ and $\langle 10, 0 \rangle$) that are not reachable from any concrete state satisfying $x > 6$. Moreover, while $must^-$ transitions came to the rescue in the $(x > 8)$ x:=x-4 $(x > 6)$ example, they are no longer useful when we add irrelevant variables. Assume, for example, that the statement executed in $(x > 8)$ is x:=x-4;y:=0. Since the abstraction ignores the variable y and not all the concrete states in $(x > 6)$ have $y = 0$, there are concrete states in $(x > 6)$, say $\langle 10, 1 \rangle$, that do not have a predecessor in $(x > 8)$. Accordingly, there is no $must^-$ transition in the new setting.

As hinted earlier, the idea behind our partitioned-must transitions is to restrict the universal nature of must transitions to a subset of the variables. Given a set X of *relevant variables*, we can partition the state space of the concrete system to equivalence classes such that states in the same class agree on the values of the variables in X. Consider again the $(x > 6)$ if y=0 then $\{x:=x+4;read(y)\}$ $(x > 8)$ example (see Figure 1 (i)). We argue that if we restrict attention to the set $X = \{x\}$ of relevant variables, then there is a partitioned $must^+$ transition from $(x > 6)$ to $(x > 8)$ in the following sense. For every concrete state $\langle x, y \rangle$ in $(x > 6)$, there is a concrete state $\langle x', y' \rangle$ in $(x > 8)$ such that all the states in the equivalence class of $\langle x', y' \rangle$ have a predecessor in the equivalence class of $\langle x, y \rangle$. Indeed, $x' = x + 4$ is such that all the states in $\{x + 4\} \times \mathbb{N}$ are reachable from the state $\langle x, 0 \rangle$, which is in the equivalence class of $\langle x, y \rangle$.

In general, we say that there is a $pmust^+_X$ transition from a to a' only if for every concrete state c that corresponds to a there is a concrete state c' that corresponds to a' such that there is a $must^-$ transition from the restriction of a to the equivalence class of c to the restriction of a' to the equivalence class of c'. Dually, there is a $pmust^-_X$ transition from a to a' only if for every concrete state c' that corresponds to a' there is a concrete state c that corresponds to a such that there is a $must^+$ transition from the restriction of a to the equivalence class of c to the restriction of a' to the equivalence class of c'. For example (see Figure 1 (ii)), in the $(x > 8)$ x:=x-4;y:=0 $(x > 6)$ setting, there is a $pmust^-_{\{x\}}$ transition from $(x > 8)$ to $(x > 6)$.

In the paper, we define partitioned-must transitions, characterize settings in which they are useful, and study their theoretical properties. As we show, while partitioned-must transitions exist in many realistic settings in which usual must transitions do not exist, they retain the advantages of must transitions: they are closed under transitivity, their calculation can be automated, and the three-valued semantics induced by usual must transitions is refined to a multi-valued semantics that takes into an account the set of relevant variables.

2   Preliminaries

Programs and Concrete Transition Systems. Consider a program P. Let V be the set of variables appearing in the program and variables that encode the program counter (pc), and let D be the domain of all variables (for technical simplicity, we assume that all variables are over the same domain). We model P by a concrete transition system in which each state is labeled by a valuation in $D^{|V|}$.

A *concrete transition system* (CTS) is a tuple $C = \langle S_C, I_C, \longrightarrow_C \rangle$, where S_C is a (possibly infinite) set of states, $I_C \subseteq S_C$ is a set of initial states, $\longrightarrow_C \subseteq S_C \times S_C$ is a total transition relation. Let $c \longrightarrow_C^* c'$ denote that state c' is reachable from state c via a path of transitions.

Predicate Abstraction. Let $\Phi = \{\phi_1, \phi_2, \ldots, \phi_n\}$ be a set of predicates (quantifier-free formulas of first-order logic) over the program variables V. In the CTS of the program, each concrete state c corresponds to a valuation of V. Given a program state c and formula ϕ, let $c \models \phi$ indicate that formula ϕ is true in state c (c is a model of ϕ). For a set $a \subseteq \Phi$ and an assignment $c \in D^V$, we say that c *satisfies* a iff $c \models \bigwedge_{\phi_i \in a} \phi_i$.

In predicate abstraction, we merge a set of concrete states into a single abstract state, which is defined by means of a subset of the predicates. Thus, an abstract state is given by a set of predicates $a \subseteq \Phi$.[1] We sometimes represent a by a formula, namely the conjunction of predicates in a. For example, if $a = \{(x \geq y), (0 \leq x < n)\}$ then we also represent a by the formula $(x \geq y) \wedge (0 \leq x < n)$. We define the set of concrete states corresponding to a, denoted $\gamma(a)$, as all the states c that satisfy a; that is, $\gamma(a) = \{c \mid c \models a\}$.

May and Must Transitions. Given a CTS and its (predicate) abstraction via a set of predicates Φ, a *modal transition system* (MTS) contains three kinds of abstract transitions between abstracts states a and a' ($a, a' \subseteq \Phi$, and we assume that Φ is clear from the context):

- $may(a, a')$ if there is $c \in \gamma(a)$ and a $c' \in \gamma(a')$, such that $c \longrightarrow_C c'$.
- $must^+(a, a')$ only if for every $c \in \gamma(a)$, there is $c' \in \gamma(a')$ such that $c \longrightarrow_C c'$.
- $must^-(a, a')$ only if for every $c' \in \gamma(a')$, there is $c \in \gamma(a)$ such that $c \longrightarrow_C c'$.

While *may* transitions over-approximate the transitions of the CTS, both types of *must* transitions under-approximate it. It is not hard to see that must transitions are closed under transitivity, and can therefore be used to prove reachability in the concrete system. Formally, if there is a sequence of $must^+$ transitions from a to a', denoted $must^{+*}(a, a')$, then for all $c \in \gamma(a)$, there is $c' \in \gamma(a')$ such that $c \longrightarrow_C^* c'$. The same holds for $must^-$. Formally, if there is a sequence of $must^-$ transitions from a to a', denoted $must^{-*}(a, a')$, then for all $c' \in \gamma(a')$, there is $c \in \gamma(a)$ such that $c \longrightarrow_C^* c'$.

On the other hand, may transitions are not transitive. Indeed, it may be the case that $may(a, a'), may(a', a'')$ and still for all $c \in a$ and $c'' \in a''$, we have $c \not\longrightarrow_C^* c'$.

---

[1] In the full generality of predicate abstraction, an abstract state is represented by a set of set of predicates (that is a, disjunction of conjunction of predicates). All our results hold for the more general setting.

Weakest Preconditions and Strongest Postconditions. In many applications of predicate abstraction, Ψ includes a predicate for the program counter. Accordingly, each abstract state is associated with a location of the program, and thus it is also associated with a statement. For a statement s and a predicate e over V, the *weakest precondition* $\mathrm{WP}(s, e)$ and the *strongest postcondition* $\mathrm{SP}(s, e)$ are defined as follows [Dij76]:

- The execution of s from every state that satisfies $\mathrm{WP}(s, e)$ results in a state that satisfies e, and $\mathrm{WP}(s, e)$ is the weakest predicate for which the above holds.
- The execution of s from a state that satisfies e results in a state that satisfies $\mathrm{SP}(s,e)$, and $\mathrm{SP}(s, e)$ is the strongest predicate for which the above holds.

Must transitions can be computed automatically using weakest preconditions and strongest postconditions. Indeed, statement s induces the transition $must^+(a, a')$ iff $a \Rightarrow \mathrm{WP}(s, a')$, and induces the transition $must^-(a, a')$ iff $a' \Rightarrow \mathrm{SP}(s, a)$.

3   Partitioned-Must Transitions

Recall that we consider programs with variables V over the domain D. For a set $X \subseteq V$, we define a relation $\sim_X \subseteq D^V \times D^V$ between concrete states such that $c \sim_X c'$ iff c and c' agree on the values of the variables in X. For a concrete state c, let $[c]_X = \{c' : c \sim_X c'\}$; that is, $[c]_X$ is the set of concrete states that agree with c on the values of variables in X.

We are now ready to introduce partitioned-must transitions. The idea is to partition the variables of the program to relevant (X) and irrelevant ($V \setminus X$) variables and restrict the universal quantification in must transitions to range over the equivalence classes of $\sim_X$. Formally, we have the following.

Definition 1. *Consider two abstract states a and a', and a set $X \subseteq V$.*

1. *There is a $pmust_X^+$ transition from a to a', denoted $pmust_X^+(a, a')$, only if for all $c \in \gamma(a)$ there is $c' \in \gamma(a')$ such that $must^-([c]_X \wedge a, [c']_X \wedge a')$.*
2. *There is a $pmust_X^-$ transition from a to a', denoted $pmust_X^-(a, a')$, only if for all $c' \in \gamma(a')$ there is $c \in \gamma(a)$ such that $must^+([c]_X \wedge a, [c']_X \wedge a')$.*

Example 1. Let us go back to the examples discussed in Section 1 and review them formally. Consider the transition $(x > 6)$ `if y=0 then {x:=x+4;read(y)}` $(x > 8)$. Assume that $V = \{x, y\}$, and let the domain of both variables be $\mathbb{N}$. There is a $pmust_{\{x\}}^-$ transition from $(x > 6)$ to $(x > 8)$. Indeed, for all concrete states $\langle x, y \rangle \in \gamma(x > 6)$, there exists the concrete state $\langle x + 4, y \rangle \in \gamma(x > 8)$ for which $must^-([\langle x, y \rangle]_{\{x\}}, [\langle x + 4, y \rangle]_{\{x\}})$. To see the latter, note that $[\langle x + 4, y \rangle]_{\{x\}} = \{x + 4\} \times \mathbb{N}$, and each state in $\{x + 4\} \times \mathbb{N}$ is reachable from $\langle x, 0 \rangle$, which is in $[\langle x, y \rangle]_{\{x\}}$. Thus, the partition to $\{x\}$ and $\{y\}$ circumvents the need to refer to the value of y in the destination state.

Consider the transition $(x > 8)$ `x:=x-4; y:=0` $(x > 6)$. There is a $pmust_{\{x\}}^-$ transition from $(x > 8)$ to $(x > 6)$. Indeed, for all concrete states $\langle x, y \rangle \in \gamma(x > 6)$, there exists the concrete state $\langle x + 4, y \rangle \in \gamma(x > 8)$ for which $must^+([\langle x + 4, y \rangle]_{\{x\}}, [\langle x, y \rangle]_{\{x\}})$. To see the latter, note that $[\langle x + 4, y \rangle]_{\{x\}} = \{x + 4\} \times \mathbb{N}$.

Executing the statement x:=x-4;y:=0 from a state in $\{x+4\} \times \mathbb{N}$ results in the state $\langle x, 0 \rangle$, which is in $[\langle x, y \rangle]_{\{x\}} = \{x\} \times \mathbb{N}$. Thus, also here, the partition to $\{x\}$ and $\{y\}$ circumvents the need to refer to the value of y in the destination state.

$\qquad\qquad\qquad\qquad\qquad\qquad\qquad\qquad\qquad\qquad\qquad\qquad\qquad\qquad$ □

Example 1 demonstrates cases in which $must^+$ and $must^-$ transitions do not exist but partitioned-must transitions do exist. Below we characterize such cases in general:

- The abstraction refers to variables in X only, and the statement involves an assignment to variables in $V \setminus X$. Here, there is no $must^-$ transition, but there is a $pmust_X^-$ transition. The example $(x > 8)$ x:=x-4;y:=0 $(x > 6)$ is emblematic of this case.
- The abstraction refers to variables in X only, and the statement involves guards on the variables in $V \setminus X$. The range of the guarded variables in the post state is not restricted to these that satisfy the guard (due to nondeterminism or the infiniteness of the domain). Here, there is no $must^+$ transitions, but there is a $pmust_X^+$ transition. The example $(x > 6)$ if y=0 then $\{$x:=x+4; read(y)$\}$ $(x > 8)$ is emblematic of this case. An example of a similar nature but with more restricted nondeterminism is

$$(x > 6) \text{ if y is odd then } \{\text{x:=x+4; (skip|y:=y-1)}\} \, (x > 8).$$

Here, not all concrete states $\langle x, y \rangle \in \gamma(x > 6)$ have a successor in $\gamma(x > 8)$, but for all concrete states $\langle x, y \rangle \in \gamma(x > 6)$, there exists the concrete state $\langle x + 4, y \rangle \in \gamma(x > 8)$ for which $must^-([\langle x, y \rangle]_{\{x\}}, [\langle x + 4, y \rangle]_{\{x\}})$. Indeed, the nondeterministic assignment guarantees that all values of y have a pre-state with an odd value. As a last example for this case, consider

$$(x > 6) \text{ if y>=10 then } \{\text{x:=x+4; y:=y-10}\} \, (x > 8).$$

Here, the program is deterministic, and still, the fact $\mathbb{N}$ is infinite, thus y can take any value that is greater than or equal to 0, implies that all values of y in the post-state are covered by values greater than or equal to 10 in the pre-state.
- The abstraction refers to all variables, but for these in X, it over-approximates the value in the post-state and for these in $V \setminus X$ it over-approximates the value in the pre-state. While there are no $must^+$ or $must^-$ transitions, there are $pmust_X^+$ and $pmust_{V \setminus X}^-$ transitions. A typical example for this case is

$$(x > 6, y > 8) \text{ x:=x+4;y:=y-4 } (x > 8, y > 6).$$

We now show that partitioned-must transitions are closed under transitivity. For two abstract states a and a' and a set of variables $X \subseteq V$, we use $pmust_X^{+*}(a, a')$ to indicate that there is a (possibly empty) sequence of $pmust_X^+$ transitions from a to a'. Formally, there are $a_1, a_2, \ldots, a_n$ such that $a = a_1$, $a_n = a'$, and for all $1 \leq i < n$, we have that $pmust_X^+(a_i, a_{i+1})$. The notation $pmust_X^{-*}(a, a')$ is defined similarly as the transitive closure of $pmust_X^-$ transitions.

Proposition 1. [transitive closure] *Consider two abstract states a and a', and a set $X \subseteq V$.*

1. *If $pmust_X^{+*}(a, a')$, then for all $c \in \gamma(a)$ there exists $c' \in \gamma(a')$ such that $must^{-*}([c]_X \wedge a, [c']_X \wedge a')$.*
2. *If $pmust_X^{-*}(a, a')$, then for all $c' \in \gamma(a')$ there exists $c \in \gamma(a)$ such that $must^{+*}([c]_X \wedge a, [c']_X \wedge a')$.*

Proof: We prove the forward case, the backwards case is dual. Assume that $pmust_X^{+*}(a, a')$. Let $a_1, a_2, \ldots, a_n$ be such that $a = a_1$, $a' = a_n$, and for all $1 \leq i < n$, we have $pmust_X^+(a_i, a_{i+1})$. We prove that for all $c_1 \in \gamma(a_1)$ there is $c_n \in \gamma(a_n)$ such that $must^{-*}([c_1]_X \wedge a_1, [c_n]_X \wedge a_n)$. The proof proceeds by induction on the length of the sequence of transitions (i.e., $n - 1$). If $n = 1$, the sequence is empty and the requirement follows from the definition of $*$. Assume that the claim holds for sequences of length n, and consider a sequence of length $n+1$. By the induction hypothesis, for all $c_1 \in \gamma(a_1)$ there is $c_n \in \gamma(a_n)$ such that $must^{-*}([c_1]_X \wedge a_1, [c_n]_X \wedge a_n)$. Since $pmust_X^{+*}(a_n, a_{n+1})$, then for all $c_n \in \gamma(a_n)$ there is $c_{n+1} \in \gamma(a_{n+1})$ such that $must^-([c_n]_X \wedge a_n, [c_{n+1}]_X \wedge a_{n+1})$. By the transitivity of $must^-$, we can conclude that $must^{-*}([c_1]_X \wedge a_1, [c_{n+1}]_X \wedge a_{n+1})$. $\qquad\square$

Traditional $must^+$ and $must^-$ transitions can be viewed as the two *polar* cases of partitioned must transitions. Formally, we have the following:

Proposition 2. *For all abstract states a and a', the following hold.*

1. *$must^+(a, a')$ iff $pmust_V^+(a, a')$ iff $pmust_\emptyset^-(a, a')$.*
2. *$must^-(a, a')$ iff $pmust_\emptyset^+(a, a')$ iff $pmust_V^-(a, a')$.*

Proof: We prove the forward case, the backwards case is dual. When $X = V$, the relation $\sim_X$ relates each state only with itself. Thus, $pmust_V^+(a, a')$ iff for all $c \in \gamma(a)$ there is $c' \in \gamma(a')$ such that $must^-(c, c')$. Since for concrete states, we have $must^-(c, c')$ coincides with $c \longrightarrow_C c'$, it follows that $must^+(a, a')$ iff $pmust_V^+(a, a')$.

When $X = \emptyset$, the relation $\sim_X$ relates all states in D^V. Thus, the condition $must^+([c]_X \wedge a, [c']_X \wedge a')$ is independent of c and c' and is equivalent to $must^+(a, a')$. $\qquad\square$

Remark 1. There are abstract states a and a' such that $must^+(a, a')$ and $must^-(a, a')$ and the only sets X for which $pmust_X^+(a, a')$ or $pmust_X^-(a, a')$ are the polar ones.

To see this, consider Boolean variables x and y and let $a = a' = true$. The transition `if x=y then skip else swap(x,y)` induces a $must^+$ as well as a $must^-$ transition from a to a'. The four possible partitions of $\{x, y\}$ and the partitioned transitions they induce are described in Figure 2. As described there, there is no $pmust_{\{x\}}^+$, $pmust_{\{x\}}^-$, $pmust_{\{y\}}^+$, or $pmust_{\{y\}}^-$ transition from a to a'.

Example 2. We demonstrate the usefulness of partitioned-must transitions with a variant of the well-known algorithm for calculating the greatest-common-divisor of two positive integers. Consider the function `gcd` described in Figure 3.

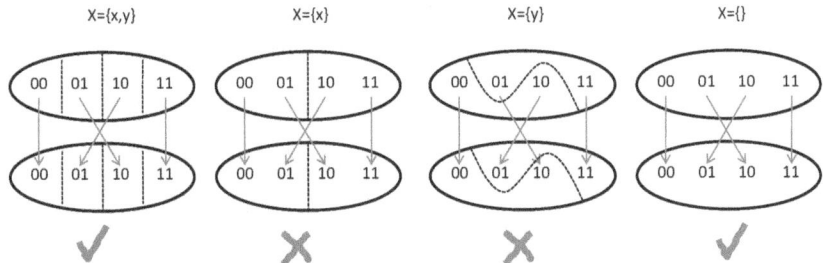

Fig. 2. Existence and nonexistence of a partitioned-must transition

```
gcd(x,y) {
  (1)    assume(x>0);
  (2)    assume(y>0);
  (3)    int t:=0;
  (4)    while (x!=y) do if (x>y) then x:=x-y;t:=t+1
                                    else y:=y-x
}
```

Fig. 3. The function gcd

In addition to the variables x and y whose gcd is calculated, the function maintains a variable t that counts the number of iterations in which $x > y$. Consider an abstraction that refers to x, y, and the program counter pc. Consider the abstract state $a = (pc = 4 \wedge x > 0 \wedge y > 0 \wedge x \neq y)$. We would like to show that all values of x, y, and pc that satisfy a are successors of other values that satisfy a. Thus, whenever we are in the loop with $x \neq y$, we have a predecessor in the loop with $x \neq y$. An attempt to prove the above with $must^-$ transitions fails: since the abstraction ignores the value of t, concrete states that satisfy a and in which $t = 0$ may not have a predecessor that satisfy a (as they may be reachable only from states visited before the execution of the loop, and in which $pc \neq 4$). Hiding the variable t, however, we can prove the above by showing that $pmust^-_{\{x,y,pc\}}(a,a)$. To see the latter, observe that for all $\langle x, y, t, pc \rangle \in \gamma(a)$, we have that $must^+([\langle x + y, y, t, pc \rangle]_{\{x,y\}}, [\langle x, y, t, pc \rangle]_{\{x,y\}})$. Indeed, satisfying a guarantees that $pc = 4$, and the execution of the statement in $pc = 4$ from the values $\langle x+y, y, t, 4 \rangle$, which satisfy a, results in values $\langle x, y, t, 4 \rangle$.

Now, consider the abstract state $b = (pc = 4 \wedge x > 0 \wedge y > 0 \wedge x = y)$, for which all corresponding concrete states cause the while loop to terminate. We would like to show that all values of x, y, and pc that satisfy b are successors of other values that satisfy a. Thus, whenever we are in the loop with $x = y$, we have a predecessor in the loop with $x \neq y$. Again, an attempt to prove the above with $must^-$ transitions fails: since the abstraction ignores the value of t, concrete states that satisfy b and in which $t = 0$ may not have a predecessor that satisfies the $pc = 4$ conjunct in a. Hiding the variable t, however, we can prove the above by showing that $pmust^-_{\{x,y,pc\}}(a,b)$. To see the latter, observe that for all $\langle x, y, t, pc \rangle \in \gamma(b)$, we have that $must^+([\langle x, 2x, t, pc \rangle]_{\{x,y\}}, [\langle x, y, t, pc \rangle]_{\{x,y\}})$. Finally, by the transitivity of

$pmust_X^-$ transitions, we can conclude that whenever we are about to leave the loop with $x = y$, and for any desired iteration count i, we can go back i transitions and stay in the loop with $x \neq y$. □

4   Calculation of Partitioned-Must Transitions

As Example 2 shows, the calculation of partitioned-must transitions may not be easy. In this section we show that this calculation can be automated. We start with $pmust_X^+$ transitions.

Theorem 3. *Consider two abstract states a and a' and a set $X \subseteq V$. Let s be the statement executed in a. The following are equivalent.*

1. *$pmust_X^+(a, a')$.*
2. *For all $c \in \gamma(a)$ there is $c' \in \gamma(a')$ such that $([c']_X \wedge a') \Rightarrow \mathrm{SP}(s, [c]_X \wedge a)$.*
3. *For all $c \in \gamma(a)$, there is an equivalence class θ of $\sim_X$ such that $\theta \wedge a'$ is satisfiable and $(\theta \wedge a') \Rightarrow \mathrm{SP}(s, [c]_X \wedge a)$.*

Proof: We prove that both (1) and (3) are equivalent to (2). We start by proving that $(1) \leftrightarrow (2)$. By Definition 1, $pmust_X^+(a, a')$ iff for all $c \in \gamma(a)$ there is $c' \in \gamma(a')$ such that $must^-([c]_X \wedge a, [c']_X \wedge a')$. By the definition of $must^-$ transitions, the latter holds iff $([c']_X \wedge a') \Rightarrow \mathrm{SP}(s, [c]_X \wedge a)$, and we are done.

It is left to prove that $(2) \leftrightarrow (3)$. Assume first that (2) holds. Thus, for all $c \in \gamma(a)$ there is $c' \in \gamma(a')$ such that $([c']_X \wedge a') \Rightarrow \mathrm{SP}(s, [c]_X \wedge a)$. Then, given $c \in \gamma(a)$, the set $\theta = [c']_X$ is an equivalence class of $\sim_X$ such that $\theta \wedge a'$ is satisfiable (say, by c'), and $(\theta \wedge a') \Rightarrow \mathrm{SP}(s, [c]_X \wedge a)$. Assume now that (3) holds. Thus, for all $c \in \gamma(a)$ there is an equivalence class θ of $\sim_X$ such that $\theta \wedge a'$ is satisfiable and $(\theta \wedge a') \Rightarrow \mathrm{SP}(s, [c]_X \wedge a)$. Let c' be such that c' satisfies $\theta \wedge a'$. Since θ is an equivalence class of $\sim_X$, we have that $[c']_X \Rightarrow \theta$. Hence, c' is such that $c' \in \gamma(a')$ and $([c']_X \wedge a') \Rightarrow \mathrm{SP}(s, [c]_X \wedge a)$. □

We can now use Theorem 3 to describe a first-order logic formula that is valid iff the conditions for the existence of a $pmust_X^-$ transition are satisfied. Describing the formula, we use $\boldsymbol{x}$ and $\boldsymbol{y}$ (possibly primed) to denote the variables in X and $V \setminus X$, respectively. For a predicate a over V, we use $a(\boldsymbol{x}, \boldsymbol{y})$ to indicate that the assignment of the variables in V (described in $\boldsymbol{x}$ and $\boldsymbol{y}$ together) satisfy a. Finally, when we use $\boldsymbol{x}$ as a predicate, it is satisfied by assignments to V that agree with $\boldsymbol{x}$ on the variables in X.

Proposition 3. *There is a $pmust_X^+$ transition from a to a' only if the following formula is valid.*

$$\forall \boldsymbol{x} \forall \boldsymbol{y} [a(\boldsymbol{x}, \boldsymbol{y}) \rightarrow \exists \boldsymbol{x}'((\exists \boldsymbol{y}'.a'(\boldsymbol{x}', \boldsymbol{y}')) \wedge (\forall \boldsymbol{y}'.(a'(\boldsymbol{x}', \boldsymbol{y}') \rightarrow \mathrm{SP}(s, \boldsymbol{x} \wedge a))))].$$

Proof: The formula states that for all states $c \in \gamma(a)$ (these are the universally quantified variables in $\boldsymbol{x}$ and $\boldsymbol{y}$, when they satisfy the left-hand side of the $a(\boldsymbol{x}, \boldsymbol{y}) \rightarrow \ldots$ implication), there is an equivalence class of $\sim_X$ (these are the existentially quantified variables in $\boldsymbol{x}'$) that satisfies the condition in item (3) of Theorem 3: the intersection of the equivalence class with a' is not empty (there is an assignment $\boldsymbol{y}'$ to the variables in $V \setminus X$ such that $a'(\boldsymbol{x}', \boldsymbol{y}')$), and every assignment in the intersection (that is, every $\boldsymbol{y}'$ that is combined with $\boldsymbol{x}'$ and for which $a'(\boldsymbol{x}', \boldsymbol{y}')$) satisfies $\mathrm{SP}(s, \boldsymbol{x} \wedge a)$. □

We now describe a similar reasoning for $pmust_X^-$ transitions. The proof is similar to the one detailed in the proofs of Theorem 3 and Proposition 3.

Theorem 4. *Consider two abstract states a and a' and a set $X \subseteq V$. Let s be the statement executed in a. The following are equivalent.*

1. $pmust_X^-(a, a')$.
2. *For all $c' \in \gamma(a')$ there is $c \in \gamma(a)$ such that $([c]_X \wedge a) \Rightarrow WP(s, [c']_X \wedge a')$.*
3. *For all $c' \in \gamma(a')$ there is an equivalence class θ of $\sim_X$ such that $\theta \wedge a$ is satisfiable and $(\theta \wedge a) \Rightarrow WP(s, [c']_X \wedge a')$.*

Proposition 4. *There is a $pmust_X^-$ transition from a to a' only if the following formula is valid.*

$$\forall \boldsymbol{x}' \forall \boldsymbol{y}' [a'(\boldsymbol{x}', \boldsymbol{y}') \rightarrow \exists \boldsymbol{x}((\exists \boldsymbol{y}.a(\boldsymbol{x}, \boldsymbol{y})) \wedge (\forall \boldsymbol{y}.(a(\boldsymbol{x}, \boldsymbol{y}) \rightarrow WP(s, \boldsymbol{x}' \wedge a'))))].$$

When the predicates of the abstraction contain only variables appearing in X, reasoning is simplified. We discuss this case in Section 6, where we also show the simplified version of the formulas described in Propositions 3 and 4 for the general case. In particular, in Example 6 there, we describe the automation of the reasoning required for the gcd function discussed in Example 2.

5   Applications

In this section we discuss applications of partitioned-must transitions. Essentially, our applications are these in which one is interested in *weak reachability* in the abstract system. For two abstract states a and a', we say that a' is weakly reachable from a iff there are concrete state $c \in \gamma(a)$ and $c' \in \gamma(a')$ such that c' is reachable from c. While weak reachability quantifies the states in $\gamma(a)$ and $\gamma(a')$ existentially, we cannot use may transitions in order to detect it, as may transitions are not closed under transitivity. Thus, the way to go is to check whether $must^{+*}(a, a')$ or $must^{-*}(a, a')$. The fragility of must transitions with respect to irrelevant variables can then prevent the detection of weak reachability, and we suggest to use partitioned-must transition instead. Below we detail the applications in falsification and verification of temporal-logic specifications.

5.1   Linear-Time Falsification

In *linear-time model checking*, we check whether all the computations of a given program P satisfy a specification ψ, say an LTL formula. In the automata-theoretic approach to model checking [Kur94, VW94], one constructs an automaton $\mathcal{A}_{\neg \psi}$ for the negation of ψ. The automaton $\mathcal{A}_{\neg \psi}$ is usually a nondeterministic Büchi automaton, where a run is accepting iff it visits a set of designated states infinitely often. The program P is faulty with respect to ψ if the product of $\mathcal{A}_{\neg \psi}$ with the program contains a fair path – one that visits the set of designated states infinitely often.

The product of $\mathcal{A}_{\neg \psi}$ with an MTS M_P that abstracts P is an MTS that retains the type of transitions in M_P. We assume that each atomic proposition in the LTL formula is a predicates over the variables, e.g., $x > 4$, $x = y$, etc. The alphabet of $\mathcal{A}_{\neg \psi}$ is then subsets of these predicates. The transitions in the product of $\mathcal{A}_{\neg\psi}$ and M_P are then such that for two abstract states a and a' of M_P and two states q and q' of $\mathcal{A}_{\neg\psi}$, we have that there is a transition of type β (say, β is $pmust_X^+$) from the state $\langle a, q \rangle$ of the product to the state $\langle a', q' \rangle$ of the product iff there is a β-transition from a to a' and there is a transition $\langle q, \sigma, q' \rangle$ of $\mathcal{A}_{\neg\psi}$ such that $a \Rightarrow p$, for all $p \in \sigma$.

Since the product retains the type of transitions of the MTS, the less underapproximating the abstraction is, the more we are likely to detect errors. When ψ is a safety property, $\mathcal{A}_{\neg\psi}$ can be replaced by an automaton accepting finite bad prefixes [KL06], and detection can be reduced to weak reachability in the product. In the general case, we have to find a concrete state that is reachable from itself. The latter cannot be reduced to two weak reachability queries (indeed, the same concrete state has to "glue" the prefix of the lasso with its repeated part, and the same concrete state has to "glue" the repeated parts), but can be reduced to the type of reachability implied by the closure of partitioned-must transitions. Formally, we have the following.

Theorem 5. *Consider the MTS M obtained by taking the product of $\mathcal{A}_{\neg\psi}$ and M_P. Let a_{init} and a_{acc} be states of M such that a_{init} is initial and a_{acc} is accepting. Consider a set $X \subseteq V$. If $pmust_X^{+\,*}(a_{init}, a_{acc})$ and $pmust_X^{+\,*}(a_{acc}, a_{acc})$, or $pmust_X^{-\,*}(a_{init}, a_{acc})$ and $pmust_X^{-\,*}(a_{acc}, a_{acc})$, then P violates ψ.*

In Section 5.2, we describe a multi-valued semantics for μ-calculus that is based on partitioned-must transitions and show, for example, that if $pmust_X^{+\,*}(a_{init}, a_{acc})$ and $pmust_X^{+\,*}(a_{acc}, a_{acc})$, then we can strengthen the conclusion in Theorem 5 to "for every concrete state c that corresponds to a_{init}, at least one state in $[c]_X$ violates ψ". Nevertheless, the main contribution of partitioned-must transition is not the ability to strengthen the conclusion, but the fact they are applicable in cases usual must transitions fail.

5.2 A Multi-valued Semantics

Since abstraction hides information, the truth value of temporal-logic formulas with respect to states of a MTS may not be definite. According to the three-valued semantics for MTS [GJ02], the value of a formula θ in abstract state a is $\mathbf{T}$, denoted $[a \models \theta] = \mathbf{T}$, only if all the concrete states in $\gamma(a)$ satisfy θ. Likewise, $[a \models \theta] = \mathbf{F}$, only if all the concrete states in $\gamma(a)$ do not satisfy θ. Sometimes, neither case holds, or our reasoning is not sufficiently strong to infer that one of the cases hold [BG00], in which case the value of θ in a is unknown, denoted $[a \models \theta] = \bot$. Since must transitions underapproximate the transitions of the concrete system, they are used in the three-valued semantics for proving existential properties. Formally, $[a \models \exists\bigcirc\theta] = \mathbf{T}$ iff there is a' such that $must^+(a, a')$ and $[a' \models \theta] = \mathbf{T}$. For logics with backwards modalities, reasoning is the same, with $must^-$ transitions.

By partitioning the variables to relevant (X) and irrelevant ones, we can refine the three-valued semantics to one that takes the partition into an account. We say that an abstract state a X-satisfies a formula θ, denoted $[a \models \theta] \sqsupseteq \mathbf{T}_X$, only if for each state $c \in \gamma(a)$, at least one state in $[c]_X \wedge a$ satisfies θ. Likewise, a does not X-satisfy a formula θ, denoted $[a \models \theta] \sqsupseteq \mathbf{F}_X$, if for each state $c \in \gamma(a)$, at least one state in $[c]_X \wedge a$ does not satisfy θ. Note that the conditions for values $\mathbf{T}_{X_1}$ and $\mathbf{T}_{X_2}$, for

$X_1 \neq X_2$, are not mutually exclusive, and so are the conditions for the values $\mathbf{T}_X$ and $\mathbf{F}_X$. This is why we use the $\sqsupseteq$ notation in the definition of the semantics. Formally, the values are taken from the domain $2^V \times 2^V$, where a pair $\langle P, N \rangle \subseteq 2^V \times 2^V$ consists of a *positive set*: all maximal sets $X \subseteq V$ for which $[a \models \theta] \sqsupseteq \mathbf{T}_X$ and a *negative set*: all maximal sets $X \subseteq V$ for which $[a \models \theta] \sqsupseteq \mathbf{F}_X$. Saying that $[a \models \theta] \sqsupseteq \mathbf{T}_X$ means that at least one of the sets in P contains X, and similarly for $\mathbf{F}_X$ and N. Note that when $P = \emptyset$, the positive set is unknown, and similarly for N.

When $X = V$, we have that $[c]_X = \{c\}$. Accordingly, the values $\mathbf{T}_V$ and $\mathbf{F}_V$ coincide with the standard $\mathbf{T}$ and $\mathbf{F}$ values from the three-valued semantics. Also, when $X = \emptyset$, we have that $[c]_X = D^V$. Accordingly, the values $\mathbf{T}_\emptyset$ and $\mathbf{F}_\emptyset$ coincide with the existential $\mathbf{T}_\exists$ and $\mathbf{F}_\exists$ values from the six-valued semantics studied in [BKY05]. Finally, it is interesting to note that the semantics is monotonic, in the sense that if $[a \models \theta] \sqsupseteq \mathbf{T}_X$ and $X' \subseteq X$, then $[a \models \theta] \sqsupseteq \mathbf{T}_{X'}$. Thus, our semantics is a natural refinement of the existential semantics in [BKY05].

As with the existential semantics, however, the weakness of the $\mathbf{T}_X$ and $\mathbf{F}_X$ values is the fact that their conjunction does not correspond to meet in the $(2^V, \subseteq)$ lattice, and results in $\bot$. An exception is the T_V value, where $T_V \wedge T_X = T_X$, for all $X \subseteq V$. Since our main motivation for partitioned-must transitions is reachability, and reachability corresponds to a least fixed point in which the main Boolean operator is a disjunction, the above weakness is not too discouraging. Still, the significance of the semantics here is mainly theoretical, and its goal is to give a logical counterpart of partitioned-must transitions.

Formally, the value of a μ-calculus formula θ in a state a of a MTS is defined by induction on the structure of θ as follows. We describe the semantics for *full μ-calculus*, which has both forward ($\exists \bigcirc$) and backwards ($\exists \ominus$) modalities. We assume a μ-calculus in which each atomic proposition is a predicate over the variables, e.g., $x > 4$, $x = y$, etc. We refer to the set of variables appearing in the atomic proposition p by $var(p)$.

$$[a \models p] \sqsupseteq \begin{cases} \mathbf{T}_X & \text{if } (var(p) \subseteq X \text{ and } a \models p) \text{ or} \\ & (var(p) \not\subseteq X \text{ and } [c]_X \wedge a \wedge p \text{ is satisfiable for all } c \in \gamma(a)), \\ \mathbf{F}_X & \text{if } (var(p) \in X \text{ and } a \models \neg p) \text{ or} \\ & (var(p) \notin X \text{ and } [c]_X \wedge a \wedge \neg p \text{ is satisfiable for all } c \in \gamma(a)). \end{cases}$$

$$[a \models \neg \theta] \sqsupseteq \begin{cases} \mathbf{T}_X & \text{if } [a \models \theta] \sqsupseteq \mathbf{F}_X, \\ \mathbf{F}_X & \text{if } [a \models \theta] \sqsupseteq \mathbf{T}_X. \end{cases}$$

$$[a \models \theta \wedge \theta'] \sqsupseteq \begin{cases} \mathbf{T}_X & \text{if } [a \models \theta] \sqsupseteq \mathbf{T}_V \text{ and } [a \models \theta'] \sqsupseteq \mathbf{T}_X. \\ \mathbf{F}_X & \text{if } [a \models \theta] \sqsupseteq \mathbf{F}_V \text{ and } [a \models \theta'] \sqsupseteq \mathbf{F}_X. \end{cases}$$

$$[a \models \theta \vee \theta'] \sqsupseteq \begin{cases} \mathbf{T}_X & \text{if } [a \models \theta] \sqsupseteq \mathbf{T}_X \text{ or } [a \models \theta'] \sqsupseteq \mathbf{T}_X. \\ \mathbf{F}_X & \text{if } [a \models \theta] \sqsupseteq \mathbf{F}_X \text{ or } [a \models \theta'] \sqsupseteq \mathbf{F}_X. \end{cases}$$

$$[a \models \exists \bigcirc \theta] \sqsupseteq \begin{cases} \mathbf{T}_X & \text{if there is } a' \text{ such that } pmust_X^+(a, a') \text{ and } [a' \models_X \theta] \sqsupseteq \mathbf{T}_X, \\ \mathbf{F}_V & \text{if for all } a' \text{ such that } may(a, a'), \text{ we have that } [a' \models_X \theta] \sqsupseteq \mathbf{F}_V. \end{cases}$$

$$[a \models \exists \ominus \theta] \sqsupseteq \begin{cases} \mathbf{T}_X & \text{if there is } a' \text{ such that } pmust_X^-(a', a) \text{ and } [a' \models_X \theta] \sqsupseteq \mathbf{T}_X, \\ \mathbf{F}_V & \text{if there is } a' \text{ such that } may(a', a) \text{ and } [a' \models_X \theta] \sqsupseteq \mathbf{T}_V. \end{cases}$$

Note that when $var(p) \subseteq X$, we have that $[c]_X \wedge a \wedge p$ is satisfiable for all $c \in \gamma(a)$ iff $a \models p$. Thus, the partition to two cases in the base case does not suggest a different semantics for each case and only suggests a simplified check for the case

$var(p) \subseteq X$. Note also that for refuting existential properties (equivalently, verifying universal properties) we proceed with usual may transitions, which corresponds to the case $X = V$. For the fixed-point operators, the closure of partitioned-must transitions under transitivity guarantees we can iterate the local $\exists\bigcirc$ and $\exists\ominus$ modalities, as in the usual three-valued semantics to μ-calculus [BG04]. Note that in the special case of CTL and CTL* formulas, this amounts to letting existential path formulas range over $pmust_X^+$ and $pmust_X^-$ paths [SG03].

6   Choosing the Relevant Variables

In this section we discuss the choice of the relevant variables. We first show that some of our previous results can be simplified in case the abstraction refers only to variables in X. Then, we show that the choice of the relevant variables need not be global, and extend the transitive closure of partitioned-must transitions to cases in which different transitions along the computation require different relevant variables.

6.1   An Abstraction Based on X

For a set $X \subseteq V$, we say that an abstraction is *based on* X if all the predicates in Φ refer only to variables in X. When our abstraction is based on X, then for all abstract states a and for all $c \in \gamma(a)$, we have $[c]_X \subseteq \gamma(a)$. Accordingly, in the definition of partitioned-must transitions, we can replace $[c]_X \wedge a$ and $[c']_X \wedge a'$ by $[c]_X$ and $[c']_X$, respectively. Consequently, the characterization in Propositions 3 and 4 can be simplified as follows:

Proposition 5. *Let a and a' be abstract states in an abstraction that is based on X. Then,*

- $pmust_X^+(a, a')$ *only if* $\forall \boldsymbol{x}[a(\boldsymbol{x}) \rightarrow \exists \boldsymbol{x'}.a'(\boldsymbol{x'}) \wedge (\boldsymbol{x'} \rightarrow SP(s, \boldsymbol{x}))]$.
- $pmust_X^-(a, a')$ *only if* $\forall \boldsymbol{x'}[a'(\boldsymbol{x'}) \rightarrow \exists \boldsymbol{x}.a(\boldsymbol{x}) \wedge (\boldsymbol{x} \rightarrow WP(s, \boldsymbol{x'}))]$.

Example 6. The function gcd described in Example 2 is based in $\{x, y, pc\}$. Hence, the existence of the $pmust_{\{x,y,pc\}}^-$ transitions demonstrated there follows from the validity of the following formulas (since a and b fix pc to 4, we ignore it in the formulas).

- $pmust_{\{x,y,pc\}}^-(a, a)$ iff
  $\forall x', y'[a(x', y') \rightarrow \exists x, y.(a(x, y) \wedge [(x > y \wedge x \neq 2y) \vee (x < y \wedge y \neq 2x)])]$.
- $pmust_{\{x,y,pc\}}^-(a, b)$ iff
  $\forall x', y'[b(x', y') \rightarrow \exists x, y.(a(x, y) \wedge [(x > y \wedge x = 2y) \vee (x < y \wedge y = 2x)])]$.

$\square$

When the specification we want to check involves only predicates that appear in the abstraction, then $var(p) \subseteq X$ for all atomic propositions. Accordingly, for sets X such that the abstraction is based on X, the base case of the multi-valued semantics described in Section 5.2 can be simplified, as $[a \models p] \sqsupseteq \mathbf{T}_X$ if $a \models p$ and $[a \models p] \sqsupseteq \mathbf{F}_X$ if $a \models \neg p$.

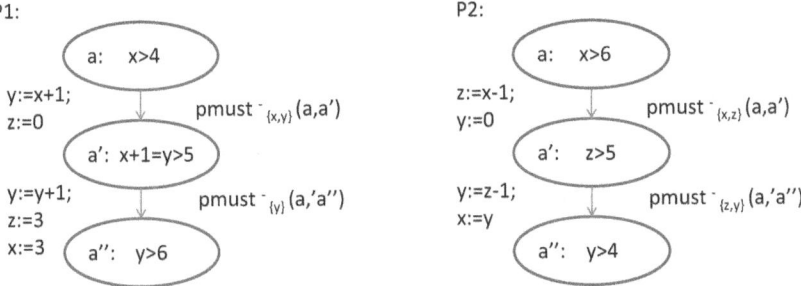

Fig. 4. Existence and nonexistence of dynamic transitive closure

6.2   Choosing X

Recall that our motivation is to detect weak reachability in the concrete system. Proposition 1 shows that partitioned-must transitions are closed under transitivity and can therefore be used for showing weak reachability. The theorem, however, assumes one set X with respect to which we partition all the transitions along the path. Below we generalize the proposition to a dynamic choice of sets according to which the transitions are partitioned.

Proposition 6. [dynamic transitive closure] *Let $a_1, a_2, \ldots, a_n$ be a sequence of abstract states.*

1. *If there is a sequence $X_1 \subseteq X_2 \subseteq \cdots \subseteq X_{n-1} \subseteq V$ such that for all $1 \leq i < n$, we have that $pmust^+_{X_i}(a_i, a_{i+1})$, then for every concrete state $c_1 \in \gamma(a_1)$, there is a concrete state $c_n \in \gamma(a_n)$, such that $must^{-*}([c_1]_{X_1} \wedge a_1, [c_n]_{X_{n-1}} \wedge a_n)$.*
2. *If there is a sequence $V \supseteq X_1 \supseteq X_2 \cdots \subseteq X_{n-1}$ such that for all $1 \leq i < n$, we have that $pmust^-_{X_i}(a_i, a_{i+1})$, then for every concrete state $c_n \in \gamma(a_n)$, there is a concrete state $c_1 \in \gamma(a_1)$, such that $must^{-*}([c_1]_{X_1} \wedge a_1, [c_n]_{X_{n-1}} \wedge a_n)$.*

The proof of the proposition proceeds by an induction on n and is similar to the proof of Proposition 1.

Remark 2. It is shown in [Bal04] that weak reachability in a framework with no partitioned-must transitions follows from a sequence of $must^-$ transitions followed by a sequence of $must^+$ transitions. By Proposition 2, $must^+(a, a')$ iff $pmust^+_V(a, a')$ and $must^-(a, a')$ iff $pmust^+_\emptyset(a, a')$. Likewise, since $must^+(a, a')$ iff $pmust^-_\emptyset(a, a')$ and $must^-(a, a')$ iff $pmust^-_V(a, a')$, it is also a special case of the dynamic transitive closure of $pmust^-$ transitions.

Example 7. Consider the program P_1 appearing in Figure 4. Since $pmust^-_{\{x,y\}}(a, a')$ and $pmust^-_{\{y\}}(a', a'')$, we can conclude that for every concrete state c' satisfying $y > 6$ there is a concrete state c satisfying $x > 4$ such that all the states satisfying $x > 4$ and that agree with c on the values of x and y can reach states that satisfy $y > 6$ and agree with c' on the value of y. Indeed, if $c' = \langle x, y, z \rangle$, then we can take $c = \langle y - 1, 0, 0 \rangle$.

Note that nor $pmust^-_{\{y\}}(a, a')$ neither $pmust^-_{\{x,y\}}(a', a'')$. Thus, the dynamic choice of relevant variables is essential.

Consider now the program P_2 in the figure. It requires a dynamic choice of relevant variables that does not satisfy the conditions of Proposition 6, as $\{z, y\} \not\subseteq \{x, y\}$. This is unfortunate, as it is true that for every concrete state c' satisfying $y > 4$ there is a concrete state c satisfying $x > 6$ such that $must^+([c]_{\{x\}}, [c']_{\{y\}})$. The cause of this inapplicability of Proposition 6 is the fact that the assignments in the program correspond to renaming of the variables. To see this, consider a program P'_2 in which the only variables are x and y, the abstract states are $(x > 6)$, $(x > 5)$, and $(x > 4)$, and statements are obtained from these of P_2 by renaming z to x in the first and second transitions and renaming y to x and x to y in the second transition. Then, we can use $pmust^-_{\{x\}}$-transitions in order to prove that for every concrete state $c' \in \gamma(a'')$, there is concrete state $c \in \gamma(a)$ such that $must^+([c]_{\{x\}}, [c']_{\{x\}})$.   □

References

[Bal04]   T. Ball. A theory of predicate-complete test coverage and generation. In *3rd International Symposium on Formal Methods for Components and Objects*, 2004.

[BG00]   G. Bruns and P. Godefroid. Generalized model checking: Reasoning about partial state spaces. In *Proc. 11th International Conference on Concurrency Theory*, volume 1877 of *Lecture Notes in Computer Science*, pages 168–182, 2000.

[BG04]   G. Bruns and P. Godefroid. Model checking with 3-valued temporal logics. In *31st International Colloquium on Automata, Languages and Programming*, volume 3142 of *Lecture Notes in Computer Science*, pages 281–293, 2004.

[BKY05]   T. Ball, O. Kupferman, and G. Yorsh. Abstraction for falsification. In *Proc. 17th CAV*, LNCS 3578, pages 67–81, 2005.

[CC77]   P. Cousot and R. Cousot. Abstract interpretation: a unified lattice model for the static analysis of programs by construction or approximation of fixpoints. In *Proc. 4th ACM POPL*, pages 238–252, 1977.

[Dij76]   E.W. Dijksta. *A Discipline of Programming*. Prentice-Hall, 1976.

[GJ02]   P. Godefroid and R. Jagadeesan. Automatic abstraction using generalized model checking. In *Proc. 14th CAV*, LNCS 2404, pages 137–150, 2002.

[KL06]   O. Kupferman and R. Lampert. On the construction of fine automata for safety properties. In *Proc. 4th ATVA*, LNCS 4218, pages 110–124, 2006.

[Kur94]   R.P. Kurshan. *Computer Aided Verification of Coordinating Processes*. Princeton Univ. Press, 1994.

[LT88]   K.G. Larsen and G.B. Thomsen. A modal process logic. In *Proc. 3th LICS*, 1988.

[LX90]   K.G. Larsen and L. XinXin. Equation solving using modal transition systems. In *Proc. 5th LICS*, pages 108–117, Philadelphia, June 1990.

[SG03]   S. Shoham and O. Grumberg. A game-based framework for CTL counterexamples and 3-valued abstraction-refinement. In *Proc. 15th CAV*, LNCS 2725, pages 275–287, 2003.

[SG04]   S. Shoham and O. Grumberg. Monotonic abstraction-refinement for CTL. In *Proc. 10th TACAS*, LNCS 2988, pages 546–560, 2004.

[VW94]   M.Y. Vardi and P. Wolper. Reasoning about infinite computations. *I & C*, 115(1):1–37, November 1994.

The Constraint Database Approach to Software Verification[*]

Peter Revesz

Max Planck Institut für Informatik
University of Nebraska-Lincoln
revesz@cse.unl.edu

Abstract. Based on constraint database techniques, we present a new approach to software verification. This new approach has some similarity to abstract interpretation that uses various widening operators; therefore, we call the new approach l-u widening. We show that our l-u widening leads to a more precise over-approximation of the invariants in a program than comparable previously proposed widening operators based on difference-bound matrices, although l-u widening can be computed as efficiently as the other widening operators. We show that constraint database techniques can compute non-convex program invariants too. Finally, we give a compact representation of addition-bound matrices, which generalize difference-bound matrices.

1 Introduction

Software verification is a basic concern of computer science, hence many different approaches were proposed for it, including data flow analysis, abstract interpretation [5,13,19], model checking [1,3,8,22], predicate abstraction [12], and mathematical induction. Today there are many examples of successful applications of these approaches to the verification of digital circuits and programs.

Software verification would be easy if we could compute the precise semantics of programs. For a procedural program, the semantics means that we find for each line of the program an invariant, which is the set of possible values of the variables that may be used at that line. While a precise computation is not possible in general, an over-approximation or under-approximation is possible. Abstract interpretation relies on a kind of over-approximation. More recently, constraint database researchers proposed for *constraint query languages* [17,18,20,21,28], which simplify *constraint logic programs* [15,4,9,16], alternative methods to over-approximate or under-approximate the semantics [26,27]. Via well-known translations among the various programming languages, the approximation results in constraint databases imply approximation results for the semantics of the more traditional procedural programs. The idea of translating from procedural programs to constraint query languages or constraint logic programs occurs in

[*] This research was supported in part by a Humboldt Research Fellowship from the Alexander von Humboldt Foundation.

B. Cook and A. Podelski (Eds.): VMCAI 2007, LNCS 4349, pp. 329–345, 2007.
© Springer-Verlag Berlin Heidelberg 2007

Delzanno and Podelski [8], Fribourg and Richardson [11], and Fribourg and Olson [10]. However, these papers did not use the latest approximation results. For example, [11] relied on the result that the least fixpoint semantics of Datalog (Prolog without function symbols and negation) with integer gap-order constraint programs can be precisely evaluated [25].[1]

In this paper we present a general approach of applying the constraint database approximation to software verification, extending earlier work in [2]. The constraint database approximations are different from *abstract interpretation* methods, which seem closest to them among the well-known software verification approaches. To further clarify their relationships, we introduce a new method between the constraint database approximations in [26,27] and abstract interpretation. We call this new method *l-u-widening*. We show that *l-u widening* is more precise than other widening operators proposed for abstract interpretation. On the other hand, program semantics approximations based on *l-u widening* can be more efficiently computed than program semantics approximations based on the constraint database techniques in [26,27] can be computed.

The rest of this paper is organized as follows. Section 2 gives a brief review of constraints, abstract interpretation, and difference bound matrices. It also describes addition-bound matrices which are similar to difference-bound matrices. Section 3 presents our new *l-u widening* operator and its use in approximating the semantics of programs. Section 4 reviews the earlier constraint database approximation methods and applies them to some sample programs. Section 5 presents an outline of the constraint database approach to software verification. Section 6 describes a novel compact representation of addition-bound matrices. This representation can be efficient for computer implementations. Finally, Section 7 discusses some related and future work.

2   Basic Concepts

2.1   Constraints

We use the following basic or *atomic constraints*:

$$
\begin{array}{ll}
\textbf{Lower Bound}: & x \geq b \\
\textbf{Upper Bound}: & -x \geq b \\
\textbf{Difference}: & x - y \geq b \\
\textbf{Addition}: & \pm x \pm y \geq b \\
\textbf{Linear}: & c_1 x_1 + \ldots + c_n x_n \geq b
\end{array}
$$

where x, y and the x_is are integer or rational variables and b, called the *bound*, and the c_is are integer constants.

---

[1] A gap-order is a constraint of the form $x - y \geq c$ or $\pm x \geq c$ where x and y are integer or rational variables and c is a non-negative integer constant.

Note: For uniformity, we prefer to always use constraints that end with "$\geq b$." We make some exceptions when other forms are clearer. For example, we use equalities of the form $x = b$ as a shorthand for $(x \geq b) \wedge (-x \geq -b)$. Some authors use the terms *potential constraint* and *sum constraint*. A *potential constraint* of the form $x - y \leq b$ translates to the difference constraint $y - x \geq -b$, and a *sum constraint* of the form $\pm x \pm y \leq b$ translates to the addition constraint $\pm x \pm y \geq -b$ with changed signs for x and y. Therefore, any result on potential constraints and sum constraints can be trivially translated to results on difference or addition constraints and vice versa.

2.2   Abstract Interpretation

Abstract interpretation finds *invariants* associated with specific program locations, such that each invariant is an over-approximation of the set of possible values of the program variables at that location, and that the invariants cannot be extended further by additional abstract execution of the program. Each invariant can be compactly described as some constraint on the program variables, for example, conjunctions of linear equations and inequalities, if the program variables are all rational numbers.

Abstract interpretation methods typically use a *widening operator*. Common widening operators use the domains of intervals [6] or polyhedra [7,19]. During an abstract execution of the program, the widening operator repeatedly updates a constraint M that describes the current value of the invariant associated with a program location with a new constraint N that describes an additional set of possible values of the program variables at that location. This happens when due to some program loop we reenter the same location again.

To keep things computationally feasible, the widening operator cannot just take $M \cup N$ as the new value of the invariant. Instead, it calculates a *convex* region, that is, a conjunction of linear inequality constraints that includes both M and N. In addition, when we use widening operators, we need to avoid an infinite number of repeated applications of the widening operators. The following clever idea guarantees that: *Preserve those constraints of M that are implied by N.* This looks attractive, because if M contains k linear inequalities, then at most k widening operators can be performed on M.

2.3   Addition-Bound Matrices

Miné [23] represents a conjunction of lower bound, upper bound, and sum constraints over variables $V = \{x_1, \ldots, x_n\}$ by a conjunction of potential constraints over variables $V^+ = \{x_1^+, x_1^-, \ldots, x_n^+, x_n^-\}$, that is, every variable has a positive form x_i^+ equivalent to x_i and a negative form x_i^- equivalent to $-x_i$.

Rephrasing Miné's idea, a conjunction of lower bound, upper bound and addition constraints C over variables $V = \{x_1, \ldots, x_n\}$ can be represented by a conjunction of difference constraints over variables $V^+ = \{x_1^+, x_1^-, \ldots, x_n^+, x_n^-\}$, as follows:

$$
\begin{aligned}
x \geq b &\equiv x^+ - x^- \geq 2b \\
-x \geq b &\equiv x^- - x^+ \geq 2b \\
x + y \geq b &\equiv x^+ - y^- \geq b \\
x - y \geq b &\equiv x^+ - y^+ \geq b \\
-x + y \geq b &\equiv x^- - y^- \geq b \\
-x - y \geq b &\equiv x^- - y^+ \geq b
\end{aligned}
$$

Now a conjunction of difference constraints can be simplified as follows. If the conjunction contains two difference constraints of the form $x - y \geq b$ and $x - y \geq c$ where $b > c$, then we can delete the second constraint, because it is already implied by the first constraint. By this simplification, there is at most one constraint with the left hand hide $x - y$, for any pair of variables x and y. We apply this simplification to the conjunction of difference constraints that result after our translation.

The conjunction of difference constraints C over variables $\{x_1, \ldots, x_n\}$ can be represented by an $n \times n$ *Addition-Bound Matrix* M, which is defined as follows:

$$
M[i,j] = \begin{cases} b & \text{if } (x_i - x_j \geq b) \in C \\ -\infty & \text{otherwise} \end{cases}
$$

Note: Rather confusingly, it is common to call *Difference-Bound Matrices (DBMs)* those matrices that represent conjunctions of potential constraints C and are actually defined as having entry b if $x_i - x_j \leq b$ is in C and $+\infty$ otherwise. We use the term *Addition-Bound Matrix (ABM)* because we ultimately represent by ABMs conjunctions of addition, lower bound, and upper bound constraints over V, although not directly as we first translate these constraints to conjunctions of difference constraints over V^+.

Example 1. Consider the following conjunction of lower bound, upper bound, and addition constraints over the variables x and y:

$$
-x \geq -25, \quad y \geq 3, \quad x - y \geq 4, \quad x + y \geq 10, \quad -x - y \geq -40
$$

These can be translated into the following difference constraints over the variables x^+, x^-, y^+, y^-:

$$
x^- - x^+ \geq -50, \quad y^+ - y^- \geq 6, \quad x^+ - y^+ \geq 4, \quad x^+ - y^- \geq 10, \quad x^- - y^+ \geq -40
$$

This set of difference constraints can be represented by the following ABM:

	x^+	x^-	y^+	y^-
x^+	$-\infty$	$-\infty$	4	10
x^-	-50	$-\infty$	-40	$-\infty$
y^+	$-\infty$	$-\infty$	$-\infty$	6
y^-	$-\infty$	$-\infty$	$-\infty$	$-\infty$

This simple representation of ABMs will suffice to describe the main theorems of the paper. Later in Section 6, we outline a more compact ABM representation that may lead to a more efficient computer implementation.

2.4 Operations on ABMs

Next we define some basic operators on ABMs.

Definition 1. Let M and N be two ABMs. Then the min of M and N, written as $M \vee N$, is defined as follows.

$$[M \vee N]\,[i,j] = \min(M[i,j], N[i,j])$$

Alternatively, we can write the above as:

$$[M \vee N]\,[i,j] = \left\{ \begin{array}{ll} M[i,j] & \text{if } M[i,j] \leq N[i,j] \\ N[i,j] & \text{if } N[i,j] \leq M[i,j] \end{array} \right\}$$

Miné's widening operator on DBMs [23] can be rephrased on ABMs as follows.

Definition 2. Let M and N be two ABMs. Then the *widening* of M by N, written as $M \triangledown N$, is defined as follows.

$$[M \triangledown N]\,[i,j] = \left\{ \begin{array}{ll} M[i,j] & \text{if } M[i,j] \leq N[i,j] \\ -\infty & \text{if } N[i,j] < M[i,j] \end{array} \right\}$$

Example 2. Let M be as in Example 1, and let N be the following ABM:

	x^+	x^-	y^+	y^-
x^+	$-\infty$	$-\infty$	15	10
x^-	-60	$-\infty$	$-\infty$	$-\infty$
y^+	$-\infty$	7	$-\infty$	2
y^-	$-\infty$	$-\infty$	$-\infty$	$-\infty$

In this case $M \vee N$ is:

	x^+	x^-	y^+	y^-
x^+	$-\infty$	$-\infty$	4	10
x^-	-60	$-\infty$	$-\infty$	$-\infty$
y^+	$-\infty$	$-\infty$	$-\infty$	2
y^-	$-\infty$	$-\infty$	$-\infty$	$-\infty$

while $M \triangledown N$ is:

	x^+	x^-	y^+	y^-
x^+	$-\infty$	$-\infty$	4	10
x^-	$-\infty$	$-\infty$	$-\infty$	$-\infty$
y^+	$-\infty$	$-\infty$	$-\infty$	$-\infty$
y^-	$-\infty$	$-\infty$	$-\infty$	$-\infty$

3   The l-u-Widening Operator

We say matrix M has domain D if all entries of M are in D. If all entries of M are $\geq l$ and $\leq u$ or $-\infty$, where l and u are some integer constants, then the domain of M is $\{-\infty\} \cup \{l, l+1, \ldots, u-1, u\}$. (The domain of M should not be confused with the domain of the variables which are integer or rational numbers.)

We now introduce the *l-u-widening* operator.

Definition 3. Let $l < 0$ and $u > 0$ be two integer numbers. Let M and N be two ABMs such that the domain of M is $\{-\infty\} \cup \{l, l+1, \ldots, u-1, u\}$. Then the *l-u-widening* of M by N, written as $M \lozenge_{l,u} N$, is defined as follows.

$$[M \lozenge_{l,u} N][i,j] = \left\{ \begin{array}{lll} M[i,j] & \text{if} & M[i,j] \leq N[i,j] \\ N[i,j] & \text{if} & l \leq N[i,j] < M[i,j] \\ -\infty & \text{if} & N[i,j] < l \leq M[i,j] \end{array} \right\}$$

Example 3. Let us continue Example 2 and find $M \lozenge_{-50,50} N$, the *l-u-widening* of M and N with $l = -50$ and $u = 50$.

	x^+	x^-	y^+	y^-
x^+	$-\infty$	$-\infty$	4	10
x^-	$-\infty$	$-\infty$	$-\infty$	$-\infty$
y^+	$-\infty$	$-\infty$	$-\infty$	2
y^-	$-\infty$	$-\infty$	$-\infty$	$-\infty$

3.1   Properties of l-u-Widening

In this section we compare the precision of the widening and l-u-widening operators. Let $\mathcal{S}$ be the solution space of an ABM or union of ABMs. We have the following.

Theorem 1. For any $l < 0$ and $u > 0$, the following holds:

$$\mathcal{S}(M \cup N) \subseteq \mathcal{S}(M \vee N) \subseteq \mathcal{S}(M \lozenge_{l,u} N) \subseteq \mathcal{S}(M \triangledown N).$$

Proof. By Definition 1, each entry of $M \vee N$ is smaller than the corresponding entry in either M or N. Hence $\mathcal{S}(M) \subseteq \mathcal{S}(M \vee N)$ and $\mathcal{S}(N) \subseteq \mathcal{S}(M \vee N)$ hold. Therefore, $\mathcal{S}(M \cup N) \subseteq \mathcal{S}(M \vee N)$ also must hold.

By Definition 3, the *minimum, widening* and *l-u-widening* operators behave the same when $M[i,j] \leq N[i,j]$. When $N[i,j] < M[i,j]$ then there are two cases. In the first case, when $l \leq N[i,j]$, then the l-u-widening operator behaves like the *minimum* operator and returns $N[i,j]$, and if $N[i,j] < l$, then it behaves like the *widening* operator and returns $-\infty$. Therefore, $\mathcal{S}(M \vee N) \subseteq \mathcal{S}(M \lozenge_{l,u} N) \subseteq \mathcal{S}(M \triangledown N)$ must hold. □

Definition 4. Given a program P, and values $l < 0$ and $u > 0$, the result of evaluating its least fixed point using l-u-widening is written as $P^{l,u}$.

The following is the main l-u-approximation theorem.

Theorem 2. Let $l < 0$ and $u > 0$ be integer constants. For any program P with m lines and n variables the following holds.

$$lfp(P) \subseteq W^{l,u}$$

where $lfp(P)$ is the least fixed point of P. Further, $W^{l,u}$ can be computed using $O(|u - l|mn^2)$ time.

Proof. We start evaluating P. For each new line L_i of P, when we find the first ABM for it, we change all entries greater than u to u and call the resulting ABM M_i. Then whenever a new ABM N is found for line L_i, we update M_i to be the result of $M_i \Diamond_{l,u} N$. This ensures that the domain of each M_i is $\{-\infty\} \cup \{l, l + 1, \ldots, u-1, u\}$ throughout the approximate evaluation. In each iteration at least one entry in at least one of the M_is must decrease. Moreover, each entry can decrease at most $|u - l|$ times and each M_i has n^2 entries. Since there are m number of M_is, the total number of iterations is at most $|u-l|mn^2$. It is also clear that the approximate evaluation is always computing an upper approximation of the actual least fixed point. $\qquad\square$

The computational complexity of the l-u-widening operator is similar to that of Miné's widening operator, which needs $O(mn^2)$ iterations. If the values of u and l are fixed constants, then the use of the two widening operators will have the same complexity. However, there are reasons to vary the values of l and u, because we can also get tighter approximations using increasingly smaller values of l or larger values of u. That is, we can show the following.

Theorem 3. For each program P and constants $l_1, l_2, u_1,$ and u_2 such that $l_1 \leq l_2 < 0 < u_2 \leq u_1$, the following condition holds:

$$W^{l_1,u_1} \subseteq W^{l_2,u_2}$$

3.2 A Simple Program with Goto Statements

Consider the following simple program fragment.

```
1 a = 0
2 a = a + 1
3 if a > 2 then   goto 6
4 if a = 2 then   goto 7
5 goto 2
6
7
```

Let us see how this widening operator works on this program. Let $L_{i,j}$ be the invariant at the beginning of line i at the jth entry of that line. Initially all $L_{i,0}$ are empty. $L_{2,1} = \{a = 0\}$ (which, like all equalities, is just a shorthand for a conjunction of two inequalities, namely in this case $\{0 \leq a \leq 0\}$), and $L_{3,1} = \{a = 1\}$. Lines 3 and 4 have false if conditions and do not change the value of a, hence $L_{4,1} = L_{5,1} = \{a = 1\}$. The execution of line 5 takes us back to the beginning of line 2 with no change in a. This is the second entry to line 2, hence $L_{2,2} = L_{2,1} \triangledown L_{5,1} = \{a = 0\} \triangledown \{a = 1\} = \{a \geq 0\}$. When $a = a + 1$ is executed, this yields $a \geq 1$. We enter line 3 for the second time. By widening we get $L_{3,2} = L_{3,1} \triangledown \{a \geq 1\} = \{a = 1\} \triangledown \{a \geq 1\} = \{a \geq 1\}$. We enter the if statement and find that $L_{3,2} \wedge (a > 2) = (a \geq 1) \wedge (a > 2) = a > 2$. That is, our invariant (or rather our current best estimate of the possible values of the program variable a at the beginning of line 3) and the condition of the if statement overlap on $a > 2$, which clearly is a nonempty set. Hence we enter line 6 with $L_{6,1} = \{a > 2\}$. This example can be summarized in the table below.

Invariants Obtained by Widening

Line	1st Entry	2nd Entry
2	$0 \leq a \leq 0$	$0 \leq a$
3	$1 \leq a \leq 1$	$1 \leq a$ if condition $a > 2$ true goto 6
4	$1 \leq a \leq 1$	
5	$1 \leq a \leq 1$	

However, the above program analysis is wrong. Actually, the program can never enter line 6. When we first get to line 5, $a = 1$. Hence when we get back to line 2 and execute $a = a + 1$, then $a = 2$. Therefore the if condition of line 3 will fail, and the program goes on to line 4. The if condition of line 4 will be true, hence we go to line 7 and never enter line 6.

Clearly, the invariant analysis is not precise enough. The inductive generalization that the widening operator applies (for example, in the above program from $a = 0$ and $a = 1$ to $a \geq 0$) is often very useful and powerful, but it has to be applied more judiciously. At the present, there are only some limited techniques in the abstract interpretation area to get around the above problem. For example, we may establish a priori a set of constraints K and widen M up-to K only, but finding a suitable K is easier said than done. For example, if K contains $\{a \leq 3\}$, then we may widen $a = 0$ and $a = 1$ to $0 \leq a \leq 3$, but then the program analysis would be still incorrect.

Now let us see how the *l-u widening* works on the same program with $l = -5$ and $u = 5$. The crucial difference is that on the second entry to line 2, we obtain $L_{2,2} = L_{2,1} \lozenge_{-5,5} L_{5,1} = \{a = 0\} \lozenge_{-5,5} \{a = 1\} = \{0 \leq a \leq 1\}$. When $a = a + 1$ is executed, this yields $1 \leq a \leq 2$. We enter line 3 for the second time and get $L_{3,2} = L_{3,1} \lozenge_{-5,5} \{1 \leq a \leq 2\} = \{1 \leq a \leq 2\}$. We enter the if statement but find that $L_{3,2} \wedge (a > 2)$ is unsatisfiable. Therefore. we continue to line 4 and find that $L_{4,2} = L_{4,1} \lozenge_{-5,5} \{1 \leq a \leq 2\} = \{1 \leq a \leq 2\}$. W enter the if statement and find that $L_{4,2} \wedge a = 2$ is satisfiable. Hence we go to line 7. The invariants found by the *l-u widening* are summarized in the table below.

Invariants Obtained by l-u Widening

Line	1st Entry	2nd Entry
2	$0 \leq a \leq 0$	$0 \leq a \leq 1$
3	$1 \leq a \leq 1$	$1 \leq a \leq 2$ if condition $a > 2$ false
4	$1 \leq a \leq 1$	$1 \leq a \leq 2$ if condition $a = 2$ true goto 7
5	$1 \leq a \leq 1$	

3.3 The Subway Train Example

Let us consider the following subway train speed regulation system described by Halbwachs [13]. Each train detects beacons that are placed along the track and receives a "second" signal from a central clock.

Let b and s be counter variables for the number of beacons and second signals received. Further, let d be a counter variable that describes how long the train is applying its brake. The goal of the speed regulation system is to keep $| b - s |$ small while the train is running.

The speed of the train is adjusted as follows. When $s + 10 \leq b$, then the train notices it is early and applies the brake as long as $b > s$. Continuously braking causes the train to stop before encountering 10 beacons.

When $b + 10 \leq s$ the train is late and will be considered late as long as $b < s$. As long as any train is late, the central clock will not emit the second signal.

The following program implements the subway train regulation using parallel case statements. In a parallel case statement one of the cases is selected randomly. If the condition of the selected case statement is false, then another is selected and executed. This repeats until one of the cases succeeds.

Train(b,s,d)
```
1 ONTIME
  begin parallel
2       if b − s > −9 then s = s + 1 goto ONTIME
3       if b − s = −9 then s = s + 1 goto LATE
4       if b − s < 9   then b = b + 1 goto ONTIME
5       if b − s = 9   then b = b + 1 goto BRAKE
  end parallel
6 LATE
  begin parallel
7       if b − s < −1 then b = b + 1 goto LATE
```

8   **if** $b - s = -1$ **then** $b = b + 1$ **goto** ONTIME
   end parallel
9 STOPPED
   begin parallel
10   **if** $b - s > 1$ **then** $s = s + 1$ **goto** STOPPED
11   **if** $b - s = 1$ **then** $s = s + 1$ **goto** ONTIME
   end parallel
12 BRAKE
   begin parallel
13   **if** $b - s > 1$ **then** $s = s + 1$ **goto** BRAKE
14   **if** $b - s = 1$ **then** $s = s + 1$, $d = 0$ **goto** ONTIME
15   **if** $d < 9$ **then** $b = b + 1$, $d = d + 1$ **goto** BRAKE
16   **if** $d \leq 9$ **then** $b = b + 1$, $d = 0$ **goto** STOPPED
   end parallel

Suppose we know that the subroutine *Train* can be called with any values where $b = s$ and $d = 0$. We need to find all the possible values of the variables b, s and d in all lines of the program.

Note that variable d is changed only in the parallel case statement after BRAKE. When we exit the BRAKE region and go to either ONTIME or STOPPED, then d is reset to 0. Hence d always remains 0 outside of the BRAKE region. This simplifies the analysis for the other three cases. With only variables b and s, each conjunction of difference constraints can be represented in the form:

$$c_1 \leq b \leq c_2, \quad c_3 \leq s \leq c_4, \quad c_5 \leq b - s \leq c_6$$

where c_1, c_2, c_3, c_4, c_5, c_6 are constants that may be omitted.

$L_{1,1} = \{0 \leq b - s \leq 0\}$
line 2 causes return to ONTIME with $\{-1 \leq b - s \leq -1\}$
line 3 fails
line 4 causes return to ONTIME with $\{1 \leq b - s \leq 1\}$
line 5 fails
$L_{1,2} = L_{1,1} \nabla (\{-1 \leq b - s \leq -1\} \sqcup \{1 \leq b - s \leq 1\}) = \{-1 \leq b - s \leq 1\}$

$\vdots$
$L_{1,9} = \{-9 \leq b - s \leq 9\}$
line 2 causes return to ONTIME with $\{-9 \leq b - s \leq 8\}$
line 3 causes entry to LATE with $\{-10 \leq b - s \leq -10\}$
line 4 causes return to ONTIME with $\{-8 \leq b - s \leq 9\}$
line 5 causes entry to BRAKE with $\{10 \leq b - s \leq 10\}$
$L_{1,10} = L_{1,9}$

$L_{6,1} = \{-10 \leq b - s \leq -10\}$
line 7 causes return to LATE with $\{-9 \leq b - s \leq -9\}$
line 8 fails
$L_{6,2} = L_{6,1} \nabla \{-9 \leq b - s \leq -9\} = \{-10 \leq b - s \leq -9\}$

$\vdots L_{6,10} = \{-10 \le b - s \le -1\}$
line 7 causes return to LATE with $\{-10 \le b - s \le -2\}$
line 8 causes return to ONTIME with $\{-1 \le b - s \le -1\}$
$L_{6,11} = L_{6,10}$
$L_{1,11} = L_{1,10}$

$L_{12,1} = \{10 \le b - s \le 10, \; d = 0\}$
line 13 causes return to BRAKE with $\{9 \le b - s \le 9, \; d = 0\}$
line 14 fails
line 15 causes return to BRAKE with $\{11 \le b - s \le 11, \; d = 1\}$
line 16 causes entry to STOPPED with $\{11 \le b - s \le 11, \; d = 0\}$
$L_{12,2} = L_{12,1} \triangledown (\{9 \le b - s \le 9, \; d = 0\} \sqcup \{11 \le b - s \le 11, \; d = 1\} = \{9 \le b - s \le 11, \; 0 \le d \le 1\}$

$\vdots$line 16 causes entry to STOPPED with $\{2 \le b - s \le 20, d = 0\}$
$L_{12,10} = \{1 \le b - s \le 19, \; 0 \le d \le 9\}$

$L_{9,1} = \{2 \le b - s \le 20, d = 0\}$
line 10 causes return to STOPPED with $\{1 \le b - s \le 19, d = 0\}$
line 11 fails
$L_{9,2} = L_{9,1} \triangledown \{1 \le b - s \le 19, d = 0\} = \{1 \le b - s \le 20, d = 0\}$
line 10 causes return to STOPPED with $\{1 \le b - s \le 19, d = 0\}$
line 11 causes return to ONTIME with $\{0 \le b - s \le 0, d = 0\}$
$L_{9,3} = L_{9,2}$
$L_{1,11} = L_{1,10}$

The table below shows the result of the invariants that can be found using $l = -20$ and $u = 20$.

Invariants Obtained by l-u Widening

Brake	Late	Ontime	Stopped
$1 \le b - s \le 19$	$-10 \le b - s \le -1$	$-9 \le b - s \le 9$	$1 \le b - s \le 20$
$0 \le d \le 9$	$0 \le d \le 0$	$0 \le d \le 0$	$0 \le d \le 0$

It is possible to prove that these values match the actual semantics of the program.

4   Non-convex Invariants

In the constraint database area, researchers have founds methods for finding over-approximations and under-approximations of the least fixpoint semantics of Datalog programs. The over-approximation yields for each relation a disjunction of conjunctions of atomic constraints. In this sense the approximation is different from widening operators that always yield a conjunction of atomic constraints.

Definition 5. Given any conjunction $\mathcal{C}$ of addition constraints and integer $l < 0$, let $\mathcal{C}'$ be the result of deleting from $\mathcal{C}$ any constraint where the bound is less than l. Further, let $\mathcal{C}''$ be the result of replacing in $\mathcal{C}$ any bound with less than l with l.

It is easy to see that $\mathcal{C}'$ is an over-approximation and $\mathcal{C}''$ is an under-approximation of $\mathcal{C}$. Further, this leads to the following evaluation idea.

Definition 6. Given a program P and value $l < 0$, the result of evaluating its least fixed point by always rewriting after each rule application any conjunction of constraints $\mathcal{C}$ into a $\mathcal{C}'$ (or $\mathcal{C}''$) as in Definition 5 is written as $P^{l,u}$ (respectively, $P_{l,u}$).

The following is the main theorem that we can adopt.

Theorem 4. Let $l < 0$ be any integer constant. For any program P the following holds.

$$P_{l,u} \subseteq lfp(P) \subseteq P^{l,u}$$

Further, $P_{l,u}$ and $P^{l,u}$ can be computed in finite time.

The bottom up evaluation in Theorem 4 is slower than the *l-u widening* approach. However, it can lead to a more precise over-approximation or under-approximation than the *l-u widening approach*.

Example 4. Consider the following program.

```
1 x = 1,   y = 1
2 x = x + 1,   y = y + 2x - 1
3 goto 2
```

For the above program, it is easy to see that for each entry i of line 2, we have:

$$L_{2,i} = \{x = i,\ y = i^2\}.$$

Recall that each equality is the conjunction of a lower and an upper bound atomic constraint. That is,

$$L_{2,i} = \{x \geq i,\ -x \geq -i,\ y \geq i^2,\ -y \geq -i^2\}.$$

Hence when we evaluate the semantics of this program using $l = -10$, we obtain the following over-approximation:

$$L_{2,i} = \{x = i,\ y = i^2 : 1 \leq i \leq 3\} \cup \{x = i,\ y \geq i^2 : 4 \leq i \leq 10\} \cup \{x \geq 11,\ y \geq 121\}$$

This formula is the union of three parts. Clearly, the first part corresponds to the actual semantics for $1 \leq i \leq 3$. The second part is an over-approximation needed because for $4 \leq i \leq 10$ we can only express the upper bounds $y \geq i^2$ but cannot express the lower bounds $-y \geq -i^2$ needed to have a precise evaluation matching the actual semantics. The third part is needed because for any $i = 11$ we can express neither the lower bound $-x \geq i$ nor the lower bound $-y \geq -i^2$. Finally, note that for any $i \geq 12$, the conjunction of the constraints $x \geq i$ and $y \geq i^2$ are more restrictive than the third part.

5   Verification

Suppose that we need to check that certain *error states* never occur during any execution of a program. The error states are expressed as a quantifier-free formula of the variables used in the program. Each satisfying assignment of values to the variables is an error that needs to be avoided. Next we outline a general constraint database approach to the verification of programs.

1. Translate the program P into a transition system T.
2. Translate T into a Datalog program that always derives conjunctions of addition constraints.
3. Find an over-approximation of the least fixed point semantics of the Datalog program.
4. Check that the over-approximation and the error states do not intersect.
5. If the answer is "yes", then return "'safe"', else goto 1 and try a smaller l.

Step (1) is well-known in the software verification area. Step (2) is explained in Chapter 5 of [28], to which we refer for the details. Step (3) follows Theorems 2 and 4 with more details in [28]. The over-approximation algorithm is implemented within the MLPQ constraint database system [29], which is available from the website: `cse.unl.edu/~revesz`. Step (4) requires to test the satisfiability of the over-approximation and the error states. Finally, Step (5) is just a repetition of the previous steps in case the check is inconclusive. In the MLPQ system the user can specify any negative l value.

In the above outline, the translations to transition system and to Datalog are required only to take a direct advantage of the already implemented constraint database systems such as MLPQ. Those who are familiar with abstract interpretations with widening operators may skip the translations steps and consider an invariant analysis similar to abstract interpretation with the widening operator replaced by *l-u widening* or the non-convex approximation.

Example 5. Consider again the subway train example. The Datalog with addition constraint program that is equivalent to the subway train control program is described in [2]. Let $\mathcal{E}$, the error states, be as follows:

$$\mathcal{E} = \{b, s \ : \ |b - s| > 20\}.$$

It can be checked that the over-approximation found for the subway train and $\mathcal{E}$ have no common solution. Hence the subway train program is safe to use.

Example 6. Consider again the program in Example 4. This program can be translated into the following constraint Datalog program.

$$Line2(x, y) \; : -- \; x = 1, \; y = 1.$$
$$Line2(x', y') : -- \; Line2(x, y), \; x' = x + 1, \; y' = y + 2x' - 1.$$
$$Line3(x, y) \; : -- \; Line2(x, y), \; x' = x + 1, \; y' = y + 2x' - 1.$$

We can calculate the over-approximation of the above Datalog program similar to Example 4. It is interesting to see how the bottom up evaluation terminates. In the 11th application of the second rule (which corresponds to the 12th entry of line 2 in the original program), the bottom up evaluation finds that $\exists x, y \; x' = x + 1, \; y' = y + 2x' - 1, \; x \geq 11, \; y \geq 121 \; = \; x' \geq 12, y' \geq 144$. Before adding this to the set of already existing ABMs for Line2, we need to replace x' by x and y' by y. The replacement yields $x \geq 12, y \geq 144$, which is more restrictive than $x \geq 11, y \geq 121$, the previously added ABM. Hence it is not added to the set of ABMs for *Line2* and the evaluation terminates.[2]

Let the error states $\mathcal{E}$ be as follows:

$$\mathcal{E} = \{y \; : \; y \geq 10, \; -y \geq -15\}.$$

This is a region where y is between 10 and 15 inclusively. It can be easily checked that the over-approximation of $L_{2,1}$ in Example 4 and $\mathcal{E}$ have no common solution. Hence the program can never enter the error states.

6   An Efficient Representation of ABMs

Without loss of generality we can fix an order of the variables and assume that in all addition constraints of the form $x - y \geq b$ or $-x + y \geq b$, x is earlier than y, and in all addition constraints of the form $x + y \geq b$ and $-x - y \geq b$ x is earlier than y or $x = y$. We can represent lower bound constraints of the form $x \geq b$ by $x + x \geq 2b$ and and upper bound constraints of the form $-x \geq b$ by $-x - x \geq 2b$.

Then we can represent $x - y \geq b$ and $x + y \geq b$ constraints by a matrix L as follows:

$$L[i, j] = \begin{cases} b & \text{if } (x_i - x_j \geq b) \in C \text{ and } i < j \\ b & \text{if } (x_j + x_i \geq b) \in C \text{ and } j \leq i \\ -\infty & \text{otherwise} \end{cases}$$

Similarly, we can represent $-x + y \geq b$ and $-x - y \geq b$ constraints by a matrix U as follows:

$$U[i, j] = \begin{cases} b & \text{if } (-x_i + x_j \geq b) \in C \text{ and } i < j \\ b & \text{if } (-x_j - x_i \geq b) \in C \text{ and } j \leq i \\ -\infty & \text{otherwise} \end{cases}$$

---

[2] This is a simplification of the bottom up evaluation, because within the ABMs constraints of the form $x \geq b$ are represented by $x^+ - x^- \geq 2b$ as described in Section 2.3.

Note that the above is equivalent to the following:

$$U[i,j] = \begin{cases} b & \text{if } (x_i - x_j \leq -b) \in C \text{ and } i < j \\ b & \text{if } (x_j + x_i \leq -b) \in C \text{ and } j \leq i \\ -\infty & \text{otherwise} \end{cases}$$

For example, the ABM in Example 1 can be represented by the following matrices. L is:

$$\begin{array}{c|cc} & x & y \\ \hline x & -\infty & 4 \\ y & 10 & 6 \end{array}$$

and U is:

$$\begin{array}{c|cc} & x & y \\ \hline x & -50 & -\infty \\ y & -40 & -\infty \end{array}$$

The above representation with matrices L and U requires only $2n^2$ matrix entries, while Miné's representation requires $4n^2$ matrix entries. Moreover, since the corresponding entries in L and U are lower and upper bounds of the same $x_i - x_j$ or $x_j + x_i$, they can be put together as follows:

$$\begin{array}{c|cc} & x & y \\ \hline x & [-\infty, 50] & [4, +\infty] \\ y & [10, 40] & [6, +\infty] \end{array}$$

Therefore, each ABM can be represented using a matrix with only n^2 entries that are intervals.

7   Related and Future Work

Pratt [24] gave efficient algorithms for testing the satisfiability and the implication problem for conjunctions of potential constraints. Harvey and Stuckey [14] gave a polynomial algorithm for the implication problem in the case of conjunctions of sum constraints with integer variables. An open problem is to improve the complexity of the algorithm in [14]. Currently, we are working on updating the MLPQ system to the more efficient ABM representation described in Section 6. Another open problem is to find conditions when the over-approximation and the under-approximation of the program semantics are the same, resulting in a precise evaluation.

References

1. ALUR, R., COURCOUBETIS, C., HALBWACHS, N., HENZINGER, T., HO, P.-H., NICOLLIN, X., OLIVERO, A., SIFAKIS, J., AND YOVINE, S. The algorithmic analysis of hybrid systems. *Theoretical Computer Science 138*, 1 (1995), 3–34.

2. ANDERSON, S., AND REVESZ, P. Verifying the incorrectness of programs and automata. In *Proc. 6th International Symposium on Abstraction, Reformulation, and Approximation* (2005), vol. 3607 of *Lecture Notes in Computer Science*, Springer-Verlag, pp. 1–13.

3. CLARKE, E. M., GRUMBERG, O., AND PELED, D. A. *Model Checking*. MIT Press, 1999.

4. COLMERAUER, A. Note sur Prolog III. In *Proc. Séminaire Programmation en Logique* (1986), pp. 159–174.

5. COUSOT, P. Proving program invariance and termination by parametric abstraction, Lagrangian relaxation and semidefinite programming. In *Sixth International Conference on Verification, Model Checking and Abstract Interpretation (VMCAI'05)* (Paris, France, LNCS 3385, Jan. 17–19 2005), Springer, Berlin, pp. 1–24.

6. COUSOT, P., AND COUSOT, R. Abstract interpretation: A unified lattice model for static analysis of programs by construction or approximation of fixpoints. In *Proc. ACM Principles on Programming Languages* (1977), ACM Press, pp. 238–252.

7. COUSOT, P., AND HALBWACHS, N. Automatic discovery of linear restraints among variables of a program. In *Proc. ACM Principles on Programming Languages* (1978), ACM Press, pp. 84–97.

8. DELZANNO, G., AND PODELSKI, A. Model checking in CLP. In *2nd International Conference on Tools and Algorithms for the Construction and Analysis of Systems* (1999), vol. 1579 of *Lecture Notes in Computer Science*, Springer-Verlag, pp. 74–88.

9. DINCBAS, M., VAN HENTENRYCK, P., SIMONIS, H., AGGOUN, A., GRAF, T., AND BERTHIER, F. The constraint logic programming language chip. In *Proc. Fifth Generation Computer Systems* (Tokyo, Japan, 1988), pp. 693–702.

10. FRIBOURG, L., AND OLSÉN, H. A decompositional approach for computing least fixed-points of Datalog programs with Z-counters. *Constraints 2*, 3–4 (1997), 305–36.

11. FRIBOURG, L., AND RICHARDSON, J. D. C. Symbolic verification with gap-order constraints. In *Proc. Logic Program Synthesis and Transformation* (1996), vol. 1207 of *Lecture Notes in Computer Science*, pp. 20–37.

12. GODEFROID, P., HUTH, M., AND JAGADEESAN, R. Abstraction-based model checking using modal transition systems. In *12th International Conference on Concurrency Theory* (2001), pp. 426–440.

13. HALBWACHS, N. Delay analysis in synchronous programs. In *Proc. Conference on Computer-Aided Verification* (1993), pp. 333–46.

14. HARVEY, W., AND STUCKEY, P. A unit two variable per inequality integer constraint solver for constraint logic programming. In *Proc. Australian Computer Science Conference (Australian Computer Science Communications)* (1997), pp. 102–11.

15. JAFFAR, J., AND LASSEZ, J. L. Constraint logic programming. In *Proc. 14th ACM Symposium on Principles of Programming Languages* (1987), pp. 111–9.

16. JAFFAR, J., AND MAHER, M. Constraint logic programming: A survey. *J. Logic Programming 19/20* (1994), 503–581.

17. KANELLAKIS, P. C., KUPER, G. M., AND REVESZ, P. Constraint query languages. In *Proc. ACM Symposium on Principles of Database Systems* (1990), pp. 299–313.

18. KANELLAKIS, P. C., KUPER, G. M., AND REVESZ, P. Constraint query languages. *Journal of Computer and System Sciences 51*, 1 (1995), 26–52.

19. KERBRAT, A. Reachable state space analysis of lotos specifications. In *Proc. 7th International Conference on Formal Description Techniques* (1994), pp. 161–76.

20. KUPER, G. M., LIBKIN, L., AND PAREDAENS, J., Eds. *Constraint Databases.* Springer-Verlag, 2000.
21. MARRIOTT, K., AND STUCKEY, P. J. *Programming with Constraints: An Introduction.* MIT Press, 1998.
22. MCMILLAN, K. *Symbolic Model Checking.* Kluwer, 1993.
23. MINÉ, A. The octagon abstract domain. In *Proceedings Analysis, Slicing and Transformation* (2001), IEEE Press, pp. 310–319.
24. PRATT, V. Two easy theories whose combination is hard. *MIT Technical Report* (1977).
25. REVESZ, P. A closed-form evaluation for Datalog queries with integer (gap)-order constraints. *Theoretical Computer Science 116*, 1 (1993), 117–49.
26. REVESZ, P. Datalog programs with difference constraints. In *Proc. 12th International Conference on Applications of Prolog* (1999), pp. 69–76.
27. REVESZ, P. Reformulation and approximation in model checking. In *Proc. 4th International Symposium on Abstraction, Reformulation, and Approximation* (2000), B. Choueiry and T. Walsh, Eds., vol. 1864 of *Lecture Notes in Computer Science*, Springer-Verlag, pp. 124–43.
28. REVESZ, P. *Introduction to Constraint Databases.* Springer-Verlag, 2002.
29. REVESZ, P., CHEN, R., KANJAMALA, P., LI, Y., LIU, Y., AND WANG, Y. The MLPQ/GIS constraint database system. In *ACM SIGMOD International Conference on Management of Data* (2000).

Constraint Solving for Interpolation

Andrey Rybalchenko[1,2] and Viorica Sofronie-Stokkermans[2]

[1] Ecole Polytechnique Fédérale de Lausanne
[2] Max-Planck-Institut für Informatik, Saarbrücken

Abstract. Interpolation is an important component of recent methods for program verification. It provides a natural and effective means for computing separation between the sets of 'good' and 'bad' states. The existing algorithms for interpolant generation are proof-based: They require explicit construction of proofs, from which interpolants can be computed. Construction of such proofs is a difficult task. We propose an algorithm for the generation of interpolants for the combined theory of linear arithmetic and uninterpreted function symbols that does not require a priori constructed proofs to derive interpolants. It uses a reduction of the problem to constraint solving in linear arithmetic, which allows application of existing highly optimized Linear Programming solvers in black-box fashion. We provide experimental evidence of the practical applicability of our algorithm.

1 Introduction

Interpolation [5] is an important component of recent methods for program verification. It provides a natural and effective means for computing separation between the sets of 'good' and 'bad' states. Such separations provide a basis for powerful heuristics for the discovery of relevant predicates for predicate abstraction with refinement and for the over-approximation in model checking, see e.g. [6,10,11,12,16,17,18,26].

The applicability of interpolation-based verification methods crucially depends on the employed procedure for interpolant generation. The existing algorithms for interpolant generation are proof-based: They require explicit construction of proofs, from which interpolants can be computed (resolution proofs in propositional logic, proofs for linear inequalities over the reals, or in the combined theory of linear arithmetic with uninterpreted function symbols [14,21,17]). Explicit construction of such proofs is a difficult task, which hinders the practical applicability of interpolants for verification. In fact, the existing tools for the generation of interpolants over linear arithmetic and uninterpreted function symbols only handle the difference bound-fragment of arithmetic constraints [11,17]. One of the consequences of this limitation is that no program whose correctness depends on a predicate over three or more variables can be handled by the method described in [7].

We propose an algorithm for the generation of interpolants for the combined theory of linear arithmetic and uninterpreted function symbols that does not

B. Cook and A. Podelski (Eds.): VMCAI 2007, LNCS 4349, pp. 346–362, 2007.

require a priori constructed proofs to derive interpolants. It uses a reduction of the problem to constraint solving in linear arithmetic. Thus, the algorithm allows application of existing highly optimized Linear Programming solvers in black-box fashion, which leads to a practical implementation.

The main contributions of the paper are the following.

- First, we describe an algorithm LI for the generation of interpolants for linear arithmetic only, which is based on a reduction to constraint solving. The algorithm LI has the following advantages:
  - it allows to handle directly strict and non-strict inequalities,
  - it can be implemented using a Linear Programming solver as a black box.
- Second, we present an algorithm LIUIF for generating interpolants in combination of linear arithmetic with uninterpreted function symbols, following the hierarchical style of [23,24]. It applies the algorithm LI as a subroutine.
- We provide experimental evidence of the applicability of this constraint based interpolant generation.

Our implementation is integrated into the predicate discovery procedure of the software verification tools BLAST [7] and ARMC [20]. Our experiments with BLAST on Windows device drivers provide a direct comparison with the existing tool FOCI [17], and show promising running times in favour of the constraint based approach. Our method can handle systems which pose problems to other interpolation-based provers: It allowed us, for instance, to apply ARMC to verify safety properties of train controller systems [19], which required inference of predicates with both strict and nonstrict inequalities, and it allows us to verify examples that require predicates over up to four variables.

Related work. Our algorithm differs from the existing methods for the interpolant generation [11,12,17,26] in the following key points. Being constraint based, our algorithm does not require a priori constructed resolution proof to derive an interpolant. However, it is possible to construct such a proof using non-negative linear combinations of inequalities computed by our algorithm.

Our method for the synthesis of interpolants for the combined theory of linear arithmetic and uninterpreted function symbols follows the hierarchical style of [23,24] and uses the interpolant construction method for linear arithmetic as a black-box. The algorithm presented in this paper, on which our implementation is based, differs from that in [24], being tuned to our constrained based approach.

In fact, our method for generating interpolants for linear arithmetic can be used as a black box procedure also in other contexts, e.g. for the method for constructing interpolants in combinations of theories over disjoint signatures proposed in [26] or for the interpolant generation method for the combinations of linear arithmetic, uninterpreted function symbols, lists, and sets with cardinality constraints, which uses a reduction to the invariant generation in linear arithmetic and uninterpreted function symbols [12]. Conversely, our method for the synthesis of interpolants for the combined theory of linear arithmetic and uninterpreted function symbols can use any method for interpolant construction for linear arithmetic.

The "split" prover [11] applies a sequent calculus for the synthesis of interpolants whose linear arithmetic part is restricted to difference bounds constraints with a user-defined constraint on the bound. In contrast, our implementation is constraint-based and handles full linear arithmetic. Its extension to accommodate user-defined constraints is a subject of ongoing work.

Our algorithm constructs linear arithmetic interpolants in a way similar to constraint-based invariant and ranking function generation methods based on Farkas' lemma and linear programming, see e.g. [2,3,4]. We use its extension (Motzkin's transposition theorem) to handle strict inequalities. In the terminology of linear programming, interpolants are hyperplanes that separate strictly disjoined convex hulls and contain only common variables of the hulls.

Structure of the paper. We introduce the necessary preliminaries in Section 2. We describe the algorithm LI for the synthesis of constrained interpolants in linear arithmetic in Section 3, and its extension LIUIF for the handling of uninterpreted function symbols in Section 4. We briefly describe our implementation and experimental results in Section 5.

2   Preliminaries

In what follows we will use the following notations:

Linear constraints over rational and real spaces. We write $Ax < a$ and $Ax \leq a$ for systems (conjunctions) of strict and non-strict inequalities, respectively. We write $Ax \leqslant a$ for a system that may contain inequalities of both kinds. We refer to such systems as *mixed* ones. Given $Ax \leqslant a$, we write $A^{\mathsf{lt}}x < a^{\mathsf{lt}}$ and $A^{\mathsf{le}}x \leq a^{\mathsf{le}}$ for the systems that contain strict and non-strict inequalities from $Ax \leqslant a$, respectively. A row vector λ with m_A elements defines a linear combination of inequalities from $Ax \leqslant a$. The vector λ has sub-vectors λ^{lt} and λ^{le} that correspond to strict and non-strict inequalities from $Ax \leqslant a$, respectively. We have $\lambda A = \lambda^{\mathsf{lt}}A^{\mathsf{lt}} + \lambda^{\mathsf{le}}A^{\mathsf{le}}$ and $\lambda a = \lambda^{\mathsf{lt}}a^{\mathsf{lt}} + \lambda^{\mathsf{le}}a^{\mathsf{le}}$. We write $A_{|k}$ for the k-th column of a matrix A. We write $A^k x \leqslant a^k$ to refer to a system of inequalities with index k. Given a vector i we write i^{T} to denote its transposition.

We note that precise handling of strict inequalites is required for interpolation problems over rationals/reals, which occur in the verification of real time and hybrid systems. Consider the unsatisfiable conjunction $x < 0$ and $x \geq 0$, where x ranges over rationals/reals. The relaxation of $x < 0$ to non-strict inequality $x \leq 0$ leads to the loss of unsatisfiability. The strengthening of $x < 0$ to $x \leq -1$ may result in the interpolant $x \leq -1$ which is not an interpolant for the original problem, since $x < 0$ does not imply $x \leq -1$.

Extensions with uninterpreted functions. Let Σ be a set of (new) function symbols. Let T_0 be one of the theories $LI(\mathbb{Q})$ (linear rational arithmetic) or $LI(\mathbb{R})$

(linear real arithmetic). with signature $\Pi_0 = (\Sigma_0, \mathsf{Pred})$. We denote by $LI(\mathbb{Q})^{\Sigma}$ the extension of $\mathbb{Q}$ with the uninterpreted function symbols in Σ. $LI(\mathbb{R})^{\Sigma}$ is defined similarily. In what follows, the definitions are given for the case of linear rational arithmetic. Similar definitions can also be given for $LI(\mathbb{R})^{\Sigma}$. A model $\mathcal{M}$ of $LI(\mathbb{Q})^{\Sigma}$ is a model of $LI(\mathbb{Q})$ with universe M and with a function $f_{\mathcal{M}} : M^n \to M$ for each $f \in \Sigma$ with arity n. No additional constraints are imposed on the properties of these functions (i.e. they are free).

Truth, satisfiability and entailment w.r.t. a theory. Let $\mathcal{T}$ be a theory (that is, a set of models in a given signature Σ). Truth and satisfiability of a first-order formula in a given model are defined in the standard way. Let ϕ and ψ be formulae over the signature Σ. We say that ϕ *is true w.r.t.* $\mathcal{T}$ (denoted $\models_{\mathcal{T}} \phi$) if ϕ is true in all models of $\mathcal{T}$; ϕ *entails* (or *implies*) ψ w.r.t. $\mathcal{T}$ (denoted $\phi \models_{\mathcal{T}} \psi$) if ψ is true in all models of $\mathcal{T}$ in which ϕ is true; ϕ *is satisfiable w.r.t.* $\mathcal{T}$ if there exists a model of $\mathcal{T}$ in which ϕ is true. If ϕ is false in all models of $\mathcal{T}$, we say that ϕ is unsatisfiable. Note that ϕ is unsatisfiable iff $\phi \models_{\mathcal{T}} \bot$, where $\bot$ stands for false.

Interpolants. A theory $\mathcal{T}$ has interpolation if, for all formulae ϕ and ψ in the signature of $\mathcal{T}$, if $\phi \models_{\mathcal{T}} \psi$ then there exists a formula I containing only symbols which occur in both ϕ and ψ such that $\phi \models_{\mathcal{T}} I$ and $I \models_{\mathcal{T}} \psi$. An alternative formulation in the model-checking literature is:

> If $\phi \wedge \psi \models_{\mathcal{T}} \bot$ then there exists a formula I containing only symbols which occur in both ϕ and ψ such that $\phi \models_{\mathcal{T}} I$ and $\psi \wedge I \models_{\mathcal{T}} \bot$.

First order logic has interpolation [5]. However, even if ϕ and ψ are very simple (e.g. quantifier-free or conjunctions of atoms), I may still be an arbitrary formula. In many applications it is important to find *simple* interpolants: for instance, if ϕ and ψ are quantifier-free formulae, we are often interested in the existence of *quantifier-free* interpolants. We say that a theory $\mathcal{T}$ has *quantifier-free* interpolants if for all quantifier-free formulae A and B:

> If $\mathsf{A} \wedge \mathsf{B} \models_{\mathcal{T}} \bot$ there exists a quantifier-free formula I over the common variables of A and B such that $\mathsf{A} \models_{\mathcal{T}} I$ and $I \wedge \mathsf{B} \models_{\mathcal{T}} \bot$.

3   Linear Interpolants

In this section we present an algorithm LI (Linear Interpolation) for the interpolant generation for linear arithmetic (with both strict and non-strict inequalities). We show the algorithm in Figure 1.

The input of LI consists of two mixed systems of inequalities $Ax \leqslant a$ and $Bx \leqslant b$ that are mutually disjoint, i.e. the conjunction $Ax \leqslant a \wedge Bx \leqslant b$ is not satisfiable. The output of the algorithm is a linear interpolant $ix \lhd \delta$, where $\lhd \in \{\leqslant, <\}$.

The algorithm proceeds by constructing linear programming problems and solving these problems using an off-the-shelf linear programming solver. The

input
> $Ax \leqslant a$ and $Bx \leqslant b$: systems of strict and non-strict inequalities,
> where $Ax \leqslant a \wedge Bx \leqslant b$ is unsatisfiable

output
> $ix \triangleleft \delta$: interpolant, where $\triangleleft \in \{\leq, <\}$

vars
> Φ: auxiliary constraint
> λ: vector defining linear combination of inequalities in $Ax \leqslant a$
> $\lambda^{lt}, \lambda^{le}$: sub-vectors of λ defining linear combination of
>   *strict* and *non-strict* inequalities in $Ax \leqslant a$, respectively
>   (in particular, $\lambda A = \lambda^{lt} A^{lt} + \lambda^{le} A^{le}$ and $\lambda a = \lambda^{lt} a^{lt} + \lambda^{le} a^{le}$)
> μ, μ^{lt}, μ^{le}: analogous to λ, λ^{lt}, and λ^{le}

begin
> $\Phi := \lambda \geq 0 \wedge \mu \geq 0 \wedge i = \lambda A \wedge \delta = \lambda a \wedge \lambda A + \mu B = 0$
> **if** exist λ, μ, i, δ satisfying $\Phi \wedge \lambda a + \mu b \leq -1$ **then**
>   (∗ 1st branch ∗)
>   **return** $ix \leq \delta$
> **else if** exist λ, μ, i, δ satisfying $\Phi \wedge \lambda a + \mu b \leq 0 \wedge \lambda^{lt} \neq 0$ **then**
>   (∗ 2nd branch ∗)
>   **return** $ix < \delta$
> **else if** exist λ, μ, i, δ satisfying $\Phi \wedge \lambda a + \mu b \leq 0 \wedge \mu^{lt} \neq 0$ **then**
>   (∗ 3rd branch ∗)
>   **return** $ix \leq \delta$

end.

x	A	a	λ	A^{lt}	A^{le}	a^{lt}	a^{le}	λ^{lt}	λ^{le}
$n \times 1$	$m_A \times n$	$m_A \times 1$	$1 \times m_A$	$m_{A^{lt}} \times n$	$m_{A^{le}} \times n$	$m_{A^{lt}} \times 1$	$m_{A^{le}} \times 1$	$1 \times m_{A^{lt}}$	$1 \times m_{A^{le}}$

Fig. 1. Algorithm LI for the synthesis of linear interpolants. The table shows dimensions of matrices and vectors used in the algorithm. The dimensions for $Bx \leqslant b$, μ, μ^{lt}, and μ^{le} are fixed in a similar fashion.

solver is treated as a black box. The structure of the problems reflects the different cases why the conjunction $Ax \leqslant a \wedge Bx \leqslant b$ is unsatisfiable, following Motzkin's transposition theorem [22]. The proofs of Theorems 2 and 3 provide a formal explanation of the correspondence.

Theorem 1 ((Motzkin's) transposition theorem [22]). *Let A and B be matrices and let a and b be column vectors. Then there exists a vector x with $Ax < a$ and $Bx \leq b$, if and only if for all row vectors $y, z \geq 0$:*

- *if $yA + zB = 0$ then $ya + zb \geq 0$; and*
- *if $yA + zB = 0$ and $y \neq 0$ then $ya + zb > 0$.*

Example 1. We simulate the algorithm LI on the following unsatisfiable conjunction of mixed systems of inequalities

$$z < 0 \wedge x \leq z \wedge y \leq x \quad \text{and} \quad y \leq 0 \wedge x + y \geq 0.$$

We assume an additional constraint that the resulting interpolant must not contain the variable y. We translate the inequalities into the matrix representation.

$$\underbrace{\begin{pmatrix} 0 & 0 & 1 \\ 1 & 0 & -1 \\ -1 & 1 & 0 \end{pmatrix}}_{A} \begin{pmatrix} x \\ y \\ z \end{pmatrix} \leqslant \underbrace{\begin{pmatrix} 0 \\ 0 \\ 0 \end{pmatrix}}_{a} \qquad \underbrace{\begin{pmatrix} 0 & 1 & 0 \\ -1 & -1 & 0 \end{pmatrix}}_{B} \begin{pmatrix} x \\ y \\ z \end{pmatrix} \leqslant \underbrace{\begin{pmatrix} 0 \\ 0 \end{pmatrix}}_{b}$$

We split the mixed system $Ax \leqslant a$ into the strict part $A^{lt}x < a^{lt}$ and the non-strict part $A^{le}x \leq a^{le}$.

$$\underbrace{(0\,0\,1)}_{A^{lt}} \begin{pmatrix} x \\ y \\ z \end{pmatrix} < \underbrace{(0)}_{a^{lt}} \qquad \underbrace{\begin{pmatrix} 1 & 0 & -1 \\ -1 & 1 & 0 \end{pmatrix}}_{A^{le}} \begin{pmatrix} x \\ y \\ z \end{pmatrix} \leq \underbrace{\begin{pmatrix} 0 \\ 0 \end{pmatrix}}_{a^{le}}$$

The system $Bx \leqslant b$ is equal to its non-strict part $B^{le}x \leq b^{le}$. The strict part of $Bx \leqslant b$ is empty.

Let $i = (i_x\ i_y\ i_z)$ and δ be the unknown coefficients that define the interpolant $i\binom{x}{y}{z} \vartriangleleft \delta$, where $\vartriangleleft$ is either the strict $<$ or non-strict $\leq$ inequality relation symbol. The algorithm computes the values for the unknown coefficients and determines the relation $\vartriangleleft$.

Let $\lambda = (\lambda_1\ \lambda_2\ \lambda_3)$ and $\mu = (\mu_1\ \mu_2)$ be the linear combinations of the inequalities of the first and the second system, respectively. We have $\lambda^{lt} = (\lambda_1)$ and $\lambda^{le} = (\lambda_2\ \lambda_3)$. The values of λ and μ determine the interpolant.

The guard of the first branch of LI is unsatisfiable. The guard of the second branch is satisfiable; we compute the valuations $\lambda = (1\ 1\ 0)$ and $\mu = (1\ 1)$ together with the interpolant's coefficients $i = (1\ 0\ 0)$ and $\delta = 0$. Since $\lambda^{lt} = (1)$, we have that $\vartriangleleft$ is the strict inequality relation symbol. The resulting interpolant is $x < 0$. □

For the completeness of the exposition, we show that two mutually unsatisfiable systems of mixed inequalities have an interpolant that is a single inequality. This inequality may be strict or non-strict.

Theorem 2 (Linear interpolants for mixed linear inequalities). *Given mutually unsatisfiable systems $Ax \leqslant a$ and $Bx \leqslant b$ of strict and non-strict inequalities, there exists a linear inequality interpolant $ix \vartriangleleft \delta$, where $\vartriangleleft \in \{\leq, <\}$.*

The correctness of the algorithm LI is stated in the following theorem.

Theorem 3 (Algorithm LI: Soundness and completeness). *The algorithm LI is sound and complete: It always produces a linear interpolant, by taking the 1st, 2nd or 3rd branch.*

3.1 Interpolants for Disjunctions

We obtain an algorithm for the synthesis of constrained interpolants for disjunctions of mixed systems

$$\bigvee_k A_k x \leqslant a_k \quad \text{and} \quad \bigvee_l B_l x \leqslant b_l$$

by taking the disjunction of convex hulls

$$\bigvee_k \bigwedge_l i_{kl} x \leqslant \delta_{kl}$$

that consists of interpolants $i_{kl} x \leqslant \delta_{kl}$ for each pair of disjuncts $A_k x \leqslant a_k$ and $B_l x \leqslant b_l$. The constraints above are in *disjunctive normal form*: both formulae for which the interpolant is computed are disjunctions of conjunctions. In applications we sometimes need to compute constrained interpolants for conjunctions of non-unit clauses, i.e. for formulae in *conjunctive normal form*. For this we can use standard methods discussed e.g. in [17] or [26]: in a DPLL-style procedure partial interpolants are generated for the unsatisfiable branches and then recombined using ideas of Pudlák [21].

4   Extension with Uninterpreted Function Symbols

So far, we have presented an algorithm for the generation of interpolants in the theory of linear arithmetic. Our application domains mentioned in the introduction include software model checking and verification of timed and hybrid systems. They naturally motivate an extension of the interpolant-generation algorithm to combination of linear arithmetic with additional theories.

In this section we consider the extension with free functions, which is useful for conservative approximation of non-arithmetic expressions. The algorithm we propose is based on a hierarchical calculus for reasoning in certain extensions of theories (which we called *local extensions*) [23]. This calculus makes it possible to reduce checking satisfiability of quantifier-free formulae w.r.t. the extension, to checking satisfiability of formulae in the 'base theory'. Any extension of a theory with uninterpreted function symbols falls into this class. As the notion of local theory extension is not needed in the present context, all relevant results will be presented for the special case of extensions of linear rational and real arithmetic with free function symbols. For the sake of simplicity, we will use as running example $LI(\mathbb{Q})$. All results can be used as well for $LI(\mathbb{R})$. However, many of the results presented here also hold for more general extensions. Such generalizations were presented in [24].

We begin by giving the main idea of the hierarchical calculus for extensions with free function symbols in [23] (Section 4.1). Based on this, in Section 4.2 we present a hierarchical method for generating interpolants in such extensions.

Notation. Everywhere in what follows let Σ be a set of (new) function symbols. We denote by $LI(\mathbb{Q})^\Sigma$ the extension of $\mathbb{Q}$ with the uninterpreted function symbols in Σ. We refer to the function symbols in Σ as extension functions. To distinguish them from constraints in linear arithmetic, we denote conjunctions of (unit) literals over this extended signature using a special font ($A \wedge B$).

4.1   A Hierarchical Calculus

Let Σ be a set of uninterpreted function symbols, let $LI(\mathbb{Q})^\Sigma$ be the extension of linear rational arithmetic $LI(\mathbb{Q})$ with the uninterpreted function symbols in Σ. Given a disjunction $\phi(x_1, \ldots, x_n)$ of conjunctions of atomic formulae over the signature of $LI(\mathbb{Q})^\Sigma$, we want to check whether

$$LI(\mathbb{Q})^\Sigma \models \forall x_1 \ldots \forall x_n \phi(x_1, \ldots, x_n),$$

i.e., whether ϕ holds in each model of $LI(\mathbb{Q})^\Sigma$ and for all possible assignments of values in this model to the variables $x_1, \ldots, x_n$. Equivalently, we can test whether there exists a model and a possible assignment to the variables $x_1, \ldots, x_n$ in it for which $\neg\phi$ becomes true, i.e. checking whether $\neg\phi(x_1, \ldots, x_n)$ is satisfiable. Thus, proving truth w.r.t. all models and valuations can be reduced to proving satisfiability of sets of clauses w.r.t. $LI(\mathbb{Q})^\Sigma$.

Let $G(c_1, \ldots, c_n)$ be a set of quantifier-free clauses with variables $c_1, \ldots, c_n$[1] in the signature of $LI(\mathbb{Q})^\Sigma$. To check the satisfiability of $G(c_1, \ldots, c_n)$ w.r.t. $LI(\mathbb{Q})^\Sigma$ we can proceed as follows:

Step 1: Flattening and purification. G is purified and flattened by introducing fresh variables for the arguments of the extension functions as well as for the subterms $t = f(g_1, \ldots, g_n)$ starting with extension functions $f \in \Sigma$, together with corresponding definitions $c_t = t$. We obtain a set of clauses $G_0 \wedge D$, where D consists of unit clauses of the form $f(c_1, \ldots, c_n) = c$, where $c_1, \ldots, c_n, c$ are variables and $f \in \Sigma$, and G_0 contains clauses without function symbols in Σ.

Step 2: Reduction to testing satisfiability in $LI(\mathbb{Q})$. By the locality of any extension with free function symbols [23], we know that we can reduce the problem of testing satisfiability of G w.r.t. $LI(\mathbb{Q})^\Sigma$ to a satisfiability test in $LI(\mathbb{Q})$ as shown in Theorem 4.

Theorem 4 ([23]). *With the notations above, the following are equivalent:*
(1) $G \models_{LI(\mathbb{Q})^\Sigma} \bot,$
(2) $G_0 \wedge D \models_{LI(\mathbb{Q})^\Sigma} \bot,$
(3) $G_0 \wedge N_0 \models_{LI(\mathbb{Q})} \bot, where$

$$N_0 = \bigwedge \{ \bigwedge_{i=1}^n c_i = d_i \rightarrow c = d \mid f(c_1, \ldots, c_n) = c \in D, f(d_1, \ldots, d_n) = d \in D \}.$$

is the set of functionality axioms corresponding to the terms occurring in D.

Problem (3) in Theorem 4 is a satisfiability problem for quantifier-free clauses in linear rational arithmetic. We thus reduced, hierarchically, the problem of testing

---

[1] In what follows we are concerned with satisfiability of such clauses; the variables in $G(c_1, \ldots, c_n)$ are implicitly existentially quantified. In the automated reasoning literature, existential variables are replaced by constants, using skolemization; thus one can replace the variables in $G(c_1, \ldots, c_n)$ by (Skolem) constants. In what follows we refer to them as variables. However, the notation we chose reminds that these existentially quantified variables can, in fact, be regarded as "constants".

the satisfiability of the set of quantifier-free clauses G in $LI(\mathbb{Q})^{\Sigma}$ to the problem of testing the satisfiability of a set of quantifier-free constraints in $LI(\mathbb{Q})$.

Complexity. Flattening and purification can be done in linear time; the growth of the formulae is linear. The size of the satisfiability problem in $LI(\mathbb{Q})$ obtained by the translation above is quadratic in the number of extension terms in the input formula. Hence, the complexity of the procedure is of order $k(n^2)$, where n is the size of the input formula and $k(m)$ is the complexity of the problem of testing the satisfiability of sets of ground clauses in $LI(\mathbb{Q})$ for an input of size m.

Remark. If G is a set of unit clauses then the procedure mimics the Nelson-Oppen procedure for combination of $LI(\mathbb{Q})$ with the theory of free function symbols in Σ within the prover for linear arithmetic. (Due to the convexity of linear arithmetic, we can always find a clause in N_0 whose premises are implied by G. The clause is replaced with its conclusion and the procedure is repeated until a set of unit clauses is obtained.) Thus, exchange of equalities between shared variables needs not be done explicitly. The complexity of the method is similar to that of the Nelson-Oppen combination of convex theories.

The following example illustrates the method.

Example 2. Let $G = \mathsf{A} \wedge \mathsf{B}$, where

$$\mathsf{A}: \quad g(a) = c + 5 \wedge f(g(a)) \geq c + 1,$$
$$\mathsf{B}: \quad h(b) = d + 4 \wedge d = c + 1 \wedge f(h(b)) < c + 1.$$

We show that $\mathsf{A} \wedge \mathsf{B}$ is unsatisfiable in $LI(\mathbb{Q})^{\{f,g,h\}}$ as follows:

Step 1: Flattening and purification. We purify and flatten the formulae A and B by replacing the terms starting with f with new variables. We obtain the following purified form:

$$\mathsf{A}_0: \quad a_1 = c + 5 \wedge a_2 \geq c + 1, \qquad\qquad D_A: \quad a_1 = g(a) \wedge a_2 = f(a_1),$$
$$\mathsf{B}_0: \quad b_1 = d + 4 \wedge d = c + 1 \wedge b_2 < c + 1, \quad D_B: \quad b_1 = h(b) \wedge b_2 = f(b_1).$$

Step 2: Hierarchical reasoning. By Theorem 4 we have that $\mathsf{A} \wedge \mathsf{B}$ is unsatisfiable in $LI(\mathbb{Q})^{\{f,g,h\}}$ iff $\mathsf{A}_0 \wedge \mathsf{B}_0 \wedge N_0$ is unsatisfiable in $LI(\mathbb{Q})$, where N_0 corresponds to the consequences of the congruence axioms for those ground terms which occur in the definitions $D_A \wedge D_B$ for the newly introduced variables.

Def	G_0	N_0
$D_A: a_1{=}g(a) \wedge a_2{=}f(a_1)$	$\mathsf{A}_0: a_1 = c + 5 \wedge a_2 \geq c + 1$	$N_0: b_1{=}a_1 \rightarrow b_2{=}a_2$
$D_B: b_1{=}h(b) \wedge b_2{=}f(b_1)$	$\mathsf{B}_0: b_1 = d + 4 \wedge d = c + 1 \wedge b_2 < c + 1$	

To prove that $\mathsf{A}_0 \wedge \mathsf{B}_0 \wedge N_0$ is unsatisfiable, note that $\mathsf{A}_0 \wedge \mathsf{B}_0 \models a_1 = b_1$. Hence, $\mathsf{A}_0 \wedge \mathsf{B}_0 \wedge N_0$ entails $a_2 = b_2 \wedge a_2 \geq c + 1 \wedge b_2 < c + 1$, which is inconsistent.

4.2   Hierarchical Interpolation in $LI(\mathbb{Q})^{\Sigma}$

We show how this hierarchical calculus can be used to generate interpolants for extensions with free function symbols.

Assume that $\mathsf{A} \wedge \mathsf{B} \models_{LI(\mathbb{Q})^{\Sigma}} \bot$, where A and B are two sets of ground clauses. Our goal is to find an *interpolant*, that is a quantifier-free formula I, containing only variables and uninterpreted function symbols which are common to A and B such that

$$\mathsf{A} \models_{LI(\mathbb{Q})^{\Sigma}} I \quad \text{and} \quad I \wedge \mathsf{B} \models_{LI(\mathbb{Q})^{\Sigma}} \bot .$$

For the sake of simplicity we first restrict to sets A and B of unit clauses, i.e. to conjunctions of ground literals. Our goal is to reduce the search for the interpolant of $\mathsf{A} \wedge \mathsf{B}$ in $LI(\mathbb{Q})^{\Sigma}$ to:

(i) constructing an interpolant I_0 in $LI(\mathbb{Q})$,
(ii) using I_0 to construct an interpolant for $\mathsf{A} \wedge \mathsf{B}$ (by appropriate substitutions).

Flattening and purification do not influence the existence of interpolants [24]: If I_0 is an interpolant of the flattened forms $(\mathsf{A}_0 \wedge D_A) \wedge (\mathsf{B}_0 \wedge D_B)$ of A_0 and B_0, then the formula $\overline{I}_0$, obtained from I_0 by replacing, recursively, all newly introduced variables with the terms in the original signature which they represent, is an interpolant for $\mathsf{A} \wedge \mathsf{B}$. Therefore we can restrict w.l.o.g. to finding interpolants for the *purified and flattened* set of formulae $(\mathsf{A}_0 \wedge D_A) \wedge (\mathsf{B}_0 \wedge D_B)$.

By Theorem 4, $\mathsf{A}_0 \wedge D_A \wedge \mathsf{B}_0 \wedge D_B \models_{LI(\mathbb{Q})^{\Sigma}} \bot$ if and only if $\mathsf{A}_0 \wedge \mathsf{B}_0 \wedge N_0 \models_{LI(\mathbb{Q})} \bot$, where $N_0 = \bigwedge \{ \bigwedge_{i=1}^{n} c_i = d_i \rightarrow c = d \mid f(c_1, \ldots, c_n) = c, f(d_1, \ldots, d_n) = d \in D \}$. By definition, $N_0 = N^A \wedge N^B \wedge N_{\text{mix}}$, where N^A only contains variables from A_0 (it is A-pure), N^B only contains variables from B_0 (it is B-pure), and $N_{\text{mix}} = \bigwedge \{ \bigwedge_{i=1}^{n} a_i = b_i \rightarrow a = b \mid f(a_1, \ldots, a_n) = a \in (D_A \setminus D_B), f(b_1, \ldots, b_n) = b \in (D_B \setminus D_A) \}$. The clauses in N_{mix} are mixed, i.e. contain combinations of A-local and B-local variables. Thus, the equivalence in Theorem 4 cannot be used directly for generating a ground interpolant.

Example 3. Consider the reduction to the base theory in the previous example. The clause $a_1 = b_1 \rightarrow a_2 = b_2$ of N_0 contains both A-local and B-local variables.

Idea. The idea of our approach is to separate mixed instances N_{mix} of congruence axioms in N_0, into an A-part and a B-part. We show that if $\mathsf{A} \wedge \mathsf{B} \models_{LI(\mathbb{Q})^{\Sigma}} \bot$ then we find a set T of terms in the signature of $LI(\mathbb{Q})^{\Sigma}$ containing only variables and extension functions common to A and B, which allows us to separate the instances of functionality axioms in N_{mix} into a part N_{sep}^A consisting of instances of functionality axioms for extension terms occurring in A and T, and a part N_{sep}^B consisting of instances with terms occurring in B and T. We show that such a separation does not lead to the loss of unsatisfiability, i.e. that the conjunction

$$(\mathsf{A}_0 \wedge N_A \wedge N_{\text{sep}}^A) \wedge (\mathsf{B}_0 \wedge N_B \wedge N_{\text{sep}}^B)$$

has no model where the extension functions may be partial, but in which all terms in D_A, D_B, and T are defined.

Example 4. Consider the reduction to the base theory in the example given in Section 4.1. The clause $a_1 = b_1 \rightarrow a_2 = b_2$ of N_{mix} can be replaced with a conjunction of A-pure and B-pure clauses as follows:

Note that $A_0 \wedge B_0 \models a_1 = b_1$. It is easy to see that there exists a term t (namely $t = c + 5$) containing only variables common to A_0 and B_0 such that $A_0 \models_{LI(\mathbb{Q})} a_1 = t$ and $B_0 \models_{LI(\mathbb{Q})} t = b_1$. Let $T = \{t\} = \{c + 5\}$. We show that instead of using the mixed clause $a_1 = b_1 \rightarrow a_2 = b_2$, we can use, without loss of unsatisfiability, the flattened and purified instances N_{sep}^A and N_{sep}^B of the functionality axioms corresponding to terms in A and T, resp. B and T:

$$N_{\text{sep}}^A = \{a_1 = c + 5 \rightarrow a_2 = c_{f(c+5)}\}, \quad N_{\text{sep}}^B = \{c + 5 = b_1 \rightarrow c_{f(c+5)} = b_2\}.$$

(We introduced a new constant $c_{f(c+5)}$ for $f(c + 5)$, together with its definition $D_T : c_{f(c+5)} = f(c + 5)$.) We can thus replace N_0 with the instances of the congruence axioms N_{sep}^A and N_{sep}^B, now separated into an A-part and a B-part. It is now sufficient to compute an interpolant in $LI(\mathbb{Q})$ for

$$(A_0 \wedge N_{\text{sep}}^A) \wedge (B_0 \wedge N_{\text{sep}}^B).$$

To compute the interpolant, note that $A_0 \wedge N_{\text{sep}}^A$ is logically equivalent to $A_0 \wedge a_2 = c_{f(c+5)}$, and $B_0 \wedge N_{\text{sep}}^B$ is logically equivalent to $B_0 \wedge b_2 = c_{f(c+5)}$. The conjunction $(A_0 \wedge a_2 = c_{f(c+5)}) \wedge (B_0 \wedge b_2 = c_{f(c+5)})$ is unsatisfiable. An interpolant is $I_0 : c_{f(c+5)} \geq c + 1$. Thus, $A_0 \wedge a_2 = c_{f(c+5)} \models I_0$ and $B_0 \wedge b_2 = c_{f(c+5)} \wedge I_0 \models \bot$.

Let $I = (f(c+5) \geq c+1)$ be obtained by replacing the newly introduced constant $c_{f(c+5)}$ with the term it denotes (namely $f(c + 5)$). It is easy to see that:

$$A_0 \wedge D_A \models_{LI(\mathbb{Q})\{f,g,h\}} A_0 \wedge (a_2 = f(c + 5)) \models_{LI(\mathbb{Q})\{f,g,h\}} I,$$
$$B_0 \wedge D_B \models_{LI(\mathbb{Q})\{f,g,h\}} B_0 \wedge (b_2 = f(c + 5)) \models_{LI(\mathbb{Q})\{f,g,h\}} \neg I.$$

Thus, I is an interpolant for $(A_0 \wedge D_A) \wedge (B_0 \wedge D_B)$, hence also for $A \wedge B$.

The method. Assume that $A_0 \wedge D_A \wedge B_0 \wedge D_B \models_{LI(\mathbb{Q})^{\Sigma}} \bot$. Then $A_0 \wedge B_0 \wedge N_0 \models_{LI(\mathbb{Q})} \bot$, where $N_0 = N^A \wedge N^B \wedge N_{\text{mix}}$, the clauses in N^A are A-pure, those in N^B are B-pure, and those in $N_{\text{mix}} = \bigwedge \{ \bigwedge_{i=1}^n a_i = b_i \rightarrow a = b \mid f(a_1, \ldots, a_n) = a \in (D_A \backslash D_B), f(b_1, \ldots, b_n) = b \in (D_B \backslash D_A) \}$ contain combinations of A-local and B-local variables.

Our goal is to replace N_{mix} with the conjunction of an A-pure and a B-pure part, $N_{\text{sep}}^A \wedge N_{\text{sep}}^B$, of instances of the functionality axioms. The correctness of the method relies on the following properties of linear arithmetic: convexity with respect to equality atoms (Lemma 1) and separability of entailed inequalities (Lemma 2).

Lemma 1. *Linear arithmetic over $\mathbb{R}$ or over $\mathbb{Q}$ is convex w.r.t. equality atoms, i.e. for each conjunction Γ of literals and for every set of equalities $s_i = t_i$, $i \in \{1, \ldots, n\}$, if $\Gamma \models \bigvee_{i=1}^n s_i = t_i$ then $\Gamma \models s_j = t_j$ for some $j \in \{1, \ldots, n\}$.*

Lemma 2. *Let $Ax \leq a$ and $Bx \leq b$ be two conjunctions of constraints in linear arithmetic, and let x_i and x_j, where $i,j \in \{1, \ldots, n\}$, appear in $Ax \leq a$ and $Bx \leq b$, respectively.*

(1) If $Ax \leq a \wedge Bx \leq b$ implies $x_i \leq x_j$ then there exists a linear expression t over variables that are common to $Ax \leq a$ and $Bx \leq b$ such that $Ax \leq a$ implies $x_i \leq t$ and $Bx \leq b$ implies $t \leq x_j$ [26].

(2) If $Ax \leq a \wedge Bx \leq b$ implies $x_i = x_j$ then there exists a linear expression t over variables that are common to $Ax \leq a$ and $Bx \leq b$ such that $Ax \leq a \wedge Bx \leq b$ implies $x_i = t$ and $t = x_j$.

We show that N_{mix} can be replaced with the conjunction of an A-pure and a B-pure part, $N^A_{\text{sep}} \wedge N^B_{\text{sep}}$, of instances of the functionality axioms, at the price of having to take into account additional terms over the shared signature of A and B not occurring in A $\wedge$ B.

Theorem 5 ([24]). *Let A_0 and B_0 be conjunctions of literals in the signature of $LI(\mathbb{Q})$ such that $A_0 \wedge B_0 \wedge N \models_{\mathcal{T}_0} \bot$, for a set $N = N^A \cup N^B \cup N_{\text{mix}}$ of flattened instances of congruence axioms. There exists a set T of $\Sigma_{LI(\mathbb{Q})}$-terms containing only variables common to A_0 and B_0, and possibly common newly introduced variables in a set Σ_c such that*

$$A_0 \wedge B_0 \wedge (N^A \wedge N^B) \wedge N_{\text{sep}} \models_{\mathcal{T}_0} \bot,$$

where $N_{\text{sep}} = \bigwedge\{((\bigwedge^n_{i=1} c_i = t_i \rightarrow c = c_{f(t_1,\ldots,t_n)}) \wedge (\bigwedge^n_{i=1} t_i = d_i \rightarrow c_{f(t_1,\ldots,t_n)} = d)) \mid \bigwedge^n_{i=1} c_i = d_i \rightarrow c = d \in N_{\text{mix}}\} = N^A_{\text{sep}} \wedge N^B_{\text{sep}}$

and $c_{f(t_1,\ldots,t_n)}$ are new variables in Σ_c (considered to be common) introduced for the terms $f(t_1, \ldots, t_n)$.

A direct consequence of Theorem 5 is the possibility of hierarchically generating interpolants in $LI(\mathbb{Q})^\Sigma$.

Corollary 1 ([24]). *Assume that $(A_0 \wedge D_A) \wedge (B_0 \wedge D_B) \models_{LI(\mathbb{Q})^\Sigma} \bot$, and let $N_0, N^A, N^B, N_{\text{mix}}, N^A_{\text{sep}}, N^B_{\text{sep}}$ be as before. Then:*

(1) There exists a formula I_0 containing only variables which occur both in A_0 and B_0 such that $(A_0 \wedge N^A \wedge N^A_{\text{sep}}) \models_{LI(\mathbb{Q})} I_0$ and $(B_0 \wedge N^B \wedge N^B_{\text{sep}}) \wedge I_0 \models_{LI(\mathbb{Q})} \bot$.

(2) The ground formula I obtained from I_0 by recursively replacing every variable c_t introduced in the separation process with the term t is an interpolant for $(A_0 \wedge D_A) \wedge (B_0 \wedge D_B)$, i.e.:

(i) I contains only variables and extension functions common to A and B;

(ii) $A_0 \wedge D_A \models_{LI(\mathbb{Q})^\Sigma} I$ and $B_0 \wedge D_B \wedge I \models_{LI(\mathbb{Q})^\Sigma} \bot$.

By Theorem 5 and Corollary 1 we know that if A and B are conjunctions of literals in linear arithmetic and uninterpreted function symbols such that A $\wedge$ B is unsatisfiable then there exists an interpolant; its existence is not influenced by the choice of the separating terms in the set T. The method terminates; its complexity is discussed in [24], and depends on the complexity of computing separating terms in linear arithmetic, and on the complexity of computing interpolants for conjunctions of *clauses* in LI. In order to compute an interpolant for $(A_0 \wedge N^A \wedge N^A_{sep}) \wedge (B_0 \wedge N^B \wedge N^B_{sep})$ one can use, for instance, the method discussed in Section 3.1.

We now present an alternative approach, in which the computation of the interpolant is interleaved with the separation process. The idea is described in the algorithm in Figure 2. The algorithm is based on Theorem 5 and Corollary 1, but contains several optimizations, which allow performing simultaneously the separation into an A-pure and a B-pure part and the interpolant construction. Termination and correctness of the algorithm are proved in what follows.

Theorem 6. *The algorithm in Figure 2 terminates and returns an interpolant I of* $A \wedge B$.

In spite of the fact that the procedure for computing interpolants for linear arithmetic is called as a "black box", and that our method does not require the existence of an a priori constructed resolution proof for building the interpolant, the complexity of the algorithm described in Figure 2 is comparable to that of other methods for interpolant generation which construct interpolants from proofs [11,12,17,26]. The complexity depends linearly on the length of the proof (which in this case is built 'online'). In addition, the complexity of the procedure used for "separating" equalities needs to be taken into account.

Theorem 7. *Assume that we start from an implementation such that in* $LI(\mathbb{Q})$ *for a formula of length* m:
  (a) *interpolants can be computed in time* $g(m)$,
  (b) *P-interpolating terms can be computed in time* $h(m)$,
  (c) *entailment can be checked in time* $k(m)$.
Then the method described above allows to compute an interpolant in time of order $n^2 \cdot (k(n^2)+h(n^2))+g(n^2)+l$.

Problems (a)–(c) can be solved in polynomial time for sets of unit clauses [22] and in NP for sets of clauses [25]. Due to the specific form of the axioms in N_0 which need to be taken into account (Horn, with all premises being equalities), the sets of clauses which occur in the problems we consider may fall into tractable classes [13], for which satisfiability can be tested in polynomial time.

5   Experiments

We implemented the presented algorithms in a tool called CLP-PROVER.[2] Although the presented algorithms are correct for both rational and real spaces, our implementation handles only rationals, which is due to the applied constraint solver [8]. CLP-PROVER is built in SICStus Prolog [15], which is a Constraint

---

[2] CLP-PROVER homepage: `http://mtc.epfl.ch/~rybalche/clp-prover/`.

input

$Ax \leq a$ and $Bx \leq b$: constraints in matrix form (obtained from flattening and purifying conjunctions A and B of (unit) literals in linear arithmetic and uninterpreted function symbols such that A $\wedge$ B is unsatisfiable)

D : definitions for fresh variables created by flattening and purification of A and B

N_0 : instances of functionality axioms for functions from D

output

I: the resulting interpolant

local vars

I_0, I_1, I_2 : partial interpolants; t_i^-, t_i^+: separating terms

begin

> **if** $N_0 \neq \emptyset$ **then**
>
> > choose $C : \bigwedge_{i=1}^{n} c_i = d_i \rightarrow c = d$ from N_0
> > such that $Ax \leq a \wedge Bx \leq b \models_{LI(\mathbb{Q})} \bigwedge_{i=1}^{n} c_i = d_i$
> > (assume C is an instance of the functionality axiom for $f \in \Sigma$)
> >
> > **for** each $i \in \{1, \ldots, n\}$ **do**
> > > compute t_i^+ and t_i^- over A-B-common variables such that
> > > $Ax \leq a \models_{LI(\mathbb{Q})} c_i \leq t_i^+$ and $Bx \leq b \models_{LI(\mathbb{Q})} t_i^+ \leq d_i$ and
> > > $Ax \leq a \models_{LI(\mathbb{Q})} c_i \geq t_i^-$ and $Bx \leq b \models_{LI(\mathbb{Q})} t_i^- \geq d_i$
> >
> > **done**
> >
> > $I_0 := $ false
> > $I_1 := $ true
> > **for** each $k := $ index within $\{1, \ldots, n\}$ such that $t_k^+ \neq t_k^-$ **do**
> > > $I_0 := I_0 \vee t_k^+ > t_k^-$
> > > $I_1 := I_1 \wedge t_k^+ = t_k^-$
> > > $Ax \leq a := Ax \leq a \wedge t_k^+ = t_k^-$
> > > $Bx \leq b := Bx \leq b \wedge t_k^- = t_k^+$
> >
> > **done**
> >
> > $t := $ fresh variable; $D := D \cup \{t = f(t_1^+, \ldots, t_n^+)\}$
> > $Ax \leq a := Ax \leq a \wedge c = t$
> > $Bx \leq b := Bx \leq b \wedge t = d$
> > $I_2 := $ result of recursively applying the procedure
> > > for the new $Ax \leq a$, $Bx \leq b$ and D, and $N_0 \backslash \{C\}$
> >
> > $I := I_0 \vee (I_1 \wedge I_2)$ where each definition from D is applied
>
> **else**
> > $ix \leq \delta := $ result of applying LI on $Ax \leq a$ and $Bx \leq b$
> > $I := ix \leq \delta$ where each definition from D is applied
>
> **endif**
> **return** "interpolant I"

end.

Fig. 2. Algorithm LIUIF for the synthesis of constrained interpolants for linear arithmetic and uninterpreted function symbols. LIUIF uses the algorithm LI as a subroutine.

Table 1. Experimental evaluation on examples from BLAST distribution. (Memory consumption was not an issue.) 'Solving LI-part' is the time spent on solving the system of constraints that defines an interpolant in linear arithmetic. 'Applying axioms' is the time spent on testing entailment of premises of functionality axiom instances. 'Total solving' is the total time spent on constraint solving. 'Total' is the total time spent in CLP-PROVER, which includes parsing, computation of constraint systems, constraint solving, etc.

Example	Number of queries	CLP-PROVER time (s)				FOCI time (s)
		Solving LI part	Applying axioms	Total solving	Total	
`ntdrivers/kbfiltr.i`	139	0.13	0.02	0.15	0.46	0.55
`ntdrivers/diskperf.i`	747	0.38	0.21	0.59	2.68	3.72
`ntdrivers/floppy.i`	1082	0.61	0.36	0.97	3.97	4.91
`ntdrivers/cdaudio.i`	1060	2.23	0.20	2.43	4.92	4.80

Logic Programming (CLP) system [9]. In particular, the CLP scheme requires that the constraint solver infers all equalities that are implied by the constraint store. This allows for an efficient implementation of the instantiation of functionality axioms, see the "choose C" step in Figure 2. We integrated CLP-PROVER into the predicate discovery procedure of the software verification tools BLAST [7] and ARMC [20]. The integration with ARMC is two-way, namely, interpolants generated by CLP-PROVER are used by ARMC to compute abstraction. The interface to BLAST is only used for comparing with the existing interpolating theorem prover FOCI [17].

Our experiments with BLAST on Windows device drivers provide a direct comparison with the FOCI tool, which is also integrated into BLAST. We used a 3 GHz Linux PC, BLAST 2.0 and applied CLP-PROVER on 3,000 interpolation problems that are also passed to FOCI. The table shows that a constraint-based implementation can provide support for full linear arithmetic with competitive running time.

We applied ARMC to verify safety properties of train controller systems [19]. These examples depend crucially on the ability of our algorithm to handle strict inequalities directly. The running times were similar to the experiments with BLAST. Additionally, we applied ARMC to verify absence of array bounds violations (90 checks) for a compact (200 LOC) but intricate C program that performs singular value decomposition. CLP-PROVER spends 190 ms on constraint solving for 457 interpolation problems, and computes interpolants over up to four variables. Unfortunately, we could not compare the running times for these experiments with FOCI since the latter does not support strict inequalities (whose relaxation immediately leads to unacceptable loss of precision), and is restricted to the difference bounds fragment of linear arithmetic (i.e. predicates containing four variables cannot be discovered).

6   Conclusion and Ongoing Work

We presented a constraint-based algorithm for the synthesis of interpolants in linear arithmetic and interpreted function symbols. Our algorithm does not require a priori constructed proofs to derive interpolants, which is a difficult task. The algorithm uses a reduction to constraint solving problem in linear arithmetic, which can be efficiently solved by using a Linear Programming tools in a black-box fashion. Our experiments provide evidence for the practical applicability of the algorithm.

In ongoing work, we are exploring the constraint based setup to accommodate user-defined constraints on the form of the generated interpolant, which has promising applications in software verification. In particular, we would like to compute interpolants that are elements of a predefined abstract domain relevant for static analysis, see e.g. [1].

Acknowledgements. We thank Friedrich Eisenbrand for valuable discussions.

This work is supported in part by the German Research Foundation (DFG) as a part of the Transregional Collaborative Research Center "Automatic Verification and Analysis of Complex Systems" (SFB/TR 14 AVACS), by the German Federal Ministry of Education and Research (BMBF) in the framework of the Verisoft project under grant 01 IS C38.

References

1. B. Blanchet, P. Cousot, R. Cousot, J. Feret, L. Mauborgne, A. Miné, D. Monniaux, and X. Rival. A static analyzer for large safety-critical software. In *PLDI'2003: Programming Language Design and Implementation*, pages 196–207. ACM Press, June 7–14 2003.
2. A. R. Bradley, Z. Manna, and H. B. Sipma. Linear ranking with reachability. In *CAV'2005: Computer Aided Verification*, volume 3576 of *LNCS*, pages 491–504. Springer, 2005.
3. M. Colón, S. Sankaranarayanan, and H. Sipma. Linear invariant generation using non-linear constraint solving. 420-432. In *CAV'2003: Computer Aided Verification*, volume 2725 of *LNCS*, pages 420–432. Springer, 2003.
4. P. Cousot. Proving program invariance and termination by parametric abstraction, lagrangian relaxation and semidefinite programming. In *VMCAI'2005: Verification, Model Checking, and Abstract Interpretation*, volume 3385 of *LNCS*, pages 1–24. Springer, 2005.
5. W. Craig. Linear reasoning. A new form of the Herbrand-Gentzen theorem. *J. Symb. Log.*, 22(3):250–268, 1957.
6. J. Esparza, S. Kiefer, and S. Schwoon. Abstraction refinement with Craig interpolation and symbolic pushdown systems. In *TACAS'2006: Tools and Algorithms for the Construction and Analysis of Systems*, volume 3920 of *LNCS*, pages 489–503. Springer, 2006.
7. T. A. Henzinger, R. Jhala, R. Majumdar, and K. L. McMillan. Abstractions from proofs. In *POPL'2004: Principles of Programming Languages*, pages 232–244. ACM Press, 2004.

8. C. Holzbaur. *OFAI clp(q,r) Manual, Edition 1.3.3.* Austrian Research Institute for Artificial Intelligence, Vienna, 1995. TR-95-09.

9. J. Jaffar and S. Michaylov. Methodology and implementation of a CLP system. In *ICLP'1987: Int. Conf. on Logic Programming*, volume 1. MIT Press, 1987.

10. R. Jhala and K. L. McMillan. Interpolant-based transition relation approximation. In *CAV'2005: Computer Aided Verification*, volume 3576 of *Lecture Notes in Computer Science*, pages 39–51. Springer, 2005.

11. R. Jhala and K. L. McMillan. A practical and complete approach to predicate refinement. In *TACAS'2006: Tools and Algorithms for the Construction and Analysis of Systems*, volume 3920 of *LNCS*, pages 459–473. Springer, 2006.

12. D. Kapur, R. Majumdar, and C. G. Zarba. Interpolation for data structures. In *FSE'2006: Foundations of Software Engineering*. ACM, 2006. To appear.

13. M. Koubarakis. Tractable disjunctions of linear constraints: Basic results and applications to temporal reasoning. *Theoretical Computer Science*, 266(1-2): 311–339, 2001.

14. J. Krajíček. Interpolation theorems, lower bounds for proof systems, and independence results for bounded arithmetic. *J. Symb. Log.*, 62(2):457–486, 1997.

15. T. I. S. Laboratory. *SICStus Prolog User's Manual.* Swedish Institute of Computer Science, PO Box 1263 SE-164 29 Kista, Sweden, October 2001. Release 3.8.7.

16. K. L. McMillan. Interpolation and SAT-based model checking. In *CAV'2003: Computer Aided Verification*, volume 2725 of *LNCS*, pages 1–13. Springer, 2003.

17. K. L. McMillan. An interpolating theorem prover. *Theor. Comput. Sci.*, 345(1):101–121, 2005.

18. K. L. McMillan. Lazy abstraction with interpolants. In *CAV'2006: Computer Aided Verification*, volume 4144 of *LNCS*, pages 123–136. Springer, 2006.

19. R. Meyer, J. Faber, and A. Rybalchenko. Model checking duration calculus: A practical approach. In *ICTAC'2006: Int. Colloq. on Theoretical Aspects of Computing*, volume 4281 of *LNCS*, pages 332–346. Springer, 2006.

20. A. Podelski and A. Rybalchenko. ARMC: the logical choice for software model checking with abstraction refinement. In *PADL'2007: Practical Aspects of Declarative Languages*, LNCS. Springer, 2007. to appear.

21. P. Pudlák. Lower bounds for resolution and cutting plane proofs and monotone computations. *J. Symb. Log.*, 62(3):981–998, 1997.

22. A. Schrijver. *Theory of Linear and Integer Programming.* John Wiley & Sons Ltd., 1986.

23. V. Sofronie-Stokkermans. Hierarchic reasoning in local theory extensions. In *CADE'2005: Int. Conf. on Automated Deduction*, volume 3632 of *LNCS*, pages 219–234. Springer, 2005.

24. V. Sofronie-Stokkermans. Interpolation in local theory extensions. In *IJCAR'2006: Int. Joint Conf. on Automated Reasoning*, volume 4130 of *LNCS*, pages 235–250. Springer, 2006.

25. E. Sontag. Real addition and the polynomial hierarchy. *Information Processing Letters*, 20(3):115–120, 1985.

26. G. Yorsh and M. Musuvathi. A combination method for generating interpolants. In *CADE'2005: Int. Conf. on Automated Deduction*, volume 3632 of *LNCS*, pages 353–368. Springer, 2005.

Assertion Checking Unified

Sumit Gulwani[1] and Ashish Tiwari[2],[⋆]

[1] Microsoft Research, Redmond, WA 98052
sumitg@microsoft.com
[2] SRI International, Menlo Park, CA 94025
tiwari@csl.sri.com

Abstract. We revisit the connection between equality assertion checking in programs and unification that was recently described in [7]. Using
a general formalization of this connection, we establish interesting connections between the complexity of assertion checking in programs and
unification theory of the underlying program expressions. In particular,
we show that assertion checking is: (a) PTIME for programs with nondeterministic conditionals that use expressions from a strict unitary theory,
(b) coNP-hard for programs with nondeterministic conditionals that use
expressions from a *bitary* theory, and (c) decidable for programs with
disequality guards that use expressions from a convex finitary theory.
These results generalize several recently published results and also establish several new results. In essence, they provide new techniques for
backward analysis of programs based on novel integration of theorem
proving technology in program analysis.

1   Introduction

We use the term *equality assertion*, or simply *assertion*, to refer to an equality
between two program expressions. The *assertion checking* problem is to decide
whether a given assertion always holds at a given program point. In general,
assertion checking is an undecidable problem. Hence, assertion checking is typically performed over some sound abstraction of the program. In this paper, we
give algorithms as well as hardness results for the assertion checking over classes
of useful program abstractions.

Consider, for example, the program shown in Figure 1. All assertions shown
in the program are valid (assuming that all variables are integer variables and
that there is no overflow). Observe that to prove the validity of the assertions
$a = b$ and $y = 2x$, we need to reason about the multiplication operator. Since
full reasoning about the multiplication operator is in general undecidable, we
can use some sound abstraction of the multiplication operator. One option is to
model the multiplication operator as a binary uninterpreted function.[1] Such a

---

[⋆] The second author was supported in part by the National Science Foundation under
grant ITR-CCR-0326540.
[1] An uninterpreted function f of arity n satisfies only one axiom: If $e_i = e_i'$ for $1 \leq i \leq n$, then $f(e_1, \ldots, e_n) = f(e_1', \ldots, e_n')$.

B. Cook and A. Podelski (Eds.): VMCAI 2007, LNCS 4349, pp. 363–377, 2007.

model is sufficient to prove the validity of the assertion $a = b$. In Section 4, we show how to use unification algorithm for uninterpreted functions to obtain a polynomial time algorithm for verifying the validity of such assertions.

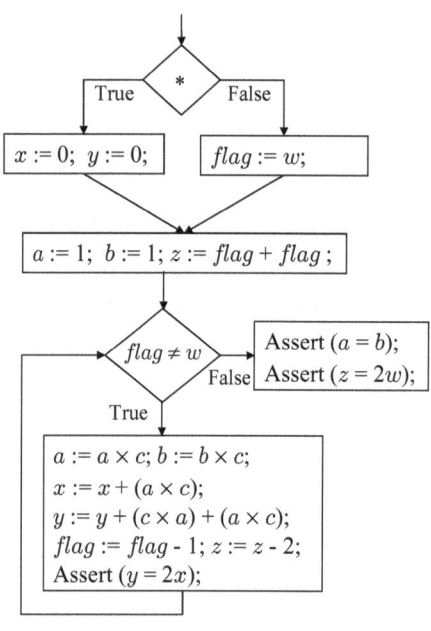

Fig. 1. An example program

Modeling the multiplication operator as an uninterpreted function is not sufficient to prove the validity of the assertion $y = 2x$, which requires reasoning about the commutative nature of the multiplication operator. Hence, if we abstract the multiplication operator as a commutative function, we can prove validity of the second assertion (as well as the first assertion). However, this requires us to work with program expressions that involve a combination of linear arithmetic and a commutative operator. In Section 5, we show that in general, assertion checking on programs with such program expressions is coNP-hard. However, the good news is that this problem is still decidable, as we show in Section 6. Also observe that the validity of the assertion $y = 2x$ requires the knowledge of the loop guard $flag \neq w$ inside the loop. Our algorithm in Section 6 can also reason about disequality guards and can hence prove the validity of such assertions.

The assertion $z = 2w$ involves discovering the loop invariant $z = 2 \times flag$ and reasoning about the equality guard $flag = w$. Reasoning about such linear arithmetic expressions in presence of equality guards has been shown to be undecidable in general [13]. This indicates that the decidability results in this paper are *tight* and that one would need incomplete heuristics, such as the one described in Section 7, to reason about arbitrary conditionals. We formalize the notion of reasoning about disequality guards as opposed to reasoning about equality guards by making all conditionals non-deterministic, and introducing Assume nodes, as described in Section 2.1.

The main appeal of this work is that all technical results are derived using the basic link between assertion checking for programs whose expressions are from some theory $\mathbb{T}$ and unification in the theory $\mathbb{T}$ (Section 3). An assertion holds at a program point if it evaluates to true in every run of the program. Every run of a program returns a valuation of the program variables. This valuation can be seen as a substitution. If every such substitution makes an assertion *true*, then each substitution would also validate some maximally general $\mathbb{T}$-unifier of the assertion. Using this basic principle, we show that unification algorithms can be

Unification type of theory of program expressions	Complexity of assertion checking	Examples	Generalizes
Strict Unitary	PTIME	ℓa, uf	[6,12,13]
Bitary	coNP-hard	$\ell a + uf$, c	[7]
Finitary-Convex	Decidable	$\ell a + uf + c + ac$	[12,7]

Fig. 2. Summary of results in this paper. If the program model consists of nodes (a)-(d) from Figure 3 and the theory underlying the program expressions belongs to the class given in Col 2, then its assertion checking problem has time complexity given in Col 3. Row 1 requires some additional minor technical assumptions. Row 4 holds even for disequality guards. Col 4 contains examples of theories for which the corresponding result holds:- ℓa: Linear Arithmetic, uf: Uninterpreted Functions, c: Commutative Functions, ac: Associative-Commutative Functions, The symbol + denotes combination of theories. Last column gives references whose results are generalized by our result.

used to strengthen assertions during assertion checking using backward analysis. Quite interestingly, the same basic principle also helps us show hardness results in some cases. While this basic principle was presented in an earlier paper [7], its fundamental role in uniformly deriving PTIME , coNP-hardness, and decidability results for assertion checking has been explicated in only this paper.

In particular, the main contributions of this paper are the following general results that relate the *complexity* of assertion checking in programs with the *unification type* of the theory of program expressions. These results are also summarized in Figure 2.

(1) We describe a generic PTIME algorithm for assertion checking in programs when the program expressions are from a strict unitary theory (Section 4).

(2) We introduce the notion of a bitary theory, and prove that several interesting theories (e.g., commutative functions) are bitary. Intuitively, a bitary theory is one that can encode disjunction. We prove that assertion checking in programs whose program expressions are from a bitary theory is coNP-hard (Section 5).

(3) We describe a generic algorithm for assertion checking in programs when the program expressions are from a finitary convex theory, thereby proving decidability. We prove that the (rich) theory of combination of linear arithmetic with functions that are uninterpreted, commutative, or associative-commutative (AC) is finitary and convex (Section 6). The significance of such functions lie in the fact that they can be used to model important properties of otherwise hard to reason about program operators. For example, commutative functions can be used to model floating-point operators (which do not obey associativity), and AC functions can be used to model bit-wise operators.

The above results uniformly generalize several known results [6,7,13,12], and also provide several new results. All prior results on the complexity of assertion checking have been for specific abstractions. For example, in an earlier paper [7] we showed that intraprocedural assertion checking in the combination of linear arithmetic and uninterpreted functions was coNP-hard, but decidable, using a

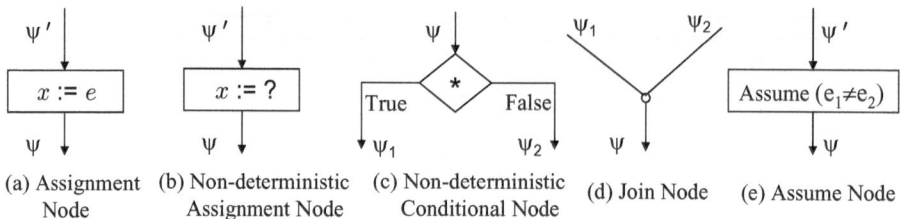

Fig. 3. Flowchart nodes in our abstracted program model

unification based approach. The results in this paper go much beyond one or two specific program abstractions and apply to intra- and inter-procedural analysis of wide classes of program abstractions. They can be used to quickly classify the hardness of these analyses for new abstractions.

The results in this paper establish closer connections between program analysis and theorem proving. The traditional way of using theorem proving in program analysis has been via decision procedures. In this usage scenario, decision procedures are used to discharge verification conditions generated from programs annotated with loop invariants. In this paper, theorem proving technology is more tightly integrated in program analysis to make it more precise and efficient, even in the absence of loop-invariant annotations.

The results in this paper should also be viewed in the context of developing new algorithmic techniques for performing *backward* analysis of programs. This paper shows that standard unification algorithms can be used during backward analyses of programs. Finally, although this paper focuses solely on backward analysis, we believe that our observations enable new ways of combining both forward and backward analyses using theorem proving technology to improve overall efficiency and precision [5].

2   Preliminaries

2.1   Program Model

We assume that each procedure in a program is abstracted using the flowchart nodes shown in Figure 3. In the assignment node, x refers to a program variable while e denotes some expression in the underlying abstraction. We refer to the language of such expressions as the *expression language of the program*. Following are examples of the expression languages for some abstractions that we refer to in this paper:

- Linear arithmetic: $e ::= y \mid c \mid e_1 \pm e_2 \mid c \times e$
  Here y denotes some variable while c denotes some arithmetic constant.
- Uninterpreted functions: $e ::= y \mid f(e_1, \ldots, e_n)$
  Here f denotes some uninterpreted function of arity n.

- Commutative Functions $e ::= y \mid f(e_1, e_2)$
  Here f denotes a commutative function.
- Combination of linear arithmetic and uninterpreted functions:
  $$e ::= y \mid c \mid e_1 \pm e_2 \mid c \times e \mid f(e_1, \ldots, e_n)$$

A non-deterministic assignment $x :=?$ denotes that the variable x can be assigned any value. Such non-deterministic assignments are used as a safe abstraction of statements (in the original source program) that our abstraction cannot handle precisely.

A join node has two incoming edges. Note that a join node with more than two incoming edges can be reduced to join nodes each with two incoming edges.

Non-deterministic conditionals, represented by $*$, denote that the control can flow to either branch irrespective of the program state before the conditional. They are used as a safe abstraction of guarded conditionals, which our abstraction cannot handle precisely. We abstract away the guards in conditionals because otherwise the problem of assertion checking can be easily shown to be undecidable even when the program expressions involves operators from simple theories like linear arithmetic [13] or uninterpreted functions [12] (in which case our result in Section 4 would not be possible, and the result in Section 5 would become trivial). This is a very common restriction for a program model while proving preciseness of a program analysis for that model.

However, (for our result in Section 6) we do allow for assume statements of the form $\mathtt{Assume}(e_1 \neq e_2)$, which we also refer to as *disequality guards*. Note that a program conditional of the form $e_1 = e_2$ can be reduced to a non-deterministic conditional and assume statements $\mathtt{Assume}(e_1 = e_2)$ (on the true side of the conditional) and $\mathtt{Assume}(e_1 \neq e_2)$ on the false side of the conditional. Hence, the presence of disequality guards in our program model allows for partial reasoning of program conditionals.

2.2   Unification Terminology

A *substitution* σ is a mapping that maps variables to expressions such that for every variable x, the expression $\sigma(x)$ contains variables only from the set $\{y \mid \sigma(y) = y\}$. A substitution mapping σ can be (homomorphically) lifted to expressions such that for every expression e, we define $\sigma(e)$ to be the expression obtained from e by replacing every variable x by its mapping $\sigma(x)$. Often, we denote the application of a substitution σ to an expression e using postfix notation as $e\sigma$. We sometimes treat a substitution mapping σ as the following formula, which is a conjunction of non-trivial equalities between variables and their mappings, i.e., $\bigwedge_x x = x\sigma$.

A substitution σ is a *unifier* for an equality $e_1 = e_2$ (in theory $\mathbb{T}$) if $e_1\sigma = e_2\sigma$ (in theory $\mathbb{T}$). A substitution σ is a unifier for a set of equalities E if σ is a unifier for each equality in E. A substitution σ_1 is *more-general* than a substitution σ_2 if there exists a substitution σ such that $x\sigma_2 = (x\sigma_1)\sigma$ for all variables x.[2] A

---

[2] The more-general relation is reflexive, i.e., a substitution is more-general than itself. All equalities are interpreted modulo theory $\mathbb{T}$.

set C of unifiers for E is *complete* when for any unifier σ for E, there exists a unifier $\sigma' \in C$ that is more-general than σ. The reader is referred to [1] for an introduction to unification theory.

We use the notation $\mathtt{Unif}(E)$, where E is some conjunction of equalities E, to denote the formula that is a disjunction of all unifiers in some complete set of unifiers for E. (If E is unsatisfiable, then E does not have any unifier and $\mathtt{Unif}(E)$ is simply *false*.)

Example 1. Consider the equality $f(x)+f(y) = f(a)+f(b)$ over theory of combination of linear arithmetic and unary uninterpreted function f. The substitution $\{x \mapsto a, y \mapsto b\}$ is a unifier for it. A complete set of unifiers, however, contains two unifiers, viz. $\{x \mapsto a, y \mapsto b\}$ and $\{x \mapsto b, y \mapsto a\}$. Hence,

$$\mathtt{Unif}(f(x) + f(y) = f(a) + f(b)) = (x = a \wedge y = b) \vee (x = b \wedge y = a)$$

Theories can be classified based on the cardinality of complete set of unifiers for its equalities as follows.

Unitary Theory. A theory $\mathbb{T}$ is said to be *unitary* if for all equalities $e = e'$ in theory $\mathbb{T}$, there exists a complete set of unifiers of cardinality at most 1, that is, there is a unique most-general unifier. We define a unitary theory to be *strict* if for any sequence of equations $e_1 = e_1', e_2 = e_2', \ldots$, the sequence of most-general unifiers $\mathtt{Unif}(e_1 = e_1'), \mathtt{Unif}(e_1 = e_1' \wedge e_2 = e_2'), \ldots$ contains at most n distinct unifiers where n is the number of variables in the given equations.[3] The theory of linear arithmetic and the theory of uninterpreted functions are both strict unitary.

Bitary Theory. We define a theory $\mathbb{T}$ to be *bitary* if there exists an equality $e = e'$ in theory $\mathbb{T}$ such that $y \mapsto z_1$ and $y \mapsto z_2$ form a complete set of unifiers for $e = e'$, where y, z_1 and z_2 are some variables. In other words, $\mathtt{Unif}(e = e')$ is $y = z_1 \vee y = z_2$. In addition, we require a technical side condition that for new variables y' and z_1', it is the case that $\mathtt{Unif}(e = e[y'/y, z_1'/z_1])$ and $\mathtt{Unif}(e' = e'[y'/y, z_1'/z_1])$ are both $y = y' \wedge z_1 = z_1'$.

The theories of a commutative function, combination of linear arithmetic and a unary uninterpreted function, and combination of two associative-commutative functions are all bitary (as proved in Section 5.2). Intuitively, bitary theories are theories that can encode disjunction.

Finitary Theory. A theory $\mathbb{T}$ is said to be *finitary* if for all equalities $e = e'$ in theory $\mathbb{T}$, there exists a complete set of unifiers of finite cardinality. Note that every unitary theory is, by definition, finitary. Hence, the theories of linear arithmetic and uninterpreted functions are both finitary. The theory of combination of linear arithmetic and uninterpreted functions is also finitary (as proved in [7]). In this paper, we show that the more general theory of combination of linear arithmetic, uninterpreted functions, commutative functions, and associative-commutative functions is also finitary (Section 6.2).

---

[3] This is an ascending (unifier) chain condition.

```
1 if (*) { x := a; y := b; }
2 else { x := b; y := a; }
3 endif
4 while (*) {
5     x := fx; y := fy;
6     a := fa; b := fb;
7 }
8 assert(x + y = a + b);
```

(a) Program

pc	Assertion at pc	
	w/o unification	w/ unification
7	$x + y = a + b$	$x = a + b - y$
4	$x + y = a + b \wedge$	$(x = a \wedge y = b) \vee$
	$fx + fy = fa + fb \wedge \cdots$	$(x = b \wedge y = a)$
1	non-termination	$true$

(b) Backward Analysis

1	$true$
3	$(x = a \wedge y = b) \sqcup (x = b \wedge y = a)$
	$= (x + y = a + b)$
7	$true$

(c) Forward Analysis

Fig. 4. This figure illustrates the advantage of using unification in backward analysis. The assertion on line 7 of program in Figure (a) is true. Standard backward analysis based procedure, illustrated in Figure (b) Column 1, fails to prove the assertion because it fails to terminate across the loop. Forward analysis in Figure (c) requires *join* computation. Unless we unreasonably assume that the join operator returns the *infinite* set of facts [9], $\bigwedge_i f^i x + f^i y = f^i a + f^i b$, it also fails. When using unification to strengthen assertions in backward analysis, as in Figure (b) Column 2, the fixpoint terminates and we can prove the assertion.

A theory is said to be *convex* if whenever $e_1 = e_1' \vee e_2 = e_2'$ is valid in the theory, then either $e_1 = e_1'$ is valid in the theory or $e_2 = e_2'$ is valid in the theory. The above-mentioned finitary theories are also convex.

3 Connection Between Unification and Assertion Checking

A backward analysis based on weakest precondition computation involves computing assertions at intermediate and initial program points that guarantee that a given assertion holds at a given program point. A unification procedure can be used to strengthen and simplify such assertions. The formula $\text{Unif}(E)$ logically implies E, but it is, in general, not equivalent to E. Since it is often "simpler" than E, we may wish to replace $\text{assert}(E)$ by $\text{assert}(\text{Unif}(E))$ at intermediate points during backward analysis. This process is *sound*, that is, if $\text{Unif}(E)$ is an invariant, then clearly E will also be an invariant. (See Figure 4 for an example.) But this process is not *complete* in general, that is, if we fail to prove that $\text{Unif}(E)$ is an invariant, then we can not conclude anything about E. The basic result formally stated in Lemma 1 and Lemma 2 is that, *in many useful abstractions*, we do *not* lose completeness by this replacement. For instance, unification preserves completeness and helps prove the assertion in the example of Figure 4.

Lemma 1 ([7]). *Let π be any location in a program that is specified using nodes (a)-(d) of Figure 3 and expressions from a theory $\mathbb{T}$. An equality $e = e'$ holds at π iff $\text{Unif}_{\mathbb{T}}(e = e')$ holds at π (assuming $\text{Unif}_{\mathbb{T}}(e = e')$ is a finite disjunction).*

The proof of this lemma is fairly simple and is given in full version of the paper [8].

The key insight is that *runs* of a program are just substitutions and if every run validates an assertion, then every run should also validate some maximally general unifier of that assertion.

We use this soundness and completeness preserving strengthening of assertions in Section 4 as part of a generic PTIME backward analysis procedure for assertion checking in a certain class of programs. Surprisingly, we use this same result to also show *hardness* of assertion checking for another class of programs in Section 5. This simplifies, and simultaneously generalizes, the proof of hardness of assertion checking for a specific theory [7].

We can generalize Lemma 1 as follows to also work in the presence of disequality guards.[4]

Lemma 2. *Let π be a location in a program specified using nodes (a)-(e) of Figure 3 with expressions from a convex finitary theory $\mathbb{T}$. Let ϕ_i be some conjunction of equalities. Then, $\bigvee_i \phi_i$ holds at π iff $\bigvee_i \mathtt{Unif}(\phi_i)$ holds at π.*

The proof of Lemma 2 is given in full version of the paper [8]. In Section 6, we argue that the standard backward analysis procedure for assertion checking, *if enhanced by unification based assertion strengthening*, yields a *decision procedure* for a large class of programs.

4   PTIME Decidability for Strict Unitary Theories

In this section, we prove PTIME complexity (by describing a polynomial-time algorithm) for the problem of assertion checking when the expression language of the program comes from a strict unitary theory, and the flowchart representation of the program is abstracted using nodes (a)-(d) shown in Figure 3.

This PTIME complexity result generalizes two earlier known results for theories of linear arithmetic and uninterpreted functions (both of which are unitary theories). Gulwani and Necula gave a polynomial-time algorithm for discovering all assertions of bounded size when the program model consists of nodes (a)-(d) and the expression language consists of uninterpreted functions, thereby proving PTIME complexity of assertion-checking for such programs [6]. Müller-Olm, Rüthing, and Seidl [12] have also pointed out that assertion checking on program with nodes (a)-(d) using the uninterpreted symbols' abstraction (Herbrand equalities) is in PTIME. Muller-Olm and Seidl [13] proved PTIME complexity for assertion checking of programs with nodes (a)-(d) and expression language of linear arithmetic by simplifying Karr's algorithm [11].

4.1   Algorithm

Our algorithm for assertion checking is based on weakest precondition computation. It represents invariants (that need to be satisfied for the assertion to

---

[4] We remark here that the program nodes for which unification does not preserve completeness, viz. *positive guards*, are exactly responsible for *undecidability* of assertion checking for many abstractions.

be true) at each program point by a formula that is either *false*, *true*, or a conjunction of equalities of the form $e = e'$.

Suppose the goal is to check whether an assertion $e_1 = e_2$ is an invariant at program point π. The algorithm performs a backward analysis of the program computing a formula ψ at each program point such that ψ must hold at that program point for the assertion $e_1 = e_2$ to be true at program point π. This formula is computed at each program point from the formulas at the successor program points in an iterative manner. The algorithm uses the transfer functions described below to compute these formulas across the flowchart nodes shown in Figure 3. The algorithm declares $e_1 = e_2$ to be an invariant at π iff the formula computed at the beginning of the program after fixed-point computation is *valid*.

Initialization: The formula at all program points except π is initialized to *true*. The formula at program point π is initialized to be $e_1 = e_2$.

Assignment Node: See Figure 3 (a). The formula ψ' before an assignment node $x := e$ is obtained from the formula ψ after the assignment node by substituting x by e in ψ, i.e. $\psi' = \psi[e/x]$.

Non-deterministic Assignment Node: See Figure 3 (b). The formula ψ' before a non-deterministic assignment node $x :=?$ is obtained from the formula ψ after the non-deterministic assignment node by substituting program variable x by some fresh variable (which does not occur in the program and substitution ψ), i.e. $\psi' = \psi[y/x]$.

Join Node: See Figure 3 (c). The formulas ψ_1 and ψ_2 on the two predecessors of a join node are same as the formula ψ after the join node, i.e. $\psi_1 = \psi$ and $\psi_2 = \psi$.

Non-deterministic Conditional Node: See Figure 3 (d). The formula ψ before a non-deterministic conditional node is obtained by taking the conjunction of the formulas ψ_1 and ψ_2 on the two branches of the conditional, and then pruning away the redundant equations using the `Unif` procedure.

$$\psi = \texttt{UPrune}(\psi_1 \wedge \psi_2)$$

We say an equation $e = e'$ is *redundant* with respect to a formula ψ if $\texttt{Unif}(\psi)$ is a unifier for $e = e'$. The function $\texttt{UPrune}(\psi)$ sequentially checks if each equation $e = e'$ in ψ is redundant with respect to $\psi - \{e = e'\}$ and removes the redundant ones. Thus, $\texttt{Unif}(\psi)$ and $\texttt{Unif}(\texttt{UPrune}(\psi))$ are equivalent.

Fixed-point Computation: In the presence of loops in procedures, the algorithm goes around each loop until the formulas computed at each program point in two successive iterations of a loop have *equivalent unifiers*, or if any formula becomes unsatisfiable.

Correctness. The correctness of the algorithm follows from the interesting connection between program analysis and unification theory stated in Lemma 1. Specifically, Lemma 1 implies the correctness of pruning and the fixpoint detection steps. It shows that the formula computed by our algorithm before a flowchart node is the weakest precondition of the formula after that node. The correctness of the algorithm now follows from the fact that the algorithm starts with the correct assertion at π and iteratively computes the correct weakest precondition at each program point in a backward analysis.

Complexity. Termination of the fixed-point computation in polynomial time relies on the unitary theory being strict. The following theorem states the complexity of the algorithm.

Theorem 1. *Let* $\mathbb{T}$ *be a strict unitary theory. Suppose that* $T_{\texttt{Unif}}(n)$ *is the time complexity for computing the most-general* $\mathbb{T}$*-unifier of equations given in a shared representation.*[5] *Then the assertion checking problem for programs of size* n *that are specified using nodes (a)-(d) and whose expressions are from theory* $\mathbb{T}$*, can be solved in time* $O(n^4 T_{\texttt{Unif}}(n^2))$.

Proof. Since the program is of size n, the number of variables is bounded by n. Due to the strictness condition, each node in the flowchart changes at most n times. Since there are at most n nodes, there are at most n^2 changes. For each change, we may have to visit all n nodes once. Hence, there are n^3 node visits. In any such visit, `UPrune` is the most complex operation we could perform. In this operation, there are at most $2n$ equations to check for redundancy. The size of each equation, in shared representation, is bounded by n. This is because some path in the program itself contains a representation for the expression in an equation. Thus, pruning takes at most $2n(T_{\texttt{Unif}}(n^2))$ time. Hence the overall time complexity is $O(n^4(T_{\texttt{Unif}}(n^2) + T_{\texttt{Valid}}(n^2)))$.   □

The above complexity result is conservative because it is based on a generic argument. It can be improved for specific theories, but that is not the focus of this paper.

4.2   Examples of Strict Unitary Theories

If the most-general $\mathbb{T}$-unifiers do not contain any *new variables*, then clearly any chain of increasingly less general substitutions, $\sigma_1, \sigma_1\sigma_2, \sigma_1\sigma_2\sigma_3, \ldots$, will have at most n distinct elements since each new distinct element will necessarily instantiate one uninstantiated variable. This is the case for the theory of linear arithmetic and uninterpreted symbols. The theory of Abelian Groups is unitary, but the most-general unifiers contain new variables. However, using a different argument it can be checked that this theory also satisfies the *strictness* condition.

5   coNP-Hardness for Bitary Theories

In this section, we first show that the problem of assertion checking, when the expression language of the program comes from a bitary theory, is coNP-hard, even

---

[5] We assume that the $\mathbb{T}$-unification procedure returns *true* when presented with an equation that is valid (true) in $\mathbb{T}$.

$\text{Check}_{\mathbb{T}}(\alpha_1, \ldots, \alpha_m, x)$

    % Let $e = e'$ be an equality in theory $\mathbb{T}$ s.t. $\text{Unif}(e = e')$ is $y = z_1 \vee y = z_2$.

    $e_1 := e[{}^x\!/y, {}^{\alpha_1}\!/z_1, {}^{\alpha_2}\!/z_2]; \quad e'_1 := e'[{}^x\!/y, {}^{\alpha_1}\!/z_1, {}^{\alpha_2}\!/z_2];$

    for $j = 1$ to $m - 2$ do

        $e_{j+1} := e[{}^{e_j}\!/y, {}^{e'_j}\!/z_1, {}^{e_j[\alpha_{j+2}/x]}\!/z_2]; \quad e'_{j+1} := e'[{}^{e_j}\!/y, {}^{e'_j}\!/z_1, {}^{e_j[\alpha_{j+2}/x]}\!/z_2];$

    $\text{Assert}(e_{m-1} = e'_{m-1});$

Fig. 5. A procedure that checks whether $(x = \alpha_1) \vee \ldots \vee (x = \alpha_m)$

when the program is loop-free and the flowchart representation of the program only involves nodes (a)-(d). In the second part of this section, we show that several interesting theories are bitary, thereby establishing that the problem of assertion checking when program expressions are from any of those theories is coNP-hard.

Gulwani and Tiwari [7] showed that the assertion checking problem is coNP-hard when the expression language involves combination of linear arithmetic and uninterpreted functions and when the program model consists of nodes (a)-(d). This section nontrivially generalizes the core idea of the proof of [7], by combining it with the unification connection (Lemma 1), to give a simple characterization of programs for which assertion checking is coNP-hard. This is used to obtain hardness results for several new and unrelated theories.

5.1 Reduction from 3-SAT

Let $e = e'$ be the equality in theory $\mathbb{T}$ that has $y \mapsto z_1$ and $y \mapsto z_2$ as its complete set of unifiers. The key observation in proving the coNP-hardness result is that a disjunctive assertion of the form $x = \alpha_1 \vee x = \alpha_2$ can be encoded as the non-disjunctive assertion $e_1 = e'_1$, where $e_1 = e[{}^x\!/y, {}^{\alpha_1}\!/z_1, {}^{\alpha_2}\!/z_2]$ and $e'_1 = e[{}^x\!/y, {}^{\alpha_1}\!/z_1, {}^{\alpha_2}\!/z_2]$. The procedure $\text{Check}_{\mathbb{T}}(\alpha_1, \ldots, \alpha_m, x)$ in Figure 5 generalizes this encoding to the disjunctive assertion $x = \alpha_1 \vee \ldots \vee x = \alpha_n$. The unsatisfiability problem can be easily reduced to the problem of checking a disjunctive assertion of the form $x = y_1 \vee \ldots \vee x = y_n$ (where $x, y_1, \ldots, y_n$ are variables). This implies the following theorem (detailed proof in full version of the paper [8]).

Theorem 2. *Assertion checking is coNP-hard for (even loop-free) programs specified using nodes (a)-(d) with expressions from the language of a bitary theory.*

5.2 Examples of Bitary Theories

We present a few examples of bitary theories, by presenting a witness equation $e = e'$ for each theory. It is easily verified that $y \mapsto z_1$ and $y \mapsto z_2$ form a complete set of unifiers for $e = e'$ in each theory. Moreover, e and e' can also be verified to satisfy the technical side condition in each case.

The theory of a *commutative function* f can be shown to be bitary using the following equality:

$$f(f(y, y), f(z_1, z_2)) \;=\; f(f(y, z_1), f(y, z_2)) \tag{1}$$

The theory of *combination of linear arithmetic and a unary uninterpreted function f* is also bitary. The following equality is a witness:

$$f(f(y) + f(y)) + f(f(z_1) + f(z_2)) = f(f(y) + f(z_1)) + f(f(y) + f(z_2)) \quad (2)$$

The theory of *combination of an AC function g and a unary uninterpreted function f* is also bitary. The following equality shows this.

$$g(f(g(y,y)), f(g(z_1, z_2))) = g(f(g(y, z_1)), f(g(y, z_2))) \quad (3)$$

The theory of *combination of two AC functions f and g* is also bitary as shown by the following equality, where c is some constant or a fresh variable distinct from y, z_1 and z_2.

$$g(f(g(y,y), c), f(g(z_1, z_2), c)) = g(f(g(y, z_1), c), f(g(y, z_2), c)) \quad (4)$$

6   Decidability for Finitary Convex Theories

In this section, we first describe a generic algorithm (thereby proving decidability) for assertion checking when the expression language of the program comes from a finitary theory that is convex, and the flowchart representation of the program consists of nodes (a)–(e) shown in Figure 3. In the second part of this section, we show that the (rich) theory of combination of linear arithmetic, uninterpreted functions, commutative functions, associative-commutative functions is finitary and convex. This establishes the decidability of assertion checking over this theory.

Our result here generalizes, using a uniform framework, the result of Müller-Olm, Rüthing, and Seidl [12] about decidability of checking validity of Herbrand equalities in the presence of disequality guards. It also subsumes our earlier result [7] of decidability of assertion checking for programs whose nodes are restricted to Nodes (a)–(d) and whose expression language involves combination of linear arithmetic and uninterpreted functions. Our new general decidability result is nontrivial since the abstract lattice (underlying the abstractions based on convex finitary theories) often has infinite height, which implies that a standard forward propagation algorithm without widening [3] cannot terminate in a finite number of steps.

6.1   Algorithm

The algorithm is based on weakest precondition computation and is similar to the one described in Section 4. It computes (in a backward analysis) a formula ψ at each program point π such that the formula ψ must hold at π for the given assertion to be true. The formula ψ computed at each program point is either false or a disjunction of conjunction of equalities of the form $x = e$ such that each disjunct represents a valid substitution. Müller-Olm, Rüthing, and Seidl [12] have used a similar representation.

The initialization and the transfer functions for assignment and join nodes are exactly same as the one for the algorithm described in Section 4. We describe the transfer functions for the remaining nodes below.

Non-deterministic Conditional Node: See Figure 3 (d).
The formula ψ before a non-deterministic conditional node is obtained by taking the conjunction of the formulas ψ_1 and ψ_2 on the two branches of the conditional, and invoking Unif on each resulting disjunct.

$$\psi = \bigvee_{i,j} \text{Unif}(\psi_1^i \wedge \psi_2^j), \text{ where } \psi_1 = \bigvee_i \psi_1^i \text{ and } \psi_2 = \bigvee_j \psi_2^j$$

Assume Node: See Figure 3 (e).
The formula ψ' before an assume node $e_1 \neq e_2$ is obtained from the formula ψ after the assume node as: $\psi' = \psi \vee \text{Unif}(e_1 = e_2)$

Correctness and Termination. The correctness of the algorithm is an easy consequence of Lemma 2, which shows that unification can be used to strengthen assertions without any loss in soundness or precision. The proof of termination of the algorithm is similar to the proof of termination for the special case of the combined theory of linear arithmetic and uninterpreted functions [7], and is described in full version of the paper [8]. Hence, the following theorem holds.

Theorem 3. *Let $\mathbb{T}$ be a convex finitary theory. Then, assertion checking is decidable for programs specified using nodes (a)-(e) with expressions from the language of $\mathbb{T}$.*

6.2   Examples of Finitary Convex Theory

In this section, we prove that the (rich) theory of combination of linear arithmetic, uninterpreted functions, commutative functions, associative-commutative functions is finitary and convex. Let $\mathbb{T}_{LA}, \mathbb{T}_{UF}, \mathbb{T}_C, \mathbb{T}_{AC}$ denote respectively the theories of linear arithmetic, uninterpreted functions, commutative functions, and associative-commutative functions *over disjoint signatures*. Let $\mathbb{T}_{All} = \mathbb{T}_{LA} \cup \mathbb{T}_{UF} \cup \mathbb{T}_C \cup \mathbb{T}_{AC}$. The theory $\mathbb{T}_{All}$ is convex because it is equational. We now use the following well-known result [1] to show that $\mathbb{T}_{All}$ is finitary.

Proposition 1 ([1]). *Let $\mathbb{T}_1, \ldots, \mathbb{T}_n$ be non-trivial equational theories over disjoint signatures that are finitary for $\mathbb{T}_i$-unification with linear constant restrictions. Then $\mathbb{T}_1 \cup \cdots \cup \mathbb{T}_n$ is finitary for elementary unification.*

For a theory $\mathbb{T}$, if unification with constants is finitary, then unification with linear constant restriction, which is more restrictive, is also finitary. Unification with constants is unitary for $\mathbb{T}_{UF}$ and $\mathbb{T}_{LA}$, whereas it is finitary for $\mathbb{T}_C$ and $\mathbb{T}_{AC}$. Therefore, it follows from Proposition 1 that $\mathbb{T}_{All}$ is finitary for elementary unification. Since $\mathbb{T}_{UF}$ is included in $\mathbb{T}_{All}$, it follows that $\mathbb{T}_{All}$ is finitary for general unification as well. In fact, an algorithm to generate the complete set of unifiers in $\mathbb{T}_{All}$ can be obtained using the generic methodology for combining unification algorithms [1].

7   Discussion

Handling Positive Guards. The results in this paper have uniformly assumed that there are no *assume* nodes with positive equalities. In the presence of positive assume nodes, we lose precision if we use unification to replace a weaker assertion by a stronger assertion. This loss in precision is not surprising since the presence of *positive guards* can cause assertion checking to become *undecidable* for several abstractions [13,12].

In practice, heuristics can be used to deal with positive guards. For instance, the precondition ψ' before a program node `Assume(x=y)` can be obtained from the formula ψ after the assume node as follows: $\psi' \equiv \psi \vee \psi[x/y] \vee \psi[y/x]$. This simple heuristic allows us to prove the assertion $z = 2w$ in the example given in Figure 1. This suggests that the unification based backward analysis procedure proposed in this paper can be effective in practice.

Backward vs. Forward Analysis. Our algorithms for assertion checking are based on backward analysis of programs. Cousot [4] formalized the semantics of sound backward analyses as computing an over-approximation of the set of program states obtained by pushing the negation of the goal backwards, which is equivalent to under-approximation of the set of program states obtained by pushing the goal backwards assuming that the abstract domain is closed under negation. However, abstract domains are, in general, not closed under negation, as is the case for all the equality based abstract domains that we consider in this paper. Also, most of these domains do not have precise transfer functions for forward analysis. Hence, there is no automatic recipe to construct algorithms for performing forward or backward analysis of arbitrary abstract domains. This paper shows how to perform precise backward analysis over a large class of abstract domains by using unification algorithms from corresponding logical theories.

For problems considered in this paper, it may be argued that backward analyses are better than forward analyses over corresponding program abstractions in terms of efficiency. This is because performing *precise* assertion checking requires forward analysis to discover *all* facts at each program point, since it is a-priori not clear which facts would be useful to prove the assertion that occurs later in the code. For some of the program abstractions described in this paper (in Section 6), the underlying abstract lattices have infinite height. Hence, forward analyses over those abstractions would not terminate unless widening techniques are used, which would lead to imprecision. However (as surprising as it may be) the backward analyses that we describe in Section 6 terminate over the same abstractions since they only attempts to decide the validity of given assertions (which are finite in number). Figure 4 presents one such example.

Connections Between Program Analysis and Theorem Proving. This paper contributes to the broader goal of transferring results from the theorem proving community to the world of program analysis. We had earlier shown that forward program analysis can be made more precise and efficient by a tighter coupling with theorem proving technology [9]. In particular, we showed how to use results from Nelson-Oppen combination of decision procedures to generate a more powerful forward analysis by combination of different forward analyses. This paper demonstrates that unification procedures are useful in improving the efficiency of backward analysis. Unification algorithms have earlier been used in type inferencing [10]. Type inferencing itself can be seen as an abstract interpreter [2]. The results of this paper can be seen as generalizing this basic use of unification in type checking to program analysis over richer abstract domains. Using *backward analysis enhanced with unification*, we showed here that the unification type of a theory determines the complexity of the assertion checking problem for the corresponding abstraction.

8 Conclusion

Unification theory plays a significant role in assertion checking. The unification type of a theory–unitary, bitary, or finitary–is critical in determining the complexity of the assertion checking problem–PTIME, coNP-hard, or decidable–modulo some minor assumptions on the theories and certain restrictions on the program models. These results uniformly generalize several known results and also yield several new ones (see Figure 2). We believe the connections between theorem proving and program analysis developed in this paper can lead to significant new research in both the communities and increase cross-fertilization.

References

1. F. Baader and W. Snyder. Unification theory. In *Handbook of Automated Reasoning*, volume I, chapter 8, pages 445–532. Elsevier Science, 2001.
2. P. Cousot. Types as abstract interpretations. In *POPL*, pages 316–331, 1997.
3. P. Cousot and R. Cousot. Abstract interpretation: A unified lattice model for static analysis of programs by construction or approximation of fixpoints. In *4th Annual ACM Symposium on POPL*, pages 234–252, 1977.
4. P. Cousot and R. Cousot. Refining model checking by abstract interpretation. *Automated Software Engineering*, 6(1):69–95, 1999.
5. S. Gulwani and N. Jojic. Program verification as inference in belief networks. Technical Report MSR-TR-2006-98, Microsoft Research, July 2006.
6. S. Gulwani and G. C. Necula. A polynomial-time algorithm for global value numbering. In *Static Analysis Symposium*, volume 3148 of *LNCS*, pages 212–227, 2004.
7. S. Gulwani and A. Tiwari. Assertion checking over combined abstraction of linear arithmetic & uninterpreted functions. In *ESOP*, volume 3924 of *LNCS*, Mar. 2006.
8. S. Gulwani and A. Tiwari. Assertion checking unified. (MSR-TR-2006-99), July 2006.
9. S. Gulwani and A. Tiwari. Combining abstract interpreters. In *PLDI*, June 2006.
10. R. Hindley. The principal type-scheme of an object in combinatory logic. *Trans. Amer. Math. Soc.*, 146:29–60, 1969.
11. M. Karr. Affine relationships among variables of a program. In *Acta Informatica*, pages 133–151. Springer, 1976.
12. M. Müller-Olm, O. Rüthing, and H. Seidl. Checking Herbrand equalities and beyond. In *VMCAI*, volume 3385 of *LNCS*, pages 79–96. Springer, Jan. 2005.
13. M. Müller-Olm and H. Seidl. A note on Karr's algorithm. In *31st International Colloquium on Automata, Languages and Programming*, pages 1016–1028, 2004.

Invariant Synthesis for Combined Theories*

Dirk Beyer[1], Thomas A. Henzinger[2],
Rupak Majumdar[3], and Andrey Rybalchenko[2,4]

[1] Simon Fraser University, Surrey, B.C., Canada
[2] EPFL, Lausanne, Switzerland
[3] University of California, Los Angeles, USA
[4] Max-Planck-Institut für Informatik, Saarbrücken, Germany

Abstract. We present a constraint-based algorithm for the synthesis of invariants expressed in the combined theory of linear arithmetic and uninterpreted function symbols. Given a set of programmer-specified invariant templates, our algorithm reduces the invariant synthesis problem to a sequence of arithmetic constraint satisfaction queries. Since the combination of linear arithmetic and uninterpreted functions is a widely applied predicate domain for program verification, our algorithm provides a powerful tool to statically and automatically reason about program correctness. The algorithm can also be used for the synthesis of invariants over arrays and set data structures, because satisfiability questions for the theories of sets and arrays can be reduced to the theory of linear arithmetic with uninterpreted functions. We have implemented our algorithm and used it to find invariants for a low-level memory allocator written in C.

1   Introduction

The classical approach to the verification of temporal safety properties of programs requires the construction of *inductive invariants* [9, 16] at each program point, that is, assertions that are true on every program execution reaching that point, and moreover, that are closed under the strongest postcondition operator. Automation of this construction is the main challenge in program verification.

One promising approach for automated invariant computation is *template-based*, where the user specifies a parameterized form of the invariant, and a constraint-based analysis generates relationships on the parameters such that every instantiation of the parameters satisfying the relationships guarantees that the resulting assertions are indeed inductive invariants. This approach has been successfully applied to numerical invariants [5, 6, 13, 19, 20, 21], using constraint solving in linear or nonlinear arithmetic. Unlike dataflow analysis techniques, which achieve low running time and convergence at the cost of lost precision (e.g., by widening [7]), the template-based techniques are sound and complete

* This research was sponsored in part by the grants NSF-CCF-0427202 and NSF-CCF-0546170.

B. Cook and A. Podelski (Eds.): VMCAI 2007, LNCS 4349, pp. 378–394, 2007.

modulo the templates used: if there is an inductive invariant expressible using the template, then the methods guarantee to synthesize such an invariant.

Unfortunately, the application of these techniques have been confined so far to numerical domains, where linear-programming based techniques, or decision procedures for the theories of rationals/reals, provide natural constraint solvers. In practice, program verification uses more general predicate domains, for example, combinations of linear arithmetic and equality with uninterpreted functions [1, 8, 11, 18, 10]. Uninterpreted functions are especially useful for modeling memory (for example, dereference operations and field accesses can be modeled as uninterpreted functions).

We present a constraint-based invariant synthesis algorithm for the combined domain of linear arithmetic and uninterpreted functions. Given invariant templates in the language of parameterized linear arithmetic and uninterpreted functions, our algorithm instantiates the parameters such that the resulting assertions are inductive invariants. Moreover, if such an instantiation exists, then the algorithm will find it. The key technical idea of our approach is *hierarchic theory combination* [23], whereby the uninterpreted function terms are compiled away to produce arithmetic constraints. The compilation instantiates "enough" functionality axioms to ensure that functions produce equal outputs for equal inputs. In the worst case, a factorial number of constraint-satisfaction problems in linear arithmetic with parametric coefficients needs to be solved.

Our technique enables us to construct invariants for programs that manipulate pointers. Furthermore, using recent results that reduce theories of data structures such as arrays and sets to the combined theory of linear arithmetic and uninterpreted functions [2, 14], we obtain an invariant-generation technique for templates that involve arrays and set data structures.

We have implemented our algorithm for invariant synthesis and applied it to generate invariants for a simplified low-level memory allocator used in an OS kernel. Our tools infer invariants that contain both arithmetic operations and memory operations (address-of and pointer dereferencing), which are approximated by uninterpreted function symbols. Heuristics for automatically searching through the space of candidate templates are left for future work.

2   Example

We illustrate our approach with the small example shown in Fig. 1. We want to prove the assertion at the end of the while loop. One way to prove an assertion ϕ in a program is to find an *inductive assertion map*, that is, a function η that maps every program location to a set of states such that (I0) the initial location of the program is marked true, (I1) for each edge $\ell \to \ell'$ of the control flow graph marked with operation op, we have $\mathrm{SP}(\eta.\ell, \mathsf{op}) \models_{\mathrm{LI+UIF}} \eta.\ell'$, and (I2) $\eta.\ell_\phi \models_{\mathrm{LI+UIF}} \phi$ for the location ℓ_ϕ of the assertion. Here $\models_{\mathrm{LI+UIF}}$ denotes the implication in the theory used to write invariants and program statements, which is linear arithmetic combined with uninterpreted function symbols in our case.

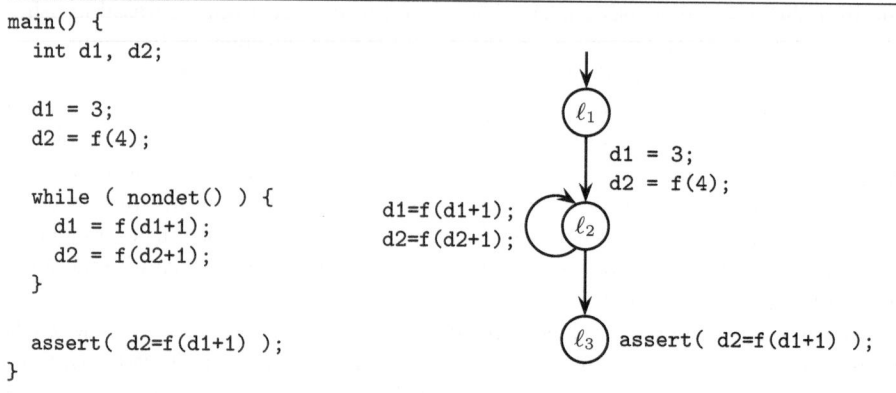

```
main() {
   int d1, d2;

   d1 = 3;
   d2 = f(4);

   while ( nondet() ) {
      d1 = f(d1+1);
      d2 = f(d2+1);
   }

   assert( d2=f(d1+1) );
}
```

Fig. 1. Example program [10] and its control-flow graph. The invariant to prove is asserted at the location ℓ_3.

SP denotes the strongest postcondition operation. For ease of exposition, we shall concentrate on the loop invariant at the location ℓ_2 in the example.

We shall use a template-based technique to infer inductive invariant maps, that is, the user provides a parameterized expression denoting the shape of the invariant, and our inference technique finds instantiations of the parameters that result in an inductive invariant map. For the example, we assume that the template ψ for the loop invariant is

$$\psi: \quad c_{d1}\mathtt{d1} + c_{d2}\mathtt{d2} + c_f f(c_{fd1}\mathtt{d1} + c_{fd2}\mathtt{d2} + c_{fd}) = c_d,$$

where c_* are parameters to be instantiated. This fixes the form of the invariant to a linear equality between a constant and a linear term where the function f occurs once with a linear argument. We use ψ' to denote the primed version of the template, where the program variables $\mathtt{d1}$ and $\mathtt{d2}$ are replaced by their primed versions $\mathtt{d1}'$ and $\mathtt{d2}'$. The primed variables denote the updated values of variables.

Given a template, our algorithm generates a set of constraints between the parameters that must be satisfied for any parameter instantiation to be an invariant. Condition (I1) requires that the template is true when the loop is entered for the first time

$$\mathtt{d1}' = 3 \wedge \mathtt{d2}' = f(4) \models_{\text{LI+UIF}} \psi', \tag{1}$$

and that it must be preserved under the loop iteration

$$\psi \wedge \mathtt{d1}' = f(\mathtt{d1} + 1) \wedge \mathtt{d2}' = f(\mathtt{d2} + 1) \models_{\text{LI+UIF}} \psi'. \tag{2}$$

Condition (I2) requires that the invariant implies the desired assertion

$$\psi \models_{\text{LI+UIF}} \mathtt{d2} = f(\mathtt{d1} + 1). \tag{3}$$

We now translate each implication into a constraint over the template parameters. This translation is the crucial part of our algorithm, and it computes a

Table 1. Purified terms and corresponding definitions for the program in Fig. 1

Fresh	Definition
v	$f(c_{fd1}d1 + c_{fd2}d2 + c_{fd})$
w	$f(c_{fd1}d1' + c_{fd2}d2' + c_{fd})$
x	$f(d1 + 1)$
y	$f(d2 + 1)$
z	$f(4)$

constraint system that has a solution if and only if there exist a valuation of the parameters that yields a desired inductive invariant.

The first step in the translation process is *purification*, which introduces fresh variables for non-arithmetic subterms and stores their definitions. We purify the template and the assertions that describe the program, which produces linear arithmetic assertions together with a set of definitions for the fresh variables. For our template, purification produces the new template

$$c_{d1}d1 + c_{d2}d2 + c_f v = c_d,$$

where v is a new variable whose definition is

$$v = f(c_{fd1}d1 + c_{fd2}d2 + c_{fd}).$$

We show the definition of fresh variables that are created by purification in Table 1.

Now, each implication (1), (2), and (3) is passed to a function CONSEC, which translates the implications into constraints in linear arithmetic. We informally describe how CONSEC transforms the implication (2). The other cases are similar.

We observe that reasoning about implication (2) requires handling of functionality axioms, that is, the proof of the implication may rely on the fact that the function f produces the same outputs for the same inputs. Since some assertions in (2) are parameterized, we do not know *a priori* which instances of the functionality axioms may appear in the proof. The function CONSEC finds such instances automatically, which are in this case

$$\text{if } d1 + 1 = c_{fd1}d1 + c_{fd2}d2 + c_{fd} \text{ then } x = v,$$
$$\text{if } d2 + 1 = c_{fd1}d1' + c_{fd2}d2' + c_{fd} \text{ then } y = w.$$

Given these axiom instances, we can focus on the following version of the implication (2) that now holds in linear arithmetic:

$$c_{d1}d1 + c_{d2}d2 + c_f v = c_d \ \wedge \ d1' = x \ \wedge \ d2' = y \ \wedge \ x = v \ \wedge \ y = w$$
$$\models_{LI} \tag{4}$$
$$c_{d1}d1' + c_{d2}d2' + c_f w = c_d.$$

Note that (4) is equivalent to (2) under the assumption that the latter is provable by using the above axiom instances, but (4) does not require any reasoning about uninterpreted function symbols. CONSEC translates (4) by applying

Farkas' lemma of *linear programming*, which states that (4) holds if the consequent of the implication can be obtained from the antecedents by taking a linear combination thereof.

Additionally, CONSEC needs to justify that its choice of the above axiom instances is valid. Let φ denote the (purified) left-hand side of (4) without the conjuncts $x = v$ and $y = w$ that arise from the axiom instances, that is, $\varphi \equiv c_{d1}d1 + c_{d2}d2 + c_{f}v = c_{d} \wedge d1' = x \wedge d2' = y$. To justify the choice of the above axiom instances, CONSEC includes constraints that the premise of the first instance follows from φ, and that the premise of the second instance follows from φ conjoined with $x = v$:

$$\varphi \models_{\mathrm{LI}} d1 + 1 = c_{fd1}d1 + c_{fd2}d2 + c_{fd}$$
$$\varphi \wedge x = v \models_{\mathrm{LI}} d2 + 1 = c_{fd1}d1' + c_{fd2}d2' + c_{fd}. \tag{5}$$

The justification of both facts translates to arithmetic constraints on template coefficients, again by applying Farkas' lemma.

We solve the conjunction of the constraints that encode the validity of implications (4) and (5) together with the constraints for similar implications obtained by translating (1) and (3) into linear arithmetic under particular choice of axiom instances. The resulting parameter instantiation below defines the loop invariant $d2 - f(d1 + 1) = 0$.

c_{d1}	c_{d2}	c_{f}	c_{fd1}	c_{fd2}	c_{fd}	c_{d}
0	1	-1	1	0	1	0

3   Preliminaries

Constraints. Let x be a set of variables, and let a *state* be a valuation of the variables from x. We shall represent sets of states using (quantifier-free) first order formulas with free variables from x.

A *signature* $\Sigma = (F, P)$ for a first order theory consists of a set of function symbols F and a set of predicate symbols P. We assume that the arity of function and predicate symbols are encoded in their names. A constant is a function of arity zero. For a signature $\Sigma = (F, P)$, the set of Σ-terms over x is the smallest set such that (1) each free variable is a Σ-term, (2) each constant symbol $u \in F$ is a Σ-term, and (3) $f(t_1, \ldots, t_n)$ is a Σ-term, given $f \in F$ is a function symbol of arity n, and each t_i is a Σ-term, for $i = 1, \ldots, n$. The set of Σ-atoms is the smallest set such that (1) $s = t$ is a Σ-atom if s and t are Σ-terms, and (2) $p(t_1, \ldots, t_n)$ is a Σ-atom for a predicate symbol $p \in P$ of arity n and each t_i is a Σ-term, for $i = 1, \ldots, n$. The set of Σ-constraints is the smallest set such that each Σ-atom is a Σ-constraint, and $\neg\varphi$ and $\varphi \wedge \psi$ are Σ-constraints whenever φ and ψ are Σ-constraints. Finally, the set of Σ-formulas is the smallest set containing the Σ-atoms that is closed under conjunction, disjunction, and negation. Semantics of formulas is given using Σ-models in the usual way [3].

In this paper, we assume a constraint language of linear arithmetic and uninterpreted functions. That is, in addition to the usual arithmetic operations, we assume that the language has a set of *uninterpreted function symbols* that can be used as primitive operations. Formally, our signature consists of the constant c for each $c \in \mathbb{Q}$, the functions $+$ and $-$, together with a set of uninterpreted function symbols, and the predicate $\leq$.

A Σ-theory is a set of Σ-formulas that is closed under logical consequences. The *satisfiability problem* for a Σ-theory T asks, given a Σ-formula φ, whether some model of the theory T satisfies φ. The theory of *linear arithmetic* (LI) is the theory of the structure of the rationals $\langle \mathbb{Q}, 0, 1, +, \leq \rangle$. The theory of *equality with uninterpreted functions* (UIF) is the theory of equality together with the axiom

$$\forall c_1, \ldots, c_n, d_1, \ldots, d_n : \bigwedge_{i=1}^{n} c_i = d_i \;\rightarrow\; f(c_1, \ldots, c_n) = f(d_1, \ldots, d_n),$$

for each uninterpreted function symbol f of arity n. We refer to the right-hand side of the above implication as the *head* of the axiom. Given two terms $f(c_1, \ldots, c_n)$ and $f(d_1, \ldots, d_n)$ we write $c \approx d$ to denote the premise $\bigwedge_{i=1}^{n} c_i = d_i$ of the corresponding axiom. We write $\models_{\mathrm{LI}}$ and $\models_{\mathrm{LI+UIF}}$ to denote implication in the theory of linear arithmetic and in its combination with uninterpreted function symbols, respectively.

In the following, we work in the combined theory of linear arithmetic and equality with uninterpreted functions, denoted LI+UIF. We reason about LI+UIF using the hierarchic approach [23]. This approach allows one to reduce the reasoning about certain combinations of base and extension theories to the reasoning in the base theory. The reduction is performed by introducing instantiations of the axioms of the extension theory to the base theory. In particular, the combination of linear arithmetic and uninterpreted function symbols admits hierarchic combination [23].

Theorem 1. *[18, 23] The satisfiability problem for LI+UIF is decidable.*

Control Flow Graphs. We assume an abstract representation of programs by transition systems [16]. A *program* $\mathsf{P} = (x, \mathsf{locs}, \ell_0, \mathcal{T}, \mathsf{Good})$ consists of a set x of variables, a set locs of *control locations*, an initial location $\ell_0 \in \mathsf{locs}$, a set $\mathcal{T}$ of *transitions*, and a constraint Good over the variables from x that describes the 'good' states. Each transition $\tau \in \mathcal{T}$ is a tuple (ℓ, ρ, ℓ') where $\ell, \ell' \in \mathsf{locs}$ are control flow locations, and ρ is a constraint over free variables from $x \cup x'$, where the variables from x' denote the values of the variables from x in the next state.

A *state* of the program P is a valuation of the variables from x. The set of all states is written $\mathsf{val}.x$. We shall represent sets of states using constraints. A *computation* of the program P is a sequence $\langle m_0, s_0 \rangle \langle m_1, s_1 \rangle \ldots \langle m_k, s_k \rangle \in (\mathsf{locs} \times \mathsf{val}.x)^*$ where $m_0 = \ell_0$ is the initial location and for each $i \in \{0, \ldots, k-1\}$, there is a transition $(m_i, \rho, m_{i+1}) \in \mathcal{T}$ such that $(s_i, s_{i+1}) \models_{\mathrm{LI+UIF}} \rho$. A state s is reachable at ℓ if $\langle \ell, s \rangle$ appears in some computation. A program is *unsafe* if some state $s \notin \mathsf{Good}$ is reachable.

Invariants. An *invariant* at a location $\ell \in$ locs of P is a set of states containing the states reachable at ℓ. An *invariant map* is a mapping η from locs to LI+UIF constraints such that the following conditions hold:

(**I0: Initiation**) for the entry location ℓ_0, we have $\eta.\ell_0 = \textit{true}$.

(**I1: Inductiveness**) for each $\ell, \ell' \in$ locs such that $(\ell, \rho, \ell') \in \mathcal{T}$, we have $\eta.\ell \wedge \rho \models_{\text{LI+UIF}} \eta.\ell'$. Here, $\eta.\ell'$ is the constraint obtained by substituting variables from x' for the variables from x in $\eta.\ell$.

(**I2: Safety**) for each $\ell \in$ locs we have $\eta.\ell \models_{\text{LI+UIF}}$ Good.

The *invariant synthesis* problem is to construct an invariant map for a given program. For ease of exposition, we assume that an invariant map assigns an invariant to each program location. For efficiency, one can require invariants to be defined only over a program *cutset*, i.e., a set of program locations such that every syntactic cycle in the control flow graph passes through some location in the cutset.

4   Invariant Synthesis for LI+UIF

We now describe our algorithm for invariant synthesis for linear arithmetic and uninterpreted function symbols. Our algorithm follows the constraint-based approach [6, 20, 19, 21, 13], which has already provided successful algorithms for the synthesis of linear and non-linear invariants and ranking functions. Our algorithm extends the applicability of invariant generation to the combination of linear arithmetic and uninterpreted function symbols. First, we briefly describe the constraint-based approach, and outline our method of handling uninterpreted function symbols. Then, we provide a formal description of our algorithm.

Constraint-based Invariant Synthesis. The constraint-based approach to invariant generation reduces the computation of an invariant to a constraint solving problem. The approach consists of three steps. First, a *template* assertion that represents an invariant is fixed in an *a priori* chosen language. The parameters in the template are the unknown coefficients that determine the invariant. Second, a set of *constraints* over these parameters is defined which encodes the definition of the invariant. This means that every solution to the constraint system yields an inductive invariant. Third, an *invariant* is obtained by solving the resulting constraint system.

4.1   Invariant Templates

An *invariant template* is an *a priori* fixed parameterized assertion over the program variables. It identifies the unknown parameters, and restricts the "dimensions" of the invariant, e.g., the number of conjuncts and the number of function applications. This means that the form of the template determines the form of the resulting invariant.

We provide the formal definition of the invariant template for a given set of program variables and functions symbols. Let c range over the set of integer constants, v over the set of program variables, f over a fixed set of uninterpreted functions symbols, and α over a fixed set of template parameters. The following grammar defines the set of constraint templates:

$$
\begin{aligned}
\text{Terms} \quad & t ::= v \mid f(e_1, \dots, e_n) \\
\text{Expressions } & e ::= c \mid c \times t \mid \alpha \times t \mid e_1 + e_2 \mid e_1 - e_2 \\
\text{Constraints } & i ::= e \leq c \mid e_1 = e_2 \\
\text{Templates} \quad & \xi ::= i \mid i \wedge \xi
\end{aligned}
$$

An invariant template is a finite conjunction of inequalities. An invariant is *expressible* by the invariant template if there exists a valuation of the template parameters that yields the invariant. Our algorithm computes invariants that are expressible by a given template.

4.2   Algorithm

The invariant synthesis algorithm $\textsc{Inv}(\text{LI}+\text{UIF})$ takes as input a program and a template map that assigns an invariant template to each program location. The algorithm computes an invariant map that assigns an invariant to each program location, if there exists an invariant that is expressible by the given invariant template. The algorithm is shown in Fig. 2. It applies an auxiliary function $\textsc{Consec}$ shown in Fig. 3. The function $\textsc{Consec}$ generates constraints between the parameters in the invariant template that ensure the conditions **(I0)**, **(I1)**, and **(I2)**. (We assume that the template map assigns *true* to the initial location ℓ_0, thus **(I0)** is satisfied.) Any satisfying assignment to these constraints gives an instantiation of the invariant template that is an invariant. Next, we describe each step of the algorithm.

Purification. We first purify all (sub-) terms that appear in the invariant templates, and in the program representation. A formula (or constraint) is *purified* if the only atom with an uninterpreted function is of the form $x = f(t_1, \dots, t_n)$ where x is a variable and $t_1, \dots, t_n$ are linear terms. A purified formula may be obtained by replacing each subterm of the form $f(e_1, \dots, e_n)$ by a fresh variable, and recording the corresponding definition. This step creates a map pur that records the correspondence between terms and their purified versions, and a map def that keeps the definitions for fresh variables.

Constraint Generation. We create the constraints by applying the function $\textsc{Consec}$. The function $\textsc{Consec}$ computes a constraint on the parameters of the templates φ_{pre} and φ_{post} over program variables and primed program variables, respectively, for a transition relation ρ. Let *Params* be the set of parameters that appear in the templates φ_{pre} and φ_{post}. The output of $\textsc{Consec}$ is the constraint over *Params* such that the implication

$$
\varphi_{\text{pre}} \wedge \rho \models_{\text{LI}+\text{UIF}} \varphi_{\text{post}} \tag{6}
$$

is valid for some valuation of *Params* if and only if such a valuation satisfies the constraint.

---

function INV(LI+UIF)
input
    Program P = $(x, \mathsf{locs}, \ell_0, \mathcal{T}, \mathsf{Good})$
    tmpl: invariant template map
local
    Params: set of parameters that appear in the invariant templates
    pur: purification map that assigns purified LI-terms to LI+UIF-terms
    def: set of definitions for fresh variables created by purification
    Φ := constraint over parameters of invariant templates
output
    inv: invariant map from locs to invariants, which is an instantiation of tmpl
begin
    Params := parameters that appear in invariant templates
    pur, def := purification of $\{\mathsf{tmpl}(\ell) \mid \ell \in \mathsf{locs}\} \cup \{\mathsf{Good}\} \cup \mathcal{T}$
    $\Phi := 0 \leq 1$
    foreach $(\ell, \rho, \ell') \in \mathcal{T}$ **do**
        $\Phi := \Phi \wedge$ CONSEC(pur(tmpl(ℓ)), pur(ρ), pur(tmpl(ℓ')), def)
    done
    foreach $\ell \in \mathsf{locs}$ **do**
        $\Phi := \Phi \wedge$ CONSEC(pur(tmpl(ℓ)), $0 \leq 1$, pur(Good), def)
    done
    if $\exists Params : \Phi$ **then**
        let $\mu : Params \rightarrow \mathbb{Q}$ be a satisfying assignment of Φ
        foreach $\ell \in \mathsf{locs}$ **do**
            inv(ℓ) := tmpl(ℓ) where parameters are instantiated by μ
                    and fresh variables replaced by definitions in def
        done
        return "Invariant map: inv."
    else
        return "No invariant expressible by template tmpl exists."
end.

Fig. 2. Algorithm INV(LI+UIF) for the synthesis of invariants in linear arithmetic and uninterpreted function symbols. The auxiliary function CONSEC is shown in Fig. 3.

CONSEC takes as inputs three linear arithmetic assertions and a set of definitions for fresh variables. The first assertion

$$(P\,P_{\mathsf{pre}})\left(\begin{smallmatrix} x \\ x_{\mathsf{pre}} \end{smallmatrix}\right) \leq p$$

represents the purified version of φ_{pre}, and is given over the program variables x and a vector of the corresponding fresh variables x_{pre}. The second assertion

$$(R\,R'\,R_{\mathsf{rel}})\left(\begin{smallmatrix} x \\ x' \\ x_{\mathsf{rel}} \end{smallmatrix}\right) \leq r$$

function CONSEC
input

$(P P_{\text{pre}}) \left(\begin{smallmatrix} x \\ x_{\text{pre}} \end{smallmatrix} \right) \leq p$: purified template for pre-location with fresh variables x_{pre}

$(R R' R_{\text{rel}}) \left(\begin{smallmatrix} x \\ x' \\ x_{\text{rel}} \end{smallmatrix} \right) \leq r$: purified transition relation with fresh variables x_{rel}

$(Q Q_{\text{post}}) \left(\begin{smallmatrix} x' \\ x_{\text{post}} \end{smallmatrix} \right) \leq q$: purified template for post-location with fresh variables x_{post}

Def: set of definitions for fresh variables x_{pre}, x_{rel}, and x_{post}

local

Φ: auxiliary constraint over the template parameters P, P_{pre}, p and Q, Q_{post}, q that encodes an implication induced by a particular sequence of axiom instances

fresh : fresh variables defined by Def

output

Ψ: consecution constraint over the template parameters P, P_{pre}, p and Q, Q_{post}, q

begin

$\Psi := 1 \leq 0$

fresh $:= x_{\text{pre}} \cup x_{\text{rel}} \cup x_{\text{post}}$

Inst $:= \{ c \approx d \to c = d \mid c, d \in$ fresh and $c = f(c_1, \ldots, c_n) \in$ Def and $d = f(d_1, \ldots, d_n) \in$ Def$\}$

foreach $n \in \{0, \ldots, |\text{Inst}|\}$ **do**

$\{ c^i \approx d^i \to c^i = d^i \}_{i=1}^{n} :=$ select sequence of n axiom instances from Inst

$(E_{\text{pre}} E_{\text{rel}} E_{\text{post}}) \left(\begin{smallmatrix} x_{\text{pre}} \\ x_{\text{rel}} \\ x_{\text{post}} \end{smallmatrix} \right) \leq e :=$ inequality representation of $\bigwedge_{i=1}^{n} c^i = d^i$

$\Phi := \exists \Lambda \in \mathbb{Q}_{\geq 0}^{|q| \times (|p| + |r| + |e|)} :$

$$\Lambda \begin{pmatrix} P & 0 & P_{\text{pre}} & 0 & 0 \\ R & R' & 0 & R_{\text{rel}} & 0 \\ 0 & 0 & E_{\text{pre}} & E_{\text{rel}} & E_{\text{post}} \end{pmatrix} = \begin{pmatrix} 0 & Q & 0 & 0 & Q_{\text{post}} \end{pmatrix} \wedge \Lambda \begin{pmatrix} p \\ r \\ e \end{pmatrix} \leq q$$

foreach $k \in \{1, \ldots, n\}$ **do**

$(F_{\text{pre}} F_{\text{rel}} F_{\text{post}}) \left(\begin{smallmatrix} x_{\text{pre}} \\ x_{\text{rel}} \\ x_{\text{post}} \end{smallmatrix} \right) \leq f :=$ inequality representation of $\bigwedge_{i=1}^{k-1} c^i = d^i$

$(G G_{\text{pre}} G_{\text{rel}} G_{\text{post}}) \left(\begin{smallmatrix} x \\ x_{\text{pre}} \\ x_{\text{rel}} \\ x_{\text{post}} \end{smallmatrix} \right) \leq g :=$ purified representation of $c^k \approx d^k$

$\Phi := \Phi \wedge \exists \Lambda \in \mathbb{Q}_{\geq 0}^{|g| \times (|p| + |r| + |f|)} :$

$$\Lambda \begin{pmatrix} P & 0 & P_{\text{pre}} & 0 & 0 \\ R & R' & 0 & R_{\text{rel}} & 0 \\ 0 & 0 & F_{\text{pre}} & F_{\text{rel}} & F_{\text{post}} \end{pmatrix} = \begin{pmatrix} G & 0 & G_{\text{pre}} & G_{\text{rel}} & G_{\text{post}} \end{pmatrix} \wedge \Lambda \begin{pmatrix} p \\ r \\ f \end{pmatrix} \leq g$$

done

$\Psi := \Psi \vee \Phi$

done

return Ψ

end.

Fig. 3. Function CONSEC computes a constraint over the template parameters which encodes the consecution condition for a given transition relation and invariant templates for the pre- and post-locations

represents the purified version of the transition relation ρ, and is given over the program variables x, their primed versions x', and a vector of the corresponding fresh variables x_{rel}. The third assertion

$$(QQ_{\mathsf{post}}) \left(\begin{smallmatrix} x' \\ x_{\mathsf{post}} \end{smallmatrix} \right) \leq q$$

is similar to the first one, where the program variables x are substituted by their primed versions x'. The resulting constraint Ψ over the parameters P, P_{pre}, p and Q, Q_{post}, q is satisfiable if and only if implication (6) is valid for some valuation of the parameters.

The constraint computed by the function CONSEC captures all sequences of instantiations of functionality axioms that may potentially appear in a proof of implication (6). For each such a sequence, which can be empty, we introduce a disjunct that encodes two conditions. The first condition says that the implication holds in the theory of linear arithmetic once all axioms from the sequence are applied. The second condition justifies the application of each axiom in the sequence. We take the disjunction of constraints computed for each sequence, which encodes the choice of an arbitrary sequence.

In algorithm INV(LI+UIF), we call CONSEC to capture the constraints **(I1)**, and **(I2)**. First, for each transition we compute the consecution constraint that ensures the closure under the application of the transition relation. Then, we encode the condition that the resulting invariant is sufficiently strong, i.e., it only contains 'good' states.

Correctness. We state the correctness of the algorithm INV(LI+UIF) in the following theorems.

Theorem 2 (Soundness of Inv(LI+UIF)). *The algorithm* INV(LI+UIF) *computes an invariant map that is expressible by a given invariant template.*

Proof. We show that the resulting map inv satisfies the consecution condition. The proof that inv also satisfies the initiation and strength conditions is similar.

Let φ_{pre} and φ_{post} be invariant templates instantiated by the algorithm. We show that the implication (6) holds. Let Ψ be the constraint that is computed by applying CONSEC on the input that corresponds to the transition relation ρ. The valuation of template parameters that defines inv satisfies Ψ. Let Φ be a disjunct of Ψ that is satisfied. We assume that Φ corresponds to the following sequence of instances of the functionality axioms:

$$c^1 \approx d^1 \rightarrow c^1 = d^1, \ldots, c^n \approx d^n \rightarrow c^n = d^n.$$

Let $(PP_{\mathsf{pre}})\left(\begin{smallmatrix} x \\ x_{\mathsf{pre}} \end{smallmatrix}\right) \leq p$, $(RR'R_{\mathsf{rel}})\left(\begin{smallmatrix} x \\ x' \\ x_{\mathsf{rel}} \end{smallmatrix}\right) \leq r$, and $(QQ_{\mathsf{post}})\left(\begin{smallmatrix} x' \\ x_{\mathsf{post}} \end{smallmatrix}\right) \leq q$ be the purified version of φ_{pre}, ρ, and φ_{post}, respectively.

The first conjunct of Φ ensures that the following implication holds, by Farkas' lemma [22]:

$$(PP_{\mathsf{pre}})\left(\begin{smallmatrix} x \\ x_{\mathsf{pre}} \end{smallmatrix}\right) \leq p \wedge (RR'R_{\mathsf{rel}})\left(\begin{smallmatrix} x \\ x' \\ x_{\mathsf{rel}} \end{smallmatrix}\right) \leq r \wedge \bigwedge_{i=1}^{n} c^i = d^i \models_{\mathsf{LI}} (QQ_{\mathsf{post}})\left(\begin{smallmatrix} x' \\ x_{\mathsf{post}} \end{smallmatrix}\right) \leq q.$$

This implication means that the above sequence of instances of functionality axioms is sufficient to prove the implication. The remaining conjuncts of Φ ensure that the axiom instances are applicable, because their premises are satisfied. This follows from the implications below, which are encoded by the remaining conjuncts of Φ. For each $k \in \{1, \ldots, n\}$ we have

$$(PP_{\mathsf{pre}})\left(\begin{smallmatrix} x \\ x_{\mathsf{pre}} \end{smallmatrix}\right) \leq p \ \wedge \ (RR'R_{\mathsf{rel}})\left(\begin{smallmatrix} x \\ x' \\ x_{\mathsf{rel}} \end{smallmatrix}\right) \leq r \ \wedge \ \bigwedge_{i=1}^{k-1} c^i = d^i \ \models_{\mathsf{LI}} \ c^k \approx d^k.$$

Since purification preserves satisfiability, we conclude that the invariant φ_{pre} is closed under the transition relation ρ by the invariant φ_{pre}.   □

Theorem 3 (Completeness of Inv(LI+UIF)). *The algorithm* Inv(LI+UIF) *computes an invariant map if it is expressible by a given invariant template.*

Proof. Let inv be an invariant map that satisfies the invariant template. We show that the consecution constraint computed by the function Consec is satisfiable. The proof that it is also satisfiable in conjunction with initiation and strength constraints is similar.

Let φ_{pre} and φ_{post} be assertions such that for a transition relation ρ the implication (6) holds. By Theorem 5 in [23] we have that the following implication is valid in the theory of linear arithmetic for some sequence of instances of functionality axioms. Furthermore, these instances are only created for the terms that appear in the assertions φ_{pre}, φ_{post}, and ρ. Let

$$c^1 \approx d^1 \rightarrow c^1 = d^1, \ldots, c^n \approx d^n \rightarrow c^n = d^n$$

be such a sequence. Since purification preserve the satisfiability, we conclude that the conjuncts of Φ encode that (i) the purified version of the assertion φ_{post} is implied by the purified version of $\varphi_{\mathsf{pre}} \wedge \rho$ in conjunction with heads $\bigwedge_{i=1}^{n} c^i = d^i$ of functionality axiom instances from the sequence, and (ii) for each $k \in \{1, \ldots, n\}$ the premise $c^k \approx d^k$ of each axiom instance is implied by $\varphi_{\mathsf{pre}} \wedge \rho$ in conjunction with the axiom heads $\bigwedge_{i=1}^{k-1} c^i = d^i$ applied so far. All implications hold in the theory of linear arithmetic. Hence, the constraint computed by Consec is satisfiable.   □

We obtain the following corollary of Theorems 2 and 3.

Corollary 1. *The existence of a LI+UIF-invariant map that is expressible by a given template is decidable.*

Complexity and Optimizations. Let n be the number of applications of function symbols in the template and in the program description. The algorithm Inv(LI+UIF) needs to solve at most $n!$ quantifier elimination problems for rational/real arithmetic constraints of the second degree, where the size of each problem is linear in program description and quadratic in n. The time complexity of each problem is exponential in its size [4].

```
int alloc() {
    assume (kfreelist != 0 && *(kfreelist + 4) == RESERVED);
                    // First page is always reserved.
    prev = kfreelist; curr = *kfreelist; permission = curr + 4;
    while(curr!=0 && *permission == RESERVED) {
        prev = curr; curr = *curr;
        permission = curr + 4;
    }
    L1: assert( *(prev + 4) == RESERVED );
    L2: assert( *prev == curr );
    if (curr!=0) *prev = *curr;
    return curr;
}
```

Fig. 4. A kernel allocator. Our algorithm automatically constructs the loop invariant `*(prev+4)-curr+perm-RESERVED==4 && perm==curr+4`, which implies the first assertion, and the invariant `*prev==curr`, which implies the second assertion.

We observe that the construction of the constraint that considers all possible axiom sequences can be done lazily, i.e., we consider new sequences only if the previously discovered ones do not yield a desired invariant map. Such a lazy construction is crucial for practical applicability of INV(LI+UIF), since in many cases only short sequences consisting of at most a pair of axioms suffice.

5   Experiences

We have implemented algorithm INV(LI+UIF) in Sicstus Prolog [15] with linear programming solver [12] and applied it to the verification of low level memory allocators in an operating system. We apply a heuristics that prefers shorter candidate sequences of axiom instances to longer ones while lazily constructing constraints. The invariant templates need to be supplied manually. Solving of non-linear constraints was done by heuristic instantiation of the values for Λ, cf. Fig. 3, and subsequent solving of the resulting linear constraint.

Figure 4 shows a simplified low level memory allocator used in an OS kernel. The variable `kfreelist` is the head of a free list of memory pages. Each memory block contains a pointer to the next free block and also a permission bit that says whether the block can be given to a user process. The permission bit is accessed using address arithmetic by adding 4 bytes to the base address of the memory block. For simplicity, we have removed the type casts from the example code and also ignore overflow issues. We assume that the free list has at least one block and the first block is reserved by the kernel.

The while loop iterates over the free list, looking for the first unreserved free block. This block is returned. The iteration uses two pointers, `curr` pointing to the current block, and `prev` pointing to the previous block. We want to prove the assertion L1, which states that pointer `prev` points to a reserved block, and assertion L2, which states that the next block from pointer `prev` is the block pointed to by `curr` (or null). The invariant requires both linear arithmetic (for the address arithmetic) and uninterpreted functions (for the dereferences).

Assertion L1: Our invariant synthesis for proving the first assertion required 3.25 s on a 1.7 GHz Linux laptop. The tool tried 105 axiom sequences. Considering sequences of length at most one was sufficient. We used a template that is a conjunction of two equalities[1] (where $ref(\cdot)$ denotes the address-of operator and $der(\cdot)$ is the dereference operator):

$$c^1_{\text{prev}}\texttt{prev} + c^1_{\text{curr}}\texttt{curr} + c^1_{\text{perm}}\texttt{perm} + c^1_{\text{RESERVED}}\texttt{RESERVED}+$$
$$c^1_{\text{ref}}\,ref\,(c^1_{\text{refprev}}\texttt{prev} + c^1_{\text{refcurr}}\texttt{curr} + c^1_{\text{refperm}}\texttt{perm} + c^1_{\text{refRESERVED}}\texttt{RESERVED} + c^1_{\text{ref}})+$$
$$c^1_{\text{der}}\,der\,(c^1_{\text{derprev}}\texttt{prev} + c^1_{\text{dercurr}}\texttt{curr} + c^1_{\text{derperm}}\texttt{perm} + c^1_{\text{derRESERVED}}\texttt{RESERVED} + c^1_{\text{der}}) = c^1$$

$$\wedge$$

$$c^2_{\text{prev}}\texttt{prev} + c^2_{\text{curr}}\texttt{curr} + c^2_{\text{perm}}\texttt{perm} + c^2_{\text{RESERVED}}\texttt{RESERVED} = c^2.$$

This template leads to the loop invariant

$$-\texttt{curr} + \texttt{perm} - \texttt{RESERVED} + der(\texttt{prev} + 4) = 4 \ \wedge\ -\texttt{curr} + \texttt{perm} = 4.$$

Assertion L2: For the second assertion we used a template that contains only the first conjunct from the template above, and we obtained the loop invariant

$$-\texttt{curr} + der(\texttt{prev}) = 0.$$

Our implementation computed an invariant that implies the second assertion in 1.28 s, which required enumeration of 44 axiom sequences.

We are working on scaling our algorithm to larger programs. The main complexity arises because invariants can be Boolean combinations of atomic facts.

6   Applications to Data Structures

We now present applications of algorithm INV(LI+UIF) to the synthesis of invariants in programs that use abstract data structures. The key technical idea is that of a *reduction function*. Let $\varSigma$ and $\varOmega$ be signatures with $\varOmega \subseteq \varSigma$. Let T be a $\varSigma$-theory and R an $\varOmega$-theory, such that $R \subseteq T$. We say T *reduces* to R if there is a computable map from $\varSigma$-formulas to $\varOmega$-formulas such that when applied to a $\varSigma$-formula φ, we get an $\varOmega$-formula φ^* such that φ and φ^* are T-equivalent, that is, $\models_T \varphi \leftrightarrow \varphi^*$, and φ^* is R-satisfiable iff φ is T-satisfiable.

Given a theory T and a reduction function from T to LI+UIF, we can extend the algorithm INV(LI+UIF) to generate invariants over T from templates that contain symbols from the theory T in the following way. The intuitive idea is that we first apply the reduction function to reduce templates in the theory T

---

[1] The implementation supports direct handling of equality and inequality constraints.

to templates in the theory LI+UIF and then apply the invariant generation algorithm for LI+UIF. The resulting invariant is an invariant also for the theory T. Technically, the purification step is identical, while in CONSEC, we apply the reduction function to each definition and then generate the constraints for the resulting formula using the theory LI+UIF. We omit the technical details.

We now show that reduction functions to LI+UIF exist for two interesting theories: the array property fragment and the theory of sets.

Arrays. The theory of arrays has a signature Σ_{array} with the function symbols read and write together with the axiom [17]:

$$\text{read}(\text{write}(a, i, e), i) = e,$$
$$i \neq j \implies \text{read}(\text{write}(a, i, e), j) = \text{read}(a, j),$$
$$(\forall\, i)(\text{read}(a, i) = \text{read}(b, i)) \implies a = b.$$

The variables in the second position of read and write are the *index variables*.

Let I be a set of index variables, which we assume are distinct from the program variables. An *array property* [2] is a universally quantified formula

$$\forall I : \varphi(I) \to \psi(I),$$

where the formula $\varphi(I)$ is a constraint on the index variables and $\psi(I)$ may contain array operations indexed by variables from I. Both $\varphi(I)$ and $\psi(I)$ are syntactically restricted. The index guard $\varphi(I)$ is a Boolean expression over linear arithmetic inequalities over I and the program variables such that each inequality is one of the following:

- a comparison $i \leq j$ between two index variables $i, j \in I$,
- a comparison $i \leq e$ or $e \leq i$ between an index variable $i \in I$ and a linear expression e over program variables.

The value guard $\psi(I)$ is restricted in the following way w.r.t. the usage of the universally quantified index variables I. Every occurrence of such a variable i must be in the index position of a read operation $\text{read}(a, i)$ for some array a. Additionally, no nested read operations that are allowed in $\psi(I)$. The *array property fragment* is the combination of linear arithmetic, uninterpreted function symbols, and array property formulas.

Sets. The theory of sets (with finite cardinality constraints) has a signature Σ_{set} containing the constant symbols $\emptyset$ (empty set) and $\Bbbk$ (full set), the binary function symbols $\cup$ (union), $\cap$ (intersection), and $\setminus$ (difference), the unary function symbol $\{\cdot\}$ (singleton), and the binary predicate symbol $\in$ with the standard semantics. In addition it has, for each natural number k, the unary predicate symbols $|\cdot| \geq k$ and $|\cdot| = k$. The element domain is assumed to be finite. The theory T_{set} is the set of all Σ_{set}-sentences that are true in all standard set-structures.

We use the following results on reductions, proved in [2, 14].

Theorem 4 (Reductions to LI+UIF).

1. [2] *The set of formulas in the array property fragment reduces to LI+UIF.*
2. [14] *The quantifier-free theories of arrays and sets reduce to LI+UIF.*

From the theorem, and the discussion on invariant generation, we get the following corollary.

Corollary 2. *The existence of a T-invariant map that is expressible by a given template is decidable, where T is the theory of arrays, sets, or formulas in the array property fragment.*

7 Conclusion

We presented an algorithm for the synthesis of invariants in the theory of linear arithmetic and uninterpreted function symbols. While expressive, in that many interesting aspects of program behavior can be modeled in (or reduced to) this logic, our technique is ultimately limited by the large space of possible templates that the user must search to provide good templates. In particular, the search space usually becomes too big in the presence of disjunctions in invariant templates. We leave the identification of heuristics for the property-guided construction of invariant templates for future work.

Acknowledgments. We thank Viorica Sofronie-Stokkermans for valuable discussions on hierarchic theory combination.

References

1. T. Ball and S. K. Rajamani. The SLAM project: Debugging system software via static analysis. In *Proc. POPL*, pages 1–3. ACM, 2002.
2. A. R. Bradley, Z. Manna, and H. B. Sipma. What's decidable about arrays? In *Proc. VMCAI*, LNCS 3855, pages 427–442. Springer, 2006.
3. C. C. Chang and H. J. Keisler. *Model Theory.* North-Holland, 3rd edition, 1990.
4. G. E. Collins. Quantifier elimination for real closed fields by cylindrical algebraic decomposition. In *Automata Theory and Formal Languages*, LNCS 33, pages 134–183. Springer, 1975.
5. M. Colón, S. Sankaranarayanan, and H. B. Sipma. Linear invariant generation using non-linear constraint solving. In *Proc. CAV*, LNCS 2725, pages 420–432. Springer, 2003.
6. P. Cousot. Proving program invariance and termination by parametric abstraction, Lagrangian relaxation and semidefinite programming. In *Proc. VMCAI*, LNCS 3385. Springer, 2005.
7. P. Cousot and R. Cousot. Comparing the Galois connection and widening/narrowing approaches to abstract interpretation. In *Proc. PLILP*, LNCS 631, pages 269–295. Springer, 1992.
8. C. Flanagan, K. R. M. Leino, M. Lillibridge, G. Nelson, J. B. Saxe, and R. Stata. Extended static checking for Java. In *Proc. PLDI*, pages 234–245. ACM, 2002.

9. R. W. Floyd. Assigning meanings to programs. In *Mathematical Aspects of Computer Science*, pages 19–32. AMS, 1967.
10. S. Gulwani and A. Tiwari. Combining abstract interpreters. In *Proc. PLDI*, pages 376–386. ACM, 2006.
11. T. A. Henzinger, R. Jhala, R. Majumdar, and G. Sutre. Lazy abstraction. In *Proc. POPL*, pages 58–70. ACM, 2002.
12. C. Holzbaur. *OFAI clp(q,r) Manual, Edition 1.3.3*. Austrian Research Institute for Artificial Intelligence, Vienna, 1995. TR-95-09.
13. D. Kapur. Automatically generating loop invariants using quantifier elimination. In *Proc. Deduction and Applications*, volume 05431. IBFI Schloss Dagstuhl, 2006.
14. D. Kapur and C. Zarba. A reduction approach to decision procedures. Technical Report TR-CS-2005-44, University of New Mexico, 2005.
15. T. I. S. Laboratory. *SICStus Prolog User's Manual*. Swedish Institute of Computer Science, PO Box 1263 SE-164 29 Kista, Sweden, October 2001. Release 3.8.7.
16. Z. Manna and A. Pnueli. *Temporal verification of reactive systems: Safety*. Springer, 1995.
17. J. McCarthy. Towards a mathematical science of computation. In *Proc. IFIP Congress*, pages 21–28. North-Holland, 1962.
18. G. Nelson. Techniques for program verification. Technical Report CSL81-10, Xerox Palo Alto Research Center, 1981.
19. S. Sankaranarayanan, H. B. Sipma, and Z. Manna. Constraint-based linear-relations analysis. In *Proc. SAS*, LNCS 3148, pages 53–68. Springer, 2004.
20. S. Sankaranarayanan, H. B. Sipma, and Z. Manna. Non-linear loop invariant generation using Gröbner bases. In *Proc. POPL*, pages 318–329. ACM, 2004.
21. S. Sankaranarayanan, H. B. Sipma, and Z. Manna. Scalable analysis of linear systems using mathematical programming. In *Proc. VMCAI*, LNCS 3385, pages 25–41. Springer, 2005.
22. A. Schrijver. *Theory of Linear and Integer Programming*. Wiley, 1986.
23. V. Sofronie-Stokkermans. Hierarchic reasoning in local theory extensions. In *Proc. CADE*, LNCS 3632, pages 219–234. Springer, 2005.

Author Index

Lecture Notes in Computer Science

For information about Vols. 1–4274

please contact your bookseller or Springer